DITHYRAMB
TRAGEDY AND COMEDY

CORINTHIAN VASE IN THE FITZWILLIAM MUSEUM
CAMBRIDGE

DITHYRAMB
TRAGEDY AND COMEDY

BY

A. W. PICKARD-CAMBRIDGE, M.A.
Fellow of Balliol College, Oxford

OXFORD
AT THE CLARENDON PRESS

Oxford University Press, Great Clarendon Street, Oxford OX2 6DP

Oxford New York

Athens Auckland Bangkok Bogota Bombay
Buenos Aires Calcutta Cape Town Dar es Salaam
Delhi Florence Hong Kong Istanbul Karachi
Kuala Lumpur Madras Madrid Melbourne
Mexico City Nairobi Paris Singapore
Taipei Tokyo Toronto Warsaw

and associated companies in
Berlin Ibadan

Oxford is a trade mark of Oxford University Press

Published in the United States by
Oxford University Press Inc., New York

ISBN 0-19-814227-7

1 3 5 7 9 10 8 6 4 2

Printed in Great Britain
on acid-free paper by
Bookcraft (Bath) Ltd.,
Midsomer Norton

PREFACE

MUCH has been written during the last thirty
years upon the origins and early history of
the Greek Drama. The conclusions reached by
some of the writers appeared to me to be so speculative and even incredible, that I began the Studies, of
which the results are summed up in this volume,
with the object of examining the evidence, and
ascertaining what conclusions it would really justify.
The result has too often been to show that no conclusions are possible, least of all some of those which
have been put forward; and although I hope that
these Studies will be found to yield some positive
results, it must be admitted that they are in a measure
critical; an unkind reader might describe them as

> Proving false all written hitherto,
> And putting us to ignorance again.

This, however, if faithfully done, may itself be a
modest service to scholarship. For the ingenuity and
the imaginative power which the writers, to whom
I refer, possess in a far higher degree than myself,
I have the most sincere respect and gratitude. I have
learned from them more than I can estimate. But
I think it is one of the most important tasks of
scholarship at the present moment—at least in regard
to these subjects—to ascertain what can really
be said to be proved or probable, and to draw the
line sharply between history on the one hand, and

attractive and interesting speculation, not founded upon evidence, on the other. It is with this end in view that these chapters have been written. They do not profess to be literary essays, but simply a dispassionate attempt to ascertain historical truth or probability by methods as logical as the subject permits.

It is more than twenty-five years since I began working on these lines. The duties of a very busy life have often caused the work to be suspended for long periods, and the War and its effects have made it impossible to prepare the results for publication until now. In consequence of this, some of the conclusions reached in these pages have been anticipated by writers who have been able to publish them before me, and I have tried duly to acknowledge their priority; but I may sometimes have omitted to do so, where my view was already determined and expressed in lectures, before I saw their work; any such omission is not intentional, and will, I trust, be forgiven. In any case, no opinion is the worse for having been independently formed by two or more students.

It is unfortunate that the authorities for the early history of the Greek Drama and Choral Lyric are for the most part late, and the information which they give very fragmentary. Aristotle, acute as he is in the discovery of principles and the logical classification of types, shows little interest in history, apart from his services in connexion with the inscriptional record. The work of his successors in the Peripatetic School, and of the Alexandrian and Per-

gamene scholars, survives almost entirely in the form
of passing remarks, scholia and lexicographical notices
in writers of much later date, in which much nonsense
is mixed with much that seems to be sound. Nevertheless, the tradition which filtered into such notices
was, at least in part, the work of scholars of great
industry, ability, and discernment, and it is dangerous
to disregard definite statements made by scholiasts,
lexicographers, and writers on literary and social
history (such as Athenaeus), unless the supposed error
can itself be accounted for and good reason found for
setting the disputed statement aside. I have, so far
as I was able, tried to test the strength of each
particular piece of evidence, as it came under discussion; and I have generally acted on the principle
that statements which combine to suggest a coherent
and intrinsically probable hypothesis, consistent with
whatever certainties there may be, or representing
a fairly steady tradition, may be provisionally accepted;
and that a hypothesis so formed, though it may not
be proved, is likely to be nearer the truth than one
based on *a priori* assumptions and indifferent to the
literary evidence. But I recognize that one of the
greatest needs of scholarship at the present time is
a fresh, detailed and critical account of the tradition
of literary history from the fourth century B.C. to the
twelfth century A. D., tracing, as well as can be done,
the filiation of the different authorities. Some in-
valuable work has already been done, such as that of
Wilamowitz on the Lyric poets; of Kaibel on the
Prolegomena περὶ κωμῳδίας; of Römer on the Scholia

to Aristophanes; of Rohde, Bapp, Wagner, and others on the sources of Pollux, Suidas, and Athenaeus; of Flickinger on Plutarch; and Körte's sketch (in Pauly-Wissowa) of the authorities for the history of Greek Comedy. But these and other detached discussions cover only a fraction of the ground, and on many points the several scholars reach conflicting conclusions. A more complete account would be a fine task for a small group of younger scholars: but it would need many years of hard work.

I hope I shall not be taken to task for daring to suggest, more than once, that the painters of vases may have been exercising their imagination, and that the greatest caution is needed in accepting the evidence of vase-paintings as proof of the existence or the characteristics of particular rituals or performances. I have also felt bound to insist that accounts given of the religious or dramatic ritual and ideas of peoples far removed from the Greek can prove nothing as to the performances and ritual of the Greeks themselves, and that the evidence for the nature of the latter must be drawn from Greece and Greece only, whatever interesting analogies may afterwards be discerned.

Two remarks of a personal character must be made:

(1) The whole of Chapters I and II were in print when news came of Sir William Ridgeway's death. A considerable part of those chapters is occupied with criticism of his views, and I had not expected that my treatment of them would pass without some rejoinder from so vigorous a controversialist. I greatly

dislike a controversy in which reply is impossible;
but my present criticism follows closely the lines of
my discussion of his book in the *Classical Review*,
shortly after its appearance, and to that he did from
time to time make some brief answers, to which
I have been careful to refer; and, on the whole, it
seemed not unfair to let the chapters go forward as
they stood. But I cannot help expressing my great
admiration for the learning and the indomitable spirit
of my antagonist, and my sense of the great loss which
his death brings to scholarship.

(2) I owe so much to the writings and the example
of Professor Gilbert Murray, that I have hesitated
long before publishing a rather lengthy criticism
(pp. 185 ff.) of a theory to which, as I know, he attaches
some importance. But I know also that no one is
more ready than he to welcome discussion, or more
generous to those who differ from him. I have
therefore given my view for what it is worth, and
I hope that any unintentional misrepresentation of
his position may be forgiven and corrected.

It may be that the readers of these Studies (if there
are any) will think that the labour expended on them
might have been more profitably laid out. I have
no quarrel with this view. The highest function of
Greek scholarship is to renew perpetually the love
and the intelligent appreciation of the greatest writers
of Greece, and towards this the present book makes
little positive contribution. But it may be pleaded
that these Studies were partly prompted by the belief
that the great dramatic poets were being set in a

wrong light by some of the theories which are here discussed, since these professed to be not merely an account of origins, but also, in some measure, an interpretation of the poems; and from this point of view these discussions may prove to be not entirely irrelevant to the right appreciation of the poems themselves; while the fact that some of the theories criticized are being actively taught in schools and colleges (as is proved by the answers offered in examinations year after year) shows that the time for the discussion of them has not gone by.

The greater part of this volume has to do with the earliest stages in the history of Greek Tragedy, Satyric Drama, and Comedy. But the discussion in regard to Tragedy necessarily involves the history of the Dithyramb, and the first chapter is an attempt to collect and discuss such information as is available upon this obscure subject. I hope that at least this may save some trouble to future students.

I had intended to offer, with these chapters, a further series of studies, partly upon matters connected with the Greek Theatre and its history, partly upon the history of Attic Comedy; but it is so uncertain when these will be completed, and indeed whether they will be completed at all, that it seems better to publish the present volume by itself.

My special thanks are due to the Trustees of the Jowett Memorial Fund, without whose help these Studies could not have been completed. I wish the work were more worthy of the Trustees' generosity.

A. W. P.-C.

CONTENTS

[1] A full analysis is given at the beginning of each chapter.

LIST OF ILLUSTRATIONS

I

THE DITHYRAMB

ANALYSIS OF CHAPTER I

I. *The Dithyramb and Dionysus* (pp. 5–14).

    1. Literary evidence of connexion with Dionysus (pp. 5–8).

    2. Evidence of the festivals at which Dithyramb was performed (pp. 8–10).

    3. Application of ' Dithyrambus' as a proper name (pp. 10, 11).

    4. Some arguments of Sir William Ridgeway (pp.12–14).

II. *The name Διθύραμβος. The Dithyramb and Phrygia* (pp. 14–18)

    1. The ancient derivation of the name (p. 14).

    2. Modern views on the derivation (pp. 14–16).

    3. Professor Calder's view.   The Dithyramb and Phrygia (pp. 16–18).

    4. Double use of the name (p. 18).

III. *The Dithyramb from Archilochus to Pindar* (pp. 18–32).

    1. Archilochus (pp. 18, 19).

    2. Arion (pp. 19–22).

    3. Lasos (pp. 22–25).

    4. Simonides (pp. 25–28).

    5. Discussion of the fragment of Pratinas (pp. 28–32).

IV. *Pindar, Bacchylides and others* (pp. 32–47).

    1. Pindar (pp. 32–39).

    2. Praxilla (p. 39).

    3. Lamprocles (pp. 39, 40).

    4. Bacchylides (pp. 40–45).

    5. Minor Composers (pp. 45–47).

V. *Dithyramb at Athens* (pp. 47–53).

    1. Summary of the early history of Dithyramb (pp. 47, 48).

    2. The dithyrambic dance (pp. 48–50).

    3. Costume of the dances (p. 50).

    4. The flute-player (p. 51).

    5. The dithyrambic contest (pp. 51–53).

CORRIGENDA

PAGE

23, last line, *after* διερριμμένοις *insert* χρησάμενος

87, line 6, *for* first *read* fifth

91, last line, *for* 28 *read* 283

92, line 12, for *Phoenissae* read *Pleuroniae*
    line 20, before (fr. 11) read *Phoenissae*

123, in quotation from Il. **xviii.** 49 ff., *for* πέλετο *read* πλῆτο

124, line 11, *for* § 14 *read* § 4

134, note 3, line 4, *for* means ' by the *read* means by ' the

142, line 1, *after* Athens *insert* along the road

145, note 2, *for* § 7 *read* § 79 ; and add *in Euerg.*, § 69.

204, lines 14 and 24, *for* Polydorus *read* Polymestor

225, line 7 of quotation, *for* κώμους *read* κώμας

229, line 20, *for* Apries *read* Osiris

236, line 19, *for* Athenians *read* Athenaeus

246, line 8 of quotation, *for* ιαππαπαῖ *read* ἱππαπαῖ

254, note 3, line 1, for *Rom.* read *Kom.*

256, line 6 from bottom, for *laena* read *lena*

284, line 7, *delete* comma *after* tradition

288, note 1, line 3, *for* 1473/2 *read* 473/2

313, line 8 from bottom, *for* (4 ll.) *read* (11 ll.)

368, line 14, *for* Epicharmus' *read* Xenophanes'

386, lines 7, 8, *delete* both of the Pygmies and

395, last line but one, *for* Πίθων *read* Πιθών or Πίθων

I

THE DITHYRAMB

The historical treatment of the dithyramb is rendered difficult by the defectiveness of our information in regard to its character before the fifth century B. C., and by the doubt which exists, whether many of the statements made by Plutarch and Athenaeus, as well as by scholiasts and *grammatici* generally, are true of the dithyramb of the first two-thirds of that century, or only of the greatly altered dithyramb which succeeded it. It is also disputed whether the most considerable of the poems which have come down to us under the name, the Dithyrambs of Bacchylides, would have been called by the name at all in his own time.

We have therefore to take the evidence piece by piece and discuss its value.

I

The Dithyramb and Dionysus.

§ 1. The earliest mention of dithyramb is found in a fragment of Archilochus of Paros, who probably flourished in the first half of the seventh century B. C.:

> ὡς Διωνύσοι᾽ ἄνακτος καλὸν ἐξάρξαι μέλος
> οἶδα διθύραμβον, οἴνῳ ξυγκεραυνωθεὶς φρένας.

Here the dithyramb is distinctly called 'the fair strain of Dionysus'. Its special connexion with Dionysus throughout its history is sufficiently attested, and would not require discussion but for the attempt made by Sir William Ridgeway to disprove it. The importance of the passage of Archilochus lies in the fact that, whereas it might be possible (though hardly plausible) to argue that later references to the connexion of the dithyramb with Dionysus were due to the

well-known performances at the Dionysiac festivals at
Athens, and that at these festivals the dithyramb was really
an alien accretion, no such suggestion can be made in regard
to the words of Archilochus; and when Sir William Ridgeway[1]
claims to explain 'why it is that the earliest dithyrambs of
which we hear were grave and solemn hymns rather than rude,
licentious vintage-songs', he is trying to explain something
which is not a fact at all; for the earliest dithyramb of
which we hear was a Dionysiac song which required plenty
of wine to make it 'go'.

Sir William Ridgeway remarks[2] that Archilochus ' does not
say that when sober he would not have sung a dithyramb in
honour of some other god or hero'. No doubt the possibility
is not logically excluded; but there is nothing in the passage
to suggest it; and his translation of the passage, 'how to
lead a fair strain in honour of Dionysus, a dithyramb' seems
much less natural (if not actually less correct) than 'how to
lead the dithyramb, the fair strain of Dionysus'.

Two other passages are worth quoting. Pindar (*Olymp.*
xiii. 18) asks

$$\tau a\grave{\iota} \ \Delta\iota\omega\nu\acute{\upsilon}\sigma o\upsilon \ \pi\acute{o}\theta\epsilon\nu \ \grave{\epsilon}\xi\acute{\epsilon}\phi a\nu\epsilon\nu$$
$$\sigma\grave{\upsilon}\nu \ \beta o\eta\lambda\acute{a}\tau a \ \chi\acute{a}\rho\iota\tau\epsilon\varsigma \ \delta\iota\theta\upsilon\rho\acute{a}\mu\beta\wp ;$$

Again Sir William Ridgeway is doubtless right in saying
that the passage does not necessarily *confine* the dithyramb
to Dionysus; but it is surely a very forced interpretation which
makes the βοηλάτης διθύραμβος a peculiar (Dionysiac) species
of an intrinsically non-Dionysiac dithyramb. It seems more
natural to take βοηλάτης here as a general epithet of
dithyramb, and the whole expression as referring to the
well-known association of the dithyramb with Dionysus.
The passage certainly gives no support to Sir William
Ridgeway's theory of the original connexion of dithyramb
with hero-worship.

As regards the exact meaning of βοηλάτης there is room
for some difference of opinion. The scholiast on Plato, *Rep.*

---

[1] *Origin of Tragedy*, p. 38.
[2] *Dramas and Dramatic Dances*, p. 45.

394 c, states that the winner of the first prize for dithyramb
received a bull; and as the statement follows the words
εὑρεθῆναι μὲν τὸν διθύραμβον ἐν Κορίνθῳ ὑπὸ Ἀρίονός
φασιν, he may, like Pindar, be referring to the Corinthian
custom. Or again, both the scholiast and Pindar may have
in mind the Athenian contest, which was well known throughout the Greek world by 464 B.C., the date of the ode, and
before which a bull was offered. Sir William Ridgeway's
explanation of the word by reference to the incidents of
a sacrifice to Dionysus by the Kynaethaeis in Arcadia[1] seems
more far-fetched; and the suggestion of Reitzenstein[2] that
Pindar's βοηλάτης is the equivalent of βουκόλος, and means
an attendant upon, or worshipper of, Dionysus, the bull-god,
hardly seems to take into account the force of ἐλαύνω, with
which βοηλάτης is connected by derivation. The word βοηλάτης seems much more appropriately used of the driving of the
bull to the altar, or the driving of it off as a prize. It has
hardly the gentle force of βουκόλος, 'tending the bull'.

The second passage is fragm. 355 of Aeschylus, which is
quoted by Plutarch[3] to illustrate the peculiar appropriateness
of dithyrambs to the worship of Dionysus, as of paeans to that
of Apollo:

μιξοβόαν πρέπει
διθύραμβον ὁμαρτεῖν
σύγκωμον Διονύσῳ.

Here the special association of the dithyramb with Dionysus
is clearly implied.

A passage in Plato's *Laws*, iii, p. 700 b, may also be quoted:
καὶ τούτῳ δὴ τὸ ἐναντίον ἦν ᾠδῆς ἕτερον εἶδος—θρήνους δέ τις
ἂν αὐτοὺς μάλιστα ἐκάλεσεν—καὶ παίωνες ἕτερον, καὶ ἄλλο,
Διονύσου γένεσις, οἶμαι, διθύραμβος λεγόμενος. The word οἶμαι
probably shows that the phrase is a playful (perhaps sceptical)
allusion to the suggested derivation of the name διθύραμβος
from the double birth of Dionysus;[4] and the passage does
not, as is often supposed, give any certain ground for think-

---

[1] Paus. VIII. xix.   [2] *Epigramm und Skolion*, p. 207.
[3] *De Ei apud Delphos*, p. 388 e.   [4] See below, p. 14.

ing that the only proper subject of dithyramb was the narrative of the birth,[1] though this was doubtless one of its common themes;[2] but it is good evidence for the connexion of the dithyramb with the god.

Two passages included among the remains of Simonides have sometimes been adduced in support of the Dionysiac character of the dithyramb, but cannot be quite safely used for this purpose. The interpretation of a phrase which occurs in one of them, fragm. 172 (Bergk, ed. iv), Διωνύσοι' ἄνακτος βουφόνον . . . θεράποντα, as = διθύραμβον is too uncertain, as the passage in which it is quoted (Athen. x, p. 456 c) shows, though the interpretation would hardly have been offered but for the special connexion of the dithyramb with Dionysus. In the other, fragm. 148, a very beautiful and instructive poem, probably not by Simonides himself, but dating from about 485 B.C., the reference is plainly to the Dionysiac festival at Athens in particular, and does not attest any general connexion. But the evidence of these passages is not required.

The specially Dionysiac character of dithyramb (despite its performance, of which more will be said later, at the festivals of certain other gods) is assumed by grammarians, scholiasts, and lexicographers;[3] but in view of the existence of better evidence, such as has been given above, there is no need to quote them at length.

§ 2. The fact, just alluded to, that the dithyramb was performed not only at the festivals of Dionysus, in Athens and elsewhere, but also on certain other occasions, is scarcely a valid obstacle to the belief in its primarily Dionysiac character.

In classical times the most important non-Dionysiac festivals of which it certainly formed a regular part were those of

---

[1] Similarly when Euripides, *Bacch.* 523 ff., in telling the story of the birth from the thigh of Zeus, makes Zeus address Dionysus as Διθύραμβε, he is doubtless alluding to the popular derivation of the word rather than to the special subject of the song.

[2] See below, p. 33, on Pindar, fr. 75.

[3] e. g. Pollux, i. 38; Proclus, *Chrest.* 344-5; Cramer, *Anecd. Ox.* iv. 314; Zenob. v. 40; Suidas, s. v. διθύραμβος, &c.

FIG. 1. KRATER AT ST. PETERSBURG

FIG. 2. KRATER IN BRITISH MUSEUM

APOLLO AND DIONYSUS AT DELPHI

Apollo. At Delphi, indeed, the regular performance of dithyrambs in winter is connected with the fact that three months of winter were there sacred to Dionysus, ᾧ τῶν Δελφῶν οὐδὲν ἧττον ἢ τῷ Ἀπόλλωνι μέτεστιν.[1] But at Delos also κύκλιοι χοροί were performed. These may have been associated, though the evidence is not very clear,[2] with the regular annual θεωρίαι, or sacred missions, from Athens. A series of inscriptions,[3] which runs from about 286 to 172 B.C., shows that during that period there were competitions between choruses of boys (i. e. probably dithyrambic choruses) at the Dionysia and Apollonia in Delos.

But the chief regular performances of dithyramb, apart from Dionysiac festivals, were those at the Thargelia at Athens. (These were given under regulations somewhat different from those in force at the Dionysia, as will be explained later.[4]) To these performances there are many references in literature and inscriptions.[5] The tripods won by the victorious poets at the Thargelia were set up in the temple of the

---

[1] Plut. *de Ei ap. Delph.*, p. 388 e, f. The view of Dr. A. B. Cook (*Zeus*, vol. ii, pp. 233–267) that Dionysus was actually anterior to, and partially displaced by, Apollo at Delphi, seems hardly to be justified by the evidence. Figs. 1 and 2 illustrate the presence of Dionysus at Delphi.

[2] Paus. IV. iv, § 1, says, Ἐπὶ δὲ Φίντα τοῦ Συβότα [i. e. in the eighth century B.C.] πρῶτον Μεσσήνιοι τότε τῷ Ἀπόλλωνι εἰς Δῆλον θυσίαν καὶ ἀνδρῶν χορὸν ἀποστέλλουσι, but he calls the song which Eumelus wrote for this chorus an ἆσμα προσόδιον, so that it may not have been strictly a dithyramb. Thucyd. iii. 104, records the re-institution in 426/5 B.C. of the traditional practice of sending choruses from Athens and the islands to compete at Delos, but does not mention dithyrambs by name. Strabo, xv, p. 728, refers to the Delian dithyrambs of Simonides (see below, p. 27) but does not mention such θεωρίαι expressly. Callimachus, *Hymn to Delos*, 300 ff., connects the κύκλιοι χοροί at Delos with the Athenian θεωρίαι. (He associates them with the music of the cithara, instead of the flute, by which dithyrambs were normally accompanied; but the cithara had come into occasional use for this purpose by the third century B.C., and the Delian performances of this date may have differed in some ways from those of the classical period.)

[3] Collected by Brinck, *Diss. Philol. Halenses*, vii, pp. 187 ff.

[4] See below, pp. 52, 53.

[5] e. g. Antiphon, περὶ τοῦ χορευτοῦ § 11 ; Lysias, xxi, §§ 1, 2 ; Aristot. *Ath. Pol.* 56, § 3 ; Suidas, s. v. Πύθιον; *C. I. A.* ii. 553, 1236, 1251, &c.

Pythian Apollo, erected by Peisistratus, to whom the development of the Thargelia as a popular festival may possibly have been due.

The performance of dithyrambs at Apolline festivals may perhaps be accounted for by the close association of Dionysus with Apollo at Delphi, and the interest shown by the Delphian oracle in propagating the cult of Dionysus in Greece; once established at Delphi, the dithyramb would naturally be adopted in the worship of Apollo elsewhere. But it may partly have been a natural result of the desire to enhance the attractiveness of popular festivals, by adding performances which appealed to the people, even if they were originally appropriated to other celebrations. This may account also for the isolated mentions of dithyrambs at the Lesser Panathenaea,[1] and at the Prometheia and Hephaesteia,[2] evidently as a regular part of the festival and provided by χορηγοί.

Plutarch (or a pseudo-Plutarch)[3] records the institution by Lycurgus, late in the fourth century B.C., of a festival in honour of Poseidon at the Peiraeus, including an ἀγὼν κυκλίων χορῶν οὐκ ἔλαττον τριῶν. An inscription,[4] dated A.D. 52/3, may possibly indicate the performance of a dithyramb to Asclepius at Athens in that year, though this interpretation is not certain.[5] But the essentially Dionysiac character of the dithyramb, down to a late date, is confirmed by the strong contrasts which are drawn between it and the Apolline paean, —the 'enthusiastic' nature of the words, rhythms, and music of the one, and the sobriety of the other.[6]

§ 3. When we examine the uses of the word Διθύραμβος as a proper name, we obtain strong confirmation of the primarily Dionysiac character of the dithyramb. The name is used of Dionysus[7] alone of the gods—with one exception. For

---

[1] Lysias, l. c.   [2] C. I. A. 553, later than 403/2 B. C.

[3] Vit. X. Orat., p. 842 a.   [4] C. I. A. iii. 68 b.

[5] See below, p. 79. The attempt of Brinck (Diss. Hal. vii, pp. 85, 177) to refer the words of the inscription to gymnastic contests is very unconvincing.

[6] Plut. de Ei, l. c.; Proclus, l. c.; Suidas, s. v. διθύραμβος; Athen. xiv, p. 628 a, b, &c.

[7] e. g. Eur. Bacchae, 527; the Delphic Paean to Dionysus; Hephae-

Athenaeus[1] tells us that at Lampsacus the names Θρίαμβος and Διθύραμβος were given to Priapus. But why? Because Priapus was there identified with Dionysus (τιμᾶται δὲ παρὰ Λαμψακηνοῖς ὁ Πρίηπος, ὁ αὐτὸς ὢν τῷ Διονύσῳ, ἐξ ἐπιθέτου καλούμενος οὗτος, ὡς Θρίαμβος καὶ Διθύραμβος).

The name (in the form ΔΙΘΥΡΑΜΦΟΣ) occurs as that of a Silenus, who is playing the lyre, on an Attic vase[2] of good red-figured style; but the Silenus is leading a Dionysiac κῶμος, and doubtless takes his name from the Dionysiac revel-song,

FIG. 3.   Silenus named Διθύραμβος.

as (on other vases) female attendants on the god are called Τραγῳδία or Κωμῳδία. The fact that (according to Herodotus)[3] the most famous of the men of Thespiae who fell at Thermopylae was Διθύραμβος Ἁρματίδεω is curious, but does not bear on our present point.

stion, περὶ ποιήμ. vii, p. 70 (Consbr.); *Etym. Magn.* 274. 44.   Θρίαμβος is used of Dionysus in Fragm. Lyr. Adesp. 109 (Bergk) Ἴακχε Θρίαμβε, σὺ τούτων χοραγέ. Compare also Pratinas, fragm. 1, Θρίαμβε Διθύραμβε κισσόχαιτ' ἄναξ; Arrian, *Anab.* vi. 28; Plut. *Vit. Marcell.* 22; Athen. xi, p. 465 a (quoting Phanodemus of the fourth century B. C.).

[1] i, p. 30 b.

[2] Fig. 3. See Heydemann, *Satyr- u. Bakchen-namen*, pp. 21, 36; Fränkel, *Satyr- u. Bakchen-namen*, pp. 69, 94.   See below, pp. 50, 150.

[3] vii. 227.

§ 4. Thus, on a general review of the evidence, it appears that the balance of probability is against Sir William Ridgeway's theory that 'at no time was the dithyramb any more the exclusive property of Dionysus than the paean was that of Apollo';[1] in fact the dithyramb, though freely transferred to festivals of other gods, and especially to those of Apollo, was primarily and continuously regarded as Dionysiac.

The fact, of which Sir William Ridgeway makes a good deal, that many dithyrambs about which we have information dealt with hero-stories, does not in any way disprove this. If his belief[2] that these dithyrambs (or any of them) were *addressed to* heroes had any foundation, it might help him; but it has none. There is no evidence whatever that dithyrambs were ever performed as part of the worship of heroes,[3] though they often dealt with their stories, when performed in the festivals of Dionysus and (secondarily) of other gods such as Apollo. There is nothing in this to disprove their Dionysiac character: the themes of the dithyramb, as of other literary forms, were doubtless extended in range as time went on; but it began in Greece, so far as our evidence goes, as a revel song after wine, not as funereal or commemorative of the dead. If at any time it had funereal associations, it was in a pre-Hellenic stage of its development[4]; there is absolutely no trace of such associations in Greece.

But, Sir William Ridgeway argues,[5] 'even if it were true that tragedy proper arose out of the worship of Dionysus, it would no less have originated in the worship of the dead, since Dionysus was regarded by the Greeks as a hero (i.e. a man turned into a saint) as well as a god'; and he appears to imply[6]

---

[1] Sir William Ridgeway thinks that the paean was not specially associated with Apollo ; with regard to this also, the facts seem to be against him : but this is not the place to argue the point.

[2] *Dramas and Dram. dances*, p. 216.

[3] Asclepius (see pp. 10, 79) was frequently regarded as a god.

[4] This would be the case if Professor Calder's theory (see below, p. 16) were true.

[5] *Dramas*, &c., pp. 5, 6. The argument mentions Tragedy, but is obviously intended to apply also to the Dithyramb, out of which Tragedy was supposed to have sprung.   [6] Ibid., p. 47.

that if dithyramb included Dionysus among its themes it was because he was a hero. The arguments which he uses to support this view consist of (1) the fact that Dionysus had an oracle among the Bessi on Mt. Pangaeum [1] 'as had the old heroes Trophonius and Amphiaraus at Lebadea and Oropus respectively'. But gods also had oracles. (2) Two passages of Plutarch. The first of these (*Quaest. Graec.* ch. 36) contains the invocation of the women of Elis, which, as given in the MSS., reads:

ἐλθεῖν ἥρω Διόνυσ'
Ἀλείων ἐς ναὸν
ἁγνὸν σὺν χαρίτεσσιν,
ἐς ναὸν τῷ βοείῳ ποδὶ θυών,
ἄξιε ταῦρε, ἄξιε ταῦρε.

But most scholars agree that there is no vocative form ἥρω, and though Dr. A. B. Cook's emendation ἧρ' ὦ (i.e. ἧρι with the -ι elided) is not easy to accept, the passage is probably corrupt and is certainly not one to build upon.[2]

In the other passage (*De Iside et Osiride*, ch. 35) Plutarch is trying to prove the identity of Osiris and Dionysus,[3] and writes: ὁμολογεῖ δὲ καὶ τὰ Τιτανικὰ καὶ Νυκτέλια τοῖς λεγομένοις Ὀσίριδος διασπασμοῖς καὶ ταῖς ἀναβιώσεσι καὶ παλιγγενεσίαις· ὁμοίως δὲ καὶ περὶ τὰς ταφάς. Αἰγύπτιοί τε γὰρ Ὀσίριδος πολλαχοῦ θήκας, ὥσπερ εἴρηται, δεικνύουσι, καὶ Δελφοὶ τὰ τοῦ Διονύσου λείψανα παρ' αὐτοῖς παρὰ τὸ χρηστήριον ἀποκεῖσθαι νομίζουσι· καὶ θύουσιν οἱ Ὅσιοι θυσίαν ἀπόρρητον ἐν τῷ ἱερῷ τοῦ Ἀπόλλωνος ὅταν αἱ Θυιάδες ἐγείρωσι τὸν Λικνίτην. But this gives no ground for thinking that Dionysus, though treated in certain cults as a chthonic power or a vegetation-god who

[1] See below, p. 184.

[2] Even if we read ἥρω (or ἥρως, which is a possible emendation), the word need not mean a 'hero' in Sir W. Ridgeway's sense. It might be simply an honorific title, as in Homer: and in fact we know from Paus. VI. xxvi, § 1 that the people of Elis worshipped Dionysus as a God—θεῶν δὲ ἐν τοῖς μάλιστα Διόνυσον σέβουσιν Ἠλεῖοι. The view of S. Wide (*Archiv. Rel.* 1907, pp. 262 ff.), that ἥρως means a chthonic power generally is hardly tenable. (See Farnell, *Greek Hero-cults*, pp. 15, 16.) I see that in *Zeus*, vol. ii, p. 823, Dr. Cook abandons his proposal.

[3] On the identification of Osiris and Dionysus, see below, p. 207.

died and lived again, was ever regarded as a ' hero ', in the sense
of a man turned into a saint. Crusius [1] and Rohde [2] notice that
a feast in which the Dionysiac Θυιάδες took part was named
ἡρωίς, and that Hesychius has the two glosses : 'Ηρόχια· τὰ
Θεοδαίσια, and Θεοδαίσιος· ὁ Διόνυσος. But these facts do
not prove that Dionysus was ever thonght of as a 'hero', though
they illustrate his connexion, in certain cults, with the world
of the dead. The ἡρωίς was probably in some respects (as
Rohde's note suggests) parallel to the Anthesteria, in which
Dionysus was connected with a chthonic cult; but its ' special
subject ', as we learn from Plutarch,[3] was Σεμέλης ἀναγωγή,
and the ' heroine ' was Semele.[4]

II

The name Διθύραμβος.   The Dithyramb and Phrygia.

§ 1. The attempts to throw light upon the original
character of the dithyramb by reference to the derivation of
the name have so far led to no satisfactory results. It is
generally recognized that the derivation which was evidently
the popular one in antiquity,[5] and which made διθύραμβος the
song of the god who, having been born a second time, came
' through two doors ', is philologically impossible, though it is
evidence of the association of both name and song with Dionysus. The same difficulty attaches to the other derivations
which interpret δῑ- as ' double ', e. g. those which refer to the
double flute, or that given in the *Etymologicum Magnum* ὅτι
ἐν διθύρῳ ἄντρῳ τῆς Νύσης ἐτράφη.

§ 2. If we pass over various fantastic suggestions made in
antiquity, we find that most scholars agree in connecting
διθύραμβος, θρίαμβος, and *triump(h)us*. (The meaning of
διθύραμβος and θρίαμβος, whether in application to the song

---

[1] Pauly-Wissowa, *Real-Enc.* v. 1212.   [2] *Psyche*, ii, p. 45.

[3] *Quaest. Graec.*, ch. 12 (p. 293 c) : see Nilsson, *Gr. Fest.*, pp. 286 ff.

[4] A more recent attempt of Sir William Ridgeway to make Dionysus
out a hero is discussed later (ch. ii, pp. 182 ff.).

[5] It is implied in Eur. *Bacch.* 523 ff., and is given by many *grammatici*,
&c.

or the god, is identical.) [1] Probably the syllable -αμβ- in
these words should be considered along with the same syllable
in ἴθυμβος, ἴαμβος, and perhaps Κάσαμβος (Herod. vi.
73), Λυκάμβης (Archilochus, &c.), Σάραμβος (Plat. *Gorg.*
518 b), Σήραμβος (Paus. vi. x, § 9), Ὀπισάμβω (Soph. fr. 406,
Pearson).[2] In these the syllable may well mean 'step' or
' movement', and if θρίαμβος, as is possible, means the 'three-
step' dance (cf. *tripudium*), δι-θύραμβος may be a modified
form of δι-θρίαμβος, the δι- denoting connexion with a god.
Similarly ἴθυμβος will be the 'forward-step'; Λυκάμβης the
man with the wolf's gait: ἴαμβος possibly the 'two-step'.[3]

The association of a ' three-step' movement with dithyramb
is only a matter of conjecture ; but this conjecture seems to be
easier than that of Dr. A. B. Cook [4] that the word is connected with the root θορ-, ' leap' and so ' beget', and that the
' dithyramb was properly the song commemorating the union
of Zeus with Semele, and the begetting of their child Dionysus'.
The ancients seem to have regarded the dithyramb as commemorating the birth, rather than the begetting, of the god,
and it is not really certain whether even this was at first its
special or only theme. Miss Harrison's interpretation of
Διθύραμβος as ' the song that makes Zeus leap or beget' has
even less probability, philological or historical. There is

---

[1] For the god, see above, p. 10. For the song, cf. Cratinus fr. 36 (*ap.*
Suid. s. v. ἀναρύτειν) ὅτε σὺ τοὺς καλοὺς θριάμβους ἀναρύτουσ' ἀπηχθάνου :
where the reference is probably to Cratinus' introduction of a dithyramb
at the beginning of his Βουκόλοι, and the words were probably addressed
to the poet's Muse. (I cannot agree with Miss Harrison, Proleg. p. 444,
that there is a special significance in the utterance of the θρίαμβοι by
a female figure.)

[2] Cf. also σαλάμβη, χηράμβη, &c. But all these words require further
investigation.

[3] I owe this suggestion to Professor J. A. Smith, who thinks that the
ἴ of ἴαμβος may be a form of ϝι = *bis*. Ἴαμβος appears, not only in its
well-known sense, but also in a fragment of Arctinus' Ἰλίου Πέρσις as the
proper name of a warrior, and Hesychius cites it as ὄνομα πόλεως περὶ
Τροίαν. The Schol. on Nicand. *Ther.* 484 (Keil's ed. p. 39) gives Ἄμβας
as the name of a son of Metaneira. In view of the connexion of Ἰάμβη
with Metaneira, it is tempting to emend to Ἰάμβας.

[4] *Zeus*, vol. i, pp. 681-2 ; cf. J. E. Harrison, *Themis*, p. 204.

no suggestion of any such purpose or magical significance about any dithyramb of which any record is preserved.[1] Miss Harrison writes, indeed, much about the ritual of the dithyramb; but it can hardly have escaped the notice of attentive readers that there is absolutely no record of any such ritual as she imagines, and that the only dithyrambic ritual known in actual records is the cyclic dance of fifty performers at Athens and elsewhere. (Her idea that there was a ritual of group-initiation lying behind the story of the double-birth of Dionysus, which is supposed to be the special subject of dithyramb, seems also to be entirely unsupported by actual evidence,[2] and Sir William Ridgeway's reply [3] to her on this point appears to be quite satisfactory.)

It may be added that the derivation from the root θορ- throws no light on θρίαμβος.

§ 3. An entirely new theory of the derivation of the name has been given by Professor W. M. Calder.[4] He has found a Phrygian word δίθρερα or δίθρεψα, which is interpreted to mean a tomb with double-doors; and he suggests that this, combined with the termination -αμβος (possibly, like -υνθος and others, an Anatolian termination), passed into Greek as διθύραμβος, and meant a dirge or grave-song. (He takes -ambos to mean primarily 'god', but it would make little difference to the theory if it meant 'step' or 'dance'.) His view is that the cult of Dionysus, originally an Anatolian deity associated with graves, passed into Greece by various

---

[1] The only passage which could suggest that dithyramb had a magical value is very late—Proclus, *Chrest.* xiv, where it is described as εἰς παραίτησιν κακῶν γεγραμμένος. But, after all, prayer is not magic; nor is the revel-song after drinking, and Proclus himself says that the dithyramb arose ἀπὸ τῆς κατὰ τοὺς ἀγροὺς παιδιᾶς καὶ τῆς ἐν τοῖς πότοις εὐφροσύνης. Further, the text is very uncertain, and some scholars take the words εἰς παραίτησιν κακῶν γεγραμμένος as referring to the Paean, of which they are strictly true. (See Crusius, in Pauly-W. *Real-Enc.* v, 1207.)

[2] The same must be said of the similar theory of Dr. E. Rostrup (*Attic Drama in the light of Theatrical History*).

[3] *Dramas*, &c., pp. 43-4.

[4] *Class. Rev.* xxxvi (1922), pp. 11 ff. He has been kind enough to amplify his theory in a letter to me.

routes—into Crete, where it gave rise to the cult of Zagreus; across the Aegean by the islands (Lesbos, Paros, Naxos); and into Thrace, where the chthonic elements in the cult remained important; and that it was thus (probably by the island-route) that the dithyramb came to Greece.

The theory is in accordance with the fact that the musical mode specially employed in dithyramb was the Phrygian. There was a tradition that the Phrygian and Lydian ἁρμονίαι came to Greece with Pelops from Asia Minor; Athenaeus,[1] who records the tradition, quotes a fragment of Telestes of Selinus (circ. 400 B.C.) as follows:

> πρῶτοι παρὰ κρατῆρας Ἑλλάνων ἐν αὐλοῖς
> συνοπαδοὶ Πέλοπος ματρὸς ὀρείας
> Φρύγιον ἄεισαν νόμον
> τοὶ δ' ὀξυφώνοις πηκτίδων ψαλμοῖς κρέκον
> Λύδιον ὕμνον.

But no further details are traceable, and the historical basis of the legend of Pelops [2] is not sufficiently certain to admit any safe conjectures as to the value of the tradition. All that can be said is that if this type of hymn and music was originally Phrygian, it is easy to understand its finding its way to Paros and Naxos, and that as Dionysus, in whose worship it was performed, was certainly a god of the Thraco-Phrygian tribes, the tradition is quite likely to have a basis of truth.

But though Professor Calder's theory thus gains somewhat in probability, the difficulties in the way of it are still considerable, for

(1) The evidence for the meaning assigned to the Phrygian

---

[1] xiv, p. 626 a.

[2] Pelops is sometimes in legend a Phrygian, sometimes a Lydian, but more often the former than the latter. He is Phrygian in Herod. VII. viii, Bacchyl. vii. 53, and Soph. *Ai.* 1292; Lydian in Pindar, *Olymp.* i. 24; ix. 9: cf. a very interesting note by Professor Gilbert Murray, *The Rise of the Greek Epic*[3], p. 48. Gruppe (*Gr. Myth.* i. 653) thinks that the legend of Tantalus and Pelops was originally Greek, and was transported to Asia Minor with the Ionian migration: but this seems to be very uncertain, and hardly affects the point in regard to the origin of the dithyramb and the Phrygian ἁρμονία.

C

word is not very complete. The word is only proved to mean a 'monument or some sepulchral attribute or characteristic'; the interpretation as 'a tomb with two doors' rests on the analogy of some other forms in which Phrygian inserted a *ρ̃*.

(2) There is no independent evidence of any connexion of the dithyramb with tombs; and though cults do change remarkably when transplanted, it is hard to see how such a dirge can have been transformed into the riotous song of Archilochus. Herodotus[1] does indeed mention a Thracian tribe which celebrated the death of any of its members with rejoicings; but this is too remote from Archilochus' drinking-bouts to help us much. At present, therefore, it only seems possible to suspend judgement and hope for further evidence.

§4. The double use of the name, for a song and for the god himself, has given rise (as has the double use of the name 'Paean') to the question which use has the priority. Those who derived the name from the supposed circumstances of the birth of the god, evidently regarded it as primarily the name of the god, afterwards transferred to the song in his honour. (They would doubtless have held the same view in regard to the Linos-song.) If, on the other hand, the word includes a root meaning 'step' or 'movement', it must first have been the name of the song. It would, however, take us too far to discuss the view of those scholars who think that the idea of the god grew out of the emotional experience of the Bacchic revellers at the time when dithyramb was a revel-song and dance, and that they so named the power which they felt to be in and among them. There are grave difficulties in this view, and at best it can be no more than a conjecture.

III

From Archilochus to Pindar.

§1. We may now return to the fragment of ARCHILOCHUS. The lines appear to imply a revel-song led off by one of a band of revellers, and they tell us no more. They do not suggest

---

[1] v. iv. The tribe was that of Γέται οἱ ἀθανατίζοντες.

a literary composition, but rather the singing or shouting of
some well-known traditional words, or perhaps some improvisation by the ἐξάρχων, with a traditional refrain in which the
band of revellers joins, as the mourners join in the θρῆνος in
the last book of the *Iliad* :[1]

$$\pi\alpha\rho\grave{\alpha} \; \delta^{\prime} \; \epsilon\hat{\iota}\sigma\alpha\nu \; \mathring{\alpha}o\iota\delta o\grave{\upsilon}s$$
$$\theta\rho\acute{\eta}\nu\omega\nu \; \mathring{\epsilon}\xi\acute{\alpha}\rho\chi o\upsilon s, \; o\tilde{\iota} \; \tau\epsilon \; \sigma\tau o\nu o\acute{\epsilon}\sigma\sigma\alpha\nu \; \mathring{\alpha}o\iota\delta\grave{\eta}\nu$$
$$o\mathring{\iota} \; \mu\grave{\epsilon}\nu \; \mathring{\alpha}\rho^{\prime} \; \mathring{\epsilon}\theta\rho\acute{\eta}\nu\epsilon o\nu, \; \mathring{\epsilon}\pi\grave{\iota} \; \delta\grave{\epsilon} \; \sigma\tau\epsilon\nu\acute{\alpha}\chi o\nu\tau o \; \gamma\upsilon\nu\alpha\hat{\iota}\kappa\epsilon s.$$

Athenaeus quotes the lines of Archilochus in proof of the
connexion of the dithyramb with οἶνος and μέθη,[2] and adds
a line from the *Philoctetes* of Epicharmus (fr. 132).

$$o\mathring{\upsilon}\kappa \; \mathring{\epsilon}\sigma\tau\iota \; \delta\iota\theta\acute{\upsilon}\rho\alpha\mu\beta os \; \mathring{o}\kappa\chi^{\prime} \; \mathring{\upsilon}\delta\omega\rho \; \pi\acute{\iota}\eta s,$$

which at any rate shows that the drunken dithyramb persisted
for a century and half or so after Archilochus.[3] It may have
been some such dithyramb that Cratinus introduced at the
beginning of his Βουκόλοι (a play on a Dionysiac subject).[4]

§2. But the dithyramb as a literary composition was, so
far as our evidence goes, the creation of ARION, who lived at
Corinth during the reign of Periander (about 625–585 B. C.).
For we need hardly consider seriously the question mentioned
by Pseudo-Plut. *de Mus.*, ch. x, p. 1143 e whether the Paeans of
Xenocritus (or Xenocrates) of Locri Epizephyrii, a poet older
than Stesichorus, may not really have been dithyrambs,
because they dealt with heroic themes. The question appears
to imply a later conception of dithyramb than can be ascribed

---

[1] i. e. xxiv. 720.   See also below, pp. 123 ff.

[2] Athen. xiv, p. 628 a.   He has just cited a statement of Philochorus
ὡς οἱ παλαιοὶ οὐκ ἀεὶ διθυραμβοῦσιν, ἀλλ᾽ ὅταν σπένδωσι, τὸν μὲν Διόνυσον ἐν
οἴνῳ καὶ μέθῃ, τὸν δὲ Ἀπόλλωνα μεθ᾽ ἡσυχίας καὶ τάξεως μέλποντες.

[3] There seems to be no justification for the statement of Wilamowitz
(*Einl. in die Trag.*, p. 63) that the dithyramb of Archilochus and
Epicharmus was a solo. Ἐξάρξαι implies a chorus or band of revellers
who at least join in the singing.

[4] Hesych. s. v. πῦρ παρέγχει· Κρατῖνος ἀπὸ διθυράμβου ἐν Βουκόλοις ἀρχό
μενος: cf. Cratin. fr. 36 (K.), ὅτε σὺ τοὺς καλοὺς θριάμβους ἀναρύτουσ᾽ ἀπηχθάνου.
The fact that Ecphantides used the address Εὔιε κισσόχαιτ᾽ ἄναξ, χαῖρε is
not enough (as some have supposed) to show that he also introduced
a dithyramb into Comedy.

to the seventh century.¹ Nor does any ancient writer ascribe
dithyrambs to Stesichorus, who lived (approximately) between
640 and 560 B. C., though he wrote largely on heroic themes.²
In fact his poems seem to have been accompanied by the
cithara, not, like the early dithyrambs, by the flute.³ To infer
from the fragment of the Oresteia,⁴

$$\tau \acute{a}\delta\epsilon \ \chi\rho\grave{\eta} \ X\alpha\rho\acute{\iota}\tau\omega\nu \ \delta\alpha\mu\acute{\omega}\mu o\tau\alpha \ \kappa\alpha\lambda\lambda\iota\chi\acute{o}\rho\omega\nu \ \acute{v}\mu\nu\epsilon\hat{\iota}\nu$$
$$\Phi\rho\acute{v}\gamma\iota o\nu \ \mu\acute{\epsilon}\lambda o s \ \acute{\epsilon}\xi\epsilon\upsilon\rho\acute{o}\nu\tau\alpha s \ \acute{a}\beta\rho\hat{\omega}s \ \mathring{\eta}\rho o s \ \acute{\epsilon}\pi\epsilon\rho\chi o\mu\acute{\epsilon}\nu o\iota o,$$

that the poems of Stesichorus generally were performed in
spring and to Phrygian music (like the dithyramb) would be
to generalize far too boldly from an isolated quotation.

With regard to Arion there are great difficulties which will
best be discussed in connexion with Tragedy.⁵ But the words in
our authorities which refer beyond question to dithyramb are
capable of a fairly certain interpretation. Herodotus,⁶ who
is, no doubt, the source from which Suidas and others drew,
speaks of Arion as διθύραμβον πρῶτον ἀνθρώπων τῶν ἡμεῖς
ἴδμεν ποιήσαντά τε καὶ ὀνομάσαντα καὶ διδάξαντα ἐν Κορίνθῳ—
a statement which Suidas reproduces in the words καὶ πρῶτος
χορὸν στῆσαι (sc. λέγεται) καὶ διθύραμβον ᾆσαι καὶ ὀνομάσαι
τὸ ᾀδόμενον ὑπὸ τοῦ χοροῦ. Arion, that is, first produced
a chorus which kept to a definite spot (e.g. a circle round
an altar) instead of wandering like revellers at random ;
and he made their song a regular poem, with a definite
subject from which it took its name. The words need

¹ The writer of the de Mus. does not say who raised the question.
After quoting the account given of Thaletas by Glaucus of Rhegium,
who wrote περὶ τῶν ἀρχαίων ποιητῶν about the end of the fifth, or begin-
ing of the fourth, century B. C., he continues : καὶ περὶ Ξενοκρίτου δέ, ὃς ἦν
τὸ γένος ἐκ Λοκρῶν τῶν ἐν Ἰταλίᾳ, ἀμφισβητεῖται εἰ παιάνων ποιήτης γέγονεν.
ἡρωικῶν γὰρ ὑποθέσεων †πράγματα ἐχουσῶν ποιητὴν γεγονέναι φασὶν αὐτόν.
διὸ καί τινας διθυράμβους καλεῖν αὐτοῦ τὰς ποιήσεις. πρεσβύτερον δὲ τῇ ἡλικίᾳ
φησὶν ὁ Γλαῦκος Θαλήταν Ξενοκρίτου γενέσθαι. The remarks about Xenocritus
are plainly a parenthesis, derived from an unspecified source, and
inserted by the writer in his summary of Glaucus' account of Thaletas.
² See Vürtheim, Stesichoros Fragmente u. Biographie, pp. 103-5.
³ Suid. (s. v.) ἐκλήθη δὲ Στησίχορος ὅτι πρῶτος κιθαρῳδίᾳ χορὸν ἔστησεν,
and Quintil. x. 1, § 62 'epici carminis onera lyra sustinentem '.
⁴ Fr. 37 (Bergk⁴), 14 (Diehl).   ⁵ See below, pp. 131 ff.   ⁶ i. 23.

not mean, as Sir William Ridgeway assumes, that he first
gave the name 'dithyramb' to a performance: that would
be obviously false, since Archilochus did this long before, and
Herodotus is likely to have known this; Archilochus was a well-
known author at least to the Athenians of the fifth century.
They mean that he first gave his dithyrambs names, as
dealing with definite subjects. We shall shortly find the
great dithyrambic writers similarly naming their poems—
'Memnon', Θρασὺς Ἡρακλῆς, Ἠΐθεοι ἢ Θησεύς, &c.,—and
Arion, we must suppose, was the first to do this.

Pindar's allusion,[1] already quoted, to the creation of the
literary dithyramb at Corinth shows that it was still performed as part of the worship of Dionysus.

The words in Suidas' notice which precede those quoted
above, viz. λέγεται καὶ τραγικοῦ τρόπου εὑρέτης γενέσθαι,
probably do not refer to dithyramb at all, but to the invention by Arion of the musical τρόπος which was afterwards
appropriated by tragedy. Aristides Quintilianus [2] expressly
distinguishes the διθυραμβικὸς τρόπος from the τραγικός and
the νομικός, and it is doubtful whether the Phrygian ἁρμονία
was regularly employed for the τραγικὸς τρόπος. (Cf. Pseudo-
Plut. *de Mus.* xvii, ἀλλὰ μὴν [sc. οὐκ ἠγνόει Πλάτων] καὶ ὅτι
προσόδια καὶ παιᾶνες, καὶ μέντοι ὅτι καὶ τραγικοὶ οἶκτοί ποτε
ἐπὶ τοῦ Δωρίου τρόπου ἐμελῳδήθησαν καί τινα ἐρωτικά.) The
words which follow the statement about the dithyramb in
Suidas' notice, viz. καὶ Σατύρους εἰσενεγκεῖν ἔμμετρα λέγοντας, will also be shown, in a later chapter, to have, in all
probability, no reference to dithyramb.

The scholiast on Pindar, *Olymp.* xiii. 19 explains Pindar's
words as referring to Arion;[3] but he, or another, writing on
l. 25 of the same ode, is not unnaturally perturbed by the fact

---

[1] *Olymp.* xiii. 18: see above, p. 6.

[2] p. 29: ὁ μὲν οὖν νομικὸς τρόπος ἐστὶ νητοειδής, ὁ δὲ διθύραμβος μεσοειδής,
ὁ δὲ τραγικὸς ὑπατοειδής.

[3] ἢ οὕτως ἀκουστέον· αἱ τῶν Διονύσου διθυράμβων ἐν Κορίνθῳ ἐφάνησαν
χάριτες, τουτέστι τὸ σπουδαιότατον τῶν Διονύσου διθυράμβων ἐν Κορίνθῳ πρῶτον
ἐφάνη· ἐκεῖ γὰρ ὡράθη ὁ χορὸς ὀρχούμενος· ἔστησε δὲ αὐτὸν πρῶτος Ἀρίων ὁ
Μηθυμναῖος, εἶτα Λᾶσος ὁ Ἑρμιονεύς. (Of course this scholium has no independent value.)

that in other places Pindar spoke of Naxos or of Thebes as the
scene of the invention of dithyramb. Pindar had doubtless
many patrons to please, and these places may well have been
early homes of the dithyramb, perhaps in its pre-literary
forms. But the tradition recorded by Herodotus, even though
he writes 150 years after the event, strongly supports the claim
of Corinth and of Arion to have converted the dithyramb into
a form of poetry. It is of some importance also that Proclus
found the same tradition in Aristotle; [1] and on the whole it
may be accepted with very fair confidence.

§ 3. Although Arion himself came from Methymna in Lesbos,
his choruses must have been composed of the inhabitants of
Dorian Corinth.[2] At a rather later date (in the time of
Polycrates, i. e. shortly after the middle of the sixth century)
we are told by Herodotus [3] that the people of Argos, which
was also Dorian, ἤκουον μουσικὴν εἶναι Ἑλλήνων πρῶτοι.
Whether Lasos of Hermione in Argolis was or was not of
Dorian stock is unknown. The people of Hermione,
Herodotus [4] informs us, were not Dorians by origin, but
Dryopes; how far they kept themselves apart from their
Dorian neighbours we cannot tell. In any case it is to Lasos
that the next important step in the history of the dithyramb
appears to have been due, though the notices in regard to
him are very unsatisfactory.

He was born, according to Suidas, in the fifty-eighth
Olympiad (548–5 B. C.). His wit and wisdom do not here
concern us; [5] but there are two things which seem to have been

---

[1] Cf. Proclus, *Chrest*. xii εὑρεθῆναι δὲ τὸν διθύραμβον Πίνδαρος ἐν Κορίνθῳ
λέγει· τὸν δὲ ἀρξάμενον τῆς ᾠδῆς Ἀριστοτέλης Ἀρίονα λέγει· ὃς πρῶτος τὸν
κύκλιον ἤγαγε χορόν. The proposal by Val. Rose (*Aristoteles pseudepigraphus*,
pp. 615 ff.) to substitute Ἀριστοκλῆς (latter half of second century B. C.) for
Ἀριστοτέλης in this and other passages is sufficiently answered by Bapp,
Leipz. Studien, viii (1885), pp. 95–6, who shows that the substitution is
only justified in certain special cases.

[2] Wilamowitz, *Einl. in die gr. Trag.*, p. 63, notes that the population
of Methymna itself, as is shown by inscriptions, was not wholly Aeolic.

[3] iii. 131.   [4] viii. 43.

[5] See Diog. L. I. i. 14; Stob. *Flor.* 29, 70 (Gaisf.); Hesych. s. v. λασί-
σματα, &c.

definitely associated with his name—the institution of dithyrambic contests at Athens, and some elaboration of the rhythms and the range of notes employed in the music of the dithyramb.

As to the former, Lasos was at Athens in the time of Hipparchus, son of Peisistratus, and detected the attempt of Onomacritus to insert forged verses among the oracles of Musaeus.[1] Suidas, as we read the notice in the MSS., says of him that διθύραμβον εἰς ἀγῶνα εἰσήγαγε, though it is difficult not to be attracted by Professor Garrod's brilliant emendation [2] (in view of a passage of Pseudo-Plutarch, quoted below) διθυραμβώδεις ἀγωγὰς εἰσήγαγεν. There is, however, a further hint of Lasos' connexion with dithyrambic competitions in Aristophanes (*Wasps*, 1409–11), where a reminiscence may be preserved of an actual contest between Lasos and Simonides:

> μὰ Δί', ἀλλ' ἄκουσον ἤν τί σοι δόξω λέγειν.
> Λᾶσός ποτ' ἀντεδίδασκε, καὶ Σιμωνίδης·
> ἔπειθ' ὁ Λᾶσος εἶπεν, "ὀλίγον μοι μέλει."

Lasos may therefore have helped to introduce dithyrambic contests under the tyrants, and this may have led some writers wrongly to ascribe the invention of κύκλιοι χοροί to him (e. g. Schol. on Aristoph. *Birds*, 1403, Ἀντίπατρος δὲ καὶ Εὐφρόνιος ἐν τοῖς ὑπομνήμασί φασι τοὺς κυκλίους χοροὺς στῆσαι πρῶτον Λᾶσον τὸν Ἑρμιονέα, οἱ δὲ ἀρχαιότεροι, Ἑλλάνικος καὶ Δικαίαρχος, Ἀρίονα τὸν Μηθυμναῖον, Δικαίαρχος μὲν ἐν τῷ περὶ Διονυσιακῶν ἀγώνων, Ἑλλάνικος δὲ ἐν τοῖς Καρνεονίκαις [3]).

With regard to the musical innovations made by Lasos, the Pseudo-Plutarch [4] writes as follows: Λᾶσος δ' ὁ Ἑρμιονεὺς εἰς τὴν διθυραμβικὴν ἀγωγὴν μεταστήσας τοὺς ῥυθμοὺς καὶ τῇ τῶν αὐλῶν πολυφωνίᾳ κατακολουθήσας πλείοσί τε φθόγγοις καὶ διερριμμένοις εἰς μετάθεσιν τὴν προϋπάρχουσαν ἤγαγε

---

[1] Herod. vii. 6.   [2] *Class. Rev.* xxxiv, p. 136.

[3] This emendation for Κραναϊκοῖς may be regarded as certain. Hellanicus seems to have written in the latter part of the fifth century; Dicaearchus lived circ. 347-287 B.C., Euphronios in the third century B.C.; Antipatros is unknown.

[4] *De Mus.* xxix, p. 1141 b, c.

μουσικήν. There is no reason to think that διθυραμβικὴ
ἀγωγή means the non-antistrophic structure, which came in at
a later date. The reference is more probably to the *tempo* or
pace at which the words were sung.[1] Perhaps Lasos increased the rapidity of the delivery, and his example was
followed by later composers; and if, in addition, he increased
the range and variety of the notes employed, taking full
advantage of the possibilities of the flute, he may have inaugurated that predominance of the music over the words
against which, as we shall see, Pratinas shortly afterwards
protested.

Statements in scholia, &c., that Lasos was the teacher of
Pindar, or of Simonides, may merely be due to a desire to set the
various poets in some relation to one another—the mistaken
attempt thus to humanize chronology being one of the causes
of the frequent unreliability of such notices. Suidas adds,
without giving any authority, that Lasos was the first to write
a prose work περὶ μουσικῆς.[2] He was also famous in antiquity
for having indulged his dislike for sibilants by composing ᾠδαὶ
ἄσιγμοι, one of which was a hymn to Demeter of Hermione, and
another was called Κένταυροι.[3] The opening lines of Pindar's
dithyramb Θρασὺς Ἡρακλῆς make it almost certain that one
at least of these was a dithyramb, and as the *Demeter* was
composed in the Aeolian or Hypodorian mode, the dithyramb
must have been the Κένταυροι: but the only certain fact about
the contents of his dithyrambs is the wholly unimportant one
recorded by Aelian,[4] that he called a young lynx by the name
of σκυμνός.

[1] Cf. Aristid. Quint., p. 42, ἀγωγὴ δέ ἐστι ῥυθμικὴ χρόνων τάχος ἢ βραδύτης.
οἷον ὅταν τῶν λόγων σωζομένων, οὓς αἱ θέσεις ποιοῦνται πρὸς τὰς ἄρσεις,
διαφόρως ἑκάστου χρόνου τὰ μεγέθη προφερώμεθα : i. e. if the relative lengths
of θέσις and ἄρσις are preserved, but both are taken faster or slower, then
there is a difference of ἀγωγή.

[2] Wilamowitz, *Pindaros*, p. 112, does not accept this; but thinks that
precepts of his survived into later days ; and this may well be the truth.

[3] Athen. x, p. 455 c; xiv, p. 624 e. Athenaeus' authorities were
Clearchus (a pupil of Aristotle) and Heracleides Ponticus (circ. 340 B.C.).
Many other references may be found in *Oxyrh. Pap.* xiii, p. 41.

[4] *N. H.* vii. 47.

In view of the attribution of dithyrambic contests to the initiative of Lasos, it is somewhat puzzling to find that the Parian Marble [1] definitely ascribes the first χοροὶ ἀνδρῶν—dithyrambs sung by a chorus of men—to a year which may be 510/9 or 509/8 B.C., and states that the first victory was won by HYPODICUS of Chalcis. It is, however, at least possible that this refers to the first victory at the Dionysia as organized under the democracy, and as distinct from such contests as may have been arranged by the tyrants with the assistance of Lasos. There is no evidence of musical and poetic contests at Athens before the time of Peisistratus.[2]

Navarre [3] states that in the sixth century dithyramb was performed by a choir and a narrator who recounted incidents in the passion of Dionysus in answer to questions. It would be interesting to know how this is proved.

No date can be assigned to BACCHIADAS of Sicyon, whose victories with a chorus of men on Mt. Helicon (i. e. probably at Thespiae) are recorded by Athenaeus; [4] but the record refers to an early period.

§ 4. SIMONIDES was probably the most famous and successful of all the ancient writers of dithyrambs. In an extant epigram he claims to have won fifty-six dithyrambic victories :

> ἓξ ἐπὶ πεντήκοντα, Σιμωνίδη, ἤραο ταύρους
> καὶ τρίποδας, πρὶν τόνδ' ἀνθέμεναι πίνακα·
> τοσσάκι δ' ἱμερόεντα διδαξάμενος χορὸν ἀνδρῶν
> εὐδόξου Νίκας ἄγλαον ἅρμ' ἐπέβης.[5]

---

[1] Epoch 46. The Marble gives the name of the archon as Lysagoras. Scholars are divided as to whether this is a mason's error for Isagoras, or whether Lysagoras may be taken to be the name of the archon of 509/8, who is otherwise unknown. See Wilamowitz, *Arist. u. Athen.* i, p. 6, and *Hermes*, xx, p. 66 ; Munro, *Class. Rev.* xv, p. 357. Reisch (Pauly-W., *Real-Enc.* iii, col. 2431) gives the date as 508/7, but I do not know why.

[2] See Reisch, *de Musicis Graecorum certaminibus*, ch. ii.

[3] *Rev. Étud. Anc.* 1911, p. 246.

[4] xiv, p. 629 a. Perhaps the text is wrong, and παῖδας should be read for ἄνδρας : see Reisch, *de Mus. Graec. cert.*, p. 57.

[5] Frag. 145 (Bergk [4]) = *Anth. Pal.* vi. 213.

It is not stated that all these victories were won in Athens and it is doubtful whether this can have been the case, even when all possible occasions of dithyrambic performances are taken into the reckoning. The date of the epigram may have been the same as that of Epig. 147, which was written in 477/6 B.C. to be inscribed beneath the tripod won by the victorious tribe, when the poet was eighty years old:

> ἦρχεν Ἀδείμαντος μὲν Ἀθηναίοις, ὅτ᾽ ἐνίκα
> Ἀντιοχὶς φυλὴ δαιδάλεον τρίποδα·
> Ξεινοφίλου δὲ τόθ᾽ υἱὸς Ἀριστείδης ἐχορήγει
> πεντήκοντ᾽ ἀνδρῶν καλὰ μαθόντι χορῷ.
> ἀμφὶ διδασκαλίῃ δὲ Σιμωνίδη ἕσπετο κῦδος
> ὀγδωκονταέτει παιδὶ Λεωπρέπεος.

It is remarkable that in the first of these two epigrams of Simonides fifty-six victories are all stated to have been won with χοροὶ ἀνδρῶν: and this suggests (though it does not answer) the question whether the choruses of boys may not have been a later institution than the choruses of men.

It is generally agreed that Epig. 148, attributed to 'Bacchylides or Simonides'[1] is at any rate not by the latter, but there is no doubt of its early date, circ. 485 B.C.,[2] and it is important for the light which it throws on the customs connected with dithyrambic performances.[3] It commemorates the victory of an otherwise unknown poet, Antigenes, representing the Acamantid tribe.[4]

> πολλάκι δὴ φυλῆς Ἀκαμαντίδος ἐν χοροῖσιν Ὧραι
> ἀνωλόλυξαν κισσοφόροις ἐπὶ διθυράμβοις
> αἱ Διονυσιάδες, μίτραισι δὲ καὶ ῥόδων ἀώτοις
> σοφῶν ἀοιδῶν ἐσκίασαν λιπαρὰν ἔθειραν,

---

[1] Bergk iii⁴, pp. 496–7 : Wilamowitz, *Sappho u. Simonides*, pp. 218 ff.

[2] Wilamowitz, l. c., p. 222. Reisch (Pauly-W., *Real-Enc.* iii, col. 2384) says 'Ende des 5 Jhdts. ?', but gives no reasons.

[3] See below, p. 50.

[4] I cannot agree with Wilamowitz in thinking that the victory was the first victory of the tribe ; the epigram seems far more likely to mean that it was the latest of them. No convincing emendation of the corrupt l. 6 has been suggested.

οἳ τόνδε τρίποδα σφίσι μάρτυρα Βακχίων ἀέθλων
†ἔθηκαν· κείνους† δ' Ἀντιγένης ἐδίδαξεν ἄνδρας.
εὖ δ' ἐτιθηνεῖτο γλυκερὰν ὄπα Δωρίοις Ἀρίστων
Ἀργεῖος ἡδὺ πνεῦμα χέων καθαροῖς ἐν αὐλοῖς·
τῶν ἐχορήγησεν κύκλον μελίγηρυν Ἱππόνικος,
Στρούθωνος υἱός, ἅρμασιν ἐν Χαρίτων φορηθείς,
αἳ οἱ ἐπ' ἀνθρώπους ὄνομα κλυτὸν ἀγλαάν τε νίκαν
θῆκαν, ἰοστεφάνων θεῶν ἕκατι Μοισᾶν.

Unfortunately no fragment of Simonides that is certainly
dithyrambic survives.[1] Strabo mentions a dithyramb of
Simonides called *Memnon* in a passage[2] which has given rise
to some controversy:—ταφῆναι δὲ λέγεται Μέμνων περὶ
Πάλτον τῆς Συρίας παρὰ Βαδᾶν ποταμόν, ὡς εἴρηκε Σιμωνίδης
ἐν Μέμνονι διθυράμβῳ τῶν Δηλιακῶν. The natural meaning
of this would be that Strabo found this statement about the
burial of Memnon in a dithyramb of Simonides—either, simply,
one of those written for performance at Delos or perhaps one
of a collection, such as Wilamowitz[3] supposes to have existed,
of those composed for Delos. There are no facts which render
either of these alternatives difficult, and Wilamowitz seems to
be interpreting Strabo in a scarcely justifiable manner when
he claims that the expression implies that Strabo knew that
there was nothing properly dithyrambic about the poem. It
should, however, be noticed that the best MS. reading of
Strabo's text is Δαλιακῶν, for which scholars have proposed
many emendations; and the difficulty of explaining why any
scribe should have changed the comparatively familiar Δηλιακῶν
into Δαλιακῶν remains, though it does not affect the main point,
the ascription to Simonides of a dithyramb called *Memnon*. A
conjecture of M. Schmidt[4] tries to bring Memnon into con-

---

[1] The conjecture of W. Schmid and others (see *Oxyrh. Pap.* xiii, p. 27)
that the 'Danae' was a dithyramb rather than a θρῆνος appears to have
no foundation.

[2] xv, p. 728.

[3] *Textgesch. der gr. Lyr.*, p. 38; he goes beyond the evidence, however,
in citing Paus. IV. xxxvii as proof of the existence of such a collection.
In his *Einl. in die gr. Trag.*, p. 64, he denies the value of Strabo's
statement entirely, but without giving reasons.

[4] *Diatribe in Dith.*, p. 132.

nexion with Dionysus, on the strength of a story mentioned by Servius[1] to the effect that Priam obtained Memnon's aid by the gift of a golden vine to Tithonus, so that in a sense Memnon's death was due to Dionysus ; but this is very far-fetched.

A poem by Simonides called *Europa* was mentioned by Aristophanes of Byzantium [2] (who noted that in it the poet called the bull both μῆλον and πρόβατον [3]). That the *Europa* was a dithyramb appears to be assumed by Bergk,[4] though it does not seem that any evidence exists. But whatever may be the truth about the *Europa*, the mention of the *Memnon* gives reason to think that the dithyrambs of Simonides, like those of Arion, Pindar, and Bacchylides, dealt with definite and special divine or heroic subjects, though it is likely enough that Dionysus was appropriately recognized at some point in the poem.

§ 5. We obtain some remarkable evidence as regards the character of the dithyramb at this period in the long fragment of Pratinas,[5] which has been treated with great ingenuity by Professor H. W. Garrod.[6] There can now be little doubt that the fragment is part of the chorus of a satyric play,[7] and it is clear that it attacks violently the growing predominance of the flute accompaniment over the words of the dithyramb, applying many insulting epithets to the offend-

---

[1] On Virg. *Aen.* i. 489.

[2] B. C. E. Miller, *Mélanges de Litt. grecque*, p. 430.

[3] Cf. Eustath. *Il.* 877, 37.   [4] *Poet. Lyr.* iii[4], p. 399.

[5] ap. Athen. xiv, p. 617 b.   [6] *Class. Rev.* xxxiv, pp. 129 ff.

[7] This view is first found in K. O. Müller, *Kl. deutsche Schriften*, i, p. 519 (1847), and is repeated in his *Gesch. der gr. Lit.* ii[2], p. 39 ; it has been adopted by Blass, Girard, and others. The description of it as a ὑπόρχημα does not preclude its being part of a play : obviously odes of various types might find appropriate places in drama ; many scholars regard some of the odes of Sophocles as hyporchemes, and Tzetzes speaks of the ὑπορχηματικόν as an element in Tragedy. Becker, *de Pratina* (1912), though holding the fragment to belong to an independent poem, compiles a good deal of evidence to prove that it was danced by satyrs. His comparisons between it and the *Cyclops* of Euripides are particularly interesting.

ing instrument. I give (in the main) Professor Garrod's text:[1]

τίς ὁ θόρυβος ὅδε; τί τάδε τὰ χορεύματα;
τίς ὕβρις ἔμολεν ἐπί Διονυσιάδα πολυπάταγα θυμέλαν;
ἐμὸς ἐμὸς ὁ Βρόμιος· ἐμὲ δεῖ κελαδεῖν, ἐμὲ δεῖ παταγεῖν,
ἀν' ὄρεα σύμενον μετὰ Ναιάδων,
5 ἅτε κύκνον ἄγοντα ποικιλόπτερον μέλος.
τὰν ἀοιδὰν κατέστασε Πιερὶς * *
βασίλειαν· ὁ δ' αὐλὸς ὕστερον χορευέτω·
καὶ γάρ ἐσθ' ὑπηρέτας.
κώμῳ μόνον θυραμάχοις
10 τε πυγμαχίαις νέων θέλει παροίνων
ἔμμεναι στρατηλάτας.
παῖε τὸν φρυνεοῦ ποικίλου πνοιὰν [2]
ἔχοντα, φλέγε τὸν ὀλεσισίαλον κάλαμον λαλοβαρύοπα παρα-
μελορυθμοβάταν
θῆτα τρυπάνῳ δέμας πεπλασμένον.[3]
15 ἠνιδοῦ· ἅδε σοι δεξιὰ καὶ ποδὸς
διαρριφά, θριαμβοδιθύραμβε
κισσόχαιτ' ἄναξ, ἄκουε τὰν ἐμὰν Δώριον χορείαν.

The first difficulty is to determine the date to which the fragment is to be assigned. It seems natural to think of it as referring to the changes introduced by Lasos, and if so it is not likely to be much later than 500 B. C., by which time, as is practically certain, Pratinas had introduced satyric drama from Phlius into Athens.[4] But Professor Garrod is inclined to assign it to a date about 468 B. C., and to explain it as re-

---

[1] I do not here discuss the metrical aspect of the passage, which offers great difficulties. Professor Garrod here differs widely from Wilamowitz (*Sappho and Simonides*, pp. 132 ff.).

[2] 'With the voice of a spotted toad' is intelligible as an insulting expression about the flute, without any such reference to Phrynichus as Prof. Garrod sees. The lower notes of a flute, badly played, may well be so described; and there is no other hint of Phrynichus as a composer of dithyrambs.

[3] This seems better than ῥυπαροτρυπάνως δέμας πεπλασμένον (read by Prof. Garrod).

[4] See below, pp. 92 ff.

ferring to the innovations of Melanippides,[1] whose appearance
he regards as roughly synchronous with the *floruit* of his
senior contemporary, Diagoras of Melos, placed under that
year by Eusebius. The decision depends upon the interpretation of passages of Athenaeus and Pseudo-Plutarch, which are
unfortunately not easy to explain. Athenaeus introduces the
fragment of Pratinas with the words: Πρατίνας δὲ ὁ Φλιάσιος,
αὐλητῶν καὶ χορευτῶν μισθοφόρων κατεχόντων τὰς ὀρχήστρας,
ἀγανακτήσας (Wilam. for ἀγανακτεῖν τινας) ἐπὶ τῷ τοὺς αὐλητὰς
μὴ ξυναυλεῖν τοῖς χοροῖς, καθάπερ ἦν πάτριον, ἀλλὰ τοὺς χοροὺς
ξυνᾴδειν τοῖς αὐληταῖς, ὃν οὖν εἶχε θυμὸν κατὰ τῶν ταῦτα
ποιούντων ὁ Πρατίνας ἐμφανίζει διὰ τοῦδε τοῦ ὑπορχήματος.
The Pseudo-Plutarch[2] reads (in the MSS.) as follows:
Λᾶσος δ᾽ ὁ Ἑρμιονεὺς εἰς τὴν διθυραμβικὴν ἀγωγὴν μεταστήσας
τοὺς ῥυθμοὺς καὶ τῇ τῶν αὐλῶν πολυφωνίᾳ κατακολουθήσας,
πλείοσί τε φθόγγοις καὶ διερριμμένοις χρησάμενος, εἰς μετάθεσιν τὴν προυπάρχουσαν ἤγαγε μουσικήν. ὁμοίως δὲ καὶ Μελανιππίδης ὁ μελοποιὸς ἐπιγενόμενος οὐκ ἐνέμεινε τῇ ὑπαρχούσῃ
μουσικῇ, ἀλλ᾽ οὐδὲ Φιλόξενος οὐδὲ Τιμόθεος· οὗτος γάρ, ἑπτα-
φθόγγου τῆς λύρας ὑπαρχούσης ἕως εἰς Τέρπανδρον τὸν Ἀντισ-
σαῖον, διέρριψεν εἰς πλείονας φθόγγους. ἀλλὰ γὰρ καὶ αὐλητικὴ
ἀφ᾽ ἁπλουστέρας εἰς ποικιλωτέραν μεταβέβηκε μουσικήν. τὸ
γὰρ παλαιόν, ἕως εἰς Μελανιππίδην τὸν τῶν διθυράμβων ποιητήν, συμβεβήκει τοὺς αὐλητὰς παρὰ τῶν ποιητῶν λαμβάνειν
τοὺς μισθούς, πρωταγωνιστούσης δηλονότι τῆς ποιήσεως, τῶν δὲ
αὐλητῶν ὑπηρετούντων τοῖς διδασκάλοις· ὕστερον δὲ καὶ τοῦτο
διεφθάρη.

It is difficult to think that the author of the second passage
can have written it as it stands; for, though there appears to
be little justification for the transposition of certain sections
in Weil and Reinach's edition, it is unlikely that the author
would have written εἰς Μελανιππίδην τὸν τῶν διθυράμβων
ποιητήν only a very few lines after Μελανιππίδης ὁ μελοποιός. There would have been no need for a new description

---

[1] In the discussion which follows it is assumed that there was only
one Melanippides, and that the 'elder Melanippides' is a fiction of
Suidas. (See Rohde, *Rhein. Mus.* xxxiii, pp. 213–14; and below, p. 55.)

[2] *de Mus.* chs. xxix, xxx (1141 c, d).

of the poet so soon; and as the sentence ὁμοίως δὲ καὶ Μελανιππίδης ὁ μελοποιός κτλ. appears to be quite in place—Lasos
began the process, Melanippides carried it further—it is probable that the words ἕως εἰς Μελανιππίδην τὸν τῶν διθυράμβων
ποιητήν should be bracketed,[1] as one among the many inter-
polations in this treatise. But if so, no reason remains for
seeing a reference to Melanippides in the passages of Athenaeus
and Pseudo-Plutarch, the common source of which, as Professor Garrod says, was probably Aristoxenus, and was better
reproduced by the Pseudo-Plutarch ;[2] these passages, and the
fragment of Pratinas, may quite well refer to Lasos.[3]

It is to be noticed also that the fragment attributed to
Pherecrates, which the Pseudo-Plutarch quotes to illustrate
his statements, plainly regards the innovations of Melanippides as affecting the lyre, not the flute: and this accords well
with the passage of Pseudo-Plutarch which deals with the
lyre, from ὁμοίως δὲ καὶ Μελανιππίδης to εἰς πλείονας φθογγούς
and returns to the flute with the words, ἀλλὰ γὰρ καὶ αὐλητική.

There is, moreover, a slight improbability in the supposition
that Pratinas was alive and composing as late as 468 B. C. In
467 his Παλαισταὶ Σάτυροί was brought out by his son
Aristias,[4] and it is at least likely that he died before this.

We may therefore provisionally, though without claiming

---

[1] Not, however, for the reasons given by Weil and Reinach—that
Melanippides attacked the art of flute-playing in his *Marsyas*, and is
therefore unlikely to have given it prominence in his practice. Poets
are not always so consistent.

[2] Athenaeus' phrase αὐλητῶν . . . τὰς ὀρχήστρας is scarcely intelligible,
though the encroachments of the flute may have been connected with
the rise of professionalism and virtuosity. I agree with Professor Garrod
that Athenaeus must be referring to a period in the history of lyric
ἀγῶνες, not (as Smyth supposes) to the appearance of 'some hired flute-
players and choreutae' on a particular occasion.

[3] There is no independent evidence as to the payment of the flute-
player, except that in Demosthenes' day he was certainly paid by the
choregus.

[4] Argt., *Sept. c. Theb.* We know of no instance of a competitor in
Tragedy or Satyric Drama bringing out the work of another during his
lifetime, though this was often done in the case of Comedy.

absolute certainty, interpret the protest of Pratinas as directed against the excessive importance assigned to the flute by Lasos.

Wilamowitz regards the fragment as itself a dithyramb, and line 3 is certainly easier if spoken by a dithyrambic chorus, and if ἐμέ = 'the dithyrambic chorus and not the flute'. But it is not impossible in the mouth of any chorus :—'it is I, the chorus, and not the instrument, that have the right &c.' (In any case there is some confusion between the chorus round the altar, and the θίασος of nymphs and satyrs in the mountains.) If the piece were itself a dithyramb, it is not easy to see what the circumstances of its performance were. Did it follow immediately on, or break into, a dithyramb in the new manner? On the whole, Professor Garrod's view seems easier, that 'we have a satyric drama, in which, at the point where our fragment begins, some one has just brought to an end a lyric strain easily apprehended by the audience as a parody of the "New Rhythmic"'. (No inference can be drawn either way from τὰν ἐμὰν Δωρίαν χορείαν. The dithyramb was composed in the Phrygian mode; but the flute-players may have been Dorian, as Pratinas himself must have been.)

IV

Pindar, Bacchylides and others.

§ 1. PINDAR (518–442 B.C.), to whom two 'books' of dithyrambs were attributed, is described by scholiasts and others as a pupil of Lasos, to whom he was committed by the flute-player Scopelinus ; others said that he was taught at Athens by Agathocles or Apollodorus or both. We cannot check these statements. But we have some striking fragments of his dithyrambs.

One is quoted by Dionysius of Halicarnassus [1] as an illustration of the severe style, the αὐστηρὰ ἁρμονία. The text and

---

[1] de Comp. Vb. xxii.

the exact interpretation are sometimes uncertain; the text
here given, except in one or two words, is that of Schroeder.[1]

ἴδετ' ἐν χορόν, 'Ολύμπιοι,
ἐπί τε κλυτὰν πέμπετε χάριν, θεοί
πολύβατον οἵ τ' ἄστεος ὀμφαλὸν θυόεντα
ἐν ταῖς ἱεραῖς 'Αθάναις
5 οἰχνεῖτε πανδαίδαλόν τ' εὐκλέ' ἀγοράν.
ἰοδέτων λάχετε στεφάνων τὰν ἐαρίδρεπτον
λοιβάν· Διόθεν τέ με σὺν ἀγλαΐᾳ
ἴδετε πορευθέντ' ἀοιδᾶν
δεύτερον ἐπὶ κισσοδέταν θεόν,
10 Βρόμιον ὅν τ' 'Εριβόαν τε βροτοὶ καλέομεν,
γόνον ὑπάτων μὲν πατέρων μελπέμεν
γυναικῶν τε Καδμεϊᾶν [ἔμολον].
ἐναργέα δ' ἐμὲ σάματ' οὐ λανθάνει,
φοινικοεάνων ὁπότ' οἰχθέντος 'Ωρᾶν θαλάμου
15 εὔοδμον ἐπάγῃσιν ἔαρ φυτὰ νεκτάρεα.
τότε βάλλεται, τότ' ἐπ' ἀμβρόταν χθόν' ἐραταὶ
ἴων φόβαι, ῥόδα τε κόμαισι μίγνυται,
ἀχεῖ τ' ὀμφαὶ μελέων σὺν αὐλοῖς,
ἀχεῖ τε Σεμέλαν ἑλικάμπυκα χοροί.

It was written for performance at Athens; but the common
belief (supported by Christ and Wilamowitz) that it was for
performance in the Agora rather than in a Dionysiac theatre
is not proved by the fact that the gods of the Agora are first
addressed.[2] The whole expression is evidently a comprehensive one for the gods of Athens, and would be quite appropriate
in a Dionysiac orchestra or in any site in Athens. It is plain
that the Athenian dithyramb was a spring performance; there
is no trace of the winter-dithyramb, such as was performed at
Delphi; and clearly Semele was one of its traditional themes.
The language and ideas are simple, when compared with the
more highly-wrought passages of Pindar's Epinikian odes; but
it is noticeable how few substantives go without an ornamental

---

[1] Edition of 1923; fragm. 75, pp. 412–13.
[2] Christ's attempt (edition of 1896) to date the poem before 472 B. C.
on this ground is sufficiently answered by Smyth, *Melic Poets*, p. 360.

or descriptive epithet, and some have two (πολύβατον ὄμφαλον
θυόεντα, πανδαίδαλον εὐκλέα ἀγοράν); in the last part, which
tells of 'the flowers that bloom in the spring', the effect is
perhaps a little cloying.

At first sight it is hard to follow Dionysius when he takes
the poem as representative of the αὐστηρὰ ἁρμονία, but
Dionysius refers not to what we should call the 'tone' of the
poem, but to a certain roughness or want of euphony in the
juxtaposition of letters and syllables,[1] very difficult for our
ears to detect, though Dionysius unkindly says that it is plain
to all who have μετρίαν αἴσθησιν περὶ λόγους. He speaks of
the lines as 'slow in their time-movement' (ἀναβέβληταί τε
τοῖς χρόνοις καὶ διαβέβηκεν ἐπὶ πολὺ ταῖς ἁρμονίαις), but the
reference is once more to the relative length of time required
for the pronunciation of different collocations of letters; to a
modern reader the effect produced by the abundance of resolved
feet is one of rapidity and even of hurry. It is generally
stated that the fragment is written in μέλος ἀπολελυμένον,—
non-antistrophic verse; but the fragment is only of about the
same length as the first strophe of the Θρασὺς Ἡρακλῆς ἢ
Κέρβερος,[2] and may well be the first strophe of an antistrophic
poem. There is, in fact, no sufficient ground for attributing
non-antistrophic compositions to Pindar.

There are also extant three short fragments [3] of another
dithyramb written by Pindar for Athens:

76 ὦ ταὶ λιπαραὶ καὶ ἰοστέφανοι καὶ ἀοίδιμοι
  Ἑλλάδος ἔρεισμα, κλειναὶ Ἀθᾶναι,
  δαιμόνιον πτολίεθρον.

77 ὅθι παῖδες Ἀθαναίων ἐβάλοντο φαεννὰν
  κρηπῖδ' ἐλευθερίας.

[1] Dionysius works out these points in great detail, but it would be
beside the present purpose to discuss them here.

[2] This is noticed by Grenfell and Hunt, Oxyrh. Pap. xiii, p. 28.

[3] They are respectively quoted by the Schol. on Aristoph. Ach. 674,
Plut. Vit. Themist. viii (with reference to the battle of Artemisium), and
Plut. de Glor. Athen. vii. The ascription of frs. 77 and 78 to the same
poem as fr. 76 is based by Christ on the similarity of metre and subject.
Wilamowitz, Pindaros, p. 272, is doubtful about the reference of fr. 78 to
Athens.

78   κλῦθ' Ἀλαλά, Πολέμου θύγατερ,
      ἐγχέων προοίμιον, ᾷ θύεται
      ἄνδρες ὑπὲρ πόλιος τὸν ἰρόθυτον θάνατον.

It was on account of the praise of Athens contained in this
dithyramb that the Athenians richly rewarded the poet, and
(perhaps at a later date) set up a statue to him.[1]
Two fragments, one of which certainly,[2] the other probably,[3]
comes from a dithyramb, refer to the story of Orion, whose
origin is stated by Strabo [4] to have been described in a dithyramb. The first (fr. 72) alludes to Orion's attack upon Merope,
daughter of Oenopion, under the influence of wine :

      ἀλόχῳ ποτὲ θωραχθεὶς ἔπεχ' ἀλλοτρίᾳ
      Ὠαρίων.

The second (fr. 74) mentions Pleione, the Pleiad whom he
assaulted :

            τρεχέτω δὲ μετὰ
      Πληιόναν, ἅμα δ' αὐτῷ κύων λεοντοδάμας.

The remaining fragments of Pindar's dithyrambs, apart
from those discovered at Oxyrhynchus, need no comment.
They are as follows :

No. 80   Κυβέλα μᾶτερ θεῶν

    81   σέ δ' ἐγὼ παρὰ μιν [5]
          αἰνέω μέν, Γηρυόνα, τὸ δὲ μὴ Δὶ φίλτερον
          σιγῷμι πάμπαν· οὐ γὰρ εἰκὸς τῶν ἐόντων
          ἁρπαζομένων παρὰ ἑστίᾳ καθῆσθαι
          καὶ κακὸν ἔμμεν.

    82   τὰν λιπαρὰν μὲν Αἴγυπτον ἀγχίκρημνον.

    83   ἦν ὅτε σύας τὸ Βοιώτιον ἔθνος ἔνεπον.

It is also recorded that ἐν τῷ πρώτῳ τῶν Διθυράμβων Pindar
ascribed the origin of dithyramb to Thebes ; [6] that he played
upon the words διθύραμβος and λῦθι ῥάμμα (the cry of Zeus

---

[1] Paus. I. viii, § 4.   As to the date of the statue, see Wilamowitz, l. c.,
p. 273.
[2] *Etym. Magn.* 460. 35.   [3] Schol. Pind. *Nem.* ii. 17.   [4] ix, p. 404.
[5] παρὰ μίν, i. e. παρὰ τὸν Ἡρακλέα, Schol. Aristid. iii. 409.
[6] Schol. Pind. *Olymp.* xiii. 25.

at the second birth of Dionysus);[1] and that he used a heteroclite plural διθύραμβα,[2] and the word παλιναίρετος (of a building destroyed and rebuilt).[3]

It is probable that Boeckh was right in ascribing to a dithyramb fr. 156 :

> ὁ ζαμενὴς ὁ χοροιτύπος
> ὃν Μαλεάγονος ἔθρεψε Ναΐδος
> ἀκοίτας Σιληνός.

But by far the most striking dithyrambic fragment is that found at Oxyrhynchus ; a few lines of it were previously known. It was entitled Θρασὺς Ἡρακλῆς ἢ Κέρβερος, and was written for Thebes. The text as given by Grenfell and Hunt is as follows (brackets being omitted where the supplements are certain) :[4]

> πρὶν μὲν εἷρπε σχοινοτένειά τ' ἀοιδὰ
> διθυράμβων
> καὶ τὸ σὰν κίβδαλον ἀνθρώποισιν ἀπὸ στομάτων,
> διαπέπτα[νται δὲ νῦν ἱροῖς] πύλ[αι κύ-
> 5 κλοισι νέαι ⏝ ⏑ – εἰδότες
> οἵαν Βρομίου τελετὰν
> καὶ παρὰ σκᾶπτον Διὸς Οὐρανίδαι
> ἐν μεγάροις ἱστάντι. σεμνᾷ μὲν κατάρχει
> ματέρι παρ' μεγάλᾳ ρομβοὶ τυπάνων,
> 10 ἐν δὲ κέχλαδον κρόταλ' αἰθομένα τε
> δᾷς ὑπὸ ξανθαῖσι πεύκαις,
> ἐν δὲ Ναΐδων ἐρίγδουποι στοναχαὶ
> μανίαι τ' ἀλαλαί τ' ὀρίνεται ριψαύχενι
> σὺν κλόνῳ.
> 15 ἐν δ' ὁ παγκρατὴς κεραυνὸς ἀμπνέων
> πῦρ κεκίνηται τό τ' Ἐνναλίου
> ἔγχος, ἀλκάεσσά τε Παλλάδος αἰγὶς
> μυρίων φθογγάζεται κλαγγαῖς δρακόντων.
> ρίμφα δ' εἷσιν Ἄρτεμις οἰοπόλος ζεύ-   antistr. α'

---

[1] Etym. Magn. 274. 50, &c.   [2] Herodian ii. 626. 35 ff. L.
[3] Harpocr., p. 232, &c.
[4] Wilamowitz, Pindaros, p. 343, has also a few useful notes on the text.

20 ξαισ' ἐν ὀργαῖς
Βακχίαις φῦλον λεόντων ἀ[γροτέρων Βρομίῳ·
ὁ δὲ κηλεῖται χορευούσαισι καὶ θη-
ρῶν ἀγέλαις· ἐμὲ δ' ἐξαίρετον
κάρυκα σοφῶν ἐπέων
25 Μοῖσ' ἀνέστασ' Ἑλλάδι καλλ[ιχόρῳ
εὐχόμενον βρισαρμάτοις ὅ[λβον τε Θήβαις,
ἔνθα πόθ' Ἁρμονίαν φάμα γα[μετὰν
Κάδμον ὑψηλαῖς πραπίδεσ[σι λαχεῖν κεδ-
νάν· Διὸς δ' ἄκουσεν ὀμφάν,
30 καὶ τέκ' εὔδοξον παρ' ἀνθρώπο[ις γενεάν.
Διόνυσ', . θ . . . . τ . γ
ματέ[ρος?
πει . . .

Lines 1–5 (and 23–4) contrast the archaic long-drawn dithyramb with Pindar's new style. As the editors have pointed out, the fact that the present fragment is antistrophic disposes of the idea (generally accepted when lines 1–3 were only known in isolation) that Pindar was introducing the composition of dithyrambs in a non-antistrophic form, and rejecting the 'long-drawn' succession of strophes and antistrophes or of triads. The reference to τὸ σὰν κίβδηλον is doubtless (as Athenaeus and Dionysius state) to the ᾠδαὶ ἄσιγμοι of Lasos, and (though the expression remains difficult), the least objectionable translation seems to be 'formerly the song of dithyrambs issued long drawn out, and the san (i. e. sigma) issued as base coin from the lips of men', i. e. the use of the sound was so discredited that Lasos actually rejected it. Pindar may have introduced a shorter form of dithyramb than that of Lasos, but in fact we cannot be certain to what exactly σχοινοτένεια refers.

The greater part of the fragment (which is but the introduction to a narrative now lost) describes 'what manner of festival of Bromius the celestials by the very sceptre of Zeus celebrate in their halls'. Unfortunately the defectiveness of the text leaves in obscurity the connexion of this description with the new type of dithyramb; but the suggestion which has been made, that the new type was modelled on the heavenly festival of Bromius, cannot really be sustained. The heavenly festival, in which each god showed his enthusiasm in his own characteristic way, was evidently a much more varied performance than we ever find denoted by the word 'dithyramb'; it includes elements which belong, not to the dithyramb, but to the trieteric orgies in which the worship and the instruments belonging to the Great Mother were combined with those of Dionysus. (The same is the case in the first chorus of Euripides' *Bacchae*, which Miss Harrison,[1] apparently with little justification, describes as in part a dithyramb. What Greek poem was ever in part of one species, in part of another? Nor is there any reason to consider the third chorus of the play, ll. 519 ff., a dithyramb, even though the birth of Dionysus is described in it, and Zeus is said to have addressed him as Διθύραμβε.)

In the same papyrus are traces of two other dithyrambs. The first, probably composed for Argos, was clearly antistrophic, and the extant words suggest that its subject was Perseus and his exploits; the other was perhaps written for Corinth,[2] but is so fragmentary that neither its subject nor its structure can be made out.

The Pindaric dithyramb was thus, so far as our evidence goes, an antistrophic composition dealing with special themes taken from divine and heroic legend, but still maintaining its particular connexion with Dionysus, who is celebrated, apparently at or near the opening of the song, whatever its subject. Dithyrambs written for the Great Dionysia at Athens might naturally have the characteristics of songs of spring.

As regards the language, the extant fragments hardly explain Horace's lines:[3]

> seu per audaces nova dithyrambos
> verba devolvit numerisque fertur
> lege solutis.

Horace may be mistakenly attributing the μέλος ἀπολελυ-

---

[1] *Themis*, p. 130.   [2] Wilamowitz, *Pindaros*, p. 372, disputes this.
[3] *Odes*, IV. ii. 10 ff.

μένον to Pindar;[1] or he may be referring to other metrical
licences, such as the freedom which Pindar displays in regard
to resolved feet. The fragments do not give us many bold
compounds, but this may be an accident.

§ 2. During Pindar's time there flourished also PRAXILLA of
Sicyon; Eusebius gives the date when she was, or became,
well known as 450 B.C. She wrote poems on a variety of
heroic subjects, as well as Παροίνια or Σκόλια,[2] and owing
to the bathos of the third line of a speech of Adonis in one
of her poems[3] a proverb arose, ἠλιθιώτερος τοῦ Πραξίλλης
Ἀδώνιδος. It does not appear on what grounds Smyth[4] takes
the *Adonis* of Praxilla to have been a dithyramb, and
says that 'the earliest form of dithyramb was in dactylic
hexameters, which were revived in the fifth century'.
The only extant line which is actually ascribed to a dithyramb of Praxilla is a hexameter verse quoted by Hephaestion[5] as παρὰ Πραξίλλῃ ἐν διθυράμβοις ἐν ᾠδῇ ἐπιγραφομένῃ
Ἀχιλλεύς,

> ἀλλὰ τεὸν οὔποτε θυμὸν ἐνὶ στήθεσσιν ἔπειθον.

But Crusius[6] may be right in thinking that the words ἐν ᾠδῇ
ἐπιγραφομένῃ Ἀχιλλεύς are a correction of ἐν διθυράμβοις,
and that the latter is inaccurate.

§ 3. Another contemporary of Pindar and, like him, a pupil
of Agathocles at Athens, was LAMPROCLES the master in music
of Damon, who was the teacher of Pericles and Socrates—
(The song, Παλλάδα περσέπολιν δεινάν, which was thought

---

[1] Probably Pseudo-Censorinus, ch. 9 (*Gramm. Lat.* vi, p. 608, Keil),
took him to mean this, when he states that Pindar 'liberos etiam nume-
ris modos edidit'.

[2] Wilamowitz, *Einl. in die gr. Trag.*, p. 71, thinks that the fact that
she wrote drinking songs proves that she was a ἑταίρα. Does it?

[3] Zenob. iv. 21 says ἐν τοῖς μέλεσι, Cod. Coisl. ἐν τοῖς ὕμνοις. The lines
are: κάλλιστον μὲν ἐγὼ λείπω φάος ἠελίοιο, | δεύτερον ἄστρα φαεινὰ σεληναίης
τε πρόσωπον, | ἠδὲ καὶ ὡραίους σικύους καὶ μῆλα καὶ ὄγχνας. (Smyth aptly
compares the beautiful fragment 481 of Menander.)

[4] *Melic Poets*, p. 348.

[5] *de Metris*, ch. ii, p. 9 (Consbr.)

[6] Pauly-W., *Real-Enc.* v. 1214.

old-fashioned at the time of Aristophanes *Clouds*,[1] was
ascribed by some to Lamprocles, by others to Phrynichus. I
can see no reason why Diehl, in his new edition of the
Anthologia Lyrica, should include it among the dithyrambic
fragments.) The only dithyrambic fragment of Lamprocles
consists of a few words, quoted by Athenaeus,[2] connecting the
name of the Pleiades with Πελειάδες:—Λαμπροκλῆς δ' ὁ
διθυραμβοποιὸς καὶ ῥητῶς αὐτὰς εἶπεν ὀμωνυμεῖν ταῖς περιστε-
ραῖς ἐν τούτοις·

αἴτε ποταναῖς
ὁμώνυμοι πελείασιν αἴθερι νεῖσθε.

§ 4. We may now pass to BACCHYLIDES, who was writing
perhaps from about 481 to 431 B.C. The poems which are
numbered xiv–xix in the papyrus are there called dithyrambs,
and it may be assumed that they were so classed by the
Alexandrian scholars on whose work the MS. must have de-
pended. (The dithyrambs are in the alphabetical order of the
initial letters of their titles, and as these only go down to *I*,
they doubtless formed part of a larger collection.) But it has
been disputed in what sense they were dithyrambs. Were they
actually written for performance by a κύκλιος χορός? Some
of them appear to be on too slight a scale for what seems to
have been (at least with some composers) a grand form of
composition, if we may judge by the openings of Pindar's
dithyrambs contained in the two longer fragments, and by the
fact that one of these fragments, after some thirty lines, has
not yet come in sight of what we know to have been the main
subject of the poem. In truth, however, we know too little
of the usual scale of the dithyramb to have any right to
generalize about it.

The longest of the dithyrambs of Bacchylides, the one
called Ἤϊθεοι ἢ Θησεύς (No. xvi) is affirmed by Jebb[3] and
others to have been a paean. This, however, is probably
a mistake. The word παιάνιξαν in l. 128 is part of the narra-

---

[1] ll. 967 ff. and schol. ad loc., &c. In all the scholia it is always called
an ᾆσμα, with no suggestion of dithyramb.

[2] xi, p. 491 c.   [3] p. 223 of his edition of Bacchylides.

tive, and gives no ground for thinking that the poem in which the narrative was contained is a paean. The invocation to Apollo in the last three lines is a natural prayer for victory to the god of Delos, where probably the poem was sung [1] — a god, moreover, to whom poets by custom appealed for victory; and dithyrambs as well as paeans were sung by choruses sent to Delos from other cities. [2] (The citation of the poem as a dithyramb by Servius has obviously no independent weight, but merely repeats the class-description of the poem which had been current long before him.)

But were the poems classed as dithyrambs simply because they contained mainly heroic narrative? Plato, [3] perhaps nearly a century later, thought of the the dithyramb as mainly narrative, though this does not mean that he would have classed any narrative lyric poem as a dithyramb. The Pseudo-Plutarch [4] or his authorities, and others to whom he alludes, thought of dithyramb as mainly dealing with heroic themes. But what evidence have we that the Alexandrian scholars, to whom probably the ascription of the title 'Dithyrambs' to these six poems is due, treated as dithyrambs poems which were not written for performance as dithyrambs, simply because they contained heroic narrative? The evidence of notices and quotations in scholia &c., which must have been largely based on the work of Alexandrian scholars, suggests that the different kinds of lyric poem were still kept distinct, and gives no ground for supposing that the Alexandrians did

---

[1] It cannot be taken as certain that it was composed for performance at Delos, but it would at least have been appropriate for this purpose (see Jebb's note on l. 130, p. 390); and this seems more likely than the idea of Comparetti (*Mélanges Weil*, p. 32) that it was written for a chorus of Ceans admitted to competition at Athens. There is no recorded parallel to the supposed admission.

[2] See above, p. 9. For a later period (the third century B. C.) the evidence of inscriptions is abundant.

[3] *Republ.* iii, p. 394 c. Plato does not intend his remark to be taken too strictly : ἡ δὲ δι' ἀπαγγελίας αὐτοῦ τοῦ ποιητοῦ· εὕροις δ' ἂν αὐτὴν μάλιστά που ἐν διθυράμβοις. The later dithyramb, which had begun to prevail in his time, included much μίμησις.

[4] *de Mus*, ch. x, p. 1143 e. See above, p. 20.

not know which were dithyrambs and which were not. That No. xv was a dithyramb in the strict sense—one of those performed at Delphi when Apollo was supposed to be absent and the paean was silent,[1] the contents of the poem leave no room to doubt.

On the whole, the balance of probability seems to be in favour of accepting these poems as really dithyrambs, intended to be sung by κύκλιοι χοροί, whether at Athens or elsewhere, despite the differences of scale which they present, and which may possibly be due to a difference in the customs of the several festivals. It will be best first to examine each separately, and then to consider any common characteristics which can be discerned.

The first (xiv) is entitled Ἀντηνορίδαι ἢ Ἑλένης ἀπαίτησις. Menelaus and Odysseus are sent to Troy to demand the restoration of Helen, and are hospitably received by Antenor and his wife Theano, who is priestess of Athena, and is apparently (at the beginning of the poem) opening the doors of her temple to them. The poem is defective, but in the latter part, which is well preserved, Antenor brings the envoys before the assembled Trojans; Menelaus speaks in praise of justice and gives a warning against ὕβρις, and there the poem ends. It did not, apparently, any more than the other dithyrambs of Bacchylides, tell a complete story. On the ground that Antenor and Theano had fifty sons (as stated by the scholiast on *Il.* xxiv. 496), Jebb suggests that they may have been represented by the chorus of fifty. This raises the question, how far the dithyrambic chorus bore a dramatic character—whether, in fact, it ever represented any one but the performers themselves. There is no reason why in the present piece it should have done so. The piece is narrative throughout and would gain nothing by being sung by a chorus impersonating some of the characters in the story. Indeed if Jebb is right (in his note on l. 37 ff.) in thinking that the sons of Antenor are spoken of in the third person (ἆγον), they cannot also have been the narrators; but in fact the subject of ἆγον is unknown, and the Antenoridae do not figure in the extant fragments at all,

---

[1] Plutarch, *de Ei ap. Delph.*, ch. ix.

though they must have done so somewhere in the poem. The poem consists of three triads in dactylo-epitrite metre, and the language is quite free from the excitement or enthusiasm which is supposed to be associated with dithyramb, and which appears in some degree in the dithyrambic fragments of Pindar.

No. xv (for which the first editor conjecturally supplies the title 'Ἡρακλῆς) consists of a single triad in a complex and somewhat puzzling metre containing an introductory apostrophe to Apollo, in whose absence from Delphi during the winter dithyrambs were performed—the present one among them, and a very brief treatment of the story of Heracles and Deianeira, breaking off before the crisis, and giving more of allusion than of direct narrative. The poet looks forward to Apollo's return, when the paeans will begin again.[1]

No. xvi, 'Ἠΐθεοι ἢ Θησεύς, is the longest and most beautiful of the dithyrambs. It has been argued above that it is probably a dithyramb in reality, and not a paean, and was composed for a chorus from Ceos to sing at Delos, rather than (as Comparetti supposed) at Athens. Like No. xiv, it begins abruptly, but the story is more complete and the poem better rounded off. It tells how Minos sailed with Theseus and the seven youths and maidens sent from Athens as an offering to the Minotaur, and how Theseus resented the insult offered by Minos to Eriboea, accepted his challenge that he should plunge into the deep, the abode of his father Poseidon, and returned safely. The poem consists of two long triads in a metre which has proved very difficult to analyse, though Jebb rightly notes its appropriateness to a rapid and striking narrative.

It is in regard to No. xvii, entitled Θησεύς, that the greatest difficulties arise. It consists of four metrically similar logaoedic strophes, the first and third spoken by a chorus of Athenians,

---

[1] There is no mention of Dionysus in the extant words of the poem; but his name may have come in the first strophe, which is very defective. Kuiper (*Mnemosyne*, liii, pp. 344 ff.) proposes a series of emendations, introducing a reference to Dionysus, though his proposals are not very satisfactory. But that the poem was a dithyramb there can be no doubt. On the metre, see Wilamowitz, *Griech-Verskunst*, pp. 423 ff.

the second and fourth by Aegeus, the reputed father of
Theseus; it is a lyric dialogue in dramatic form, and is unique
in extant Greek literature. The chorus asks the king why the
people have been summoned to arms, and the king in reply
tells them of the reported approach of an unknown youth,
who has slain the monsters that infested the country,—Sinis,
the Erymanthian boar, Cercyon, Procoptes; and in answer to
further questions, describes his appearance. There are no
introductory words before or between the speeches, and
though its content is the representation of a brief mythical
episode, it is a great strain of language to speak of the poem
as 'virtually a narrative'; and it is hard to relate it to those
among which it stands. There is no evidence to show whether
it was performed by a soloist and chorus, or whether it was
sung by a chorus or two semi-choruses throughout, the change
of speakers (who are not indicated in the papyrus) being marked
only by a pause. Nor is there anything to tell us whether
the performers were masked, unlike those of the regular
dithyramb. It is not easy to follow Comparetti, when he
suggests that we have here a dithyramb like those of the days
before Thespis, with a chorus and ἐξάρχων. So late a 'reversion
to type' is hardly likely; and the ἐξάρχων in this poem is more
completely distinct from the chorus than the ἐξάρχων in primitive tragedy seems to have been before the time of Thespis.[1]
It is more attractive and plausible to suppose that we may have
here an experimental anticipation or adoption by Bacchylides of
that introduction of solo parts into the dithyramb, which was
taken up by the newer school, some of whom he must have
overlapped in time. But there is no ancient poem in regard
to which our imperfect knowledge is more tantalizing.

The occasion of the poem is unknown; but the subject is an
Athenian one, and the last words are complimentary to Athens
(φιλαγλάους Ἀθάνας), so that the poem was probably intended
for performance there; and the legendary connexion of
Theseus with the Thargelia supports Jebb's conjecture that it
may have been written for that festival.

No. xviii, entitled Ἰω, was written for the Athenians. It

---

[1] See below, pp. 109, 123 ff.

consists of a single triad (fifty lines) in which iambic, trochaic, and dactylic rhythms are combined. It was probably written for a Dionysiac festival, as the climax of the very brief narrative or rather allusion to the story of Io is the descent of Dionysus from Io, through Cadmus and Semele, ἃ τὸν ὀρσιβάκχαν | τίκτεν Διόνυσον, lord of garlanded choruses.

The last poem, No. xix, the ῎Ιδας, dealing with the story of Idas and Marpessa, was written for Sparta, but is represented only by a slight fragment.

Besides these poems, we know from the scholiast on Pindar, *Pyth.* i. 100, that Bacchylides wrote a dithyramb in which the mission sent by the Greeks to bring Philoctetes from Lemnos was mentioned; and a few words survive of another dithyramb[1] referring to the consecration of Mantinea to Poseidon.

The dithyrambs of Bacchylides have all in common the fact that they treat in a somewhat detached but picturesque manner a scene taken from legend, sometimes both beginning and ending *in mediis rebus*; in one only (No. xviii) is there any direct reference to Dionysus, though his worship at Delphi is clearly in mind in another (No. xv). The language is rarely if ever 'audacious'; there are few bold or elaborate compounds, and little ecstasy or excitement, except perhaps in the ᾿Ηίθεοι ἢ Θησεύς, though the language has an extraordinary gracefulness of its own. It is noticeable also how large a proportion of the poems is occupied by speeches in the first person; and though (except in No. xvii) these are woven into a narrative, they give the poems a dramatic quality like that which Aristotle finds and praises in Homer.

§ 5. It is not worth while to spend time over the names of KEKEIDES and KEDEIDES. An inscription[2] referring to the middle or later part of the fifth century records a victory of Kedeides at the Thargelia; and the scholiast on Aristophanes, *Clouds*, 983–4 (ἀρχαῖά γε καὶ Διπολιώδη καὶ τεττίγων ἀνάμεστα | καὶ Κηκείδου καὶ Βουφονίων) says that Kekeides was ἀρχαῖος διθυραμβογράφος, οὖ μέμνηται Κρατῖνος ἐν Πανόπταις. (No doubt the person mentioned was an old-fashioned contemporary

---

[1] Schol. Pind. *Olymp.* xi. 83.   [2] *C. I. G.* i. 334a.

of Cratinus.) These are all the facts, and on these it is not wise to identify Kekeides and Kedeides, nor to identify Kedeides either with KYDIDES (the rival of Lamprocles for the credit of composing the song Τηλέπορόν τι βόαμα, and described by the scholiast on Aristoph. *Clouds*, 967 as a κιθαρῳδός of Hermione), or with KYDIAS whom Plato[1] and Plutarch[2] mention as an erotic poet of the first half of the fifth century; still less to emend any or all of these names where they occur, as some scholars freely do.

It is possible that ION of Chios should be referred to the earlier rather than the later school of dithyrambic poets, if (as seems probable from Aristoph. *Peace*, 834–7) he died before 421 B.C.; but two fragments which are ascribed by scholars to dithyrambs—the first[3] on account of its subject, the second[4] for no better reason than that διθυράμβων comes first in the description of the poet by the scholiast who quotes the words (Ἴων ὁ Χῖος διθυράμβων καὶ τραγῳδίας καὶ μελῶν ποιητής· ἐποίησεν δὲ ᾠδὴν ἧς ἡ ἀρχή . . .)—show a certain floridity of style. They are as follows:

(1)   Ἄδαμον
παῖδα, ταυρωπόν, νέον οὐ νέον, ἥδιστον πρόπολον
βαρυγδούπων ἐρώτων, οἶνον ἀερσίνοον,
ἀνθρώπων πρύτανιν.

(2)   ἀοῖον ἠεροφοίταν
ἀστέρα μείναμεν ἀελίου λευκοπτέρυγα πρόδρομον.

We are told[5] that in one of Ion's dithyrambs Antigone and Ismene were said to have been burned to death in the temple of Hera by Laodamas, son of Eteocles; and in another[6] he told how Thetis had summoned Aegaeon from the deep to protect Zeus.

PANTACLES may also have belonged to the earlier school. The speaker of Antiphon's Oration περὶ τοῦ χορευτοῦ mentions that he drew Pantacles by lot as his poet at the Thargelia,

---

[1] *Charmid.* 155 d.   [2] *de Fac. in orbe Lun.*, ch. xix.
[3] Athen. ii, p. 35 e.
[4] Schol. on Aristoph. *Peace*, 833–7.   [5] Arg. ad Soph. *Antig.*
[6] Referred to by Schol. Apoll. Rhod. i. 1165.

when choregus, and the scholiast adds that Aristotle's Διδασκαλίαι showed that there was such a poet. (The speech is dated
before 415 B.C. by Drerup, Keil, &c.) The name also occurs
in a fragmentary inscription (*C. I. A.* i. 337) containing a dithyrambic record, but the date is lost.

NICOSTRATUS is also known from an inscription (*C. I. A.* i.
336), probably of a date not long before the end of the fifth
century, to have won a victory with a boys' chorus for the
Oeneid tribe. But it is not known to what school he may
have belonged.[1]

V

Dithyramb at Athens.

It will be convenient at this point to summarize the probable
history of the dithyramb down to (or a little beyond) the
middle of the fifth century B.C., before discussing the transition from the earlier to the later type.

§ 1. The dithyramb probably originated in Phrygia, or at
least among Thraco-Phrygian peoples, and came to Greece
with the cult of Dionysus. We hear of it first as a riotous
revel-song at Paros; Naxos and Thebes were apparently
among its early homes, but we do not know what form it took
in either place. As a literary composition dithyramb was the
creation of Arion at Corinth, and it seems (like the music of
the flute which accompanied it) to have been at first specially
cultivated in Dorian lands, but to have attained its full literary
development in connexion with the Dionysiac festivals at
Athens,—first under the tyrants, when Lasos of Hermione was
active, and then under the democracy, the first dithyrambic
victory at a democratic festival being won by Hypodicus of
Chalcis about the year 509 B.C.

It is noteworthy how many of the composers of dithyrambs
for the Athenian festivals, including all the most famous, were
of non-Athenian birth,—by no means all Dorians, but composing in a dialect containing Dorian elements,[2] though always
to music of the Phrygian type, and with the flute as the

---

[1] Vid. Brinck, *Diss. Hal.* vii, p. 101; Reisch, *de Mus. Gr. Cert.*, p. 31.

[2] See below, pp. 146 ff.

accompanying instrument. (During the period under review
no attempt appears to have been made to introduce any other
mode or instrument.) Both the Phrygian mode, and the music
of the flute, are described by Aristotle[1] as ὀργιαστικὰ καὶ
παθητικά. How did this orgiastic and passionate music suit
the comparatively quiet language which characterizes the
dithyrambs of Bacchylides, and even those of Pindar, though
in the fragments of the latter there is a certain imaginative
richness? It may be suggested that as the dithyramb was
further removed from the Bacchic revel to which it had
at first belonged, and became part of the celebration of an
orderly civic festival, the wildness of the music may have
abated. The subjects certainly ceased to be necessarily
Dionysiac,[2] though perhaps the absence of all allusions to
Dionysus in some of Bacchylides' dithyrambs was exceptional;
and the performance of dithyrambs in connexion with the
worship of Apollo may have tended to introduce a certain
sobriety into them, though down to a late date, as Plutarch
shows, the contrast between the dithyramb and the paean
remained strong and significant. But these are only conjectures; and it must be admitted that our evidence, and
particularly our knowledge of Greek music at this period, is
not sufficient to convert them into anything better.

So far as the extant remains are concerned, there is no
reason (apart from the one exceptional poem of Bacchylides)
to doubt Plato's statement that the story was presented, not
dramatically, but δι' ἀπαγγελίας αὐτοῦ τοῦ ποιητοῦ.

§ 2. At Athens the dithyramb was danced and sung by a
chorus of fifty men or boys. The name κύκλιος χορός, which
always means dithyramb, was probably derived from the
dancers being arranged in a circle, instead of in rectangular
formation as dramatic choruses were.[3] (The circle may have

---

[1] *Politics*, VIII. vii, p. 1342 a, b.

[2] Zenob. v. 40 explains the proverb Οὐδὲν πρὸς τὸν Διόνυσον primarily
with reference to dithyramb; the confusions in his account will be discussed later (see below, p. 167).

[3] Athen. v, p. 181 c definitely contrasts τετράγωνοι and κύκλιοι χοροί.
Wilamowitz, *Einl. in die gr. Trag.*, pp. 78, 79, thinks that the κύκλιος

been formed round the altar in the orchestra.) There is no
reason to doubt (though the fact is never expressly stated)
that the performances took place in the theatre.[1]

A dance especially associated with the dithyramb was the
τυρβασία. We do not know that it was the only one;
Hesychius describes it as ἀγωγή τις τῶν διθυραμβικῶν, which
looks as if he knew of other dithyrambic measures; Pollux [2]
says simply, τυρβασία δὲ ἐκαλεῖτο τὸ ὄρχημα τὸ διθυραμβικόν.
The meaning of the word τυρβασία is unknown. Some have
tried to connect the syllable τυρ- with the -θυρ- of διθύραμβος,
but this appears very doubtful. Solmsen [3] explains the
syllable as it occurs in Σάτυρος, Τίτυρος, &c., in a way which
makes both words mean 'ithyphallic'; but it is doubtful
whether this idea can be applied to the dithyrambic dance,
which, so far as our evidence goes, was never ithyphallic, nor
danced by satyrs. Others with much greater probability
connect the word with τυρβάζω, τύρβα and other words which
seem to imply confusion, riot, or revelry.[4] (That Hesychius
uses the word ἀγωγή seems to imply that he is thinking of the
rapidity of the movement.) Pausanias [5] mentions a feast in
Argolis called τύρβη: πρὸς δὲ τοῦ Ἐρασίνου ταῖς κατὰ τὸ ὄρος
ἐκβολαῖς Διονύσῳ καὶ Πανὶ θύουσι, Διονύσῳ δὲ καὶ ἑορτὴν
ἄγουσι καλουμένην τύρβην, and it has been suggested that this
means that the τυρβασία was Peloponnesian and Doric in
origin; but though this is likely enough to have been the
case, we do not know that the τυρβασία or the dithyramb

χορός was so called because it took place in the round orchestra and was
a 'round' dance, while in drama the σκηνή afforded a rectilinear back-
ground. This hardly seems to explain τετράγωνοι adequately; but the
question whether the circle was actually round an altar requires an
archaeological discussion which must be postponed till later (see Bethe,
Hermes, lix, p. 113).

[1] Navarre, *Dionysos*, p. 10, says that Pericles transferred them to his
newly-built Odeum. But the relevant passage in Plut. *Per.*, ch. 13, is
most naturally interpreted as referring entirely to the Panathenaic
contests.

[2] iv. 104.   [3] *Indogerm. Forsch.* xxx (1912), pp. 32 ff.

[4] This would suit the dithyramb of Archilochus.

II xxiv, § 6.

formed any part of the feast referred to, and so the argument
fails.

Some scholars[1] have supposed that the occurrence of TYPBAϹ
as the name of a Silenus on an Attic amphora preserved at
Naples[2] shows that the dithyrambic τυρβασία was danced
in satyr-dress. But the name may simply mean ' riotous ';
there is no suggestion of dithyramb about the scene depicted;
and the use of the name is probably no more significant than
that of Διθύραμφος attached to a satyr on a vase already
mentioned,[3] or that of names such as Τραγῳδία, Κωμῳδία,
'Εφυμνία, &c., for Bacchants on other vases. (It could not be
inferred from these that tragedy, &c., were performed by a
chorus dressed in fawn-skins, like the Bacchants.)

§ 3. The epigrams, written by or ascribed to Simonides,
which tell us something of the performances at Athens in that
poet's day, have already been quoted.[4] The dancers were
crowned with flowers and ivy, but there is no suggestion
either here or elsewhere that they wore masks. The dramatic
character of one dithyramb of Bacchylides, and the introduction
at a later date by Philoxenus of solos in character, certainly
do not necessarily imply the use of masks, least of all their use
in the earlier period. The belief that the original performers
of Arion's dithyrambs were masked rests on the idea that they
were disguised as satyrs, and this, as will be shown later,[5] is
almost certainly a misinterpretation of Suidas' notice. It is
much more likely that the literary dithyramb was the modification of a revel in which the revellers did not pretend to be
any other than themselves—human worshippers of Dionysus,
and in which they were crowned with flowers and ivy (like
revellers at a feast),[6] but not masked.

---

[1] See Nilsson, *Gr. Feste*, p. 303.

[2] See Heydemann, *Satyr- u. Bakchen-namen*, pp. 19, 39 ; Fränkel, *Satyr-
u. Bakchen-namen*, pp. 69, 103. Two Satyrs—Tyrbas and (probably)
Simos—and three Bacchants, two of whom are called Ourania and
Thaleia, are playing round Marsyas with his flute and Olympus with
his lyre. The scene is plainly fanciful and has nothing to do with
dithyramb. In Xen. *Cyneg.* vii. 5 Τύρβας is the name of a dog.

[3] See above, p. 11.   [4] pp. 25-27.   [5] See below, p. 133.

[6] See below, p. 234.

§ 4. The flute-player, who during the earliest period was
hired by the poet, and, though important, was secondary to
him,[1] stood in the midst of the dancers.[2] It was only when
the music had become predominant that the choregus became
responsible for the flute-player. It appears from Aristophanes
(*Birds*, 1403–4) that the choregi (each representing his tribe)
must have had a choice between the rival poets :

ταυτὶ πεποίηκας τὸν κυκλιοδιδάσκαλον
ὃς ταῖσι φυλαῖς περιμάχητός εἰμ' ἀεί;

and the arrangement was probably the same at the Thargelia
as at the Dionysia. A passage of Antiphon [3] suggests that
the choregi drew lots for the order of choice ; the choregus
who drew tenth place would of course have no choice (ἐπειδὴ
χορηγὸς κατεστάθην εἰς Θαργήλια καὶ ἔλαχον Παντακλέα
διδάσκαλον—presumably because only Pantacles was left) : [4]
and in the time of Demosthenes (and probably earlier) they
certainly drew lots for the order of choice among the flute-
players.[5]

§ 5. The contest between the dithyrambic choruses at
Athens, was, as has been said, a tribal one. At the Dionysia
each chorus was drawn entirely from one of the ten tribes,
and as five choruses of men and five of boys competed, all ten
tribes took part.[6] The choregi were nominated by the tribal

---

[1] Plut. *de Mus.* xxx ; Pratinas, fr. 1 : see above, p. 28.

[2] Schol. on Aeschines *in Timarchum*, § 10 (Bekker in *Abh. Akad.
Berl.* 1836, p. 228) ἐν τοῖς χοροῖς δὲ τοῖς κυκλίοις μέσος ἵστατο αὐλητής.

[3] *Or.* vi, § 11.

[4] Cf. Xen. *Mem.* III. iv, § 4 καὶ μὴν οὐδὲ ᾠδῆς γε ὁ ᾿Αντισθένης οὐδὲ χορῶν
διδασκαλίας ἔμπειρος ὢν ὅμως ἐγένετο ἱκανὸς εὑρεῖν τοὺς κρατίστους ταῦτα.

[5] Dem. *in Meid.* §§ 13, 14. From Isaeus v, § 36, it appears that a
similar drawing of lots for choice took place in the tribal contests of
πυρριχισταί, and that it was a great disadvantage to be drawn last.

[6] Schol. in Aesch. *in Tim.* § 10 ἐξ ἔθους ᾿Αθηναῖοι κατὰ φυλὰς ἵστασαν
ν' παίδων χορὸν ἢ ἀνδρῶν, ὥστε γενέσθαι δέκα χορούς, ἐπειδὴ καὶ δέκα φυλαί.
διαγωνίζονται δ' ἀλλήλοις διθυράμβῳ, φυλάττοντος τοῦ χορηγοῦντος ἑκάστῳ
χορῷ τὰ ἐπιτήδεια. ὁ δ' οὖν νικήσας χορὸς τρίποδα λαμβάνει, ὃν ἀνατίθησι τῷ
Διονύσῳ. λέγονται δ' οἱ διθύραμβοι χοροὶ κύκλιοι καὶ χορὸς κύκλιος. There is
a special difficulty in regard to the record in *C. I. A.* ii. 971 d
(i, Wilhelm, *Urk. dram. Aufführ.*, p. 30), according to which the same

officials and appointed by the archon, subject to the possibility
of an appeal by means of a challenge to ἀντίδοσις. (Aeschines
(*in Tim.* § 11) states that the choregus for a boys' chorus had
to be over forty years of age; but this rule cannot always
have been observed; the speaker of Lysias' 21st Oration can
hardly have been over twenty-five years old.) The victory was
primarily that of the tribe;[1] but the great didascalic inscription[2] shows that in the official records of dithyrambic victories
at the Dionysia throughout the fifth and fourth centuries the
name of the choregus was also mentioned; the name of the
poet, and in the fourth century that of the flute-player, were
recorded on tribal and private choregic monuments, but not
in the official records. The prize won by the victorious tribe
was a tripod, which was dedicated to Dionysus, with an
appropriate monumental setting, by the choregus. (The best-
known extant specimens are the monuments of Lysicrates and
Thrasyllus.) There is no doubt that the poet whose work was
awarded the first prize received a bull.[3] The mention in the
epigram of Simonides of Νίκας ἅρμα, and the words of
Epigram 148,[4] ἅρμασιν ἐν Χαρίτων φορηθείς have suggested to
some scholars that the poet was escorted home in a chariot by
a festal procession, his head crowned with ribands and roses
(μίτραισι δὲ καὶ ῥόδων ἀώτοις | σοφῶν ἀοιδῶν ἐσκίασαν λιπαρὰν
ἔθειραν), and there is nothing improbable about this, though
the references to the chariot *may* be metaphorical.

At the Thargelia also (as at the Prometheia and Hephaesteia[5])
the contest was tribal; but at the Thargelia each choregus
represented two tribes,[6] and on the extant inscriptions the

tribe in 336/5 B. C. supplied both a boys' and a mens' chorus. But this
may have been an accidental dislocation: comp. Brinck, *Diss. Phil. Hal.*
vii, p. 86; Reisch in Pauly-W. iii, col. 2432. There is no sign of any
such irregularity in the period now under consideration.

[1] Cf. Lysias, *Or.* iv, § 3; Dem. *in Meid.* § 5.   [2] *C. I. A.* ii. 971.

[3] Simon. fr. 145 (see above, p. 25). Whether the Schol. on Plato,
Rep., p. 399 (see p. 7) refers to Athens is uncertain; it states that the
second prize was an amphoreus of wine, the third a goat, which was led
away smeared with wine-lees.

[4] See above, p. 26.   [5] *C. I. A.* ii. 556.

[6] Aristot. *Athen. Pol.* lvi, § 3.

choregus, not the tribe, is mentioned as victor, though the names of the tribes which he represented are recorded (e.g. Ἐρυξίας Ἐρυξιμάχου Κυδαθηναιεὺς ἐχορήγει Πανδιονίδι Ἐρεχθηίδι παιδῶν). The tripods were erected in the temple of Apollo Pythius. In the fifth century the tribe which provided a choregus appears to have drawn lots for its partner among the five tribes which provided none, but at a later date it is most likely that the same two tribes always worked together, providing the choregus alternately.[1] Lysias[2] affords interesting evidence as to the cost of a dithyrambic chorus. The magnificence expected evidently varied with the festival. The speaker states that a chorus of men at the Thargelia in 411/410 B.C. cost him 2,000 drachmae, and a similar chorus at the Great Dionysia, in the next year, 5,000 drachmae, including the cost of the tripod; while a κύκλιος χορός at the Lesser Panathenaea in 409/408 B.C. cost only 300 drachmae. A chorus of boys for a festival (not named) in 405/404 cost him more than fifteen minae (1,500 drachmae). Demosthenes[3] states that a chorus of men cost much more than a tragic chorus (on which Lysias' client spent 3,000 drachmae),—partly, no doubt, on account of the larger number of its members. Brinck[4] offers various conjectures to account for the very small expenditure on the chorus at the Lesser Panathenaea: ʻaut numerus choreutarum minor fuit, aut tota exornatio minus magnifica quam Dionysiis, aut utrumque statuendum est.ʼ But we have no evidence, and this is the only mention of a cyclic chorus at this festival.

VI

The Later Dithyramb.

§ 1. By the last quarter of the fifth century B.C. the change which had been taking place gradually in the literary and social atmosphere of Athens was practically complete, and the character of the later dithyramb is closely connected with this

---

[1] See Brinck, op. cit., pp. 89, 90. The evidence consists in the conjunction of the same tribes in inscriptions recording victories in years not far apart; but it is not quite conclusive.

[2] *Or.* xxi, §§ 1, 2.   [3] *in Meid.*, § 156.   [4] op. cit., p. 75.

change.[1] The younger generation were impatient of the old-
fashioned discipline and literature; the lyric poetry of the
older writers—Stesichorus, Pindar, and others,—a knowledge
of which seems to be assumed in his audience by Aristophanes,
was no doubt read by cultivated persons, but became gradually
more and more unfamiliar and out of date; no lyric poetry of
any importance was composed apart from the dithyrambs,
νόμοι, and paeans required for performance at festivals; from
the festivals themselves the religious interest was probably
fast disappearing, and it is natural that in these also the desire
for novelty and freedom should find expression. Aristophanes
naturally regards the change as an abandonment of discipline,
order, and sound educational ideas; but there is no doubt that
it was popular, and Euripides clearly sympathized with it.

§ 2. In a fragment from a play called Χείρων and doubtfully
ascribed to Pherecrates[2] (the poet of the Old Comedy, who

---

[1] An admirable account of the tendencies of the time is given by
Wilamowitz, *Textgesch. der gr. Lyriker*, pp. 11–15.

[2] Athen. viii, p. 364 a, quoting another fragment, describes it as τὰ
εἰρημένα ὑπὸ τοῦ τὸν Χείρωνα πεποιηκότος, εἴτε Φερεκράτης ἐστὶν εἴτε Νικόμαχος
ὁ ῥυθμικὸς ἢ ὅστις δήποτε. Nicomachus ὁ ῥυθμικός was a contemporary of
Aristoxenus (near the end of the fourth century B. C.), and Athen. is
probably confusing him with another Nicomachus, almost certainly a
poet of the Old Comedy, to whom Eratosthenes ascribed the Μεταλλεῖς,
also attributed to Pherecrates (Harpocr. s. v. Μεταλλεῖς· ἔστι δὲ καὶ δρᾶμα
Φερεκράτους Μεταλλεῖς, ὅπερ Νικόμαχόν φησι πεποιηκέναι ᾿Ερατοσθένης ἐν
ἑβδόμῳ περὶ τῆς ἀρχαίας κωμῳδίας); cf. Meineke, *Com. Fr.* i, p. 76. Meineke
himself thinks that the play may have been by the comic poet Plato, on
the ground (surely insufficient) of the writer's use of στρόβιλος of musical
extravagances—a use ascribed to Plato by the grammarian Phrynichus.
Wilamowitz (*Timotheus*, p. 74) thinks that the poem can hardly have been
written for the stage, but does not say why. A greater difficulty in the
way of ascribing it to Pherecrates lies in the fact that Philoxenus, who
is supposed to be criticized in the last part of it, can hardly have become
sufficiently famous in the lifetime of Pherecrates to be thus treated; and
the criticism can hardly be earlier than 400 B.C. But the passage
appears to be a criticism of the poets quite in the vein of the Old
Comedy, both in its conservatism and its language, whoever wrote it.
Unfortunately the text is in bad condition. It deals almost entirely
with the music of the cithara, not that of the flute, and is only important
for the present purpose as illustrating the general tendency of the time.

flourished, roughly speaking, from about 438 B. C. until after
421), Μουσική complains to Δικαιοσύνη of the injuries inflicted
upon her by the new lyric poets, and mentions the special mis-
demeanours of each. The beginnings of the mischief are traced
to MELANIPPIDES, a native of Melos. Suidas distinguishes
two poets of the name, making the earlier the grandfather of
the later; but there are great difficulties in this, and Rohde [1]
is probably right (though his arguments are not all equally
convincing) in concluding that Suidas misunderstood his
authorities, and that there was but one Melanippides, who was
active from about 480 B. C. onwards, and died at the court of
Perdiccas in Macedonia sometime between 454 [2] and 413.
(There are plenty of other instances of the duplication of poets
by Suidas, e. g. Nicomachus, Phrynichus, Crates, Timocles,
Sappho.) His fame is attested by Xenophon,[3] who makes
a certain Aristodemus, conversing with Socrates, place
him as a dithyrambic poet in a position corresponding to
that of Homer, Polycleitus, and Zeuxis in their respective
arts.

The principal change in the dithyramb which was ascribed
to Melanippides was the introduction of ἀναβολαί or lyric
solos—at least they were probably always solos—in which no
antistrophic arrangement was observed. The change was
doubtless designed to secure a more realistic expression of
emotion, which does not return to the same point antistro-
phically, as it were, at fixed intervals: and Aristotle [4] connects
the abandonment of the antistrophic form with the mimetic
character of the new dithyramb. The words in Pseudo-Plutarch
de Musica [5] which connect the rise of the flute-player into undue prominence with Melanippides are probably an interpo-

---

[1] *Rhein. Mus.* xxxiii, pp. 213-4.

[2] Rohde says 436, when Perdiccas became sole monarch. But he may
have invited Melanippides while still sharing the throne.

[3] *Memor.* I. iv, § 3.

[4] *Probl.* xix. 15 διὸ καὶ οἱ διθύραμβοι, ἐπειδὴ μιμητικοὶ ἐγένοντο, οὐκέτι
ἔχουσιν ἀντιστρόφους, πρότερον δὲ εἶχον. The context suggests that he
refers to the introduction of dramatic solo-parts.

[5] See above, pp. 30-1.

lation as they stand; but they may have had some basis of
fact; and if he did elaborate the music of the flute, as he
certainly did that of the lyre, his object may again have been
the vivid portrayal of emotion, since the emotional character
of the flute was strongly felt.

Of course there was criticism. A contemporary attack,
probably, is recorded by Aristotle:[1] ὁμοίως δὲ καὶ αἱ περίοδοι
αἱ μακραὶ οὖσαι λόγος γίγνεται καὶ ἀναβολῇ ὅμοιον, ὥστε
γίγνεται ὃ ἔσκωψεν Δημόκριτος ὁ Χῖος εἰς Μελανιππίδην
ποιήσαντα ἀντὶ τῶν ἀντιστρόφων ἀναβολάς,

> οἵ τ' αὐτῷ κακὰ τεύχει ἀνὴρ ἄλλῳ κακὰ τεύχων,
> ἡ δὲ μακρὰ 'ναβολὴ τῷ ποιήσαντι κακίστη.

The fragment ascribed to Pherecrates accuses Melanippides
of making poetry slack or effeminate, though here the
reference is, probably, not specifically to his dithyrambs, since
the criticism is directed against some change made by the poet
in the number of the strings of the lyre, the nature of which
the corrupt text does not enable us to understand.[2] The scanty
remains of Melanippides include fragments of a *Danaides*, a
Marsyas, and a *Persephone*. Smyth speaks of these as dithyrambs, and they may have been such, but there is no certain
ground for stating that they were. The fragment of the
Marsyas represents Athena as flinging away the flute in disgust
at its effect on the beauty of her cheeks:

> ἁ μὲν Ἀθάνα
> ὄργαν' ἔρριψέν θ' ἱερᾶς ἀπὸ χειρός,
> εἶπέ τ'. Ἔρρετ' αἴσχεα, σώματι λύμα,
> οὔ με τᾷδ' ἐγὼ κακότατι δίδωμι.

About this a pretty controversy seems to have arisen, a later
dithyrambic poet, Telestes, denying that the goddess did any
such thing (see below).

---

[1] *Rhet.* III. ix. 1409 b 25 ff.

[2] The uncertainty of the text also makes it impossible to place any
confidence in the statement, based on Pseudo-Plut. *de Mus.* xv. 1136 c,
that some writers ascribed to Melanippides the introduction of the
Lydian ἁρμονία in the flute-accompaniment of the ἐπικήδειον.

The lines from the *Persephone* contain only a piece of etymology :

καλεῖται δ', εἵνεκ' ἐν κόλποισι γαίας
ἄχε' εἶσιν προχέων
Ἀχέρων.

The passage from the *Danaides* is the longest extant : [1]

οὐ γὰρ ἀνθρώπων φόρευν μορφὰν †ἐνεῖδος†,
οὐ δίαιταν τὰν γυναικείαν ἔχον,
ἀλλ' ἐν ἁρμάτεσσι διφρούχοις ἐγυμνάζοντ' ἂν εὖ,
δι' ἄλσεα πολλάκι θήραισιν φρένα τερπόμεναι,
ἤθ' ἱερόδακρυν λίβανον εὐώδεις τε φοίνικας κασίαν τε
    ματεῦσαι,
τέρενα Σύρια σπέρματα.

(In l. 1, Dobree conjectures μορφᾶεν εἶδος, comparing Pind. *Isthm.* vii. 22, ἰδεῖν τε μορφάεις.)

Two fragments from a poem or poems not named are conjecturally ascribed to dithyrambs by Hartung on account of their theme, viz. :

πάντες δ' ἀπεστύγεον ὕδωρ,
τὸ πρὶν ἐόντες ἀΐδριες οἴνου,
τάχα δὴ τάχα τοὶ μὲν ἀπ' ὦν ὄλοντο,
τοὶ δὲ παράπληκτον χέον ὀμφάν,

and (another piece of etymology) :

ἐπώνυμον, δέσποτ', οἶνον Οἰνέως.

Clement of Alexandria quotes the supposed testimony of Melanippides to the immortality of the soul :

κλῦθί μοι, ὦ πάτερ, θαῦμα βροτῶν,
τᾶς ἀειζώου μεδέων ψυχᾶς.

(The words were perhaps addressed to Dionysus.)   The only remaining extant fragment is about Eros :

γλυκὺ γὰρ θέρος ἀνδρὸς ὑποσπείρων πραπίδεσσι πόθον.

But it is quite possible that none of these quotations is from a dithyramb, and they are not sufficient to afford any idea of

---

[1] The subject and text are very uncertain.

the poet's style. One or two of them show some amount
of resolution of feet, but it is an exaggeration to say, as
Smyth does, this constitutes an important modification of the
ancient severity of style. The fragments do not justify any
generalization.

It is only necessary to mention in passing DIAGORAS of
Melos, the famous freethinker, who was a little senior to his
fellow-countryman Melanippides, and was exiled from Athens
for the 'atheism' shown in his ridicule of the Eleusinia.
Sextus Empiricus (ix. 402) describes him as διθυραμβοποιός, ὥς
φασι, τὸ πρῶτον γενόμενος ὡς εἴ τις ἄλλος δεισιδαίμων, and the
two fragments which survive of him (not from dithyrambs) show
that as a poet he could express himself with orthodox piety;
but his poetry was probably of little significance, and was
known even to ancient scholars only from the mention of it
by Aristoxenus. (All that is known of him is discussed by
Wilamowitz, *Textgesch. der. gr. Lyriker*, pp. 80–4.) He may
not have favoured the innovations made by Melanippides.

Of HIERONYMUS nothing is known apart from a passing
allusion in Aristophanes' *Clouds*, 349, which the scholiast
explains by reference to his immoral life. He must have been
contemporary with the new school.

§ 3. The movement begun by Melanippides continued. The
music became more and more elaborate, and (though we
cannot fix any precise date) the modes appropriate to each
several kind of lyric came to be abandoned; the composers,
so Plato tells us,[1] were influenced by the passion for
novelty which was displayed by popular audiences. Plato is
writing, probably, towards the middle of the fourth century,
but his words were clearly intended to apply to the new
school as a whole. μετὰ δὲ ταῦτα προϊόντος τοῦ χρόνου,
ἄρχοντες μὲν τῆς ἀμούσου παρανομίας ποιηταὶ ἐγίγνοντο φύσει
μὲν ποιητικοί, ἀγνώμονες δὲ περὶ τὸ δίκαιον τῆς Μούσης καὶ τὸ
νόμιμον, βακχεύοντες καὶ μᾶλλον τοῦ δέοντος κατεχόμενοι ὑφ'
ἡδονῆς, κεράννυντες δὲ θρήνους τε ὕμνοις καὶ παίωνας διθυράμβοις, καὶ αὐλῳδίας δὴ ταῖς κιθαρῳδίαις μιμούμενοι, καὶ
πάντα εἰς πάντα συνάγοντες, μουσικῆς ἄκοντες ὑπ' ἀνοίας

---

[1] *Laws*, iii. 700 d.

καταψευδόμενοι ὡς ὀρθότητα μὲν οὐκ ἔχοι οὐδ᾽ ἡντινοῦν μουσική, ἡδονῇ δὲ τῇ κρίνοντος, εἴτε βελτίων εἴτε χείρων ἂν εἴη τις, κρίνοιτο ὀρθότατα. τοιαῦτα δὴ ποιοῦντες ποιήματα, λόγους τε ἐπιλέγοντες τοιούτους, τοῖς πολλοῖς ἐνέθεσαν παρανομίαν εἰς τὴν μουσικὴν καὶ τόλμαν ὡς ἱκανοῖς οὖσιν κρίνειν. ὅθεν δὴ τὰ θέατρα ἐξ ἀφώνων φωνήεντ᾽ ἐγένοντο, ὡς ἐπαΐοντα ἐν μούσαις τό τε καλὸν καὶ μή, καὶ ἀντὶ ἀριστοκρατίας ἐν αὐτῇ θεατροκρατία τις πονηρὰ γέγονεν. The same mixture of musical styles by the writers whom we are about to consider is censured by Dionysius of Halicarnassus.[1] οἱ δέ γε διθυραμβοποιοὶ καὶ τοὺς τρόπους μετέβαλλον, Δωρίους τε καὶ Φρυγίους καὶ Λυδίους ἐν τῷ αὐτῷ ᾄσματι ποιοῦντες, καὶ τὰς μελῳδίας ἐξήλλαττον, τότε μὲν ἐναρμονίους ποιοῦντες, τότε δὲ χρωματικάς, τότε δὲ διατόνους, καὶ τοῖς ῥυθμοῖς κατὰ πολλὴν ἄδειαν ἐνεξουσιάζοντες διετέλουν, οἵ γε δὴ κατὰ Φιλόξενον καὶ Τιμόθεον καὶ Τελέστην· ἐπεὶ παρά γε τοῖς ἀρχαίοις τεταγμένος ἦν καὶ ὁ διθύραμβος.

The fragment ascribed to Pherecrates places Kinesias and Phrynis next to Melanippides among the corruptors of poetry and music.

Of PHRYNIS little is known. He came from Mitylene, and was son of Kamon. The tale that he was a slave, and cook in the household of the tyrant Hiero, was probably an invention. (As Suidas says, if it had been true, it would surely have been mentioned by the comic poets who attacked him for enfeebling the ancient music.) The characteristic feature of his music seems to have consisted of 'twists and twirls'—καμπαὶ δυσκολόκαμπτοι as Aristophanes[2] calls them; but most of the notices about him[3] refer to his alterations in the νόμος and in the κιθάρα by which it was accompanied; there is little reason to connect him with dithyramb; and if, as Suidas' notice suggests, he early gave up the flute for the cithara, this is natural enough. That his innovations did not go to extremes is indicated by the delight of Timotheus at defeating him, and so securing the triumph of his own newer style.

KINESIAS, son of Meles, was primarily a dithyrambic poet.

[1] *de Comp. Vb.* xix.　　　　　　　　　　[2] *Clouds*, 970-1.
[3] Suidas, s. v.; Pseudo-Plut. *de Mus.* ch. vi; Pollux, IV. lx; Aristotle, *Met.* i. 993 b 16. Cf. Wilam. *Timotheus*, pp. 65-7.

Whether or not there were two poets of the name, as Aristotle is said [1] to have stated in his Διδασκαλίαι, is uncertain; [2] but there was evidently only one of any significance, and he flourished in the last quarter of the fifth century. He attracted the onslaughts of contemporary comic poets and others as much by his personal peculiarities and his defiance of religious conventions as by his dithyrambs. He was very tall and thin, and (so it was said) wore stays to hold himself together. Lysias [3] made it a great point against a defendant that he was supported by Kinesias, who was guilty of outrageous acts against religion, and had founded a kind of 'Thirteen Club' (κακοδαιμονισταί) which dined on 'unlucky' days. The language of Pherecrates does not give a very clear idea of the offences of Kinesias, but suggests that he composed everything ' the wrong way round '—like the reflections in a mirror :

> Κινησίας δέ μ' ὁ κατάρατος Ἀττικός,
> ἐξαρμονίους καμπὰς ποιῶν ἐν ταῖς στροφαῖς,
> ἀπολώλεχ' οὕτως, ὥστε τῆς ποιήσεως
> τῶν διθυράμβων, καθάπερ ἐν ταῖς ἀσπίσιν,
> ἀρίστερ' αὐτοῦ φαίνεται τὰ δεξιά.

Aristophanes, in a delightful scene in the Birds,[4] which is too long to quote and too good to abridge, ridicules the ἀναβολαί of Kinesias, with their multiplication of meaningless epithets (perhaps spun out to fit the accompaniment), and it is probably he who is specially referred to in the Clouds, 333 ff.:

> κυκλίων τε χορῶν ᾀσματοκάμπτας, ἄνδρας μετεωροφένακας,
> οὐδὲν δρῶντας βόσκουσ' ἀργούς, ὅτι ταύτας μουσοποιοῦσιν κτλ.[5]

An allusion to Kinesias in the Ecclesiazusae shows that he must have lived on into the fourth century. Plato [6] speaks of him as one who was guided by the pleasure of his audience, instead of caring for their edification. But none of his work has come down to us, except the two words Φθιῶτ' Ἀχιλλεῦ

[1] Schol. on Aristoph. Birds, 1379.   [2] Cf. Brinck, op. cit., p. 110.
[3] ap. Athen. xii, p. 551 e.   [4] ll. 1373-1404.
[5] Comp. also Frogs, 336, 1437 ; Gerytades, fr. 149, 150; Eccles. 329, 330.   [6] Gorg. 501 e.

which he is said to have repeated *ad nauseam*. (Strattis
wrote a whole comedy about him, and addressed the words to
Kinesias himself.[1])

§ 4. But the most famous and influential of the new school
were Philoxenus and Timotheus.

PHILOXENUS was a native of Cythera. The Parian Marble
gives the dates of his birth and death as 436/435 and 380/
379 B.C. respectively. Unfortunately the records about him
show that he was early confused with Philoxenus of Leucas,
the author of the Δεῖπνον, a gastronomical poem in hexameters
quoted in Plato's *Phaon* and elsewhere, and sometimes wrongly
ascribed to the poet of Cythera; while some of the anecdotes
which make the latter a gourmand may have been transferred
to him from his namesake of Leucas.[2]

Philoxenus (the dithyrambic poet) was for some time at the
court of Dionysius of Syracuse, who enjoyed his company at
and after dinner; but he engaged in an intrigue with Galatea,
the concubine of Dionysius, and the tyrant sent him to the
quarries, where a cavern was long afterwards shown as his
prison.[3] Nothing daunted, the poet there composed his most
famous dithyramb, the *Cyclops*, in which the blinded Cyclops,
in love with Galatea, represented the short-sighted Dionysius.[4]
Apparently the Cyclops sang a solo to the lyre in the course
of the poem, and this implies a great change in the ancient
form of the dithyramb, as well as the introduction of an
instrument hitherto strange to it.[5]

---

[1] Athen. xii, p. 551 d ff. Comp. also Harpocr. and Suid. s. v. Κινησίας;
Plut. *de Glor. Ath.* v, p. 348 b; *Quaest. Conviv.* VII. iii, p. 712 a; *de Aud.
poet.* iv, p. 22 a; Philodemus, περὶ εὐσεβείας, p. 52 (Gomperz); *C.I.A.* ii.
1253. It appears from Aristoph. *Frogs*, 153, that Kinesias composed a
πυρρίχη, but Crusius (Pauly-W., *Real-Enc.* v, col. 1217) gives no justification for saying that he included it in a dithyramb. (Athen. xiv, p. 631 a,
distinguishes a less martial type of πυρρίχη, Dionysiac in character, from
the Spartan war-dance known by the name; but he does not make clear
of what date he is speaking.)

[2] See Wilamowitz, *Textgesch. der gr. Lyr.*, pp. 85 ff.

[3] Aelian, *Var. Hist.* xii. 44.

[4] Diodor. xv. 6; Athen. i, p. 6 e; Schol. Aristoph. *Plut.* 290, &c.

[5] The belief, however, that Timotheus and Philoxenus increased the
number of the chorus (Luetcke, *de Graecorum dithyrambis*, p. 60) appears

The Pseudo-Plutarch [1] quotes as from Pherecrates (whose criticisms of other poets, placed in the mouth of Μουσική, immediately precede) some lines which are textually imperfect, but give a general sense which is plain enough. He writes: καὶ Ἀριστοφάνης ὁ κωμικὸς μνημονεύει Φιλοξένου καί φησιν ὅτι εἰς τοὺς κυκλίους χοροὺς μέλη εἰσήγαγεν. ἡ δὲ Μουσικὴ λέγει ταῦτα·

> ἐξαρμονίους ὑπερβολαίους τ' ἀνοσίους
> καὶ νιγλάρους, ὥσπερ τε τὰς ῥαφάνους ὅλην
> καμπῶν με κατεμέστωσε.

(i. e. the poet indulged in shrill meaningless sounds with frequent 'runs' or trills. The pun in καμπῶν is expressive, but untranslatable). Unfortunately the passage has been much vexed by the critics. Westphal and Reinach are not content to take μέλη as 'solos', and in fact it is not easy to do so; they would read προβατίων αἰγῶν τε μέλη, after Aristophanes' *Plutus*, 290 ff.; but it seems at least as likely that some word meaning 'solos' (e. g. μονῳδικά, as suggested by Westphal) may have dropped out. But further, the lines themselves are inserted by some editors among those referring to Timotheus in the quotation which precedes (after the words ἐκτραπέλους μυρμηκίας).[2] Westphal conjectures that they were accidentally omitted by the scribe, and afterwards inserted in the wrong place, and a marginal note added by some one, ἡ δὲ Μουσικὴ λέγει ταῦτα. This is not impossible; but it cannot be said that such a supposition is necessary.

A much more favourable view of Philoxenus appears in a fragment of Antiphanes' Τριταγωνιστής,[3] a play which may have appeared at any time after Philoxenus' death:

> πολύ γ' ἐστὶ πάντων τῶν ποιητῶν διάφορος
> ὁ Φιλόξενος, πρώτιστα μὲν γὰρ ὀνόμασιν
> ἰδίοισι καὶ καινοῖσι χρῆται πανταχοῦ.
> ἔπειτα τὰ μέλη μεταβολαῖς καὶ χρώμασιν

to rest entirely on the false reading ὀλιγοχορείαν (for ὀλιγοχορδίαν), in Pseudo-Plut. *de Mus.* xii, p. 1135 d.

[1] *de Mus.* xxx. 1142 a.

[2] The lines are printed below, p. 65.   [3] Athen. xiv, p. 643 d.

ὡς εὖ κέκραται. θεὸς ἐν ἀνθρώποισιν ἦν
ἐκεῖνος, εἰδὼς τὴν ἀληθῶς μουσικήν.
οἱ νῦν δὲ κισσόπλεκτα καὶ κρηναῖα καὶ
ἀνθεσιπότατα μέλεα μελέοις ὀνόμασιν
ποιοῦσιν ἐμπλέκοντες ἀλλότρια μέλη.

The last lines suggest that the mixture of ἁρμονίαι, which Plato notes as characteristic of the new school, was not regularly practised by Philoxenus. We know, however, from Aristotle [1] that he did try to compose a dithyramb, the Μῦσοι, in the Dorian mood, but found the tradition too strong for him and slipped back into the Phrygian.

The *Cyclops* was wittily parodied by Aristophanes in the *Plutus*; [2] but only a few lines of the original survive:

 fr. 6. συμβαλοῦμαί τι μέλος ὑμῖν εἰς ἔρωτα.

(The ascription of this to the *Cyclops* is not certain, but very probable.[3])

 fr. 8. (The Cyclops to Galatea.)

  ὦ καλλιπρόσωπε
  χρυσοβόστρυχε Γαλάτεια,
  χαριτόφωνε, θάλος ἐρώτων.

 fr. 9. (Odysseus speaks.)

  οἵῳ μ' ὁ δαίμων τέρατι συγκαθεῖρξεν.

 fr. 10. (The Cyclops to Odysseus.)

  ἔθυσας ; ἀντιθύσῃ.

It is not safe to attempt to reconstruct the actual words of Philoxenus from Aristophanes' parody; but the sense of one or two lines is preserved in two passages quoted by Bergk, viz : (1) the scholiast on Theocr. xi. 1 : καὶ Φιλόξενος ποιεῖ τὸν Κύκλωπα παραμυθούμενον ἑαυτὸν ἐπὶ τῷ τῆς Γαλατείας ἔρωτι καὶ ἐντελλόμενον τοῖς δελφῖσιν, ὅπως ἀγγέλλωσιν αὐτῇ ὅτι ταῖς Μούσαις τὸν ἔρωτα ἀκεῖται : and (2) Plutarch, *Symp. Quaest.* I. v, § 1, ὅπου καὶ τὸν Κύκλωπα Μούσαις εὐφώνοις ἰᾶσθαί φησι τὸν ἔρωτα Φιλόξενος. (Dionysius fancied himself as a poet.)

---

[1] Pol. VIII. vii, p. 1342 b 9.   [2] 290 ff.
[3] See Bergk, *Gr. Lyr.* iii⁴, pp. 610-11.

Of the strange words used by Philoxenus we have a hint in a fragment[1] of Antiphanes' Τραυματίας, from which he seems to have used the phrase οἶνον τὸν ἀρκεσίγυιον; and in the scholia on Aristophanes, Clouds, 335, where the scholiast, in stating (what is chronologically impossible) that Aristophanes is parodying Philoxenus' use of στρεπταιγλᾶν, may have in mind some actual use of the word by Philoxenus.

Philoxenus engaged the well-known flute-player Antigenidas to accompany his works.[2]

The stories about the poet do not here concern us; but a witty account of his last hours (implying a high appreciation of his work) by the comic poet Machon[3] is worth quoting in part, whatever truth there may be in it (for here too the reputation of his namesake may have invaded his own). According to Machon he died from indigestion after eating almost the whole of a fine cuttlefish; the doctor who attended him told him that death was near, and asked for his last wishes: the poet replied:

τέλος ἔχει τὰ πάντα μοι,
ἴατρε, φησί, καὶ δεδιῴκηται πάλαι·
τοὺς διθυράμβους σὺν θεοῖς καταλιμπάνω
ἠνδρωμένους καὶ πάντας ἐστεφανωμένους,
οὓς ἀνατίθημι τοῖς ἐμαυτοῦ συντρόφοις
Μούσαις—Ἀφροδίτην καὶ Διόνυσον ἐπιτρόπους.
ταῦθ' αἱ διαθῆκαι διασαφοῦσιν· ἀλλ' ἐπεὶ
ὁ Τιμοθέου Χάρων σχολάζειν οὐκ ἐᾷ,
οὐκ τῆς Νιόβης, χωρεῖν δὲ πορθμίδ' ἀναβοᾷ,
καλεῖ δὲ μοῖρα νύχιος, ἧς κλύειν χρεών
ἵν' ἔχων ἀποτρέχω πάντα τἀμαυτοῦ κάτω,
τοῦ πουλύποδός μοι τὸ κατάλοιπον ἀπόδοτε.

§ 5. TIMOTHEUS of Miletus lived, roughly speaking, from 450 to 360 B.C. The Parian Marble gives the date of his death when ninety years old as 357, or a year between that and 365 B.C. (editors are not agreed as to which). Suidas says that he lived ninety-seven years. The date of his birth must thus have fallen between 462 and 447. Probably the later

---

[1] Fr. 207.   [2] Suid. s. v. Ἀντιγενίδης.   [3] Quoted by Athen. viii, p. 341.

date assigned to his death, viz. 357 B. C., is the correct one,
if there is any accuracy in the note of Suidas which connects
him with Philip of Macedon (ἦν δὲ ἐπὶ τῶν Εὐριπίδου χρόνων
τοῦ τραγικοῦ, καθ' οὓς καὶ Φίλιππος ὁ Μακέδων ἐβασίλευσεν—
a strange remark as it stands, but not without its parallels in
Suidas).

He seems to have gone beyond all his contemporaries and
predecessors in innovation, and to have made a boast of it, his
first great triumph being his victory over Phrynis, whom he
regarded as old-fashioned. Two extant fragments [1] illustrate
the spirit of the man:

(1) μακάριος ἦσθα Τιμόθεος, εὖτε κῆρυξ
    εἶπε, "νικᾷ Τιμόθεος
    Μιλήσιος τὸν Κάμωνος τὸν Ἰωνοκάμπταν."

(2) οὐκ ἀείδω τὰ παλεά, καινὰ γὰρ ἀμὰ κρείσσω.
    νέος ὁ Ζεὺς βασιλεύει,
    τὸ πάλαι δ' ἦν Κρόνος ἄρχων·
    ἀπίτω Μοῦσα παλαιά.

He was not popular in Athens. The audience on one occasion hissed his newfangled music, but Euripides consoled him,
ὡς ὀλίγου χρόνου τῶν θεατῶν ὑπ' αὐτῷ γενησομένων,[2] and the
lyrics of Euripides himself show some of the features which
are ascribed to the new school of lyric poets.

In the fragment ascribed to Pherecrates Μουσική complains
of the outrages committed by Timotheus against her:

M. ὁ δὲ Τιμόθεός μ', ὦ φίλτατε, κατορώρυχε
    καὶ διακέκναιχ' αἴσχιστα.

Δ.   ποιὸς οὑτοσὶ
    ὁ Τιμόθεος;

M.   Μιλήσιός τις Πυρρίας·
    κακά μοι πάρεσχεν οἷς ἅπαντας οὓς λέγω
    παρελήλυθεν, ἄγων ἐκτραπέλους μυρμηκίας,[3]
    κἂν ἐντύχῃ πού μοι βαδιζούσῃ μόνῃ
    ἀπέδυσε κἀνέλυσε χορδαῖς δώδεκα.

---

[1] The text is given as printed by Wilamowitz, *Timotheus*, p. 74.
[2] Plut. *An sit seni*, &c., p. 23.
[3] See p. 62 for other lines which may belong here.

Much that we are told of Timotheus relates primarily to his work as a composer of νόμοι, and the increase which he made in the number of the strings of the lyre. The stories connected with this are fully discussed by Wilamowitz in his edition of the *Persae*, the extant portion of which gives a very clear idea of the νόμος as composed by Timotheus, and is of particular interest for students of the dithyramb, because one of the charges which critics made against him [1] was that he composed νόμοι in the style of dithyrambs. By this nothing complimentary was intended; the predominance of music over the words was such that the words were composed to fit the notes and degenerated greatly, elaborate periphrases taking the place of straightforward or genuinely poetical expression. Thus in the *Cyclops*—it is not known whether this was a dithyramb or a νόμος—there were such lines as:

ἔγχευε ⟨δ'⟩ ἐν μὲν δέπας κίσσινον μελαίνας
σταγόνος ἀμβρότας ἀφρῷ βρύαζον·
εἴκοσιν δὲ μέτρ' ἐνέχευ', ἀναμίσγων
αἷμα Βακχίου νεορρύτοισι δακρύοισι Νυμφῶν.

It was Timotheus also who was responsible for the strange phrase 'the cup of Ares' (meaning a shield) which Aristotle [2] gives as an instance of metaphor κατὰ τὸ ἀνάλογον. Similarly Anaxandrides quotes his expression ἐν πυρικτίτῳ στέγῃ for 'in a cooking-vessel'. (This is like Lewis Carroll's 'dreams of fleecy flocks, pent in a wheaten cell' for 'mutton-pies'.) We may doubtless regard the elaborate and almost nonsensical language of parts of the *Persae*, with its strange compound words, as instances of Timotheus' dithyrambic style. Plato and Aristotle [3] both speak of compound words as especially characteristic of dithyrambs, and many other writers emphasize this, among them Aristophanes: [4]

ΟΙ. ἄλλον τιν' εἶδες ἄνδρα κατὰ τὸν ἀέρα
      πλανώμενον πλὴν σαυτόν;
ΤΡ.   οὔκ, εἰ μή γέ που
      ψυχὰς δύ' ἢ τρεῖς διθυραμβοδιδασκάλων.

---

[1] Pseudo-Plut. *de Mus.* iv, p. 1132 e.   [2] *Poet.* xxi, 1457 b 22.
[3] Plato, *Cratylus*, 409 c, d; Aristot. *Poet.* xxii, *Rhet.* III. iii.
[4] *Peace*, 827 ff.

ΟΙ. τί δ' ἔδρων;

ΤΡ. ξυνελέγοντ' ἀναβολὰς ποτώμεναι,
τὰς ἐνδιαεριανερινηχέτους τινάς.

(There was a proverb,[1] καὶ διθυράμβων νοῦν ἔχεις ἐλάττονα.) The same point is noticed by Demetrius:[2] ληπτέον δὲ καὶ σύνθετα ὀνόματα, οὐ τὰ διθυραμβικῶς συγκείμενα, οἷον "θεοτεράτους πλάνας", οὐδὲ "ἀπτέρων δορύπορον στράτον": and by Philostratus:[3] λόγων δ' ἰδέαν ἐπήσκησεν οὐ διθυραμβώδη καὶ φλεγμαίνουσαν ποιητικοῖς ὀνόμασι, with the scholiast *ad loc.*:— διθυραμβώδη συνθέτοις ὀνόμασι σεμνυνομένην καὶ ἐκτοπωτάτοις πλάσμασι ποικιλλομένην· τοιοῦτοι γὰρ οἱ διθύραμβοι, ἅτε Διονυσίων τελετῶν ἀφωρμημένοι. Similarly Dionysius of Halicarnassus,[4] criticizing a phrase of Plato, says ψόφοι ταῦτ' εἰσὶ καὶ διθύραμβοι, κόμπον ὀνομάτων πολύν, νοῦν δὲ ὀλίγον ἔχοντες.

(In connexion with the λέξις διθυραμβική, it is convenient here to notice the theory of G. Meyer,[5] who, in a long discussion on the subject, argues that Aristotle, in speaking of διπλᾶ ὀνόματα as appropriate to dithyrambs, means διπλᾶ in the strict sense of 'double', i. e. composed of two elements and no more, and that the 'dithyrambic style' is not characterized by very long compounds, which are sometimes a sign of intense feeling, and are quoted in criticism, not of the λέξις, but of the music of the new dithyrambic poets. He thinks that the words which were really regarded as characteristic of dithyramb were compounds which involved an incongruous combination of elements, or a mere jingle of sound. Certainly the incongruousness of the compounds is conspicuous in most of the examples which he assembles, and most of them are only double, not multiple words; but his explanation of some passages, and especially of Plato's *Cratylus*, 409 b, is not convincing, nor is his account of the long compounds in Timotheus' *Persae*—which is rightly assumed to be a specimen of dithyrambic style—as passionate or invective, but not dithyrambic. A discussion of the individual words with which he deals

---

[1] Schol. on Aristoph. *Birds*, 1393.   [2] *de Interpr.* § 91.
[3] *Vit. Apoll.* I. xvii.
[4] *de Adm. vi dic. Dem.* vii; cf. xxix, and *Ep. ad Pomp.* ii, p. 762.
[5] *Philologus*, Suppl.-Bd. xvi. 3, pp. 153 ff.

would take us too far, but there appears to be a good deal of 'special pleading' in his arguments.)

A great part of the lyrics of Timotheus were ἀπολελυμένα—free from the trammels of strophe and antistrophe, and so seemed to old critics to be like ἐκτράπελοι μυρμηκίαι.

Among the dithyrambs of Timotheus were (1) Αἴας Ἐμμανής, a performance of which at Athens, after the composer's death, is attested by Lucian;[1] (2) Ἐλπήνωρ, which won a victory 320/19 B.C., also long after Timotheus' death, with Pantaleon of Sicyon as flute-player, and a chorus of boys;[2] (3) Ναύπλιος, in which the attempt to represent a storm by means of the flute roused the ridicule of the flute-player Dorion, who said that he had seen a bigger storm in a boiling saucepan;[3] (4) Σεμέλης Ὠδίς, in which the cries of the goddess were realistically imitated, not without ludicrous results;[4] (5) Σκύλλα, the lament of Odysseus in which was criticized by Aristotle[5] as degrading to the hero; the same poem is probably alluded to in the last chapter of the *Poetics*:—οἱ φαῦλοι αὐληταί . . . ἕλκοντες τὸν κορυφαῖον ἂν Σκύλλαν αὐλῶσιν.[6]

§ 6. It is difficult, with so little first-hand evidence, to estimate the real value and importance of the new movement in music and poetry which is represented by the composers whom we have been considering. On the one hand, it was clearly a movement in the direction of freedom and adequacy of expression, a revolt against stereotyped forms which had come to be felt artificial. In this respect it may have resembled some modern movements in music, such as that which was inaugurated by Wagner. On the other hand it was perverted by the passion for μίμησις in the sense of mere reproduction of sounds (often non-musical sounds) and other effects; for the more perfectly and, as it were, mechanically the artist reproduces his object, the less he seems to have the right to call himself an artist at all. Art is not so simple a thing as that. Further, the want of restraint shown by the new poets

---

[1] *Harmonides*, § 1.   [2] *C. I. A.* ii. 1246; Brinck, op. cit., p. 248.
[3] Athen. viii, p. 338 a.   [4] Ib., p. 352 b; Dio Chrys. 78. 22.
[5] *Poet.* xv, 1454 a 30.   [6] ib. xxvi, 1461 b 31.

was felt to be a kind of degeneracy: and there can be little
doubt that Timotheus, and perhaps some of his contemporaries,
did not know where to stop, and often became ludicrous, both
in sound and language,—the more so because the excessive
predominance of the music tended to make the libretto vapid
and silly. The impression made by the *Persae* is that the
writer could not himself distinguish between expressions of
real beauty (such as he sometimes uses), and expressions
which were simply grotesque or ridiculous. This deficiency
in taste is not rare in Alexandrian writers also.

It is well to notice that practically all of these writers,
though they obtained considerable vogue in Athens, were
natives of other cities; and while tragedy continued to be
almost exclusively Athenian, dithyramb, though regularly
performed at the festivals of Athens, was almost entirely the
work of strangers.

§ 7. A number of other poets of this period—mainly of the
fourth century—are known by name, and one or two by some
fragments.

KREXOS is mentioned by the Pseudo-Plutarch [1] along with
Timotheus as one of the new school, and again [2] in a rather
obscure passage, which may indicate that he introduced
recitative, or some kind of instrumentally-accompanied speaking, into dithyramb. (ἔτι δὲ τῶν ἰαμβείων τὸ τὰ μὲν λέγεσθαι
παρὰ τὴν κροῦσιν τὰ δ' ᾄδεσθαι Ἀρχίλοχόν φασι καταδεῖξαι,
εἶθ' οὕτω χρήσασθαι τοὺς τραγικοὺς ποιητάς, Κρέξον δὲ λαβόντα
εἰς διθυράμβων χρῆσιν ἀγαγεῖν.) Philodemus [3] states τὸ τοῦ
Κρέξου ποίημα, καίπερ οὐκ ὂν ἀνάρμοστον, πολὺ σεμνότερον
φαίνεσθαι τοῦ μέλους προστιθέντος.

POLYIDUS of Selymbria is stated by the Parian Marble to
have flourished at a date which falls between 398 and 380 B.C.;
Diodorus [4] ranks him with the famous dithyrambic poets of
the early fourth century, and says that he was also a painter.
The Pseudo-Plutarch [5] makes a depreciatory reference to his
flute-music, which appears to have been an inconsistent patch-

---

[1] *de Mus.* xii, p. 1135 c.   [2] ib. xxviii, p. 1141 a.
[3] *de Mus.*, p. 74.   [4] xiv. 96.   [5] op. cit. xxi, p. 1138.

work (ἀποπεφοιτήκασιν εἴς τε τὰ καττύματα καὶ εἰς τὰ Πολυίδου
ποιήματα). Whether the *Iphigencia* of Polyidus, mentioned
by Aristotle,[1] was a dithyramb (as Tièche conjectures) there
is no evidence to show. The only other fact known about
him is that he described Atlas as a Libyan shepherd, turned
to stone by Perseus.

TELESTES of Selinus also belongs to the beginning of the
fourth century. The Parian Marble dates his (presumably
first) victory in 402/1 B.C. Some fragments of his reply, in
the *Argo*, to Melanippides' statements about Athena's rejection
of the flute are preserved by Athenaeus, and may be quoted
in default of any better specimens of the dithyramb of this
period:

(1) ὅν σοφὸν σοφὰν λαβοῦσαν οὐκ ἐπέλπομαι νόῳ
    δρυμοῖς ὀρείοις ὄργανον
    δίαν Ἀθάναν δυσόφθαλμον ἄχος ἐκφοβηθεῖσαν αὖθις ἐκ
      χερῶν βαλεῖν,
    νυμφαγενεῖ χειροκτύπῳ φηρὶ Μαρσύᾳ κλέος.
    τί γάρ νιν εὐηράτοιο κάλλεος ὀξὺς ἔρως ἔτειρεν,
    ᾇ παρθενίαν ἄγαμον καὶ ἄπαιδ᾽ ἀπένειμε Κλώθω;
    ἀλλὰ μάταν ἀχόρευτος
    ἅδε ματαιολόγων φάμα προσέπταθ᾽ Ἑλλάδα μουσοπόλων
    σοφᾶς ἐπίφθονον βροτοῖς τέχνας ὄνειδος.

(2) The praise of αὐλητική,

    ἃν συνεριθοτάταν Βρομίῳ παρέδωκε, σεμνᾶς
    δαίμονος ἀερόεν πνεῦμ᾽ αἰολοπτερύγων σὺν ἀγλαᾶν ὠκύ-
    τατι χειρῶν.

The same theme was taken up in the *Asclepius*:

    ἢ Φρύγα καλλιπνόων αὐλῶν ἱερῶν βασιλῆα
    Λῦδον ὃς ἥρμοσε πρῶτος
    Δωρίδος ἀντίπαλον μούσης νόμον αἰολόμορφον
    πνεύματος εὔπτερον αὔραν ἀμφιπλέκων καλάμοις.

Another fragment, on the importation of the Phrygian mode
from Asia by Pelops, has already been quoted:[2] and there are

---

[1] *Poet.* xvi, 1455 a 6.   [2] See above, p. 17.

four lines on the stringed instrument called μάγαδις from the
Hymenaeus, which was also a dithyramb:

> ἄλλος δ' ἄλλαν κλαγγὰν ἱεὶς
> κερατόφωνον ἠρέθιζε μάγαδιν,
> ἐν πενταράβῳ χορδᾶν ἀριθμῷ
> χεῖρα καμψιδίαυλον ἀναστρωφῶν τάχος.

The fragments do not give a high idea of Telestes' style; but
his compositions long retained their popularity, and they were
among the works sent for by Alexander, along with the plays
of the great tragic poets and the dithyrambs of Philoxenus,
when he felt, in the far East, the need of literature.[1]

ANAXANDRIDES of Cameirus, the comic poet, also wrote a
dithyramb, if there is any truth in a story told by Chamaeleon,[2]
who says that διδάσκων ποτὲ διθύραμβον Ἀθήνησιν εἰσῆλθεν
ἐφ' ἵππου καὶ ἀπήγγειλέν τι τῶν ἐκ τοῦ ἄσματος.

DICAEOGENES, the tragic poet, also (according to Harpocra-
tion and Suidas) composed dithyrambs.

LICYMNIUS of Chios is mentioned by Aristotle,[3] along with
Chaeremon the tragic poet, among the ἀναγνωστικοί[4] whose
works were in a style well suited for reading; and his dithyrambs are once mentioned by Athenaeus.[5] He was also a
rhetorician.

TELESIAS of Thebes is described[6] as a contemporary of
Aristoxenus, and must therefore belong to the latter half of
the fourth century. He was quoted by Aristoxenus as a sad
example of one who, brought up in the old school, that of
Pindar and the ancients, fell away to the theatrical and
variegated music of a later day; but he had been so well
brought up that his attempt to compose in the style of
Philoxenus was a failure.

---

[1] Plut. *Alex.* viii.   [2] In Athen. ix, p. 374 a.
[3] *Rhet.* III, p. 1413 b 12.
[4] Crusius (*Festschr. für Gomperz*, pp. 381 ff.) shows that this does not
mean they were not designed or not suitable for performance, but that
they were written in a γραφικὴ λέξις, which did its work without requiring
much assistance from ὑπόκρισις.
[5] xiii, p. 603 d.   [6] Pseudo-Plut. *de Mus.* xxxi.

ARCHESTRATUS is mentioned in an inscription found in Plutarch,[1] who (quoting Panaetius) showed that although Demetrius of Phalerum had identified the 'Aristides' named in it with the hero of the Persian Wars, the inscription was really proved by the form of the letters to be post-Euclidean. The words were: Ἀντιοχὶς ἐνίκα, Ἀριστείδης ἐχορήγει, Ἀρχέ στρατος ἐδίδασκεν.

Inscriptions provide a list of names of dithyrambic poets, of whom little or nothing is known except that they were victorious at Athens in the fourth century or not long afterwards: Aristarchus, Philophron (384/3 B.C.), Pamphilus of Hagnus (366/5 B.C.), Eucles (from 365/4 B.C. onwards: he was several times successful at the Thargelia), Paideas (who won a victory at Salamis early in the fourth century), Nicomachus, Lysiades of Athens (352–333 B.C.: he is the poet commemorated on the monument of Lysicrates), Epicurus of Sicyon (for whom Chares, the condottiere, was choregus in 344/3 B.C.), Charilaus of Locri (328/7 B.C.), Karkidamos (320/19 B.C.), Hellanicus of Argos (after 308 B.C.), Eraton of Arcadia (circ. 290 B.C.), and Theodoridas of Boeotia (circ. 281 B.C.). The list again contains many non-Athenian names.

§ 8. It has already been noticed[2] that in the choragic monuments of the fourth century the name of the flute-player is generally given, as well as those of the choregus and the poet. In the first half of the century it usually follows that of the poet; in the latter half it actually precedes it—a strong testimony to the growing importance of the music.[3]

The names of some celebrated flute-players are known to us. In the fifth century Pronomus of Thebes (where the art was especially cultivated) had been particularly famous; an epigram[4] recounts that

Ἑλλὰς μὲν Θήβας προτέρας προύκρινεν ἐν αὐλοῖς,
Θῆβαι δὲ Πρόνομον, παῖδα τὸν Οἰνιάδου.

---

[1] *Aristid.* i. [2] See above, p. 52.
[3] The evidence for this is conveniently collected by Reisch in Pauly-W. *Real-Enc.* iii. 2435 b.
[4] *Anth. Pal.* xvi. 28; cf. Paus. IX. xii, § 4.

Alcibiades took lessons from Pronomus, and his music, as well as that of Sacadas of Argos, was played to the workmen who were rebuilding Messene at the bidding of Epaminondas. His son, Oeniades, is mentioned as playing at Athens for Philophron, who won a victory in 384/3 B.C.[1]

Among the well-known flute-players of the fourth century were Antigenidas and Dorion, who seem to have founded rival schools;[2] and Telephanes of Samos, who played for Demosthenes on the occasion of the assault upon him by Meidias. He was buried at Megara,[3] and is commemorated in an extant epigram:[4]

'Ορφεὺς μὲν κιθάρᾳ πλεῖστον γέρας εἵλετο θνητῶν,
  Νέστωρ δὲ γλώσσης ἡδυλόγου σοφίῃ,
τεκτοσύνῃ δ' ἐπέων πολυΐστωρ θεῖος "Ομηρος,
  Τηλεφάνης δ' αὐλοῖς, οὗ τάφος ἐστὶν ὅδε.

Others were Chrysogonus (son of the younger Stesichorus); Timotheus of Thebes; Euius, who played at Alexander's wedding-feast at Susa in 324 B.C.;[5] Ismenias and Kaphisias. Most of them were Thebans. Didymus[6] tells the quaint story that at a musical competition arranged by Philip shortly before he lost his eye at Methone, Antigenidas, Chrysogonus and Timotheus all played music representing the Cyclops.

A fragment of Amphis[7] illustrates the eagerness of competing tribes to get a good flute-player, as well as the enthusiasm with which the audience welcomed novel musical effects. Some conjecture that the passage of Menander,[8] which notices that the chorus was largely composed of dummies, with a few singers only, refers to dithyramb. This is doubtful; but, if it is true, it emphasizes all the more strongly the importance of the instrumentalist.

It was perhaps partly in consequence of the great importance of the flute-player that old dithyrambs, which gave an opportunity for the exhibition of his skill, were now performed,

---

[1] For other Theban flute-players, see Reisch, *de Mus. Graec. Cert.*, p. 58.
[2] Pseudo-Plut. *de Mus.* xxi, 1138 a, b.   [3] Paus. I. xliv, § 6.
[4] *Anth. Pal.* vii. 159.   [5] Athen. xii, p. 538 f.
[6] Comment. on Dem. (*Berl. Klass. Texte*, i, p. 59).
[7] Fr. 14 (K.).   [8] Fr. 165 (K.).

any interest in the words having become secondary.[1] Thus
Timotheus of Thebes won a victory at Athens with the Αἴας
ἐμμανής of Timotheus of Miletus many years after the death
of the latter. The practice of performing old music was
perhaps common outside Athens. There is an interesting
illustration of this at a later date in an inscription [2] of about
193 B.C. at Teos, set up there by the people of Cnossos in
gratitude to the citizens of Teos for sending two envoys,
Herodotus and Menecles, to visit Crete; of whom Menecles
gave several performances to the lyre of the works of Timotheus
and Polyidus and the old Cretan poets, καθὼς προσῆκεν ἀνδρὶ
πεπαιδευμένῳ.

Apart from the use of ἀναβολαί either instead of, or as an
introduction to, strophes and antistrophes—an introduction (so
we gather from Aristotle [3]) often as irrelevant to the subject of
the poem as the prooemion of an epideictic oration was to the subject of the speech—little can be said of the form of the fourth-
century dithyramb. Probably the conventional practice of
ending with a prayer was retained.[4] There may have been
various experiments as regards the accompaniment; Timotheus
had used the cithara on occasion instead of the flute; and with
the mixture of musical modes, to which Plato objected, there
was naturally less conservatism as regards instruments; but a
passage of Athenaeus [5] which is cited by Crusius [6] to prove
the use of castanets does not appear to refer to dithyramb.
Probably the repetition of syllables to fit the music (parodied
by Aristophanes in the *Frogs*, and adopted by Euripides and
also in the Delphian Hymns) was common in dithyrambs,[7]
though there is no proved instance of it.

---

[1] The rise of the διδάσκαλος or chorus-trainer, distinct from the poet,
was also probably the result of this performance of the works of deceased
composers: see Reisch in Pauly-W. *Real-Enc.* v. 404.

[2] *C. I. G.* iii. 3053. [3] *Rhet.* III. xiv.

[4] Aristid. *Rom. Enc.* i, p. 369 (Dind.) κράτιστον οὖν ὥσπερ οἱ τῶν
διθυράμβων τε καὶ παιάνων ποιηταί, εὐχήν τινα προσθέντα οὕτω κατακλεῖσαι τὸν
λόγον.

[5] xiv, p. 636 d. [6] In Pauly-W. *Real-Enc.* v. 1223.

[7] See Crusius, *Die delphischen Hymnen* (*Philologus*, Suppl.-Bd., liii,
p. 93).

§ 9. Before leaving the fourth century we may note the
records of dithyrambic performances at Eleusis, where a certain
Damasias, son of Dionysius of Thebes, provided two choruses,
τὸν μὲν παιδῶν, τὸν δὲ ἀνδρῶν, for the local Dionysia at his
own expense, and was publicly thanked and commemorated in
an extant inscription ;[1] at Salamis, the flute-player being
Telephanes and the poet Paideas ;[2] and at the Peiraeus, where
(as has already been noticed)[3] performances κυκλίων χορῶν οὐκ
ἔλαττον τριῶν were ordered by a law of the orator Lycurgus to
be given (and this is remarkable) at a festival of Poseidon,
and prizes were established of 10, 8, and 6 minae for the
victors. There are also inscriptions recording choruses of
boys and men at Ceos in the fourth century, and the sending
of a chorus of boys from the island to Delos.[4] Cyclic choruses
at the Dionysia at Iasos are recorded at about the time of
Alexander.[5] The cyclic contests at Delphi are mentioned in
the Paean of Philodamus to Dionysus.[6] At Thebes Epamein-
ondas was choregus to a chorus of boys accompanied by the
flute.[7] About the end of the century inscriptions mention
cyclic choruses at Halicarnassus, and, not long afterwards,
choruses of boys at Chios.[8]

VII

The Dithyramb after the Fourth Century B.C.

In the records of dithyramb after the fourth century Athens
does not hold as important a place as before. This may be
largely an accident ; but many other centres of musical and
dramatic activity had sprung up, partly at the courts of the
successors of Alexander, partly at new festivals such as the

[1] *C. I. A.* iv. 2. 574 b (*Eph. Arch.* iii, p. 71).
[2] *C. I. A.* ii. 1248.   [3] Above, p. 10.
[4] Halbherr, *Mus. Ital. di antich. class.* i. ii, pp. 207–8.
[5] *C. I. G.* 2671.
[6] l. 135 ; see Fairbanks, *Study of the Greek Paean*, p. 143 ; Powell,
Collect. Alex., p. 169.
[7] Plut. *Vit. Aristid.* i.   [8] *Bull. Corr. Hell.* v. 212 and 300.

Soteria at Delphi. An inscription[1] which records the victories
of Nicocles of Tarentum, an eminent citharist at the beginning
of the third century, includes festivals in every part of Greece.
The inscription is of special interest as recording a dithyrambic
victory at the Lenaea. At what period dithyrambs began to
be performed at this festival is uncertain ; it is clear from a
passage of Demosthenes[2] that there was no such performance
in the middle of the fourth century. It is further noticeable
that in this performance the instrument was the cithara and
not the flute. The age seems to have liked festivals which
included a great variety of performances. Contests of soloists,
both vocal and instrumental, were added to the choral competitions, and conjurers and all sorts of entertainers got their
turn.

At Athens the chief external change was the substitution
of a publicly appointed *agonothetes* for the choregus, and
the payment of his expenses by the state. The change took
place, probably, about fifteen years before the end of the fourth
century, and among the poets who performed under this
system were Eraton and Lysippus of Arcadia, Hellanicus of
Argos, Theodoridas and Pronomus (the younger) of Thebes.[3]
There is no extant mention of dithyrambs at the Thargelia
after 325/4 B.C.

It is probable that the festival of the Soteria at Delphi was
first celebrated about 276 B.C.,[4] and the important series of
inscriptions relating to it belongs approximately to the years
272–269 B.C.[5] The festival commemorated the defeat of the
Gauls near Delphi, and in the third year of every Olympiad
it was combined with the Pythia. The performances included
ἄνδρες αὐληταί and παῖδες αὐληταί.[6] The choruses of men

---

[1] *C. I. A.* ii. 1367.   [2] *in Meid.*, § 10.   [3] See above, p. 72.

[4] There is, however, a good deal of controversy as to the exact year,
which it would be beside the point to discuss here : cf. Roussel, *Bull.
Corr. Hell.* xlvii. 1 ff. ; *Suppl. Epigr. Gr.* ii. 260 ; *The Year's Work in
Class Stud.* 1925, p. 26 (for refs.).

[5] Pomtow, *Jahrb. f. klass. Phil.* xliii (1897), pp. 819 ff. ; Capps, *Trans.
Am. Phil. Ass.* xxxi (1900), p. 125.

[6] There can be no doubt that these expressions regularly signified
dithyrambic choruses of men and boys, accompanied by the flute.

and boys consisted each of fifteen members only; a number of
διδάσκαλοι are mentioned, but it is not certain whether they
were poets or only chorus trainers. The choruses mentioned
in an inscription referring to the winter Soteria, probably after
the middle of the second century, seem to have consisted of
very few choreutae—probably only three, including a ἡγέμων
παῖς or ἡγέμων ἀνδρῶν—and this does not look like dithyramb.[1] No doubt the performances of choral works at festivals
had fallen by this time mainly into the hands of professionals,
as inscriptions show; and there may have been a tendency
in this direction in the fourth century, when, as Aristotle
mentions,[2] the singers in tragic and comic choruses were often
the same; and virtuosity may have come to be as important
in singing as in flute-playing. Athenaeus[3] mentions a dithyramb of Theodoridas of Syracuse, about the latter half of the
third century B.C., called Κένταυροι, in which occurred the
words

$$\pi ί σ σ α \ \delta' \ ἀπὸ \ γραβίων \ ἔσταζεν$$

(γραβίων being a synonym for λαμπάδων).

From Delos comes a series of inscriptions[4] which run from
286 to 172 B.C., and show that at the Delian Dionysia and
Apollonia two choruses of boys, each provided with two
choregi, competed with each other. It is not known whether
the regular mission of choruses to Delos from Athens and
other cities was continued during this period.

Inscriptions also show that choruses of men and boys performed at Miletus in the third century B.C., and at Teos and
Samos in the second.[5] In the Samian inscriptions the choregi

Brinck (*Diss. Philol. Hal.*, pp. 75, 76) disposes of the idea of Boeckh
and others (a terrible idea in any case) that the phrase referred to bodies
of flute-players performing together. (The boys' fife-band was a horror
unknown to Greece. Polybius, xxx. 13, quotes the order of Anicius that
the flute-players should perform ἅμα πάντας as an instance of his want
of intelligence.)

[1] See Reisch, *de Mus. Gr. cert.*, p. 105.
[2] *Pol.* III. iii, p. 1276 b.   [3] xv, p. 699 f.
[4] Brinck, op. cit., pp. 187 ff.; Reisch, op. cit., pp. 64–7.
[5] All these are collected by Brinck, pp. 207–16. An inscription of
unknown date from Teos records the victory there of a poet with a

are mentioned, and in one of them the flute-player Satyrus,
but there is no mention of poets, and the performance was
probably confined to old works. An inscription from Assos
(ascribed by Boeckh to the third century B.C.)[1] orders some
one to be crowned for his merits at the Dionysia αὐλητῶν τῇ
πρώτῃ ἡμέρᾳ. A passage of the historian Callixenus of
Rhodes[2] gives evidence of choruses of boys and men at a
festival celebrated by Ptolemy Philadelphus at Alexandria,
with tripods as prizes for the choregi—nine cubits high for
boys' choruses, twelve for the mens'.

Polybius[3] (writing in the second century), in a remarkable
passage, records the regular performance by the Arcadians of
lyric choruses, apparently including dithyrambs, as a unique
feature of their social life : παρὰ γοῦν μόνοις Ἀρκάσιν οἱ παῖδες
ἐκ νηπίων ᾄδειν ἐθίζονται κατὰ νόμον τοὺς ὕμνους καὶ παιᾶνας,
οἷς ἕκαστοι κατὰ τὰ πάτρια τοὺς ἐπιχωρίους ἥρωας καὶ θεοὺς
ὑμνοῦσι. μετὰ δὲ ταῦτα τοὺς Τιμοθέου καὶ Φιλοξένου νόμους
μανθάνοντες χορεύουσι κατ᾽ ἐνιαυτὸν τοῖς Διονυσιακοῖς αὐληταῖς
ἐν τοῖς θεάτροις, οἱ μὲν παῖδες τοὺς παιδικοὺς ἀγῶνας, οἱ δὲ
νεανίσκοι τοὺς τῶν ἀνδρῶν. (Polybius' terminology is not very
exact, but the reference in the last two clauses must be to
dithyrambs, though the Arcadians may have sung the νόμοι of
these composers as well. The expression χορεύουσι τοῖς
Διονυσιακοῖς αὐληταῖς shows the importance of the flute-
player.)

Finally, there are inscriptions from Orchomenos recording
victories of synchoregi (acting two together) who had been
victorious with choruses of men, probably about 175 B.C., and
other inscriptions from the same place, assigned by Reisch to
the earlier half of the first century B.C., record the successes
of both mens' and boys' choruses, accompanied by the flute,
the victories of the leading boys and men (i. e. probably of the

dithyramb called *Andromeda*, which he himself accompanied on the
cithara ; another dithyramb performed at Teos was called *Persephone*
(*Bull. Corr. Hell.* iv, pp. 177, 178).

[1] *Invest. at Assos*, i, p. 137 (ed. J. T. Clarke).
[2] Athen. v, p. 196 ff., *esp.* 198 c.
[3] IV. xx.

principal singer in each chorus) being also mentioned. A much mutilated inscription from Chaeroneia [1] refers also to a chorus of men.

VIII

Dithyramb in the Imperial Period.

The information about dithyramb in imperial times is very fragmentary, and consists solely of a few inscriptions. Two fragments of a dedication at Athens to Asclepius,[2] in A. D. 52/3, are perhaps rightly taken to refer to a dithyrambic victory among other things; but it does not appear to be legitimate to infer that the dithyramb was performed in honour of Asclepius. (He might well be thanked for the victory, if he had given the choregus or the poet the necessary health.) It is remarkable that the tripod dedicated is itself called by the name 'dithyramb'. The fragments are as follows:

(1) Διονυσόδωρος ἦρχε, Δεξικλῆς μ' ὅτε
    νείκης ἄεθλον ἔλαβεν ἠϊθέων χορῷ.

(2) ἄρχων Διονυσόδωρος Εὐκάρπου τέχνης
    πάσης με κῦδος κωμικῆς τραγικῆς χορῶν
    τὸν δειθύραμβον τρίποδα θῆκ' Ἀσκληπίῳ.

Another inscription [3] of about A. D. 100 thanks the archon and agonothetes of the Dionysia at Athens on behalf of the Oeneid tribe for his services to the tribe; the circumstances are not very clear, but apparently Philopappus had paid the expenses of the Oeneid tribe in the contest: ἡ Οἰνηὶς φυλὴ διὰ τῶν εὖ ἀγωνισαμένων χορῷ Διονυσιακῷ τὸν ἄρχοντα καὶ ἀγωνοθέτην Γάιον Ἰούλιον Ἀντίοχον Ἐπιφάνη Φιλόπαππον Βησαιέα τῆς εἰς ἑαυτὴν εὐεργεσίας ἕνεκα. ἐδίδασκε Μοιραγένης, ἐχορήγει Βούλων, οἱ Μοιραγένους Φυλάσιοι. ἐπεστάτει Μένανδρος Φυλάσιος, ηὔλει Φίλητος Μενίσκου Κολωνῆθεν, ἐχόρευον (a list of about twenty-five names from different tribes follows), ἐμελοποίει Μουσικό[ς]. It is noticeable that the chorus is only half the size of the classical κύκλιος χορός,

---

[1] Reisch, op. cit., p. 109, note [1].
[2] *C. I. A.* iii. 68 b.   See above, p. 10.   [3] *C. I. A.* iii. 78.

and is not drawn entirely from one tribe; it was doubtless a professional body. A similar act of generosity on the part of Philopappus is recorded by Plutarch:[1] ἐν δὲ τοῖς Σαραπίωνος ἐπινικίοις, ὅτε τῇ Λεοντίδι φυλῇ τὸν χορὸν διατάξας ἐνίκησεν, ἐστιωμένοις ἡμῖν ἅτε δὴ καὶ φυλέταις οὖσι δημοποιητοῖς, οἰκεῖοι λόγοι τῆς ἐν χειρὶ φιλοτιμίας παρῆσαν. ἔσχε γὰρ ὁ ἀγὼν ἐντονωτάτην ἅμιλλαν, ἀγωνοθετοῦντος ἐνδόξως καὶ μεγαλοπρεπῶς Φιλοπάππου τοῦ βασιλέως ταῖς φυλαῖς ὁμοῦ πάσαις χορηγοῦντος.

An inscription[2] of the second century A. D. shows that the contest had been abandoned, and that all the choregi joined in one show and one monument: ὁ δῆμος ἐνίκα· Λούκιος Φλάυιος Φλάμμας Κυδαθηναιεὺς ἦρχε.

πάντες χοραγοὶ πᾶς τε φυλέτας χορὸς
ἄγαλμα δήμῳ Κέκροπος ἐστάσαντό με
ἑκούσιοι μεθέντες ἐξ ἀγωνίας
ὡς μὴ φέροι τις αἶσχος ἀποκισσούμενος.
ἐγὼ δ' ἑκάστῳ τόσσον εὐκλείας νέμω
καθ' ὅσσον αὐτῷ ξυνὸς ὢν ὀφείλομαι.

The Dorian elements in the language in this inscription seem to require explanation.[3]

In other inscriptions[4] either the δῆμος or a number of tribes (six in C. I. A. iii. 82) are mentioned as 'victorious', and this again implies the abandonment of any contest. In another,[5] a letter, perhaps of Antoninus Pius, written to a congress of τεχνῖται Διονύσου, seems to refer to the performance of many dithyrambs at the Great Dionysia.

IX

Conclusion.

Thus the history of the dithyramb proves to be a somewhat puzzling and disappointing affair. No complete dithyramb, except those of Bacchylides, survives, and those, in their quiet

---

[1] *Symp. Quaest.* I. x, p. 628 a, b.   [2] *C. I. A.* iii. 80 (Kaibel, *Epigr.* 927).
[3] They occur also in *C. I. A.* iii. 82.
[4] *C. I. A.* iii. 81 (much mutilated), 82, 82 a.   [5] *C. I. A.* iii. 34 a.

gracefulness seem to belong almost to another world from the fragments of Pindar, in which the spirit of Dionysus is at least discernible. It is the dithyramb of the Pindaric period which it would be most worth while to know; of the later dithyramb the extant fragments are perhaps enough.

It is unsatisfactory also that we have to depend for our facts, to a large extent, upon writers in whose critical and historical capacity it is not possible to have any confidence. The author of *de Musica*, ascribed to Plutarch, drew largely upon Glaucus of Rhegium and Aristoxenus (who could themselves take advantage of a continuous, though not necessarily pure, stream of tradition); but he is spoiled for us by the difficulty of discovering his source for many particular statements. Athenaeus preserves much valuable material, but the filiation of his sources is a matter upon which those who have studied them persistently disagree. Nothing can give us a much greater degree of certainty, unless fortune restores to us the works of Chamaeleon or some similar 'researcher'.

It is even more unsatisfactory that we have practically no evidence of the spirit in which the dithyramb, as a form of religious celebration, was regarded during the classical period. After the jolly drinking song of Archilochus passes out of view, we are not told whether the light-heartedness of early days was still attached to it, or whether it was solemn, as tragedy was.[1] There may conceivably have been a difference in this respect between the winter dithyramb at Delphi, when Apollo was away, and Dionysus was perhaps thought of in his gloomier aspects, and the spring dithyramb at Athens. There is not, however, any ground for connecting dithyramb in Greece with any chthonic ritual, Dionysiac or other, and it is very significant that there is no trace of dithyramb at the Anthesteria.[2] The Pindaric fragments are brilliant and cheerful enough. The contrast between the dithyramb and the

---

[1] There is no justification for speaking of the τραγικοὶ χοροί at Sicyon in the time of Cleisthenes as 'dithyrambs'. Herodotus must have known well enough what dithyrambs were, and he could have called these χοροί by that name, had it been appropriate (see below, p. 137).

[2] Despite M. Schmidt and Crusius (Pauly-W. *Real-Enc.* v. 1207).

paean, drawn by Plutarch,[1] dates from a time long after the
fusion of Dionysus with Zagreus and the development of his
mysteries in Greece, and Plutarch is perhaps somewhat fanciful when he tries to prove the appropriateness of the dis-
tracted music (evidently that of the later dithyramb) with the
experiences attributed to the mystic deity : Διόνυσον δὲ καὶ
Νυκτέλιον καὶ Ἰσοδαίτην ὀνομάζουσι, καὶ φθοράς τινας καὶ
ἀφανισμούς, εἶτα ἀποβιώσεις καὶ παλιγγενεσίας, οἰκεῖα ταῖς
εἰρημέναις μεταβολαῖς αἰνίγματα καὶ μυθεύματα περαίνουσι·
καὶ ᾄδουσι τῷ μὲν διθυραμβικὰ μέλη παθῶν μεστὰ καὶ μεταβολῆς πλάνην τινα καὶ διαφόρησιν ἐχούσης ... τῷ δὲ παῖανα.
There is no hint elsewhere of any association of the dithyramb with the mystic cults referred to, and indeed Plutarch
himself does not assert it, but only compares the contorted
music of the dithyramb with the perplexed experiences of the
god—a comparison of very little value, and probably far removed from the minds of the composers of the music.   We
cannot tell what Proclus meant by saying (if he did say it)
that the dithyramb was κοινότερος and εἰς παραίτησιν κακῶν
γεγραμμένος, and it is at least probable that the passage is corrupt.[2]   So far as we can see, the religious significance rather
rapidly went out of dithyramb, as the words became unimportant or degenerate, and it became what may be called
' concert-music ', such as the Oratorio was in the nineteenth
century.   In the latest stages of its history it seems to be
quite secularized.   But for the present we must be content to
be ignorant of much which we should like to know.

[1] de Ei apud Delphos, 388 e ff.   [2] See above, p. 16.

II

THE ORIGINS OF GREEK TRAGEDY

ANALYSIS OF CHAPTER II

The Origins of Greek Tragedy

I

The earliest known Greek Tragedy and its Character.

It is convenient to begin the discussion of the origins of
Greek Tragedy with a statement of known facts at the
earliest point at which a clear view is possible, and to work
backwards from that point. The earliest extant Greek
tragedy is the *Supplices* of Aeschylus. This was performed
soon after the beginning of the first century B.C., as part of
a trilogy of three plays dealing with parts of the same mythical story; to these was appended a satyric play which perhaps
treated the same legend in a lighter fashion. Such at least is
a probable account of the facts: the early date is virtually
proved by the structure and character of the play, and the position of the play as part of a trilogy by its obvious lack of any
conclusion to its story, coupled with the fact that Aeschylus
certainly composed one other play, and probably two—the
Aegyptii and *Danaides* [1]—on the same story; and a mention of
a satyric play, the *Amymone*, of which the Danaid so named
must have been the heroine, completes the evidence.

The *Supplices* differs from all other extant Greek tragedies
in the large proportion of the play which is assigned to the
chorus, the very small part taken by the second actor, and
the simplicity (even at times the crudity) of the treatment of
the actor's part. These points are undisputed.

But on the important question of the size of the chorus
there is less agreement. On the one hand the number of the
Danaids is consistently given in legend as fifty, and in line 321
Aegyptus, the father of their would-be husbands, is described as

---

[1] There seems to be no evidence for Hermanns' conjecture that the
Θαλαμοποιοί dealt with this story. The ascription of the Αἰγύπτιοι to this
Trilogy follows a conjecture of Dindorf, which at least has the name of
the play in its favour.

πεντηκοντάπαις. Wilamowitz and others, who believe that all
fifty Danaids appeared in the chorus, enlarge on the magnificence of the whole spectacle—the fifty with their attendants
(making a hundred in all), the king of Argos with chariots
and a great retinue ; and, later in the play, the herald with
a force (probably of black Nubians) attempting to carry the
Danaids off, and the king with a larger force to prevent it.
But with what ancient theatrical arrangements would such
crowds have been possible ? and by what steps did the much
less spectacular and crowded drama of the greater part of the
classical period supersede this magnificent and impressive forerunner ? It seems more likely—though Wilamowitz is content
simply to say that it is absurd—that the fifty were represented by a much smaller number (probably twelve).[1] It is
a remarkable thing that the chorus in the *Supplices* never
speak of themselves as fifty in number, and though Aegyptus
is described in passing as πεντηκοντάπαις, it does not necessarily follow that all his sons appeared in the chorus of the
Aegyptii, as some have conjectured. The belief that it was so is .
generally connected by those who hold it with the theory that
the tragic chorus originated from the cyclic dithyramb; but
it will be seen later that this is itself more than doubtful. As
it is, neither theory can be used to support the other without
a *petitio principii*, and the question of the number of the
chorus in the *Supplices* must at least be left open. The statement of Pollux [2] that the tragic chorus was composed of fifty
persons until Aeschylus so terrified the audience with his fifty
Eumenides that the number was restricted, is obviously fabu-
lous—like the story [3] that the same terrifying effect made
him so unpopular that he had to leave Athens ; and it is contradicted by the virtual certainty that the *Agamemnon* had
a chorus of twelve. In all probability the idea that tragedy

---

[1] There is no evidence for the conjecture of Reisch (Pauly-W. *Real-
Enc.* iii. 2320) that the number of fifty was made up by *personae mutae*,
and it may be doubted whether this form of deception would have been
employed at this early date, though it is found in Menander's time (see
above, p. 73).

[2] iv. 110.   [3] *Vit. Aeschyli.*

at first had a chorus of fifty either originated from the passage
of Aristotle (to be discussed later) which derives tragedy from
dithyramb, or else was actually an inference from the facts
that legend spoke of fifty Danaids, and that both Phrynichus
and Aeschylus composed a *Danaides* and an *Aegyptii*.

However this may be, we have in the *Supplices* a play largely
lyrical, serious in subject and tone, and unconnected with
Dionysus in subject; and, speaking generally, the last-men-
tioned characteristic holds good generally of the drama of the
early part of the fifth century: Dionysiac subjects might be
chosen, but plainly had no preference. Now and then a contemporary subject was selected. Chorus and actors wore
masks. The linguistic basis of the dialogue was Attic, with
a sprinkling of epic and (in a smaller degree) of Doric forms
and words; the lyrics were further removed from Attic by
their more unrestricted use of forms and words which belong
to epic or non-dramatic lyric poetry; and, in particular, the use
of the long a in place of η, a use common to all the Greek
dialects except Ionic and Attic, was regular. (The special
problem of the relation of the language of tragedy to Doric
will be discussed later.)

It is not known whether in the early part of the fifth
century composition in trilogies or tetralogies was normal.
That it was a common practice of Aeschylus himself is certain;
but apart from Aeschylus very few trilogies or tetralogies are
definitely recorded,—the Λυκουργεία of Polyphradmon,[1] the
Πανδιονίς of Philocles,[2] and the Οἰδιποδεία of Meletus.[3]

[1] Arg. Aesch. *Sept. c. Theb.*

[2] Schol. Ar. *Birds*, 281, on the authority of Aristotle's Διδασκαλίαι.

[3] Schol. Plat. *Laws* x, 893 a 14, also on Aristotle's authority. The attempt
of Mr. R. J. Walker (in his book on Sophocles' *Ichneutae*) to prove that
Sophocles and Euripides composed in tetralogies is entirely unconvincing. But Robert (*Oedipus*, pp. 396 ff.) makes out a strong case for his
view that there was a certain connexion of subject between the *Chrysippus*,
Oenomaus, and *Phoenissae* of Euripides, which were performed together
in 410 B.C. It seems that composition in connected tetralogies or
trilogies was mainly a speciality of Aeschylus, and that he himself
may not always have practised it. (The attempt of Donaldson, *Theatre
of the Greeks*, pp. 118-19, to explain the group of plays of which the
Persae was one as a trilogy or tetralogy seems to be very speculative.)

The last play of each group of four was, throughout the classical period—with only one or two known exceptions, such as the *Alcestis* of Euripides—a satyric play. This was like tragedy in its general form, being a joint performance of chorus and actors, all wearing masks; but the chorus invariably represented satyrs—creatures half man, half beast, led by Silenus, and associated especially (and often in the plays) with Dionysus, but frequently also with other gods or with certain heroes. Their costume was indecent; there was a good deal of vigorous dancing, and the language and gestures were often obscene. The plot represented those parts of ancient legends which were grotesque in themselves or which could be made so by burlesquing them. The satyric play was an integral part of the poet's work for the prize in the competition at the Dionysia.

Such are the facts, stated in outline, in regard to tragedy and satyric drama, early in the fifth century. We have now to trace the history of these forms of art backwards, so far as our information allows us.

II

Phrynichus, Pratinas, Choerilus.

§ 1. The information which we have in regard to PHRYNICHUS, a slightly senior contemporary of Aeschylus—his first victory is dated 511 B.C.,—suggests that his tragedies were of the same type as the early work of Aeschylus himself; that the lyric element predominated and was of very high literary merit; that his treatment of his actors was crude, and that he was quite free from any restriction to Dionysiac subjects. The main evidence on these points can be very shortly stated.

Aristophanes [1] warmly praises his lyrics:

ἔνθεν ὡσπερεὶ μέλιττα
Φρύνιχος ἀμβροσίων μελέων ἀπεβόσκετο καρπὸν ἀεὶ
φέρων γλυκεῖαν ᾠδάν.

[1] *Birds*, 748 ff. Cf. *Wasps*, 220.

He appears to have invented many new varieties of choral dance : Plutarch [1] writes of him : καίτοι καὶ Φρύνιχος ὁ τῶν τραγῳδιῶν ποιητὴς περὶ αὐτοῦ φησιν ὅτι

σχήματα δ᾽ ὄρχησις τόσα μοι πόρεν, ὅσσ᾽ ἐνὶ πόντῳ
κύματα ποιεῖται χείματι νὺξ ὀλοή.

But the simplicity of his handling of his actors was such that Aristophanes [2] scoffed at the spectators who could stand either it or the comparatively artless management of Aeschylus in his early days, who

τοὺς θεατὰς
ἐξηπάτα μώρους λαβὼν παρὰ Φρυνίχῳ τραφέντας.

(Probably Phrynichus, like Aeschylus, improved as he went on. In the *Phoenissae*, in 476 B. C., he adopted the second actor, the invention of Aeschylus.[3])

The variety of his subjects is indicated by the titles of his plays. The *Pleuroniae* was drawn from the story of Meleager and Oeneus and the Calydonian boar-hunt ; the *Aegyptii* and *Danaides* from that of the Danaids ; the *Antaeus* and *Alcestis* (the latter probably a satyric play) [4] from the Heraclean cycle ; the *Actaeon* from Attic legend ; the Μιλήτου ἅλωσις (if that was the title) [5] and the *Phoenissae* from contemporary history.[6]

Suidas states that Phrynichus was μαθητὴς Θέσπιδος τοῦ πρώτου τὴν τραγικὴν εἰσενέγκαντος—which can hardly be in-

---

[1] *Symp. Quaest.* VIII. ix, § 3.   [2] *Frogs*, 910 ff.

[3] Wilamowitz (*Einl.*, p. 92) thinks of the Μιλήτου ἅλωσις as more of an oratorio than a drama ; it can, he thinks, have had no action. But really we have no evidence as to the extent to which Phrynichus developed the dramatic possibilities of his single actor.

[4] See Schol. on Virg. *Aen.* vi. 694 ; Wilamowitz, *Einl.*, p. 92.

[5] Suidas does not mention this title, but does mention a play called Δίκαιοι ἢ Πέρσαι ἢ Σύνθωκοι—which suggests a chorus of Persian elders. The conjecture that Δίκαιοι may be a corruption of Λακαῖοι, the name of a Persian clan, seems to be very speculative.

[6] It is not necessary for the present purpose to discuss Dr. Verrall's interesting but scarcely tenable theory that the *Persae* of Aeschylus is an improved version of the *Phoenissae* of Phrynichus (*The Bacchants of Eur.*, pp. 28 ff.).

terpreted in a literal sense, if (as seems likely) Thespis was
already exhibiting plays about 560 B.C.; that he was εὑρετὴς τοῦ
τετραμέτρου—which is absurd in itself, but may possibly mean
that he first introduced speeches in the tetrameter metre;[1] and
that he first γυναικεῖον πρόσωπον εἰσήγαγεν ἐν σκηνῇ—a statement which we cannot check.

Some meagre fragments show that Phrynichus was a master
of poetic language, with some of the pomp and richness of
Aeschylus, e. g.:

　　Alcestis (fr. 2)　σῶμα δ' ἄθαμβες γυιοδόνητον
　　　　　　　　　　τείρει . . .

　　Phoenissae (fr. 5)　στρατός ποτ' εἰς γῆν τήνδ' ἐπιστρωφᾷ ποδὶ
　　　　　　　　　　"Ταντος ἦν ἔναιεν ἀρχαῖος λεώς·
　　　　　　　　　　πεδία δὲ πάντα καὶ παράκτιον πλάκα
　　　　　　　　　　ὠκεῖα μάργοις φλὸξ ἐδαίνυτο γναθοῖς.

　　　　　　(fr. 6)　　　　κρυερὸν γὰρ οὐκ
　　　　　　　　　　ἤλυξεν μόρον, ὠκεῖα δέ νιν φλὸξ κατεδαίσατο
　　　　　　　　　　δαλοῦ περθομένου ματρὸς ὑπ' αἰνᾶς κακο-
　　　　　　　　　　μαχάνου.

　　　　　　(fr. 11)　ψαλμοῖσιν ἀντίσπαστ' ἀείδοντες μέλη.

Incert. fab. (fr. 13) λάμπει δ' ἐπὶ πορφυρέαις παρῇσι φῶς ἔρωτος.

Phrynichus then seems, in all essentials, to have resembled
Aeschylus as he was at the beginning of his career.[2] He
doubtless made improvements in tragedy, but whose work
was it that he improved upon? The scanty information
which we have about Pratinas and Choerilus helps us but
little.

§ 2. PRATINAS is the subject of a puzzling and confused
notice in Suidas. He is described as Φλιάσιος, τραγικός·

---

[1] Even this is hard to reconcile with Aristotle's statements about the
tetrameter as the original metre of tragedy (*Poet.* iv, 1449 a 22), though
we do not know who his authority was.

[2] Suidas has a notice of another Phrynichus, son of Melanthas,
described as Ἀθηναῖος τραγικός· ἔστι δὲ τῶν δραμάτων αὐτοῦ καὶ τάδε·
Ἀνδρομέδα, Ἠριγόνη. ἐποίησε καὶ πυρριχάς. But nothing is said of
his date, and Suidas may be confusing the various poets of this
name.

ἀντηγωνίζετο δὲ Αἰσχύλῳ τε καὶ Χοιρίλῳ ἐπὶ τῆς ἑβδομη-
κοστῆς Ὀλυμπιάδος (i. e. 499–496 B. C.). καὶ πρῶτος ἔγραψε
Σατύρους . . . καὶ δράματα μὲν ἐπεδείξατο ν´ ὧν σατυρικὰ λβ´.
ἐνίκησε δὲ ἅπαξ. His name was evidently connected by
tradition especially with satyric drama; this appears also
from Dioscorides' epigram on Sositheus,[1]

ἐκισσοφόρησε γὰρ ὡνὴρ
ἄξια Φλιασίων, ναὶ μὰ χορούς, Σατύρων,

and from Pausanias,[2] who shows that his memory was kept
alive in his native town: ἐνταῦθα ἔστι καὶ Ἀριστίου μνῆμα τοῦ
Πρατίνου· τούτῳ τῷ Ἀριστίᾳ Σάτυροι καὶ Πρατίνᾳ τῷ πατρί εἰσι
πεποιημένοι πλὴν τῶν Αἰσχύλου δοκιμώτατοι. He cannot have
exhibited at Athens entirely under the system which was
regular in the fifth century, and under which each poet produced three tragedies and one satyric play, if thirty-two of
his fifty plays were satyric, as Suidas states;[3] but if, as is
possible, this system only came into force just before the
beginning of the century, he may at first have exhibited under
conditions which allowed poets to offer tragedies and satyric
plays in any proportion.

[Unfortunately it is impossible to say at what date the
system referred to came into use. It may have been when
state-regulated choregia was introduced; the laying of re-
sponsibility on the shoulders of individuals would necessitate
some understanding as to what each was responsible for, in
order that the competition might be a fair one. Before this
a poet might well take his own risks. Competitions appear, as
we shall see,[4] to have been instituted about 534 B. C., and

[1] *Anth. Pal.* vii. 707 (second century B. C.). Pratinas is also obscurely
alluded to in the same writer's epigram on Sophocles (vii. 37).

[2] II. xiii, § 5.

[3] The suggestion of Capps that Pratinas may have composed satyric
plays for other poets to present with their trilogies, and that the dis-
proportionate number of his satyric plays may thus be accounted for, is
ingenious, but is not sufficiently substantiated by the fact that his son
Aristias in 467 B. C. completed his group of plays with a satyric play of
Pratinas, who may have been dead by that date. But possibly all the
thirty-two satyric plays were not performed at Athens.

[4] See below, p. 107.

possibly there was some reorganization of the festival after the expulsion of the tyrants. The great inscription *C. I. A.* ii. 971; iv. 971, which gives the record of the victories at the City Dionysia, seems, though the heading is imperfect,[1] to have begun its record 'in the year in which there first were κῶμοι to Dionysus'. Capps and Wilhelm reconstruct the lost beginning of the inscription in such a way as to make the record begin with the year 502/1 B. C. or thereabouts, and the natural date for the beginning would be the date at which the state made new regulations for the festival, and introduced the choregic system.[2] Capps and Wilhelm assume that the word κῶμοι is used in the heading of the inscription in a wide sense to cover the whole festival, just as Euripides[3] mentions the Hyacinthia by the name κῶμοι 'Υακίνθου, and it is perhaps more probable that, in such a general heading, it should mean this, than that it should refer to the κῶμος as an element in the festival distinct from the dithyrambs, tragedies, and comedies, as in the Law of Euegorus, quoted by Demosthenes;[4] but of course it is not certain. Nor is it certain whether, as they think probable, only two columns of 140 lines preceded that to which the first extant portion of the inscription belonged ; and on this assumption the initial date which they propose depends. Their calculations are also liable to uncertainty[5] owing to their assumption that (apart from the first introduction of the dithyrambic chorus of men in 509 B. C., and that of comedy in 486) the contests followed the same lines throughout the missing period (e. g. in the year of the sack of Athens by the Persians). Nor can we entirely exclude the possibility that the record itself began in 509 B. C.,

[1] The heading may have been οἵδε νενικήκασιν ἀφ' οὗ πρῶτ]ον κῶμοι ἦσαν τῶ[ι Διονύσῳ ἐν ἄστει.

[2] Possibly (though this is only a conjecture) the introduction of satyric plays by Pratinas from Phlius, by bringing a new element into the tragic competitions, itself necessitated new regulations, and the system under which Aeschylus competed may have been the result.

[3] *Helena*, 1469.

[4] *in Meid.*, § 10 καὶ τοῖς ἐν ἄστει Διονυσίοις ἡ πομπὴ καὶ οἱ παῖδες καὶ ὁ κῶμος καὶ οἱ κωμῳδοὶ καὶ οἱ τραγῳδοί.

[5] This is pointed out by Wilamowitz, *Gött. Gel. Anz.* 1906, pp. 624-6.

after the overthrow of the tyranny; and in that case three columns, not two, may have been lost. But their view, dating the beginning of the system which we are discussing about 502/1 B. C., has at least great likelihood, and the corrections which more exact knowledge would necessitate would probably not be great. The fact that the tradition of the early writers on Greek literature (as found in Suidas and others) preserved some dates for Thespis, Choerilus, Phrynichus, &c., certainly does not disprove the suggested initial date of this inscription, as Wilamowitz appears to think. The recorders of the tradition need not have got their information from this inscription.]

The words (in the notice of Suidas) πρῶτος ἔγραψε Σατύρους cannot mean anything but that, in the opinion of Suidas or his unknown authority, Pratinas was the first to compose satyric plays of the type known in the fifth century. (The word Σατύρους is used in the same sense as Σάτυροι in the passage of Pausanias quoted above, and in many other places.[1]) Professor Murray's suggestion [2] that the words of Suidas mean that Pratinas was the first to write set words for the satyr-revellers is hardly consistent with the statement, also found in Suidas,[3] that it was Arion who brought in σατύρους ἔμμετρα λέγοντας.

The new satyric plays must have been brought into the Dionysia alongside of the tragedies which had presumably become regular since 534 B. C.[4] Professor Flickinger [5] thinks that Pratinas' work is to be explained as an attempt to restore the Dionysiac character of the festival. 'After tragedy had lost its exclusively Bacchic themes and had considerably de-

---

[1] This tradition probably appears also in Pseudo-Acron. Schol. Hor. *Ars P.* 216 'Cithara monochordos fuit; deinde paulatim dextra laevaque addentes . . . ponebant tragoediis satyrica dramata, in quibus salva maiestate secundum Pratinae (MS. Cratini) institutionem. Is enim Athenis, Dionisia dum essent, satyricam fabulam induxit.'

[2] In J. E. Harrison, *Themis*, p. 344.   [3] See below, p. 133.

[4] I find the attempt of Mr. R. J. Walker (*Addenda Scenica*, p. 13) to show that Pratinas composed satyric plays in trilogies entirely unconvincing, as also his speculations (Sophocles, *Ichneutae*, pp. 249–69) about the poet's tragedies and metres.

[5] *Greek Theater*, pp. 23, 24.

parted from its original character, Pratinas endeavoured to
satisfy religious conservatism by introducing a new manner of
production, which came to be called satyric drama. This was
a combination of the dramatic dithyramb of his native Phlius,
which of course had developed somewhat since the day of
Arion and Epigenes, and of contemporary Attic tragedy '. But
this goes far beyond the evidence. We have no information at all as to the object which Pratinas may have had in
view ; it is at least equally possible that both he and Thespis
simply came to Athens to try their luck as entertainers ; there
is not a particle of evidence about any dithyramb at Phlius,
nor do we know anything of dithyrambs or of satyric plays
by Epigenes or of the development of dithyramb between
Arion and Lasos. (The actual evidence in regard to Epigenes
and the statements bearing upon the supposed religious
conservatism of the Athenians will be considered later.[1])

We know nothing of the tragedies of Pratinas. In the
Argument to the *Seven against Thebes* we read that
Aristias won the second prize Περσεῖ Ταντάλῳ ⟨Ἀνταίῳ⟩[2]
Παλαισταῖς τοῖς Πρατίνου πατρός : but it is quite likely that
only the last play, which was satyric, was by Pratinas.
Athenaeus[3] records the title Δυσμαίναι ἢ Καρυατίδες as that
of a play of Pratinas, and it has been conjectured that
Δυσμαίναι may be a false reading for Δυμαίναι or Δυμανίαι,—
Dymanian maidens of Karyai, dancing at the festival of
Artemis there,—and so may = Καρυατίδες. Others think
that Δυσμαίναι here = Μαινάδες,[4] and this seems quite likely.
The long fragment from a satyric play of Pratinas has already
been discussed.[5]

[1] See pp. 138, 146, 166-168.
[2] I accept Professor H. W. Garrod's convincing emendation (*Class.
Rev.* xxxiv, p. 130).
[3] ix. 392 f.   [4] Cf. Hesych. Δυσμαίναι· αἱ ἐν Σπάρτῃ χοριτίδες βάκχαι.
[5] See above, p. 29. It is uncertain whether any work of Pratinas
survived into the fourth century B. C. Pseudo-Plut. *de Mus.* xxxi says that
Aristoxenus recorded that Telesias of Thebes had learned the works of
Pindar and Dionysius of Thebes καὶ τὰ Λάμπρου καὶ τὰ Πρατίνου : but there
is a reading Κρατίνου, which may be right. The context shows that
Aristoxenus was thinking of music, and the songs (and presumably the

§ 3. CHOERILUS, according to Suidas, was a native of Athens who composed 160 plays, from 523 B. C. onwards, won thirteen victories, competed in the first years of the fifth century against Aeschylus and Pratinas, and κατά τινας τοῖς προσωπείοις καὶ τῇ σκευῇ τῶν στόλων ἐπεχείρησε. Eusebius places his *floruit* in 482 B. C., and the 'Life of Sophocles' (a doubtful authority) makes him compete against Sophocles in 468. Only one of his plays, the *Alope*, is known by name. The two fragments quoted by grammarians as instances of metaphor—γῆς ὀστοῖσιν ἐγχριμφθεὶς πόδα, and γῆς φλέβες—suggest the same type of language as was sometimes used by Phrynichus and Aeschylus.

It has been usual to explain by reference to this Choerilus the line quoted by Plotius,[1] as a specimen of the *metrum Choerileum*,

ἡνίκα μὲν βασιλεὺς ἦν Χοιρίλος ἐν σατύροις

and to suppose that it means that he was famous for his satyric plays. But Reisch[2] has suggested a different explanation of the line. The expression βασιλεῦ Σατύρων, where it occurs in a fragment of Hermippus,[3] has no reference to drama; and Cratinus[4] scoffs at a certain Choerilus who was a servant and helper of Ecphantides, the author of a comedy called Σάτυροι. It may be this Choerilus to whom the line of Plotius refers.

III

Thespis.

§ 1. The evidence in regard to Thespis is both more full and more interesting, though the points upon which anything like certainty is possible are few. It will be convenient first of all to collect the more important passages:

MARMOR PARIUM (under a year about 534 B.C.). Ἀφ᾽ οὗ Θέσπις ὁ ποιητὴς [ὑπεκρίνα]το πρῶτος, ὃς ἐδίδαξε [δρ]ᾶ[μα ἐν

---

tunes) of Cratinus were famous (see Aristoph. *Knights*, 529–30). The corruption would be the converse of that noticed in Pseudo-Acron (above, p. 95, n. 1). [1] de Metris (Keil, *Grammatici Lat.* vi, p. 508).

[2] *Festschr. für Gomperz*, p. 461.   [3] Fragm. 46 (K.).

[4] Fragm. 335 (K.). See below, p. 291.

ἄ]στ[ει καὶ ἆθλον ἐ]τέθη ὁ [τ]ράγος, ἔτη **ΗΗ**Ⴈ[ΔΔ], ἄρχοντος
Ἀθ[ήνησι ...]ναίου τοῦ προτέρου.

Notes. (1) The inscription is restored by different scholars with
sundry variations in detail, but there is complete agreement as
to ascription to Thespis of a victory at this date, with the goat
as a prize.

(2) Wilamowitz[1] may be right in inserting the name of
Thespis in Eusebius, *Can. Ol.* 61. 3 (i. e. 534/3 B.C.). Ξενοφάνης
φυσικὸς ⟨καὶ Θέσπις⟩ τραγῳδοποιὸς ἐγνωρίζετο. But when Eusebius,
Can. Ol. 47. 2 (591/0 B. c.) states that τοῖς ἀγωνιζομένοις παρ᾽ Ἕλλησι
τράγος ἐδίδοτο, ἀφ᾽ οὗ καὶ τραγικοὶ ἐκλήθησαν, this is probably an
attempt to synchronize Thespis and Solon at a date when the
latter was at his ἀκμή.[2] Professor Flickinger thinks that Eusebius
refers here to tragedy at Sicyon.[3]

DIOSCORIDES, *Anth. Pal.* vii. 411.

Θέσπιδος εὕρεμα τοῦτο· τὰ δ᾽ ἀγροιῶτιν ἀν᾽ ὕλαν
παίγνια, καὶ κώμους τούσδ᾽ ἔτι μειοτέρους
Αἰσχύλος ἐξύψωσεν κτλ.

ID. *Anth. Pal.* vii. 410.

Θέσπις ὅδε, τραγικὴν ὃς ἀνέπλασα πρῶτος ἀοιδὴν
κωμήταις νεαρὰς καινοτομῶν χάριτας,
Βάκχος ὅτε τρυγικὸν κατάγοι χορόν, ᾧ τράγος †ἄθλων†
χὤττικὸς ἦν σύκων ἄρριχος ἆθλον ἔτι·
οἱ δὲ μεταπλάσσουσι νέοι τάδε· μύριος αἰὼν
πολλὰ προσευρήσει χἄτερα· τἀμὰ δ᾽ ἐμά.

Notes. (1) There are many emendations besides τρυγικόν for the
corrupt MSS. reading τριτθύν in l. 3.

(2) Compare Plutarch, *de cupid. div.* viii, p. 527 d ἡ πάτριος τῶν Διονυσίων ἑορτὴ τὸ παλαιὸν ἐπέμπετο δημοτικῶς καὶ ἱλαρῶς· ἀμφορεὺς οἴνου
καὶ κληματίς, εἶτα τράγον τις εἷλκεν, ἄλλος ἰσχάδων ἄρριχον ἠκολούθει
κομίζων, ἐπὶ πᾶσι δ᾽ ὁ φαλλός.

HORACE, *de Arte Poet.* 275-7.

Ignotum tragicae genus invenisse Camoenae
dicitur et plaustris vexisse poemata Thespis,
quae canerent agerentque peruncti faecibus ora.

---

[1] *Homer. Unters.* vii. 248.　　　[2] See below, p. 107.　　　[3] See p. 137, n. 1.

CLEM. ALEX. *Strom.* i, § 79. Ναὶ μὴν ἴαμβον ἐπενόησεν Ἀρχίλοχος ὁ Πάριος, χωλὸν δὲ ἴαμβον Ἱππῶναξ ὁ Ἐφέσιος, καὶ τραγῳδίαν μὲν Θέσπις ὁ Ἀθηναῖος, κωμῳδίαν δὲ Σουσαρίων ὁ Ἰκαριεύς.

ERATOSTHENES, *Erigone.* (Fragm. ap. Hygin. *de Astr.* ii. 4).[1] Ἰκάριοι τόθι πρῶτα περὶ τράγον ὠρχήσαντο.

ATHENAEUS, ii, p. 40 a, b. ἀπὸ μέθης καὶ ἡ τῆς κωμῳδίας καὶ ἡ τῆς τραγῳδίας εὕρεσις ἐν Ἰκαρίῳ τῆς Ἀττικῆς εὑρέθη καὶ κατ' αὐτὸν τῆς τρύγης καιρόν.

EUANTHIUS, *de Com* i.[2] Quamvis igitur retro prisca volventibus reperiatur Thespis tragoediae primus inventor etc.

DONATUS, *de Com.* v.[3] Thespis autem primus haec scripta in omnium notitiam protulit; postea Aeschylus secutus prioris exemplum locupletavit; de quibus Horatius etc.

PLUTARCH, *Solon*, ch. xxix. ἀρχομένων δὲ τῶν περὶ Θέσπιν ἤδη τὴν τραγῳδίαν κινεῖν καὶ διὰ τὴν καινότητα τοὺς πολλοὺς ἄγοντος τοῦ πράγματος, οὔπω δ' εἰς ἅμιλλαν ἐναγώνιον ἐξηγμένου, φύσει φιλήκοος ὢν καὶ φιλομαθὴς ὁ Σόλων ... ἐθεάσατο τὸν Θέσπιν αὐτὸν ὑποκρινόμενον, ὥσπερ ἔθος ἦν τοῖς παλαιοῖς. μετὰ δὲ τὴν θέαν προσαγορεύσας αὐτὸν ἠρώτησεν, εἰ τοσούτων ἐναντίον οὐκ αἰσχύνεται τηλικαῦτα ψευδόμενος. φήσαντος δὲ τοῦ Θέσπιδος μὴ δεινὸν εἶναι τὸ μετὰ παιδιᾶς λέγειν τὰ τοιαῦτα καὶ πράττειν, σφόδρα τῇ βακτηρίᾳ τὴν γῆν ὁ Σόλων πατάξας "ταχὺ μέντοι τὴν παιδιάν" ἔφη "ταύτην ἐπαινοῦντες καὶ τιμῶντες εὑρήσομεν ἐν τοῖς συμβολαίοις".[4]

DIOG. LAERT. iii, § 56. ὥσπερ δὲ τὸ παλαιὸν ἐν τῇ τραγῳδίᾳ πρότερον μὲν μόνος ὁ χορὸς διεδραμάτιζεν, ὕστερον δὲ Θέσπις ἕνα ὑποκριτὴν ἐξεῦρεν ὑπὲρ τοῦ διαναπαύεσθαι τὸν χορόν, καὶ δεύτερον Αἰσχύλος, τὸν δὲ τρίτον Σοφοκλῆς, καὶ συνεπλήρωσεν τὴν τραγῳδίαν· οὕτω καὶ τῆς φιλοσοφίας ὁ λόγος κτλ.

---

[1] For the reading, see Hiller, *Eratosth. Carm. Reliquiae*, pp. 105 ff.
[2] Kaibel, *Fragm. Com. Graec.* i, p. 62.
[3] ibid., p. 68.
[4] The note in Diog. L. i, § 59 (Life of Solon)—καὶ Θέσπιν ἐκώλυσε τραγῳδίας διδάσκειν, ὡς ἀνωφελῆ τὴν ψευδολογίαν—obviously comes from the same source.

THEMISTIUS, *Orat.* xxvi, p. 316 d. *ἀλλὰ καὶ ἡ σεμνὴ τραγῳδία μετὰ πάσης ὁμοῦ τῆς σκευῆς καὶ τοῦ χοροῦ καὶ τῶν ὑποκριτῶν παρελήλυθεν εἰς τὸ θέατρον; καὶ οὐ προσέχομεν Ἀριστοτέλει ὅτι τὸ μὲν πρῶτον ὁ χορὸς εἰσίων ᾖδεν εἰς τοὺς θεούς, Θέσπις δὲ πρόλογόν τε καὶ ῥῆσιν ἐξεῦρεν, Αἰσχύλος δὲ τρίτον ὑποκριτὴν καὶ ὀκρίβαντας, τὰ δὲ πλείω τούτων Σοφοκλέους ἀπελαύσαμεν καὶ Εὐριπίδου;*

Note. Many scholars think that τρίτον ὑποκριτήν is a false reading; but as Aeschylus certainly did adopt the third actor, after the introduction of him by Sophocles, Themistius may have found the statement in some form in Aristotle, and also the assertion about ὀκρίβαντες.

ATHENAEUS i, p. 22 a. *φασὶ δὲ καὶ ὅτι οἱ ἀρχαῖοι ποιηταί, Θέσπις, Πρατίνας, Φρύνιχος, ὀρχησταὶ ἐκαλοῦντο διὰ τὸ μὴ μόνον τὰ ἑαυτῶν δράματα ἀναφέρειν εἰς ὄρχησιν τοῦ χοροῦ, ἀλλὰ καὶ ἔξω τῶν ἰδίων ποιημάτων διδάσκειν τοὺς βουλομένους ὀρχεῖσθαι.*

SUIDAS. *Θέσπις· Ἰκαρίου πόλεως Ἀττικῆς, τραγικὸς ἐκκαιδέκατος ἀπὸ τοῦ πρώτου γενομένου τραγῳδοποιοῦ Ἐπιγένους τοῦ Σικυωνίου τιθέμενος, ὡς δέ τινες, δεύτερος μετὰ Ἐπιγένην. ἄλλοι δὲ αὐτὸν πρῶτον τραγικὸν γενέσθαι φασί. καὶ πρῶτον μὲν χρίσας τὸ πρόσωπον ψιμυθίῳ ἐτραγῴδησεν, εἶτα ἀνδράχνη ἐσκέπασεν ἐν τῷ ἐπιδείκνυσθαι, καὶ μετὰ ταῦτα εἰσήνεγκε καὶ τὴν τῶν προσωπείων χρῆσιν ἐν μόνῃ ὀθόνῃ κατασκευάσας. ἐδίδαξε δὲ ἐπὶ τῆς πρώτης καὶ ξ' Ὀλυμπιάδος* [i.e. 536/5–532/1 B.C.]. *μνημονεύονται δὲ τῶν δραμάτων αὐτοῦ Ἄθλα Πελίου ἢ Φόρβας, Ἱερεῖς, Ἤϊθεοι, Πενθεύς.*

As regards the works of Thespis, two other passages should be noticed:

DIOG. LAERT. v, § 92. (Life of Heraclides Ponticus.) *φησὶ δ' Ἀριστόξενος ὁ μουσικὸς καὶ τραγῳδίας αὐτὸν* (i. e. Heraclides) *ποιεῖν καὶ Θέσπιδος αὐτὰς ἐπιγράφειν.*

ARISTOPHANES, *Wasps*, 1478–9:

> *ὀρχούμενος τῆς νυκτὸς οὐδὲν παύεται*
> *τἀρχαῖ' ἐκεῖν' οἷς Θέσπις ἠγωνίζετο.*

Schol. Θέσπις· ὁ κιθαρῳδός, οὐ γὰρ δὴ ὁ τραγικός.

To these passages should be added the following, which give some evidence of traditions in regard to tragedy before Thespis:

PSEUDO-PLAT. *Minos*, p. 321 a.   ἡ δὲ τραγῳδία ἐστὶ παλαιὸν ἐνθάδε, οὐχ ὡς οἴονται ἀπὸ Θέσπιδος ἀρχομένη, οὐδ' ἀπὸ Φρυνίχου, ἀλλ', εἰ ἐθέλεις ἐννοῆσαι, πάνυ παλαιὸν αὐτὸ εὑρήσεις ὂν τῆσδε τῆς πόλεως εὕρημα.

POLLUX iv. 123.   ἐλεὸς δ' ἦν τράπεζα ἀρχαία, ἐφ' ἣν πρὸ Θέσπιδος εἷς τις ἀναβὰς τοῖς χορευταῖς ἀπεκρίνατο.

ETYMOL. MAGN. (s. v. θυμέλη).   ἡ τοῦ θεάτρου μεχρὶ νῦν ἀπὸ τῆς τραπέζης ὠνόμασται, παρὰ τὸ ἐπ' αὐτῆς τὰ θύη μερίζεσθαι, τούτεστι τὰ θυόμενα ἱερεῖα.   τράπεζα δ' ἦν, ἐφ' ἧς ἑστῶτες ἐν τοῖς ἀγροῖς ᾖδον, μήπω τάξιν λαβούσης τραγῳδίας.

ISIDOR., *Origg.* xviii. 47.   et dicti thymelici, quod olim in orchestra stantes cantabant super pulpitum quod thymele vocabatur.

ATHENAEUS, xiv, p. 630 c.   συνέστηκε δὲ καὶ σατυρικὴ πᾶσα ποίησις τὸ παλαιὸν ἐκ χορῶν, ὡς καὶ ἡ τότε τραγῳδία· διόπερ οὐδὲ ὑποκριτὰς εἶχον.

Note. The statement is probably, though not certainly, taken from Aristocles περὶ χορῶν, which is quoted earlier in the chapter.

EUANTHIUS *de Com.* ii.[1]   Comoedia fere vetus ut ipsa quoque olim tragoedia simplex carmen, quemadmodum iam diximus, fuit, quod chorus circa aras fumantes nunc spatiatus, nunc consistens, nunc revolvens gyros, cum tibicine concinebat. sed primo una persona est subducta cantoribus, quae respondens alterius choro locupletavit variavitque rem musicam; tum altera, tum tertia, et ad postremum crescente numero per auctores diversos personae pallae cothurni socci et ceteri ornatus atque insignia scenicorum reperta.

§ 2. Unhappily there is scarcely a point in these passages which has not been, or might not be, the subject of controversy, and it is very difficult to trace back some of the statements made in them to any reputable source, so that the true line between credulity and undue scepticism is often hard to draw.

---

[1] Kaibel, *Fragm. Com. Graec.* i, p. 63.

It has been doubted, in the first place, whether 'Thespis' is not an assumed name, appropriate to a poet, but actually derived from such passages of the *Odyssey* as the following:

τοῦ δ' ὑπερωιόθεν φρεσὶ σύνθετο θέσπιν ἀοιδὴν
κούρη Ἰκαρίοιο   (i. 328–9),

or αὐτίκ' ἐγὼ πᾶσιν μυθήσομαι ἀνθρώποισιν
ὡς ἄρα τοι πρόφρων θεὸς ὤπασε θέσπιν ἀοιδήν
                                               (viii. 497–8),

or ἢ καὶ θέσπιν ἀοιδόν, ὅ κεν τέρπησιν ἀείδων   (xvii. 385).

But for the present we may be content to use the traditional name.

The connexion of Thespis with Icarius or Icaria in Attica [1] is mentioned by Athenaeus and Suidas, and is generally taken to be proved by the line of Eratosthenes quoted above. But whether Eratosthenes ought to be cited in this context at all depends upon the interpretation of the words περὶ τράγον ὠρχήσαντο. Hyginus,[2] to whom we owe the line, gives not a hint of tragedy, and thinks of it as referring to ἀσκωλιασμός. Icarius, according to his story, received the vine from father Liber, with instructions as to its cultivation, and then, 'cum sevisset vitem et diligentissime administrando floridam †falce† fecisset, dicitur hircus in vineam se coniecisse et quae ibi tenerrima folia videret decerpsisse; quo facto Icarium irato animo tulisse eumque interfecisse et ex pelle eius utrem fecisse ac vento plenum praeligasse et in medium proiecisse suosque sodales circa eum saltare coegisse; itaque Eratosthenes ait . . .'

Now Hiller [3] is puzzled, naturally enough, at Eratosthenes' saying περὶ τράγον, *circa caprum*, instead of *super utrem*; and so he thinks that Hyginus or his authority (a commentator on Aratus) has misinterpreted Eratosthenes, and that the latter was really speaking of the dance round a goat sacrificed (or to be sacrificed) on the altar of Dionysus—a dance from which

---

[1] It does not appear to have been suggested as yet that the connexion is really derived from *Odyssey* i. 329.

[2] *Astron.* II. iv. Cf. Theophrastus ap. Porphyr. *de abst.* ii. 10 αἶγα δ' ἐν Ἰκαρ⟨ί⟩ῳ τῆς Ἀττικῆς ἐχειρώσαντο πρῶτον, ὅτι ἄμπελον ἀπέθρισεν.

[3] *Eratosth. carm. reliqq.*, pp. 107 ff.

tragedy is assumed to have sprung—and that it was a dance
round the whole goat, not round its inflated skin only. But
after all, whoever quoted Eratosthenes in the first instance
must have had the poet's work before him, and must have
known what he was talking about; Virgil,[1] speaking of
ἀσκωλιασμός in Attica as a form of revenge upon the goat,
gives no hint of tragedy; there is no difficulty in supposing
that the peasants while using the skin for ἀσκωλιασμός,
may also have danced round this and other portions of
the unfortunate animal; and the phrase περὶ τράγον, if not
absolutely exact, would represent the facts well enough for
poetry.[2]

It is therefore very unsafe to read into Eratosthenes the
tradition which brings Thespis from Icaria, or to regard his
words as referring to the origin of tragedy at all.[3] But if so,
the earliest extant authority for the tradition is Athenaeus;
and we do not know what his source was. Crusius [4] thinks
that it was Seleucus (who lived in the first half of the first
century A.D.); but Seleucus is only quoted in a later section
of the chapter for a quite different point. It may have been
Chamaeleon's treatise περὶ Θέσπιδος, and if so we should get
back to the end of the fourth century B.C.; but Athenaeus
does not say that it was so.

[It is only necessary to refer in passing to an extraordinary
theory recently propounded by Eisler in a work entitled
*Orphisch-dionysische Mysterien-Gedanken in der christlichen
Antike* with reference to the story of Icarius. It is suggested
that ἀσκωλιασμός was really a primitive way of pressing the
wine from the grapes—filling a goatskin with them and jumping
on it so that the juice leaked out, and that the τρυγῳδία—the
vintage song (connected with τρυγάω, τρύγη, rather than with
τρύξ)—which was primarily a lament for such πάθη of

---

[1] *Georg.* ii. 380 ff.

[2] It may be suspected (if the suggestion is not too frivolous) that
those who play at ἀσκωλιασμός are more often *circa* than *supra utrem*.

[3] Maass, *Analect. Eratosth.*, p. 114, actually speaks of a tragic chorus
with Icarius as choregus.

[4] Comment. in Plut. *de prov. Alex.*, § 30.

Dionysus Botrys (the god identified with the grapes),[1] was thus closely connected from the first with τραγῳδία, the lament for the πάθη of the slain goat,—slain in revenge for its destruction of vines. It is sufficient to note that there is no proof whatever of the existence of such a method of wine-pressing in Greece; that in the story of Icarius the ἀσκός was *vento plenus*;[2] that τρυγῳδία never seems to be applied to anything remotely akin to a lament, or indeed to anything but comedy, in classical times; and that if the goat was slain as an enemy, the lament for its πάθη would be rather surprising. We need not pursue the theory into its many ramifications.[3] One or two aspects of it will be referred to elsewhere.]

§ 3. The remark of Athenaeus which connects the origin of tragedy with Icaria derives both comedy and tragedy from μέθη, intoxication; and seems to imply the theory, which is found elsewhere, of a common origin of both, tragedy being regarded as virtually an offshoot from comedy, and the original performance as connected with the grape-harvest. Dioscorides also (if the reading τρυγικόν is correct) suggests

---

[1] Whether this view derives any real support from the further suggestions that the Linos song is a lament for the torn flax, and the Adrastus song at Sicyon for the poppy or the gourd may be left to the reader to decide.

[2] Nearly all the Greek explanations of ἀσκωλία, &c., in scholiasts and lexicographers agree as to this. One scholium (on Aristoph. *Plut.* 1129) says, ἀσκὸν γὰρ οἴνου πληροῦντες ἐνὶ ποδὶ ⟨ἐπὶ⟩ τοῦτον ἐπήδων καὶ ὁ πηδήσας ἆθλον εἶχε τὸν οἶνον. (The notices are conveniently collected by Headlam-Knox, *Herodas*, p. 390.) The performance may, as some anthropologists think, have been a charm against violent winds. Another says that the ἀσκός was filled with air for the game, but with wine when given as a prize to the competitor who managed to keep his footing on it; and this may be the solution of the discrepancies; or the game may not always have been played in the same way. See Herzog, *Philologus*, lxxix (1924), pp. 401-4, 410-11.

[3] Thus Dionysus Μελαναιγίς represents the wine in the black goat-skin. In Dithyramb (for the name of which a new derivation is provided) the bull takes the place of the goat; this is the aristocratic form of the ceremony; for heroes, ἀσκὸς βοὸς ἐννεώροιο (*Od.* x. 19), took the place of the goat-skin which sufficed for ordinary men : and so on.

that the scene of Thespis' performance was the vintage-festival, and Horace's *peruncti faecibus ora* possibly involves the same idea. Other passages imply a similar tradition. It appears in a longer form in Plutarch, *de Proverbiis Alexandrinorum*, § 30. The text is corrupt, but its general drift is clear: τὰ μηδὲν πρὸς τὸν Διόνυσον· τὴν κωμῳδίαν καὶ τὴν τραγῳδίαν ἀπὸ γέλωτος εἰς τὸν βίον φασὶ παρελθεῖν. καὶ ⟨γὰρ⟩ κατὰ καιρὸν τῆς συγκομιδῆς τῶν γεννημάτων παραγενομένους τινὰς ἐπὶ τὰς ληνοὺς καὶ τοῦ γλεύκους πίνοντας ποιήματά τινα σκώπτειν καὶ γράφειν, διὰ τὸ πρότερον εἰς κωμῳδίαν καλεῖσθαι. [Crusius proposes to read: πίνοντας σκώπτειν, ὕστερον δὲ σκωπτικὰ ποιήματά τινα καὶ γράφειν, ἃ διὰ τὸ πρότερον ἐν κώμαις ᾄδεσθαι κωμῳδίαν καλεῖσθαι.] ἤρχοντο δὲ συνεχέστερον εἰς τὰς κώμας τὰς Ἀττικὰς γύψῳ τὰς ὄψεις κεχρισμέναι καὶ ἔσκωπτον ⁕ ⁕ ⁕ τραγικὰ παρεισφέροντες ⟨ἐπὶ τὸ⟩ αὐστηρότερον μετῆλθον ⁕ ⁕ ⁕ ταῦτα οὖν καὶ ἐπεὶ τῷ Διονύσῳ πολέμιόν ἐστιν ὁ τράγος ἐπισκώπτοντες ἔλεγον ⁕ ⁕ ⁕ ἐπὶ τῶν ἀνοικεῖά τισι προσφερόντων.

The same theory lies behind a passage in the *Etymologicum Magnum* [1] on tragedy: ἢ ἀπὸ τῆς τρυγὸς τρυγῳδία· ἦν δὲ τὸ ὄνομα κοινὸν καὶ πρὸς τὴν κωμῳδίαν, ἐπεὶ οὔπω διεκέκριτο τὰ τῆς ποιήσεως ἑκατέρας· ἀλλ' εἰς αὐτὴν ἐν ἦν τὸ ἄθλον, ἡ τρύξ. ὕστερον δὲ τὸ μὲν κοινὸν ὄνομα ἔσχεν ἡ τραγῳδία· ἡ δὲ κωμῳδία ὠνόμασται κτλ. The theory is found in practically the same words in the commentary of Ioannes Diaconus on Hermogenes.[2]

The ' basket of figs ' which is mentioned as part of the prize by Dioscorides and Plutarch (in the passage from the *De cupiditate divitiarum*) also probably implies an autumn or late-summer festival; they are not likely to have been dried figs.

If Crusius' textual suggestions on Plutarch's explanation of the proverb are accepted—and something like them appears necessary—Plutarch's story has points of contact with an account of the origin of comedy in some nocturnal excursions of rustics into the city, which is found in the scholia on Dionysius Thrax, Tztezes, and in an anonymous writer on

[1] 764. 10 ff.   [2] *Rhein. Mus.* lxiii, p. 150 ; see below, p. 132.

comedy found in certain MSS. of Aristophanes; [1] and Kaibel [2] thinks that the common source of all these is a lost book of the *Chrestomathia* of Proclus; but the treatise ascribed to Plutarch is earlier than Proclus, and, whether the work be that of Plutarch or not we do not know from what source it drew. It must not be forgotten that Aristotle himself spoke of tragedy as being originally ludicrous or 'satyric' in its language: and so far the tradition may be true (we shall recur to the point later). In view of the distinction which Aristotle makes between the origins of comedy and those of tragedy, it would not be right to ascribe to him the belief that both arose out of a τρυγῳδία such as the writers who have been quoted suggest: but it is at least possible that this theory itself arose out of mistaken interpretations of the *Poetics*, since (at least in some of these writers) the same common source is alleged for all three forms of drama, tragic, comic, and satyric. Such a misinterpretation might be further encouraged by the mention of Thespis' 'waggons', when connected with the σκώμματα ἐκ τῶν ἁμαξῶν which were part of some kinds of κῶμος, though the resemblance is only superficial. The fact that Thespis at one period hung flowers over his face, like certain φαλλοφόροι described by Semus of Delos,[3] might also be adduced in support of the theory; but such a disguise is common in mummers' performances everywhere, and could not really be used as evidence of original identity. (To the waggons we shall return.)

The only conclusion which seems legitimate is that, on the one hand, there *may* once have been an undifferentiated performance involving both serious and grotesque elements out of which both tragedy and comedy could be evolved—such a performance as in fact still takes place (or did take place until recently) in parts of the modern Greek world: [4] but that, on the other hand, there is no sufficient proof of it, since the tradition may well be due to false inferences from Aristotle, and the

---

[1] Kaibel, *Fragm. Com. Graec.*, i, p. 12: see below, p. 281.

[2] *Die Prolegomena περὶ κωμῳδίας*, pp. 12 ff.

[3] See below, pp. 231, 234.

[4] See below, p. 163, and references there given.

word τρυγῳδία (applied in classical times to comedy) is very
likely simply a parody-word [1] based on the name τραγῳδία,
which was certainly not derived from it, and was undoubtedly
primitive. If, as is quite possible, tragedy was originally an
autumn performance (though the connexion of this date with
the derivation from τρυγῳδία is suspicious), it may well have
been converted into a spring celebration at the time of the organization of the Great Dionysia by Peisistratus; though there is
no independent evidence of any such change, and tragedy is
not likely to have arisen from anything like the type of κῶμος
with which the beginnings of comedy were probably connected.[2]

§ 4. As regards the date of Thespis, there is no reason for
doubting that the compiler of the record on the Parian Marble,
which is generally trustworthy, had some ground for placing
his victory—doubtless his first victory in a public competition
at Athens—about 534 B.C., at the time when Peisistratus was
organizing or reorganizing the Great Dionysia, and for saying
that he won a goat as his prize. The tradition, recorded by
Plutarch, of his controversy with Solon may be true, if the
event took place late in Solon's life—e.g. in 560 B.C.—and (as
Plutarch says) before the institution of contests. A certain
suspicion attaches to any anecdote which brings famous
persons into relation with Solon, in view of the existence of
stories chronologically impossible, connecting Solon with
Croesus and with Amasis.[3] But in the present instance there
is no such impossibility, and the story is quite in keeping
with what we know of Solon's independence of judgement.

Sir William Ridgeway [4] places an interpretation upon
Plutarch's words which can be sufficiently met by reference to

---

[1] See below, pp. 164, 284.

[2] Some scholars conjecture that the Peripatetic School (basing their
theory on their inferences from Aristotle) may have been responsible for
the ascription of tragedy and comedy to an identical origin, and that the
points of resemblance noted in the statements of Suidas, &c., may have
been invented by them. But there is no sufficient evidence of this.

[3] Thus Nilsson, *Neue Jahrb.* xxvii (1911), p. 611, thinks that the story
is an invention.

[4] *Origin of Trag.*, p. 61.

the actual passage. Arguing in defence of his theory that
tragedy arose among the tombs, he suggests that the plays of
Thespis were not Dionysiac but heroic, and that the innovation made by him and condemned by Solon consisted in the
removal of these plays from the hero-tomb and the performance of them at other spots. But Plutarch tells us quite
clearly what it was that upset Solon, and it was something
entirely different, viz. that Thespis told such falsehoods before
so large a crowd. (Perhaps, like Plato, he regarded impersonation as a kind of deceit.) There is not a shadow of
evidence for Sir William Ridgeway's statement that a 'performance, which he would have regarded as fit and proper
when enacted in some shrine of the gods or at a hero's tomb,
not unnaturally roused his indignation when the exhibition
was merely for sport . . . and not at some hallowed spot'. For
all we know, the performance of Thespis (if, as the tradition
suggests, it had something to do with the worship of Dionysus)
may have been at a hallowed spot.

The various theories which Suidas records as to the place
of Thespis in the series of early tragic poets—sixteenth after
Epigenes, next after Epigenes, or first of all—show the uncertainty of the traditions. We shall return to Epigenes, who,
if he was performing at Sicyon early in the sixth century,
may have been long enough before Thespis to allow of fifteen
known poets between them.[1] Those who knew of no such
poets, but had heard of Epigenes, placed the two first and
second on the list; those who held to the strong tradition that Thespis invented tragedy placed him first, and
probably either ignored Epigenes or said that what he wrote
was something else. The difference of date (if Plutarch's
story is true) between Thespis' first appearance at Athens and

---

[1] Suidas speaks of Ἀλκαῖος Ἀθηναῖος (s. v.) as τραγικός, ὅν τινες θέλουσι
πρῶτον τραγικὸν γεγονέναι, and Mr. R. J. Walker (in his book on Sophocles'
Ichneutae, pp. 294 ff.) tries to pick out of the fragments assigned to
Alcaeus *Comicus* some, which (when sufficiently emended) might be
ascribed to Alcaeus *Tragicus*. But his argument is not to be taken
seriously. The confusion in which Suidas lay in regard to poets of the
name Alcaeus is shown by his other notices s. v.

his first victory in a contest, would also give rise to divergent views. These views are not history, and all that we can feel fairly confident about is the victory in or near the year 534 B. C.

§ 5. What can be gathered from our authorities as to the kind of tragedy that Thespis wrote ? There is substantial agreement between Diogenes Laertius, Themistius, and others that Thespis introduced speeches by a ὑποκριτής into a performance which had hitherto been given by a chorus alone, and Themistius makes Aristotle responsible for this view. There is no passage to this effect in the extant works of Aristotle ; in the *Poetics* he ascribes the second actor to Aeschylus (though in some lost work he may also have mentioned the adoption by Aeschylus of the third) ; the first actor he evidently regards as being the ἐξάρχων of the dithyrambic chorus, now separated from the rest, but he does not mention Thespis as the author of the change. This, however, is no conclusive proof that he did not think of the first actor as the invention of Thespis, and Hiller[1] is perhaps too ready to discredit Themistius' ascription of this view to Aristotle. The suggestion that Themistius is merely paraphrasing the *Poetics* loosely, and supplying the name of Thespis on his own authority, is disproved by the mention of ὀκρίβαντες, of which the *Poetics* says nothing. He may possibly be referring to some passage in the lost περὶ ποιητῶν. What authority Diogenes Laertius used is unknown.

It is, of course, impossible to exclude absolutely the possibility that the tradition which Diogenes and Themistius record may be based on a 'combination' by ancient writers who had before them the writings of Aristotle and some stories about Thespis. But the tradition—that Thespis introduced an actor who impersonated a legendary or historical character, and gave him a prologue and one or more set speeches to deliver instead of leaving him to improvise his remarks—is in itself probable enough. The importance of the change is obvious; and if it was really Thespis who

---

[1] *Rhein. Mus.* xxxix, pp. 321–38.

created the actor, the description of him as the first tragic poet or the inventor of tragedy is sufficiently explained and justified.

If we can assume that Aristotle [1] is referring to the work of Thespis when he says λέξεως δὲ γενομένης αὐτὴ ἡ φύσις τὸ οἰκεῖον μέτρον εὗρε, we must infer that the ῥήσεις which Thespis introduced were probably in the iambic trimeter, not in the trochaic tetrameter metre; and it is at least probable that the use of the iambic metre for this purpose, which was fully established by the time of Aeschylus' *Supplices*, began sometime before.

According to Plutarch, Thespis took the actor's part himself. If Bywater [2] and others [3] are right in stating that the word ὑποκριτής does not mean ' one who answers the chorus ', but rather ' the spokesman ' who interprets the poet's text to the public, and that the term must have acquired this sense at the time when, by a division of labour, the poet left the acting to others, instead of being himself the performer of his pieces (as he originally was, according to Aristotle),[4] it would be interesting to know whether Thespis, as actor, gave himself, or received, any technical name; but of this there is no record.

§ 6. Suidas states that, when acting, Thespis at first disguised his face with white lead, but afterwards hung purslane over his face, and finally introduced masks of linen. But what the words ἐν μόνῃ ὀθόνῃ mean is uncertain; they perhaps mean ' of linen only, not of cork or wood ', rather than ' of linen

---

[1] *Poet.* iv. 1449 a 22.   [2] *Aristotle's Poetics*, p. 136.

[3] Heimsoeth, *de voce ὑποκριτής*, and Sommerbrodt, *Scaenica*, pp. 259, 289; but see Curtius's reply, *Rhein. Mus.* xxiii. 255 ff. It seems fairly clear that while ὑποκρίνεσθαι and ὑποκριτής were used in Homer and at least down to Plato's time (e. g. *Timaeus*, p. 72 b) of the interpretation of dreams and omens, it is very difficult to get away from the meaning ' answer' even in Homer, and impossible afterwards. By the fourth century the meanings ' act', ' actor' (without any consciousness of either derivation) are regularly current; and there is nothing which can enable us to decide from which of the early senses—' interpret' or ' answer '—the application of the word to the actor's part is derived.

[4] *Rhet.* III. i, p. 1403 b 23.

without paint or colouring'. Nothing is said about the
costume of his chorus.

Sir William Ridgeway[1] argues that the statement that
Thespis originally painted his face with white lead or wore a
white mask indicates that he was acting the part of the ghost
of a deceased hero—an argument adduced in support of his
peculiar theory of the origin of tragedy. To this Dr. Farnell
gives a sufficient reply.[2] 'Are we then to infer that the
primitive fathers of Greek drama, starting with hero-parts,
and wishing to act the deeds of Achilles and Agamemnon, could
not pretend to be the living men of the past, but only the dead
men, so that the ghost of Achilles would be represented fighting the ghost of Hector? Was the early Greek mimetic dance
a dance of ghosts? Did the medieval passion-play represent
the real saint or the ghost of the saint? This interpretation
of the whitened face or the white mask has consequences so
weird that we must distrust it and try to imagine others.
And, in any case, if the record is trustworthy at all, it would
only attest the reminiscence that white masks were among the
occasional properties of the early Attic stage.' At the same time
it is not certain that the masks were white, as we have seen;[3]
and the purslane has still to be explained. Is not the simple
explanation that a primitive actor is mainly concerned to disguise his own face, so that the fact that 'this is just Bottom'
may not obtrude itself, and that these three experiments in
disguise—paint, flowers (like those which some modern mummers hang over their faces), and simple masks—were very
natural ones to make? The fact that Thespis (if the record

[1] *Origin of Tragedy*, p. 89.

[2] *Hermathena*, 1913, p. 12. I am grateful to Dr. Farnell for permission
to quote his words here and elsewhere.

[3] P. Girard (*Rev. Ét. Grecques*, 1891, p. 169) conjectures that Thespis
may have introduced the white colour to represent women, using wine-
lees for men, following the example of the vase-painters of the sixth
century B. C., who (led by the Athenian painter Eumares) painted women's
faces white, men's faces red. This is ingenious: but so far as we have
any evidence on the subject, it is to the effect that Phrynichus first
introduced female masks (see above, p. 92), and Girard does not really
meet this difficulty.

is true) only arrived at masks after trying other experiments
does not square with the assertions of some anthropologists who regard masks as essentially bound up with primitive
drama on account of their magical significance : and that they
always had such a significance may well be held doubtful ; [1] but
that question may be postponed for later discussion. What is
really unfortunate is that we do not know who Suidas'
authority may have been ; it may have been Chamaeleon, but
it may not ; and the historical value of the statement cannot
now be tested.[2]

It is, however, worth while to remark that there is not
a word in any of the notices about Thespis to suggest that his
performers or any of them were disguised as satyrs. Certainly his actor cannot have been, if the story of his disguises
is true ; and of his choruses we are told nothing. The oft-
repeated statement that he employed a satyr-chorus rests on
inferences from statements of Aristotle,[3] which, as will be
argued later, are far from conclusive.

The tradition recorded by Horace that Thespis took his
plays about on wagons, to be acted by persons who were
peruncti faecibus ora is hardly consistent with Suidas' account
of his disguises, unless either the latter were later improvements on wine-lees, or unless Horace refers only to the

[1] Dr. E. Rostrup (*Attic Tragedy in the Light of Theatrical History*,
pp. 76 ff.) has a peculiar and, as it seems to me, a quite untenable
theory about Thespis' masks and the beginnings of tragedy generally.
I may refer to what I have said of this in the *Class. Rev.* for 1924,
p. 202.

[2] Plut. *de prov. Alex.*, § 30 (quoted above, p. 105) says that the
performers in the processions which were supposed to be the common
origin of Comedy and Tragedy used gypsum to disguise their faces.

[3] Aristotle's statement that the earliest tragedies had short plots and
grotesque diction may itself be due to his theory that tragedy developed
out of satyr-play. This will be considered later. But if Thespis, in
addition to his iambic ῥήσεις, used the trochaic tetrameter freely (e. g. in
dialogue), this might be felt to have a comic effect, cf. Ar. *Rhet.* III. viii,
1408 b 36 ὁ τροχαῖος κορδακικώτερος· δηλοῖ δὲ τὰ τετράμετρα, ἐστὶ γὰρ ῥυθμὸς
τροχαῖος τὰ τετράμετρα. Aeschylus of course succeeded in employing the
metre without any such effect, by the adoption (as in the case of the
iambic trimeter) of stricter rules than those followed for comic purposes.

FIG. 4. Dionysiac Procession

I

appearance of the chorus; we have already seen that it seems to be connected with the belief in an original autumn performance, and that Dioscorides possibly had the same tradition, at least as regards the wine-lees. If, however, Dioscorides is rightly interpreted as meaning that Thespis presented Dionysus at the head of a chorus, and if the statement is true (and Dioscorides is not a sufficiently good authority to guarantee this), it is improbable that Dionysus should have been disguised with white lead, which (as we must concede to Sir William Ridgeway) would give a very inappropriate complexion to the god, especially in that company. But Horace and Dioscorides may quite well be wrong as regards the wine-lees, and may be confusing the origins of tragedy with the κῶμοι which gave rise to comedy.

If there is any truth in Horace's words it may be that Thespis, like travelling players at fairs down to the present day, took his plays about on wagons to local Dionysiac festivals, and like them stood on the end of the wagon to act (with his chorus dancing round it,) and used the covered part of it as his σκηνή to dress up in. But that it is pure speculation, and it is more likely that Horace is thinking confusedly of the wagons in processions of a riotous or comic type, with their σκώμματα ἐκ τῶν ἀμαξῶν.

It is, however, necessary to discuss briefly the supposed confirmation of the wagons by certain vase-paintings. Three black-figured Attic scyphi,[1] probably painted in the last years of the sixth century, present a procession in which the figure of Dionysus is seated in a wagon partly transformed into the shape of a ship, with a satyr standing in the car at each end, blowing a double flute, and two satyrs drawing the car. Various human worshippers take part in the procession—one a canephoros, another bearing a censer, most of them carrying branches of vine-leaves—and they lead a bull, doubtless to the sacrifice. Dionysus holds in his hand a vine which overshadows the car. The procession appears in its completest form on the scyphus at Bologna (fig. 4); that in the British Museum (figs. 5 and 6) is essentially similar, but is

[1] Figures 4–7.

FIG. 5

FIG. 6

SCYPHUS IN THE BRITISH MUSEUM (B. 79)

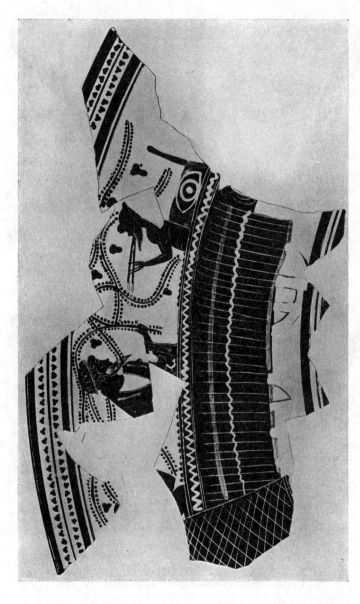

Fig. 7. SCYPHUS IN ATHENS

much damaged. (Two λήκυθοι [1] present a similar procession, without Dionysus and the car, and with a trumpeter at the head; but it is hardly safe to assume, as Frickenhaus does, that they represent the same ceremony as the scyphi. Many sacrificial processions must, apart from the naval car, have presented similar features.)

It is claimed by Bethe [2] that the Bolognese scyphus—he had not examined the others—presents to us the drama as conducted by Thespis, and that we have here the visible interpretation of Horace's *plaustris vexisse poemata*. But it is surely plain that what is represented is not a play, but a κῶμος in procession to a sacrifice; and there is) suggestion of actor and chorus in the grouping. Frickenhaus [3] who has discussed these vases and others of kindred subject very fully, believes that they represent the procession in which Dionysus Eleuthereus was escorted to the temple close by the theatre at the beginning of the Great Dionysia, and explains the ship-shaped car by the fact that the sailing season opened with the Dionysia.[4] There are difficulties in the way of this view, which it is not necessary to discuss fully here,[5] but it is safe

[1] Figs. 8–10 represent one of these (in the British Museum). The other (in Athens) is figured by Heydemann, *Gr. Vasenb.*, pl. xi. 2.

[2] *Proleg. zur Gesch. des Theaters*, pp. 45-6. See also Dieterich, *Arch-Rel.*, 1908, pp. 173-4.

[3] *Jahrb. Arch.* xxvii (1912), pp. 61 ff. Other vases presenting Dionysus in a ship date from at least half a century earlier than those discussed above.

[4] Theoph. *Char.* iii. 3. The ἀδολέσχης tells you τὴν θάλασσαν ἐκ Διονυσίων πλόϊμον εἶναι. But this does not really carry with it any information about the naval car.

[5] e. g. as to the time of year; there were no vine-leaves to overshadow the car at the time of the City Dionysia: and there is a difficulty in the bringing of the god on a ship in a procession which was intended to reproduce the original bringing of his image by road from Eleutherae. Other arguments against Frickenhaus' interpretation of the vases as referring to the Great Dionysia are given by Nilsson, *Jahrb. Arch.* xxxi (1916), pp. 332-6, and some of these appear to be conclusive, though his own explanation of the vases by reference to the Anthesteria is less convincing. It is possible that the vases represent imaginatively the original arrival of Dionysus in Athens, and not any procession actually held in the sixth century; the worship of Dionysus may have come to

to reject the attempts to justify the belief in the wagons of
Thespis by means of these vases.

§ 7. Suidas gives us the titles of Thespis' plays: Ἆθλα Πελίου
ἢ Φόρβας, Ἱερεῖς, Ἤϊθεοι, Πενθεύς. Of these the first is not,
the last is, a Dionysiac subject. The others may or may not
have been. We do not know whence Suidas got the titles,
and all statements about the plays of Thespis are rendered
doubtful by the allegation made by Aristoxenus against
Heracleides Ponticus, that he forged plays in the name of
Thespis. Nor can we tell how long the real plays remained
known in Athens itself. Horace [1] seems to think of them as
still open to Roman students in the third century B.C.:

> Serus enim Graecis admovit acumina chartis,
> et post Punica bella quietus quaerere coepit
> quid Sophocles et Thespis et Aeschylus utile ferrent.

But there is no confirmation of the idea that Roman poets
imitated Thespis, and Horace is not always accurate. The
name of Thespis would scan more easily than that of Euripides,
from whom the Romans borrowed largely.

The lines quoted above from Aristophanes' *Wasps* [2] have often
been taken as a proof of a knowledge of choruses of Thespis
in 422 B.C., but our suspicions are aroused by the scholiast and
by Suidas, who (on whatever authority) say that it is not the
tragic poet who is meant, but a citharode of the same name.

Sophocles is said by Suidas to have written a prose treatise

Attica in the first instance by sea, whether direct from Thrace or from
elsewhere; and legends of Dionysus as a sea-farer are well known, e. g.
Hom. *Hymn* vii and Hermippus fr. 63 (K.). (Comp. a festival at Smyrna
described by Philostratus, *Vit. Soph.* I. xxv πέμπεται γάρ τις μηνὶ Ἀνθεστη-
ριῶνι μεταρσία τριήρης ἐς ἀγοράν, ἣν ὁ Διονύσου ἱερεὺς οἷον κυβερνήτης εὐθύνει
πείσματα ἐκ θαλάττης λύουσαν). The well-known Kylix of Exekias (Gerhard,
Auserl. Vasenb. I, pl. 49; Buschor, *Greek Vase-painting*, Engl. tr., fig. 93)
represents the same idea; but Dionysus has not yet landed, and so his
boat is not on wheels.

[1] *Epp.* II. i. 161–3.

[2] If the Phrynichus of l. 1490 is the tragic poet, this would so far
support the belief that the tragic Thespis is alluded to in l. 1479; but
most editors think it is a different Phrynichus, and the point cannot be
conclusively settled.

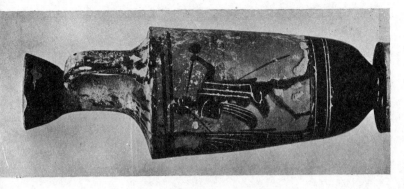

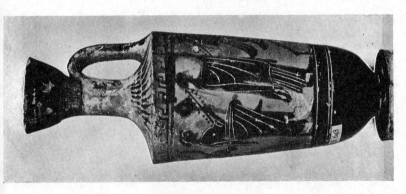

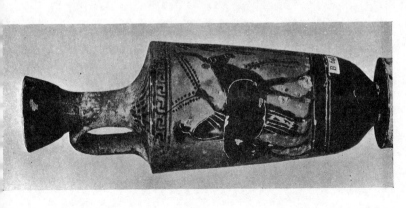

Figs. 8–10. LEKYTHUS IN BRITISH MUSEUM

on the chorus, λόγον καταλογάδην περὶ τοῦ χοροῦ πρὸς Θέσπιν καὶ Χοιρίλον ἀγωνιζόμενος. But Suidas' statements are frequently anachronistic, and this may simply be one of the countless confusions contained in his lexicon. That Sophocles should have competed against Thespis and Choerilus in a regular dramatic contest is impossible. Mr. R. J. Walker[1] makes the ingenious suggestion that ' Sophocles' work was a dialogue in which Thespis, Choerilus, and himself were the disputants '; and if this were the case we should be almost obliged to infer that Sophocles had personal knowledge of the plays of Thespis; but this cannot be regarded as more than a possibility, and not a very probable one, particularly as elaborated in detail by Mr. Walker.

It may be added that the existence of a tradition, alluded to in the Pseudo-Platonic *Minos*[2] (probably written shortly after the time of Aristotle), that Phrynichus was the originator of tragedy, is strong circumstantial evidence that no genuine plays of Thespis were extant late in the fourth century.[3] It is indeed just possible to suppose that works of Thespis were extant, but that they were not counted as true tragedies, owing to their grotesqueness; and Bentley thought that they were merry and satirical, mainly on the strength of Plutarch's state-ment[4] that it was Phrynichus and Aeschylus who made the plot tragic—ὥσπερ οὖν Φρυνίχου καὶ Αἰσχύλου τὴν τραγῳδίαν εἰς μύθους καὶ πάθη προαγόντων ἐλέχθη, Τί ταῦτα πρὸς τὸν Διόνυσον, οὕτως ἔμοιγε κτλ. But it may be doubted whether Plutarch was entirely correct. The language of Thespis may have been in some ways rude and grotesque ; but the story of Pentheus (assuming that Thespis treated it) must always have been tragic. (Probably he did treat it. Even if Heracleides did forge plays in the name of Thespis, he is likely to have followed tradition as regards their titles.)

Four extant fragments are ascribed to Thespis by the writers who quote them, but none of them can be regarded as genuine. Nauck (following Bentley) is certainly right in assigning a late

[1] *Sophocles' Ichneutae*, pp. 305 ff. [2] p. 321 a.
[3] This was pointed out by Bentley (*Phalaris*, p. 215).
[4] *Symp.* I. i. 5.

date (probably the second century A.D.) to the fourth; the third echoes a Platonic belief; the other two are single lines, of which one is probably corrupt. Mr. R. J. Walker's attempt [1] to rewrite the fragments and to defend their genuineness in their new form is not likely to convince many readers. Perhaps Heracleides is responsible for the first three passages; or again, Wilamowitz may be right [2] in his conjecture that revised versions of Thespis' plays may have been in existence, and that Aristoxenus is libelling Heracleides. But there is no positive evidence that there were such versions.

§ 8. Among the passages quoted above are some which seem to take us back beyond Thespis. The speaker in the *Minos*, who is evidently aware that he is uttering a paradox, need not be seriously considered. Athenaeus (perhaps quoting Aristocles, who wrote in the second century B.C.) states that the earliest satyric poetry was choral, as also ($\overset{\text{\"o}}{\omega}\sigma\pi\epsilon\rho$ $\kappa\alpha\iota$) the earliest tragedy—which seems to show that he regarded them as originally distinct.

The most interesting statement is that of Pollux, who speaks of a table called $\epsilon\lambda\epsilon\delta\varsigma$ on which in the days before Thespis $\epsilon\iota\varsigma$ $\tau\iota\varsigma$ used to mount and answer the chorus. A somewhat similar statement, but without the mention of the word $\epsilon\lambda\epsilon\delta\varsigma$, is found in the *Etymologicum Magnum*; the writer of this note is probably using Pollux himself or the same source as Pollux, but by using the word $\hat{\eta}\delta\sigma\nu$ shows either that he thought of the $\tau\rho\alpha\pi\epsilon\zeta\alpha$ as used by the chorus (which is not likely, if he had ordinary common sense), or that he thought that the $\epsilon\iota\varsigma$ $\tau\iota\varsigma$ addressed the chorus in lyrics, as in the later $\kappa\sigma\mu\mu\delta\varsigma$. (The difficulties in regard to the word $\theta\upsilon\mu\epsilon\lambda\eta$ in this connexion will be discussed later.[3]) Isidore probably follows the same tradition.

Now if, as is quite probable, Thespis added a single actor to a pre-existent lyric performance, and so created tragic drama, it is very likely that there was a time $\pi\rho\delta$ $\Theta\epsilon\sigma\pi\iota\delta\sigma\varsigma$ when one of the singers, presumably the leader or $\epsilon\xi\alpha\rho\chi\omega\nu$, separated himself from the rest and engaged in lyric 'question and

---

[1] *Sophocles' Ichneutae*, ch. ix.   [2] *Neue Jahrb.* xxix, p. 468.
[3] See below, pp. 175 ff.

answer' with his companions. Aristotle might well think of
the next step loosely as the transformation of this responding
ἐξάρχων into an actor impersonating a definite character, and
say (assuming as he does that tragedy originated from
dithyramb) that tragedy arose ἀπὸ τῶν ἐξαρχόντων τὸν διθύραμβον; and though the *Etymologicum Magnum* and Isidore
have no independent value, Pollux and Aristotle hang together
fairly well so far.

But the use of the word ἐλεός by Pollux, as the name of the
table referred to, has aroused some suspicion. The word, in
the form ἐλεόν, meant properly, as Pollux says elsewhere,[1] a
cook's chopping-block—ἐπίξηνον, ὃ ἡ νέα κωμῳδία ἐπικόπανον
καλεῖ, τὸ δ' αὐτὸ παρὰ τοῖς παλαιοῖς ἐλεὸν ἐκαλεῖτο. In the
Iliad, ix. 215, it is evidently a carving table: αὐτὰρ ἐπεί ῥ'
ὤπτησε καὶ εἰν ἐλεοῖσιν ἔχευε, as also in *Odyssey* xiv. 432; and
in Aristophanes' *Knights*, 152, ἐλεόν is the chopping-block of
the sausage seller.

On these facts two questions arise : (1) what reason have
we to think that Pollux knew the names of the 'stage-
properties' of the days before Thespis? (2) what evidence is
there to confirm the idea, which seems to be in the minds of
Pollux and of the writer of the note in the *Etymologicum
Magnum* that one of the choreutae jumped on the table upon
which sacrificial victims were cut up, and indulged in lyric
dialogue with the chorus ?

As to the first question we can only agree with Hiller [2] that
it is very unlikely that Pollux had any such knowledge.
Hiller may be right in supposing that Pollux may have got
the word from some comedy in which the early stage was
contemptuously described by the word ἐλεός, in contrast with
the magnificence of later days, and in which the words πρὸ
Θέσπιδος were loosely used for ' early ', and that he took this
as a record of fact. But in default of further evidence, we
can only note this conjecture and pass on.

As to the second question, there is nothing inherently improbable in the idea suggested, and it may well be true.

---

[1] vi. 90. So also, less clearly, in x. 101.
[2] *Rhein. Mus.* xxxix, pp. 321–38.

Nothing is more likely than that Thespis should have taken in hand a pre-existing extempore speaker, talking to the chorus as he chose to do at the moment, and have made him deliver regularly composed speeches in character. But the only attempt to find confirmatory evidence appears to be that of Dr. A. B. Cook,[1] who refers to a number of vase-paintings, of which one series proves the frequent existence of a table standing beside sacrificial altars, the other shows that in certain kinds of musical performance or contest the competitor or performer stood on a somewhat similar low table or platform. (Both series go back into the sixth century B.C.) Unfortunately neither can be shown to have any connexion with such dramatic or semi-dramatic choral performances as those with which we are now concerned, though some of the first, and perhaps of both, series represent the ritual of Dionysus.[2] There is no trace of a chorus. (It is not necessary to follow Dr. Cook's very interesting paper into minor points.) We are left, therefore, only with the general probability and the very uncertain evidence.

§ 9. To what then does the tradition about Thespis amount? We can only say that he was regarded, in the general belief of writers later than Aristotle, as the inventor of tragedy; that this was further explained (possibly in accordance with a statement of Aristotle himself) to mean that he introduced an actor, distinct from the chorus, to deliver a previously composed prologue and set speech; that his first performance may have been at Icaria, and in the autumn; that the date of his first victory at Athens was about 534 B.C. and that it was probably won at the city Dionysia in the spring; that he may have been performing there, before the organization of dramatic competitions, as early as 560 B.C.; that he is credited with certain experiments in facial disguise; that the statements about the form and style of his work are probably based on Aristotle's account of

---

[1] *Class. Rev.* ix (1895), pp. 370 ff.

[2] A red-figured vase in the Naples Museum (*Mon. dell' Ist.* vi. 37), reproduced also by Farnell, *Cults*, v, p. 256, pl. xli, shows a table standing by the altar of Dionysus; but it would hardly serve for the lightest actor, and the scene has no connexion with drama.

the development of tragedy; that, apart from this account, there is no reason for supposing that his plays were of the satyric type; and, finally, that we have no information about the earlier performances on which he may have improved, except what is afforded by late and unverifiable statements, in which, nevertheless, there is nothing improbable. No hint is given to us anywhere as to the date at which the chorus, as well as the actor, came to represent a definite group of persons belonging to some legendary time.

But so much that is reported or conjectured about Thespis and early tragedy is either definitely based on Aristotle, or may be supposed with great probability to be an interpretation of his statements, that our next task must be a careful discussion of these statements.

IV

Aristotle on the Origin of Tragedy.

§ 1. The following are the passages of the *Poetics* which have to be considered:

Ch. iii (p. 1448 a 29 ff.). διὸ καὶ ἀντιποιοῦνται τῆς τε τραγῳδίας καὶ τῆς κωμῳδίας οἱ Δωριεῖς (τῆς μὲν γὰρ κωμῳδίας οἱ Μεγαρεῖς ... καὶ τῆς τραγῳδίας ἔνιοι τῶν ἐν Πελοποννήσῳ) ποιούμενοι τὰ ὀνόματα σημεῖον· αὐτοὶ μὲν γὰρ κώμας τὰς περιοικίδας καλεῖν φασιν, Ἀθηναίους δὲ δήμους ... καὶ τὸ ποιεῖν αὐτοὶ μὲν δρᾶν, Ἀθηναίους δὲ πράττειν προσαγορεύειν.

Ch. iv (p. 1449 a 9 ff.). γενομένης δ' οὖν ἀπ' ἀρχῆς αὐτοσχεδιαστικῆς—καὶ αὐτὴ καὶ ἡ κωμῳδία καὶ ἡ μὲν ἀπὸ τῶν ἐξαρχόντων τὸν διθύραμβον, ἡ δὲ ἀπὸ τῶν τὰ φαλλικὰ ἃ ἔτι καὶ νῦν ἐν πολλαῖς τῶν πόλεων διαμένει νομιζόμενα—κατὰ μικρὸν ηὐξήθη προαγόντων ὅσον ἐγίγνετο φανερὸν αὐτῆς· καὶ πολλὰς μεταβολὰς μεταβαλοῦσα ἡ τραγῳδία ἐπαύσατο, ἐπεὶ ἔσχε τὴν αὐτῆς φύσιν. καὶ τό τε τῶν ὑποκριτῶν πλῆθος ἐξ ἑνὸς εἰς δύο πρῶτος Αἰσχύλος ἤγαγε καὶ τὰ τοῦ χοροῦ ἠλάττωσε καὶ τὸν λόγον πρωταγωνιστὴν παρεσκεύασε· τρεῖς δὲ καὶ σκηνογραφίαν Σοφοκλῆς. ἔτι δὲ τὸ μέγεθος· ἐκ μικρῶν μύθων καὶ λέξεως γελοίας διὰ τὸ ἐκ σατυρικοῦ μεταβαλεῖν ὀψὲ ἀπεσεμνύνθη, τό τε μέτρον ἐκ τετραμέτρου

ἰαμβεῖον ἐγένετο. τὸ μὲν γὰρ πρῶτον τετραμέτρῳ ἐχρῶντο διὰ
τὸ σατυρικὴν καὶ ὀρχηστικωτέραν εἶναι τὴν ποίησιν, λέξεως δὲ
γενομένης αὐτὴ ἡ φύσις τὸ οἰκεῖον μέτρον εὗρε· μάλιστα γὰρ
λεκτικὸν τῶν μέτρων τὸ ἰαμβεῖόν ἐστιν ... ἔτι δὲ ἐπεισοδίων
πλήθη. καὶ τὰ ἄλλα ὡς ἕκαστα κοσμηθῆναι λέγεται, ἔστω
ἡμῖν εἰρημένα· πολὺ γὰρ ἂν ἴσως ἔργον εἴη διεξιέναι καθ'
ἕκαστον.

Ch. v (p. 1449 a 38 ff.). αἱ μὲν οὖν τῆς τραγῳδίας μεταβάσεις
καὶ δι' ὧν ἐγένοντο οὐ λελήθασιν, ἡ δὲ κωμῳδία διὰ τὸ μὴ
σπουδάζεσθαι ἐξ ἀρχῆς ἔλαθεν· καὶ γὰρ χορὸν κωμῳδῶν ὀψέ
ποτε ὁ ἄρχων ἔδωκεν, ἀλλ' ἐθελονταὶ ἦσαν. ἤδη δὲ σχήματά
τινα αὐτῆς ἐχούσης οἱ λεγόμενοι αὐτῆς ποιηταὶ μνημονεύονται.
τίς δὲ πρόσωπα ἀπέδωκεν ἢ προλόγους ἢ πλήθη ὑποκριτῶν καὶ
ὅσα τοιαῦτα, ἠγνόηται.

There is no need to quote here the passage (Ch. iv, p. 1448 b
25 ff.) in which the derivation of the serious subjects of
Tragedy from Homer is described, and the passage quoted
from ch. iii will be considered later. Our present difficulties
are concerned with the other two passages.

§ 2. Aristotle gives no hint of his sources; but we may be
sure that (in compiling his Διδασκαλίαι) he had access to
official records as far back as they went, and we have seen
that they may have begun in the last years of the sixth century.[1]
He knows all about the changes made by Aeschylus and
Sophocles; 'and presumably he believed that he knew, in
regard to tragedy, who it was that introduced πρόσωπα and
προλόγους, as well as πλήθη ὑποκριτῶν, though in ch. iv he
says nothing of πρόσωπα,[2] or of πρόλογοι except in so far as

---

[1] Above, p. 94. Kranz, *Neue Jahrb.* 1919, pp. 148 ff., appears to take
a very exaggerated view of the written sources open to Aristotle for the
history of tragedy; most of the works earlier than Aristotle, the titles
of which he quotes, cannot be shown to have covered this particular
ground; and it is hardly justifiable to treat what were perhaps only
passing allusions (by Eucleides, Ariphrades, &c.) as evidence of the
existence of good sources.

[2] Flickinger (*Greek Theater*, p. 35), following a suggestion of Capps,
renders πρόσωπα 'characters'. Presumably this means impersonations
of definite personages, whereas before the speaker had been merely the
ἐξάρχων of a body of worshippers. If so, πρόσωπα will be contrasted with

they are covered by the phrase λέξεως γενομένης. But we do
not know whence he derived this knowledge, and the last words
of ch. iv seem to show that he was not professing to give a full
or critical account, but only recording ὡς ἕκαστα κοσμηθῆναι
λέγεται, so far as his purpose required.

So much, however, is clear. Before Aeschylus instituted a
second actor, there must have been a first; and it cannot be
doubted that Aristotle thought of this actor as the ἐξάρχων of
the dithyramb, now made independent of the chorus. Now
what does the word ἐξάρχων mean? It does not mean
necessarily quite the same thing as κορυφαῖος or *chorus*-leader.
It does mean the leader of the whole performance.[1] But this
leader, though closely connected with his chorus and joining
in one song with them, was not necessarily of the same nature
or even of the same sex. The passages which best illustrate
the meaning of the word are the following:

Il. xxiv. 720 :

> παρὰ δ' εἷσαν ἀοιδοὺς
> θρήνων ἐξάρχους, οἵ τε στονόεσσαν ἀοιδὴν
> οἱ μὲν ἄρ' ἐθρήνεον, ἐπὶ δὲ στενάχοντο γυναῖκες.

Il. xviii. 49 :

> ἄλλαι δ' αἱ κατὰ βένθος ἁλὸς Νηρηΐδες ἦσαν·
> τῶν δὲ καὶ ἀργύφεον πέλετο σπέος· αἱ δ' ἅμα πᾶσαι
> στήθεα πεπλήγοντο. Θέτις δ' ἐξῆρχε γόοιο.

Ibid. 316 :

> τοῖσι δὲ Πηλεΐδης ἀδινοῦ ἐξῆρχε γόοιο.

the ἐξάρχοντες τὸν διθύραμβον of the previous chapter. But the usual
translation, 'masks', is probably right; cf. τὸ γελοῖον πρόσωπον, 'the comic
mask', at the beginning of ch. v. The use of πρόσωπα for 'persons',
'characters' seems to be considerably later than Aristotle, and such
evidence as there is suggests that masks were not essential to either
tragedy or comedy in their earliest stages. See pp. 111, 112.

[1] I cannot agree with Bywater's identification of the ἐξάρχων with the
poet or διδάσκαλος. The poet may often have been his own ἐξάρχων, but
not *qua* poet or composer. When Bywater quotes (p. 134) the saying of
Archilochus (see above, p. 5), he omits the last words, οἴνῳ συγκεραυνωθεὶς
φρένας. Archilochus may have led off the revel-song in that state; it may
be doubted if he composed it so, or indeed if it was 'composed' at all.

(In these three passages we have evidently a θρῆνος of a conventional form, in which the chorus join in a refrain of lamentation. But how easily the part of the ἐξάρχων might lead to speech-making is shown by the speeches of Thetis and Achilles in the last two passages.)

Il. xviii. 603 :

πολλὸς δ' ἱμερόεντα χορὸν περιίσταθ' ὅμιλος
τερπόμενοι, μετὰ δέ σφιν ἐμέλπετο θεῖος ἀοιδὸς
φορμίζων· δοιὼ δὲ κυβιστητῆρε κατ' αὐτοὺς
μολπῆς ἐξάρχοντες ἐδίνευον κατὰ μέσσους.

Pausan. v. xviii, § 14 πεποίηνται δὲ καὶ ᾄδουσαι Μοῦσαι καὶ Ἀπόλλων ἐξάρχων τῆς ᾠδῆς, καί σφισιν ἐπίγραμμα γέγραπται,
Λατοΐδας οὗτος τάχ' ἄναξ ἑκάεργος Ἀπόλλων,
Μοῦσαι δ' ἀμφ' αὐτόν, χαρίεις χορός, αἷσι κατάρχει.[1]

Now the ἐξάρχων must have been transformed into an actor, when he delivered a speech (not a song), in which the chorus did not join in—the change attributed to Thespis—and when he became, not merely the leading one of a non-dramatic body of worshippers, such as were the performers of dithyramb, but the impersonation of some divine or heroic character. (Aristotle does not mention Thespis here, though Themistius quotes him as doing so elsewhere; the omission is certainly strange, if Thespis was the first to start the series of improvements carried further by Aeschylus and Sophocles.)

But the ἐξάρχων who thus became an actor was, according to Aristotle, the ἐξάρχων of the dithyramb; and though the cyclic dithyramb, as we know it in the fifth century, had a coryphaeus but no ἐξάρχων, the dithyramb in its earlier form of revel-song certainly had an ἐξάρχων, such as was Archilochus. From what kind or stage of dithyramb did Aristotle think that tragedy was derived? And with this is bound up the further question, what did he think of the relation of dithyramb and tragedy to satyric drama? It is at this point that the task of discovering his meaning becomes almost hopeless. For διὰ τοῦ ἐκ σατυρικοῦ μεταβαλεῖν may mean either ' through its ceasing to be satyric drama,' or ' through

---

[1] See also Addenda, p. 417 below.

its passing out of a shape in which it was grotesque'; and
σατυρικήν in the next sentence can similarly be taken either
literally or metaphorically.[1] Accordingly we cannot tell
whether Aristotle means that tragedy developed out of a
dithyramb danced by persons made up as satyrs, or only that
it developed out of a dithyramb which had an ἐξάρχων, and
that in its early stages its language was grotesque. Most
scholars have no doubt that the former was his meaning, and
Bywater,[2] though cautious, evidently inclines to that opinion;
and since the metaphorical use of σατυρικός cannot be shown
to be as early as the fourth century B.C., the balance of
probability is in favour of the literal interpretation, though it
cannot be held to be beyond dispute.

But this being granted, what is the historical value of
Aristotle's statement? His words may be treated in various
ways.

(1) They may be accepted without question as historically
true. This is, on the whole, the inclination of Bywater, who
is convinced that Aristotle knew more about the early history
of tragedy than he chose, for his special purpose, to tell his
readers. 'It is clear from Aristotle's confession of ignorance
as to comedy in 1449 a 37 that he knows more of the history of
tragedy than he actually tells us, and that he is not aware of
there being any serious lacuna in it.' Is this really so certain?
In the passage referred to he is not speaking of the earliest
development or the origin of the two forms of art, but of
certain definite points—regarding masks, prologues, increased
number of actors, &c. These points, he says, he knows in the
case of tragedy; but he does not indicate that he knows more
about even these than he tells us in ch. iv (except as regards
πρόσωπα, which he does not mention in that chapter); and we
do not know what evidence can have been available as to the
transition stages between the purely lyric performance and

---

[1] The metaphorical use of the word (of which Gomperz, Reisch, and
others believe Aristotle's phrases to be examples) is illustrated by
Lucian, Προλαλιά ὁ Διόνυσος, § 5 οἰόμενοι γὰρ σατυρικὰ καὶ γελοῖα καὶ
κομιδῇ κωμικὰ παρ' ἡμῶν ἀκούσεσθαι τοιαῦτα πεπιστεύκασιν.

[2] *Poetics*, p. 38.

tragedy proper; he may well have been theorizing about this. Wilamowitz,[1] however, goes further than Bywater, and regards it as unjustifiable even to attempt to go behind Aristotle. Tragedy developed out of a dithyramb danced by satyrs: Aristotle says so, and that is enough. (This satyr-dithyramb, he thinks, was the creation of Arion, and was introduced into Athens under Peisistratus.) The μικροὶ μῦθοι are supposed to be illustrated by the *Supplices*, *Persae*, and *Prometheus* of Aeschylus, and traces of the λέξις γελοία are found in the last scene of the *Supplices*. (The last point it is quite impossible to concede; the scene cannot be called comic or ' satyric ' in any sense; and further, the *Supplices* and *Prometheus* at least are parts of trilogies, and their plots cannot be treated in isolation.)

But in fact the difficulties in the way of the literal acceptance of Aristotle are serious. There is absolutely no support for it in any early evidence (the statements in regard to Arion which bear on this point are late and will be considered below); the character of the earliest extant remains of tragedy is against it; it involves the rejection of the statement that it was Pratinas who πρῶτος ἔγραψε σατύρους, with the evidence confirmatory of it; and, above all, it is extraordinarily difficult to suppose that the noble seriousness of tragedy can have grown so rapidly, or even at all, out of the ribald satyric drama; nor is there any parallel to such a development.

(2) It has been suggested that when Aristotle speaks of dithyramb, he does not refer to the cyclic dithyramb in the strict sense.

(*a*) He may be using the word, it is said, in the sense in which it was loosely used later, covering any lyric poems dealing with ὑποθέσεις ἡρωικαί,[2] and may have in mind the development of tragedy out of such performances as were current at Sicyon in the sixth century B.C. in honour of Adrastus and of Dionysus.[3]

Now it is quite probable, as we shall see, that the lyric portions of tragedy were greatly influenced by Peloponnesian

---

[1] *Einl. in die gr. Trag.*, pp. 49 ff.; *Neue Jahrb.* xxix (1912), pp. 467 ff.

[2] Pseudo-Plut. *de Mus.*, ch. x. See above, p. 20, n. 1.

[3] See below, pp. 135 ff.

choral lyric of a type which died out after the development of
tragedy itself, and it is just possible that Aristotle may have
thought of this as a kind of dithyramb; but it is not very
likely. For it is improbable that the εἴδη of poetry were less
distinct in Aristotle's mind than they were in those of (e.g.)
the Alexandrian scholars; dithyramb was still a living thing
in his own day and long afterwards; and there is no ground
for dating back to his time the inaccurate use of the word
mentioned in the Pseudo-Plutarchean *de Musica*.[1] The only
account of the performances at Sicyon calls them τραγικοὶ
χοροί, not dithyrambs. As regards Arion's lyric compositions
more will be said later.

(*b*) Some scholars are inclined to attribute to him, and to
regard as likely in itself, a belief in a primitive kind of
dithyramb from which both tragedy and the dithyramb
of Pindar and Simonides originated. To satisfy the text of
Aristotle such a dithyramb must have been satyric, or, at least,
grotesque—which is discordant with the character both of
tragedy and of the Pindaric dithyramb; we have certainly no
reason to think that Archilochus (whose works must have
been known to Aristotle) and his companions masqueraded in
satyr-dress; and as for the intrinsic probability of this theory,
the facts that the cyclic dithyramb was, until a comparatively
late period, an entirely undramatic song, delivered by performers who retained their own personality, and that the
organization of the chorus was different from that of tragedy,
make a common origin very unlikely.[2]

In any case, therefore, it seems certain that by dithyramb
Aristotle means the cyclic dithyramb. How it became possible
for him to connect this with tragedy we shall see immediately.

---

[1] Wilamowitz, ap. Tycho von Wilamowitz-Möllendorf, *Dramatische
Technik von Sophocles*, p. 314, affirms that dithyramb meant for Ar., as for
the dithyrambic poets and the 'eidographoi', simply choral poems with
narrative contexts, and quotes Plato, *Rep.* iii. 394 c. But what Plato
says is that narrative is specially found in dithyrambs, not that any
narrative lyric is a dithyramb. Dieterich (*Arch. f. Rel.* xi, p. 164) states
dogmatically that in Aristotle's time διθύραμβος included all choral lyric.
It certainly did not include the νόμος (when this was choral) or the
paean.   [2] See above, p 48.

(3) We may suppose that Aristotle is theorizing. He found existing in his own day, side by side with tragedy, the satyric drama, in many ways like the tragic in form, but more primitive and uncivilized in tone; and also a dithyramb which by his own day had become semi-dramatic or mimetic, and included solos as well as choral song; and he must have heard of the primitive revel-song, the dithyramb of Archilochus, with its ἐξάρχων. What could be more natural than to suppose that tragedy developed out of dithyramb by the transformation of an ἐξάρχων or soloist into a full-fledged actor? And since the more crude and primitive may naturally be supposed to precede the more artistic, satyric drama might be regarded as an early stage of tragedy which succeeded in surviving even after tragedy had developed. If so, the plots of early tragedy must have been short, like those of the satyric drama, and the language grotesque.[1] In the same way he may have conjectured, from the existence of phallic elements in the Old Comedy, and the survival of phallic dances at processions in his own day, that comedy must have originated from primitive phallic performances.

Now this is a perfectly possible interpretation of Aristotle, and it accounts for all that he says.[2] But unhappily it robs his statements of all historical value. We shall see later that, even as regards Comedy, it is very doubtful whether he is strictly correct; as regards Tragedy the difficulties of his view will shortly become plain. We have, in short, to admit with regret that it is impossible to accept his authority without question, and that he was probably using that liberty of theorizing which those modern scholars who ask us to accept

[1] There can of course be no doubt that Aristotle did think that the language was originally grotesque. Sir William Ridgeway's argument to the contrary (*Origin of Gk. Drama*, pp. 5 and 57), on the ground that Aristotle speaks of tragedy as the successor of epic, will not bear examination. It is quite plain from Aristotle's language that it is in respect of its themes that he regards tragedy as the successor of epic; he says nothing, in the passage in question, about epic diction. (On the grotesqueness, see above, p. 117.)

[2] This is also in substance the view of Nilsson, *Neue Jahrb.* xxvii, pp. 609 ff.

him as infallible have certainly not abandoned. It follows that we are no longer obliged to derive tragedy from satyric drama, but can at least hold it to be probable that, twenty or thirty years after Thespis had won his notable victory with a tragedy at Athens, Pratinas brought into Athens a more primitive kind of play, with a satyr-chorus, from Phlius, and assimilated it to tragedy in certain respects; and that about the end of the sixth century the two kinds of performances were given their place, along with dithyramb, in a reorganized festival.

§ 3. With regard to other points in Aristotle's account, little need be said. The large use made of the trochaic tetrameter in early tragedy is illustrated by the *Persae* of Aeschylus, in which it is the principal metre of the dialogue, as distinct from the long set speeches. It is not clear at what point Aristotle thought the language of tragedy ceased to be grotesque. He cannot have thought of the language of Aeschylus as grotesque, nor, probably, of that of Phrynichus; and we do not know what he may have thought about Thespis. If, as is likely, he regarded the change of style as connected with the introduction of the iambic metre, he must have thought of these changes as taking place before the fifth century; for it seems impossible to accept the view put forward by Sir William Ridgeway [1] that he must have been thinking of the first half of that century itself. Sir William Ridgeway's statement that 'the change from the short to the long plot was posterior to the first appearance of Aeschylus in 499 B.C.' cannot be tested; for 'short' and 'long' are relative terms, and we know nothing of the length of plots before Aeschylus. But he adds that the change of metre to iambic was also the work of Aeschylus, since 'Phrynichus used the tetrameter almost solely'. There is no evidence of this except the plainly false statement in Suidas that Phrynichus *invented* the tetrameter; and in fact a number of iambic lines (and, as it happens, no tetrameters) are quoted from Phrynichus.

Sir William Ridgeway appears, further, to connect the change in diction to which Aristotle refers with a supposed

---

[1] *Dramas and Dramatic Dances*, pp. 3-4.

substitution of non-satyric plays for satyric. ' Whatever was
the modification referred to by Aristotle's words respecting the
satyric drama, this could not have taken place before the first
half of the fifth century before Christ,[1] the very period
when tragedy was shaking itself free from the satyric drama,[2]
which was finally supplanted by the melodramas, such as the
Alcestis, which in 438 B.C. took the place of a satyric drama
in a tetralogy of Euripides. For as the Greek term *tragoedia*
included both serious and "sportive tragedy" (the satyric
drama), so long as the truly tragic trilogy was followed by
a coarse satyric drama tragedy had not freed itself from
"ludicrous diction" and attained to her full dignity. Aristotle,
therefore, is not referring to the first beginnings of tragedy in
the sixth century, but to the state in which Aeschylus found
it and from which he lifted it.' It would be hard to find a
more confused and inaccurate series of observations than this.
What 'melodramas' besides the *Alcestis* were substituted for
satyric plays? Wilamowitz mentions the *Inachus* of Sophocles
as a possible example; there is no evidence of others. Aristotle
cannot be referring to this substitution, and in any case
Aeschylus had nothing to do with any such change. Nor can
we suppose that Aristotle regarded tragedy as not having
' attained her full dignity ' until the satyric play was discarded;
such a supposition would rule out (e. g.) the *Oresteia*.

Again, did the term *tragoedia* include satyric drama? when
is the latter ever called by the name? Sir William Ridgeway
quotes a passage of Demetrius,[3] but this certainly does not prove
it. The passage runs: τραγῳδία δὲ χάριτας μὲν παραλαμβάνει
ἐν πολλοῖς, ὁ δὲ γέλως ἐχθρὸς τραγῳδίας. οὐδὲ γὰρ ἐπενόησεν ἄν

---

[1] In *Class. Quart.* vi (1912), p. 244, Sir William Ridgeway argues that
ὀψέ in 1449 a 20 must mean what it does in 1449 b 1, χορὸν κωμῳδῶν
ὀψέ ποτε ὁ ἄρχων ἔδωκεν, viz. a date between 500 and 450 B.C. But ὀψέ
is a relative term: it must mean ' late in the process of development ' in
both cases; but the actual date may well have been (and doubtless was)
different in the case of the two arts.

[2] Sir William Ridgeway appears to think (*Class. Quart.*, l. c.) that ἐκ
σατυρικοῦ μεταβαλεῖν can be translated ' to discard the satyric play '. This
is surely impossible.

[3] Περὶ ἑρμηνείας, § 169.

τις τραγῳδίαν παίζουσαν, ἐπεὶ σάτυρον γράψει ἀντὶ τραγῳδίας. This only says that if a man tried to write a ‘sportive’ tragedy, the result would be a satyric play, not a tragedy; implying that a satyric play could *not* be called τραγῳδία ; and in any case Demetrius, whoever he was, is too late to be of any value as evidence that the name τραγῳδία could cover satyric drama in the time either of Aeschylus or of Aristotle. The argument that because the changes mentioned in Aristotle's sentence about the numbers of ὑποκριταί follow the chronological order, the next sentence must do the same, needs no refutation.[1] But fortunately we may agree with Sir William Ridgeway's view that tragedy was not derived from satyric drama, without adopting his exegesis of Aristotle.

V

Arion.

In the preceding section it has been argued that it is not possible to rely upon Aristotle's account of the early development of tragedy, according to which it grew out of a dithyramb danced by satyrs. But that account is commonly supposed to be confirmed, first, by the tradition in regard to Arion, who is regarded as the creator of just that kind of satyric dithyramb which is required; secondly, by the name τραγῳδία itself, which is supposed to indicate a song of goat-like satyrs ; and thirdly, by some of the interpretations offered of the proverb, Οὐδὲν πρὸς τὸν Διόνυσον. Accordingly it is necessary first to examine carefully the traditions with regard to Arion and that Peloponnesian ‘tragedy’ which is supposed to bridge the gulf between Arion and Thespis or Phrynichus.

It will be useful in the first place to collect the more important passages which deal with Arion.[2]

HERODOTUS i. 23. ἐτυράννευε δὲ ὁ Περίανδρος Κορίνθου· τῷ δὴ λέγουσι Κορίνθιοι (ὁμολογέουσι δέ σφι Λέσβιοι) ἐν τῷ

---

[1] Flickinger (*Class. Phil.* viii, p. 264) points out other defects in Sir William Ridgeway's theory—particularly the inaccuracy of his chronological procedure.　　　[2] See also above, pp. 20–22.

βίῳ θῶμα μέγιστον παραστῆναι, Ἀρίονα τὸν Μηθυμναῖον ἐπὶ δελφῖνος ἐξενειχθέντα ἐπὶ Ταίναρον, ἐόντα κιθαρῳδὸν τῶν τότε ἐόντων οὐδενὸς δεύτερον, καὶ διθύραμβον πρῶτον ἀνθρώπων τῶν ἡμεῖς ἴδμεν ποιήσαντά τε καὶ ὀνομάσαντα καὶ διδάξαντα ἐν Κορίνθῳ. (The story of the circumstances of his voyage on the dolphin's back follows.)

SUIDAS. Ἀρίων· Μηθυμναῖος, λυρικός, Κυκλέως υἱός, γέγονε κατὰ τὴν κή Ὀλυμπιάδα· τίνες δὲ μαθητὴν Ἀλκμᾶνος ἱστόρησαν αὐτόν. ἔγραψε δὲ ᾄσματα· προοίμια εἰς ἔπη β'. λέγεται καὶ τραγικοῦ τρόπου εὑρετὴς γενέσθαι, καὶ πρῶτος χορὸν στῆσαι καὶ διθύραμβον ᾆσαι καὶ ὀνομάσαι τὸ ᾀδόμενον ὑπὸ τοῦ χοροῦ, καὶ Σατύρους εἰσενεγκεῖν ἔμμετρα λέγοντας. φυλάττει δὲ τὸ ὦ καὶ ἐπὶ γενικῆς.

PROCLUS, Chrest. xii. εὑρεθῆναι δὲ τὸν διθύραμβον Πίνδαρος ἐν Κορίνθῳ λέγει· τὸν δὲ ἀρξάμενον τῆς ᾠδῆς Ἀριστοτέλης Ἀρίονα λέγει· ὃς πρῶτος τὸν κύκλιον ἤγαγε χορόν.

(On the proposal to read Ἀριστοκλῆς here, vid. supra p. 22.)

IOANNES DIACONUS, Comm. in Hermogenem (Rabe, Rhein. Mus. lxiii (1908), p. 150). τῆς δὲ τραγῳδίας πρῶτον δρᾶμα Ἀρίων ὁ Μηθυμναῖος εἰσήγαγεν, ὥσπερ Σόλων ἐν ταῖς ἐπιγραφομέναις Ἐλεγείαις ἐδίδαξε. Δράκων δὲ ὁ Λαμψακηνὸς δρᾶμά φησι πρῶτον Ἀθήνησι διδαχθῆναι ποιήσαντος Θέσπιδος.

The place of Arion in the history of the dithyramb has been discussed in the preceding chapter.[1] Despite the story of the dolphin, and the probably fictitious name which is ascribed to his father, there is no sufficient reason for doubting the poet's existence.[2] The really difficult problem raised by the notices is whether the words of Suidas, λέγεται—λέγοντας, all refer to one type of performance, as is

[1] pp. 19 ff.

[2] The name Κυκλεύς seems to be invented with reference to the κύκλιος χορός. Suidas mentions similar fictitious parents of Phrynichus, who was certainly real. A brief statement of the case against the real existence of Arion will be found in Smyth's Greek Melic Poets, pp. 205 ff., and adequate references are there given. I do not pursue the subject here, because whether an individual named Arion existed or not, there is no ground for doubting that the developments of the poetic art ascribed to him took place in Corinth about the time mentioned.

generally assumed, or to three. The words which definitely
refer to the dithyramb are plainly a paraphrase of Herodotus;
the statements with regard to the τραγικὸς τρόπος and the
satyrs must come from some other source. If the whole
sentence refers to one type of performance, these statements
may be a badly expressed inference by Suidas (or the authority
on whom he drew) from Aristotle's *Poetics*, ch. iv : [1] tragedy,
according to Aristotle, arose from the dithyramb and was
satyric; if, therefore, Arion invented the dithyramb, he must
have invented tragedy and introduced satyrs.

But it does not seem natural to interpret the three statements as referring to the same performance. The sentence
quoted from Proclus shows that what was traditionally
ascribed to Arion was the invention of the κύκλιος χορός, which
is nowhere associated with a satyr chorus in any record about
it; and if the τραγικὸς τρόπος [2] and the employment of satyrs
are one and the same thing, why are they separated by remarks
about the dithyramb ? Besides this, the words τραγικὸς τρόπος
have a quite definite technical meaning in Greek writers about
literature and music, viz. the tragic style or mode in music
(e. g. Aristid. Quintil., p. 29 ὁ μὲν οὖν νομικὸς τρόπος ἐστὶ
νητοειδής, ὁ δὲ διθυραμβικὸς μεσοειδής, ὁ δὲ τραγικὸς ὑπατοειδής).
There is no warrant for interpreting the words as referring to
the supposed tragic dress, the goat- or satyr-costume. It
seems much more likely that Suidas found traditions ascribing
three different things to Arion. He invented the musical
mode which was afterwards adopted by tragedy—possibly in
connexion with some such kind of ‘tragic choruses’ as we shall
presently find at Sicyon; he reduced the dithyramb to order,
and made his dithyrambs poems with definite subjects and
names; and he modified the satyr-dances, which he probably
found already in existence, by making the satyrs speak verses.[3]

---

[1] This has also been suggested by Nilsson, *Neue Jahrb.* xxvii (1911),
p. 610.

[2] For reasons against taking τραγικός as ‘goat-like’, i. e. satyric, as has
sometimes been suggested, see below, p. 137.

[3] This interpretation of the passage was suggested by Reisch, *Festschr.
für Gomperz*, p. 471, in 1902, and he has of course the first claim to be

(εἰσενεγκεῖν is a word commonly used of 'bringing on the scene', 'bringing before the public', &c., and should not be treated as if it meant 'introduced into tragedy or dithyramb'.)

The passage in the commentary of John the Deacon (a writer of unknown date) on Hermogenes' Περὶ μεθόδου δεινότητος to some small extent confirms the belief that some step towards tragedy (as distinct from dithyramb) was taken by Arion. He says that Solon had stated in his elegies that the first δρᾶμα τῆς τραγῳδίας was produced by Arion, though Dracon of Lampsacus[1] had said that the first tragic drama was produced at Athens by Thespis. The authority of John the Deacon of course carries no weight in itself; and he retails some of the foolish theories about the origin of comedy which are found in several other writers, as well as the tradition that comedy and tragedy arose out of a common ancestor called τρυγῳδία.[2] But he shows a considerable acquaintance with classical poetry (some of it now lost), and there is no reason to doubt that he is quoting an actual poem of Solon, known to him (or to his source).

The words τῆς τραγῳδίας δρᾶμα are of course his own, and the word τραγῳδία will not go into elegiacs. But τραγῳδοί and its parts will; or again, Flickinger[3] may possibly be right in his conjecture that the word which Solon used was δρᾶμα— originally a non-Attic word, probably derived from Peloponnesian sources—and that the words τῆς τραγῳδίας are an explanation by John or his source.[4] But if John is right, we have

considered the author of it; but I find that I proposed it myself in my lectures a year or two before that.

[1] For Dracon of Lampsacus, who is unknown, Wilamowitz (*Neue Jahrb.* xxix, p. 470) would substitute the name of Charon of Lampsacus, one of the historians earlier than Herodotus.

[2] See above, p. 105-107.

[3] *Greek Theater*, p. 8; cf. also his paper in *Classical Philology*, viii, p. 266. I cannot, however, think that (as he suggests) Solon being incensed with Thespis was glad to ascribe the origination of tragedy (if this is what he means 'by the place of honour') to another. The idea of asking which of several claimants originated tragedy is surely post-Solonian.

[4] Dr. Farnell is of course right in saying (*Hermath.* xvii. 20) that the

a tradition dating back almost, if not quite, to Arion's own lifetime, that he produced something which was sufficiently on
the lines of the tragic choruses of later days to be called by the
same name by later writers; and it may be that this use of
the name δρᾶμα, which is never applied to dithyramb, dates
from Arion or from his time. At least we can infer that
tradition knew of two experiments, an earlier by Arion at
Corinth, a later by Thespis in Attica, both of which were
regarded by different persons as steps, not, so far as we can
judge, towards the cyclic dithyramb or the satyric drama, but
towards tragedy. There is no reason to suppose that Arion's
work was dramatic in the sense that it included actors impersonating gods or heroes; it was probably purely lyric;
the chorus *may* have impersonated some group of characters
and been so far dramatic, but there is no proof that they
did so.

VI

Sicyon and Hero-Drama.

§ 1. If it is conceded that (as has been urged in the preceding
sections) the σάτυροι ἔμμετρα λέγοντες are not to be regarded
as the forerunners of tragic ὑποκριταί, it will also be generally
granted that any τραγῳδία composed by Arion is likely to
have been purely lyric; and this is confirmed by the fact that
Herodotus,[1] when he speaks of τραγικοὶ χοροί performed at
Sicyon, not very long after the time of Arion, gives no hint of
their having been anything but χοροί: for it is surely natural
to connect Arion's τραγικὸς τρόπος and δρᾶμα τῆς τραγῳδίας
with these τραγικοὶ χοροί of a neighbouring town. But the
passage of Herodotus has been the centre of so much controversy that it must be discussed at length. It occurs in a
narrative about Cleisthenes, who was tyrant of Sicyon during

question can only be solved by the recovery of Solon's *ipsissima verba*.
But his suggestion that John may be quoting something that Hermogenes
said is disproved by reference to the passage of Hermogenes upon which
he is commenting.

[1] v. 67.

most of the first third of the sixth century. Being at war
with Argos (which claimed supremacy over Sicyon), Cleisthenes
resolved to expel the worship of the Argive hero Adrastus,[1]
who had a ἡρῷον in the market-place at Sicyon. As the oracle
refused to sanction this, he contrived a device (as Herodotus
quaintly says) to make Adrastus withdraw of his own accord.
He sent to Thebes, and brought in thence the hero Melanippus,
who had been in life Adrastus' greatest enemy. ἐπείτε δέ οἱ τὸ
τέμενος ἀπέδεξε, θυσίας τε καὶ ὁρτὰς Ἀδρήστου ἀπελόμενος
ἔδωκε τῷ Μελανίππῳ. οἱ δὲ Σικυώνιοι ἐώθεσαν μεγαλωστὶ
κάρτα τιμᾶν τὸν Ἄδρηστον . . . τά τε δὴ ἄλλα οἱ Σικυώνιοι
ἐτίμων τὸν Ἄδρηστον καὶ δὴ πρὸς τὰ πάθεα αὐτοῦ τραγικοῖσι
χοροῖσι ἐγέραιρον, τὸν μὲν Διόνυσον οὐ τιμῶντες, τὸν δὲ
Ἄδρηστον. Κλεισθένης δὲ χοροὺς μὲν τῷ Διονύσῳ ἀπέδωκε,
τὴν δὲ ἄλλην θυσίην Μελανίππῳ.[2]

We shall probably be right in thinking that in introducing
the worship of Dionysus into popular festivals, Cleisthenes
was pursuing a policy like that of Peisistratus,[3] who afterwards did this in Athens, and of Periander, who had doubtless
encouraged Arion at Corinth: and if it is true that Arion
introduced 'tragic' choruses in Corinth, it is probable, as has
already been suggested, that those of Sicyon would be more or
less similar.

But there is no agreement among scholars as to the meaning

---

[1] It is unnecessary to discuss the suggestion of Eisler (*Orphisch-
Dionys. Myst.-Gedanken*, p. 243) that Ἀδρηστός means 'ripe' (cf. ἀδρέω,
ἀδρός, &c.), and that as Σικυών = garden of gourds or melons, the
lamentations for Adrastus were for the death of the ripe gourd or
melon. (Formerly Sicyon had been called Μηκώνη, and Adrastus must
have been the ripe poppy.) Eisler thinks that Cleisthenes' innovation
was connected with a transition from market-gardening to vine-growing.
I am not convinced by the etymology or the inferences.

[2] Cf. Themistius, *Or*. 27, p. 406 καὶ τραγῳδίας εὑρεταὶ μὲν Σικυώνιοι,
τελεσιουργοὶ δὲ Ἀττικοὶ ποιηταί. We do not know whether Themistius had
any other authority besides that of Herodotus.

[3] The theory of W. Schmid (*Zur Gesch. des gr. Dithyrambos*, 1900) that
Cleisthenes was trying to reconcile the aristocratic families (who worshipped their heroic ancestors by means of τραγικοὶ χοροί at their tombs)
with the people, whom he supposes to have been worshippers of Dionysus
in the country districts, appears to rest on no evidence.

of τραγικοῖσι here. Those who think that Arion instituted
a dithyramb danced by satyrs in goat-dress—the τραγικὸς
τρόπος, according to this interpretation—and that tragedy is
the performance of the 'goat-men' or satyrs, take τραγικοῖσι
here also to mean 'satyric', 'in goat-dress'. Now not only is
it almost inconceivable that these tragic choruses, having
reference to the sufferings of the hero, should have been
performed by ithyphallic demons with the limbs of goats, but
it seems also very improbable that Herodotus, the friend of
Sophocles, living in the great period of Greek tragedy, should
have used the word in any sense but 'tragic', or should have
meant by τραγικοῖσι χοροῖσι anything but 'choruses like those
of tragedy'; he is not likely to have reverted to the etymological sense 'goat-like' or 'relating to the goat'. Τραγικός
means 'tragic' in Aristophanes, e. g. in the *Peace*, 136–7 :

οὐκοῦν ἐχρῆν σε Πηγάσου ζεῦξαι πτερόν,
ὅπως ἐφαίνου τοῖς θεοῖς τραγικώτερος,

and in fr. 149 (from the *Gerytades*), where Meletus is described
as an ambassador ἀπὸ τῶν τραγικῶν χορῶν. (The use is
parallel to that of κωμικός, which almost invariably means
'connected with comedy', not 'connected with the κῶμος'.) In
fact it is not until very late that we find the word used with
reference to the goat; e. g. Plutarch, *Pyrrhus*, ch. xi ἐγνώσθη
δὲ τῷ τε λόφῳ διαπρέποντι καὶ τοῖς τραγικοῖς κέρασιν : Lucian,
Ἀλεκτρυών, § 10 ὁ γοῦν πώγων μάλα τραγικὸς ἦν εἰς ὑπερβολὴν
κουριῶν (not an absolutely certain instance): Longus, *Soph.*
iv. 17 καὶ ἅμα ὑπεκρίνετο τὴν τραγικὴν δυσωδίαν μυσάττεσθαι.
(In Plato's *Cratylus*, 408 c, where Plato is speaking of Pan, the
use of the word is a deliberate pun : οὐκοῦν τὸ μὲν ἀληθὲς αὐτοῦ
λεῖον καὶ θεῖον καὶ ἄνω οἰκοῦν ἐν τοῖς θεοῖς· τὸ δὲ ψεῦδος κάτω
ἐν τοῖς πολλοῖς τῶν ἀνθρώπων καὶ τραχὺ καὶ τραγικόν· ἐνταῦθα
γὰρ πλεῖστοι οἱ μῦθοί τε καὶ τὰ ψεύδη ἐστί, περὶ τὸν τραγικὸν
βίον.)

There is, indeed, no ground for supposing that these choruses
were called τραγικοί early in the sixth century at Sicyon itself,
or that Herodotus knew this to be the case.[1] What Herodotus'

---

[1] Flickinger (*Class. Phil.* viii, p. 274; *Gk. Theater*, p. 15) suggests that
the name originated at Sicyon, when the newly introduced worship of

expression probably means is that he found evidence of
choruses at Sicyon, relating to the sufferings of Adrastus, 150
years or so before his own time, and observing that they were
more or less like the choral odes of tragedy in his own day,
naturally called them τραγικοὶ χοροί. Unfortunately Herodotus tells us nothing of the subject of these choruses after
their transference to Dionysus; but they quite probably
continued to be οὐδὲν πρὸς τὸν Διόνυσον.[1]

Epigenes of Sicyon, who is mentioned in one or two very
late notices[2] as the first tragic poet (Thespis being only the
sixteenth) may have been a composer of such tragic choruses
under the régime of Cleisthenes. The evidence, for what it is
worth, suggests that the festival for which he composed was a
festival of Dionysus, but that he treated non-Dionysiac subjects.
I can see no sufficient evidence for the suggestion advanced by
Professor Flickinger[3] that the people of Sicyon, when the
worship of Dionysus was introduced, expected a satyr-chorus
(such as Arion had instituted at Corinth) as an essential part
of that worship, and that it was because Epigenes gave them
a human chorus that they exclaimed "οὐδὲν πρὸς τὸν Διόνυσον",
though it does seem to be true that there is no reason for
thinking that the choruses at Sicyon were satyric. The truth
is that (as we shall see later) nothing worth calling evidence
can be extracted from the various explanations offered of this
proverb.

§ 2. The words of Herodotus afford, at first sight, a strong
argument in favour of the theory of Sir William Ridgeway[4]
that tragedy originated in performances at the tombs of
deceased heroes, and was afterwards transferred to Dionysus;
for here we have a definite transference of τραγικοὶ χοροί from
a hero to Dionysus. But we have no other; and it is going
far beyond the evidence to infer from this that the villages of

Dionysus brought the goat-prize with it. This is ingenious, but we
know nothing of such a prize at Sicyon.

[1] See below, pp. 167–8.

[2] Suidas, s. v. Θεσπίς (see above, p. 100), and s. v. Οὐδὲν πρὸς τὸν Διόνυσον
(see below, p. 168).

[3] *Class. Phil.* viii, p. 274.   [4] *Orig. of Gk. Dr.*, pp. 26, &c.

Attica had each its own local hero, and that upon these local festivals the worship of Dionysus was superimposed, and absorbed their tragic performances. Moreover, the transference at Sicyon was the arbitrary act of a tyrant, done with a special political motive, not a natural religious development, such as the supposed gradual absorption of hero-cults by Dionysiac would imply; and to infer from this single arbitrary act at Sicyon that such an absorption took place generally in Greece, or took place in Attica, would be most hazardous.[1] It is not to the point to prove, as Sir William Ridgeway does at some length, that there were solemn lamentations, as well as various kinds of contests, &c., at hero-tombs all over Greece, and that the dead were carefully propitiated; or even to prove (and this can very rarely be done, if at all) that there were dramatic or mimetic performances at the tombs. We require some proof that the Dionysiac festivals at Athens (and elsewhere) got *their* dramatic performances from this source, and the proof offered is not sufficient.

There is, in fact, no evidence that at Sicyon itself there was any dramatic representation of the sufferings of Adrastus. Τραγικοὶ χοροί doubtless involved appropriate gestures—the raising of the hands in lamentation, perhaps; almost all Greek dancing and music did so; but nothing dramatic, no impersonation or representation of the hero's story, is involved in this. Nor, as far as our information goes, were the other ritual θρῆνοι which are recorded dramatic, such as the laments for Achilles in Elis,[2] at Croton[3] and at Rhoeteum,[4] for Medea's

---

[1] Some scholars, and esp. Robert (*Oedipus*, pp. 141–2), think that the transference may have been made easier by the fact (as they regard it) that Adrastus was a personage of much the same character as Dionysus—a suffering and dying god. This is hardly proved, and the fact that (according to Paus. II. xxiii, § 1) the sanctuaries of Adrastus and Dionysus were adjacent to one another at Argos cannot really be held to confirm the idea; the juxtaposition need have had no such reason. Sir William Ridgeway's idea (*Dramas*, &c., p. 6) that Dionysus was himself regarded as a hero has already been referred to (above, pp. 13–14). See also below, pp. 182 ff.

[2] Paus. IV. xxiii, § 3.   [3] Lycoph. *Alex*. 859.

[4] Philostr. *Her*. 20, 22.

children at Corinth,[1] for Leucothea at Thebes,[2] and for Hippolytus at Troezen.[3] Such laments Herodotus would probably
have called 'tragic' in view of their tone and their resemblance to the tragic choruses of the Attic drama; but evidence
that they involved dramatic elements is entirely wanting.[4]

Sir William Ridgeway's argument for a belief in mimetic
performances at the tombs of heroes partly rests on a record
in Pausanias.[5] A certain Leimon, so the story went, had been
killed by Artemis in punishment for the murder of Skephros,
and at the tomb the priestess of Artemis pursued some one, as
Artemis had pursued Leimon (ἅτε αὐτὴ τὸν Λειμῶνα ἡ Ἄρτεμις).
But there is no suggestion in the Greek of Pausanias that the
priestess impersonated Artemis, or that there was any drama
at all. The ritual pursuit and bloodshed (real or feigned) is a
common form of agrarian magic, and it is 'putting the cart
before the horse' to treat it as the acting of a story. The
ritual was doubtless there long before the story, and the latter
is simply (like countless other stories) an aetiological myth,[6]
invented to account for the ritual. Further, such pursuits are
not peculiar to hero-worship, and traces of them are found in
the worship of Dionysus himself;[7] nor is it without significance
that the festival at Tegea at which the pursuit of Leimon took
place was not really a hero-festival, but a feast of Apollo
Agyieus.

It should be added that when Sir William Ridgeway
goes on to assert that at Sicyon the θυμέλη of Dionysus
superseded the tomb of Adrastus, he is (to use the happy
expression of Dr. Farnell)[8] 'soaring on the wings of fancy

[1] ib. 20–1; Paus. II. iii, § 7 ; Schol. Eur. *Med.* 273, 1359, &c.

[2] Plut. *Apophth. Lac.*, p. 228 e.   [3] Eur. *Hipp.* 1435–7.

[4] Some of these paragraphs (and others in this volume) are quoted
with little alteration from my review of Sir William Ridgeway's book in
Class. Rev. xxvi (1912), pp. 52 ff. Some of the same points will be found
in Nilsson's paper in *Neue Jahrb.* xxvii (1911), and in Dr. Farnell's review
in *Hermathena*, xvii. With the latter I am almost wholly in agreement.

[5] Paus. VIII. liii, §§ 2 ff.

[6] Farnell, l. c., p. 8, takes the same view and gives other instances ; cf.
also Nilsson, l. c., p. 614, and *Gr. Feste*, pp. 166 ff.

[7] See Farnell, *Cults*, v, p. 231, note b.   [8] *Hermath.*, l. c., p. 8.

into the region of the unrecorded'. In fact, Herodotus tells
us that though the τραγικοὶ χοροί were transferred [1] to
Dionysus, Cleisthenes gave τὴν ἄλλην θυσίην Μελανίππῳ,
and if there was a θυμέλη there at all, presumably Melanippus
got it.

Sir William Ridgeway does indeed [2] adduce one strange
argument to show that in Athens itself there was a transference
of choruses to Dionysus. It is not easy to follow, but it seems
to be this: The Anthesteria was a festival of the dead, at
which cyclic choruses were performed; and lest it should be
supposed that these cyclic choruses were in honour of Dionysus,
we are to remember that ' on the first day of the City Dionysia
cyclic choruses danced round the altar of the Twelve Gods in
the Agora, which plainly shows that such cyclic dances were
by no means confined to Dionysus ', but were pre-Dionysiac,
and were transferred from the dead to Dionysus. But (1) it
is not certain that the Anthesteria was originally and primarily
a festival of the dead. Sir William Ridgeway says that Miss
Harrison has proved it; but there is much to be said for
Dr. Farnell's view,[3] according to which the festival was
primarily Dionysiac, and the addition to it of chthonic ritual
is otherwise explained. In any case the undoubted presence
of Dionysiac elements in the festival makes it possible that
the supposed choruses belonged to these. (2) It is very
doubtful indeed if there were cyclic choruses at the Anthesteria.
The suggestion that there were such choruses was originally
made by M. Schmidt,[4] but rested upon arguments so weak
that their author only put them forward in the most tentative
manner; and they are really not worth repeating. (3) As the
'cyclic choruses' on the first day of the City Dionysia, to
which Sir William Ridgeway refers, were part of a Dionysiac
festival, we can hardly say that they were non-Dionysiac,
wherever they were held. But in fact there is no evidence
that these χοροί, which were an incident in the great pro-

---

[1] I agree with Ridgeway (*Origin of Gk. Dr.*, p. 28) that ἀπέδωκε cannot
here mean 'restored', as if they had belonged to Dionysus there before.

[2] *Origin of Gk. Dr.*, p. 50.   [3] *Cults*, v, pp. 214 ff.

[4] *Diatribe in Dithyrambum*, pp. 202 ff.

cession which escorted the statue of Dionysus from Athens to
Eleutherae, were 'cyclic' choruses at all. Xenophon,[1] the only
authority, does not suggest it: καὶ ἐν τοῖς Διονυσίοις δὲ οἱ
χοροὶ προσεπιχαρίζονται ἄλλοις τε θεοῖς καὶ τοῖς δώδεκα
χορεύοντες. In any case the twelve gods were not deceased
heroes.

VII

Peloponnesian and Dorian Tragedy.

The problems in regard to the existence of some kind of
primitive 'tragedy' in the Peloponnese cannot be separated
from those raised by the claim of the Dorians (as recorded by
Aristotle) to have originated tragedy; and it may be that the
discussion will throw some light on the question how it was
that tragedy in the hands of Phrynichus and Aeschylus, despite
the simplicity or even the crudity of the dialogue, was so fine
a lyrical composition.

§ 1. It will be well to set aside at once the theory of
Welcker [2] and Boeckh [3] that there once existed an extensive
non-Athenian lyrical tragedy, of which Pindar and Simonides
were distinguished representatives, as well as the the philosophers Xenophanes and Empedocles. The arguments used to
prove this were plainly unsound, and were disproved for the
most part by G. Hermann.[4] Apart from some misinterpreted
inscriptions, the case rested almost entirely on Suidas' notice
of Pindar, ascribing τραγικὰ δράματα to him, and on the scholia
to Aristophanes' *Wasps*, 144,[5] in regard to Simonides. The
former is quite unreliable; its arithmetic will not come right
when the Isthmian and Nemean Odes (which the notice over-
looks) are taken into account; it is not improbably a conflation
from two or more sources, and the τραγικὰ δράματα mentioned

---

[1] *Hipp.* iii. 3.

[2] *Kleine Schriften*, i. 175-9, 245-7; and his edition of the trilogy,
App., p. 245.

[3] *Staatsh. Athen.*[1] ii, pp. 361 ff.; *C. I. G.* i, p. 766, ii, p. 509; cf. Lobeck,
Aglaoph., pp. 974 ff.   [4] *Opuscula*, vii, pp. 211 ff.

[5] Repeated by (or from) Suidas, s.v. Σιμωνίδης.

among Pindar's works may perhaps (as Hermann suggested) be
the dithyrambs, though δρᾶμα is never used of dithyramb in
classical Greek ; or, as is more likely still, the words may be
a late interpolation, like others in the same notice.[1] The uses
of the word τραγικός in Byzantine writers are hopelessly
loose.[2] Thus in the scholia on Aristophanes' *Plutus*, 290,
Philoxenus is called τραγικός. (διασύρει δὲ Φιλόξενον τὸν
τραγικόν· ὃς εἰσήνεγκε κιθαρίζοντα τὸν Πολύφημον : and
Φιλόξενον τὸν διθυραμβοποιὸν ἢ τραγῳδοδιδάσκαλον διασύρει·
ὃς ἔγραψε τὸν ἔρωτα τοῦ Κύκλωπος τὸν ἐπὶ Γαλατείᾳ.) There
is a similar incorrectness in Jerome,[3] 'Xenophanes physicus,
scriptor tragoediarum', and Syncellus,[4] Φωκυλίδης καὶ Ξενοφάνης τραγῳδοποιὸς ἐγνωρίζετο. The ascription of τραγῳδία
to Simonides by the scholiast may be literally true ; he may
have tried his hand at tragedy as at many other things, though
such authority is not good enough to prove it. The tragedies
ascribed to Empedocles were doubtless those of the philosopher's nephew, and may quite well have been tragedies in the
ordinary classical sense, though we know nothing of his work
except from Suidas.[5]

So the case in regard to lyric tragedy comes back to the
τραγικὸς τρόπος or δρᾶμα τῆς τραγῳδίας of Arion, and the
τραγικοὶ χοροί of Sicyon, together with the claim of the
Dorians and whatever evidence can be held to support it.

§ 2. The claim of the Dorians is recorded by Aristotle in
the following words ;[6] διὸ καὶ ἀντιποιοῦνται τῆς τε τραγῳδίας
καὶ τῆς κωμῳδίας οἱ Δωριεῖς (τῆς μὲν κωμῳδίας οἱ Μεγαρεῖς . . .

---

[1] Hiller (*Hermes*, xxi, pp. 357 ff.) gives strong reasons for this view,
and against the attempt to refer Suidas' list of Pindar's works to good
Alexandrian authority. He points out that in Demosth. *de F. L.*, § 237
δρᾶμα τραγικόν means 'tragedy', and that it is very unlikely that an
Alexandrian scholar would have used the words in a different sense from
that current in the fourth century. For later usage, cf. Aelian, *Var. H.*
xiii. 18 Διόνυσος δὲ ὁ τῆς Σικελίας τύραννος τραγῳδίαν μὲν ἠσπάζετο καὶ
ἐπῄνει καὶ οὖν καὶ δράματα ἐξεπόνησε τραγικά.

[2] See Immisch, *Rhein. Mus.* xliv, pp. 553 ff.

[3] On Olymp. lxi.   [4] p. 238.

[5] s. v. Ἐμπεδοκλῆς. For doubts about these tragedies see Diog. Laert.
viii. 58.   [6] *Poet.* iii, 1448 a 29 ff.

καὶ τῆς τραγῳδίας ἔνιοι τῶν ἐν Πελοποννήσῳ) ποιούμενοι τὰ
ὀνόματα σημεῖον· αὐτοὶ μὲν γὰρ κώμας τὰς περιοικίδας καλεῖν
φασιν, Ἀθηναίους δὲ δήμους ... καὶ τὸ ποιεῖν αὐτοὶ μὲν δρᾶν,
Ἀθηναῖοι δὲ πράττειν προσαγορεύειν.

Aristotle does not say what Dorian writers made the
claim—he may have found it recorded, as Wilamowitz suggests,
in the *Chronica* of his senior contemporary Dieuchidas of
Megara—and he expresses neither agreement nor disagreement
with it.   Some of the arguments quoted are plainly bad;
but the claim may carry some weight if any part of the statement made in support of it is true, and if there is confirmatory
evidence.

The late Mr. Herbert Richards [1] has collected and discussed
the uses of δρᾶμα and δρᾶν.   The conclusions to which the
evidence given in his article points are:

(1) that δρᾶν is not originally an Attic word, though it is
used freely in Attic poetry and in those prose writers who
admit poetical words and phrases, especially Antiphon, Thucydides, and Plato.[2]   It is also used rarely by Demosthenes—of
that later; but not at all by most of the Attic orators.   It is
also (almost certainly) not an Ionic word, and the statement
that it is Doric may well be true, though it is not actually
proved.

(2) that δρᾶν is primarily in Attic a word with a religious
colour, and is used especially of serious and solemn religious
performances.   It is very doubtful whether δρᾶμα is ever
used of comedy in classical Attic,[3]—or indeed at all until quite

---

[1] *Class. Rev.* xiv (1900), pp. 388 ff.

[2] Plato uses Sicilian words, and may have been more influenced by
Sicilian Doric than we usually recognize. In *Rep.* v, p. 451 c μετὰ τὸ ἀνδρεῖον
δρᾶμα παντελῶς διαπερανθὲν τὸ γυναικεῖον αὖ περαίνειν, where Richards thinks
the reference is to tragedy, Plato is surely alluding to the μῖμοι ἀνδρεῖοι
and γυναικεῖοι of his favourite author Sophron, and the application of
the word δρᾶμα may have seemed natural because these were Dorian
compositions.

[3] When Ecphantides speaks (in a fragment) of a δρᾶμα, it is δρᾶμα
Μεγαρικόν, i. e. of a Dorian type, even though it is comedy of which he
is thinking (comp. Xen. *Hell.* I. i, § 23—the Doric message, ἀπορίομες τί
χρὴ δρᾶν).

late; it is regularly applied to tragedy and satyric drama, both of which were less secular than comedy; and the mysteries were τὰ δρώμενα 'Ελευσῖνι.[1] Most of the uses of δρᾶν in good Attic prose (apart from writers known to have been addicted to poetical expressions) can be explained by the religious sense: it is applied (e. g.) to ritual and to murder by Demosthenes (or a pseudo-Demosthenes) in several places.[2] (To commit murder and to perform a religious service were alike perilous operations, to Greek religious ideas, and partly for the same reasons.) The ' Letter of Philip '[3] uses the word of an impious act.

It is then at least possible that δρᾶμα was originally a Doric word, and so far there is no reason to deny the Dorian claim.

§ 3. The claim may also be said to be supported by the tradition respecting Arion, who was indeed a Lesbian of Methymna (a town mainly, but not exclusively, of Aeolian population), but whose choruses must have been those of Dorian Corinth. We do not in fact know anything of Lesbian dithyrambic poetry at this date, nor have we any reason even for saying that Arion's work consisted in the introduction of Lesbian music into Corinth. When, therefore, Sir William Ridgeway says[4] that a supporter of the Dorian claim ' might just as well argue that because Handel composed the *Messiah* and many other great works in England, the English race are to be credited with the creation of the Handelian music ', he is suggesting a false parallel. Arion probably was, Handel was not, working upon pre-existing local performances.

The claim is also supported by the record of τραγικοὶ χοροί

---

[1] Paus. VIII. xv, § 1. At the same time δρᾶμα does not, like δρώμενα, imply anything mystic. (The expression τὰ δρώμενα is evidently a reverent or reticent name for a mystic rite; cf. Plut. *De Is. et Osir.*, pp. 352 c, 378 a, b; Paus. II. xxxvii, §§ 5, 6; III. xxiii, § 2, &c.) Pausanias regularly uses δρᾶν of religious rites, but not δρᾶμα. Clem. Alex. *Protrept.* ii. 12 speaks of Demeter and Kore having become δρᾶμα μυστικόν, but this is very late, and the addition of μυστικόν shows that δρᾶμα alone did not carry this connotation.

[2] *in Neaer.*, § 7; *in Aristocr.*, § 40; *in Theocrin.*, § 28.

[3] § 4. Mr. Richards is not responsible for all these instances.

[4] *Class. Rev.* xxvi (1912), p. 135.

at Sicyon in Herodotus. For even if the cult of Dionysus was only introduced by Cleisthenes, the τραγικοὶ χοροί were already there, and were celebrated in commemoration of the Dorian hero Adrastus, whom Cleisthenes drove out in order to rid the town of Argive influence.

§ 4. It is usual to adduce the dialectical peculiarities of the choruses of Attic tragedy as evidence for the Dorian claim, and the argument is not without weight; but the matter is not so simple as it is usually thought to be.

We may indeed reject at once Sir William Ridgeway's contention that 'it is difficult to believe that the Athenians would have borrowed the diction of their sacred songs from the hated Dorians, whom they would not permit to enter their sanctuaries'. The evidence [1] given for the statement contained in the last clause only records the refusal of the priestess of Athena to allow Cleomenes to enter the adyton of Athena on the Acropolis, because Dorians were not allowed to enter *that* temple (οὐ γὰρ θεμιτὸν Δωριεῦσι παριέναι ἐνθαῦτα). This phrase, which applies to one temple only, is obviously unequal to the weight of so sweeping a generalization. (Why Sir William Ridgeway, in reply,[2] should remind us 'that though the Carians admitted their kindred Lydians and Mysians into the temple of Zeus at Mylasa, they kept out all others, even though they spoke Carian' does not appear; at any rate it has nothing to do with Athens and the Dorians.) But the problem in regard to the language itself is not altogether easy. It is usual to lay stress upon the use in tragedy—mainly in the lyric portions, but also to some extent in the dialogue—of forms containing ā where Attic used η. But this use of ā was common to all dialects except Attic and Ionic, and therefore was naturally part of the lyric κοινή which seems to have grown up in the sixth century; and though it is impossible to accept the suggestion of B. Kock and (on different grounds) of Sir William Ridgeway [3] that

---

[1] Herod. v. 72.   [2] *Class. Rev.* xxvi (1912), p. 135.

[3] See esp. *The Early Age of Greece*, i, pp. 670-1. It is difficult to understand what he means by 'the absurd doctrine that the Athenians would have composed their ancient songs, which probably dated from

these forms are old Attic, they cannot be assumed to be Doric without argument.

It does, however, seem reasonable to suppose that if a number of distinctively Doric words and forms are found in Attic tragedy, then the forms containing ā for η are also probably attributable as a whole to the influence of Doric poems and speech upon the writers. The main substance of their language is Attic, with an infusion of Epic and Ionic forms, and of other dialectical forms used in lyric poetry—an infusion to be accounted for as an instance of that persistence of literary conventions in Greece which all scholars recognize: but there is a considerable number of words and forms which are distinctly Doric, some of them used in the lyric portions, some in the iambic, some in both. (The use of them in the iambic portions is best explained as a natural infiltration or infection from the lyrics; it cannot always be accounted for by metrical convenience; but poets who were writing lyric as part of the same work would naturally, even in iambics, find themselves using some of those elements of a heightened style which were regular in lyric.) [1] Among these Doric words are γαμόρος, δαρός,

a period anterior to the Dorian conquest, in a Dorian dialect'. It is not a question here of the composition of ancient songs, but of that of dithyrambs and 'tragic choruses' taken over (doubtless with their conventional dialect), not earlier than the sixth century, from non-Attic sources. We know nothing of dithyrambs anterior to the Dorian conquest, or in primitive Attica. The real difficulties, however, in the way of this theory are (1) that the peculiarities of the language of tragedy generally are certainly not old Attic, and this is clearly shown by Smyth, Thumb, &c., in answer to Rutherford (*New Phrynichus*, pp. 1–52) and others (e. g. Barlen, *De vocis a pron. in tragicorum Graecorum versibus trimetris usu*, Bonn, 1872), who had put forward the old Attic theory; and it is *pro tanto* unlikely that this one peculiarity should be : (2) that this ā is not found in any Attic known to us, and it is very improbable that it should have been preserved from pre-historic times for the use of tragedy without a written or literary tradition to preserve it. But we have no record of any ancient Attic literature, and it can be confidently asserted that there was none. Nor is there any evidence of the existence of such traditional religious poems as (Sir William Ridgeway imagines) may have preserved this one feature.

[1] This is an easier hypothesis than that of Hoffmann, *Rhein. Mus.* lxix, pp. 244 ff., that there must have been Doric as well as Ionic iambic

νάϊος, λοχαγός, κυναγός, ποδαγός, τιμάορος, συνάορος, μάκιστος, πέπαται, ὀπαδός.[1] If these and other words and forms (e. g. σφετεριξάμενοι in Æsch. *Suppl.* 38) are Doric, the common use of α for η may be traceable to the same source. The use of such forms in the lyrics of Tragedy is by no means consistent; they were doubtless employed when the poet felt the need of some greater distinction from ordinary speech; but this is natural enough. Accordingly it seems to be, at least, reasonably probable that some of the features of the language of Attic tragedy are explicable by Dorian influence;[2] and, on the whole, when we put the various indications together—δρᾶμα, Arion, Sicyon, language—the Dorian claim to have in some sense originated tragedy becomes an extremely likely hypothesis.

It is, moreover, a hypothesis which will explain the early excellence of the lyric portions of tragedy. We nowhere find a hint that Thespis was a lyric poet of any merit; but, if the hypothesis is true, it was in the compositions of Peloponnesian lyric poets—Arion, Lasos, and perhaps poets of Sicyon, now forgotten—that the early Attic tragedians, and above all Phrynichus and Aeschylus, found models of choral lyric poetry, with the music appropriate to serious themes, and were thus enabled themselves to produce work of an even higher degree of perfection. It is sometimes conjectured also that the tragic choruses of the Peloponnese may have impersonated groups of legendary characters, instead of remaining (like the performers of dithyramb) simply bodies of worshippers; but on this point there is no evidence.[3]

poetry in the sixth century, or earlier, to account for the Doric forms in the dialogue of Attic tragedy.

[1] See also J. D. Rogers, *Amer. J. Phil.* xxv (1904), pp. 285-305.

[2] On the whole question see Thumb, *Handb. der gr. Dialekte*, pp. 159-60, 369 ff.; Smyth, *Ionic Dialect*, pp. 74 ff.; Meillet, *Aperçu d'une histoire de la langue grecque* (ed. ii), ch. viii. Some useful material is collected by W. Aly, *De Aeschyli verborum copia* (Berlin, 1904). See also Addenda, p. 417 below.

[3] See above, pp. 135, 139.

VIII

Τραγῳδία, Τράγοι, ETC.

The origin and meaning of the words τραγῳδοί and τραγῳδία is, like the questions already discussed, the subject of a long-standing controversy. Τραγῳδοί (the singular is found very rarely, and only comparatively late) is presumably the earlier word of the two, τραγῳδία being derived from it; and it is clear that τραγῳδοί was used primarily of a chorus, not of actors or poets.[1] But eleven different explanations of the words are summarized by Professor Flickinger in his valuable paper on the subject,[2] and yet others have been suggested. Those which try to get away from the belief that τράγος means 'goat' may safely be disregarded,[3] and practically only three views need be seriously considered:

(1) that τραγῳδοί mean a chorus of goat-like satyrs;

(2) that it means a chorus, not representing satyrs, but clad in goatskins as an ancient dress retained for religious or antiquarian reasons;

(3) that it means a chorus dancing either for the goat as a prize or around the goat as a sacrifice.

These must be separately discussed.

§ 1. The first explanation is bound up with the belief that tragedy was historically an offshoot of satyric drama, made more dignified by the abandonment of the satyr-costume and language; and that the satyrs were in the form of creatures half man and half goat.

Now as it is Attic tragedy and satyr-play with which we are concerned, it is important to notice that the satyrs of the Athenian stage were not goat-like until a comparatively late period, and that early Attic art knows nothing of such goat-like demons. Both in the theatre and in art we find, instead, creatures that were half man, half horse. The evidence in

---

[1] The facts are given by H. Richards, *Aristophanes and others*, pp. 334 ff.; cf. also Reisch, *Festschr. für Gomperz*, p. 466.

[2] *Class. Phil.* viii, pp. 269 ff.

[3] There is also no need to refer again to the theory of Eisler, briefly discussed on pp. 103–4.

regard to this rather complex matter has been discussed many
times in recent years; it has been stated with great completeness by Kühnert,[1] and the more important points have been
discussed by Reisch,[2] Frickenhaus,[3] A. B. Cook [4] and others;
reference to the earlier discussions by Furtwängler, Loeschke,
Wernicke, A. Körte, and others is also indispensable. The
view taken below is in the main in agreement with that of
Reisch, though it was reached independently and in certain
points diverges from his opinion; but it will be convenient to
take point by point, and to state the evidence briefly.

There can be no question that popular imagination throughout the Greek world was familiar with creatures combining
a generally human form with the ears and tail, and often the
hoofs or entire legs, of the horse. They are usually ithyphallic
when they appear in early art, and there is no doubt that the
name under which they passed generally was Σιληνοί (or Σει-
ληνοί).[5] This name is found inscribed against the representations of them on a number of very early vases, which are conveniently enumerated by Dr. Cook.[6] It is tolerably clear that,
as at first conceived of, they were not associated especially with
Dionysus, but were (like the kindred Centaurs) creatures of the
wild mountain forests, the male counterparts, and at the same
time the lovers, of the nymphs,—vegetation-demons, but not in
special relation to the vine or to any other plant above the rest.

These creatures cannot be regarded as peculiar to any one
region of the Greek world. Certain facts point to their being
less familiar among early Dorian peoples than elsewhere.
'Silenus' is very rarely a proper name in Dorian countries, as
it is in others, and as 'Satyrus' is in Athens, and the figure of
the semi-equine demon seems to be wanting, or almost wanting, in the remains of early Dorian art; but there can be no
doubt as to the association of legends of Silenus with Malea in
Laconia,[7] and the name occurs as a personal name at Akragas

---

[1] Art. *Satyros* in Roscher's Lexicon. [2] *Festsch. für Gomperz* (1902).
[3] *Jahrb. Arch. Inst.* xxxii. [4] *Zeus*, i, pp. 695 ff.
[5] The orthography depends upon the view taken of the derivation;
see below, p. 152. [6] l. c., pp. 696-7.
[7] Pollux iv. 104 (speaking of Λακωνικὰ ὀρχήματα διὰ Μαλέας), Σιληνοὶ δ'

in the fifth century at least, and is found in Athens itself [1] in
the Dorian form 'Silanus', showing perhaps that the bearer of
it was of Dorian descent. There were also legends of Silenus
in Arcadia, where we are told that he was regarded as father
of Apollo Nomios.[2] We may safely state that in the sixth
century the popular conception of creatures of the semi-equine
type was spread over the Greek world. They are found on
sixth-century coins from Thasos and Lete; on archaic gems;
on the sarcophagus from Clazomenae; on an early vase from
Cameirus; on many other vases of Ionian origin, as well as
on a number of early Attic vases. The association of the
creatures with Dionysus seems to have begun in Ionia and
Attica; in the latter it soon becomes regular and almost invariable. (The evidence for these statements is clearly given
by Kühnert.)

But such creatures are not always called Σιληνοί, and there
is evidence that the name regularly applied to them in Athens
was Σάτυροι. This name itself first occurs in a fragment of
Hesiod;[3] the poet is speaking of the five daughters of a
daughter of Phoroneus,

ἐξ ὧν ο(ὐ)ρείαι Νυμφαὶ θεαὶ ⟨ἐξ⟩εγένοντο,
καὶ γένος οὐτιδάνων Σατύρων καὶ ἀμηχανοεργῶν
Κουρῆτές τε θεοὶ φιλοπαίγμονες ὀρχηστῆρες.

—a passage which suggests the same kind of wild creatures as
the horse-demons were, but gives no hint as to whether they

ἦσαν καὶ ὑπ' αὐτοῖς Σάτυροι ὑπότρομα ὀρχούμενοι. The conjecture of Reisch,
l. c., p. 463, that we may here have an anticipation of that differentiation
of Silenus from the satyrs which is otherwise supposed to be an Athenian
innovation, seems hazardous, as we do not know of what date Pollux is
speaking. For the Silenus of Malea comp. Pindar fr. ap. Paus. III. xxv,
§ 2 (fr. 156, Schroeder). It would also be unsafe to connect with the
notice of the Silenus of Malea the statement of Herodian (Lentz, vol. i,
p. 244, l. 21), λέγονται δὲ Εἴλωτες καὶ οἱ ἐπὶ Ταινάρῳ Σάτυροι, as there is no
indication what he is referring to. (He refers two or three times to a
comedy called Εἴλωτες and ascribed by Athenaeus to Eupolis, but there
may be no connexion between this and the statement quoted. May not
the statement mean simply that helots and the people of Taenarum
were nicknamed 'satyrs'?)

[1] C. I. A. i. 447.   [2] Clem. Al. Protrept., p. 24.   [3] fr. 129.

shared the nature of horse or goat. (The connexion with Phoroneus is thought by Kühnert [1] to point to the origin of the name in Argolis, but this seems an uncertain conjecture.) In Attica we find the name first on a vase of about 520 B. C., now at Würzburg, on which a horse-man is painted with a name inscribed against him which is now generally agreed to be Σάτυρος.[2] There can be no doubt that in the fifth century B. C., the names Σάτυρος and Σιληνός were interchangeable. Socrates is sometimes compared to a satyr, sometimes to a Silenus;[3] Marsyas the satyr is called a Silenus by Herodotus;[4] and, most important of all, there can no doubt that the satyr-choruses of the Attic theatre were dressed in semi-equine, not semi-caprine costume, whereas their father (or eldest brother) was called Silenus,—the word being now specialized into a proper name. (The personality of Silenus becomes more and more specialized as time goes on.[5])

What the satyrs of Arion at Corinth were like, and even whether (as seems probable) they were specially connected with Dionysus, there is no evidence to show. The horse-demons do not appear in early Corinthian art, but Arion may have introduced them from non-Corinthian sources, or the Corinthian satyrs may have had some other shape.[6] It is

---

[1] As by Furtwängler, Kl. Schr., pp. 183 ff.

[2] A few scholars still read the letters in the opposite direction and make the name Σιβύρτας (a name found in Theocr. v. 5) ; cf. Fränkel, Satyr- u. Bakchen-Namen, p. 35 ; W. Schulze, Gött. gel. Anz. (1896), p. 254. Eisler (Orph.-Dion. Myst.-Gedanken, p. 362) suggests Σατύρωψ.

[3] Xen. Symp. IV. xix ; v. vii ; Plato, Symp. 215 b, 216 d, 221 d, e.

[4] vii. 26.

[5] Solmsen, Indog. Forsch. xxx (1912), pp. 1 ff., makes it fairly certain that Σιληνός is connected with *σιλός, a by-form of σιμός, 'snub-nosed ', such forms in -ανός, -ηνός being Peloponnesian as well as Ionian ; while σάτυρος = ithyphallus. Other scholars connect Σειληνός with the Thracian ζείλα, 'wine' (Tomaschek, Die alten Thraker, II. i, p. 11: cf. Σεμέλη and Thracian ζεμελώ), or think that σιλ- is a Thracian root corresponding to the Greek κήλων = ὀχεύτης, 'stallion' (Lagercrantz, in Sertum philol. C. F. Johannson oblatum, pp. 117-21); while Eisler, l. c., p. 262) thinks that σάτυρος may be an Illyrian word (like πάτυρος for πάτηρ) = sator.

[6] There is, however, no ground for giving the name Σάτυροι (as Solmsen does) to the demons on certain Corinthian vases which will be discussed

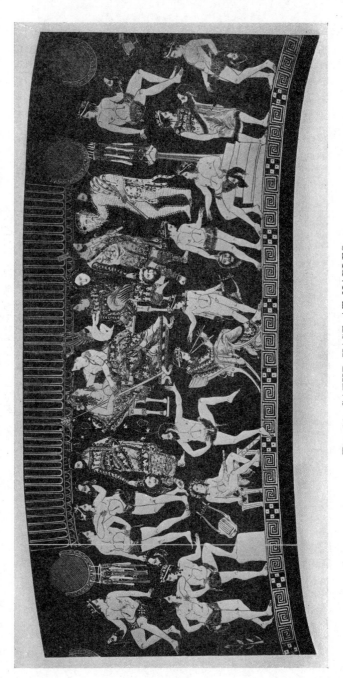

Fig. 11. SATYR VASE AT NAPLES

Fig. 12. SATYR VASE AT NAPLES

useless to speculate about this in the absence of evidence, and
even more useless to dogmatize, as some scholars do.

§ 2. That the satyr-choruses of the theatre in the fifth
century were horse-men is not seriously to be doubted. On
the celebrated vase [1] at Naples, on which a satyr-chorus is
depicted, and which belongs to about the end of the century,
the horses' tails and ears are unmistakable; and if it be
objected that most of the choreutae wear a goatskin round
the loins, it must be pointed out that one of them at least
wears linen drawers; and that the latter were one of the
regular forms of stage satyr-dress is shown by its occurrence at
about the same period on another vase,[2] representing a satyric
play in which Poseidon and Amymone were characters. It
may be added that Pollux [3] shows that there was no special
animal whose skin was appropriated for this purpose by satyr-
choruses : ἡ δὲ σατυρικὴ ἐσθὴς νεβρίς, αἰγῆ, ἣν καὶ ἰξαλῆν
ἐκάλουν καὶ τραγῆν, καί που καὶ παρδαλῆ ὑφασμένη, καὶ τὸ
θήραιον τὸ Διονυσιακόν, καὶ χλανὶς ἀνθινή, καὶ φοινικοῦν ἱμάτιον, καὶ χορταῖος χιτὼν δασύς, ὃν οἱ Σιληνοὶ φοροῦσιν. Plainly
the goatskin had no prerogative position. It was the horse's
tail and ears that were invariable and essential.

The common belief that the satyr-choruses were composed
of goat-men rests, so far as the early and the fifth-century
drama is concerned, almost entirely upon two passages from

below (pp. 261 ff.) in connexion with Comedy. The statement of Frickenhaus (*Jahrb. Arch. Inst.* xxxii, pp. 7, 8) that Arion's dithyramb was sung
by satyrs, and that he made use of Silenus, the father of the satyrs, as a
separate individual, appears to be mere guess-work. (See above, p. 133.)

[1] The best reproduction and discussion of this vase are given by
Buschor in Furtwängler-Reichold, *Griech. Vasenmalerei*, Ser. iii, pp.
132 ff., pl. 143–5, from which figs. 11 and 12 are taken. The painting
does not strictly represent (as is usually stated) the preparations for
a play, or a 'peep behind the scenes', but rather the Dionysiac θίασος
in its dramatic aspect, just as the corresponding painting on the other
side of the vase represents the θίασος in its ecstatic revel. But this does
not affect its value as evidence for the costume of the satyr-chorus.

[2] Fig. 13 ; cf. Bieber, *Das Dresdener Schauspiel-Relief*, p. 17 ; *Athen. Mitt.*
xxxvi (1911), pp. 269 ff., pl. xiii and xiv.

[3] iv. 118. It is quite uncertain to what periods the statements of
Pollux refer.

the satyric drama itself, and upon an interpretation of a celebrated vase. A number of later passages are indeed often
cited as evidence, but these really depend upon the conception
of the satyr in the Hellenistic age, when the satyr-type was
blended with that of Pan.[1] Thus the passage of the *Etymologicum magnum*[2] s. v. τραγῳδία is not evidence at all, but
only contains a series of guesses at the etymology of the
word ... ἢ ὅτι τὰ πολλὰ οἱ χοροὶ ἐκ σατύρων συνίσταντο, οὓς
ἐκάλουν τράγους, ἢ διὰ τὴν τοῦ σώματος δασύτητα ἢ διὰ τὴν
περὶ τὰ ἀφροδίσια σπουδήν· τοιοῦτον γὰρ τὸ ζῷον. ἢ ὅτι οἱ
χορευταὶ τὰς κόμας ἀνέπλεκον, σχῆμα τράγων μιμούμενοι. Of
the same type is Hesychius' τράγους· σατύρους, διὰ τὸ τράγων
ὦτα ἔχειν—which was not true of the fifth century. Both
notices, in any case, regard τράγοι as a *nickname* of satyrs, given
on account of certain special peculiarities; if the satyrs had
been thought of as in their own nature half-goat, this must
surely have been mentioned.[3]

The passages most generally quoted to prove that the satyric
play was acted by goat-like satyrs are:

(1) Plut. *de inimicorum utilitate*, p. 86 f. τοῦ δὲ σατύρου τὸ
πῦρ, ὡς πρῶτον ὤφθη, βουλομένου φιλῆσαι καὶ περιβαλεῖν ὁ
Προμηθεύς, Τράγος, ἔφη, γένειον ἄρα πενθήσεις σύ γε. (The line
quoted is commonly ascribed by scholars, on somewhat inconclusive grounds, to the Προμηθεὺς Πυρκαεύς of Aeschylus.)
This is supposed to imply a satyr of goat-like form. But two
other explanations have been offered, neither of which involves
this implication. Either, with Löschke,[4] we may suppose that
the satyr is addressed as τράγος metaphorically, owing to his
wantonness (one of the reasons for which, according to the
Etymologicum magnum, satyrs were nicknamed τράγοι); or,
perhaps better, with Shorey,[5] we may regard the expression as

---

[1] The development is traced by Furtwängler, *Ann. dell. Ist.* 1877,
p. 208 f.; and *Der Satyr aus Pergamon*, pp. 26-7 (*Kleine Schriften*,
pp. 190 ff.). [2] p. 764.

[3] The passages which show that Aelian and various grammarians
equated τίτυρος with σάτυρος, and some of them also with τράγος, are also
very late, and have no bearing on the classical and preceding periods.
They are quoted by Reisch, *Festschr. für Gomperz*, p. 453.

[4] *Athen. Mitt.* xix, p. 522. [5] *Class. Philol.* iv (1909), p. 435.

FIG. 13. FRAGMENTS OF VASE IN BONN

a proverbial one—' You'll be the proverbial goat mourning for his beard '—an expression like ὁ δ' ὄνος ὕεται, 'he is like the donkey out in the rain ', and many others quoted by Shorey. In the same way the lines from Sophocles' *Ichneutae*, addressed to the chorus-leader or to Silenus,

νέος γὰρ ὢν ἀνηρ
πώγωνι θάλλων ὡς τράγος κνήκῳ χλιδᾷς,

do not imply that the satyr addressed was not semi-equine, but only that he had a light beard, like a goat.[1]

(2) Euripides, *Cyclops*, ll. 78–82 :

θητεύω Κύκλωπι
τῷ μονοδέρκτᾳ δοῦλος ἀλαίνων
σὺν τᾷδε τράγου χλαίνᾳ μελέᾳ
σᾶς χωρὶς φιλίας.

Here, it is plain, the chorus are dressed in goatskins ; but they think the dress a hardship. They wear them not because they are goats, but because they are the shepherd slaves of Polyphemus. The expression 'this miserable goatskin' would be impossible, if the goat-dress were supposed to be their own skin ; so far from gaining in point, as Dr. A. B. Cook [2] thinks it would, it would surely lose all its point, if the satyrs were essentially goat-like. It is a confirmation of this view that (as Reisch points out) the satyrs in the picture [3] of the blinding of Polyphemus, on a vase painted (as is agreed by Kühnert and others) under Euripidean influence, are horsemen, not goat-men.

As regards other Attic vases on which goat-like beings appear, little need be said except that most of those enumerated by Wernicke [4] and by Dr. A. B. Cook [5] have no connexion with the theatre or with any performance at all ; that most of them are too late to be good evidence for the existence of goat-men in Athenian popular imagination in the sixth and early fifth centuries ; and that on none of them are the goat-

---

[1] See Frickenhaus, *Jahrb. Arch. Inst.* xxxii, pp. 9 ff., for a discussion of the passage, and Pearson's edition ad loc.

[2] *Zeus*, vol. i, p. 702.   [3] *Jahrb. Arch. Inst.* vi, p. 271, pl. vi.

[4] s. v. Pan in Roscher's *Lexicon*.   [5] *Zeus*, vol. i, pp. 698–9.

like beings called satyrs. Indeed, we have no instance of this
name applied to a goat-man in the fifth century at all. It
appears most likely that such goat-like beings entered into
Athenian ideas about the time of the Persian Wars, when
the reported appearance of the Arcadian god Pan to Pheidippides secured for him a welcome in Athens; and the goat-like
beings depicted on the vases may well, as Reisch and others
have maintained, be Pans or creatures modelled on Pan. That
the Athenians thought of a plurality of such creatures is
certain:[1] cf. Aristophanes, *Eccles.* 1069 ὦ Πᾶνες, ὦ Κορύ-
βαντες, ὦ Διοσκόρω: Schol. on Euripides' *Rhesus*, 36 Αἰσχύλος δὲ δύο Πᾶνας, τὸν μὲν Διὸς †ὸν καὶ δίδυμον†, τὸν δὲ Κρόνου:
Schol. on Theocritus iv. 62 τοὺς Πᾶνας πλείους φησίν, ὡς
καὶ Σειληνοὺς καὶ σατύρους, ὡς Αἰσχύλος μὲν ἐν Γλαύκῳ,
Σοφοκλῆς δὲ ἐν Ἀνδρομέδᾳ:[2] and Plato, *Laws*, 815 c Νύμφας
τε καὶ Πᾶνας καὶ Σιληνοὺς καὶ Σατύρους ἐπονομάζοντες.[3] It
may even be the case (as Professor Pearson thinks[4]) that the
plural name, used generically of the whole class of goat-
demons, is the earlier, and that the specialization of the individual god Pan was a comparatively late development, like
that of Silenus.[5]

But the vase upon which most controversy has turned is
the crater in the British Museum from Altemura,[6] representing, among other things, the creation of Pandora. One of the
scenes on this vase presents four goat-men and a human flute-
player. The presence of the latter, combined with the fact
that the goat-men are represented as wearing drawers, and

---

[1] Apart from Athens, Paus. VIII, xxxvii, § 2, speaks of Νύμφαι καὶ
Πᾶνες as represented in the temple of Despoina in Arcadia, five miles
from Megalopolis (comp. an epigram of Myrinus, *Anth. Pal.* vi. 108;
but this is not earlier than the first century A. D.).

[2] This is a practically certain emendation of the MSS. readings τοὺς
σατύρους . . . καὶ Πᾶνας, or καὶ σατυρίσκους τοὺς Πᾶνας, which as Pearson
shows (Soph. Fragm. i, p. 85) do not suit the text of Theocritus.

[3] Cf. also the *Culex*, ll. 94, 115.   [4] Soph. Fragm., l. c.

[5] I do not see why (as Dr. A. B. Cook, *Zeus*, i, p. 702, suggests) these
creatures should, if they are Pans or modelled on Pan, be necessarily
associated with nymphs and carry the syrinx whenever they appear.

[6] Figs. 14, 15.

Figs. 14–15. THE PANDORA KRATER IN THE BRITISH MUSEUM

probably masks, implies that the painter had some performance
in mind, or is at least representing imaginary performers,
and not merely imaginary creatures. But the performance
need not be a satyr-play; it may either itself be imaginary, or
may be based on some rustic amusement in which Pans were
represented dancing, and not on a theatrical performance. If,
however, it is based on a theatrical performance, it may be on
some comedy; there are other vases which show members of
comic choruses with their flute-player, and there were comedies
which had choruses of goats—at least the Αἶγες of Eupolis
had. (If the scenes on the vase are connected—but this is
very doubtful—the *Pandora* of Nicophon suggests itself.)
On the other side of the crater a female chorus, perhaps representing nymphs, is rehearsing its dance, with flute-player and
trainer; and below them (in the lower half of the vase) a
number of horse-men are playing. The latter are perhaps
thought of, not as performers, but as the original wild creatures;
the absence of costume does not indeed prove this (see below),
but at least suggests a distinction between this and the other
scenes. (The scene which represents the making of Pandora
does not look like a theatrical representation at all.) The vase
is, in any case, too late to be good evidence for the early
period of satyric drama; it is not earlier than about 450 B.C.

On the other hand, it has been thought that some vases on
which horse-demons appear may be reminiscent of actual
satyric plays; and if this is true, they confirm the belief that
the satyr-drama had a chorus of such creatures. Among these
is a celebrated early red-figured vase of Brygos [1] in which
Hera and Iris are assailed by horse-satyrs and Heracles is
coming to the rescue; on others satyrs are shown in various
situations along with Heracles, Perseus, or other heroes.[2]   It

---

[1] Figured in *Wiener Vorlegebl.* viii, pl. 6; Furtwängler-Reichhold, i,
pl. xlvii. 2; Kühnert, l. c., p. 467, &c. This vase must belong to a very
early date in the fifth century.

[2] Some represent the *Cyclops* of Euripides or other poets: one
(Gerhard, *A. V.* 153-4) shows the satyrs in captivity to Amycus; the
crater from Bonn, where Poseidon, Amymone, and satyrs (in costume)
appear has already been mentioned. Reisch also notices a vase of

is true that the horse-satyrs on the vases of Brygos and
Douris are represented as naked, not as men dressed in the
stage-costume of Satyrs; but this does not necessarily mean
that the scene was not suggested by the theatre, for (as
Wilamowitz has pointed out[1]) vase-painters did not invariably
copy the theatrical costume, even when presenting scenes
taken from drama; and the attitude of the satyrs to Heracles
is in accordance with the remark of Aristides,[2]—ἤδη Θέτις καὶ
Σάτυρος τῶν ἐπὶ σκηνῆς κατηράσατο τῷ Ἡρακλεῖ, εἶτά γ'
ἔκυψε προσιόντος κάτω. The scenes on these vases are just
such as the satyric drama appears to have offered, and though
the connexion cannot be proved, it is at least very likely.

We may take it then as practically certain that the choruses
of the Athenian satyric drama were of the equine, not of the
caprine type, and that there are no goat-demons in Attic art
early enough to support the opposite view. The suggestion
is often made that the early satyr-choruses in the Peloponnese
were caprine, but that when they were transferred to Athens by
Pratinas they became equine, the Athenians being familiar
with the equine type; or that, having been caprine early in
the fifth century, they gradually became equine. But there is
really no evidence to support either of these views, and we do
not know at all what the costume of Peloponnesian satyr-
choruses was. It may just as well have been equine as
caprine, even though Peloponnesian people were also familiar
with caprine demons. Suggestions of this kind are generally
due to a refusal at any cost to abandon the idea that τραγῳδοί
are singers dressed like goats,[3] and that tragedy is derived

Douris (*Brit. Mus. Cat.* iii. E 788; *Wiener Vorlegebl.* vi, pl. 4; Flickinger,
Gk. Theater, p. 31), on which there are ten horse-men, with an eleventh
dressed as a herald; its date is about 480 B.C. Most of these vases
are mentioned by Kühnert, l. c., pp. 500 ff.; cf. O. Jahn, *Philolog.* xxvii,
pp. 1 ff.

[1] *Neue Jahrb.* xxix, p. 464.

[2] Aristid. xlvii. 2. 310 (quoted by Kühnert).

[3] This, however, is not the case with Flickinger (*Gr. Theater,* p. 32),
who thinks that Pratinas changed his Dorian goat-men—(do we know
that they were goat-men ?)—into horse-men on bringing them to Athens;
that fifty or sixty years afterwards the attempt was made to introduce

from the songs of such goat-satyrs. We shall shortly consider whether such an interpretation of τραγῳδοί is necessary or probable.

§ 3. But it will be convenient first to discuss the theory that τραγῳδοί means singers dressed like goats, not as being goat-like satyrs, but for various other reasons.

Reisch,[1] while preferring the interpretation of τραγῳδοί which will be maintained later in this chapter, suggests that if τραγῳδία *must* be interpreted as τράγων ᾠδή, the τράγοι may be thought of as a collection of persons performing for ritual purposes as τράγοι, in the same way as other groups performed as ἵπποι, ταῦροι, μέλισσαι, ἄρκτοι, &c.[2] But it is not necessary, as we shall see, to take τραγῳδία as = τράγων ᾠδή, and this is fortunate, since there is no proof of the existence of such a *Kultgenossenschaft* of τράγοι. It is certainly not proved by the passage of Hesychius, which shows that αἱ κόραι Διονύσῳ ὀργιάζουσαι wore goatskins and were called τραγηφόροι: and such κοραί sometimes wore other skins instead,—those of the fox or the fawn.

Dr. E. Rostrup[3] elaborates a theory that the τράγοι were the class of young men who had just undergone initiation at puberty, and were known by an animal name; and that the χοροὶ παίδων, τραγῳδία, and χοροὶ ἀνδρῶν were the performances of three age-groups (*Altersklassen*). But all the arguments that can be drawn from the Australian Bush, Central Africa, and other remote regions can prove nothing about Greek tragedy in default of all evidence from Greece itself.

Nilsson's conjecture that the worshippers of Dionysus, having slain the god in goat form in their mystic rites, dressed up in goatskins and lamented him, and that tragedy arose

the goat-men (whence their appearance on vases at this period), but without permanent success. But this view again is devoid of sufficient evidence. We do not know what Pratinas' satyrs were like, and the vases do not justify a belief in the supposed attempt.

[1] l. c., p. 468.

[2] This is the view of Nilsson, *Neue Jahrb.* xxvii, pp. 687-8, and of Reisch himself in Pauly-W., *Real-Enc.* iii, col. 2385, s. v. Chor.

[3] *Attic Tragedy in the Light of Theatrical History.*

from these lamentations (together with certain other elements), suffers from the same defect as some other theories—that there is no record of any mystic rites of Dionysus in which this happened. In some orgiastic rites various animals, including the goat, were dismembered, but there is no trace of lamentation in connexion with these; and the goatskin was only one of various animal skins which might be worn by the participants in such orgies.

Sir William Ridgeway [1] thinks that tragedy was performed by persons who wore goatskins because these were an ancient costume which was retained in celebrating ancient heroes such as Adrastus (Herodotus' expression τραγικοὶ χοροί being interpreted as 'goat-choruses'). He tells us that 'in Peloponnesus, as well as elsewhere in Greece, and in Thrace and Crete, goatskins were the ordinary dress of the Aborigines', and that for this reason the chorus which celebrated the ancient heroes, such as Adrastus, wore the primeval dress of goatskin and was therefore fitly termed a 'goat-chorus'. The natural answer to this has been admirably expressed by Dr. Farnell.[2] 'At what time in Greece, since 1400 B.C., were goatskins the universal garb? They were not worn by the well-to-do of the age of King Minos or Agamemnon or of any of the periods of archaic art. Nor do we find actors of other races, when they wish to act the great men of old, deliberately arraying themselves in the poorest and vilest garb that may indeed have been worn by the humblest subject of King Atreus, as it is still worn by the poor Arcadian or poor Sicilian.' (Prof. Ridgeway himself says that the goatskin was 'simply regarded as the meanest form of apparel that could be worn by a slave'.) 'Primitive actors,' Dr. Farnell adds, 'acting heroic parts endeavour to dress in some conventionally heroic costumes.'

Dr. Farnell's own theory requires far more serious consideration.[3] He naturally looks for some early stages of tragedy

[1] *Orig. of Trag.*, pp. 87, 91–2.
[2] *Hermath.* xvii, p. 15.
[3] *J. H. S.* xxix (1909), p. xlvii; *Cults*, v, pp. 234 ff.; *Hermath.* xvii, pp. 21 ff.

(which was part of the worship of Dionysus of Eleutherae, after that god was introduced into Attica) to Eleutherae itself, and there he finds evidence of a ritual duel between Xanthos and Melanthos, 'fair man and black man', which (following Usener) he interprets with great probability as 'a special form of the old-world ritual fight between winter and summer or spring'. In the story of this fight Dionysus Μελαναιγίς, the god of the black goatskin,—i. e., according to the most probable interpretation, the god of the nether world,—aids Melanthos to kill Xanthos. (With this he compares the Macedonian spring-purification investigated by Usener,[1] called τὰ Ξανδικά, and celebrated in honour of a hero called Xanthos.[2]) 'This play,' he continues, 'spreading through the villages of Greece, would easily acquire variety of motives; for many villages had their local legends of some one who perished in the service of Dionysus, and who had come to be regarded as the ancestral priest-leader of the clan; he would take the part of Xanthos or Melanthos as required: and thus early tragedy could easily appear as in some sense a commemorative dirge of the heroic dead, and acquire that dirge-like character which is deeply imprinted on its earlier forms. Certainly the village of Ikaria, the reputed home of Thespis, possessed an excellent motive for primitive tragedy in the sad death of Ikarios and Erigone; and actors who had reached the point of dramatizing such stories as these would soon feel equal to any heroic subject of the sorrowful kind. At that point the necessities of the stage would compel them to drop the goatskin. Yet they might continue to be called τράγοι or τραγῳδοί, just as the girls at Brauron were called "bears" long after they had discarded the bear-skin.'

---

[1] Arch. f. Religionswiss., 1904, pp. 303 ff.

[2] The other legend about Dionysus Μελαναιγίς—that in which he maddens the daughters of Eleuther—has no immediate bearing on the present subject (Suid. s. v. Μελαναιγίς). The story of the fight of Xanthos and Melanthos is found in Schol. Aristoph. Ach. 146, and Schol. Plat. Symp., p. 208 d. Dr. A. B. Keith (J. Asiatic Soc., 1912, and Sanskrit Drama, p. 37) describes a very similar duel from India—a ritual slaying by black-man, or winter, of red-man, or summer.

M

There can really be no doubt that Dr. Farnell has correctly interpreted the Melanaegis story in itself; and his reply to Sir William Ridgeway's criticisms is so far entirely convincing.[1] But the proof that tragedy originated from this particular mumming at Eleutherae is not so satisfying. The principal difficulties appear to be these :

(1) The identification of the Dionysus Eleuthereus of the Attic theatre with the Dionysus Μελαναιγίς of the mumming at Eleutherae is not quite made out. A god might be worshipped in the same place under various names and with different rituals on different occasions. No doubt the Dionysus of the theatre was brought to Athens from Eleutherae; but was it in the form of Μελαναιγίς, and with that particular ritual? And if the first tragedy in honour of Dionysus Eleuthereus actually came from Icaria, there is the further difficulty that we know nothing of the worship of Dionysus in goatskins, or of Dionysus Μελαναιγίς at all, at Icaria. Dr. Farnell's account of the spread of the Μελαναιγίς play to Icaria (and other villages) is not of course at all impossible, but it is only conjectural.

(2) The one thing which appears to be tolerably certain about the earliest Attic tragedy is that it was mainly a choral performance. There could be no ἀγών without actors; and the first actor was introduced by Thespis, the second by Aeschylus. But the mumming at Eleutherae involves three actors and no chorus, and is all ἀγών. Even if there were bystanders included in the mumming (spectators in, and not merely of, the drama) there is no hint that they wore goat-skins—or indeed that Xanthos and Melanthos themselves did so. If there was a play in honour of Dionysus at Icaria, presenting or relating the deaths of Icarius and Erigone and performing a dance round the slain goat, there *would* have been a chorus there; and it is quite possible that the primitive tragedy of Thespis was based on some such choral dance; but in that story we find no hint of goatskin dresses worn by the dancers or of their being called τράγοι, and we have seen [2]

[1] *Hermathena*, l. c. Cf. also Nilsson, *Neue Jahrb.* xxvii, pp. 674 ff., 686 ff., and Wilamowitz, *Neue Jahrb.* xxix, pp. 472-3.   [2] p. 103.

that the bearing of the Icarian story on the origins of tragedy
is very uncertain.

It thus appears to be very difficult to accept the derivation
of tragedy from the worship of Dionysus Μελαναιγίς at
Eleutherae. But there can be little doubt that it was *some*
rustic performance—only a performance mainly choral—which
Thespis brought to Athens, and which was there rapidly
developed by the addition of actors and the infusion of high
literary quality into the lyric portions, probably under the
influence of Peloponnesian choral lyric and of the contemporary
cyclic dithyramb.

§ 4. The interpretation of τραγῳδία as the song of men in
goatskins has been thought to derive some support from the
modern performances at Viza in Thrace, described by Professor
R. M. Dawkins.[1] Some parts of the drama enacted are very
like several ancient Greek ceremonies—a φαλλοφορία and a
λικνοφορία, for instance; there is a ritual slaying and a resurrection, with some of the familiar features of agrarian magic; and
it has been suggested that we have here a dramatic ritual,
connected possibly long ago with the worship of Dionysus in
Thrace itself, his early home, and surviving almost unchanged
into modern times; and that it is ritual of just the kind which
(apart from the comparative unimportance of the 'chorus')
might be supposed to have given rise to Greek Tragedy.
Similar performances are recorded from Scyros, from Thessaly,
from Sochos in Macedonia, from Kosti on the Black Sea and
from other places, by various observers.[2] But as regards the
point which here concerns us, the fact that the performers at
Viza wore goatskins, it must be pointed out[3] that earlier
observers saw the performance conducted by men who wore
skins of the fox, the wolf, and the fawn. Any of these
animals would afford an easy means of 'dressing up', but the

---

[1] *J. H. S.* xxvi (1906), pp. 191 ff.

[2] Lawson, *Ann. B. S. A.* vi. 135 ff.; Dawkins, ibid. xi. 72 ff.; M.
Hamilton, *Greek Saints*, p. 205; Von Hahn, *Albanesische Studien*, i. 156;
cf. also Nilsson, *Neue Jahrb.* xxvii. 677 ff.; Ridgeway, *Origin of Tragedy*,
pp. 20 ff.; Headlam and Knox, *Herodas*, p. lv.

[3] This is also noticed by Ridgeway, *Dramas*, &c., p. 20.

goat would generally be the easiest to catch. (In the same
way the satyrs of the Athenian stage,[1] though keeping their
horses' tails and ears, might wear the skins of various animals.)
One feature of these modern rites, the procession, going round
and collecting gifts, has perhaps more affinity with the
primitive κῶμοι with which the origin of comedy may be
connected [2] than with anything tragic.

Whether or not these modern plays are really a survival of
primitive Dionysiac worship is a difficult question. Now that
a good many of them are known, it is less easy than it was to
refer them all to one primitive type; parts of them are
parodies of Christian ceremonial; and there is a certain improbability in the supposition of an unbroken continuity
extending over more than two thousand years.[3] But there
can be little doubt that the plays spring from a basis of rustic
ideas of very much the same kind as those which must have
promoted agrarian ritual, more or less dramatic and probably
leading up to the drama, in primitive times; and they have
therefore some interest as illustrations for classical scholars,
though they do not justify the suggested interpretation of the
word τραγῳδοί.

§ 5. If τραγῳδοί does not mean singers dressed as goats or
in goatskins, what does it mean? It may be pointed out
first [4] that, if it did bear this meaning, it would be an exception
among the compounds of ᾠδή, in which the first part of the
compound generally refers to the accompaniment or the
occasion or subject of the song. This is the case with αὐλῳδός,
κιθαρῳδός, κωμῳδός, μελῳδός. If τρυγῳδός is not a parody-
word (and therefore not to be too minutely scrutinized), it may

---

[1] See above, p. 153.   [2] See below, p. 248–250.

[3] Perhaps too much stress may be laid on this. Nilsson (l. c.) makes
out a strong case for believing that the festival of the Rosalia, as celebrated in spring in parts of the Balkan peninsula down to the present day,
is a real survival of an ancient Dionysiac festival. In this case also the
resemblance to a primitive κῶμος, of which an ἀγών formed a part, is more
striking than any resemblance to tragedy.

[4] Reisch, l. c., p. 467, presents the argument briefly and clearly, and
(though I had arrived independently at the same conclusions) I have only
added a few small points.

mean the 'singer at the vintage', just as well as the 'singer stained with wine-lees'; μονῳδός really refers to the circumstances of the song, not to the personality of the singer; ῥαψῳδός does not mean that the singer was 'a thing of shreds and patches'; and τραγῳδός may well mean (as has often been held) the 'singer at the goat-sacrifice' or (a very ancient view) the 'singer for the goat-prize'.[1] The first of these two interpretations is to some extent supported by the line of Eratosthenes, Ἰκάριοι τόθι πρῶτα περὶ τράγον ὠρχήσαντο, for, whether the immediate reference is to a 'tragic' performance, or (as is more probable) to ἀσκωλιασμός only, the story at least records a dance around a slain goat. The second is supported by the tradition that Thespis won a goat as a prize. The two may even be reconciled, if the goat was first won and then sacrificed. A more precise conclusion is impossible. (There is no record showing that a goat-sacrifice formed part of the Great Dionysia, though it may well have been a feature of the rustic festivities of Attic villages.) But either of these solutions appears to be better than those which make 'goat-singers' = 'singers celebrating the goat-god', τράγον ᾄδοντες, though this is not impossible: or (as Frickenhaus suggests) [2] 'singers (i. e. the satyr-chorus) to the accompaniment of the goat flute-player Silenus'. The latter solution breaks down, if tragedy was not derived from the satyr-chorus; and Frickenhaus' theory that Silenus was originally conceived of as goat-like seems to be quite contrary to such evidence as there is; he only acquired the more caprine attributes which differentiated him from the satyrs at a comparatively late date.

§ 6. The result of the discussion up to this point is that the conventional theory that Attic Tragedy originated from Satyric play is not proved; and that Tragedy much more probably grew out of the fusion of the rustic, but non-satyric, plays of Thespis with the choral lyric of the Dorian peoples. The attempt to go

---

[1] Euseb. *Chron.* Ol. 47. 2 τοῖς ἀγωνιζομένοις παρ᾽ Ἕλλησι τράγος ἐδίδοτο, ἀφ᾽ οὗ καὶ τραγικοὶ ἐκλήθησαν (Jerome: 'his temporibus certantibus in agone [de voce] tragus, id est hircus, praemio dabatur, unde aiunt tragoedos nuncupatos'). See above, p. 98.

[2] *Jahrb. Arch. Inst.* xxxii, p. 11.

behind Thespis can hardly succeed, with our present information; but it is very probable indeed that the themes of Tragedy became more and more varied by the inclusion, first, of the various Dionysiac legends—those of Lycurgus and Pentheus, for instance, as well as local Attic stories, such as those of Icarius, Eleuther, &c.—and then of stories which were wholly or in part οὐδὲν πρὸς τὸν Διόνυσον; and that rude plays on many subjects (perhaps mostly, but not exclusively, Dionysiac) were already being acted in Attic villages in the time of Thespis, and suggested subjects to himself. (The ease with which ritual or religious acting passes from its proper business to other themes is illustrated by the performances of the Mexican dancers described by Preuss,[1] and by the growth of the English mystery-play into a drama independent of religious subjects.[2]) The details of the early expansion of tragedy cannot be traced, nor can we tell in what particular way such stories may have been treated by a chorus with an ἐξάρχων or with a single actor; and we have at present to be content with a general view of the main lines of development.

IX

Οὐδὲν πρὸς τὸν Διόνυσον.

We have, however, to dispose of certain notices in regard to the proverb Οὐδὲν πρὸς τὸν Διόνυσον, which are supposed to support the derivation of tragedy from satyric drama.

Plut. *Symp. quaest.* i. i, § 5 ὥσπερ οὖν Φρυνίχου καὶ Αἰσχύλου τὴν τραγῳδίαν εἰς μύθους καὶ πάθη προαγόντων ἐλέχθη, τί ταῦτα πρὸς τὸν Διόνυσον; οὕτως ἔμοιγε . . .

It has already been pointed out[3] that if Plutarch intends to imply that the plays of Thespis were not tragic in subject, he can hardly be right, at least if the story of Pentheus was one

---

[1] *Neue Jahrb.* xvii (1906).

[2] Cf. Chambers, *Mediaeval Stage*, i, pp. 202–3; ii, pp. 33, 55, 70 ff., 90, 131 ff., for illustrations of the ways in which the range of characters presented in early drama may expand.

[3] See above, p. 117.

of his subjects. This passage at any rate gives no ground for
thinking that Thespis wrote satyr-plays.

Zenobius, v. 40. Οὐδὲν πρὸς τὸν Διόνυσον. Ἐπειδὴ τῶν
χορῶν ἐξ ἀρχῆς εἰθισμένων διθύραμβον ᾄδειν εἰς τὸν Διόνυσον,
οἱ ποιηταὶ ὕστερον ἐκβάντες τὴν συνήθειαν ταύτην Αἴαντας καὶ
Κενταύρους γράφειν ἐπεχείρησαν. ὅθεν οἱ θεώμενοι σκώπτοντες
ἔλεγον, Οὐδὲν πρὸς Διόνυσον. διὰ γοῦν τοῦτο τοὺς Σατύρους
ὕστερον ἔδοξεν αὐτοῖς προεισάγειν, ἵνα μὴ δοκῶσιν ἐπιλανθάνε-
σθαι τοῦ θεοῦ.

This notice seems to be a confused mixture of several
different reminiscences or traditions. (1) The Aristotelian
doctrine that tragedy was derived from dithyramb; (2) the
tradition, doubtless sound, that dithyramb and tragedy were
first occupied with Dionysiac subjects, and afterwards widened
their range;[1] (3) the theory, probably based on Aristotle,
Poetics iv, that the early Dionysiac tragedy was performed
by a satyr-chorus; (4) the change made in the Dionysiac
festival in the fourth century, when each poet, instead of producing three tragedies and a satyric play, produced tragedies
only, and *one* satyric play only was performed at the *beginning*
of the proceedings (whence προεισάγειν). Plainly this notice
is too frail a support for any theory; it certainly does not
support the theory under discussion.

Suidas s. v. Οὐδὲν πρὸς τὸν Διόνυσον. Ἐπιγένους τοῦ
Σικυωνίου τραγῳδίαν εἰς τὸν Διόνυσον ποιήσαντος, ἐπεφώνησάν
τινες τοῦτο. ὅθεν ἡ παροιμία. βέλτιον δὲ οὕτως. τὸ πρόσθεν
εἰς τὸν Διόνυσον γράφοντες τούτοις ἠγωνίζοντο, ἅπερ καὶ
σατυρικὰ ἐλέγετο. ὕστερον δὲ μεταβάντες εἰς τὸ τραγῳδίας
γράφειν, κατὰ μικρὸν εἰς μύθους καὶ ἱστορίας ἐτράπησαν, μηκέτι
τοῦ Διονύσου μνημονεύοντες. ὅθεν τοῦτο καὶ ἐπεφώνησαν. καὶ
Χαμαιλέων ἐν τῷ περὶ Θέσπιδος τὰ παραπλήσια ἱστορεῖ.

The first explanation offered appears to mean that Epigenes

---

[1] Κενταύρους may perhaps refer to the Κένταυροι of Lasus, if, as we have
seen to be probable, he wrote a dithyramb of the name. The reading
Αἴαντας has been suspected of being a corruption of Γίγαντας: but
Timotheus wrote a dithyramb entitled Αἴας ἐμμανής, and other composers
may have written about the same hero before him, or the reference may
be to tragedies.

wrote tragedy in honour of (εἰς) Dionysus—probably under the auspices of Cleisthenes—but not with reference to (πρός) Dionysiac legend; and this may be true; but it does not bear upon our present point.[1]

The second explanation seems to be based upon Aristotle's *Poetics*; Aristotle had said that the beginnings of tragedy were 'satyric', whatever he may have meant by the word; and he had laid stress upon the introduction of actors, which made μῦθοι possible. It was evidently assumed by the writers of this notice that 'satyric' could only refer to the satyric drama, which was of course Dionysiac. But we have seen that Aristotle was probably only indulging in conjecture when he derived tragedy (if he did so) from satyric drama; and Suidas (whose notice is taken almost *verbatim* from Photius) cannot carry more weight than Aristotle, his probable ultimate source; nor have we any reason to suppose that Chamaeleon, the pupil of Aristotle, was better informed than his master. (How much is covered by παραπλήσια it is impossible to say.)

In fact, what is plain from these notices is that nobody knew exactly what the real origin of the proverb was. That it arose out of the introduction of non-Dionysiac themes into performances in honour of Dionysus was agreed; but whether this was the work of Epigenes, Thespis, Phrynichus, or Aeschylus was plainly disputed; we have to do, not with history, but with guess-work,[2] and guess-work which, by making satyric drama the predecessor of tragedy (whether at Sicyon or at Athens), ignores the much more probable tradition (recorded also by Suidas) that it was Pratinas (many years after the appearance of Thespis) who πρῶτος ἔγραψε σατύρους.

---

[1] Flickinger (*Greek Theater*, p. 13) thinks that Epigenes may have written plays εἰς Διόνυσον without introducing the satyrs whom his audience would expect to find with Dionysus; this is of course only a conjecture, and perhaps not a very probable account of the origin of the proverb, but it is at least as good as those of the old *grammatici*. (See above, p. 138.)

[2] A different set of guesses is recorded by Plutarch, *de prov. Alex.*, § 30. (See above, p. 105.)

X

Special problems about Satyrs and Dionysus.

Before we dismiss the satyrs, and the theory of tragedy as the song of the goat-men, there are some minor points in connexion with them which may be briefly discussed.

§ 1. It has been assumed in the preceding pages that the satyrs and sileni were imaginary creatures of the wilds, generically akin to the centaurs and other similar beings found, in varying shapes, in the mythology or folk-lore of most Indo-Germanic peoples, and existing in the imagination of Greek peasants even down to the present day.[1] In the Vedic poems we find the Ghandarvas, who like the satyrs and their kinsmen the centaurs,[2] were drinkers of wine and lovers of the nymphs; they are, moreover, closely associated with Shiva, who is in many respects the counterpart of Dionysus; and they are as 'impossibly-behaved'—to borrow Professor Murray's happy rendering of ἀμηχανοεργοί—as the satyrs. It has already been mentioned that the folk-lore of Sweden, Russia, Germany, and other countries is familiar with similiar beings.[3] This is not the place to discuss these parallels in detail; they are mentioned in order to lay stress on the wide prevalence of these fancies, and the inadequacy of any theory about them which is confined to Greece alone, to the exclusion of other Indo-Germanic peoples.

It is therefore necessary to reject the interesting suggestion

[1] See Lawson's *Modern Greek Folk-lore*, pp. 190 ff., for an account of the Καλλικάντζαροι, who resemble the Ghandarvas down to minute details. It is disputed whether there is any etymological connexion between Ghandarvas and Κένταυροι, and also whether the Καλλικάντζαροι are a product of the native Greek mind. (See Rose, *Primitive Culture in Greece*, p. 46, for a brief statement of the view that they are of Slavonic rather than Greek origin. Mr. E. H. Sturtevant, *Class. Philol.*, 1926, p. 239, makes Κένταυρος a Thracian word, equivalent in sense to Φίλιππος.)

[2] The close relationship of the satyrs and the centaurs is well illustrated in Miss J. E. Harrison's *Prolegomena*, pp. 380 ff., though I cannot agree with some of her interpretations.

[3] See Kühner in Roscher's Lexicon, iv, pp. 513 ff.

of Leake,[1] revived by Sir William Ridgeway,[2] that the
Σάτυροι were simply the Satrae, a wild Thracian tribe devoted
to Dionysus, represented in the light in which their more
civilized Greek neighbours regarded their half-bestial ways.
This theory does not account for the existence of similar
creatures in the beliefs of other peoples, where we can find no
such conveniently named tribe by which to explain them;
and it may be added that if the satyrs were originally only
a human tribe which worshipped Dionysus, their 'supernatural' character is not explained.

§ 2. We must also dismiss the theory, favoured by Dieterich[3]
and others, that the satyrs were really ancestor-ghosts.
Dieterich supposes that there was, to begin with, a dance
of satyrs about the car of Dionysus at the Anthesteria,[4] one
day of which was devoted to the placation of the dead, while
Dionysus had the main part in the three days' celebration.
This dance, he supposes, was made into a work of art, and
freed from its association with the particular cult, by Thespis;[5]
and into the tragedy, the song of the goat-men, thus established, another feature of the Anthesteria, viz. the public
lamentation for the dead, the θρῆνος, also found its way; and
finally the whole was transferred by the tyrants to the newly
established festival, the Great Dionysia. The satyrs, he supposes, represented the spirits of the dead, who surrounded
Dionysus in his chthonic aspect. The identification of the
satyrs with the spirits of the dead is supposed to be justified
by the fact that on certain vases (and especially on one to
which Dieterich particularly refers[6]) the ἄνοδος, or resurrection from the ground of Kore, or of the earth-spirit, is represented as accompanied by dancing satyrs, surrounding the
rising goddess.

---

[1] *Travels in Northern Greece*, iii. 190.

[2] *Origin of Trag.*, pp. 12 ff., 50.

[3] *Arch. f. Rel.* xi (1908), pp. 163 ff.   [4] See above, p. 115.

[5] It has already been noticed (p. 112) that there is no evidence for the
attribution of a satyr-chorus to Thespis.

[6] Some of these vases are figured by Miss Harrison, *Proleg.*, pp. 277,
278, 640; *Themis*, pp. 419, 422.

But (1) there is not a particle of evidence to support the
idea that satyrs, or similar creatures imagined by any primitive people, ever represented the spirits of the dead. It is
hard to imagine a frame of mind in civilized or uncivilized
man, which would lead him to represent his forefathers in a
monstrous (and commonly ithyphallic) shape, with the limbs of
horses or goats. (Both forms appear on the vases on which
the ἄνοδος is depicted; but those which surround the car of
Dionysus are uniformly horse-demons, not τράγοι, and this is
not favourable to Dieterich's theory.) The satyrs dancing
round Kore surely represent simply the joy of wild nature at
her return.[1]

(2) There is not the least proof that these vases have anything to do with the Anthesteria, or represent any actual
ritual or performance.[2] The painters may well have been
exercising their imagination.

(3) There is no evidence to show that any dramatic performance was connected with the Anthesteria at Athens, with
the possible exception of the ἀγῶνες χύτρινοι—only recorded
at a very late period, and quite probably not dramatic at all,
though in some way concerned with the selection of comic
actors: still less is there evidence that the Anthesteria included
a public θρῆνος for the dead.[3] In fact the business of the last
day of the festival (Χύτροι) was not, so far as we know, one of
lamentation at all. It is still worse for the theory that the
celebrations of that day had nothing to do with Dionysus as
lord of souls, but with Hermes, the conductor of the dead;[4]
and this makes their supposed transference to the Great

---

[1] A somewhat different view of these vases is taken by Miss Harrison,
Essays and Studies presented to Wm. Ridgeway, pp. 136 ff.; but as it has
no bearing on tragedy, I do not discuss it here.

[2] Comp. a nearly allied group of vases, representing the ἄνοδος of
Dionysus and Semele (Farnell, *Cults*, v, p. 246), which hardly admits of
a ritual interpretation.

[3] See Farnell, *Cults*, v, p. 219; Haigh, *Att. Theat.*[3], p. 31. The day was
one of 'tendance' of the dead, rather than of lamentation.

[4] See Nilsson, *Stud. de Dionysiis Atticis*, p. 131. The word Διονύσῳ in
Schol. ad Aristoph. *Ach.* 1076, and in Suidas, s. v., Χύτροι appears to be
an interpolation.

Dionysia even more difficult to accept than it would have been in any case.[1]

§ 3. Too much has probably been made by some scholars of the parallel drawn by Strabo between the satyrs and the Κουρῆτες who attended upon the infant Zeus. Hesiod indeed ascribes to them the same ancestors;[2] but Hesiod's genealogies are an obviously artificial construction; it would be natural enough to couple together the two sets of 'sportive dancers'; and, in fact, all that Strabo himself does[3] is to compare the relation of the Κουρῆτες to the infant Zeus with that of the satyrs to Dionysus. After discussing at length the records of the Κουρῆτες as primitive inhabitants of Aetolia, he passes to the mythological Κουρῆτες in the following words: τὰ δ' ἀπωτέρω τῆς ὑποθέσεως ταύτης, ἄλλως δὲ διὰ τὴν ὁμωνυμίαν εἰς ταὐτὸν ὑπὸ τῶν ἱστορικῶν ἀγόμενα . . . ἐκείνων μὲν διαφέρει, ἔοικε δὲ μᾶλλον τῷ περὶ Σατύρων καὶ Σειληνῶν καὶ Βακχῶν καὶ Τιτύρων λόγῳ· τοιούτους γάρ τινας δαίμονας ἢ προπόλους θεῶν τοὺς Κουρῆτάς φασιν οἱ παραδόντες τὰ Κρητικὰ καὶ τὰ Φρύγια. The point is repeated later:[4] ὥστε οἱ Κουρῆτες ἤτοι διὰ τὸ νέοι καὶ κόροι ὄντες ὑπουργεῖν ἢ διὰ τὸ κουροτροφεῖν τὸν Δία (λέγεται γὰρ ἀμφοτέρως) ταύτης ἠξιώθησαν τῆς προσηγορίας, οἱονεὶ Σάτυροί τινες ὄντες περὶ τὸν Δία.

On the strength of this one point of contact—the service of Κουρῆτες and Σάτυροι as πρόπολοι to two different gods— it would be obviously wrong to infer that they were parallel in any other sense; and even if Miss Harrison is right in treating the Κουρῆτες as the representatives of the ancestors of the tribe, into whose company the κοῦροι were initiated—an interpretation which cannot but be held doubtful—it could not

---

[1] As Nilsson points out (*Neue Jahrb.* xxvii, p. 617 n.), it is no contradiction of the view here taken that in late times there was some ceremony or performance in the theatre at certain non-Attic Anthesteria, e. g. at Cyzicus in the third or second century B.C.; *C.I.G.* 3655, l. 20 (τοὺς δὲ πρυτάνεις στεφανῶσαι 'Απολλόδωρον τοῖς 'Ανθεστηρίοις ἐν τῷ θεάτρῳ). There is no hint of drama here, any more than in *C.I.G.* 3044, referring to the Anthesteria at Teos, circ. 470 B.C. (καθημένου τὠγῶνος 'Ανθεστηρίοισιν καὶ 'Ηρακλείοισιν καὶ Δίοισιν).

[2] See above, p. 151.   [3] x. vii, p. 466.

[4] x. xi, p. 468.

be legitimately argued that the satyrs also were to be regarded as ancestors.[1]

§ 4. The question whether Dionysus was ever thought of in the form of a goat, as well as of a bull, has been the subject of a controversy between Sir William Ridgeway[2] and Dr. Farnell.[3] The evidence collected by the latter in his *Cults of the Greek States*[4] really places beyond all doubt the fact that at a number of places Dionysus was so conceived, either on particular occasions, or as a regular object of worship,[5] and that the goat was offered to him as a sacrifice on certain occasions. (Sir William Ridgeway's statement that the goat was equally an offering made to heroes will not bear examination. It rests on the offering of a goat to Asclepius at Balagrae ; but, as Dr. Farnell points out,[6] Asclepius was very commonly worshipped as a god, and the other examples of goat-sacrifices to heroes are late and uncertain.)

It happens, indeed, that there is very little evidence of the goat as a sacrifice, or of Dionysus conceived as a goat, in connexion with the city Dionysia at Athens. There was certainly the sacrifice of a bull ; and Thespis, we are told, received the goat as a prize. This might have been a serious matter, if we were committed to the belief that τραγῳδία was the song of men dressed in goatskins as the worshippers of the goat-god. But we do not require either goat-men or goat-god to explain τραγῳδία, and in any case the name must be considerably anterior to the organization of the city Dionysia as known to us ; so that the controversy is not of great importance for the history of tragedy.

---

[1] If there is anything in the suggestion that the satyrs, attendant upon Dionysus, are parallel to the Ghandarvas in their relation to Shiva, then it is *pro tanto* likely that they were very distinct in popular belief from the Κουρῆτες, who resemble rather the Marûts, the armed dancers of Sanskrit mythology. Professor A. B. Keith (*Journ. R. Asiat. Soc.* 1909, p. 200) gives strong reasons against the view that the armed dancers in Indo-European mythology represented the souls of the dead at all.

[2] *Orig. of Trag.*, ch. ii.   [3] *Hermath.* xvii, pp. 22 ff.

[4] vol. v, pp. 165 ff., with the refs. given ; and pp. 303 ff.

[5] Cf. also A. B. Cook, *Zeus*, vol. i, pp. 672–77.

[6] *Hermath.* l. c., p. 16.

§ 5. It is impossible to trace in detail the route or routes by which the worship of Dionysus, with or without a dramatic or semi-dramatic ritual, reached Athens. Dionysus was certainly a god of the Thraco-Phrygian stock, and it is probable that he was worshipped both in Thrace [1] and in Asia Minor [2] long before he was received in Greece. His worship may have come to Greece by sea, by more than one route; and the tradition of the arrival of the god by sea persisted, as has been already noticed,[3] in Athenian art, ritual, and literature. But it may also have travelled from north overland; and there is little doubt that Delphi assisted its propagation. There are legends of his reception at Icaria, at Acharnae and at Eleutherae;[4] and while an elementary form of drama, probably at Icaria and very possibly in other Attic villages also, was the foundation of the tragedy of Thespis, the worship of the god in the Peloponnese (whither also it had travelled by unrecorded stages) contributed, in all probability, the higher lyric elements which found a place in tragedy, and also the satyr-play which was brought into Athens from Phlius. We do not know when the equine satyrs first came to be especially associated with Dionysus; probably they were originally independent of him and had existed from immemorial antiquity in the imagination of the primitive Greeks; but once attached to him, they remained his companions to the end.

XI

Further consideration of Sir William Ridgeway's theory.

It will be convenient at this point to complete our consideration of the theory that tragedy originated in hero-worship at the tomb, rather than in the worship of Dionysus, by noting

---

[1] e. g. by the Bessi, whom Herodotus especially mentions as his worshippers: cf. A. B. Cook, *Zeus*, vol. ii, pp. 268 ff., for a very interesting discussion, though I cannot follow Dr. Cook in all his conclusions.

[2] See above, ch. i, p.17 .   [3] See above, pp. 16, 115–16.

[4] Hyginus, II. iv ; Steph. Byz. s. v. Σημαχίδαι ; cf. Euseb. *Chron.* i, p. 30 ; Stat. *Theb.* xii. 623 and Schol. ; Philochorus, *ap.* Athen. ii, p. 38 c, and Paus. I. ii, § 5.

briefly such of the arguments used in support of that theory as have not already been discussed.

§ 1. Sir William Ridgeway bases an argument[1] upon certain stage properties mentioned by Pollux, iv. 123 καὶ σκηνὴ μὲν ὑποκριτῶν ἴδιον· ἡ δὲ ὀρχήστρα τοῦ χοροῦ, ἐν ᾗ καὶ ἡ θυμέλη, εἶτα βῆμά τι οὖσα, εἴτε βωμός. ἐπὶ δὲ τῆς σκηνῆς καὶ ἀγνιεὺς ἔκειτο βωμὸς πρὸ τῶν θυρῶν, καὶ τράπεζα πέμματα ἔχουσα, ἢ θεωρὶς ὠνομάζετο ἢ θυωρίς. ἔλεος δ' ἦν τράπεζα ἀρχαία, ἐφ' ἣν πρὸ Θέσπιδος εἶς τις ἀναβὰς τοῖς χορευταῖς ἀπεκρίνατο.

With this passage he compares the passage of the *Etymologicum magnum*: θυμέλη· ἡ τοῦ θεάτρου μεχρὶ νῦν ἀπὸ τῆς τραπέζης ὠνόμασται, παρὰ τὸ ἐπ' αὐτῆς τὰ θύη μερίζεσθαι, τούτεστι τὰ θυόμενα ἱερεῖα. τράπεζα δ' ἦν ἐφ' ἧς ἑστῶτες ἐν τοῖς ἀγροῖς ᾖδον μήπω τάξιν λαβούσης τῆς τραγῳδίας.

These notices appear to mean that in the orchestra stood the θυμέλη, and (perhaps beside it) a table for the cutting up of victims, used in very early times as a rude stage on which a member of the chorus conversed with the rest;[2] while on the stage stood an ἀγνιεύς-stone, with a table for offerings, in front of the palace which served as a back-scene. (Mr. A. Gow, in a learned discussion[3] of all the evidence with regard to the meaning of θυμέλη, is no doubt right in explaining the notice in the *Etymologicum magnum* as an attempt to account for the later use of θυμέλη as = 'stage' by identifying the θυμέλη with the ἐλεός.)

Sir William Ridgeway thinks that the ἀγνιεύς-stones which stood before house-doors 'were probably the grave-stones of ancient worthies'. This is absolutely contrary to all the evidence that exists about ἀγνιεύς-stones, which were the most primitive form of dedication to Apollo (dating from the aniconic period of his worship), and were placed before house-doors in order to claim the protection of the god. Yet from this mistaken interpretation of the ἀγνιεύς-stone Sir William Ridgeway argues that there has been a superimposition of the Dionysiac cult upon that of the dead; such an

---

[1] *Orig. of Trag.*, pp. 39 ff. [2] See above, pp. 118–120.
[3] *J. H. S.* xxxii (1912), pp. 213 ff.

argument plainly has no value. Dr. Farnell[1] has called attention to other mistakes in it, e.g. the assumption that the θεωρίς or θυωρίς on which fruit and cakes were offered would be more appropriate to heroes than to Dionysus. In any case there is no ground for regarding the ἀγυιεύς-stone in the theatre as primitive; it was a common property of house-fronts, and no doubt first appeared in the theatre when the palace-front became a regular or frequent back-scene—i. e. probably not till after the first third of the fifth century; and so it tells nothing of origins.

The θυμέλη, Sir William Ridgeway tells us, was originally the tomb of the hero, and only afterwards became the altar of Dionysus; and he thinks that the circular hole in the middle of the orchestra at Epidaurus and in the later Athenian orchestra may represent the βόθρος into which offerings to dead heroes were poured. Pollux cannot really help him here. The natural explanation of the words εἴτε βῆμά τι οὖσα εἴτε βωμός is surely that Pollux knew of the later use of θυμέλη for ' stage ', and also of its common use for ' altar ', and there-fore mentioned both. Sir William Ridgeway translates βωμός ' an altar or a tomb '; and it is true that in some late inscrip-tions on tombs, and also in some late epigrams in the Anthology [2] the word βωμός is applied to a tomb. But that the words βωμός and ' tomb ' were not really identical is indicated by such lines as

Αὐσόνιον δάπεδον, βωμός θ' ὅδε σῆμά τε κρύπτει [3]

and

τάφον τὸν ὄντα πλησίον, βωμόν θ' ἅμα,[4]

and βωμός is never applied to a tomb except in a context in which there is separate mention of the tomb. It is not there-fore likely that Pollux would use it to mean ' tomb ', where any reader would naturally understand it to refer to the use of θυμέλη as an altar. As to the holes in the orchestra,

---

[1] *Hermath.* xvii, pp. 12, 13.

[2] *Anth. Pal.*, App. 130, 262, 331; cf. Jacobs, *A. P.*, vol. iii, p. 922.

[3] Ep. 130.

[4] Ep. 331. In No. 262 the use of βωμός is more than half metaphorical, even if it applies to the tomb at all.

nothing definite is known—certainly not their date, which is not very early. There is at least a possibility that they were used to fix small altars in their place.[1]

Sir William Ridgeway attempts to support his view by the assertion that the 'tomb of Darius almost certainly forms the *thymele*'. There seems to be no justification for this assertion, though the question of the theatrical arrangements of Aeschylus' early period, and of the setting of the *Persae* in particular, is an extremely difficult one.[2] Nor can it help him to quote the words of the chorus in the *Choephoroe* (l. 106), αἰδουμένη σοι βωμὸν ὡς τύμβον πατρός, which only mean that the chorus held Agamemnon's tomb in as great reverence as if it were an altar. His statement[3] that the central object in the setting of the *Supplices* was a sepulchral mound is an assumption and nothing more. The dead are appealed to in l. 25, but so are the gods above (ll. 22, 24, &c.); and it is most unlikely that the dead had any share in the κοινοβωμία of the gods about which the play centres, or that the κοινοβωμία itself was planted on a tomb. χωρὶς ἡ τιμὴ θεῶν.

The result of Mr. Gow's exhaustive discussion is to show that the word θυμέλη is primarily equivalent to ἐσχάρα, a hearth or place of fire, rather than to βωμός, which implies a raised structure;[4] though θυμέλη came to be used also of βωμοί properly so called, from the mere fact of their upper surface being a θυμέλη in the strict sense. The word was certainly applied to the altar of Dionysus in the theatre; and Mr. Gow suggests that there may have been a special reason for this, because some of the ceremonies preceding the theatrical contests at the City Dionysia brought Dionysus Eleuthereus into special connexion with an ἐσχάρα, from which the Ephebi escorted his image into the theatre.[5] He conjectures that the

---

[1] See Haigh, *Attic Theatre*[3], p. 108. Petersen, *Die attische Tragödie*, p. 547, can hardly be right in denying that the orchestra contained an altar at all: but it would take too long to discuss this here.

[2] I hope to recur to this at a later date.   [3] l. c., p. 128.

[4] Cf. Pearson's note on Sophocles, Fragm. 38.

[5] *C. I. A.* ii. 470 εἰσήγαγον δὲ καὶ τὸν Διόνυσον ἀπὸ τῆς ἐσχάρας θύσαντες τῷ θεῷ: and 471 εἰσήγαγον δὲ καὶ τὸν Διόνυσον ἀπὸ τῆς ἐσχάρας εἰς τὸ θέατρον μετὰ φωτός.

altar of Dionysus in the theatre itself may originally have been an ἐσχάρα and not a βωμός. If so, this would lend some support to the idea that at the City Dionysia there was some consciousness of the chthonic aspect of Dionysus, though this could not be regarded as certain, since ἐσχάραι were not confined to chthonic powers.[1] But it could certainly not be taken to show that Dionysus himself was once a ἥρως, or that his cult was superimposed upon that of a ἥρως. It must be added that there is no evidence that the altar of Dionysus in the theatre was ever actually called an ἐσχάρα.

§ 2. The most impressive evidence in favour of the origin of tragedy in hero-worship consists in the occurrence in many plays of scenes in which a tomb-ritual is enacted, or a solemn lamentation performed; and to these must be added a few scenes in which the ghosts of the dead appear. These latter scenes are so few that in any case not much stress can be laid upon them—we have the shade of Darius in Aeschylus' *Persae*; the ghost of Clytemnestra hounding on the Furies in the *Eumenides*; the ghost of Polydorus in Euripides' *Hecuba*; and the ghost of Achilles in the lost *Polyxena* of Sophocles.[2] The imagination of the poet was certainly equal to the invention of such scenes, without the assistance of any grave-ritual; we have no independent evidence of dramatic grave-ritual in Greece in which the spirit of the deceased appeared as a character; and in the *Eumenides* and (so far as can be seen) in the *Polyxena* the appearance of the shade does not take place in response to, or in connexion with, any grave-ritual.

Apart from these appearances of ghosts, there are certainly plays in which a heroic tomb or a grave-ritual are prominent, either in the body of the play itself, as in the *Persae*, the *Choephoroe* and the *Oedipus Coloneus*, or else in the prologue or epilogue, which, nominally prophesying the origin and institution of such ritual, may sometimes, it is said, imply the actual performance of ritual in which the story of the play was dramatically presented. Such ritual, it is argued, is

---

[1] See Mr. Gow's note, l. c., p. 238.

[2] See Pearson's edition of Sophocles' Fragments, vol. ii, p. 163.

indicated in the *Helena*, in which the tomb of Proteus plays
a prominent part; in the *Hecuba*, in which Polyxena is sacrificed at the tomb of Achilles, and in the *Rhesus*: while the
lamentations for the deaths of heroes in many plays are
supposed to carry with them the same implication, that hero-
worship at the tomb was the origin of tragedy. Such plays
are the *Septem contra Thebas* and the *Choephoroe* of Aeschylus,
and many plays of Euripides,—the *Supplices*, *Andromache*,
Troades, and *Phoenissae*; together with some which have
a θρῆνος of less regular form—the *Alcestis* (in which the
farewell of the chorus to the heroine is so treated), the *Hippolytus* and the *Iphigeneia in Tauris* (in which funeral rites
are prepared for Orestes). It will be best to defer the special
consideration of these plays until we discuss the much more
carefully reasoned theory of Professor Murray, which has
some points in common with that which is now criticized, and
raises the whole question of the aetiological significance of
tragedy in a fresh form. For the present it is sufficient to
say that no such tomb-ritual can be shown to be implied in
nearly all the extant plays (nor even in some of those mentioned) without great straining of the evidence; and that as the
stories selected by tragic poets are generally stories of disaster
and death, no ritual explanation is needed to explain the
occurrence of lamentations and scenes at the tomb. What is
valuable in the theory is simply the recognition that such
scenes of mourning naturally took their form from the kind
of mourning which was in vogue in contemporary Greek life
or in the heroic age as recorded in Homer.[1] No more than
this is required to explain the κομμός and other forms of
lamentation; and the adoption in the plays of those forms of
mourning with which the Greeks were familiar—for why
should any other have been adopted?—does not prove that the
Greek drama was not Dionysiac in origin. It must be repeated that there is no evidence which will bear inspection
that the stories of the deaths of heroes were dramatically
acted at their graves, though certain ritual θρῆνοι are known

---

[1] See above, pp. 19, 123, 124.

to have been performed.[1] Tragedy no doubt did, though
originally Dionysiac, borrow many of its themes from local
hero-stories, but the particular kind of ritual from which
tragedy is stated by Sir William Ridgeway to have sprung,
exists only in his imagination.

§ 3. It will be convenient to interpolate here a note upon
some suggestions made by Dieterich [2] upon the origin of
tragedy, because they also aim at explaining the persistence of θρῆνοι in the plays. His attempt to trace these θρῆνοι
to a public lamentation at the Anthesteria has already
been discussed.[3] He further suggests that the θρῆνοι or
κομμοί of tragedy may have been modelled, if not on any
public mourning for the dead, at least on the mourning for
Kore at the time of the Eleusinian mysteries. But we know
nothing of the nature of this mourning, nor whether it had any
regular or artistic form at all; and Dieterich's conjecture cannot really derive much support from the fact that Aeschylus was
profoundly influenced in his religious attitude by the mysteries,
and was accused of revealing them in his plays. (The alleged
adoption by Aeschylus of the dress of the Eleusinian hierophant for his principal actor is a point which requires separate
discussion; but it does not carry with it any conclusions as to
the κομμοί.) It must again be said that the existence of θρῆνοι
in a tragedy needs no explanation, and that the form of them
is to be explained from Homer and from Greek funeral
customs generally.[4]

§ 4. Sir William Ridgeway supports his case for his theory
that Greek tragedy arose among the tombs by an impressive
array of descriptions of dramatic ceremonies in honour of the
dead from all over the world. In regard to these it is almost

---

[1] See above, pp. 139–40. These also may well have followed the conventional type of mourning.

[2] *Arch. f. Rel.*, 1908, pp. 181 ff.

[3] Above, p. 170.

[4] For the existence of a more or less stereotyped form of mourning in
actual Greek life, cf. Nilsson, *Neue Jahrb.* xxvii (1911), pp. 622 ff. He
quotes especially Plut. *Vit. Solon.* 21 and Plato, *Laws* xii. 947 c. He
notices (p. 619) the continuance of what is practically the Homeric form
of mourning down to the present day in Greece.

enough to refer to the comments of Nilsson (l. c.) and Farnell.[1]
It is probable that Sir William Ridgeway has misinterpreted
some of these ceremonies; but even if his interpretations were
all well-founded, they would prove nothing whatever about
Greek tragedy. Before parallels can be drawn, the things to
be compared must be separately substantiated; and we cannot
infer from ceremonies belonging to all grades of culture among
distant and unrelated peoples, and on the ground of resemblances which when investigated are very slight, that the
ceremonies of the Greeks are to be similarly explained. At
most, such parallels can be used to lend a general probability
to an explanation for which the other grounds are very strong;
and it is just these other grounds which we have seen to be
fatally weak. Accordingly, interesting as Sir William Ridgeway's compilation is, it really contributes nothing to the
solution of our present problems.[2]

§ 5. In the *Cambridge University Reporter* for 21 April,
1925, there appears a summary of a paper by Sir William
Ridgeway on ' Euripides in Macedon '. The main contention
of the paper appears to be that the *Archelaus, Bacchae,* and
Rhesus were performed at Aegae, at a festival in honour of
the deceased Macedonian kings who were buried there, and
not in honour of Dionysus.

That the *Archelaus may* have been performed at Aegae
cannot be denied, because there is no evidence to show where
it was performed. But although it is certain that Aegae
possessed a theatre (in which Philip was murdered) it was not
the only theatre in Macedonia, and it is beyond dispute that
Dium also was the scene of dramatic performances. Sir William
Ridgeway speaks of Dium ' as a most unlikely place to hold
a dramatic festival '. It does not appear why he thinks so;
but it is remarkable that among the most striking ruins of
the town are the remains of a very fine theatre. There is a
conflict of authority as to the place at which the games and
dramatic contests were held on Alexander's return from

---

[1] *Hermathena*, l. c.

[2] The same must be said of the work of Dr. E. Rostrup, *Attic Tragedy
in the Light of Theatrical History*, in so far as it follows the same method.

Greece : Diodorus [1] says they were held at Dium, Arrian,[2] at
Aegae. Now if Dium were ' a most unlikely place ' for such
contests, it would hardly have been mentioned as the scene of
them at all, unless they had really been held there : but a study
of Diodorus' actual words suggests that it was not really an
unlikely place, since Archelaus himself had instituted a
dramatic festival there : [3] διδάξας οὖν αὐτοὺς περὶ τοῦ συμφέρον-
τος καὶ παρορμήσας διὰ τῶν λόγων πρὸς τοὺς ἀγῶνας, θυσίας
μεγαλοπρεπεῖς τοῖς θεοῖς συνετέλεσεν ἐν Δίῳ τῆς Μακεδονίας,
καὶ σκηνικοὺς ἀγῶνας Διὶ καὶ Μούσαις, οὓς Ἀρχέλαος ὁ προβασι-
λεύσας πρῶτος κατέδειξε. The play Archelaus may therefore
have been performed at Dium (despite the lack of buried
kings there) at least as well as at Aegae ; but of course the
absence of evidence makes it impossible to say definitely in
what theatre any of Euripides' Macedonian plays were
presented.[4]

Towards the end of his paper, Sir William Ridgeway makes
yet another attempt to save the hero-theory of tragedy, by a
renewed effort to make Dionysus out to have been a hero.
He suggests that the Βάκχου προφήτης of the Rhesus, l. 972,
described as dwelling on the Pangaean mountain, is Dionysus ;
and he argues that Dionysus was not identical with Bacchus,
but was ' an old Thracian chief who was regarded as a re-
incarnation of Bacchus ' ; and that when he entered Greece he
was regarded only as a hero.

Now the interpretation of the passage in the Rhesus is
extremely difficult ; but Sir William Ridgeway cannot dispose
of the old view, that the Βάκχου προφήτης was Orpheus, by
the mere assertion that Orpheus ' was buried at Libethra on
Olympus, and there is no evidence that he ever expounded
Bacchus '. As regards the first point, he has overlooked the

---

[1] Diod. XVII. xvi, § 3.   [2] Arrian, Anab. I. xi.

[3] This is, of course, not certain ; but it is the natural meaning of the
words.

[4] Sir William Ridgeway's arguments for the Euripidean authorship of
the Rhesus, and for assigning it to the poet's Macedonian period, are
interesting and ingenious ; but it would be beside the point to discuss
them here.

fact, to which Maass [1] called attention long ago, that although the burial-place of Orpheus was usually said to be Leibethra under Olympus (near Dium), there was a tribe called Λειβήθριοι who lived under the Pangaean Mountain [2] and paid reverence to Orpheus. It is thus at least possible that Euripides found a tradition of Orpheus' burial there ; and since it was on the Pangaean Mountain that (according to the *Bassarai* of Aeschylus) Orpheus was slain by Maenads, it is not improbable that legend should have given him a burial-place there also. (Whether the story originally belonged to the district of Pangaeum, and was transferred to that of Olympus, or whether it travelled from the Leibethra near Olympus with the Pierians who had migrated thence to Pangaeum, makes no difference for the present purpose. On either hypothesis Euripides could have found a tradition that Orpheus was buried on the Pangaean Mountain.)

The description of Orpheus as Βάκχου προφήτης is sufficiently explained by the fact that the rites of the Orphic brotherhoods were to a great extent in honour of Bacchus or Dionysus,[3] as well as of Kore, and, unlike most forms of Greek religion, involved definite doctrines, the exposition of which would naturally be ascribed to the mythical founder. The reference to these rites founded by Orpheus in the *Rhesus*, ll. 943–4 :

> μυστηρίων τε τῶν ἀπορρήτων φανὰς
> ἔδειξεν Ὀρφεύς . . .

makes it likely that he had them in mind also in ll. 972–3, and the words σεμνὸς τοῖσιν εἰδόσιν θεός (like Pindar's words, φωνᾶντα συνετοῖσιν,[4] which refer certainly to Orphic doctrine) suggest mystic rites, such as those ascribed to Orpheus. On this interpretation the whole passage, 963 ff., hangs together

---

[1] *Orpheus*, p. 135.

[2] Himerius, *Or.* xiii. 4 Λειβήθριοι μὲν οὖν Παγγαίου πρόσοικοι Ὀρφέα τὸν Καλλίστης, τὸν Θράκιον, πρὶν μὲν δημοσιεύειν εἰς αὐτοὺς τὴν ᾠδὴν ἣν παρὰ τῆς μητρὸς τῆς Μούσης ἔμαθεν, ἐθαύμαζόν τε καὶ συνήδοντο κτλ. The assertion of Perdrizet (*Cultes et Mythes du Pangée*, pp. 29, 30) that the Pangaean Leibethrii are a fiction of Himerius seems to be purely dogmatic.

[3] Cf. Apollod. I. iii, § 2 εὗρε δὲ Ὀρφεὺς καὶ τὰ Διονύσου μυστήρια κτλ.

[4] *Olymp.* ii. 93.

well: 'Rhesus will not die, for I will persuade Kore to let him dwell on earth as a cave-god. She owes something to the relatives of Orpheus, who propagated her mysteries; and he will live like Orpheus, himself a buried god on Mount Pangaeum and revered by the initiated '.[1]

The Βάκχου προφήτης then, the buried god or hero, is Orpheus, not Dionysus. Dionysus doubtless had an oracle on Mount Pangaeum, as Herodotus states;[2] but Sir William Ridgeway is going beyond the text when he says that Dionysus was buried there. Here are Herodotus' words : Σάτραι δὲ οὐδενός κω ἀνθρώπων ὑπήκοοι ἐγένοντο, ὅσον ἡμεῖς ἴδμεν, ἀλλὰ διατελεῦσι τὸ μέχρι ἐμεῦ αἰεὶ ἐόντες ἐλεύθεροι μοῦνοι Θρηΐκων· οἰκέουσί τε γὰρ ὄρεα ὑψηλά, ἴδησί τε παντοίῃσι καὶ χιόνι συνηρεφέα, καὶ εἰσὶ τὰ πολέμια ἄκροι. οὗτοι οἱ τοῦ Διονύσου τὸ μαντήιόν εἰσι κεκτημένοι· τὸ δὲ μαντήιον τοῦτο ἔστι μὲν ἐπὶ τῶν ὀρέων τῶν ὑψηλοτάτων, Βησσοὶ δὲ τῶν Σατρέων εἰσὶ οἱ προφητεύοντες τοῦ ἱροῦ, πρόμαντις δὲ ἡ χρέωσα κατά περ ἐν Δελφοῖσι, καὶ οὐδὲν ποικιλώτερον. Dionysus need not have been supposed to be buried, in order to give oracles through a priestess, any more than Apollo at Delphi; and the undoubtedly chthonic character of his divinity in some places of his worship does not imply that he was supposed to have been once a mortal.[3]

It is difficult to agree with Sir William Ridgeway when he tries to prove that Bacchus and Dionysus were distinct, on the strength of such expressions as ὁ Βακχεῖος Διόνυσος (Hom. *Hymn to Pan*, 46), ἐπεθύμησε Διονύσῳ Βακχείῳ τελεσθῆναι (Herod. iv. 79), ὁ Βακχεῖος θεὸς ναίων ἐπ' ἄκρων ὀρέων (Soph. *O. T.* 1105). His statement that the meaning of the termina-

---

[1] Wilamowitz (*Hermes* lxi, pp. 285 ff.) objects that Orpheus was not a god. But we know too little of Orphic mysteries to deny that he was a god to the initiated (τοῖσιν εἰδόσιν); cf. Tertull. *de anim.* 2, p. 301 'plerosque auctores etiam deos existimavit antiquitas, nedum divos . . . ut Orpheum, ut Musaeum ' etc.

[2] vii. 111.

[3] I do not see the point of Sir William Ridgeway's reference to Aristotle, *de Ausc. Mir.*, p. 842 f.; the passage only shows that there was a precinct or temple of Dionysus in Crestonia, the region next to that of the Bisaltae.

tion -εῖος is ' son of ', 'sprung from' is against most of the
evidence. It cannot be so explained in words like 'Ομήρειος,
'Επικούρειος, Πυθαγόρειος, Λύκειος : much less where the
termination is not combined with a proper name (ἀνδρεῖος,
γυναικεῖος, ἀνθρώπειος, βόειος, οἰκεῖος, ἴππειος, &c.). It simply
means ' appertaining or belonging to ', ' related to ', in whatever
way. No doubt it is sometimes patronymic, as sonship is a
common kind of relation, but it is by no means always so.
Βακχεῖος itself is applied to βότρυς, νόμος, ῥυθμός, &c.; and
when we remember that the worshippers of the god were
called βάκχοι, we need not hesitate to translate the word as
used by the Hymn-writer, Herodotus, and Sophocles as ' lord
of the βάκχοι ', or ' worshipped by the βάκχοι '. The word may
possibly mean ' frenzied' or ' inspired ', when Aristophanes [1]
applies the words τὸν βακχεῖον ἄνακτα to Aeschylus. It
certainly does not mean ' son of Bacchus '.

The attempt therefore to treat Dionysus as a buried hero
and as distinct from Bacchus seems to fail on all grounds.[2]

XII

Professor Murray's Theory.

§ 1. In an Appendix to ch. viii of Miss J. E. Harrison's
Themis, Professor Gilbert Murray attempts to explain certain
recurrent forms or elements of Greek tragedy by the hypothesis that these are survivals of the forms of a spring ritual
or *dromenon* in honour of Dionysus, a ritual identified by
him with the dithyramb from which, according to Aristotle,
tragedy sprang. The fact that in nearly all extant Greek
tragedies these forms, or some of them, appear as part of the
presentation of the fortunes, not of Dionysus, but of some
hero or heroine, is explained by the hypothesis which plays so

[1] *Frogs*, 1259.
[2] For other arguments on this subject, see above, pp. 12–14. Just as
these pages were going to press, Sir William Ridgeway's paper appeared
in full in *Class. Quart.* xx (1926), pp. 1 ff., but I do not think that any
alteration in the above is called for.

large a part in *Themis*, that both Dionysus and the principal heroes of Greek legend were alike forms of what Miss Harrison and Professor Murray term the ʼΕνιαυτός-Δαίμων, who represents the cyclic death and rebirth, not merely of the year, but of the tribe, by the return to life of the heroes or dead ancestors. Such heroes, like Dionysus, we are asked to believe, had their *dromena*, essentially the same in type, and closely akin to, or identical with, such initiation-ceremonies as (on Miss Harrison's showing) were those of Kouretes. (The reader of *Themis* will find that Miss Harrison is not perfectly clear in her theory of the relation of these various rites to each other and to the dithyramb; and it is also not quite clear how far Professor Murray follows her in detail, but so far as has been stated above, his language appears to imply his agreement with her.) The forms into which tragedy falls are to be explained, according to the theory, as modifications of the forms of the original ritual of Dionysus or the ʼΕνιαυτός-Δαίμων,—the dithyramb or spring ritual; and tragedy had for its business originally, and continued to have, the representation of the αἴτιον, the supposed historical cause, of the ritual, whether Dionysiac or heroic. What then was this ritual? It will be best to quote Professor Murray's own words :

' If we examine the kind of myth which seems to underlie the various ʼΕνιαυτός celebrations, we shall find :

1. An *Agon* or Contest, the Year against its enemy, Light against Darkness, Summer against Winter.

2. A *Pathos* of the Year-Daimon, generally a ritual or sacrificial death, in which Adonis or Attis is slain by the *tabu* animal, the Pharmakos stoned, Osiris, Dionysus, Pentheus, Orpheus, Hippolytus torn to pieces (σπαραγμός).

3. A *Messenger*. For this Pathos seems seldom or never to be actually performed under the eyes of the audience . . . . It is announced by a Messenger . . . and the dead body is often brought in on a bier. This leads to

4. *Threnos* or Lamentation. Specially characteristic, however, is a clash of contrary emotions, the death of the old being

also the triumph of the new : see p. 318 f., on Plutarch's
account of the Oschophoria.

5 and 6. An *Anagnorisis*—discovery or recognition—of the slain
and mutilated Daimon, followed by his Resurrection or
Apotheosis, or, in some sense, his *Epiphany* in glory.
This I shall call by the general name *Theophany*. It
naturally goes with a *Peripeteia* or extreme change of
feeling from grief to joy.

Observe the sequence in which these should normally occur :
Agon, Pathos, Messenger, Threnos, Theophany, or, we might say,
Anagnorisis and *Theophany*.'

He illustrates the theory by applying it to three plays
of Euripides, the *Bacchae, Hippolytus*, and *Andromache*.
Now he himself points out that, in one very important point,
the theory does not apply even to them ; nor, in fact, does it
apply to any other play. There is not a single extant play in
which the epiphany is the epiphany of the god or hero who
has been slain. ' In the *Bacchae* it is Pentheus who is torn,
but Dionysus who appears as god.' Does this really matter
less, as he suggests (p. 345), because Pentheus is only another
form of Dionysus himself ?[1] If there was any consciousness
of this on the part of poet or audience the play is reduced
to a more bewildering series of riddles as regards the
personality of the characters than Dr. Verrall or Professor
Norwood ever conceived. When is Pentheus Pentheus, and
when is he Dionysus ? when is Dionysus the enemy of Pentheus, and when is he another form of him ? and how are these
transitions between *ego* and *alter ego* managed?[2] However this
may be, ' In the *Bacchae* it is Pentheus who is torn, but Dionysus who appears as god. In the *Hippolytus* it is not Hippolytus
who appears as god, but Artemis, his patroness.[3] In the *Andromache* the persons are all varied : it is Peleus and Menelaus

[1] I do not think that this is a quite accurate view, but the point is of
no importance here.

[2] There is the same difficulty with regard to Dionysus-Orpheus in
the lost *Bassarai* of Aeschylus, as interpreted by Professor Murray,
p. 349.

[3] I do not think any one has yet suggested that Hippolytus is a form
of Artemis.

who have the contest; it is Neoptolemus who is slain and mourned; it is Thetis who appears as divine.' Now this is surely a very serious difficulty. The kernel of tragedy, according to the theory, is the death and resurrection or epiphany of a slain daimon. Yet there is not one single tragedy in which the epiphany is that of the daimon or hero who has been slain, nor have we the faintest indication anywhere of any tragedy in which a slain character is resuscitated, with the possible exception of the *Alcestis*, which is more of a satyric play than a tragedy, and in which the year-daimon (if there is one) is not Alcestis but Heracles. Is it possible to come to any other conclusion than that the theory simply does not fit the facts ?

Further, it is extremely doubtful whether, in any ritual known in Greece, the representation of the death, and the representation of the resurrection of the god or other object of the cult were ever combined in the same ceremony.[1] They were, in fact, almost inevitably supposed to take place at different times of the year, if they represent the phenomena of winter and spring. Σπαραγμός is a winter ceremony, and in Greece seems to be generally trieteric: and in the σπαραγμός-rites of which we have any account no resurrection follows as the sequel to the death. Moreover, we have no hint anywhere of any tragedy in which Dionysus was torn or slain: and the Zagreus mysteries (in which, in a sense, this did happen) cannot be shown by any evidence to have any connexion whatever with tragedy, or with the dithyramb. (In any case ὠμοφαγία, the devouring of the god who has been torn or slain, is not a ceremony naturally followed by resurrection, and belongs to a different type from the vegetation-ritual of death and

---

[1] The one doubtful instance, the awakening of Liknites at Delphi, is far too uncertain to build upon. Dr. Farnell, *Cults*, v, pp. 186 ff., has a more probable explanation. The resuscitation of the ox at the Bouphonia is not a 'Resurrection', but a pretence that the ox has not been slain ; and in any case does not help us much in regard to Dionysus and the heroes. It seems to be only in such modern performances as those at Viza, &c., in which the original meaning of the ritual is forgotten, that these two are combined.

resurrection, its object being rather what is loosely called ' communion '.) It seems most probable that the supposed ritual, with which the origins of tragedy are connected by the theory under discussion, never existed in Greece at all; but it will be well to consider more in detail how far the theory serves to explain the extant remains.

2. Assuming that the original ritual contained a theophany, a περιπέτεια from sorrow to joy,[1] what does Professor Murray suppose its history to have been ? It may be objected, as he rightly sees (p. 343) that ' Our tragedies normally end with a comforting theophany ' [even this, as we shall see, appears to be an over-statement] ' but not with an outburst of joy '. ' No ', he replies, ' but it looks as if they once did. We know that they were in early times composed in tetralogies consisting of three tragedies and a satyr-play . . . The satyr-play coming at the end of the tetralogy, represented the joyous arrival of the re-living Dionysus and his rout of attendant daimones at the end of the Sacer Ludus '. The theophany then is to be looked for first in the fourth play, the satyr-play of the old tetralogy.

Now at what period is the satyr-play supposed to have represented the theophany of a slain god or hero, or indeed a theophany connected with the story of the other three plays at all ? It has been contended above [2] that the tetralogic arrangement is itself probably far from original in tragedy; but whether this is so or not, the alleged phenomenon does not take place, so far as the evidence goes, in Aeschylus. The most certain Aeschylean theophanies to which Professor Murray points all come in the third play of the trilogy—the appearances of Apollo and Athena in the *Eumenides*, of

---

[1] It is difficult to follow Dieterich, as Professor Murray does, in drawing a parallel between the Eleusinian Mysteries and Tragedy. True, there is a περιπέτεια from sorrow to joy in the mysteries. But was there any enactment of the πάθος, the rape of Kore ? (It is also rather inconvenient to use the word περιπέτεια of tragedy in two senses : Aristotle, of course, states that a περιπέτεια may be of either kind, but the περιπέτεια which he treats as characteristic of tragedy is the περιπέτεια from joy to sorrow.)

[2] pp. 89, 93 ff.

Aphrodite in the Danaid trilogy, and possibly of Zeus in the
Prometheus-trilogy, if Professor Murray's interpretation is
correct. (None of these daimones had been previously slain.)
In the Theban trilogy Oedipus really may have reappeared in
the satyric play, the *Sphinx*, but apparently Professor Murray
interprets this trilogy otherwise, and looks in the *Sphinx* for
the epiphany, not of Oedipus, but of Dionysus as the deliverer.
The interpretations suggested of other lost plays of Aeschylus
are for the most part too conjectural to serve as evidence, but
there is no suggestion of an epiphany in the satyric play of
any daimon connected with the preceding plays. If then this
ever happened, it must have been before Aeschylus. But
before Aeschylus we have no hint of tetralogies, and the very
slight indirect evidence that there is does not favour the
hypothesis of their existence.[1]

In his account of the theophanies which are extant (or can
be inferred to have happened in lost plays), Professor Murray
seems almost to give up Sophocles. In fact, nothing of the kind
happens except in the *Philoctetes*, in which in many ways the
influence of Euripides is traceable. It is above all in Euripides,
much more even than in Aeschylus, that theophanies and some
of the other forms occur more or less as they should,—of course
now within the single play, not in tetralogies. This is not
very easy to understand. Presumably the poet is supposed to
have been conscious that he was reproducing a year-god's
ritual, or at any rate something not to be tampered with; for
after an enumeration of all the extant theophanies in Euripides and a demonstration of the strong resemblance between
them, we are told that 'if this were free and original composition, the monotony would be intolerable and incomprehensible :
we can understand it only when we realize that the poet is
working under the spell of a set traditional form'. A poet
can scarcely do inartistic things under sheer compulsion without being conscious of the compulsion. But why was Aeschylus
so much less 'monotonous', and Sophocles hardly under the spell
at all, though his poetic career coincided for two-thirds of its
length with Euripides' own? Can we accept the theory when

[1] See above, p. 89.

the exceptions are so significant a proportion of the whole material?

It may be said parenthetically that the Euripidean 'monotony' does not really seem to be at all intolerable or incomprehensible; it is hard to understand how any one who has seen many Euripidean plays acted, whether in the original or in Professor Murray's own incomparable translations, can think them so. The form of the plays appears to be admirably adapted for presenting just the ideas which Euripides wished to present, and it is because his ideas, rather than any prescribed ritual, follow the same lines over and over again, that his plays are made to do so, often by very bold modifications of the legends. But it would require too long a digression to discuss this here in detail.

'Our tragedies', we are told, 'normally end with a comforting theophany'. The three trilogies of Aeschylus, the course of which is more or less clear, certainly ended in a scene of reconciliation, effected by divine interposition—by the agency of Aphrodite in the *Danaides*, of Athena in the *Eumenides*, and possibly of Zeus in the *Prometheus*-trilogy; and the same thing may have happened in some of the lost plays or trilogies. The contending claims are reconciled and given their due place in the higher unity. But it will still remain possible that this was due, not to the constraining force of a primitive ritual sequence, but to the genius and the comprehensive theological thinking of Aeschylus himself. In the *Persae* the appearance of Darius is scarcely a comforting theophany. In the *Philoctetes* of Sophocles also there is a reconciling theophany, though otherwise, as Professor Murray points out, 'the sequence is rather far from any type'. In the other plays of Sophocles there is very little to suggest a περιπέτεια from sorrow to joy. As regards Euripides, it is true that many of the extant plays end with the appearance of a god, who arranges matters conveniently, if ingloriously, and often institutes some custom familiar to fifth-century Athenians; yet it is hard to think of some of those appearances (e. g. those in the *Hippolytus* and *Bacchae*) as even a 'faded' form of περιπέτεια from sorrow to joy; and many of them can hardly have been intended to be

comforting. The viciousness and incompetence of the gods is
so plain that the tragedy is deepened unspeakably by these
theophanies ; that is, partly, why they are there; the consola-
tion offered to Hippolytus and Ion is very cold comfort, and
Ion's attitude clearly indicates this. But what it is more important to notice is that though such 'comforting theophanies',
if we are to call them so, are proportionately numerous in the
extant plays of Euripides, they were probably not characteristic
of him, if, as Aristotle says, 'most of his tragedies end in
calamity',[1] so that some of his critics complained of their
dismalness.

Further, if the original ritual always ended joyfully, it is
less easy to explain why in most tragedies the ending was in
disaster,—at least if, as seems probable, it is not legitimate to
call in the satyric play to our aid. It would be easier to explain tragedy by a ritual which had originally no happy
ending—whether in the form of a theophany or not—than to
explain why, if a happy ending was an essential part of
the original ritual, the majority of tragedies should have got
rid of it. It seems more likely that happy endings, where
they occur, should be at least in part due to the cause to which
Aristotle refers some of them—the weakness of the spectators,
who wanted to go away cheerful.

§ 3. It will be sufficient to state here in outline some of the
difficulties in regard to the supposed ritual forms, other than
the theophanies. (The application of the theory to the extant
plays individually will be considered briefly in an Appendix,
and a few illustrations only given here.) It may be said briefly
that it is only possible to find the Forms in the extant plays if
their order—Agon, Pathos, Messenger, Anagnorisis, Threnos,
Theophany,—which we were asked to observe, can be changed
to almost any extent, and the very broadest meaning given to
the terms themselves.

'Agon', for example, in Professor Murray's exposition will
cover almost any difference of opinion,—so much so that it
would scarcely be possible to conceive of any drama or work
of fiction without an 'agon' in this wide sense, apart from

---

[1] *Poetics*, xiv.

any ritual origins. In the *Supplices* of Aeschylus a song of
prayer has to do duty for the ' threnos '; there cannot be
a threnos, for there has been no ' pathos '; and the peripeteia
(if the word can be used at all of the promise given by the
king) comes in the wrong place. In the *Persae* Atossa's dream
of the contest of Europe and Asia has to do duty for the agon.
In the *Prometheus* of course an agon—in fact a series of
agones—is inextricably involved in the very idea of the play,
though we may greatly doubt if they had any ritual counterpart; the rest of the play—Prometheus' long narrative and
prophecy to Io—is very imperfectly explained by the forms.
In the *Oresteia*, as Professor Murray truly says, the sequence
in the individual plays is upset and confused : but it is difficult to understand the reason which he gives—and which
I suppose he would give for the confusion of the sequence
in the individual plays of the other trilogies—viz. that the
full theophany is reserved for the last play. Surely that,
according to the theory, is just where it ought to be, at
least if it cannot be in the satyric play, and the other
forms ought to be distributed in orderly sequence over the
whole trilogy ; but if he means that the forms are to be sought
for in a complete sequence in each play, except for the theophany, surely this should not involve such disturbance of the
order in each play that some of the forms should be omitted,
some doubled or trebled, and the sequence in fact practically
ignored. Besides this we are told that Orestes is a very
characteristic hero of the Eniautos-Daimon type,—he is reported dead (and that by σπαραγμός) and returns in triumph :
he is closely parallel to Dionysus himself, the forms of whose
ritual are supposed to be the basis of tragedy. Why then
should he above all ' always produce a peculiar disturbance in
the forms'? (p. 356.) His story, if any, ought to fit into the
traditional mould. And yet the wilful dramatist postpones
the agon in which, according to the sequence, the hero ought
to be slain, until after the hero's so-called resurrection ! Is
not the solution simply that the Orestes story is not based on
any such ritual-sequence at all?

If the theory is to be applied to trilogies at all, probably

O

it ought to be applied not to individual plays, but (as has just been suggested) to whole trilogies or tetralogies. It would perhaps be possible to reconstruct the lost second play of the Danaid trilogy in such a way as to compose a trilogy bringing in all the forms; but this would of course be mere guesswork; and it would not be easy to treat the other trilogies in the same way with any probability. As applied to individual plays of Aeschylus the theory breaks down hopelessly. Where, for instance, is the anagnorisis in the *Supplices* or the *Septem*? (The term anagnorisis appears to be very loosely applied to some scenes in other plays, for instance to the discovery of the body of Ajax, and to ' a kind of spiritual anagnorisis' in Euripides' *Electra*. It was Dieterich who set the example of using in a vague and inexact sense certain technical terms the meaning of which is clearly defined in Aristotle, who first applied them for the purposes of dramatic criticism.) Professor Murray's own analysis of the plays of Sophocles shows how remote that poet's structures are from the supposed ritual-sequence, and he has to invoke 'atrophied' messengers and 'faded' theophanies to obtain even a semblance of correspondence between the two. (The atrophied messenger in the *Ajax* foretells the pathos, which he ought, according to the sequence, to report; and the pathos obediently follows.)

The stronghold of the theory is Euripides; but again Professor Murray's own detailed analysis shows how much interpretation and conjecture is required before even Euripides' plays can be adduced in support of the theory. We have to suppose that there was some other form of Hippolytus-dromenon than any actually known, to explain the *Hippolytus*; and that the *Orestes* (and also Aeschylus' *Choephoroe*) had some more complete predecessor, in which Agamemnon actually rose from the tomb. In the *Heracles*, instead of a god, Theseus appears *ex machina* 'as it were', and we are left in some doubt where we are to find the agon; and so on, in almost every play.

§ 4. Professor Murray's theory appears to run contrary to such literary and historical evidence as there is for the origins of tragedy. The one thing which seems quite clear from such evidence is that tragedy began as a choral song; the first actor was the creation (using the word loosely) of Thespis, the second of Aeschylus, the third of Sophocles. It takes two to make a quarrel. Where was the agon before Aeschylus? (Even Aeschylus is not very skilful at first—in the *Supplices*—in handling two actors; the only passage of dialogue between the two is the brief dispute between Danaus and the Egyptian Herald.) It is very difficult under the circumstances to believe that an agon was part of the song and dance from which tragedy sprang, or that there was a messenger, announcing a pathos resulting from such an agon, before Thespis. There can hardly have been a formal agon until the second actor brought with him the possibility of a clash of interests; and when it does come, it is never so formal or persistent in shape as the agon of the Old Comedy, which, as we shall see, was really primitive. Where (as sometimes in Sophocles and commonly in Euripides) there is some formality in the dispute, this is probably a reflection of the set speeches of litigants in the law-courts, and is not due to the constraining effect of an original ritual.

§ 5. With his theory of the original ritual Forms of Tragedy, Professor Murray connects the theory that every tragedy represents the supposed αἴτιον, or historical reason, of a rite in vogue in the worship of Dionysus or in that of some hero, or occasionally the αἴτιον of some other institution. Now originally, we must suppose, the representation of the death and resurrection of Dionysus must have been ritual with an ulterior motive, not drama acted for its own sake; and the ritual sanctity or exclusiveness must have given way considerably before non-Dionysiac themes would be admitted. But when this had happened, why should the poets (if there were any at this stage) or the organizers of the representation have necessarily represented the *rituals* of heroes, instead of going to their stories, which no doubt (however aetiological in origin some may have been) were by now current in detachment from their rituals? And why should we require a *ritual* origin for every detail of non-Dionysiac plays? For so convinced is Professor Murray of the necessity of a ritual explanation that the dramatic and artistic reasons which are produced for certain scenes are not sufficient for him; but (e.g.) in order to explain the absence of a θρῆνος from the *Medea*, he has to conjecture that there was no θρῆνος in the Corinthian rite;[1] and after noticing the perfectly adequate artistic justification of the Euadne scene in Euripides' *Supplices*, he adds ' but it must, no doubt, have some ritual justification also'. Why must it?

The transition from Dionysiac to non-Dionysiac subjects evidently took place during the sixth century B.C.: all the evidence points to that date. Now this was just the time when the heroic legends were being collected and consolidated. Are not the facts sufficiently explained when we observe that just when the Dionysiac drama was being developed and popularized, as it evidently was at this time, by Peisistratus and other tyrants, a tremendous mass of legend was also being made accessible to the dramatic poets and organizers?[2] It can easily be understood how enterprising and imaginative poets should have seized on the legends, experimenting freely, and ultimately rejecting stories which did not make good plays, and so settling down (as Aristotle says)[3] to the stories of a few houses. By no means all these legends were aetiological (though no doubt some were); and it is very doubtful whether even in dealing with many of those which had been worked up from an aetiological origin the poet would have been conscious of this origin.

It is, however, desirable to deal briefly with one point upon which Professor Murray lays some stress (being so far in agreement with Sir William Ridgeway). Most plays, he rightly says, deal with the death or pathos of some hero; and he adds, 'Indeed, I think it can be shown that every extant tragedy contains somewhere towards the end the celebration of a *tabu* tomb'.[4] (The words 'every extant tragedy' seem

---

[1] In fact what we know of the Corinthian rite shows that it was quite different in several points from anything that could be inferred from the play.

[2] See below, pp. 199, 219.　　　　[3] *Poetics*, ch. xiv.

[4] I do not discuss here the justification or implications of the adjective

to be an exaggeration, but this may be passed over for the
moment.) The answer seems to be partly (as was briefly urged
in reply to Sir William Ridgeway [1]) that the most striking
stories about most heroes, ancient and modern, are connected
with their death; that in almost every tragedy in the world
there is conflict, death, and lamentation; and that if the
Dionysiac τραγικοὶ χοροί were already ' tragic '—connected,
for instance, with stories like those of Pentheus, Lycurgus,
Icarius and Erigone,—it would naturally be stories of the
deaths of heroes that poets would select; nor is there any
need to go back behind the stories to the ritual of the heroes;
for it is surely not suggested that no tragic myths would ever
have come into existence but for the desire to explain ritual.
This would be as bad as the solar theory. Even if some of
the stories were explanatory of ritual, this would not necessarily determine the literary form of the stories in their epic
shape, still less in any drama based on the epic stories.

But further, the actually and unmistakably aetiological
passages (whether referring to tomb-worship or to other
institutions) in the extant plays need some sifting.

It would appear that Aeschylus and Sophocles aetiologize
very little except about Athenian institutions. (It is not
really justifiable to treat the worship of Oedipus and his
children at Thebes as the αἴτιον of plays in which that worship
is not so much as hinted at. The *Septem* ends with a very
serious doubt whether Polynices will get any burial at all,
much less worship.) But the introduction of Athenian institutions in plays performed before an Athenian audience does
not need for its explanation the hypothesis that the whole
play is developed from the ritual of the institution.

On the other hand, aetiologizing about non-Athenian institutions was certainly a hobby of Euripides—possibly, in part
because it gave a certain element of novelty to his work, but
mainly, we may surmise, because aetiologizing was popular at
the time. For it is by no means a peculiarity of the drama at
this period; we find it in Pindar and Herodotus, and even in

tabu in this connexion. But it is a word to be used with some circum-
spection.   [1] Above, p. 179.

Thucydides. And in this popularity of aetiology we may find
a contributory cause to account for the explanation in the
dramas not only of grave-rituals, but of other institutions—
torch-processions, the Ionian tribes, the worship of Artemis at
Brauron, &c. We do not need the hypothesis that if the
institution of a hero-cult is brought in at the end of a play, it
is because the play is somehow based on the hero's ritual.

§ 6. With regard to the kind of ritual from which Tragedy
is supposed to have sprung, there is great difficulty. Professor
Murray speaks of this ritual sequence as the Dithyramb or
Spring Dromenon of Dionysus; but when we ask what this
was, we are referred to chapter vi of *Themis*. Now it is
almost impossible to discover what Miss Harrison means by
‘ Dithyramb’; the word, in her hands, seems to be applicable
to anything—the lyrics of the *Bacchae*, the ritual of the
Kouretes, a spring-song of magical fertility for the New Year,
an initiation ceremony, and a good many other things, most
of them very different from one another, and all of them quite
different from the dithyramb as known to us from literature.
But it can be safely said that neither in *Themis* nor in any
records of Greek ritual is there any trace of a ceremony called
Dithyramb on good authority and taking the form Agon,
Pathos or Sparagmos, Threnos, Anagnorisis, Resurrection;
nor does any known Dionysiac ritual contain such a combination of elements. We know little enough of the Dithyramb;
what is known has been (no doubt imperfectly) collected
in the preceding chapter; but it was nothing like what
Professor Murray and Miss Harrison require.

The other rite which is supposed to have contributed to
Tragedy is the Eleusinian. Professor Murray follows Dieterich
in comparing the prologue of Tragedy with the prorrhesis of
the hierophant before the sacred dromenon. But it is
only necessary to read the passages to see that there is
really no resemblance at all between the parody of such a
prorrhesis in the *Frogs* (354 ff.), and the prologues or introductory scenes of Tragedy. Professor Murray's allusion to
the Proagon, which was not part of the play, but a ceremony
on an earlier day, is not very easy to understand; and when

he states that 'if our knowledge were a little fuller, we should
very likely be told who πρῶτος ἔγραψε προλόγους', he forgets
that we *are* told; it was Thespis, of whom no special connexion
with Eleusis is recorded.

It should be repeated that there is no hint in any extant
evidence of any connexion between tragedy, as performed in
honour of Dionysus Eleuthereus, and the ritual of Dionysus-
Zagreus (in which, it appears, σπαραγμός did take place,
though without any resurrection). It was under Peisistratus
that the festival of Eleuthereus was organized at Athens, and
that Thespis appeared there; it was Peisistratus, probably,
who encouraged the collection by Onomacritus and the
systematic publication of epic legend;[1] it was under Peisistratus
that Onomacritus Διονύσῳ συνέθηκεν ὄργια and put together
the Orphic legend of Zagreus into something like coherent
form. If the Zagreus ritual had been also the basis of the
newly organized Tragedy—the one thing which we are *not*
told—is it likely that not a hint of it would have been preserved? It is perhaps permissible to add that the application
of the conception of the Eniautos-Daimon to Hamlet[2] and
St. John the Baptist[3] is not likely to win belief in the
soundness of Professor Murray's theory.

Note on the application of Professor Murray's theory to certain plays.

As regards the plays of Aeschylus, little need be added to what
has been said above. The real difficulty, as has been indicated,
is to know whether we are to look for traces of the Ritual Forms
in a trilogy as a whole, or in single plays. It may be doubted
whether in the last play of the Danaid trilogy Aphrodite really
founded the institution of marriage based on consent, and therefore whether the last scene gave the αἴτιον of the plays. (A little

---

[1] Whatever difficulties of detail there may be, there can be little doubt
as to the Collection of Epic poetry at this time; cf. Cauer, *Grundfr. der
Homerkritik* I[3], pp. 130 ff. Murray, *Rise of the Greek Epic.*[3] pp. 304 ff.

[2] British Academy Shakespeare Lecture, 1914.

[3] J. E. Harrison, *Class. Rev.* xxx (1916), pp. 216 ff.; see also ibid.
xxxi, pp. 1 ff., 63 f.

difficulty arises at times, because Professor Murray sometimes speaks of the ritual as the αἴτιον of the play, and sometimes of the play as representing the αἴτιον of the ritual. The two conceptions, however, are obviously not irreconcilable.) A different view of the Danaid trilogy is taken by Wilamowitz (*Interpr.*, pp. 21 ff.). No tomb is conspicuous in this trilogy; probably the forty-nine sons of Aegyptus had to be buried somehow; but it may be doubted whether they were accorded a heroic ritual either in the play or in the legend on which it was based.

In the *Persae* no one has been killed; there has been no pathos of Darius, who rises from the dead, and it is difficult to find any αἴτιον in this play. The play certainly does not explain the worship of Darius, nor is he much like a year-god.

As for the *Prometheus* trilogy, we are left in doubt whether the theophany is reserved for the third play, or whether (as is suggested on p. 357) the earthquake has to do duty for the theophany. The difficulty of making Hermes serve both as messenger (though he reports no pathos), and as disputant in an agon, is obvious.

Professor Murray assumes that the last scene of the *Septem contra Thebas* is genuine. The difficulties of this view seem to be almost insuperable (see Wilamowitz, *Interpr.*, pp. 88 ff. ; Robert, *Oidipous*, pp. 375 ff.) ; and in any case the statement that the scene gives the αἴτιον of the grave-ritual of Eteocles and Polynices is open to the objections already stated (p. 197). There is no agon in the play, unless the seven descriptions and counter-descriptions of heroes are to be called an agon, and no theophany, though this might be thought of as reserved for the *Sphinx*.

The confusion of the order and the character of the supposed Ritual Forms in the plays of the *Oresteia* is too obvious to need further comment. Professor Murray's suggestion (p. 355) that the great evocation in the *Choephoroe* may be softened down from some more complete predecessor in which Agamemnon actually rose from the tomb appears to have no evidence to support it.

When we come to Sophocles, the difficulty of detecting the Ritual Forms and finding αἴτια which will explain the plays increases.

In the *Ajax* there is no trace of any institution of ritual. Professor Murray's conjecture that the play actually contained 'some great final pomp representing the burial' is unsupported by evidence, and seems to be out of keeping with the tone of the play, which, so far as the survivors are concerned, is one of quiet resignation to fate. He reminds us that 'among the dromena of the Aianteia was a πομπή, and that the funeral bier of Ajax μετὰ πανοπλίας κατεκοσμεῖτο'. Surely the absence of the least hint of anything of this kind from the play is significant of its independence of this ritual. The simple and pathetic funeral rite foreshadowed in the play (1403 ff.) needs no ritual to explain it. The suggestion of a year-ritual in which the dead hero reappeared in the spring in the flower which was marked with his name is pretty, but hardly probable—certainly not proved by any evidence. Other points have already been dealt with (p. 194).

The *Electra* illustrates the impossibility of fitting the story of Orestes to the Ritual Forms. (See above, p. 193.)

In the *Oedipus Tyrannus* there is absolutely no hint of the death or resurrection of a hero or daimon; and Professor Murray's description of ll. 1451 ff. as 'Threnos, with suggestion of Oedipus' flight to Kithairon to become a Daimon' is surely unjustified. Oedipus only asks to go to Kithairon to die as his parents had intended he should.

> ἀλλ' ἔα με ναίειν ὄρεσιν, ἔνθα κλῄζεται
> οὑμὸς Κιθαιρὼν οὗτος, ὃν μήτηρ τέ μοι
> πατήρ τ' ἐθέσθην ζῶντε κύριον τάφον,
> ἵν' ἐξ ἐκείνων, οἵ μ' ἀπωλλύτην, θάνω.

Nothing could be more unlike Sophocles than to distract attention from the all-absorbing human tragedy presented in this play by any suggestion that Oedipus was to be a daimon after all. No doubt there was a grave of Oedipus at Eteonos—probably, as Robert argues, the only grave of him known in early times, that on the Areopagus being a much later invention; but Sophocles never hints at any worship there. On the other hand, the *Oedipus Coloneus* is much more aetiological, and the references to the connexion of Oedipus with Colonus in Athenian belief are clear enough, though whether he had any ritual at Colonus is less certain. He had no known grave there—it was to be kept a secret. As for the Forms, the last speech of Oedipus (consisting of prophecies and αἴτια, with thunder and lightning) is treated by Professor Murray as a faded theophany. The theophany therefore precedes the pathos and messenger.

The αἴτιον of the *Antigone* is thought by Professor Murray to be the same as that of the *Septem*—'some Theban hero-ritual com-

memorating the children of Oedipus and their unhallowed ends—
the buried living and the unburied dead'. But was there any
ritual, Theban or other, involving a commemoration of Antigone
and Haemon, as well as of Eteocles and Polynices? As regards
the latter Pausanias gives a brief account, which raises problems
which it would be beside the point to discuss here (Paus. ix. xviii,
§ 3). As regards Antigone he only tells us (ix. xxv, § 2) that
tradition gave the name Σῦρμα ᾿Αντιγόνης to the ground through
which she dragged Polynices' body, to cast it on to the same pyre
as that of Eteocles. The story of Haemon's death, as presented
in the play, may have been Sophocles' invention; the earlier
version makes him one of the victims of the Sphinx. One has
only to read Robert's exhaustive treatment of the legend of the
House of Oedipus to realize the freedom of invention which poets
allowed themselves, and the hazardousness of attributing to any
particular version a ritual origin.

The *Trachiniae*—or rather a section of it—contains some of the
required scenes (ll. 734 ff.); but these all have to do with the fate
of Deianeira, so that even if the appearance and burning of Heracles
can be construed as an apotheosis, the scheme of the forms is not
satisfied, and the same scene has to serve both as pathos and
epiphany. There seems to be no evidence for the suggestion
that the burning and apotheosis were represented on the stage by
Sophocles, or that Sophocles himself treated the death by fire as
an apotheosis, though no doubt the two things were sometimes
connected. As in the *Ajax* and the *Oedipus Tyrannus*, he leaves
the human tragedy unrelieved.

To the *Philoctetes*, apart from the *deus ex machina* (though
Heracles is not a slain daimon) the forms really cannot be fitted.
It is enough that Professor Murray himself finds that the sequence
is rather far from any type.

The full discussion of Professor Murray's interpretation of the
plays of Euripides by means of the forms would require a long
investigation of some of the heroic legends, and for the present
purpose a less detailed indication of the difficulties must suffice.

As regards the *Medea* it can only be said that the Corinthian rite
having reference to Medea's children had nothing in common with
the play, but presupposed the murder of the children by the
Corinthians, not by their mother; and the conjecture that there
is no threnos in the play because there was none in the Corinthian

rite is really therefore beside the mark. (On the whole subject
see Roscher's Lexicon, s. v. Medeia, and esp. Farnell, *Cults*, i,
pp. 201–4.)

The αἴτιον of the *Heracleidae* is said to be the ἄγος of Eurystheus' death and his sacred grave. These are of course referred to
at the end of the play, but it is difficult to think that the story
grew up simply as an aetiological explanation of them. The play,
however, is so incomplete that it is difficult to tell where the
balance of interest was laid. The absence of all reference to
Macaria's sacrifice after l. 629 is too brutal to have been intended
by Euripides, and we may at least suspect that she rather than
Eurystheus was the real centre of the play. But conjecture is of
little value. If Professor Murray's view is right, the messenger
precedes the agon and the pathos of Eurystheus, the ritual hero
of the play ; and Eurystheus has to serve both for the suffering
hero and the θεὸς ἀπὸ μηχανῆς.

In the *Hippolytus* Artemis establishes a θρῆνος for Hippolytus
at Troezen, and institutes the rite in accordance with which
Troezenian maidens before marriage laid a lock of their hair in
Hippolytus' temple. This is a familiar kind of hero-cult, but
contains not a hint of resurrection : and the Troezenians seem to
have felt uncomfortable about their identification of Hippolytus
(Paus. II. xxxii, §§ 1–4) with the constellation Auriga. The real
difficulty, however, is to find any evidence that he was of the
'Year-daimon' type at all : and Dr. Farnell's account of him
(*Hero-cults*, pp. 64 ff.) harmonizes all the evidence much better.
He points out (what is significant for our purpose) that there is no
reflection at all in any ritual of the σπαραγμός of Hippolytus by
the horses. As regards the appearance of the supposed 'forms'
in the play, it must surely be said that there is no θρῆνος—or if
any, not till after the epiphany (not of the slain Hippolytus, but)
of Artemis, i. e. not till the last nine lines of the play.

As regards the *Andromache* there is the same difficulty as encounters us in so many plays—the almost complete insignificance
of the supposed αἴτιον (the grave ritual of Neoptolemus) in the play
itself. The messenger's speech describes Neoptolemus' death, and
Thetis orders him to be buried at Delphi, among other elements
in the general settlement of affairs which she makes ; there is not
a hint of cult ; the object of burying him there is that the tomb
is to be Δελφοῖς ὄνειδος—an idea which would appeal to good

Athenians in the Peloponnesian War, when the oracle was no friend to Athens. The part played by Orestes (and the absent Neoptolemus) in the play is of altogether secondary interest. The difficulty of applying the forms to this play has already been noticed (above, p. 187).

In the *Hecuba* the forms are crowded into the early part of the play (centring round the death of Polyxena) with a ghost at the beginning instead of a theophany at the end (p. 354), though the latter is (according to an earlier suggestion, p. 353) represented by 'the fey and dying Thracian hero, and his announcement of the Aition of Kunos Sema'. (The hero also announces the death of Agamemnon, but that apparently is unimportant.) In all seriousness, are we to believe that the whole pathetic story of Hecuba and Polyxena or even of Hecuba and Polydorus, grew out of an aetiological explanation of the name Κυνὸς σῆμα, or that the play embodying the story introduced the Κυνὸς σῆμα at all except as a kind of convenient 'rounding off'? It explains nothing in the play.

Of the *Supplices* something has already been said (p. 196), as regards the Euadne scene. The threnos is here said to include all the play from 778 to the theophany, interrupted only by the Euadne scene.

It may be noted that none of the plays of Euripides which have been so far considered contains an anagnorisis (unless Polydorus' discovery that Hecuba has outwitted him is one), still less an anagnorisis of a slain hero or daimon. The *Heracles* on the other hand presents this feature, in Heracles' 'recognition' of the children whom he has slain. So far as we know, there was no hint of any resurrection of the children, or of any ritual connected with them, though their tomb was exhibited at Thebes in Pausanias' day (Paus. I. xli, § 1 ; IX. ix, § 2). In the play they are promised burial, but no rite. Heracles is promised worship at Athens after his death, but he has not been slain or 'recognized', and it is surely very difficult to treat the speech of Theseus as equivalent to a theophany. In the play, Theseus is king of Athens, with no touch of the supernatural about him.

The *Ion* moves on completely different lines from the supposed ritual-sequence, which does not really explain the form of the play in any degree. The play is not about death and resurrection at all. There is, of course, a conflict, as in almost every tragedy

which the world has seen (without any assistance from ritual);
but there is no pathos, and the messenger cannot really be called
a pathos-messenger ; there is only the detection of a plot (unless
the death of the birds is the pathos) ; nor is the choral ode, 1229–
1250, a threnos, but a lively anticipation of punishment. There
is a fine anagnorisis, but not one of the kind demanded by the
Ritual Sequence ; and the theophany, as in all other cases, is
not the appearance of any being who has been slain.

The form of the *Troades* is, as Professor Murray says, from
the point of view of the forms, 'in many ways peculiar'. It
starts with the theophany ; there is no anagnorisis ; and we
look in vain for an αἴτιον.

In the *Electra* Professor Murray finds (combined with the
threnos) 'a kind of spiritual Anagnorisis and Peripeteia'; this
peripeteia is certainly not from sorrow to joy, as the forms
demand : and it is surely not justifiable to treat the realization by
Orestes and Electra of the character of their act as the equivalent
of the anagnorisis of a slain daimon. The Dioscuri at the end of
the play foretell, not the origin of the Areopagus (on which point
they correct Aeschylus' deviation from the orthodox legend) but
the institution of the rule that equality of votes should give
acquittal, and explain how and where most of the persons concerned are to be buried ; but it will hardly be suggested that their
story and their place in the plot came into existence as an attempt
to explain their tombs.

In the *Iphigeneia in Tauris* and the *Helena* there is no real
pathos ; and whatever else may be dispensed with in the Ritual
Sequence, a pathos seems to be essential. The truth seems to be
that in these and some other plays (e. g. the *Ion*), so far from being
constrained by ritual forms, Euripides is striking out on quite
new lines, which are not those of Tragedy in the strictest sense.
It is difficult to miss the irony of the speech of the Dioscuri in
the *Helena*, and we need not take their aetiology too seriously.

The *Phoenissae* presents many difficult problems, which it would
take too long to discuss here, and it would be unfair to insist upon
difficulties which Professor Murray obviously feels. He also does
not discuss the structure of the play fully in this connexion. It may
be doubted whether there was an Oedipus-dromenon at all, but there
is little doubt that in the earlier versions of the story, Oedipus did
go from Thebes to Mount Cithaeron and was buried at Eteonos.

In the *Orestes*, as Professor Murray's exposition (p. 355) shows, the order of the parts is much mixed, and some are doubled.

The difficulty in regard to the *Bacchae* has already been stated (p. 187), and the *Iphigeneia in Aulis* is too incomplete to be profitably discussed. In the *Rhesus* the ritual forms will at best explain one section of the play.

Any one who reads carefully Professor Murray's own account of the emergence of the Ritual Forms from the plays can hardly come to any conclusion but one—that he is trying to find one explanation for phenomena which are too various to be explained in one way; or, in other words, that the supposed phenomenon which he is trying to explain—the intolerable and incomprehensible monotony of the plays of Euripides (not to speak of Aeschylus and Sophocles)—does not exist. Euripides does show a certain uniformity in his use of the *deus ex machina* in many of his plays: in nearly all of these there appears a strongly ironical or critical attitude towards the gods, which could be very conveniently expressed in this way, without spoiling the purely human interest of his main plot. (So far Verrall's view seems to be sound.) There also appears a tendency to connect the story of the play with living institutions of his own day, sometimes even with current events (e.g. the Dioscuri in the *Electra* go off to join in the Sicilian expedition); we may suspect that this (though not without a concealed irony) gave a flavour of piety to the endings of his plays, which would be satisfying to the old-fashioned, though most of the writers of the fifth century dabble in aetiology. But the mere recital of the plots of the plays seems enough to show that the supposed ritual sequence simply does not explain them, and can only be made to do so by the most unrestricted distortions of the sequence itself, and some very improbable general assumptions about the relations between legend, plot, and ritual.

Note on the death and sufferings of Dionysus.

The idea that the origin of tragedy is to be found in some kind of passion play representing the death or sufferings of Dionysus appears to rest in part upon what seems to be a misinterpretation (or, at least, a very doubtful interpretation) of certain passages in Herodotus. One of these, Herod. v. 67, has already been considered at length (pp. 135 ff.), and all that need be noticed here is that Herodotus does not say that the τραγικοὶ χοροί at Sicyon had to do with the πάθη of Dionysus at all, but only that the choruses which had been concerned with the πάθη of Adrastus were transferred to Dionysus. In subject they may well have been οὐδὲν πρὸς τὸν Διόνυσον, and at least one explanation of this proverb connects it with these early choruses at Sicyon (see above, p. 167).

The other passages are those in which Herodotus, identifying Osiris with Dionysus (and even interchanging the names), gives accounts of the ritual of Osiris in Egypt. In ii. 61, 132, 170 he shows that the death of Osiris was an ἄρρητον, and the mourning for him at the feast of Isis a mystic rite,—in ch. 61 at Busiris, in chs. 132, 170 at Sais: and from this it appears to be concluded that there was in Greece a mystic rite in which the death of Dionysus was enacted, the story being ἄρρητον.

In ii. 144, Herodotus, it is true, identifies Osiris with Dionysus: ″Οσιρις δέ ἐστι Διόνυσος κατὰ Ἑλλάδα γλῶσσαν. But that this identification must be taken with reserves is shown by the equation (in the same chapter) of Orus, son of Osiris, with Apollo, who must therefore (if the identification is to be taken seriously) be regarded as son of Dionysus. In fact the identification seems to have been made by Herodotus' Egyptian informants, from whom he got a good deal that was only very partially true in regard to Greek religion: this appears (e.g.) from ii. 42 θεοὺς γὰρ δὴ οὐ τοὺς αὐτοὺς ἅπαντες ὁμοίως Αἰγύπτιοι σέβονται, πλὴν ″Ισιός τε καὶ 'Οσίριος, τὸν δὴ Διόνυσον εἶναι λέγουσι· τούτους δὲ ὁμοίως ἅπαντες σέβονται. It certainly cannot be inferred from this that every rite which occurred in the worship of Osiris in Egypt occurred in that of Dionysus in Greece. Still less can this be inferred from ii. 48, where a particular festival of Osiris (Dionysus) is described: τῷ δὲ Διονύσῳ τῆς ὀρτῆς τῇ δορπίῃ χοῖρον πρὸ τῶν θυρέων σφάξας ἕκαστος διδοῖ ἀποφέρεσθαι τὸν χοῖρον αὐτῷ τῷ ἀποδο- μένῳ τῶν συβωτέων. τὴν δὲ ἄλλην ἀνάγουσι ὀρτὴν τῷ Διονύσῳ οἱ Αἰγύπτιοι πλὴν χορῶν κατὰ ταὐτὰ σχεδὸν πάντα ″Ελλησι· ἀντὶ δὲ φαλλῶν ἄλλα σφί ἐστι ἐξευρημένα, ὅσον τε πηχυαῖα ἀγάλματα νευρόσπαστα, τὰ περιφορέουσι κατὰ κώμας γυναῖκες, νεῦον τὸ αἰδοῖον, οὐ πολλῷ τέῳ ἔλασσον ἐὸν τοῦ ἄλλου σώματος· προηγέεται δὲ αὐλός,, αἱ δὲ ἔπονται ἀείδουσι τὸν Διόνυσον. διότι δὲ μέζον τε ἔχει τὸ αἰδοῖον καὶ κινέει μοῦνον τοῦ σώματος, ἔστι λόγος περὶ αὐτοῦ ἱρὸς λεγόμενος. But this feast clearly has nothing whatever to do with any mystic or dramatic death of Dionysus or mourning for him; it is a public pro- cession of the phallic type, and has nothing to do with the mystic ritual described in ii. 61, 132, 170. Herodotus *may* be comparing it with the procession at the City Dionysia in which phalli were carried, or he may not be thinking of Athens at all.

The tale of the death of Dionysus does occur in the Zagreus-legend, and no doubt was in part a tale explanatory of ritual; but there is no hint anywhere of the connexion of any public dramatic ceremony, still less of early Attic or Peloponnesian drama, with Zagreus or with Orphic ritual.

There was current also at Delphi, perhaps from the third century B.C. onwards, a peculiar form of the legend of the death of Dionysus, at the hands either of the Titans, or (after his Indian tour) of Perseus. The authorities are given in full by Dr. A. B. Cook, *Zeus*, vol. ii, pp. 218–220, and they are most confused and unsatisfactory. In one version Zeus is said to have entrusted the half-cooked limbs of Dionysus—the accounts differ as to whether they were roast or boiled—to Apollo, who buried them beside the tripod; and it is clear that Philochorus (third century B.C.) knew that there was a tomb of Dionysus at Delphi, with an inscription : ἔστιν ἰδεῖν τὴν ταφὴν αὐτοῦ ἐν Δελφοῖς παρὰ τὸν Ἀπόλλωνα τὸν χρυσοῦν. βάθρον δέ τι εἶναι ὑπονοεῖται ἡ σορός, ἐν ᾧ γράφεται, Ἐνθάδε κεῖται θανὼν Διόνυσος ἐκ Σεμέλης (Müller, *Fr. Gr. Hist.* i. 387); and an unknown poet, Deinarchus (who cannot have been much earlier than Philochorus, since he mentioned Dionysus' Indian tour, the legend of which was later than Alexander the Great), told the same story. There is no suggestion of any mourning for Dionysus at Delphi, or any dramatic ritual connected with the tomb; and if the death of the god was publicly proclaimed on the tomb, it obviously was not ἄρρητον at Delphi. We are told nothing (in this connexion) of any resurrection of the god.

XIII

Dr. A. B. Cook's theory.

§ 1. Among the many subjects treated in the first volume of his monumental work on Zeus,[1] Dr. A. B. Cook discusses the origin of Tragedy and Comedy. He starts with the Cretan ritual of Dionysus-Zagreus, and argues that Zagreus was regarded by his Cretan worshippers as Zeus reborn after being slain, and that the ritual included a yearly drama in which the worshippers performed all that the boy (Zeus or

---

[1] pp. 645 ff.

Zagreus) had done or suffered at his death ; the ritual (which included an ὠμοφαγία, a bull being in course of time substituted for the human victim) was a magical means of reviving the life of all that lives, and the worshippers came to be, through the omophagy, identified with the god.

It is not necessary to discuss here the arguments used to prove that Zagreus was Zeus reborn, though in fact the evidence appears to be very late and unsatisfactory, and Dr. Cook's thesis can hardly claim to rest on anything but a series of very ingenious conjectures. It may, however, be admitted to be quite probable that the Cretan ritual included the kind of omophagy which Firmicus Maternus (about A. D. 350) describes, though it would be more accurate to describe it as ritual than as a drama or ' passion-play '. (Of course no hard and fast line can be drawn.)

Dr. Cook passes from the Cretan ritual to the Lenaea, and argues that the ritual of the Lenaea was of the same type, except that a goat took the place of a bull; that it ended in the revelation of the god reborn, and that the passion-play thus enacted developed into Attic tragedy. On this view, Tragedy must have been connected originally with the Lenaea rather than with the Great Dionysia, and Dr. Cook exactly inverts the ordinary account, and assigns the origins of Tragedy to the Lenaea, of Comedy to the Great Dionysia. He thinks that at the Great Dionysia the union of Zeus and Semele, the begetting of Dionysus, was represented, and at the Lenaea, just ten lunar months afterwards, his birth.

We have to ask what is the evidence for this.

§ 2. The evidence for connecting a passion-play involving the death and rebirth of Dionysus with the Lenaea is hardly good enough even to prove that Semele, the mother of the reborn god as well as Dionysus himself, had a part in the festival. The Ravenna Scholion on Aristophanes, *Frogs* 479, does not prove that there was a passion-play, or that Semele figured in it, but only that at some point in the festival Iacchus was invoked as son of Semele ; [1] and whether he was

---

[1] Schol., l. c., κάλει θεόν . . . ἐν τοῖς Ληναϊκοῖς ἀγῶσιν τοῦ Διονύσου ὁ δᾳδοῦχος κατέχων λαμπάδα λέγει " καλεῖτε θεόν ", καὶ οἱ ὑπακούοντες βοῶσιν

really invoked as an infant, and not (as πλουτοδότα suggests) as a full-grown god, may well be doubted. The fact that Semele had some part in the ritual of the Lenaea at Myconos [1] does not necessarily show that the same thing happened in Athens. On one vase of the series which Frickenhaus [2] believes to represent the Lenaean ceremonial, a Maenad is carrying an infant; but it is very doubtful indeed whether the ceremonial represented is that of the Lenaea at all—the question is too complicated to discuss here [3]—and even if it is, there are only one or two vases among all those which appear to represent this ceremonial, in which the infant is depicted, and it is not at all certain that the infant *is* Dionysus.[4] It must therefore be regarded as very doubtful whether the Lenaea really represented the birth of the god at all, though it did include an invocation of Iacchus.

For the representation of his death, we are referred to a passage of Clement of Alexandria [5] and the Scholiast thereon. It is very doubtful whether the crucial word in the passage means what Dr. Cook takes it to mean. The passage is as follows:

πῇ δὴ οὖν μύθοις κενοῖς πεπιστεύκατε, θέλγεσθαι μουσικῇ τὰ ζῷα ὑπολαμβάνοντες; ἀληθείας δὲ ὑμῖν τὸ πρόσωπον τὸ φαιδρὸν μόνον, ὡς ἔοικεν, ἐπίπλαστον εἶναι δοκεῖ καὶ τοῖς ἀπιστίας ὑποπέπτωκεν ὀφθαλμοῖς. Κιθαίρων δὲ ἄρα καὶ Ἑλικὼν καὶ τὰ Ὀδρυσῶν ὄρη καὶ Θρακῶν, τελεστήρια τῆς πλάνης, ⟨διὰ⟩ τὰ μυστήρια τεθείασται καὶ καθύμνηται. ἐγὼ

"Σεμελήιε "Ιακχε πλουτοδότα" : cf. Farnell, *Cults*, v, p. 209, whose account of the Lenaea is entirely satisfactory.

[1] Dittenb. *Syll. Inscr. Gr.*³ no. 1024 (vol. iii, p. 173).
[2] Lenaeenvasen, *Winckelm.-Progr.* (1912).
[3] See Robert, *Gött. gel. Anz.* 1913, pp. 366 ff. (whose arguments against the reference to the Lenaea seem to be conclusive); Petersen in *Rhein. Mus.* lxviii (1913), pp. 239 ff., and Nilsson, *Jahrb. Arch.* xxxi, pp. 326–32. Whether Petersen and Nilsson are right in explaining the vases (though in somewhat different ways) by reference to the Anthesteria seems rather doubtful.
[4] The infant may be a human infant carried by its mother while she takes part in the worship of Dionysus.
[5] *Protrept.* i. 2. 2 (p. 4 Stählin), and Schol., p. 297 (Stählin).

μέν, εἰ καὶ μῦθός εἰσι, δυσανασχετῶ τοσαύταις ἐκτραγῳδου-
μέναις συμφοραῖς· ὑμῖν δὲ καὶ τῶν κακῶν αἱ ἀναγραφαὶ
γεγόνασι δράματα καὶ τῶν δραμάτων οἱ ὑποκριταὶ† θυμηδίας
θεάματα†. ἀλλὰ γὰρ τὰ μὲν δράματα καὶ τοὺς ληναΐζοντας
ποιητάς, τέλεον ἤδη παροινοῦντας, κιττῷ που ἀναδήσαντες,
ἀφραίνοντας ἐκτόπως τελετῇ βακχικῇ, σὺν καὶ τῷ ἄλλῳ
δαιμόνων χορῷ, Ἑλικῶνι καὶ Κιθαιρῶνι κατακλείσωμεν
γεγηρακόσιν, κατάγωμεν δὲ ἄνωθεν ἐξ οὐρανοῦ ἀλήθειαν κτλ.

Here Dr. Cook translates ληναΐζοντας 'Lenaean poets': and
the scholiast evidently thought there was a reference to the
Lenaea. His note is as follows:

ληναΐζοντας· ἀγροικικὴ ᾠδὴ ἐπὶ τῷ ληνῷ ᾀδομένη, ἢ καὶ αὐτὴ
περιεῖχεν τὸν Διονύσου σπαραγμόν. πάνυ δὲ εὐφυῶς καὶ
χάριτος ἐμπλέως τὸ κίττῳ ἀναδήσαντες τέθεικεν, ὁμοῦ μὲν τὸ
ὅτι Διονύσῳ τὰ Λήναια ἀνάκειται ἐνδειξάμενος, ὁμοῦ δὲ καὶ
ὡς παροινίᾳ ταῦτα καὶ παροινοῦσιν ἀνθρώποις καὶ μεθύουσιν
συγκεκρότηται.

But it may be doubted whether there is really any reference
to the Lenaea at all. The first part of the Scholiast's note is
evidently borrowed from somewhere else—probably from a
note on some other passage in which some song was named,
because ληναΐζοντας cannot be paraphrased by ᾠδή. (That he
wrongly connects the word with ληνός and not with λῆναι
does not here matter.) The meaning of ληναΐζοντας is
'behaving like λῆναι or Maenads'—i.e. 'frenzied', or conceivably 'inspired'—here in an ironical sense; and it has no
necessary connexion with the Λήναια (another derivative from
λῆναι). The meaning of ληναΐζειν appears from a later
passage,[1] in which Clement quotes Heracleitus' words: "ωὑτὸς
δὲ Ἅιδης καὶ Διόνυσος, ὅτεῳ μαίνονται καὶ ληναΐζουσιν", οὐ διὰ
τὴν μέθην τοῦ σώματος, ὡς ἐγὼ οἶμαι, τοσοῦτον ὅσον διὰ τὴν
ἐπονείδιστον τῆς ἀσελγείας ἱεροφαντίαν. Here the scholiast
quite rightly says: ληναΐζουσιν· βακχεύουσιν· λῆναι γὰρ αἱ
βάκχαι.[2]

[1] Ibid. ii. 34–5 (p. 26, Stählin), and Schol. on p. 307.
[2] The latter part of the first of the scholia on Clement need not be
discussed here; the scholiast, thinking that ληναΐζοντας referred to the

Even if the scholiast were right in seeing a reference to the Lenaea in the first passage, his note would only show that a chant sung at the Lenaea told of the σπαραγμός of the god, not that there was a passion-play in which the σπαραγμός was re-enacted. But in fact we do not know what the ἀγροικικὴ ᾠδή, to which his note originally referred, may have been.

For the suggestion that the supposed passion-play at the Lenaea ultimately developed into Attic Tragedy, the only evidence offered is that of Suidas' notice about Thespis. The statement that Thespis disguised his face with white lead is supposed to connect him with the Titans, the original devourers of the Cretan god, who whitened themselves with gypsum. Dr. Cook, indeed, quotes Suidas as saying that 'for the purpose of his tragedies he first smeared the faces of the performers with white lead'—'as if' (he adds) 'they were so many Titans smeared with gypsum'. But Suidas says only that he smeared *his own* face with white lead; whereas if his play were really based on the devouring of a victim by frenzied worshippers corresponding to the Titans, it should have been the faces of his chorus. Suidas is plainly speaking of the experiments in disguise which Thespis tried when he appeared as an actor distinct from the chorus, and that no special ritual significance was attached to this one is suggested by its being immediately given up.[1] But Dr. Cook also urges that the attribution to Thespis of plays called *Pentheus* and Ἆθλα Πελίου indicates that he treated the rending and devouring of Dionysus by Maenads (λῆναι) and the rejuvenation of Pelias by boiling. We have seen that the genuineness of the titles of the plays ascribed to Thespis is disputable;[2] but it is obvious that in the story of Pentheus as acted in a play Pentheus must already have been clearly distinguished from the god, as he is in Euripides,[3] and his dismemberment cannot

festival, naturally continued his note on that assumption. The crowning with ivy would be an appropriate testimony to the poet's frenzy or inspiration quite apart from the Lenaea, cf. Eur. *Bacch.* 81.

[1] See above, pp. 110 ff.   [2] See above, p. 116.
[3] See above, p. 187.

be regarded as representing that of Dionysus. It is also very doubtful whether a play entitled Ἆθλα Πελίου (whether Ἆθλα means 'contests' or 'prizes') would have included his boiling, however true it may be that a regeneration-ritual lies behind the myth of the boiling, and behind that of the cooking of Pelops, which (as a favourite tragic theme) Dr. Cook also cites in support of the view that tragedy is based on a regeneration-drama. The connexion of the other stories which Dr. Cook cites [1] (Hippolytus, Orestes, Apsyrtus) with regeneration-ritual is very thin indeed, but they need not be discussed now.[2]

On the whole, it is difficult to come to any other conclusion than that the Lenaea, though doubtless a more primitive festival and containing elements which recall those of various mysteries, cannot be shown to have involved any passion-play of the required kind,[3] and that there is no reason to disturb the traditional belief that Tragedy came to Athens from the villages of Attica and was grafted into the Great Dionysia in the middle third of the sixth century B.C.

§ 3. But, Dr. Cook tells us, the dithyramb, performed at the Great Dionysia, represented the begetting of Dionysus, as Lenaea represented his birth. The arguments for this are as follows:

(1) The two festivals were ten lunar months apart. This, however, may be due to other causes. The Anthesteria and the Rural Dionysia were also ten lunar months apart, and accordingly Dr. Cook connects these occasions also with the begetting and birth of the god. To the Anthesteria and Rural Dionysia we shall return; it need only be noticed here that the date of the latter varied in different places, and there is

---

[1] l. c. p. 680.

[2] Dr. Cook works into his discussion the line of Eratosthenes about the origin of ἀσκωλιασμός (see above, p. 102); but we have seen that it is uncertain whether this can be brought into connexion with Tragedy at all. His suggestion (p. 689) that 'ἀσκωλιασμός originated as a serious rite, designed to bring the celebrants one by one into contact with the sacred beast', as in the rite of the Διὸς κῳδίον, in which also the 'celebrants' stood on one leg on the skin, is very ingenious, though the coincidence may be a coincidence and nothing more.

[3] This is also the conclusion of Farnell, *Cults*, v, p. 176.

some reason for thinking that (e.g.) at Icaria the Rural
Dionysia took place in spring.[1]

(2) We are offered the derivation of διθύραμβος from -θορ-,
'leap' or 'beget'; but this is itself very conjectural, and can
scarcely be used as a basis of argument.[2]

(3) We are referred to Plato's description[3] of the dithyramb
as Διονύσου γένεσις, οἶμαι, διθύραμβος λεγόμενος, and we are
told that γένεσις includes γέννησις. But γένεσις certainly
cannot *exclude* 'birth'; and if the proper subject of dithyramb
were γέννησις, as distinct from the birth ten months later, it
would have to do so. The passage cannot really be treated in
this way.

(4) Dr. Cook suggests[4] a reinterpretation of the evidence
about the Pandia, a festival which immediately succeeded—or,
as he says, formed the concluding act of—the Great Dionysia,
so as to make it commemorate the union of Zeus, not with
Selene, as tradition appears to have affirmed, but with Semele.
The arguments used, though highly ingenious, are not convincing, depending, as they do, upon the making of emendations in the authorities : certainly no reliable conclusion could
be based upon such conjecture.

As to the supposed representation of the birth of Dionysus
at the Lenaea, Dr. Cook's position does not seem to be clear.
If the parallel which he draws between the Lenaean and the
Cretan ceremonies were correct, the birth ought to be a rebirth
after being slain,[5] not a normal birth consequent upon a
matrimonial union ten lunar months before. Dr. Cook can
hardly 'have it both ways'.

§ 4. There are further difficulties in the theory that the
Anthesteria (like the Great Dionysia) commemorated the begetting, the Rural Dionysia (like the Lenaea), the birth of
Dionysus, and that rudiments of Comedy can be found in the
former festival, of Tragedy in the latter.

---

[1] Haigh, *Attic Theatre*[3], p. 29; Farnell, *Cults*, v, p. 206.
[2] See above, p. 15.   [3] *Laws*, iii, p. 700 b: see above, p. 7.
[4] p. 733.
[5] Such at least seems to be Dr. Cook's view of the Cretan ritual,
pp. 645 ff.

Dr. Cook conjectures[1] that the baskets handled by the Gerairai[2] on Anthesterion 12 (the day of the Choes) contained phalloi, and that the rite performed on that day (on which alone the temple of Dionysus $Λιμναῖος$ was opened) was a phallic rite, and connected with the begetting of the god,—probably the rite which some MSS. in § 78 of the Speech against Neaera (our only authority) called $Θεόγνια$. But (1) this is almost all conjecture—though there is nothing improbable in Mr. Cook's guess as to the contents of the basket; (2) the passage gives no ground for assuming that the Theognia (or Theoinia) and the Iobakcheia, mentioned at the same time, took place on Anthesterion 12; they are only spoken of as celebrated $ἐν τοῖς καθήκουσι χρόνοις$. (3) Mr. Cook hardly succeeds in disposing of the difficulty that it was probably on Anthesterion 12 that the $ἱερὸς γάμος$ took place between Dionysus, who cannot therefore have been thought of as an infant, and the wife of the Archon Basileus. It is true that there is no direct statement to this effect in our authorities. But the indirect evidence is very strong. So solemn a ceremony must have belonged to one of the great festivals of Dionysus. The Lenaea was a mid-winter festival and an unlikely time, therefore, for the marriage of the god; the Great Dionysia was too modern for so ancient a ceremony; the Anthesteria, at the beginning of spring, would be a natural time for the $ἱερὸς γάμος$. Further, it is very difficult not to associate the solemn ceremony in the Limnaeum, described in the Speech against Neaera, with the $ἱερὸς γάμος$ in the Boukolion. Demosthenes emphasizes the necessity of the Basilissa being pure of origin and of life, and describes the oath of purity which she administers to her assistants, the $γεραιραί$, —an oath taken $ἐν κανοῖς$, such $κανᾶ$ as played a special part in an Attic marriage. All this looks like a ceremony preliminary to a marriage; and in § 73 of the Speech the administration of the oath and the sacred marriage are mentioned in the same breath,—$ἐξώρκωσέ τε τὰς γεραιρὰς τὰς ὑπηρετούσας τοῖς ἱεροῖς, ἐξεδόθη δὲ τῷ Διονύσῳ γυνή, ἔπραξε δὲ ὑπὲρ τῆς πόλεως τὰ πάτρια κτλ.$ Probably then the $γεραιραί$ accompanied the

---

[1] p. 684.   [2] Dem. *in Neaer.* 73, 78, 79.

Basilissa from the Limnaeum to the Boukolion for the marriage rite.

As to the supposed traces of Comedy at the Anthesteria, little need be said. There was a κῶμος beyond doubt, and Comedy, of course, *might* have arisen out of this; but *did* it, in any sense? There were ἀγῶνες χύτρινοι at the Anthesteria, but practically nothing is known about them.[1] Finally, Apollonius of Tyana, according to Philostratus,[2] being in Athens at the Anthesteria, ' supposed that the citizens were flocking to the theatre in order to hear solos and songs, choruses and music, such as you get in Comedy and Tragedy', but actually found that they did something else, and abused them for it! Surely this is not even the semblance of proof; and the suggestion that the pelting of Dicaeopolis at his ' Rural Dionysia ' in the *Acharnians*[3] is the relic of an original σπαραγμός of the god at that festival is difficult to take seriously. As a matter of fact it is clear that in the phallic procession organized by Dicaeopolis, Xanthias acts as phallophorus and Dicaeopolis represents the chorus or κῶμος who chant the phallic song of the god ;[4] he certainly does not represent the god. (The meaning of this scene will be more fully discussed in connexion with the origin of Comedy.)

Dr. Cook has constructed a most ingenious two-year calendar, working in the two Dionysiac years corresponding to the two pairs of festivals; but there is obviously no need to discuss this, if we cannot accept his account of the meaning of the festivals; and similarly the analogy drawn between the performances at certain festivals in the modern Greek world[5] and the supposed performances at the Lenaea only has value if the latter are independently proved, and this is just what it is hard to believe.

§ 5. Tragedy, we are told, originated at the Lenaea, Comedy at the Great Dionysia. With the origin of Comedy we shall

---

[1] See Haigh, *Attic Theatre*[3], pp. 31, 44, and above, p. 171 ; also Nilsson, *de Dionysiis Atticis*, p. 57, and O'Connor, *Chapters in the History of Actors and Acting in Ancient Greece*, pp. 54 ff.

[2] *Vit. Apoll.* iv. 21.   [3] Aristoph. *Ach.* 237 ff.

[4] See Athen. xiv. 622 c, d, and pp. 237 ff, below.   [5] pp. 694–5.

be concerned later on, and it is only necessary here to note the *non sequitur* in Dr. Cook's argument from the performance of phallic rites at the Dionysia. The argument appears to be :—the City Dionysia included phallic rites ; comedy (according to Aristotle) originated from phallic rites ; therefore comedy originated at the City Dionysia—a simple case of 'undistributed middle'. We shall see that the phallic rites which perhaps gave rise to some elements in comedy were in all probability quite different from those associated with the City Dionysia.

But Dr. Cook also argues [1] to his conclusion from the order in which the performances at the two festivals are mentioned in the Law of Euegorus (Dem. *in Meid.* § 10) and in *C.I.A.* ii. 971 ; iv. 971,—tragedy before comedy at the Lenaea, comedy before tragedy at the City Dionysia. He assumes [2] (1) that the order of enumeration is the order of performance, and not the order of importance at the two festivals ; (2) that the more primitive part of the festival was necessarily performed first. Both assumptions are very doubtful. As to (1) it is most probable that the inscriptions in question and the Law of Euegorus alike followed the order observed in the official inscriptional record made at the time of the performances ; but the order in that record would not necessarily, as Dr. Cook thinks, be that of the official *programme*—i. e. the order of the performances. The order of enumeration in an official record might well depend upon the order of importance of the several kinds of performance at the two festivals, Tragedy being originally connected with the Great Dionysia, Comedy with the Lenaea, and each being treated, at its own special festival, as the crown of the festival and mentioned last. The text of Aristophanes, *Birds*, 786 ff., implies that the comedies at the Great Dionysia were performed after the tragedies, and Dr. Cook has to emend the text in order to bring it into line with his view.[3] In view of the evidence of Aristophanes, it

---

[1] p. 683.

[2] I repeat part of this and some other arguments from my review of *Zeus* in *Cl. Rev.* xxix (1915), p. 84 ; cf. Haigh, *Attic Theatre*[3], pp. 23 ff., and for the inscriptions the Appendix to that work.

[3] The text runs : αὐτίχ' ὑμῶν τῶν θεατῶν εἴ τις ἦν ὑπόπτερος, | εἶτα πεινῶν

seems probable (though no proof is possible as regards the
first two days) that the performances from Elaphebolion 10–
14 were—on the 10th, boys' choruses and one comedy; 11th,
men's choruses and one comedy; 12th, 13th, 14th, three
tragedies, one satyric play, one comedy.

Dr. Cook's other assumption (2) seems to be quite arbitrary,
and without it his argument fails. Accretions might obviously
either precede or follow the original performance.

Dr. Cook suggests that if the supposed Lenaean drama was
the true parent of Attic tragedy, it was presumably followed
by a satyric display. He adds in a note that 'this is not
definitely recorded, but our records are very incomplete'. But
the inscriptional record of Lenaean tragedies for the years
420/19, 419/8 B.C. (*C. I. A.* ii. 972),[1] though mutilated, show
quite clearly that in those years at any rate there was no
satyric play attached to the tragedies presented by the two
competing poets: the inscription allows no room for the
mention of anything more than the tragedies. What little
evidence there is is thus distinctly against the suggestion
made. In view of this, it is not worth while to discuss
whether the vases on which satyrs are represented as assisting
or rejoicing at the Anodos of the Earth-mother are, as
Dr. Cook suggests, reminiscent of Lenaic satyr-play. There
is no positive evidence at all for any such connexion.[2]

XIV

Summary.

The result of the long investigation with which this chapter
has been occupied may be briefly summarized. As the worship
of Dionysus spread over Greece, there came with it or
developed out of it into various forms several types of performance. One of the most widespread was the dithyramb;

τοῖς χοροῖσι τῶν τραγῳδῶν ἤχθετο, | ἐκπτόμενος ἂν οὗτος ἠρίστησεν ἐλθὼν
οἴκαδε, | κᾆτ' ἂν ἐμπλησθεὶς ἐφ' ἡμᾶς αὖθις αὖ κατέπτετο. Dr. Cook has to
adopt the emendation τρυγῳδῶν. See Haigh, l. c.

[1] Haigh, l. c., p. 356.   [2] See above, p. 170.

this became a literary composition in the hands of Arion at Corinth; its history thenceforward, though it is very incompletely known, has been traced in the previous chapter. Another type was the dance of satyrs or sileni, to which Arion gave metrical form, and which doubtless continued in vogue in the north of the Peloponnese, until Pratinas brought it (in a more or less developed dramatic form) from Phlius to Athens, at the end of the sixth century; it then became partly assimilated to tragedy, and remained a constant element in the reorganized City Dionysia.

More important for humanity than either of these were those dramatic or semi-dramatic performances, which, however crude or even grotesque they may once have been, contained from the first elements of solemnity, and dealt with death and sorrow. At first they were purely choral, though probably led by an ἐξάρχων; but, perhaps in the Attic village of Icaria, Thespis created an actor's part, and brought his plays to Athens just when the spring Dionysiac festival was being reorganized and extended, and on to this festival his drama (which may have originally been performed in autumn) was grafted. This village drama met and mingled in Athens with another outcome of the solemn side of Dionysiac ritual, the lyrics which were composed to music in the τραγικὸς τρόπος invented by Arion, and were in vogue also at Sicyon and perhaps at other places; and by its union with these, and under the influence of contemporary Greek lyric poetry generally, tragedy became elevated into a supremely noble form of literature, as we see it in Aeschylus. By a singularly fortunate coincidence, the early days of tragedy fell in the time when the mass of legends, whether already in epic form or still in process of being so composed, was being collected and consolidated, and so tragedy was not confined to local or floating legend, but was given ready-made a rich store of material upon which to draw. Its literary form was improved first by the addition of a prologue and set speeches, delivered by a separate actor, to the original song and dance of the chorus; then by the addition of a second and a third speaker, in the very natural manner which is recorded.

But the attempts to explain tragedy by deriving it from dramatic representations at the tombs of deceased heroes, or by the forms of a supposed passion-play, however conceived, appear to run contrary to the evidence. Equally improbable is the belief that tragedy, even in its early stages, was ever acted by a chorus of satyrs; the evidence on the whole tends to show that dithyramb in the strict sense, satyric drama, and tragedy were always distinct, and followed each its own line of development.

It has not been possible in this discussion to deal with the archaeology of tragedy—the nature and history of the Dionysiac festivals, the costume of the actors, the character of the theatrical presentation, and the early history of the theatre. It is hoped that these and similar matters may be dealt with in another volume. In the meantime it will be convenient to undertake in regard to comedy an investigation similar to that which we have now concluded in reference to tragedy.

THE BEGINNINGS OF GREEK
COMEDY

ANALYSIS OF CHAPTER III

Appendix B. On Mr. Cornford's theory of the Origin of Attic Comedy (pp. 329–49).

III

THE BEGINNINGS OF GREEK COMEDY

I

The κῶμος.

§ 1. In discussing the origins of Greek, and particularly of
Attic, comedy, it will be convenient to take as a starting-
point the statements made by Aristotle in the *Poetics*, ch. iii,
iv, and v.

Ch. iii: διὸ καὶ ἀντιποιοῦνται τῆς τε τραγῳδίας καὶ τῆς
κωμῳδίας οἱ Δωριεῖς (τῆς μὲν γὰρ κωμῳδίας οἱ Μεγαρεῖς οἵ τε
ἐνταῦθα ὡς ἐπὶ τῆς παρ' αὐτοῖς δημοκρατίας γενομένης καὶ οἱ
ἐκ Σικελίας, ἐκεῖθεν γὰρ ἦν Ἐπίχαρμος ὁ ποιητὴς πολλῷ πρότερος ὢν Χιωνίδου καὶ Μάγνητος· καὶ τῆς τραγῳδίας ἔνιοι τῶν ἐν
Πελοποννήσῳ) ποιούμενοι τὰ ὀνόματα σημεῖον· αὐτοὶ μὲν γὰρ
κώμους τὰς περιοικίδας καλεῖν φασιν, Ἀθηναίους δὲ δήμους, ὡς
κωμῳδοὺς οὐκ ἀπὸ τοῦ κωμάζειν λεχθέντας, ἀλλὰ τῇ κατὰ
κώμας πλάνῃ ἀτιμαζομένους ἐκ τοῦ ἄστεως· καὶ τὸ ποιεῖν αὐτοὶ
μὲν δρᾶν, Ἀθηναίους δὲ πράττειν προσαγορεύειν.

What is of value in this passage is the evidence which it
gives of a tradition in Aristotle's day—he does not support or
deny it himself—that comedy originated among Dorian peoples,
and that something which could be identified by name with
comedy was found in Megara in Greece proper (between about
581 B.C. when the tyrant Theagenes was expelled, and 486, the
date of Chionides' appearance in Athens), and also in Megara
Hyblaea, where Epicharmus was composing at a considerably
earlier date than Chionides and Magnes. The value of these
traditions will be discussed later, along with other evidence ;
in anticipation it may be said that both appear to be sufficiently well founded. On the other hand the linguistic argument adduced is worthless : there can be no doubt that κωμῳδία is connected with κῶμος (κωμάζειν), not with κώμη, and

Q

that in any case κώμη was a good Attic word, at least in the
fifth century B. C., though it referred to a quarter of the city,
not to a country town or village.[1]

Ch. iv connects the subjects of comedy with the lighter
poems of the Epic age, such as the *Margites*, in which the poet
dealt not with personalities as in earlier days, but with general
topics of a humorous kind, οὐ ψόγον ἀλλὰ τὸ γελοῖον δραματο-
ποιήσας, the process being parallel to that by which tragedy
developed out of encomiastic poetry, with grand Epic as an
intermediate stage in which the interest had ceased to be
personal. This is too vague to be very valuable ; Aristotle is
obviously theorizing and propounding a logical scheme of
classification as if it were an historical order of development;
and there is in fact some doubt whether the *Margites* was
earlier than the comedy of Megara and Sicily. If there is
anything in the ascription of it (by Suidas and Proclus) to
Pigres of Halicarnassus, the uncle of the Artemisia who fought
for Xerxes, it may well not have been so.[2]

Aristotle further writes: γενομένης δ' οὖν ἀπ' ἀρχῆς αὐτοσχεδιαστικῆς—καὶ αὐτὴ (i.e. ἡ τραγῳδία) καὶ ἡ κωμῳδία καὶ ἡ μὲν
ἀπὸ τῶν ἐξαρχόντων τὸν διθύραμβον, ἡ δὲ ἀπὸ τῶν τὰ φαλλικὰ
ἃ ἔτι καὶ νῦν ἐν πολλαῖς τῶν πόλεων διαμένει νομιζόμενα—κατὰ
μικρὸν ηὐξήθη κτλ.

---

[1] See Bywater, ad loc. Bywater omits to notice Aristoph. *Lysistr.* 5
ἡ ἐμὴ κωμῆτις—an earlier instance of the Attic use than any which he
gives. [Mr. H. P. Richards (*Cl. Rev.* xiv. 201 ff.) shows that there is no
clear instance in Attic of δρᾶμα applied to Attic comedy until the time of
Plutarch, so that the part of the argument quoted by Aristotle which turns
on δρᾶμα and δρᾶν must refer to tragedy. See above, pp. 144–5.] For the
dates of Chionides and Magnes, see below, pp. 286 ff. Bywater wrongly
refers the notice in an inscription (*C. I. A.* ii. 971), recording a victory of
Magnes, to 464 B. C. : there can be no doubt that the date of the victory
was 472, though we do not know if it was his first victory (cf. Capps, *Introd.
of Comedy into City Dionysia* : Wilhelm, *Urkunden dram. Auff.*, p. 174).

[2] The ascription is perhaps a conjecture based on the facts that
(1) Pigres interpolated the *Iliad* with pentameters, (2) the *Margites* contained iambics irregularly mixed up with the hexameters (cf. Hephaest.,
p. 60, 2 Consbr.). Perhaps it was assumed that not more than one poet
was likely to have tried this kind of experiment. In the pseudo-Platonic
Alcibiad. ii, p. 147 c, the *Margites* is ascribed to 'Homer'.

If we were right in concluding above that Aristotle is con-
structing in this chapter a theory as to the origins of tragedy
and comedy, and that in deriving tragedy from dithyramb he
was probably mistaken, we cannot accept without further inquiry his derivation of comedy from phallic revelry, such as
survived in his own day in a number of cities ; [1] he may well
have seen in such revelry features common to it and to the
Old Comedy, and may not unnaturally have treated the latter
as an offshot of the cruder type of performance. As in the case
of tragedy, it is the actor's part, not that of the chorus, which
he regards as developing. We must, therefore, inquire carefully what is to be known of such phallic revelry, and test
Aristotle's theory accordingly. But first it will be convenient
to quote his statement in ch. v.

Ch. v: αἱ μὲν οὖν τῆς τραγῳδίας μεταβάσεις καὶ δι' ὧν ἐγένοντο οὐ λελήθασιν, ἡ δὲ κωμῳδία διὰ τὸ μὴ σπουδάζεσθαι
ἐξ ἀρχῆς ἔλαθεν· καὶ γὰρ χορὸν κωμῳδῶν ὀψέ ποτε ὁ ἄρχων
ἔδωκεν, ἀλλ' ἐθελονταὶ ἦσαν. ἤδη δὲ σχήματά τινα αὐτῆς
ἐχούσης οἱ λεγόμενοι αὐτῆς ποιηταὶ μνημονεύονται. τίς δὲ
πρόσωπα ἀπέδωκεν ἢ προλόγους ἢ πλήθη ὑποκριτῶν καὶ ὅσα
τοιαῦτα, ἠγνόηται. τὸ δὲ μύθους ποιεῖν ['Επίχαρμος καὶ
Φόρμις] τὸ μὲν ἐξ ἀρχῆς ἐκ Σικελίας ἦλθε, τῶν δὲ Ἀθήνησιν
Κράτης πρῶτος ἦρξεν ἀφέμενος τῆς ἰαμβικῆς ἰδέας καθόλου
ποιεῖν λόγους καὶ μύθους.

The date at which the archon can be supposed to have
granted a chorus to a comic poet was doubtless the date at
which Chionides appeared, 486 B. C. The text of the last
sentence is uncertain, but it evidently ascribed the first composition of plots of general interest to Epicharmus and Phormis
in Sicily (for even if the names are a gloss, the reference must
still be to these poets),[2] and to Crates in Athens. The last
sentence but one seems to imply the existence, in Aristotle's

---

[1] Cf. Athen. x, p. 445 a, b (speaking of Antheas of Lindos, a poet of
late but unknown date) οὗτος δὲ καὶ κωμῳδίας ἐποίει καὶ ἄλλα πολλὰ ἐν τούτῳ
τῷ τρόπῳ τῶν ποιημάτων, ἃ ἐξῆρχε τοῖς μεθ' αὐτοῦ φαλλοφοροῦσιν.

[2] Bywater, who brackets 'Επίχαρμος καὶ Φόρμις (after Susemihl), supposes
that the names originally formed part of a sentence after ἦλθε, e. g. ἦσαν
γὰρ 'Επ. καὶ Φ. ἐκεῖθεν.

belief, of a comedy earlier than that of which he had detailed
knowledge, in which there were not masks [1] nor prologues nor
several actors; an investigation of the records of phallic and
similar performances suggests that he may have had some
facts to suggest such a belief. To this investigation we may
now proceed.

§ 2. The *locus classicus* in regard to such performances is
Athenaeus xiv, pp 621 d, e, 622 a–d : παρὰ δὲ Λακεδαιμονίοις κωμι-
κῆς παιδιᾶς ἦν τις τρόπος παλαιός, ὥς φησι Σωσίβιος, οὐκ ἄγαν
σπουδαῖος, ἅτε δὴ κἂν τούτοις τὸ λιτὸν τῆς Σπάρτης μεταδιω-
κούσης. ἐμιμεῖτο γάρ τις ἐν εὐτελεῖ τῇ λέξει κλέπτοντάς τινας
ὀπώραν ἢ ξενικὸν ἰατρὸν τοιαυτὶ λέγοντα, (622 e) ὡς Ἄλεξις ἐν
Μανδραγοριζομένῃ διὰ τούτων παρίστησιν·

> ἐὰν ἐπιχώριος
> ἰατρὸς εἴπῃ "τρυβλίον τούτῳ δότε
> πτισάνης ἕωθεν", καταφρονοῦμεν εὐθέως·
> ἂν δὲ πτισάναν καὶ τρουβλίον, θαυμάζομεν.
> καὶ πάλιν ἐὰν μὲν τευτλίον, παρείδομεν.
> ἐὰν δὲ σεῦτλον, ἀσμένως ἠκούσαμεν,
> ὡς οὐ τὸ σεῦτλον ταὐτὸν ὂν τῷ τευτλίῳ.

ἐκαλοῦντο δ᾽ οἱ μετιόντες τὴν τοιαύτην παιδιὰν παρὰ τοῖς
Λάκωσι δεικηλίσται, ὡς ἄν τις σκευοποιοὺς [2] εἴπῃ καὶ μιμητάς.
(The quotation will be continued shortly.)

Sosibius appears to have lived about 300 B. C., a generation
or so after Aristotle. The performances which he described
were evidently little acted plays, very like the mimes of later
days,[3] and treated by Plutarch as virtually the same thing, in
the anecdote which he tells in the life of Agesilaus, ch. i, καί

---

[1] As already stated (pp. 122, 123), I see no reason for following Capps
and Flickinger in rendering πρόσωπα by 'characters'.

[2] σκευοποιός is used by Aristophanes, Aristotle, &c., of the maker of the
dress and general 'make-up' of the actors. See Bywater on Ar. *Poet.* vi.
1450 b 20.

[3] The theory of Thiele (*Neue Jahrb.* 1902, p. 411) that the performance
of the δεικηλίσται was a puppet-play seems to be based on no evidence
that will bear inspection, and he admits that no direct proof of it has
been found It is contradicted by Plutarch's equation of them with
μῖμοι.

ποτε Καλλιππίδης ὁ τῶν τραγῳδῶν ὑποκριτής ὄνομα καὶ δόξαν
ἔχων ἐν τοῖς Ἕλλησι καὶ σπουδαζόμενος ὑπὸ πάντων, πρῶτον
μὲν ἀπήντησεν αὐτῷ καὶ προσεῖπεν, ἔπειτα σοβαρῶς εἰς τοὺς
συμπεριπατοῦντας ἐμβαλὼν ἑαυτὸν ἐπεδείκνυτο, νομίζων ἐκεῖνον
ἄρξειν τινὸς φιλοφροσύνης, τέλος δὲ εἶπεν, " οὐκ ἐπιγιγνώσκεις
με, ὦ βασιλεῦ"; κἀκεῖνος ἀποβλέψας πρὸς αὐτὸν εἶπεν, " ἀλλ'
οὐ σύ γ' ἐσσὶ Καλλιππίδας ὁ δεικηλίκτας"; οὕτω δὲ Λακεδαι-
μόνιοι τοὺς μίμους καλοῦσι. (The point of the insult lay in
the fact that the actors of tragedy and comedy regarded the
actors of mimes with contempt; at a later date the Διονύσου
τεχνῖται never admitted them to their Society.)

The expression σκευοποιοὺς καὶ μιμητάς is partly explained
by the lexicographers' synonyms for δείκηλα, which sometimes meant the ' masks ', sometimes the 'imitation', i. e. the
performance. (Hesychius gives both πρόσωπα and also εἰκόνες,
ὁμοιώματα as equivalents of δείκηλα : other lexicographers
give εἰκάσματα, μιμήματα. The word occurs first in Herodotus ii. 171 in the sense of ' representations ': the mysteries of
Sais are said to have included δείκηλα τῶν παθέων, exhibitions
of the sufferings of Apries. The scholiast on Apoll. Rhod. i.
746 explains δεικηλίστας as τοὺς σκωπτικούς, τοὺς ἐν τῷ σκώπτειν ἄλλον τινα μιμουμένους.) It may safely be assumed that
the δεικηλίσται performed in a costume which included
masks.[1]

It happens that Plutarch[2] records a custom of Spartan boys—
apparently a part of their strange education—which suggests
that the scenes represented by the δεικηλίσται were based on real
life : καὶ φέρουσι κλέπτοντες οἱ μὲν ἐπὶ τοὺς κήπους βαδίζοντες,
οἱ δὲ εἰς τὰ τῶν ἀνδρῶν συσσίτια παρεισρέοντες εὖ μάλα πανούρ-
γως καὶ πεφυλαγμένως· ἂν δ' ἁλῷ, πολλὰς λαμβάνει πληγὰς τῇ
μάστιγι ῥαθύμως δοκῶν κλέπτειν καὶ ἀτέχνως. κλέπτουσι δὲ
καὶ τῶν σιτίων ὅ τι ἂν δύνωνται, μανθάνοντες εὐφυῶς ἐπιτίθε-

---

[1] Reich, *Mimus*, i, p. 257, n., has shown that the statement commonly
made that mime-actors wore no masks can be made with certainty only
of Roman mimes. Athen. x, p. 452 f. describes a certain Κλέων as Ἰταλικῶν
μίμων ἄριστος αὐτοπρόσωπος ὑποκριτής, and this implies that his authority
must have known of mime-actors who wore masks. The date of this
Cleon was probably early in the third century B. C. (Reich, ibid., p. 528).

[2] *Vit. Lycurg.* xvii.

σθαι τοῖς καθεύδουσιν ἢ ῥαθύμως φυλάσσουσι· τῷ δὲ ἀλόντι ζημία
πληγαὶ καὶ τὸ πεινῆν. Pollux[1] also mentions a Laconian
dance—its name was probably μιμηλική—δι' ἧς ἐμιμοῦντο τοὺς
ἐπὶ τῇ κλοπῇ τῶν ἑωλῶν κρεῶν[2] ἁλισκομένους.

Now these records are of importance, because they introduce
us to character types with which Greek comedy was familiar.
The fruit-stealer was known to Epicharmus.[3] The thief of
food of other kinds appears on one of the vases representing
the performances of the phlyakes of South Italy,[4] whose relation
to early Peloponnesian performances and to Sicilian comedy
will often be referred to hereafter; and we may find a trace
of the same character in Aristophanes' *Knights*, l. 417 ; though
the cunning stealer of food is so common a resource of low
comedy in all ages, that it would not be right to lay stress on
this character in an argument as to orgins or influence. It
is of more significance that the quack-doctor is found not only
in the passage of Alexis quoted by Athenaeus, but in Crates,
a poet of the Old Comedy, and that in Crates he speaks
Doric.[5] The doctor occurred also in the *Endymion* of
Alcaeus, and tried to cure the hero's somnolence. In a fragment of Theopompus (a poet of the later Old Comedy) a similar
character, the apothecary, is a Megarean, though whether he
is so called because the occupation was commonly followed
by Dorians, or because this was a character in Megarean
comedy, we do not know.

Whether the δεικηλίσται were phallic is not definitely stated.
The actors of mimes frequently were, and their kinsmen, the

---

[1] iv. 104.

[2] MSS. μερῶν: perhaps ἑωλομερῶν (Kühn) is the right reading. (For
the whole passage see below, p. 258.)

[3] ap. Zenob. v. 84 Σικελὸς ὀμφακίζεται·. . . . μετενήνεκται δὲ ἀπὸ τῶν Σικελῶν
τὰς ἀβρώτους ὄμφακας κλεπτόντων. Epich. fr. 239 (Kaibel).

[4] Heydemann, *Jahrb. Arch.* i, p. 273 d : Xanthias appears to be hiding
away a stolen cake.

[5] ἀλλὰ σικύαν ποτιβαλῶ τοι, καὶ τὺ λῇς ἀποσχάσω (fr. 41). The doctor was
still a character in mimes in the time of Choricius in the sixth century
A.D. (see *Rev. de Phil.* i (1887), p. 218) as he is still in Christmas
mummings. In primitive times the doctor was, probably very often, an
itinerant practitioner, and so came often to be represented as a foreigner.

Graeco-Italian phlyakes, were so regularly;[1] and it is probable
that Athenaeus thought that the δεικηλίσται were similarly
costumed. We shall return to the δεικηλίσται later.

Athenaeus continues:[2] τοῦ δὲ εἴδους τῶν δεικηλιστῶν πολλαὶ
κατὰ τόπους εἰσὶ προσηγορίαι. Σικνώνιοι μὲν γὰρ φαλλο-
φόρους αὐτοὺς καλοῦσιν, ἄλλοι δ᾽ αὐτοκαβδάλους, οἱ δὲ φλύακας,
ὡς Ἰταλοί, σοφιστὰς δὲ οἱ πολλοί· Θηβαῖοι δὲ καὶ τὰ πολλὰ
ἰδίως ὀνομάζειν εἰωθότες ἐθελοντάς.[3] ... Σῆμος δὲ ὁ Δήλιος ἐν
τῷ περὶ παιάνων, " οἱ αὐτοκάβδαλοι", φησί, " καλούμενοι ἐστε-
φανωμένοι κιττῷ σχέδην ἐπέραινον ῥήσεις. ὕστερον δὲ ἴαμβοι
ὠνομάσθησαν αὐτοί τε καὶ τὰ ποιήματα αὐτῶν. οἱ δὲ ἰθύφαλλοι", φησί, " καλούμενοι προσωπεῖα μεθυόντων ἔχουσι καὶ ἐστε-
φάνωνται, χειρῖδας ἀνθινὰς ἔχοντες· χιτῶσι δὲ χρῶνται μεσο-
λεύκοις καὶ περιέζωνται ταραντῖνον καλύπτον αὐτοὺς μέχρι τῶν
σφυρῶν. σιγῇ δὲ διὰ τοῦ πυλῶνος εἰσελθόντες, ὅταν κατὰ
μέσην τὴν ὀρχήστραν γένωνται, ἐπιστρέφουσιν εἰς τὸ θέατρον
λέγοντες·

> ἀνάγετ᾽, εὐρυχωρίαν ποι-
> εῖτε τῷ θεῷ· ἐθέλει γὰρ
> [ὁ θεὸς] ὀρθὸς ἐσφυδωμένος
> διὰ μέσου βαδίζειν.

οἱ δὲ φαλλοφόροι", φησίν, " προσωπεῖον μὲν οὐ λαμβάνουσιν,
προσκόπιον δ᾽ ἐξ ἑρπύλλου περιτιθέμενοι καὶ παιδέρωτος ἐπάνω
τούτου ἐπιτιθένται στέφανον δασὺν ἴων καὶ κιττοῦ· καυνάκας τε
περιβεβλημένοι παρέρχονται οἱ μὲν ἐκ παρόδου, οἱ δὲ κατὰ
μέσας τὰς θύρας, βαίνοντες ἐν ῥυθμῷ καὶ λέγοντες,

> σοί, Βάκχε, τάνδε μοῦσαν ἀγλαΐζομεν,
> ἁπλοῦν ῥυθμὸν χέοντες αἰόλῳ μέλει,
> καινάν, ἀπαρθένευτον, οὔ τι ταῖς πάρος
> κεχρημέναν ᾠδαῖσιν, ἀλλ᾽ ἀκήρατον
> κατάρχομεν τὸν ὕμνον.

---

[1] See Reich, ibid., i, pp. 17, 258, &c.   [2] xiv, pp. 621 f, 622.

[3] That Aristotle, *Poet.* v, speaks of primitive performers of comedy as
ἐθελονταί is doubtless only a coincidence. It could not be inferred that
he had the Theban performances in his mind. Körte, however (Pauly-W.
xi, col. 1221), suggests that ἐθελοντάς in Athen. is a gloss upon a local
Theban name which has dropped out of the text, and this is highly
probable, as the word is by no means one peculiar to Thebes.

εἶτα προστρέχοντες ἐτώθαζον οὓς [ἂν] προέλοιντο, στάδην δὲ
ἔπραττον· ὁ δὲ φαλλοφόρος ἰθὺ βαδίζων καταπασθεὶς αἰθάλῳ."
(The text at the end is uncertain : καταπασθείς is Kaibel's
emendation for καταπλησθείς.)

The date of Semus of Delos is perhaps early in the second
century B. C.[1] The passages quoted must be used with great
caution, since it is clear that Athenaeus has failed to distinguish between non-choral performances like those of the
δεικηλίσται and φλύακες, and, on the other hand, distinctly
choral performances like those of the φαλλοφόροι and ἰθύφαλλοι, which can only be said to belong to the εἶδος τῶν
δεικηλιστῶν in a very general sense. We shall see that this
distinction is of the greatest importance.

With regard to the names αὐτοκάβδαλοι and σοφισταί not
much can be said. In Aristotle's *Rhetoric* III. vii αὐτοκα-
βδάλως is opposed to σεμνῶς, and in ch. xiv αὐτοκάβδαλα may
mean ' off-hand ', ' unprepared '. In Lycophron 745 αὐτοκά-
βδαλον σκάφος is an improvised boat. In Hesychius αὐτοκάβδαλα is paraphrased by αὐτοσχέδια ποιήματα εὐτελῆ : and the
Etymologicum Magnum gives the meaning as τὸ ὡς ἔτυχε
φυραθὲν ἄλευρον (κάβος being a word for a measure of corn,
which is found in the lexicographers). The meaning as
applied to poems is clearly ' improvised ',[2] and perhaps σχέδην
(' quietly') in the text of Athenaeus should be emended to
σχεδίην (' at once ', ' off-hand ').[3] In any case improvised ῥήσεις
can hardly have been choral. The αὐτοκάβδαλοι, ivy-crowned, do
not appear to have been masked. The name σοφισταί certainly
can apply to a body of musicians or poets as well as to individuals,[4] and in Cratinus, Ἀρχίλοχοι fr. 2, it is used of poets
(οἷον σοφιστῶν σμῆνος ἀνεδιφήσατε), though whether of the
chorus of the play or not is uncertain ; in fr. 1 of Iophon it

[1] See Jacoby in Pauly-W. *Real-Enc.* ii A, col. 1357–8; Bapp, *Leipz.
Stud.* viii, pp. 99, 121.

[2] Aristotle, *Poet.* iv, regards both serious and comic poetry as
originating ultimately from αὐτοσχεδιάσματα.

[3] It and the parts of σχέδιος are used in this sense in Nicander,
Babrius, &c. (see Liddell & Scott).

[4] In Pindar, *Isthm.* iv. 25 it is used of the ἀοιδός, in Eur. *Rhesus*, 923
of Thamyris.

is used of the satyr-musicians accompanying Silenus (καὶ γὰρ
εἰσελήλυθεν | πολλῶν σοφιστῶν σμῆνος ἐξηρτημένος), and it
could probably be used of clever performers of any kind, many
or single.[1]

It is not clear what Semus meant by saying that the
αὐτοκάβδαλοι and their poems were afterwards called ἴαμβοι,
in the absence of any indication of date or place. There is no
other instance of the word ἴαμβοι being applied to persons,
though Athenaeus speaks of ἰαμβισταί at Syracuse.[2]

The ἰθύφαλλοι wore the masks of drunken-men, and garlands
on their heads; they wore also a tunic with a white stripe,[3]
and flowered (or gaily-coloured) sleeves, and a ταραντῖνον—
a fine transparent robe (mostly worn by women)—falling to the
feet. Their own costume was not phallic, but they escorted
a phallus (perhaps set on a pole) into the theatre, marching
in silently, probably through the central door in the προσκήνιον,
and then facing the audience and singing their song demand-
ing ' room for the god ', whom they escorted. Unfortunately
Semus tells us nothing of the ceremony, nor even the name of
the town, in which this performance took place: for it was
obviously a formal ceremony, not a mere revel, though not
dramatic; and this appears to differentiate it from the
behaviour of (e.g.) the festive young Athenians mentioned in
Demosthenes' Speech against Conon, who called themselves
αὐτολήκυθοι[4] or ἰθύφαλλοι, initiated themselves to 'Ιθύφαλλος,

---

[1] There seems no reason to think that the use of the word was
ironical, as Lorenz supposes, in application to performances of the εἶδος
τῶν δεικηλιστῶν. Thiele (*Neue Jahrb.* 1902, p. 409) thinks that the word
implies professionals, as distinct from the Theban ἐθελονταί: and though
this is not proved (for he seems to rely on the analogy with the
wandering teachers to whom the name of 'sophist' was given), it is not
impossible that the δεικηλίσται and σοφισταί and the Syracusan ἰαμβισταί,
and also the Graeco-Italian φλύακες, were professionals, as distinct from
the ἰθύφαλλοι, φαλλοφόροι, and αὐτοκάβδαλοι.

[2] v. 181 c καθόλου δὲ διάφορος ἦν ἡ μουσικὴ παρὰ τοῖς ῞Ελλησι, τῶν μὲν
'Αθηναίων τοὺς Διονυσιακοὺς χοροὺς καὶ τοὺς κυκλίους προτιμώντων, Συρακοσίων
δὲ τοὺς ἰαμβιστάς, ἄλλοι δὲ ἄλλο τι.

[3] For further explanation of μεσόλευκος see Reich, *Mimus*, i. 276.

[4] Dem. *in Conon.*, § 14. The meaning of αὐτολήκυθοι (see Sandys'
commentary) is probably ' men who carried their own λήκυθοι ', instead

and attacked and insulted respectable citizens in their revels. But there is little about the ἰθύφαλλοι of Semus which helps to an understanding of comedy.

Is it otherwise with the φαλλοφόροι? These wore garlands of pansies and ivy on their heads,[1] and hung flowers in front of their faces, but were not masked ; they were clad in thick wool-lined garments,[2] and marched into the orchestra, some by the parodos, some by the central doors in the προσκήνιον, keeping time and singing some iambic lines in which they profess to be offering to Bacchus an entirely new song—no doubt supposed to be improvised on the spot. They then ran up to any of the audience whom they chose to select and made fun of them. The phallophorus proper had his face disguised with soot. (Probably he carried, but did not wear, the phallus.) The words στάδην δὲ ἔπραττον seem to mean that the performers did not dance.

How far then does this account help us with regard to the origin of comedy ?

In the first place it is quite uncertain (as in the case of the ἰθύφαλλοι) of what performance Semus is speaking. Athenaeus states that φαλλοφόροι was the Sicyonian name for the εἶδος τῶν δεικηλιστῶν—a statement obviously false, for the performance of the φαλλοφόροι was choral, while that of the δεικηλίσται was not. Whether Athenaeus' authority for connecting the φαλλοφόροι with Sicyon was Semus or Sosibius or neither does not appear from the text: the quotation from Semus begins subsequently.[3] The iambic lines of the song

---

of taking slaves with them, and so 'gentlemen-tramps': cf. also Robert, *Die Masken der neueren Att. Kom.*, p. 24, n. 1, who quotes passages showing that the word connoted poverty.

[1] Cf. Plato, *Symp.* 212 e, where Alcibiades wears the same garland.

[2] For καννάκαι see Aristoph. *Wasps*, 1137, &c., and Starkie's note ad loc. They seem to have been made of thick cloth, lined with sheep-skin, and to have been worn by slaves and Orientals.

[3] Hence the suggestion of Poppelreuter (*de Com. Att. primordiis*, p. 14) that in ascribing the phallophori to Sicyon, Semus was influenced by a desire to assign a Dorian origin to comedy, after Ar. *Poet.* iii, hangs in the air. (Poppelreuter traces a similar desire in an epigram of Onestes in *Anth. Pal.* xi. 32 (date unknown).)

are not in the dialect of Sicyon, but in the conventional lyric
dialect used by Attic poets.[1] Bethe[2] calls the phallophori
'Delians', and it is of course possible that Semus was describing
what happened in his own home; but there is not much to be
said for this view, as he was apparently writing a general
treatise,[3] and need not have been thinking of Delos in
particular. Possibly the ceremony of the phallophori was of
a common type, differing little from town to town.

In the second place, there are no dramatic elements in the
ceremony. The performers impersonate no one, and remain
themselves throughout. It is true that not too much stress
must be laid upon this. For the part of the Old Comedy which
the phallophori are usually supposed to explain is the parabasis, and the parabasis may originally have been non-dramatic.
On this point it is well to be as precise as possible. The statement sometimes made that at the beginning of the parabasis
the chorus threw off their dramatic costume is an exaggeration:
at most they probably threw off only their outer garment, for
greater ease in dancing;[4] they did not throw off their masks;[5]
and while the 'anapaests' delivered by the leader are usually
(not always)[6] irrelevant to the plot, the dramatic character is
retained, as a rule, in the epirrhema and antepirrhema,
though plenty of topical allusion and personal satire are combined with it. But the parabasis does make a break in the
dramatic structure; and the fact that we can trace the steps
by which Aristophanes attempted to work it better into the
whole, suggests that if we were able to trace its development
backwards, we should find that it was originally a non-

---

[1] See above, p. 147. [2] *Proleg.*, p. 54.

[3] The quotation is from the Περὶ παιάνων of Semus, not from the Δηλιακά.

[4] e. g. *Ach.* 627; *Peace* 729; *Lysistr.* 614, 634, 662, 686. The fact that
the chorus behave similarly when the dramatic action is at its height in
Wasps 408, *Thesm.* 655, shows that their object was freedom of movement,
not freedom from their dramatic character.

[5] Cornford, *Origin of Att. Comedy*, p. 121, states that they did, but gives
no evidence, and on pp. 126, 127 he appears to take the other view.
Navarre, *Rev. Et. Anc.* 1911, p. 256, also without offering evidence, states
that the chorus laid aside their masks in the parabasis.

[6] e. g. in the *Birds*.

dramatic performance, the executants of which only acquired masks and a dramatic character when brought into union with actors of a really dramatic type and of different origin. But this does not really help us much: since the other points of contrast between the phallophori and the parabasis are very marked.

For, in the third place, it seems clear that the chorus in the parabasis danced—at least in the ode and antode, and probably throughout the epirrhematic portion,[1] whereas the phallophori στάδην ἔπραττον.

In the fourth place, the form of the phallophoric ceremony is of an entirely different type from anything that we find in the parabasis. In the latter, after the delivery of the 'anapaests', there is a perfectly formal epirrhematic structure, the ode and epirrhema being followed by an antode and antepirrhema which exactly balance them. In the former, there is nothing to suggest any such symmetry; and when we come to consider the phallic κῶμος presented in the *Acharnians* (in many ways like that described by Athenians), we shall see that the phallic hymn there sung is unlike anything in the parabasis.

Lastly, there is nothing in the parabasis, or indeed in comedy at all, to correspond to the black man who seems to be the ἐξάρχων of the phallophori, and who reminds us of the sweep or the black man (under whatever name) who is a figure in English mummings at Christmas and May-day, and in the rustic play of many other peoples.[2] If it be suggested that the black man and the phallophori correspond to the actor and chorus of comedy, it must be pointed out that though the

---

[1] See Appendix A, p. 296.

[2] It is sometimes thought that the Maypole itself began its career as a phallic emblem. Dr. Farnell (*Cults*, v, p. 211) compares the black man of the phallophori with the ψολοεῖς or 'sooty ones' in a ceremony at Orchomenus (Plut. *Quaest. Gr.* ch. 38), and the blackened figure in the modern rural dramatic performance at Viza (*J. H. S.* 1906, p. 191). I do not feel sure that the ψολοεῖς are really parallel; they seem to belong to a more serious sphere, like the Μέλανθος of Eleutherae (see above, p. 161). It is very doubtful whether the phallic κῶμος, at least in historical times, was usually more than a revel with little religious significance.

black man carried a phallic emblem, there is nothing to show that he wore the phallus, whereas the Athenian comic actor commonly (though not always) did so in the most indecent fashion.[1] In fact the actor, as we shall see, has probably quite different affinities, and his whole costume was quite different from that of the phallophori.

Accordingly we have no real points of contact between the phallophori of Semus and the Old Comedy, except that in both a chant or invocation was or might be followed by mockery of the bystanders; and the points of contrast are so marked, that though we may still connect comedy with some kind of primitive κῶμος, this particular kind helps us little. It will be best to consider next a type of phallic ceremony not unlike that described by Semus, but certainly belonging to Athens itself.

§ 3. This ceremony is that which Aristophanes connects with the Rural Dionysia, and it cannot be ruled out of consideration on the ground that the festival with which comedy was originally connected at Athens was the Lenaea.[2] This is almost certainly true: but it is at least highly probable that the festival called at Athens by the name 'Lenaea' *was* the 'Rural Dionysia' of primitive Athens itself, and corresponded to the Dionysia κατ' ἀγρούς of the rural demes.

---

[1] This has been disputed by Thiele, *Neue Jahrb.* ix, p. 421, and others; but Aristoph. *Clouds* 537 ff. is unintelligible unless the practice were at least common, and it is not likely to have been common unless it were quite primitive and at one time essential. The schol. on *Clouds* 542 is probably right in saying: ἰστέον δὲ ὅτι πάντα ὅσα ἂν λέγῃ εἰς ἑαυτὸν τείνει, τοὺς γὰρ φάλητας εἰσήγαγεν ἐν τῇ Λυσιστράτῃ, τὸν δὲ κόρδακα ἐκ τοῖς Σφηξί, τοὺς δὲ φαλακροὺς ἐν Εἰρήνῃ, τὸν δὲ πρεσβύτην ἐν Ὄρνισι, κτλ. Passages in which the wearing of the visible phallus seems certain are *Acharn.* 158, 592; *Wasps* 1343; *Lysistr.* 991, 1077, &c. Other passages in which there is little doubt of it are enumerated by Körte, *Jahrb. Arch.* viii, p. 66, and Pauly-W. *Real-Enc.* xi, col. 1219. Probably it was conventional that one or more phallic actors should appear in each play, and Aristophanes only modified the grossness of the custom without entirely abolishing it (cf. Eupolis, fr. 244 K.). There is little evidence that a phallic costume was worn by leading characters taken from life; Kinesias in the *Lysistrata* is the one extant example: it was probably confined almost entirely to typical or fictitious personages of the βωμολόχος type (see below, pp. 270 ff.).

[2] See above, p. 217.

We know that the Lenaea originally took place in or near the site of the later agora:[1] but this was almost certainly north-west of the Acropolis, and outside the most primitive city, which lay mainly to the south and south-west of the Acropolis; so that the festival in fact took place ἐν ἀγροῖς, although, when that district came to be included in the city, the rural character of the festival disappeared, and it was transferred to the theatre on the south side of the Acropolis.[2] Although, therefore, there is no direct evidence connecting a phallic procession, like that depicted by Aristophanes, with the Lenaea, but only some kind of procession in wagons, from which the riders jeered at the bystanders,[3] it is at least likely to have included a phallic κῶμος also, as the Rural Dionysia did.

In the *Acharnians*, Aristophanes shows us Dicaeopolis celebrating the Rural Dionysia, with what is obviously a skeleton procession of the phallophoric type. Dicaeopolis' daughter walks in front as κανηφόρος, with a basket probably containing the cakes and instruments for the sacrifice; Xanthias follows carrying the phallus; Dicaeopolis acts chorus [4]—he is obviously non-phallic, like the phallophori of Semus—and sings the hymn to Phales, companion of Bacchus; his wife (representing the crowd) looks down from the roof. The hymn contains, one, if not two, satirical personalities, corre-

---

[1] Cf. Haigh, *Attic Theatre*[3], App. C: but I prefer the interpretation now given of the passages quoted on p. 378 to that which I there offered.

[2] That the Lenaea was the same festival as the Rural Dionysia of other districts is also suggested by the fact that no Attic townships can be shown to have had both festivals; and, indeed, there would have been no object, from a religious or ritual point of view, in having two winter festivals of the same kind. See Farnell, *Cults*, v, p. 213.

[3] Suidas, s. v. τὰ ἐκ τῶν ἁμαξῶν σκώμματα . . . Ἀθήνησι γὰρ ἐν τῇ τῶν Χοῶν ἑορτῇ οἱ κωμάζοντες ἐπὶ τῶν ἁμαξῶν τοὺς ἀπαντῶντας ἔσκωπτόν τε καὶ ἐλοιδόρουν. τὸ δ' αὐτὸ καὶ τοῖς Ληναίοις ὕστερον ἐποίουν: and s. v. ἐξ ἁμάξης· ἡ λεγομένη ἑορτὴ παρ' Ἀθηναίοις Λήναια.

[4] Körte (in Pauly-W. xi, col. 1219) seems to regard Dicaeopolis as the ἐξάρχων, without a chorus. There is no objection to this, unless it is that the title ἐξάρχων belongs more strictly to the φαλλοφόρος proper (here Xanthias): Dicaeopolis is rather the coryphaeus. But Körte emphasizes the essential point, the entirely non-dramatic character of the κῶμος as depicted.

sponding to the mockery of the bystanders described by Semus.
What differentiates this ritual from that recorded by Semus
is that its central feature was evidently a sacrifice. It might
also appear, at first sight, as if it were a purely domestic
function. Dicaeopolis says (ll. 247 ff.) :

> καὶ μὴν καλόν γ᾽ ἔστ᾽, ὦ Διόνυσε δέσποτα,
> κεχαρισμένως σοι τήνδε τὴν πομπὴν ἐμὲ
> πέμψαντα καὶ θύσαντα μετὰ τῶν οἰκετῶν
> ἀγαγεῖν τυχηρῶς τὰ κατ᾽ ἀγροὺς Διονύσια.

But, as the context shows, this is only because he has got
his treaty all to himself, and therefore performs, all by himself
(or with a few slaves), what should really be a social or choral
ceremony ; so that the parallelism with the ritual described
by Semus holds good. In neither is there anything dramatic ;
the agents represent no-one but themselves.

At the same time, the procession in the *Acharnians* does
not really bear much more resemblance to anything in the form
of comedy than does the ceremony described by Semus. We
have a chant and in it (though not, as in the parabasis, after
it also) there are satirical allusions of a personal kind ; but
the chant itself is of a very different type from anything in
the parabasis. It has the look of those popular chants in
which stanza might follow stanza to any length, so long as the
singer's stock of personalities lasted : the only parallel to it
in Aristophanes is found in the Iacchus song in the *Frogs*
supposed to be sung in procession to Eleusis ; but there are
other instances in Greek literature,[1] and it is in any case
a very different thing from the strictly symmetrical double-
form of the parabasis. The ridicule of the bystanders, or the
satirical allusions, whether in Semus' performance or in the
Rural Dionysia of Dicaeopolis, offer a very slender thread of
connexion with comedy ; for such ridicule occurred on many

---

[1] See Cornford, l. c., p. 40, for some interesting parallels. Such chants
often have a refrain, in which the revellers join, while the leader ex-
temporizes words leading up to it. In Dicaeopolis' chant, there is no
trace of such a refrain, but the chant is of a kind which might go
on indefinitely, if it had not been broken off by the irruption of the
chorus.

different occasions in Athenian life—on the return of the
mystics from Eleusis, at the Anthesteria, at the Stenia, &c.; and,
quite apart from the ritual employment of abusive language,[1]
it may be suspected that any occasion on which Athenians
came together to watch a merry procession was unlikely to
pass without a good deal of banter between the performers
and the bystanders.[2]

It seems, therefore, at least possible that Aristotle, in
deriving comedy from the phallic processions, was once more
theorizing, not recording an ascertained historical development.
Knowing that the Old Comedy involved phallic actors, he came
to his conclusion without realizing that in all probability the
phallic actor of comedy was derived (as we shall see) from
a quite different type of performance, the Dorian mime or
farce or burlesque.

But if the phallic κῶμος as portrayed for us by Aristophanes
and Semus cannot be shown to have had much to do with
the beginnings of comedy, we are bound to ask whether any
other form of κῶμος is of more use for our purpose : for that
comedy arose out of a κῶμος in some sense the name itself
does not permit us to doubt.

§ 4. Before proceeding directly with this problem it will be
well to inquire rather more closely into its conditions. For
it is not the parabasis alone for which we have to account.
Assuming (for reasons which will appear later) that the
iambic scenes, a series of which for the most part succeed the
parabasis, are not to be explained by reference to the κῶμος,
and neglecting for the moment the prologue and all that precedes the entrance of the chorus, we find closely connected
together in an Aristophanic play (1) a scene in which the chorus
enters, not infrequently in some haste and excitement, and
which we may conveniently term the Parodos ;[3] (2) a scene of

---

[1] e. g. as recorded in Herod. v. 82. I cannot subscribe to the view
that the origin of such ridicule or abuse was always in ritual.

[2] See Nilsson, *Gr. Feste*, p. 282.

[3] The name has no ancient authority in connexion with comedy, and
different modern writers use it to cover varying portions of the first half
of a play. See Appendix A for details.

conflict, calming down to a formal debate or Agon, which ends
with the victory of one party in the dispute; (3) the Parabasis.
These scenes are all for the most part in long metres (anapaestic,
iambic or trochaic tetrameters, or occasionally Eupolideans or
long verses nearly allied), and they present in greater or less
perfection the symmetrical structure which is known as
epirrhematic,[1] and though Aristophanes (who represents the
last stage in the development of the Old Comedy) varies this
structure in many ways, and is never closely tied to strict
symmetry except in the parabasis, it is plain that he is basing
his variations on a more or less definite conventional form, and
that in the parabasis he was much more strictly bound by it.
The kind of κῶμος to which this points is one in which the
chorus enters singing and excited; a dispute arises—and is
fought out, at first violently, and then by a debate in set form;
judgement is given, and the revellers, having so far been concerned with themselves only, now address themselves to the
audience, in the conventional form of the parabasis, consisting
essentially of an address, not concerned with the subject of
the dispute, followed by an epirrhematic system (ode, epirrhema,
antode, antepirrhema), the two speeches included in this being
topical or satirical. Throughout, the division of the chorus into
two semi-choruses is easily made, and in the parabasis is regular.

Now it seems virtually certain that parodos, agon, and parabasis form one whole, and it is probably a mistake to inquire
whether the agon or the parabasis is the earliest or most
essential element, though much trouble has been expended on
this problem;[2] and there is obviously a presumption in favour
of the normal order, as found in the Old Comedy, having been
the original one. If the parabasis was once the opening of

---

[1] See later.

[2] Cf. Mazon, *Essai sur la Comp. des Com. d'Arist.*, p. 174; Zielinski,
Glied., p. 186; Kaibel in Pauly-W. *Real-Enc.* ii. 987; Poppelreuter, l. c.,
32 ff.; Körte in Pauly-W. xi. 1247. The view taken above is (so far) the
same as that of Zielinski; the arguments to the contrary appear to be
very inconclusive. The fact that the form of the agon is more liable to
vary than that of parabasis suggests that the epirrhematic form is more
essential to the latter and probably therefore originally belonged to it
and was transferred to the agon.

the performance, as some scholars suppose, it is difficult to account for the existence of a more or less regular manner of entry in the scenes preceding the debate : but there seems to be no difficulty in imagining an excited κῶμος-like entry, followed by (or bringing with it) a dispute, or in the disputants then calming down to the debating-temper, and when the debate is over, talking at large to the crowd.[1] (In the parabasis of the play they usually solicit the favour of the audience for the poet ; in the κῶμος, especially if they were expecting gifts, they would ask it for themselves.)

There is, however, a certain difficulty about the debate or dispute. For in the plays of Aristophanes the dispute is only exceptionally (in fact, only in the *Lysistrata*) a dispute between two semi-choruses ; and that this was not the original form is almost proved by the dislocation of the normal structure which is thereby entailed.[2] The dispute is either between one personage and the chorus, or between two characters, one of whom is closely connected with the chorus and is virtually their representative. Probably then the dispute may, in the original κῶμος, have been between one of the revellers and the rest, and any set debate may have been between this one and a champion or representative of the rest.

---

[1] The word παράβασις does not seem to be a real obstacle to this view. It (or the verb παραβαίνειν which is used in *Acharn.* 629, &c.) need not denote the first entrance on to the scene ; it may equally mark the point where the revellers, having so far been entirely engaged with one another, turn to address the bystanders or audience (cf. the regular use of παρέρχομαι of the orator who comes forward to address his hearers). I find it difficult to accept the view of Radermacher (Ar. *Frösche*, p. 34) that it denotes a 'march past'.

[2] The normal form of parabasis is entirely destroyed. I cannot (with Cornford, op. cit., pp. 125, &c.) treat the parabasis of the *Lysistrata*, in which two semi-choruses are opposed, as the original form of parabasis, or the parabasis as originally an agon. The *Lysistrata* is quite unique among the plays of Aristophanes in this respect ; there is nowhere else any trace of opposition within the parabasis, and the only other instance of a sharp distinction between two semi-choruses is in the ’Οδυσσεῖς of Cratinus as (not quite convincingly) reconstructed by Kaibel, *Hermes*, xxx, pp. 71 ff. (esp. 79 ff.). The division of opinion in the *Acharnians* is quite momentary.

If this is so, it is not easy to accept the solution offered by Navarre,[1] who thinks that the κῶμος which gave rise to comedy was a phallic κῶμος, such as Semus describes ; that the dispute began when the revellers began to chaff the bystanders ; that the latter produced their champion, and so the brawl arose, and, as they calmed down, the debate. This does not really correspond to the facts of the Old Comedy, in which the addresses to the bystanders do not occur until the parabasis is reached: in the agon there is no consciousness of the audience ; the κῶμος is there self-contained. Nor is it satisfactory to account for the fact that the comic chorus consisted of twenty-four members (instead of twelve as in early tragedy) by supposing that it was really a double chorus, half representing the phallic revellers, half the bystanders : for, again, there is nothing in the Old Comedy to support this idea ; the chorus generally speaks (through its leader) as a whole, and the fact that on some of the occasions when the members of a procession chaffed the bystanders (e. g. on the road to Eleusis) the latter seem to have joined in and retaliated, does not really prove anything as regards comedy. May not the explanation of the large number of the chorus lie in the nature of a κῶμος ? Twelve would make a very thin κῶμος.

Now it must be admitted without reserve that we have no direct evidence for the existence of the exact κῶμος which we want to explain the epirrhematic parts of comedy : but in truth the existence of a form so persistent in type as that of the Parados-Agon-Parabasis structure can almost itself be taken as evidence for the existence of a κῶμος of a similar type before the Old Comedy (which combines this with scenes of a quite different origin) was produced : and along with this κῶμος-sequence, we must postulate the existence of a conventional epirrhematic form—surely a very simple and natural form—associated with it.[2] This assumption, though of course it is

---

[1] *Rev. Et. Anc.* xiii (1911), pp. 245 ff.

[2] It seems unprofitable to discuss whether Sieckmann is right in supposing that the parabasis borrowed the epirrhematic form from the agon, or Körte in supposing that the agon borrowed it from the para-basis. If either borrowed, it was probably the agon, as suggested

conjectural, seems more satisfactory than the attempt to extract comedy from the phallic revel, which meets the required conditions so badly: and we may therefore provisionally suppose that comedy arose, not out of the specifically phallic element in the Lenaea (which may have been like Dicaeopolis' procession at the Rural Dionysia), but more probably out of a κῶμος associated with the festival, taking a form something like that which we have postulated.[1]

§ 5. There is however one type of κῶμος known to us which partly meets our conditions, and accounts for some elements in early Attic comedy which we have so far left out of account; and this may be thought of either as a variety of the κῶμος whose existence we have postulated above, or as another type which was also pressed into the service of comedy, and blended with the one which we have imagined. This type, which existed in Athens, as well as in other parts of the Greek world,[2] was one in which the revellers masqueraded as animals,

above (p. 241), since the strict form is only consistently preserved in the parabasis (see later, pp. 296, 300 ff.). But it may have been a conventional form used with different degrees of strictness for the whole performance. (I am not convinced by Zielinski's attempt to show (*Glied.*, pp. 235 ff.) that the epirrhematic form is derived from music in which flute and voice performed alternately.) In any case, on the assumption that comedy derives something from such a κῶμος-sequence as we have postulated, it is confirmatory of the close association with that sequence of the long tetrameter metres which the epirrhematic form employs, to find that in the plays of Aristophanes the chorus (or its coryphaeus) takes no part in the scenes in iambic trimeters in any play before the *Peace*, and when the coryphaeus does so in the *Peace*, it is still in long metres that he speaks. In and after the *Birds* he sometimes speaks in iambic trimeters.

[1] It may seem inconsistent that after rejecting the ritual-sequence by which Professor Murray would explain Tragedy, I should put forward a hypothetical κῶμος-sequence as the explanation of Comedy. But there are two differences: (1) I do not think that Professor Murray's ritual-sequence *does* explain tragedy; (2) I think there is enough evidence —it will be given below—to show that something like the κῶμος-sequence may really have existed, while I can see no such evidence for the ritual of the Eniautos-Daimon.

[2] For very early animal dances in Greece see A. B. Cook, *J. H. S.* xiv, pp. 81 ff.; Bosanquet, ibid. xxi, p. 388; Cavvadias, *Fouilles de Lycosure,*

FIG. 16. OENOCHOE IN THE BRITISH MUSEUM

FIG. 17. AMPHORA IN BERLIN

or rode on animals, or carried about an animal as, so to speak, their representative. Indeed, the practice of dressing up in the guise of animals is world-wide; in some countries it may go back to a totemistic origin; in others (or in the same) it may be connected with magic rites for securing the fertility of the ground or of the human species; and very often, probably oftener than anthropologists always allow, it may have been done just for fun, either because any religious reason for the custom had long been forgotten, or (perhaps more often) because the child in mankind dies hard.

The evidence for the existence of the animal masquerade in Athens has been well marshalled by Poppelreuter in his small but valuable dissertation *de Comoediae Atticae primordiis*, in which he uses in part material already published by Mr. Cecil Smith.[1] This evidence must be briefly recalled. In the British Museum there is a black-figured oenochoe,[2] representing a flute-player with two dancers disguised as birds; it is at least probable that the painting represents a primitive bird-chorus, the two dancers standing for the whole chorus, in accordance with the conventions of vase-painting. The date of the vase is placed roughly between 520 and 480 B.C., and the probability is thus rather in favour of its being anterior to the earliest state-recognized performance of comedy in 486 B.C.[3] Again, an amphora, now in Berlin,[4] though less striking, has also, along with a flute-player, two figures which seem to be wearing crests and wattles like cocks,[5] though there

---

p. 11, pl. iv (showing a procession of various animals headed by flute-player on robe of the goddess of Lycosura); cf. also the girls who sacrificed to Artemis at Brauron as ἄρκτοι (Schol. Ar. *Lysistr.* 645; Harp. s. v. ἀρκτεῦσαι; Suid. s. v. ἄρκτοι); and cf. Mannhardt, *Mythologische Forschungen*, pp. 143 ff., and Poppelreuter, op. cit., for illustration of this kind of dance from Germany and other countries. There are plenty of instances of such dances in which the dancers ridiculed the bystanders and prominent men as part of the performance.

[1] *J. H. S.* ii, pl. xiv, pp. 309 ff.   [2] Fig. 16.
[3] See below, p. 286.   [4] Fig. 17.
[5] Cf. Dieterich, *Pulcinella* (esp. pp. 237 ff.), for the history of the cock-costume. It would take us too far to discuss his theory that Mr. Punch is the remote descendant of the cock-masks of early Greece and Italy.

is a strong likeness to pigs about their faces; they wear long
cloaks, but these might be thrown off in dancing and reveal
a complete bird-costume or some grotesque half-animal
appearance. More interesting still is another amphora in
Berlin,[1] which was bought in Rome, and according to Panofka
probably came from Caere. It presents a flute-player in a long
robe, and facing him, three bearded men, wearing loosely the
masks of horses (their own faces appearing below) and horses'
tails, and stooping down with their hands on their knees. On
the back of each is a helmeted rider, wearing a breastplate;
the riders' hands are raised as though to strike their steeds.
The picture bears the inscription **EIOXEOXE** ('Gee-up'),
which Poppelreuter amusingly describes as *sensu carens*; the
horses doubtless understood it. Here we cannot fail to
recognize a comic procession of knights on horseback, and it
was probably just such a performance that Aristophanes
adapted to his use in the *Knights*. For as Poppelreuter (partly
following Zielinski)[2] points out, the chorus in that play certainly had steeds of some sort, and the lines (595–610) which
they address to their horses in the parabasis gain immensely
in point if the 'horses' were really men on whose backs
they were riding:

ἃ ξύνισμεν τοῖσιν ἵπποις, βουλόμεσθ' ἐπαινέσαι.
ἄξιοι δ' εἴσ' εὐλογεῖσθαι· πολλὰ γὰρ δὴ πράγματα
ξυνδιήνεγκαν μεθ' ἡμῶν, ἐσβολάς τε καὶ μάχας.
ἀλλὰ τὰν τῇ γῇ μὲν αὐτῶν οὐκ ἄγαν θαυμάζομεν,
ὡς ὅτ' ἐς τὰς ἱππαγωγοὺς εἰσεπήδων ἀνδρικῶς,
πριάμενοι κώθωνας, οἱ δὲ καὶ σκόροδα καὶ κρόμμυα·
εἶτα τὰς κώπας λαβόντες, ὥσπερ ἡμεῖς οἱ βροτοί,
ἐμβαλόντες ἀνεβρύαξαν, "ἱππαπαῖ, τίς ἐμβαλεῖ;
ληπτέον μᾶλλον. τί δρῶμεν; οὐκ ἐλᾷς, ὦ σαμφόρα;"
κτλ.

The vase is in the early black-figured style and probably
nearly a century earlier than the *Knights*, and affords good

---

[1] Fig. 18.

[2] *Gliederung der alt. att. Komödie*, p. 163. Zielinski shows that the use
of the words ἐλᾶτε, κονιορτός, &c., proves that steeds of some kind were
employed.

Fig. 18. AMPHORA IN BERLIN

evidence of the familiarity of Athens with the kind of
masquerade which appears in the play; and when we
remember how many choruses of fifth-century comedy were
disguised as animals, we can have little hesitation in finding
in the animal masquerade one of the roots of the Old Comedy.
(Magnes appears to have written *Birds, Frogs,* and *Gall-flies* : [1]
Aristophanes himself wrote the *Wasps, Birds, Frogs* and
Storks : there were the Θηρία of Crates, the *Goats* of Eupolis,
the *Ants* of Plato, the *Ants* and *Nightingales* of Cantharos,
and the *Fishes* of Archippus.[2]) Our information does not
enable us to connect such animal processions with any
particular festival: probably they could attach themselves to
any occasion of popular enjoyment; and it is perhaps not
a very extravagant supposition that they may have come to
form part of the Lenaea; and, though of course this is only
conjecture, it has not the difficulties of the attempt to extract
comedy from the phallic processions. We cannot indeed show
that any special song or any form of contest was connected
with these animal dances; for this we have to rely partly
on the analogy of the animal dances of other peoples,[3] which
certainly included satirical attacks on the bystanders; partly
on the strong probability that such merry-making would be
accompanied by song; and partly on what we know of other
varieties of the animal-κῶμος in Greek lands. Of these, the
most helpful is one to which attention has lately been recalled
by Radermacher,[4] and which is described in the scholia to
Theocritus.[5]

The description is that of a κῶμος of βουκολιασταί at

---

[1] See later, p. 289.

[2] An old Attic vase shows men riding on one part upon dolphins, on
another upon ostriches, accompanied by flute-players (Robinson, *Cat. of
Vases in Boston Museum*, No. 372; Flickinger, l. c., p. 40). On the other
hand, the dances enumerated by Athenaeus (xiv, p. 629, &c.) and
Pollux (iv. 103) under animal names—γλαῦξ, λέων, ἀλώπηξ, γέρανος, σκώψ,
&c., were probably all solo-dances, and not relevant here (cf. Reich,
Mimus, i, pp. 479 ff.).   [3] See above, p. 244, note 1.

[4] *Beitr. zur Volkskunde aus dem Gebiet der Antike*, pp. 114 ff., and
Aristoph. *Frösche*, pp. 4–14; cf. Reitzenstein, *Epigramm und Skolion*,
pp. 194 ff.   [5] Ed. Wendel, p. 2.

Syracuse, at a festival of Artemis Λυαία.¹ (In the worship of
Artemis at Syracuse various ceremonies seem to have been
held, which at Athens were associated rather with Dionysus.)
The revellers carried round a great loaf, on which all kinds of
animal shapes were fashioned, and other objects; they themselves wore stags' horns and carried hunting-spears; there
was some kind of contest of song between members of the
κῶμος, and the unsuccessful party went round the villages
jesting, collecting gifts of food, and invoking good luck on
those who gave to them. The words of the scholiast (under the
heading Εὕρεσις τῶν βουκολικῶν) are as follows: ὁ δὲ ἀληθὴς
λόγος οὗτος. ἐν ταῖς Συρακούσαις στάσεώς ποτε γενομένης καὶ
πολλῶν πολιτῶν φθαρέντων, εἰς ὁμόνοιαν τοῦ πλήθους ποτε
εἰσελθόντος ἔδοξεν Ἄρτεμις αἰτία γεγονέναι τῆς διαλλαγῆς. οἱ
δὲ ἄγροικοι δῶρα ἐκόμισαν καὶ τὴν θεὸν γεγηθότες ἀνύμνησαν,
ἔπειτα ταῖς ⟨τῶν⟩ ἀγροίκων ᾠδαῖς τόπον ἔδωκαν καὶ συνήθειαν.
ᾄδειν δέ φασιν αὐτοὺς ἄρτον ἐξηρτημένους θηρίων ἐν ἑαυτῷ
πλέονας τύπους ἔχοντα καὶ πήραν πανσπερμίας ἀνάπλεων καὶ
οἶνον ἐν αἰγείῳ ἀσκῷ, σπονδὴν νέμοντας τοῖς ὑπαντῶσι, στέ-
φανόν τε περικεῖσθαι καὶ κέρατα ἐλάφων προκεῖσθαι καὶ μετὰ
χεῖρας ἔχειν λαγωβόλον. τὸν δὲ νικήσαντα λαμβάνειν τὸν
τοῦ νενικημένου ἄρτον· κἀκεῖνον μὲν ἐπὶ τῆς τῶν Συρακουσίων
μένειν πολέως, τοὺς δὲ νενικημένους εἰς τὰς περιοικίδας χωρεῖν
ἀγείροντες ἑαυτοῖς τὰς τροφάς. ᾄδειν τε ἄλλα τε παιδιᾶς καὶ
γέλωτος ἐχόμενα καὶ εὐφημοῦντας ἐπιλέγειν·

> δέξαι τὰν ἀγαθὰν τύχαν,
> δέξαι τὰν ὑγίειαν,
> ἂν φέρομες παρὰ τᾶς θεοῦ
> ἂν † ἐκλελάσκετο † τήνα.
>
> (ἄν τ' ἐκαλέσκετο, Radermacher)

The account given by the scholiast contains many rather
obscure features, which this is not the place to discuss:² but

---

¹ Eisler (*Orph. Dion. Myst.-Ged.*, p. 260) speaks of these βουκολιασταί
as Dionysiac, on account of the wineskin which they carried. But a
wineskin would be a natural 'property' of any κῶμος. On some features
of this κῶμος see Cook, *Zeus*, vol. ii, p. 1140.

² The whole affair (despite the aetiological story attached to it) reminds
us of the companies of children collecting gifts and wishing good luck

what is clear is that we have here a κῶμος of revellers wearing an animal head-dress, including an agon among the
revellers themselves, and ending with something not unlike
the exodos of some Aristophanic comedies. We cannot show
that the Athenian animal-masqueraders held such an agon,
though it is likely enough that as they departed from the
scene they wished their friends good luck ; but a fragment of
Aristophanes' *Danaides*[1] (also noticed by Radermacher) speaks
of a time when the chorus in rough rustic garments danced
with all kinds of things good to eat packed under the arms :

ὁ χορὸς δ' ὠρχεῖτ' ἂν ἐναψάμενος δάπιδας καὶ στρωματόδεσμα,
διαμασχαλίσας αὐτὸν σχελίσιν καὶ φύσκαις καὶ ῥαφανῖσιν.

We have here a definite point of contact between the
Sicilian and Athenian κῶμοι, and the resemblance may well
have extended to other features. At least the evidence leaves
us free to maintain provisionally our conjecture that some
form of Athenian κῶμος may, like the Syracusan, have
included a kind of agon,[2] which early comic poets might

on May-morning, and the similar rounds made by early (and modern)
Greek children carrying a swallow (and singing the swallow-song) or
a crow (Phoenix of Colophon, fr. 2 : Powell, *Coll. Alex.*, p. 233). Radermacher (Ar. *Frösche*, l. c.) notices these, and also a procession, which
perhaps took place at Naxos, of young men carrying a fish. (Is it
fanciful to remember also the organ-grinder's monkey ?) In the *Anecd.
Estense*, iii (Wendel, ibid., p. 7) the story is repeated *verbatim*, but the
horns and spear are conjectured to be imitative of Pan as the shepherd's
deity. (But did Pan wear stag's horns ?) In the account of the proceedings given by Diomedes (*Gramm. Lat.* i, p. 486, Keil) the contest
took place in the theatre, but this was probably a later development.
The procession (like similar κῶμοι in other countries) was doubtless
believed really to bring good luck : see Nilsson, *Gr. Feste*, pp. 200 ff. ;
and for medieval and modern κῶμοι in Greek lands involving both an
agon and a procession collecting gifts, see Nilsson, *Neue Jahrb.* xxvii,
pp 677–82, and above, pp. 163–4 (the performance at Viza). On modern
parallels to the stag-disguise see Nilsson, *Arch. Rel.* xix. 78 ; Schneider,
ibid. xx. 89 ff., and other refs. there given.

[1] fr. 253 K. I agree with Radermacher (l. c., p. 11) as to the meaning
of διαμασχαλίσας.

[2] The fondness of the Greeks for an agon needs no proof. Navarre
(*Rev. Et. Anc.*, l. c.) regards Aristophanes' *Frogs*, l. 395, as showing that

develop. This would be more satisfactory than to suppose[1] that the agon of the Attic Old Comedy (in which the chorus always assisted, if only as judges) was borrowed from the agon as developed by Epicharmus, who, so far as we can tell, did not write choral comedy at all, and with whom the agon does not seem to have been an element in a larger structure.[2] Such an account of the earliest stages in the development of comedy would also have the advantage that, though κωμῳδία is derived from κῶμος and not from κώμη, it would recognize some measure of truth in the persistent tradition (mentioned by Aristotle and recurring down to late Byzantine times) which associated the rudiments of comedy with the village, and in the expressions used by some early *grammatici*, who also knew of a tradition of comedy as once a begging-procession. This tradition was known to Varro,[3] and is also found in Tzetzes, who, though his authority for this statement cannot be traced, sometimes preserves scraps of historical information of some value.

It is perhaps not carrying conjecture too far to suggest that such masqueraders as we have been considering may not have confined themselves to animal disguises, but may have represented (e. g.) foreigners, just as modern children (and not children only) dress up as niggers or Red Indians.[4] The

---

the γεφυρισ ός on the return from Eleusis involved a contest (evidently of wit), the victor in which was crowned with a ταινία, (Such a ταινία is found in Art in the hands of Nike.) This is possible ; but it may be that the passage is really a prayer of the chorus for the victory of the play which they were acting.

[1] With Sieckmann and others.　　[2] See below, pp. 396 ff., 404.

[3] Diomedes, *de Poemat.* ix. 2 (Kaibel, *Fragm. Com. Gr.* i, p. 57) 'Comoedia dicta ἀπὸ τῶν κωμῶν . . . itaque iuventus Attica, ut ait Varro, circum vicos ire solita fuerat et *quaestus sui causa* hoc genus carminis pronuntiabat'. Tzetzes, *Prooem. de Comoed.* (Kaibel, l. c., p. 27) περὶ ποιητῶν πολλάκις ὑμῖν ἐδιδάξαμεν καὶ περὶ τῆς ἀγοραίας καὶ ἀγυιάτιδος κωμῳδίας καὶ ἀγυρτρίδος, ὅτι τε γεωργῶν εὕρημα κτλ. Varro's authority was doubtless some Greek writer earlier than himself.

[4] Whatever may have been the case with τὰ φαλλικά, the object of which was probably at first magical or religious, it may be suspected that the psychological explanation of the κῶμος was much more often the love of fun.

choruses of Magnes included a chorus of Lydians; Aristophanes wrote a *Babylonians*, Pherecrates a *Persians*; and
these may have had their forerunners in some masquerade.
From foreigners it would not be a very great step to the
representation of groups with well-marked characteristics—
Harp-players, Acharnians, Prospaltians, and so on.

The end of the κῶμος from ;which comedy sprang was, no
doubt, the departure of the revellers, marching or dancing as
the case might be, possibly with a song of victory raised by
the party who had won the contest and perhaps shared by all.
The exodos of the comedies of Aristophanes varies in type, and
will be discussed later;[1] it is never epirrhematic, and was
probably not derived from a primitive κῶμος-sequence; but
a song of victory occurs in it several times, though it must
be admitted that it is likely that the victory of which the
song speaks is (as a rule) the anticipated victory of the
comedy over its rivals; and there are generally vivid antici-
pations of a feast. These are features which familiarity
with such a κῶμος as we have been discussing would render
natural.

The result, then, of the foregoing discussions is the hypothesis that the epirrhematic portions of the Old Comedy are an
adaptation of a native Athenian κῶμος (possibly of more than
one variety of κῶμος) in the course of which some kind of
contest developed, and in which it had become customary to
conclude with addresses, no doubt in part satirical or jesting,
to those standing by; and that in these addresses and the
chants which preceded them, as well as in the agon and the
lively entrance scene, the epirrhematic structure, employed
with varying degrees of strictness, had become conventional.
Such a hypothesis would account for this distinct and coherent section of comedy, and there is, at any rate, some
evidence for it in the facts and the passages which have been
adduced.

It should be added that Aristophanes once or twice introduces a different kind of agon from that which arises as it
were naturally out of the κῶμος, viz. the agon between such

---

[1] pp. 309-10.

abstract conceptions as the Just and Unjust Argument, and
between Poverty and Wealth. Such contests of abstractions
may also have been employed by Epicharmus,[1] and there are
instances in Alexandrian times, when the contest was virtually
a self-contained little work.[2] (It may also have been such in
Epicharmus.) Aristophanes may thus have availed himself of
what was possibly a popular form of entertainment, whether
among Dorian or other peoples.[3] If we knew for certain in
what guise such abstract conceptions appeared on the stage,
we might be able to judge whether they could be supposed to
have any connexion with the κῶμος, or whether (as seems
most likely) they belonged to the same type as the Dorian
mime : but the scholia which profess to give us this information about the Just and Unjust Argument possibly (though not
necessarily) contradict one another, and neither tells us quite
enough to be useful.[4]

It has been noticed already that Aristotle appears to have
had some notion of a primitive comedy without masks or
prologues or a number of actors. The phallophori from whom
he derived comedy probably wore no masks, as we have seen,
nor did various other kinds of κωμασταί : so that, though in
all probability some kind of masked κῶμος had most to do
with the beginnings of comedy, the notion of an unmasked
comedy was a natural one enough. The κῶμος almost certainly
can have had no prologue, and probably no actor who was
more than temporarily distinct from the general body of the
revellers; but this temporary distinctness of one (or two) of
them for the purposes of the agon would render the introduction of a regular actor easy when the κῶμος took more
definite shape as comedy. It is plain that in all this we are

---

[1] See below, pp. 396 ff.

[2] e. g. the episode in Callimachus' *Iambi* on the dispute of the Olive
and the Laurel ; and see below, p. 404.

[3] Perhaps an agon of this kind occurred in the *Persae* of Pherecrates,
but the context of the fragments is not certain.

[4] Schol. Ven. on Aristoph. *Clouds* 889 says that the two Λόγοι were
brought on in cages like fighting-cocks (ὑπόκεινται ἐπὶ σκηνῆς ἐν πλεκτοῖς
οἰκίσκοις οἱ Λόγοι δίκην ὀρνίθων μαχόμενοι). The Schol. on l. 1033 says that
ἐν ἀνδρῶν σχήματι εἰσήχθησαν.

but theorizing, as Aristotle was; but it may be that our theory is as near the truth as his; it does not claim to be more than an attempt at a more satisfactory hypothesis.

II

Dorian elements : Susarion.

§ 1. There is a considerable part of the Old Comedy which the κῶμος, whether phallic or other, is powerless to explain; and we have therefore to return to the consideration of the view which derives at least some elements in it from Dorian sources.

We have already seen [1] that the Spartan δεικηλίσται, whose virtual identity with the later mime-actors is clear from passages of Plutarch and Hesychius, gave performances which had some points in common with Attic Comedy, presenting such scenes as the advent of the itinerant physician with his nostrums, the detection of the orchard-robber or the thief who stole the meat after the feast—all of them characters in the real life of the times. We saw that the δεικηλίσται wore masks and were quite probably phallic. The mimes of later times were not specially connected with the worship of Dionysus, and there was no trace in them of satire or per-sonalities at the expense of the audience; they were short and had little or nothing in the way of a plot of connected scenes; and possibly these characteristics belonged also to the mimes of the δεικηλίσται, though there is no evidence beyond what has already been given. These performances in any case must have been really dramatic, and in character throughout; and if Attic Comedy grew from the combination of these and other more or less similar representations with the non-dramatic κῶμος, we should have an explanation of the source from which the dramatic element in comedy came.

§ 2. Another link appears to connect Attic comedy with

---

[1] See above, pp. 228 ff.

Sparta, though the precise history of the connexion is no longer to be traced.

In the course of their excavations at Sparta in 1906, the members of the British School at Athens discovered a large number of clay masks,[1] most of which appear to belong, roughly speaking, to the period between 600 and 550 B.C. They were doubtless votive copies of the actual masks worn by the performers of some ritual dance in honour of Artemis Orthia, in whose sanctuary they were found and to whom they must have been dedicated; and since the dedication of votive copies is generally a later thing than the offering of the real object, it seems fairly safe to assume that these dances existed at least in the latter part of the seventh century B.C. Among these masks are many which represent an old woman with a much wrinkled face and a very few teeth.[2] Now just such an old woman was a regular personage in Attic comedy throughout its duration, and extant comic masks, as well as the description given by Pollux of the masks of the New Comedy, illustrate the character, though it had naturally become differentiated into slightly differing types in the course of time. Such masks are figured by Robert,[3] and the important passage in Pollux (iv. 150, 151) is as follows: τὰ δὲ τῶν γυναικῶν, γραΐδιον ἰσχνὸν ἢ λυκαίνιον, γραῦς παχεῖα, γραΐδιον οἰκουρὸν ἢ οἰκετικὸν ἢ ὀξύ. τὸ μὲν λυκαίνιον ὑπόμηκες· ῥυτίδες λεπταὶ καὶ πυκναί· λευκόν, ὕπωχρον, στρεβλὸν τὸ ὄμμα. ἡ δὲ παχεῖα γραῦς παχείας ἔχει ῥυτίδας ἐν εὐσαρκίᾳ, καὶ ταινίδιον τὰς τρίχας περιλαμβάνον. τὸ δὲ οἰκουρὸν γραΐδιον σιμόν, ἐν

---

[1] The members of the School kindly showed me these when I was at Sparta in 1909, and I afterwards had the advantage of discussing the whole subject with the late Capt. Guy Dickins. A short account of the masks by Prof. Dawkins and Mr. Bosanquet is to be found in the *B. S. A. Annual*, vol. xii, pp. 324 ff., 338 ff. The relevant literary references are practically all collected by Nilsson, *Gr. Feste*, pp. 182 ff.; and in *Neue Jahrb.* xxvii, p. 273, he recognizes the importance of the Spartan masks.

[2] Figs. 19–26. I am indebted to the authorities of the British School for permission to reproduce these masks.

[3] *Die Masken der neueren Att. Kom.*, p. 47. See Figs. 27–31. Comp. Navarre, *Rev. Ét. Anc.* xvi (1914), pp. 1 ff.

Fig. 19. CLAY MASK FROM SPARTA

FIG. 20   FIG. 21

FIGS. 22–23

CLAY MASKS FROM SPARTA

FIG. 24

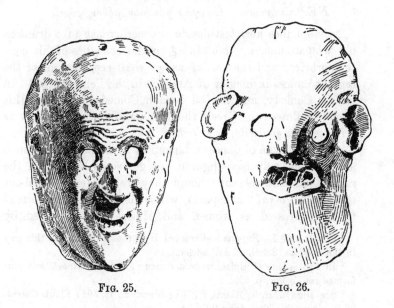

FIG. 25.   FIG. 26.

FIGS. 24–26.   Clay Masks from Sparta.

ἑκατέρᾳ τῇ σιαγόνι ἑκατέρωθεν ἀνὰ δύο ἔχει γομφίους. We
find exactly the type—wrinkled and with a few teeth—in
Aristophanes' *Plutus*, ll. 1050 ff. :

NE. ὦ Ποντοπόσειδον καὶ θεοὶ πρεσβυτικοί,
    ἐν τῷ προσώπῳ τῶν ῥυτίδων ὅσας ἔχει.
ΓΡ. ἆ ἆ,
    τὴν δᾷδα μή μοι πρόσφερ'.
XP.   εὖ μέντοι λέγει.
    ἐὰν γὰρ αὐτὴν εἷς μόνος σπινθὴρ λάβῃ
    ὥσπερ παλαιὰν εἰρεσιώνην καύσεται.
NE. βούλει διὰ χρόνου πρός με παῖσαι;
ΓΡ.   ποῖ τάλαν;
NE. αὐτοῦ, λαβοῦσα κάρυα.
ΓΡ.   παιδιὰν τίνα;
NE. πόσους ἔχεις ὀδόντας.
XP.   ἀλλὰ γνώσομαι
    κἄγωγ'· ἔχει γὰρ τρεῖς ἴσως ἢ τέτταρας.
NE. ἀπότεισον· ἕνα γὰρ γόμφιον μόνον φορεῖ.

Aristophanes also testifies to the occurrence of a drunken
old woman, dancing the κόρδαξ, in the comedies of his contemporaries,[1] and the κόρδαξ, as we shall see, was one of the
regular dances in honour of Artemis in the Peloponnese.[2] In
Greek Comedy, and in the Roman Comedy which in this
respect followed the Greek, the drunken old woman occurs as
a nurse, or a midwife, or a *laena*.[3]

As to the type of dance in honour of Artemis in which such
a character may have figured, we get some light from the
notices (textually corrupt though they are) in Hesychius about
the βρυλλιχισταί[4] at Sparta, whose dances were performed
by men dressed as women and, almost certainly, also by

[1] *Clouds* 553-6. Eupolis had treated Hyperbolus' mother in this way
in the *Maricas* (Schol. on Ar., ad loc.).

[2] In the *Sphinx* of Epicharmus a dance of Artemis Χιτωνέα was performed (see below, p. 392).

[3] See Dionys., fr. 5; Alexis, fr. 167; Menand., fr. 397; Plaut. *Curcul.*
96 ff., *Asin.* 802; Ter. *Andr.* 228, &c.

[4] βρυλλιχισταί seems the most probable form of the name, and βρύλλιχα
of that of the dance. The corruptions are easily explained.

Fig. 27

Fig. 28

Fig. 29

Fig. 30

Fig. 31

FIGS. 27–31. NEW COMEDY MASKS

women dressed as men and wearing φαλλοί. (The interchange of costumes is a device, familiar to anthropologists, for deceiving evil powers who might otherwise interfere with the sexual magic which is the purpose of such dances.[1]) The principal passages in Hesychius are these:

βρυδάλιχα· πρόσωπον γυναικεῖον παρὰ τὸ γελοῖον καὶ αἰσχρὸν περιτίθεται[2] . . . καὶ γυναικεῖα ἱμάτια ἐνδέδυται, ὅθεν καὶ τὰς † μαχρὰς †[3] βρυδαλίχας καλοῦσι Λάκωνες.

βρυλλιχισταί· οἱ αἰσχρὰ προσωπεῖα περιθέμενοι γυναικεῖα καὶ ὕμνους ᾄδοντες.

βρυαλίκται· πολεμικοὶ ὀρχησταὶ μετ' αἰδοίου·[4] Ἴβυκος καὶ Στησίχορος.

Similar (and certainly indecent) dances to Artemis, who was in early days in the Peloponnese a goddess of fertility of a primitive type, were the καλλαβίδες or καλλαβίδια of Spartan women and girls, and the dances of the κυριττοί, whom Hesychius describes as οἱ ἔχοντες τὰ ξύλινα πρόσωπα κατὰ Ἰταλίαν καὶ ἑορτάζοντες τῇ Κορυθαλίᾳ γελοιασταί.[5] The mention of Ibycus and Stesichorus confirms the belief that such dances were known in Magna Graecia, where dances in honour of Artemis were evidently familiar, and these were doubtless derived in part from the Peloponnesian mother-cities of the colonists: cf. Pollux iv. 103 τὸ δὲ ἰωνικὸν Ἀρτέμιδι ὠρχοῦντο Σικελιῶται μάλιστα· τὸ δὲ ἀγγελικὸν ἐμιμεῖτο σχήματα ἀγγέλων: and Athen. xiv, p. 629 e παρὰ δὲ Συρακοσίοις

---

[1] Cf. the *couvade*, and (at Sparta) the dressing of the bride in male attire. Cf. also Philostr. *Imag.* I. ii (p. 298, 10 ff.), where the exchange of costumes is spoken of as characteristic of certain κῶμοι.

[2] The text reads αἰσχρὸν ὀρρ . . . τιθεαι ὀρίνθῳ τὴν ὀρχήστραν καὶ γυναικ . . . ἱμάτια ἐνδέδυται. No convincing emendation has been proposed.

[3] ἀκρίδας, Wilam.

[4] πολεμικοί may be corrupt; the other words are corrections (by Lobeck and others) of ὤρχηται μὲν αἰδοίπου. Hermann emends to: πολεμικοὶ ὀρχησταί· βρυαλίκται μενέδουποι (a supposed quotation).

[5] Nilsson notes that the word κυριττοί suggests phallic dances. For women's dances to Artemis in male costume, cf. Hesych. s. v. λόμβαι· αἱ τῇ Ἀρτέμιδι θυσιῶν ἄρχουσαι ἀπὸ τῆς κατὰ παιδιὰν σκευῆς· οἱ γὰρ φάλητες οὕτω καλοῦνται. There were dances of women to Artemis Κορυθαλία at the Tithenidia at Sparta (see Nilsson, *Gr. Feste*, pp. 182 ff.).

καὶ Χιτωνέας Ἀρτέμιδος ὄρχησίς τίς ἐστιν ἴδιος καὶ αὔλησις.
ἦν δέ τις καὶ Ἰωνικὴ ὄρχησις παροίνιος. καὶ τὴν ἀγγελικὴν δὲ
πάροινον ἠκρίβουν ὄρχησιν.

A further account of early Laconian dances may be found
in Pollux iv. 104–5[1] ἦν δέ τινα καὶ Λακωνικὰ ὀρχήματα διὰ
Μαλέας. Σειληνοὶ δ' ἦσαν καὶ ὑπ' αὐτοῖς Σάτυροι ὑπότρομα
ὀρχούμενοι· καὶ ἴθυμβοι ἐπὶ Διονύσῳ, καὶ Καρυάτιδες ἐπ'
Ἀρτέμιδι.[2] καὶ βαρύλλιχα, τὸ μὲν εὕρημα βαρυλλίχου, προσ-
ωρχοῦντο δὲ γυναῖκες Ἀπόλλωνι καὶ Ἀρτέμιδι. οἱ δὲ ὑπο-
γύπωνες γερόντων ὑπὸ βακτηρίαις τὴν μίμησιν εἶχον, οἱ δὲ
γύπωνες ξυλίνων κώλων ἐπιβαίνοντες ὠρχοῦντο, διαφανῆ
ταραντινίδια ἀμπεχόμενοι. καὶ μὴν Ἐσχαρίνθον ὄρχημα, ἐπώνυμον δ' ἦν τοῦ εὑρόντος αὐλητοῦ. τυρβασίαν δ' ἐκάλουν τὸ
ὄρχημα τὸ διθυραμβικόν. μιμητικὴν (? μιμηλικὴν) ἐκάλουν
δι' ἧς ἐμιμοῦντο τοὺς ἐπὶ τῇ κλοπῇ τῶν ἑωλῶν κρεῶν[3] ἁλισκομένους. λομβρότερον δ' ἦν ὃ ὠρχοῦντο γυμνοὶ σὺν αἰσχρο-
λογίᾳ. ἦν δὲ καὶ τὸ σχιστὰς ἕλκειν,[4] σχῆμα ὀρχήσεως χορικῆς·
ἔδει δὲ πηδῶντα ἐπαλλάττειν τὰ σκέλη.

The interest of this passage is that it not only introduces the
thief of stale food and the βρύλλιχα (under a probably corrupt
name), but also a dance of old men leaning on sticks (ὑπογύ-
πωνες) ; and it is noteworthy that many of the masks found in
the precinct of Artemis Orthia are those of old men. The old
man—not infrequently with a stick—is a regular character in
the New Comedy and in Plautus and Terence ; he is to be
seen on the vases on which the performances of the Italian
phlyakes are depicted ; his long-bearded mask is among those
enumerated by Pollux iv. 144, in a description which recalls
some of the Spartan masks ; and if this character (as distinct
from the old rustic who is the hero of so many comedies of
Aristophanes) does not come out so clearly in the Old Comedy,

---

[1] I give what seems to me the best text with little discussion ; the
MSS. have many obvious corruptions. In ὑπὸ βακτηρίαις the preposition
seems simply to denote 'attendant circumstances', as it not infrequently
does in late Greek. λομβρότερον is read by Bethe for MSS. λαμπρότερον.

[2] For Καρυάτιδες see Nilsson, l. c., pp. 196 ff.

[3] MSS. μερῶν: perhaps ἑωλομερῶν (Kühn) is the right reading.

[4] What this was is uncertain. Hesych. has σχῆμα ποδός· τὰ σχίσματα,
καὶ ὀρχηστικὸν σχῆμα, but this may be corrupt.

it may be because Aristophanes deliberately gave him up,
along with other stock tricks of his contemporaries: cf.
Clouds 540 ff. :

οὐδ' ἔσκωψε τοὺς φαλακρούς, οὐδὲ κόρδαχ' εἵλκυσεν,
οὐδὲ πρεσβύτης ὁ λέγων τἄπη τῇ βακτηρίᾳ
τύπτει τὸν παρόντ' ἀφανίζων πονηρὰ σκώμματα.

The occurrence of such characters—the wrinkled and gap-
toothed old woman and the old man with his stick—in Spartan
dances does not of course prove that they got into Attic
comedy directly from that source; but it does add weight to
the other evidence for the view that some of the stock
characters of Attic comedy became familiar to the Athenians
from intercourse with Dorian peoples. Any people can easily
devise ' comic ' old men and old women, and the uglinesses and
infirmities of old age are an unfailing source of popular
merriment; but their occurrence in Attic comedy just in their
Spartan forms is at least confirmatory of the theory that
Dorian influence was responsible for some features of comedy,
and in particular for the introduction of certain character
types familiar either through performances like the later
mimes, or through well-known cult-dances.

§ 3. This theory derives further confirmation from the
regular occurrence in Attic comedy of the kordax. That it
was a common feature is plain from the passage of Aristophanes
just quoted, and the scholiasts and lexicographers describe it
as ὄρχησις κωμική. We cannot point to a definite instance of
its introduction into a play by Aristophanes himself, and if he
deliberately abjured it, as he claims to have done, this is not
surprising. (A scholiast does indeed state that it occurred in
the *Wasps*, and he must be referring to Philocleon's dance,
ll. 1487 ff.: but this is probably a mistake, as Philocleon is
evidently travestying some tragic dance.) But there can be
no doubt of its employment by Eupolis and perhaps by
Phrynichus. It was a dance associated with drunkenness and
was of a lascivious kind (Schol. on Ar. *Clouds* 540 calls it
κωμικὴ . . . ἥτις αἰσχρῶς κινεῖ τὴν ὀσφύν :[1] cf. Mnesimachus,

---

[1] Cf. Hesych. κορδακισμοί· τὰ τῶν μίμων γελοῖα καὶ παίγνια.

fr. 4 πρόποσις χωρεῖ· λέπεται κόρδαξ· | ἀκολασταίνει νοῦς μειρακίων: and Theophr. *Char.* vi treats it as a sign of ἀπόνοια, ὀρχεῖσθαι νήφων τὸν κόρδακα). Its exact nature is (perhaps fortunately) undiscoverable, as the attempts to identify with it the dances on a number of vase-paintings rest on no sufficient evidence: there was more than one kind of vulgar dance.[1] It is clear from Aristoph. *Clouds* 553–4 that the dance was associated with a drunken old woman:

Εὔπολις μὲν τὸν Μαρικᾶν πρώτιστον παρείλκυσεν
ἐκστρέψας τοὺς ἡμετέρους Ἱππέας κακὸς κακῶς,
προσθεὶς αὐτῷ γραῦν μεθύσην τοῦ κόρδακος οὔνεχ', ἣν
Φρύνιχος πάλαι πεποίηχ', ἣν τὸ κῆτος ἤσθιεν,[2]

and a passage of Pausanias (VI. xxii, § 1) shows its connexion with Artemis; it was danced in honour of Artemis Κορδάκα in Elis (προελθόντι δὲ . . . σημεῖά ἐστιν ἱεροῦ Κορδάκας ἐπίκλησιν Ἀρτέμιδος, ὅτι οἱ τοῦ Πέλοπος ἀκόλουθοι τὰ ἐπινίκια ἤγαγον παρὰ τῇ θεῷ ταύτῃ καὶ ὠρχήσαντο ἐπιχώριον τοῖς περὶ τὸν Σίπυλον κόρδακα ὄρχησιν). He derives the dance from Asia Minor, and it is true that there were similar dances in honour of the Ephesian Artemis, the Asiatic mother-goddess;[3] but the derivation was perhaps a false inference; the Peloponnesian dances were probably very primitive and were connected with the coarsely-conceived goddess of fertility who afterwards became identified with Artemis; and Ottfried Müller (followed by Schnabel) may be right in the conjecture that the later worshippers of Artemis, the goddess of chastity, tried to account for, and excuse the connexion of, such dances

---

[1] The last and most thorough attempt—that of H. Schnabel (*Kordax*, 1910)—is rightly set aside by Körte (*Deutsche Littzg.* 1910, pp. 2787–9; Bursian, *Jahresber.* clii, p. 236) and others, though his work contains much useful material. Other attempts are enumerated by Warnecke, s. v. κόρδαξ, in Pauly-Wissowa, *Real-Enc.* xi, col. 1384. I doubt if it can be inferred from the passage of Pausanias that the κόρδαξ was danced at Elis by men.

[2] Phrynichus doubtless travestied the story of Andromeda.

[3] Autocrates, fr. 1 οἷα παίζουσιν φίλαι | πάρθενοι Λυδῶν κόραι | κοῦφα πηδῶσαι κόμαν | κἀνακρουοῦσαι χεροῖν | Ἐφεσίαν παρ' Ἄρτεμιν | καλλίσταν, καὶ τοῖν ἰσχίοιν | τὸ μὲν κάτω, τὸ δ' αὖ | εἰς ἄνω ἐξαίρουσα | οἷα κίγκλος ἄλλεται.

with her, by ascribing them to a foreign source. However
that may be, the association of the dance with a drunken old
woman and with the worship of Artemis in the Peloponnese
confirms the indications already mentioned of Dorian influence
on comedy.[1]

We may add to these indications the fact that another
primitive Peloponnesian dance, the μόθων, was occasionally
introduced into Attic comedy. This dance was perhaps that
of the μόθωνες—the liberated helots of Laconia—as Ottfried
Müller conjectures:[2] Photius describes it as ὄρχημα φορτικὸν
καὶ κορδακῶδες. It is danced for a moment by the Sausage-
Seller in the *Knights* 697 ἀπεπυνδάρισα μόθωνα: and the
Scholiast's description of it seems to identify it with the
dance of the Spartan Lampito in the *Lysistrata* 82:

γυμνάδδομαι γὰρ καὶ ποτὶ πυγὰν ἄλλομαι,

and with a Spartan dance mentioned by Pollux iv. 102, in
which ἔδει ἄλλεσθαι καὶ ψαύειν τοῖς ποσὶ πρὸς τὰς πυγάς.

§ 4. A further argument (again not perfectly conclusive,
but still increasing the probability, otherwise established, that
Dorian influence must be taken into account in judging of
the origins of Attic comedy) is drawn from a comparison of
the costume of the Attic comic actor with that worn by
a number of figures which appear on Peloponnesian vases.
There is little doubt that the Attic actors commonly secured
comic effect by extravagant padding of the person, in front
and behind, the exaggerated figure being clad in a short tight-
fitting tunic, usually cut short so as to show the phallus which
was often worn.[3] (The extravagant padding was evidently

---

[1] There is no doubt that at a much later date the dance was associated
with Dionysus (Lucian, περὶ ὀρχησ. § 22 ; Προλαλιά ὁ Διόν. § 1, &c.). But
there is no evidence of any early connexion of it with him. The attempt
of Hincks (*Rév. Archéol.* xvii (1911), pp. 1–5) to find such evidence depends
on the identification with the κόρδαξ of a dance in the presence of an apparently Dionysiac personage in a panther-skin, depicted on an aryballos
in the British Museum ; but this identification is quite unproved.

[2] *Dorier*, ii, p. 338.

[3] Various kinds of upper garment, mantle, &c., might be worn as
required ; see Müller, *Bühnen-Altertümer*, pp. 249 ff. : and the comic

used in the *Clouds* 1237, 1238, where Strepsiades is mocking Pasias:

ΣΤ. ἀλσὶν διασμηχθεὶς ὄναιτ᾽ ἂν οὑτοσί.

ΠΑ. οἴμ᾽ ὡς καταγελᾷς.

ΣΤ.   ἐξ χοὰς χωρήσεται,

and in the *Frogs* 663 f., where Dionysus is certainly wearing the *προγαστρίδιον*.[1]) The costume appears also on various terra-cotta statuettes of comic actors,[2] and on an Attic vase at St. Petersburg,[3] representing a scene in a theatrical dressing-room, probably early in the fourth century, before the Attic comedians had given up the phallic costume. But it is significant that there is no trace of this costume on early Attic vases, where we should expect to find it worn by Dionysiac figures, if it were proper to the members of the retinue of Dionysus or in any way connected with his cult. His followers on the early vases are all satyrs or sileni. Nor are such figures like the human *κωμασταί* on the vases. And this absence of the costume from early Attic paintings gives point to its occurrence on a considerable number of Peloponnesian vases; the two facts together strongly suggest that the Attic stage derived the costume from a Peloponnesian source. (If it were not for these facts, it would be open to us to believe that, as padding and indecency are obvious and universal methods of obtaining a low comic effect, the

poets no doubt exercised great freedom in the matter. Some of the terra-cotta statuettes and figures on vases wear a short chiton distinct from the close-fitting vest, the name of which is unknown.

[1] He is called *γάστρων* in l. 200, and the Schol. explains : *εἰσάγουσι γὰρ τὸν Διόνυσον προγάστορα καὶ οἰδάλεον ἀπὸ τῆς ἀργίας καὶ οἰνοφλυγίας.*

[2] Bieber, pl. 69–71. Körte gives a long catalogue of these (*Jahrb. Arch. Inst.* viii, pp. 77 ff.). Most appear to belong to the fourth century : but he argues that the type of costume familiar from the Old Comedy would probably have lasted on, as long as parody and mythology, and not real life, were the subjects of the plays. The type of statuette is certainly Attic in origin. The account given above, like that of all writers on the subject since 1893, necessarily (and gratefully) takes Körte's article as its basis.

[3] Fig. 32 : the two right-hand figures are phallic in the original. (See Bieber, l. c., Abb. 124.)

Athenians would have no need to go to the Peloponnese for
them.)

The costume is found upon a sixth-century Corinthian
amphora (now in the Louvre), which has been much discussed.[1]
On the left is a flute-player, padded before and behind and
wearing a short close-fitting vest, but not phallic : and facing
him a bearded demonic figure labelled Εὔνους. Then follow
two figures carrying a wine jar : they appear to be naked ;
the right-hand one is labelled ᾿Οφέλανδρος : on the right they
are being approached by a naked and grossly phallic figure
labelled ᾿Ομρικός, with a stick in either hand ; the situation
seems to be that he is detecting the two in the theft of the

Fig. 32.   Dressing-room scene from Vase in St. Petersburg.

wine jar.[2] The names appear to be those of Dionysiac demons,
᾿Οφέλανδρος (who is semi-phallic) a giver of fertility, Εὔνους an
incarnation of goodwill, and ᾿Ομρικός probably a by-name
of Dionysus himself, as it certainly was in the form
᾿Ομβρικός (cf. Bekk. *Anec. Gr.* i, p. 224, s. v. Βάκχος. οἱ δὲ
᾿Ομβρικὸς ὑπὸ ᾿Αλικαρνάσσεων Βάκχος.   Halicarnassus was
at least partly Dorian).   That the vase represents some
kind of performance burlesquing mythological characters in
a scene of theft is often thought to be indicated by the flute-
player.   But it is at least possible that the flute-player and the
dancer form a pair apart, and that the whole is not taken

---

[1] Figured by Körte, l. c., p. 91 ; Bieber, p. 129, &c.
[2] This was conjectured by Dümmler, who figured and discussed the
vase in *Ann. dell' Inst.* 1885.

from an actual performance, but is a fancy picture of
a Dionysiac group, two of whom are amusing themselves,
while two others are detected in wine stealing by Dionysus:
the fact that the group of three are entirely naked makes it
doubtful whether the vase can be intended to reproduce an
actual performance. But this does not affect the main point—
the association of the costume with the Dionysiac demons
imagined by Corinthian artists. The only difficulty in connecting these with the Attic comic actor lies in the fact that
the figures which wear the tight vest are not phallic, while
the phallic figures are naked. This difficulty, however, grows
less, when we consider that not all Attic actors were phallic
either ; and it is at least possible that in many plays (especially
of Aristophanes) and in many Corinthian burlesques the tight-
fitting vest and the padding were considered enough. A very
similar costume, but including the phallus, appears on a black-
figured Corinthian amphoriskos of the early part of the sixth
century, representing the return of Hephaestus to heaven,
when he was brought back by Dionysus in order to liberate
Hera from the chair in which she had been imprisoned by
his devices.[1] The interpretation of the vase in detail is
disputed,[2] but it is agreed that the two phallic figures thus
costumed are supernatural or demonic. (Loeschke regards
them as demonic attendants of Dionysus ; Schnabel, with less
probability, as Dionysus and Zeus.) The subject is not
specially Dorian, and is found on Attic and other vases, not all
of which can be regarded as imitations of Corinthian pottery,
even though the Corinthian vase is the earliest representation
of the subject : but this does not diminish the importance of
the discovery of this particular costume as worn by demonic
figures in a burlesque Dionysiac scene on Dorian pottery.
(The vase does not depict a performance, but a scene in which
none the less some of the performers wear costumes like that
worn probably by actors of burlesques.[3]) The short tight

---

[1] The vase is figured by Loeschke, *Ath. Mitt.* xix, pl. viii. Cf. ibid.,
pp. 510 ff., and Bieber, Abb. 122, p. 129. For the subject see below, p. 391.

[2] See Loeschke, l. c., and Schnabel, *Kordax*, p. 55.

[3] Similar figures occur on a representation of the return of Hephaestus

vest is worn by the distorted Dionysiac figures which occur on a number of early vases—mostly of the sixth century— painted either at Corinth or under obvious Corinthian influence. On a good many vases these figures, which are dancing in pairs and sometimes carrying drinking horns, are not phallic,

FIG. 33.   Dancers on Corinthian phiale.

and the type varies somewhat while remaining generically the same.[1]

on a Corinthian vase in the British Museum, B. 42. (Figured by Walters, *Anc. Pottery*, i, pl. xxi.   Prof. Beazley informs me that this vase is real Corinthian work, not imitative as stated in the B. M. Catalogue.)

[1] Besides those specially mentioned, I have examined the originals or figures of the following: phiale, Baumeister, *Denkm.*, p. 1963, fig. 2099 (fig. 33 in this book); the dolphin shows that this scene does not reproduce an actual performance: phiale in British Museum (figs. 34, 35), not previously published: phiale, 'Εφ. 'Αρχ. 1885, pl. 7 (both these sets of figures much padded and dancing in pairs): two pinakes in Berlin, *Ant. Denkm.* i. 8. 19 a and ii. 39. 9 (both wearing the characteristic vest, and non-phallic, but neither quite like the dancers on the last two vases): phiale from Sabouroff Coll. (Furtw. i, pl. 48. 1), on which the figures wear short purple chitons, two of them spotted like one of those on the earliest Corinthian Hephaestus vase, and are only slightly padded (not all in front) (fig. 36): krater in Louvre, E. 620, Pottier, pl. 44, dancing

It seems then to be beyond question that the costume commonly worn by the Attic comic actor, with or without phallus, was particularly connected, before the fifth century, not with any Attic figures, but with the Dionysiac 'demons' represented mainly on Corinthian vases. We need not discuss whether these demonic figures are to be regarded as Dorian, or as belonging to the pre-Dorian population, but continuing to hold a place in the imagination of the Dorian settlers, as some scholars believe.[1] In the latter case they would have their origin in fancies of an earlier date than that of the introduction of Dionysiac worship into the Peloponnese (whenever this happened), but would naturally have attached themselves to that worship, as we find them attached, in a burlesque form, on some of the vases. There is no ground for expressly connecting them with Artemis,[2] though it is likely enough that there was some transference of ideas between the primitive cult of Artemis and that of Dionysus, when it arrived.

The special association of the costume with mythological mainly in pairs and slightly padded: votive plate, Benndorf, *Gr. and Sic. Vas.*, pl. 7 (very roughly executed figures, some slightly, but not conspicuously, padded, but some apparently phallic): phiale from Akrai (Benndorf, pl. 43. 1) with two figures (? women) in tight vests, and one bearded; an elderly bearded figure, perhaps Dionysus (fig. 40 opposite): aryballos in Brit. Museum (*Rev. Arch.* xvii, 1911, p. 1) with dancers in tight vests, also in presence of an elderly naked figure (? Dionysus) (figs. 37-9): stamnos in Brit. Mus. B. 44, with three bearded dancers, wearing close-fitting purple vests (fig. 41); Rayet-Collignon, *Céram*, p. 63, fig. 33 (dancing pairs, with flute-player, non-phallic). See also Addenda, p. 418 below. A similar garment appears on two grotesque figures, one on each side of a crater, on a vase (*Arch. Ztg.*, pl. 12. 1 and 13. 4; Pottier, *Vases du Louvre*, iii, D c, pl. 8) now considered to be Laconian (rather than Cyrenaic) and certainly in Peloponnesian style. Of one or two vases cited by different writers in this connexion I have been unable to see figures; several others appear to be really irrelevant to the subject. An amphora from Vulci (Roulez, *Vases de Leide*, pl. v) shows not only a dance of sixteen padded non-phallic figures in short close-fitting vests, but, as its main subject, a dance of satyrs (phallic and horse-tailed) and bacchants. I do not know whether the two types are found together on any other vase.

[1] Loeschke, *Ath. Mitt.* xix, p. 519; Bethe, *Proleg.*, pp. 48, 49, &c.

[2] The idea that these dancers are dancing the κόρδαξ is quite unproved, and this ground for connecting them with Artemis disappears.

FIGS. 34–35. CORINTHIAN PHIALE IN THE BRITISH MUSEUM

FIG. 36. CORINTHIAN PHIALE FROM SABOUROFF COLLECTION

Figs. 37–39. CORINTHIAN ARYBALLOS IN THE BRITISH MUSEUM

burlesque (and probably with dances performed in the guise of demons) is not only suggested by its occurrence in the *entourage* of Dionysus and Hephaestus, but by its reappearance in the fourth and third centuries on South Italian vases representing the performances of the φλύακες, who burlesqued mythological

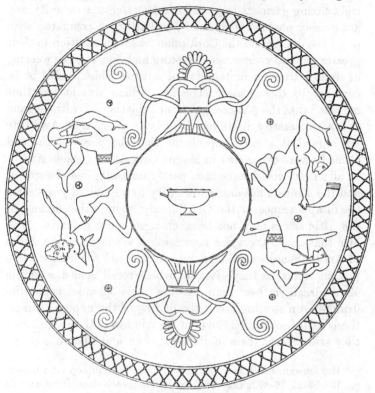

FIG. 40. Phiale from Akrai.

legends. These performances, as has already been suggested, had almost certainly descended directly from those of the Peloponnesian mother-cities of the Graeco-Italian colonies; and the inclusion of such burlesques among the types of performance which we can ascribe to the Peloponnese increases the probability that the Attic comic poets also got both the costume and the mythological burlesque, which forms so large a part of Attic comedy, from Peloponnesian sources. (Such bur-

lesque is a main part of the stock-in-trade of Epicharmus, who
lived in two Dorian colonies, Megara Hyblaea and Syracuse.)

The φλύακες-vases were enumerated and many of them
figured by Heydemann, and these have frequently been
figured since.[1] Many of the actors depicted on them wear the
tight-fitting garment (some with a short chiton over it), and
are grossly phallic; their chief peculiarity, as compared with
(e. g.) the dancers on the Corinthian vases, in addition to their
greater general coarseness of feature and figure, is the wearing
of striped trousers or 'tights' of a type which seems to be
confined to these vases. The idea which was at one time
current [2] that the φλύακες got their subjects and costume from
the Attic comedy itself has long been given up. As Körte
has argued, it is very improbable that the plays of the Old
Comedy were ever acted in Magna Graecia, or outside Athens
at all; they would have been partly unintelligible elsewhere:
and the φλύακες are dated from fifty to a hundred years after
the disappearance of the Old Comedy, though the costume of
the Attic actors may not have changed quite so early. The
idea that one of the vases represents a scene from the *Frogs*
of Aristophanes was clearly mistaken; [3] and when these vases
present scenes, as they often do, which recall comedies of the
Menandrean rather than of the Aristophanic type—the
drunken son stealing home, the finding of the exposed infant,
the boastful soldier, the lover at the window of the courtesan—
they still present them in the grotesque and phallic costume

---

[1] Heydemann, *Jahrb. Arch. Inst.* i, pp. 260 ff. ; von Salis, op. cit. ; Bieber,
pp. 138-53, pl. 76-86. Those noticed or discovered since Heydemann's
article are enumerated by Zahn in *Furtw. Reich.*, *Griech. Vasenm.* (series iii),
pp. 178 ff. ; he dates those assigned to Assteas about the middle of the
fourth century. The occurrence of a stage in many of the paintings
shows that the vases represent performances, but a literary form seems
first to have been given to this kind of performance by Rhinthon of
Tarentum (circ. 300 B.C.). Comp. Nossis' epigram (*Anth. Pal.* vii. 414)
'Ρίνθων εἴμ' ὁ Συρακόσιος | Μουσάων ὀλίγη τις ἀηδονίς· ἀλλὰ φλυάκων | ἐκ
τραγικῶν ἴδιον κισσὸν ἐδρεψάμεθα.

[2] Refs. are given by Körte, *Jahrb. Arch. Inst.* viii. 61.

[3] Heydemann, l. c., p. 283; von Salis, l. c., p. 23 ; Körte, l. c., pp. 61,
87. See also Robert, *Archaeol. Hermeneutik*, pp. 286-7.

Fig. 41. STAMNOS IN THE BRITISH MUSEUM

which the New Comedy had abandoned. But the use of this costume, both in the Old Comedy and by the φλύακες, may well be due to its having been taken by each from Peloponnesian burlesques.

Any further inference is perhaps hazardous. It certainly cannot be argued that such primitive Peloponnesian plays included any and every subject which we find on the φλύακες-vases; but Robert and von Salis may be right in thinking that Heracles (who recurs frequently on them) was a favourite figure in early Dorian burlesques,[1] Peloponnesian as well as Italian; and von Salis would add Odysseus also, though the evidence is much less strong.[2] It seems in any case reasonably safe to conjecture that both Epicharmus and the φλύακες, in their mythological travesties and their comedy of low life, were continuing the traditions of their ancient mother-cities in Greece proper.

The stage on which the φλύακες performed seems to have been a temporary affair, like that used by conjurers and early mime-actors;[3] and such a stage may also have been in use by the early Dorian players in Greece.

It has been usual, in discussing the actors' costume, to refer to some grotesque paintings on vases found at Thebes, mainly in the precinct of the Kabeiroi.[4] On these phallic figures occur, much distorted—Odysseus, Bellerophon, Cadmus, &c.; and it has been thought that these are parallel to the impersonations of the φλύακες: but Körte[5] is almost certainly right in deny-

---

[1] We shall see reason later to think that Heracles was a stock-figure in the comedy of Megara. The position occupied by Heracles as a Dorian hero makes this natural enough.

[2] von Salis also conjectures that the overloaded slave, who occurs on some of the vases and was a stock jest of the Old Comedy (cf. Aristoph. *Frogs* 13–15, and fragm. 323), may have been a character in early Dorian buffoonery; but the character is one which would occur readily to any Greek comedian. A food-stealing slave, Xanthias, is seen on one of the vases (see above, p. 230). [3] Reich, *Memoirs*, i, pp. 605–7.

[4] See Bethe, *Proleg.*, p. 58; Bieber, *Denkm.*, pp. 153–5, pl. 87, fig. 134–5, and *Ath. Mitt.* xiii, pl. 11, &c.

[5] *Neue Jahrb.* xlvii (1921), pp. 311–12. Körte criticizes deservedly the surprising statements made by Dr. Bieber on these vases.

ing this. Some of these figures are represented as naked, not as clad in tight garments, and they are not masked; they have no traceable connexion with any kind of stage-performance, and for our present purpose may be left out of account, except in so far as they illustrate the general readiness of the Greeks to travesty their mythological legends.

§ 5. We have found sufficient traces of Dorian burlesques of mythological scenes and of grotesque Dionysiac dances, both associated with the costume which was afterwards worn by the Athenian comic actor, to justify the conjecture that there was a connexion between such Dorian performances and Attic comedy. We have also found that some of the standing types of Attic comedy seem to have their fore-runners in the mime-like performances of Dorian peoples, or in dances in character, associated with Dorian ritual—the old woman, the old man with his stick, the quack-doctor, the detected food-stealer. It is possible that some further suggestions may be derived from a consideration of other types which constantly recur in Attic comedy.[1]

A considerable part of many plays of Aristophanes consists of scenes in which a person of absurd or extravagant pretensions is derided or made a fool of by a person who plays the buffoon—scenes (to use the convenient Greek terms) between an ἀλαζών and a βωμολόχος.[2] The ἀλαζών may be a sophist or philosopher—Hippo in the Πανόπται of Cratinus, Socrates in the *Clouds* of Aristophanes, and the Κόννος of Ameipsias; or a politician (Cleon), a quack-doctor or apothecary, a star-gazer (Meton), a prophet, an ecstatic poet (Cinesias, &c.), a boastful soldier (Lamachus), an elegant aesthete (Agathon)—

---

[1] I have made much use of the writings of Süss, *De personarum antiquae comoediae Atticae usu atque origine* (Bonn, 1905), and *Zur Komposition der altattischen Komödie* (*Rh. Mus.* lxiii (1908), pp. 12-38, though I am unable to agree with him on some points of detail.

[2] Cf. the *Tractatus Coislinianus* (which no doubt in this takes up points made by Aristotle), § 6 ἤδη κωμῳδίας τά τε βωμολόχα καὶ τὰ εἰρωνικὰ καὶ τὰ τῶν ἀλαζόνων : cf. Ar. *Rhet.* III. xviii. 1419 b 8 ff, *Eth. Nic.* II. vii. 1108 a 21, &c., IV. vii. 1127 a 21. Of the εἰρωνικά the extant remains give us plenty of illustrations, especially in the person of the parasite : they are full of the ἀλαζών and the βωμολόχος.

any one who feels himself to be out of the common and takes
himself too seriously. Euripides and even Aeschylus in the
Frogs have something of the ἀλαζών in them.[1] The ἀλαζών
was brought up to date or worked into the character of some
living person, with very different degrees of skill or brilliancy
by different poets and in different plays: but the regularity
of his occurrence in such scenes, and the persistence of the
type in certain forms even in the New Comedy, suggest very
strongly that the ἀλαζών was a stock-character in the older
forms of buffoonery to which Attic comedy owed much, and
that the quack-doctor of the δεικηλίσται was only one variety
of a type constant in essentials—i. e. in ἀλαζονεία, though
taking more than one shape.[2] It is some confirmation of this
view that the type is found in Epicharmus, in the fragments
of whom we shall find the quack wise-man prominent and the
μάντις mentioned; and that in another form, that of the
swaggering soldier, we find him in the representations of the
φλύακες.[3] It is natural to explain these coincidences between
Dorian and Attic comedy by a common source.

The βωμολόχος in Aristophanes generally takes one of two
forms—the old rustic and the jesting slave. His business is
much the same wherever he appears. He makes nonsense of
what another speaker says, or gives an indecent or vulgar turn
to it—sometimes taking words literally where they are not so
meant, or otherwise playing upon them; sometimes interrupt-
ing with silly or indecent remarks or anecdotes, particularly
in the agon; sometimes making asides or (quite undramatically)
addressing the audience. He also has a particular function in
the prologue—that of stating the subject of the play, request-

---

[1] Aeschylus embodies not only the characteristics of the great poet,
but some of those associated with the terrific soldier, in so far as he is
half identified with his warriors in their extravagant panoply.

[2] Süss appropriately quotes the catalogue in Aristoph. *Clouds* 331 ff.
ἴσθ' ὅτι πλείστους αὗται βόσκουσι σοφιστάς | Θουριομάντεις, ἰατροτέχνας,
σφραγιδονυχαργοκομήτας | κυκλίων τε χορῶν ᾀσματοκάμπτας, ἄνδρας μετεωρο-
φένακας | οὐδὲν δρῶντας βόσκουσ' ἀργούς, ὅτι ταύτας μουσοποιοῦσιν.

[3] e.g. on vase G, Heydemann, loc. cit. The character is recognizable
in Archilochus fr. 58 (Bergk⁴), and is found in one form or another
throughout the history of Greek comedy.

ing the goodwill of the audience, and attracting their favour by some preliminary jesting; and he is usually the principal character in those scenes of buffoonery which normally succeed the parabasis, and in which one claimant for recognition after another, whatever the degree of his ἀλαζονεία, is derided and driven away. In almost all the earlier plays of Aristophanes the βωμολόχος of the second half of the play is the old rustic or a character very like him—Dicaeopolis, Strepsiades, Trygaeus, Philocleon, Peithetaerus. In the *Acharnians* and *Clouds* the old rustic also prologizes; but in the prologue the part is more commonly taken by a slave (sometimes two slaves)[1] introduced for the purpose (as in the *Knights*, *Wasps*, *Frogs*, and *Plutus*), or by a companion of one of the principal characters—Euelpides, Kalonike, Mnesilochus—the role of the companion being perhaps a later modification of that of the slaves. As a rule (though Mnesilochus is an exception) neither slave nor companion is prominent in the second part of the play. In the preparations for the wedding or the feast with which many of the plays end, the βωμολόχος gets free play for his greed and his obscenity.

It is possible to trace the manner in which Aristophanes progresses in his handling of these types, in abating their grossness, and in working them into a plot which forms a unity. The βωμολόχος of the rustic kind, as has already been indicated, seems to belong primarily to the iambic scenes in which he makes a fool of a series of ἀλαζόνες or characters not far removed from ἀλαζόνες. It is in these iambic scenes that Dicaeopolis, Strepsiades, Trygaeus, Peithetaerus, Blepyrus, play a characteristic part; and when this type of βωμολόχος is prominent in the first half of the play, as Dicaeopolis is in the *Acharnians*, it is often in contact with some form of ἀλαζονεία (Pseudartabas, Lamachus, Euripides) that he shines, though he may also be a protagonist in the agon (as Peithetaerus is), and so form a bond of union between the essentially dissimilar epirrhematic and iambic scenes.[2] The other type,

---

[1] As regards the two slaves, see below, p. 277.

[2] Another bond of unity was the prologue, though it is possible that the primitive mimes sometimes had prologues or preliminary speeches

the slave or companion, appears, as has been said, most characteristically in the prologue, but also as the vulgar interrupter of arguments, the irreverent bystander in the agon.

Now it seems to be at least a possible explanation of these characters, that they carry on a primitive type of buffoonery, very like the mimes of later days, taken over by the Athenians from Dorian peoples. The fact that the βωμολόχος sometimes addresses the audience as the spokesman of the poet, suggests that he comes from a performance which had no chorus; for it was the chorus which had this function in epirrhematic comedy. The old rustic was probably a character in the Ἀγρωστῖνος of Epicharmus; and as at least some forms of ἀλαζονεία—the quack-doctor, the swaggering Heracles—can be traced back to Dorian mimes, the explanation is not without confirmation. Another stock character, the parasite, appears in Epicharmus, before we have any sign of him in Attic comedy; and he may also have been a well-known Dorian type. (One of the three masks for the parasites of the New Comedy, as described by Pollux, was still called Σικελικός.[1]) The jesting and disrespectful slave would be bound to get into the comedy of any Greek community; but he too may have begun to play his characteristic part in the mime-like performances of the Peloponnese.[2]

It would be absurd to pretend that these suggestions are anything but conjectures; but they are conjectures which appear to be in accordance with the few known facts.

§ 6. Thus it seems probable that while the epirrhematic scenes in the Old Comedy are mainly of Attic origin, the iambic derive most from Dorian sources. It is, however,

to the audience. (Choricius, i. 2, makes it clear that the mimes of his own day had, and the mime seems to have remained more or less the same, at least in some of its types, from first to last.)

[1] See Robert, *Die Masken*, pp. 68, 109.

[2] Some interesting comparisons of the "ἀλαζών *versus* βωμολόχος" scenes of Greek comedy with modern performances of low comedy are to be found in Reich, *Mimus*, i, p. 689, &c.; Poppelreuter, op. cit.; Cornford, op. cit., pp. 142 ff. The history of the βωμολόχος type is traced with much ingenuity, though sometimes in a highly speculative way, in Dieterich's *Pulcinella*.

impossible to trace the steps by which the two elements came to
be combined,—how a variety of Dorian character-types, realistic
scenes from ordinary life, mythological travesty,[1] a peculiar
costume, were united with the Attic κῶμος, whether the
κωμασταί were disguised as animals or not. Nor do we know
by what route the Dorian elements travelled to Attica. But
there is reason to suspect that Megara may have been a half-
way house for comedy, as it was for the traveller by land.
The question of the nature of Megarean comedy is a well-worn
one, but it needs less argument now, since Wilamowitz, the
chief of those who were inclined to deny the existence of
Megarean comedy, has long abandoned that view.[2]

The claim of the Megareans to have originated comedy,
recorded by Aristotle in the passage of the *Poetics* which
has already been quoted, is not likely to be entirely devoid of
historical foundation. Comedy arose, they said, in the time
of their democracy. This democracy lasted from the expulsion
of Theagenes, about 581 B.C. down to 424 B.C., when the
oligarchical party re-established itself with the aid of Brasidas;
but the only period which concerns us is that which precedes the
appearance of Chionides at Athens in 486 B. C. Plutarch[3] records that after the expulsion of the tyrant the Megareans for
a short time showed a spirit of moderation, but soon indulged
in extremes of liberty under the leadership of demagogues.
Such an atmosphere would be favourable enough to comedy.[4]
Wilamowitz[5] conjectures that Aristotle derived his knowledge

---

[1] Moessner (*Die Mythologie in der dorischen u. altattischen Komödie*,
pp. 49 ff.) argues that the first Attic Comedy based on mythological
travesty was the 'Οδυσσεῖς of Cratinus, but this is far from certain.

[2] Compare *Gött. Gel. Anz.* 1906, p. 619, with *Hermes*, ix (1875), pp. 319

[3] *Quaest. Gr.*, ch. 18 Μεγαρεῖς Θεαγένη τὸν τύραννον ἐκβαλόντες ὀλίγον
χρόνον ἐσωφρόνησαν κατὰ τὴν πολιτείαν, εἶτα πολλήν, κατὰ Πλάτωνα, καὶ
ἄκρατον αὐτοῖς ἐλευθερίαν τῶν δημαγωγῶν οἰνοχοούντων κτλ. (Plato is
probably not the authority for Plutarch's statement, but only the source
of the metaphor.)

[4] The national temperament of the Megareans seems to have included
a biting wit, if the saying ascribed to Pittacus is justified—Μεγαρεῖς δὲ
φεῦγε πάντας, εἰσὶ γὰρ πικροί: the ascription itself is very doubtful.

[5] *Gött. Gel. Anz.* 1906, p. 619.

of the Megarean claim from his contemporary Dieuchidas of
Megara; this is possible, but it is permissible to be sceptical of
the suggestion, which Wilamowitz next propounds, of a kind of
warfare of claims between Athenians and Dorians with regard
to the origination of literary forms—the Megareans claiming
comedy, and pretending that Susarion was a Megarean, and the
Sicyonians tragedy (as the work of Epigenes and Neophron),
while the Athenians replied with a tradition of Icarian comedy
and of Thespis performing before Solon. We shall return to
Susarion; but it is improbable that he would have been claimed
as a Megarean unless Megara were actually a very early home
of some kind of comedy. (It is perhaps not irrelevant to
notice that Megara had a cult of Artemis Ὀρθωσία,[1] who is
not likely to have been very different from the Artemis
Orthia of Sparta, and may have been worshipped by similar
cult-dances.)

Most of the very slight information which we have about
Megarean comedy is drawn from a passage from the prologue
of Aristophanes' *Wasps*, a passage of Aristotle's *Ethics*, and the
scholia on both. These must be quoted in full:

Ar. *Vesp.* 54 ff.:

> φέρε νυν κατείπω τοῖς θεαταῖς τὸν λόγον,
> 55 ὀλίγ' ἄτθ' ὑπειπὼν πρῶτον αὐτοῖσιν ταδί,
> μηδὲν παρ' ἡμῶν προσδοκᾶν λίαν μέγα,
> μηδ' αὖ γέλωτα Μεγαρόθεν κεκλεμμένον.
> ἡμῖν γὰρ οὐκ ἔστ' οὔτε κάρυ' ἐκ φορμίδος
> δούλω διαρριπτοῦντε τοῖς θεωμένοις,
> 60 οὔθ' Ἡρακλῆς τὸ δεῖπνον ἐξαπατώμενος,
> οὐδ' αὖθις ἐνασελγαινόμενος Εὐριπίδης·
> οὐδ' εἰ Κλέων γ' ἔλαμψε τῆς τύχης χάριν,
> αὖθις τὸν αὐτὸν ἄνδρα μυττωτεύσομεν.
> ἀλλ' ἔστιν ἡμῖν λογίδιον γνώμην ἔχον,
> 65 ὑμῶν μὲν αὐτῶν οὐχὶ δεξιώτερον,
> κωμῳδίας δὲ φορτικῆς σοφώτερον.

l. 61. ἐνασελγαινόμενος Herm.: ἀνασελγαινόμενος codd.:
ἀσελγανοῦμεν εἰς Εὐριπίδην van Leeuwen (after Schol. Rav. κατ'

[1] *C. I. G.* 1064.

Εὐριπίδου πολλὰ λέξομεν ἀσελγῆ). The reference (as Schol. Ven. shows) is perhaps to the treatment of Euripides in Aristophanes' Προάγων in 423 B.C.

Schol. ἢ ὡς ποιητῶν τινων ἀπὸ Μεγαρίδος ἀμούσων καὶ ἀφυῶς σκωπτόντων, ἢ ὡς τῶν Μεγαρέων καὶ ἄλλως φορτικῶς γελοιαζόντων. Εὔπολις Προσπαλτίοις· τὸ σκῶμμ' ἄσελγες καὶ Μεγαρικὸν σφόδρα. Ar. Eth. Nic. IV. iii ἐν μὲν γὰρ τοῖς μικροῖς τῶν δαπανημάτων πολλὰ ἀναλίσκει (sc. ὁ βάναυσος) καὶ λαμπρύνεται παρὰ μέλος, οἷον ἐρανιστὰς γαμικῶς ἑστιῶν καὶ κωμῳδοῖς χορηγῶν ἐν τῇ παρόδῳ πορφύραν εἰσφέρων, ὥσπερ οἱ Μεγαρεῖς. Schol. σύνηθες ἐν κωμῳδίᾳ παραπετάσματα δέρρεις ποιεῖν, οὐ πορφυρίδας. Μυρτίλος ἐν Τιτανόπασι . . . "τὸ δεῖν' ἀκούεις; Ἡράκλεις, τοῦτ' ἐστί σοι | τὸ σκῶμμ' ἄσελγες καὶ Μεγαρικὸν καὶ σφόδρα | ψυχρόν· γελᾷ ⟨γάρ, ὡς⟩ ὁρᾷς τὰ παίδια." διασύρονται γὰρ οἱ Μεγαρεῖς κωμῳδίᾳ, ἐπεὶ καὶ ἀντιποιοῦνται αὐτῆς ὡς παρ' αὐτοῖς πρῶτον εὑρεθείσης, εἴ γε καὶ Σουσαρίων ὁ κατάρξας κωμῳδίας Μεγαρεύς. ὡς φορτικοὶ τοίνυν καὶ ψυχροὶ διαβάλλονται καὶ πορφυρίδι χρώμενοι ἐν τῇ παρόδῳ. καὶ γοῦν Ἀριστοφάνης ἐπισκώπτων αὐτοῖς λέγει που, "μηδ' αὖ γέλωτα Μεγαρόθεν κεκλεμμένον." ἀλλὰ καὶ Ἐκφαντίδης παλαιότατος ποιητὴς τῶν ἀρχαίων φησί, "Μεγαρικῆς | κωμῳδίας ᾆσμ' ⟨οὐ⟩ δίειμ'·[1] αἰσχύνομαι | τὸ δρᾶμα Μεγαρικὸν ποιεῖν." δείκνυται γὰρ ἐκ πάντων ὅτι Μεγαρεῖς τῆς κωμῳδίας εὑρεταί.

Cf. also Pseudo-Diog. iii. 88 γέλως Μεγαρικός· ἐπὶ τῶν ἀώρως θρυπτόντων· ἤκμασε γὰρ ἡ Μεγαρικὴ κωμῳδία ἐπὶ χρόνον, ἣν Ἀθηναῖοι καταμωκώμενοι ἐγέλων.

(The fragment τὸ σκῶμμ' ἄσελγες κτλ. is no doubt from Eupolis' Προσπάλτιοι, not from Myrtilus. The nature of the σκῶμμα may perhaps be suggested by Aristoph. *Clouds* 539 τοῖς παιδίοις ἵν' ᾖ γέλως, where the laughter is provoked by the wearing of the phallus.)

These passages, while they show that the scholiasts had no more definitely historical knowledge of Megarean comedy

─────────

[1] ᾆσμα διείμαι codd. The right reading is quite uncertain, but this does not affect the present problem.

than ourselves, also show that in the fifth and fourth centuries there was a type of comedy not only known as ' Megarean ', but associated with Megara, and that this was vulgar and probably indecent. Aristophanes illustrates the 'laughter stolen from Megara' by (1) a pair of slaves throwing nuts out of a basket to the audience; (2) Heracles cheated of his dinner.[1] The latter obviously suggests mythological burlesque, such as was employed by Epicharmus of Megara Hyblaea and Syracuse. But the persistence of this particular theme in Attic comedy is proved by the pride which Aristophanes takes in having discarded it (*Peace* 741–2):

τούς θ᾽ Ἡρακλέας τοὺς μάττοντας καὶ τοὺς πεινῶντας ἐκείνους
ἐξήλασ᾽ ἀτιμώσας πρῶτος.

The former reminds us of the pair of slaves who open the *Knights*, the *Wasps*, and the *Peace*, though they do not act exactly in the manner described; and of the reference in *Plutus* 796 ff. to the scattering of figs and sweetmeats among the audience (a passage very like that quoted above from the *Wasps*):

ἔπειτα καὶ τὸν φόρτον ἐκφύγοιμεν ἄν.
οὐ γὰρ πρεπῶδές ἐστι τῷ διδασκάλῳ
ἰσχάδια καὶ τρωγάλια τοῖς θεωμένοις
προβαλόντ᾽ ἐπὶ τούτοις εἶτ᾽ ἀναγκάζειν γελᾶν.

In the *Peace* (962 ff.), Xanthias does, at Trygaeus' bidding, throw some of the grains of sacrificial barley to the spectators.[2] Possibly the practice was in vogue in Megarean comedy as known to Aristophanes.

Further, in the *Acharnians* 738, the Megarean speaks of the disguising of his daughters as pigs as Μεγαρικά τις μαχανά, and this may indicate, though it does not necessarily do so,

---

[1] The coupling of these two οὔτε . . . οὔτε shows that they form the explanation of Μεγαρόθεν κεκλέμμενον as distinct from the mockery of Euripides and Cleon, which are introduced by οὐδέ.

[2] I cannot accept Mr. Cornford's conjecture (pp. 101, 2) that the object of this was to make the spectators partakers in a communal meal. It seems to have been simply a rather vulgar *captatio favoris* (Ἕλληνες ἀεὶ παῖδες).

that disguise-tricks were a speciality of Megarean comedy:[1] and a fragment (fr. 2) of Theopompus speaks of the apothecary —probably own brother to the quack-doctor—as a Megarean :

> τὴν οἰκίαν γὰρ εὗρον εἰσελθὼν ὅλην
> κίστην γεγονυῖαν φαρμακοπώλου Μεγαρικοῦ.

These references are consistent (to say no more) with the conjecture that some elements in Dorian farce found their way into Athens through Megara.

Besides this, certain masks were associated with Megara. One of these was the μαίσων, though the accounts given of this are peculiarly confusing. According to Athenaeus,[2] Chrysippus derived the name from μασᾶσθαι and took it to connote gluttony, while Aristophanes of Byzantium said it was the invention of a Megarean actor named Maeson. On the whole the passages of Athenaeus and Zenobius seem to point to a definite person of the name, rather than to a character-type, corresponding to the Manducus of the Atellane farce, with whom Dieterich[3] and others identify μαίσων:[4]

---

[1] Reich, *Mimus*, i, pp. 478-9, notices the occurrence of such animal-disguises in mimes, perhaps as early as Sophron : and it is quite possible that Megarean comedy was more like mime than like choral comedy.

[2] xiv, p. 659 a ἐκάλουν οἱ παλαιοὶ τὸν μὲν πολιτικὸν μάγειρον μαίσωνα, τὸν δὲ ἐκτόπιον τέττιγα. Χρύσιππος δ' ὁ φιλόσοφος τὸν μαίσωνα ἀπὸ τοῦ μασᾶσθαι οἴεται κεκλῆσθαι, οἷον τὸν ἀμαθῆ καὶ πρὸς γαστέρα νενευκότα, ἀγνοῶν ὅτι Μαίσων γέγονεν κωμῳδίας ὑποκριτὴς Μεγαρεὺς τὸ γένος, ὃς καὶ τὸ προσωπεῖον εὗρε τὸ ἀπ' αὐτοῦ καλούμενον Μαίσωνα, ὡς Ἀριστοφάνης φησὶν ὁ Βυζάντιος ἐν τῷ περὶ προσώπων, εὑρεῖν αὐτὸν φάσκων καὶ τὸ τοῦ θεράποντος πρόσωπον καὶ τὸ τοῦ μαγείρου. καὶ εἰκότως καὶ τὰ τούτοις πρέποντα σκώμματα καλεῖται μαισωνικά ... τὸν δὲ Μαίσωνα Πολέμων ἐν τοῖς πρὸς Τίμαιον ἐκ τῶν ἐν Σικελίᾳ φησιν εἶναι Μεγάρων καὶ οὐκ ἐκ τῶν Νισαίων. The proverbial expression ἀντ' εὐεργεσίης Ἀγαμέμνονα δῆσαν Ἀχαιοί (used κατὰ τῶν ἀχαρίστων) is quoted by Zenobius ii. 11 with the words φασὶ δὲ αὐτὴν ὑπὸ Μέσωνος (= Μαίσωνος) τοῦ Μεγαρέως πεποιῆσθαι : and there does not seem to be much to support Crusius' conjecture (*Philol. Suppl.* vi. 275) that it was quoted from a comedy (perhaps of Epicharmus) in which it was spoken by Μαίσων = Manducus.

[3] *Pulcinella*, p. 87 ; cf. p. 39. The existence of types like Maccus, Bucco, Manducus, &c., outside Italy, is too readily assumed by Dieterich.

[4] There is the same difficulty about the foreign cook, τέττιξ, whom some regard as a character-type named after the cook's irrepressible

FIGS. 42–46. TERRACOTTA FIGURES AND MASK OF
NEW COMEDY CHARACTERS

but the creation of eponymous inventors was so common a
thing that the matter must remain doubtful, and it can only
be regarded as possible, not as proved, that the cook was an
early Megarean character.   The same is the case with the
slave, whose mask—or at least that which in the New Comedy
was associated with the leading slave, the θεράπων ἡγέμων —
Aristophanes of Byzantium also described as the invention of
Maeson.

Robert notices several masks and terra-cotta statuettes [1]
which (on fairly good grounds) he considers to represent the
μαίσων.   One of these is supposed to have come from Megara
itself; but all are much later than the Megarean comedy
which we are discussing, though one at least is earlier than
the New Comedy. The μαίσων and the θεράπων ἡγέμων wear
their hair in the form of the σπεῖρα, which is characteristic
of early fifth-century statues from Dorian countries; [2] and it
may be noticed in passing (as confirming in some slight degree
the presence of early Dorian elements in Attic comedy) that
Robert also dates back some other masks to the time of the
Old Comedy, e.g. those of the σφηνοπώγων type, and the
' second 'Ερμώνιος ' (of Pollux' catalogue),[3] both of which preserve the pointed beard of the fifth century; and he thinks
that as masks with such pointed beards are common on the
φλύακες-vases, both the Attic comedians and the φλύακες may
have derived them from the Dorian farce, which was an
ultimate source of both.   (The same vases also depict masks
which correspond to those of the θεράπων κάτω τριχίας of
Pollux, and at least one specimen of a mask like that of the
τέττιξ, though it is worn by a dancing silenus, not by a cook.

loquacity, while others (after Clem. Al. *Protrept.* I. i) state that there
was an actor of the name. The former view is strongly supported by
Robert, l. c., p. 72. (Fig. 46 represents the τέττιξ.)

[1] Figs. 42–5. Navarre disputes the identification of fig. 45 with the
μαίσων, perhaps rightly (*Rev. Ét. Anc.* xvi, pp. 1 ff.).

[2] Robert, ibid., p. 109. Navarre (l. c.) interprets the σπεῖρα in a different
manner from Robert, and if he is right, it is not characteristically Dorian.

[3] The first 'Ερμώνιος with its ampler beard may belong to the last
quarter of the fifth century, when Hermon, the supposed inventor of
both, was acting: see Robert, l. c., p. 63.

The masks of the πάπποι wearing beards, which were out of
fashion in the time of the New Comedy, must also, he considers, go back to earlier models.)

Some late and uncertain notes[1] are preserved about a poet,
Tolynus of Megara, who was earlier than Cratinus, and
invented the metre usually attributed to the latter. His
existence must remain very doubtful; but the tradition at
least attests a belief in Megarean comedy in the writer (whoever he was) from whom it was derived.

But in fact the tradition of Megarean comedy rests almost
entirely upon the passages of Aristophanes and Aristotle.
The evidence from other writers which goes to prove the
existence of such a tradition can add but little weight.
Perhaps the most significant indication, among these fragments
of evidence, is that which (as has been already indicated)
makes Susarion a Megarean; this would hardly have done if
there had been no such thing as an early Megarean comedy.
Our next task therefore is to examine the records in regard to
him.

§ 7. The first extant mention of Susarion is in the Parian
Marble[2] (the date of which is about 260 B.C.), under a year
which may fall anywhere between 581 and 560 B.C.: ἀφ' οὗ ἐν
Ἀθ[ήν]αις κωμῳ[δῶν χο]ρ[ὸς ηὑρ]έθη [στη]σάν[των αὐτὸν] τῶν
Ἰκαριέων, εὑρόντος Σουσαρίωνος, καὶ ἆθλον ἐτέθη πρῶτον
ἰσχάδιο[ν] ἄρσιχο[ς] καὶ οἴνου με[τ]ρητής. The restoration of the
inscription is uncertain in places, but it evidently connected
Susarion with Icaria and with the first comic chorus at Athens.

---

[1] Etym. Magn., p. 761. 47 Τολύνιον· τὸ καλούμενον Κρατίνειον μέτρον
πολυσύνθετον. καλεῖται καὶ Τολύνιον ἀπὸ τοῦ Μεγαρέως Τολύνου· ἐστὶ δὲ προ-
γενέστερος Κρατίνου. Meineke, however (Hist. Crit. i, p. 38), suggests that
the metre was really called Τελλήνειον, after Τελλῆν, a contemporary of
Epaminondas (Plut. Apophth. Epam. 20, p. 193 f.), and on this theory the
name Τόλυννος would have been invented to account for the corrupt
Τολύνιον. The conversion of Tellen into a comic poet might be easier if
his music was of a ludicrous kind, as is suggested by Leonidas' epigrams
(Anth. Pal. vii. 719), Τέλληνος ὅδε τύμβος, ἔχω δ' ὑπὸ βώλεϊ πρέσβυν | τῆνον,
τὸν πρῶτον γνόντα γελοιομελεῖν. But these speculations are very unprofitable.

[2] Ed. Jacoby, p. 13.

Clement of Alexandria also speaks of Susarion of Icaria as the inventor of comedy : [1] καὶ μὴν ἴαμβον μὲν ἐπενόησεν Ἀρχίλοχος ὁ Πάριος, χωλὸν δὲ ἴαμβον Ἱππῶναξ ὁ Ἐφέσιος, καὶ τραγῳδίαν μὲν Θέσπις ὁ Ἀθηναῖος, κωμῳδίαν δὲ Σουσαρίων ὁ Ἰκαριεύς.

For all other notices of Susarion we have only the authority of late and mostly anonymous scholiastic writers, of whose authorities we know nothing certain.[2] The story upon which several of these writers are more or less agreed is as follows : [3] Once upon a time certain rustics of Attica had been injured by some wealthy Athenians who lived in the city : they came therefore into the city at nightfall, went into the streets where their oppressors lived, and loudly proclaimed their grievances outside the doors, though without mentioning names. In the morning the neighbours, who had heard the clamour, investigated the matter, and the rulers of the city, thinking that the exposure of the oppressors, which resulted from the inquiry was a salutary thing,[4] compelled the rustics to repeat their story and their invective in the theatre (or in the market-place). For fear of being recognized by their oppressors, the

---

[1] *Strom.* i. 16, 79, p. 366 P. Kaibel (*C. G. F.*, p. 77) compares with this the Schol. in Dion. Thrac. (Cramer, *Anecd. Ox.* iv. 316) καὶ εὑρέθη ἡ μὲν τραγῳδία ὑπὸ Θέσπιδός τινος Ἀθηναίου, ἡ δὲ κωμῳδία ὑπὸ Ἐπιχάρμου ἐν Σικελίᾳ καὶ ὁ ἴαμβος ὑπὸ Σουσαρίωνος κτλ.

[2] Kaibel, *die Prolegomena περὶ κωμῳδίας*, argues with some force that a considerable number of the statements in these writers were derived from the *Chrestomathia* of Proclus (fifth cent. A. D.), but Proclus' authorities are quite unknown.

[3] Kaibel, *Com. Gr. Fr.*, pp. 12 ff. The Prolegomena which he quotes include six or seven versions of the story.

[4] Joannes Diaconus, Comm. in Hermog. (*Rh. Mus.* lxiii, p. 149), gives a different motive : μετὰ γοῦν τὸν ἀνήμερον βίον μεταβολῆς ἐπὶ τὸ βελτίον γινομένης ἀπαλλαγέντες οἱ ἄνθρωποι τῆς βαλανοφαγίας καὶ ἐπὶ γεωργίαν τραπόμενοι ἀπαρχὴν τῶν γινομένων καρπῶν τοῖς θεοῖς ἀνετίθεντο, ἡμέρας αὐτοῖς εἰς πανηγύρεις καὶ ἑορτὰς ἀπονείμαντες· καὶ ἐν ταύταις ἄνδρες σοφοὶ τὸ τῆς ἀνέσεως ἄλογον ἐπικόπτοντες καὶ βουλόμενοι τὰς πανηγύρεις λογικῆς παιδιᾶς μετέχειν τὴν κωμῳδίαν ἐφεῦρον· ἧς λόγος πρῶτον κατάρξαι τὸν Σουσαρίωνα ἔμμετρον αὐτὴν συστησάμενον. ἐνστῆναι μὲν γὰρ κατὰ τὸ σύνηθες τὰ Διονύσια, ἐν τούτῳ δὲ τῷ καιρῷ τὴν γυναῖκα τούτου μεταλλάξαι τὸν βίον· καὶ τοὺς μὲν θεατὰς ἐπιζητεῖν αὐτὸν ὡς πρὸς τὰς τοιαύτας ἐπιδείξεις εὐφυᾶ, τὸν δὲ παρελθόντα λέγειν τὴν αἰτίαν καὶ ἀπολογούμενον εἰπεῖν ταῦτα· (ll. 1–4 of the fragment follow) καὶ εἰπόντος τάδε εὐδοκιμῆσαι παρὰ τοῖς ἀκούουσι.

rustics smeared their faces with wine-lees (τρύξ) before com-
plying. Still more convinced of the salutariness of the
performance, the Athenians next encouraged poets to take up
the task of denunciation, and Susarion was the first of the
poets who did so, but all his works were lost except the few
lines to be discussed presently.

It is possible that this absurd story may preserve a grain of
genuine tradition—the origin of comedy in some kind of
κῶμος,[1] and perhaps this κῶμος may have been organized into
a display in the theatre at about the date indicated in the
Parian Marble ; but the evidence is too poor to prove anything.

One or two other writers simply mention Susarion as the
inventor of comedy without further particulars ; but Tzetzes [2]
(who is at times even more fatuous than the anonymous
scholiasts) speaks of him as a Megarean,[3] son of Philinus, who
in revenge for the desertion of his wife, entered the theatre at
the Dionysia and delivered himself of the lines ascribed to
him : [4]

ἀκούετε λέῳ· Σουσαρίων λέγει τάδε,
υἱὸς Φιλίνου Μεγαρόθεν Τριποδίσκιος·
κακὸν γυναῖκες· ἀλλ᾽ ὅμως, ὦ δημόται,
οὐκ ἔστιν οἰκεῖν οἰκίαν ἄνευ κακοῦ·
καὶ γὰρ τὸ γῆμαι καὶ τὸ μὴ γῆμαι κακόν.

These lines are quoted by some writers with, by others without,[5] the second of the five, which makes Susarion a Megarean :
but the lines are certainly not genuine. They are in Attic,
not Doric : the word δημόται suggests an Attic writer : and

---

[1] Though one of these writers (Kaib., p. 14) derives κωμῳδία from
κῶμα, because it was invented at the hour of sleep.

[2] circ. A. D. 1180 : see Kaib., p. 27. An earlier note gives the slightly
different version of John the Deacon.

[3] The Megarean tradition was known to the Schol. on Ar. *Eth.
N.* IV. vi, quoted above (p. 276), but he evidently doubts it.

[4] It is doubtless because of these lines that Schol. Dion.Thrac., p. 748 B,
and John the Deacon call him the author of metrical comedy.

[5] It is omitted by Stob. Flor. 69. 2, and Diomedes, p. 488. 26 ; it is
included by Schol. Dion. Thrac., p. 748 B (Kaib., p. 14), Tzetzes, and
John the Deacon.

probably even in the forgery the second line is an interpolation designed to reconcile the tradition of the Megarean origin
of comedy, with that of its invention by Susarion. The
sentiment and style suggest the Middle or New Comedy. It
is, in fact, very doubtful whether such a person as Susarion
existed at all; Körte [1] thinks that he was an invention, but
that the inventor made him a Megarean, and gave him a
name unlike any Attic name. Other scholars think of him as
a Megarean who migrated to Icaria—an obvious resource of
the reconciler. Of his supposed work we have no account
except the statement of an anonymous writer (or possibly, as
Kaibel thinks, of Tzetzes) that Susarion and his contemporaries introduced their characters in a disorderly manner, and
that it was Cratinus who first reduced comedy to order; and
further that they aimed only at amusement, and not at the
moral improvement of the audience.[2] (This may be intended
as a contradiction of the story of the rustics.) In any case it is
very unlikely that these earliest supposed or actual forerunners
of the Old Comedy composed literary works; they must belong
to the age of αὐτοσχεδιάσματα, and but for the spurious lines
no one would have ascribed metrical comedy to them. Whether
they used wine-lees as a disguise is as uncertain as everything
else; it would be a natural thing for κωμασταί to do: but we
here touch once more the theory of τρυγῳδία as the origin of
τραγῳδία and κωμῳδία, and of both as performed at vintage
festivals, at which (according to some of the scholiasts) a bottle
of new wine (τρύξ in its other sense) was given as a prize.[3]
The truth about this is irrecoverable; there may have been

---

[1] Pauly-W. *Real-Enc.* xi, col. 1222.

[2] Kaib., p. 18 καὶ αὐτὴ δὲ ἡ παλαιὰ αὐτῆς διαφέρει· καὶ γὰρ οἱ ἐν τῇ
Ἀττικῇ πρῶτον συστησάμενοι τὸ ἐπιτήδευμα τῆς κωμῳδίας (ἦσαν δὲ οἱ περὶ
Σουσαρίωνα) τὰ πρόσωπα ἀτάκτως εἰσῆγον. καὶ γέλως ἦν μόνος τὸ κατα-
σκευαζόμενον κτλ. Cf. Diomedes, p. 488. 23 K. (Kaib., p. 58) 'poetae primi
comici fuerunt Susarion, Mullus et Magnes. Hi veteri disciplinae
iocularia quaedam minus scite ac venuste pronuntiabant'.

[3] The Marm. Par. also mentions a basket of figs, and this too points to
autumn. Some traditions made this part of the prize for tragedy also
(see above, pp. 104 ff.). It might well be a prize for any performance,
serious or comic, of rustic origin and in simple times.

an autumn festival including both tragic and comic elements, but, as has been said, τρυγῳδία was probably in origin simply a comic parody of τραγῳδία, giving to comedy a name which was both ludicrous and also suggestive of wine and the wine-god in whose honour the performance took place.[1]

The records of Susarion, therefore, leave us with nothing of historical value, except the tradition, of an early Megarean comedy (without which there would have been no point in assigning him to Megara), and of some formless Attic comedy early in the sixth century.[2]

III

Early Athenian Comic Poets.

§ 1. The names which are associated by Diomedes with that of Susarion are those of Euetes, Euxenides, and Myllus. According to Suidas (s. v. 'Επίχαρμος) the life of Epicharmus at Syracuse coincided with the activity of Euetes, Euxenides, and Myllus at Athens,[3] seven years before the Persian Wars; i. e. they were practically contemporary with Chionides.

With regard to Euetes, the difficulty lies in the fact that the only Euetes of whom we know anything (even by con-jecture) is a tragic poet, whose name occurs in the inscriptional list of tragic poets victorious at the City Dionysia between the names of Aeschylus and Polyphradmon,[4] as having won a

---

[1] See Nilsson, *Studia de Dionysiis Atticis*, pp. 88–90 ; and for explana-tions of τρυγῳδία, Schol. on Aristoph. *Ach.* 398, 499 ; *Clouds* 296 ; Ann. *de Com.* in Kaibel, p. 7, &c.

[2] The date assigned to Susarion by the Parian Marble would make him, roughly speaking, a contemporary of Thespis, if the latter was really at Athens before the death of Solon. It is not impossible that two such persons should have come to Athens about the same time, with their performances, but it cannot be regarded as historically certain. On the suggestion of a common origin of tragedy and comedy see above, p. 107.

[3] See below (pp. 287, 353 ff.).

[4] *C. I. A.* ii. 977 a ; see Wilhelm, *Urk.*, p. 100, and Capps, *Introd. of Com. into City Dionysia*. The restoration of the name seems certain, though the first two letters are missing.

single victory; and it is strange that Suidas should mention a
tragic poet here, or that if he wished to mention one, he should
not have mentioned Aeschylus. If, on the other hand, there
was a comic poet of the name of Euetes, why should he have
been mentioned in preference to Chionides, whom Aristotle
and Suidas recognize as a landmark? These questions admit
of no certain answer.

Euxenides is mentioned nowhere except in these two
passages. Wilamowitz once conjectured[1] that the names
given by Suidas were derived from some authority who
wished to prove that Athens had comic poets as early as the
Dorians of Sicily, and invented names beginning with *Εὐ-* to
prove his case. In his later references to the subject[2] he does
not repeat this suggestion, but substitutes a rather different
one,[3] still, however, based on the assumption of a warfare
of fictions between Athenian and Dorian champions. Such
speculations must be received with great caution.

Several writers speak of a comic poet named Μύλλος, and
when we are asked to regard Μύλλος as a character-type (like
Μαίσων),[4] it is right to notice, as Wilamowitz does,[5] that
Zenobius[6] clearly distinguishes the comic poet from the
proverbial μύλλος who is supposed to constitute the character-
type. His words are: Μύλλος παντ' ἀκούων· αὕτη τέτακται
ἐπὶ τῶν κωφότητα προσποιουμένων καὶ πάντα ἀκουόντων.
μέμνηται αὐτῆς Κρατῖνος ἐν Κλεοβουλίναις. ἔστι δὲ καὶ
κωμῳδιῶν ποιητὴς ὁ Μύλλος. Arcadius (53) also mentions
Μύλλος among the disyllabic proper names ending in -λλος
and adds ποιητὴς κωμικός: both Hesychius and Photius speak
of a Μύλλος (the name is sometimes corrupted) as ποιητὴς
ἐπὶ μωρίᾳ κωμῳδούμενος: and the reference of Eustathius[7] to
an actor of the name, if not free from suspicion, at least con-

---

[1] *Hermes*, ix, p. 341.   [2] *Gött. Gel. Anz.* 1906, p. 621.

[3] See above, p. 275.

[4] Wilamowitz, *Hermes*, ix, p. 338; Capps, l. c., p. 5; Körte in Pauly-W.
Real-Enc. xi. 1227.

[5] *Gött. Gel. Anz.*, l. c.   [6] v. 14.

[7] On *Od.* xx. 106 Μύλλος κύριον ὑποκριτοῦ παλαιοῦ, ὃς μιλτωτοῖς, φασι,
προσωπείοις ἐχρήσατο.

firms the use of the word as a proper name. Wilhelm [1] knows
it as a proper name in inscriptions from Thasos and Hermione.
Accordingly, poor though the evidence is, we have to admit
the possibility of a poet of the name.[2]

§ 2. It is a relief to turn from these unprofitable names to
two poets of whom at least some facts are certain—Chionides
and Magnes. Aristotle mentions them,[3] evidently because
they were the first Attic comic poets properly so called, in
connexion with the Megarean claim to priority. His information doubtless came from official records ;[4] and these records
would begin as soon as comedy was granted a chorus by the
archon at a Dionysiac festival. Of the date of this first grant
we have two indications ; Suidas' account of Chionides, and
the great didascalic inscription *C. I. A.* ii. 971, both contain the
record of contests at the City Dionysia. The former is as
follows : Χιωνίδης· Ἀθηναῖος, κωμικὸς τῆς ἀρχαίας κωμῳδίας,
ὃν καὶ λέγουσι πρωταγωνιστὴν γενέσθαι τῆς ἀρχαίας κωμῳδίας,
διδάσκειν [5] δὲ ἔτεσιν ὄκτω πρὸ τῶν Περσικῶν. τῶν δραμάτων
αὐτοῦ ἐστὶ καὶ ταῦτα· "Ηρως, Πτωχοί, Πέρσαι ἢ Ἀσσύριοι.
The statement that he was the πρωταγωνιστής of the Old
Comedy can hardly mean anything else than that he was
victorious at the first contest,[6] and so was the first or leading

---

[1] l. c., p. 247.

[2] Those who take the word simply as an adjective (used as the name
of a type), accented μυλλός, differ as to its meaning. Wilamowitz
(*Hermes*, l. c.) and Dieterich (*Pulc.*, p. 38) took it *sensu obscaeno*, Kaibel
(*Com. Gr. Fr.* i, p. 78) as = κυλλός or στρεβλός = διεστραμμένος τὴν ὄψιν,
alio oculis alio mente conversis.

[3] *Poet.* iii ἐκεῖθεν γὰρ ἦν Ἐπίχαρμος ὁ ποιητὴς πολλῷ πρότερος ὢν Χιωνίδου
καὶ Μάγνητος. It can hardly be doubted that he refers to them also in
ch. v ἤδη δὲ σχήματά τινα αὐτῆς ἐχούσης οἱ λεγόμενοι αὐτῆς ποιηταὶ μνημονεύονται. I cannot think that Bywater is right in thinking λεγόμενοι con-
temptuous. It means simply those whose names were known, as distinct
from those who λελήθασι.

[4] See Capps, *Introd. of Comedy into City Dion.*, p. 9. (I follow Capps'
admirable discussion closely in this section.)

[5] Capps perhaps goes too far in suggesting that Suidas has actually in
mind a didascalic record, Χιωνίδης ἐδίδασκεν : διδάσκειν in this sense was
not confined to such records.

[6] The meanings of πρωταγωνιστής are fully discussed by K. Rees, *The*

representative of the art; and Suidas' dates seem generally to be connected with some important event in a writer's career, such as this victory would be. 'Eight years before the Persian Wars' may mean either 488/7 B.C., or, if the reckoning is inclusive, 487/6 B.C.[1] Either of these dates is possible, but Capps finds it easier to reconstruct the inscription mentioned on the assumption that the latter date is the correct one, and this may be provisionally accepted. This date is quite consistent with the statement that Epicharmus was composing much earlier than Chionides and Magnes, since Epicharmus must have been composing at Megara before his migration to Syracuse,[2] and may well have been writing as early as 510 B.C. It is also consistent with the most probable view of the inscription *C. I. A.* ii. 977 d (Capps) or i (Wilhelm), which gives the list of comic poets victorious at the City Dionysia in the order of their first victories.[3]

Rule of Three Actors in the Classical Greek Drama, pp. 31 ff. He rightly declines to emend πρωταγωνιστήν to πρῶτον ἀγωνιστήν (Wilamowitz) or προαγωνιστήν (Schenkl).

[1] The year of the Persian Wars is assumed to be 480/79 B.C.

[2] See below, p. 353.

[3] It is practically certain that the eighth line contained the name of Magnes; for though only the last letter of the name and the number of victories is preserved, the missing letters must have been five in number, and the number of victories, eleven, is that ascribed to Magnes by the Anonymous writer preserved in Cod. Estensis and the Aldine Aristophanes. Suidas' ascription of two victories only to Magnes is probably a simple mistake. Aristoph. *Knights* 521, says that he set up πλεῖστα χορῶν τῶν ἀντιπάλων νίκης τρόπαια: and the attempt to justify Suidas (whose numbers are very often not such as to inspire confidence) by supposing that he refers to Lenaean victories only fails, because the numbers in such literary notices of victories are always those of Dionysian and Lenaean victories together or of Dionysian alone, and Suidas elsewhere always gives the total for both festivals (see Capps, *Ann. J. Ph.* xx, p. 398); and it is now generally agreed that Lenaean contests in comedy were not state-managed and recorded before (circ.) 442 B.C. Allowing two lines for the heading of the inscription, there will have been five names before that of Magnes, and of these Chionides must have been the first. (The four intervening poets must have been so obscure that Aristotle passed them over. One of them may have been Alkimenes, as Wilhelm, p. 107, suggests; he is only mentioned by

Probably the texts of Chionides' plays were not preserved
in Aristotle's day; he can only tell us that the comedy of
these first recorded poets had already a certain form, and it is
not likely that any texts of comedies earlier than those of
Cratinus long survived their production. We do not know
what authority Suidas had for the names which he gives to
supposed plays of Chionides; Athenaeus shows that the
Πτωχοί was known to be spurious in the third century A.D.[1]
The fragments of the poems are of no importance, even if
genuine.

Magnes won a victory in 473/2 B.C.,[2] and eleven victories
in all. The statement of Suidas that he was 'Ικαρίου πόλεως,
'Αττικός, ἢ 'Αθηναῖος κωμικός, probably betrays an attempt

Suidas). Now if Magnes' victory in 473/2 B.C. (C.I.A. 971 b) were his
first we should have six victorious poets over a space of fifteen years
(487/6 B.C.–1473/2 B.C.)–a quite possible number; but in fact some of
Magnes' victories may have fallen before 473/2 B.C. Four lines below
the name of Μάγνη]s in C.I.A. ii. 977, comes a name which is almost
certainly restored as Εὐφρόν]ιος, with one victory. Euphronius won a
Dionysiac victory in 459/8 (C.I.A. 971 a), fourteen years after Magnes'
victory in 473/2; and as the four poets intervening between Magnes
and Euphronius in the list of victors won only one victory each, most
of the victories of these fourteen years must have been won by Magnes
and his predecessors, including, presumably, Chionides. The whole
record works out easily if Magnes' victory in 473/2 fell somewhat before
the middle of his career, and if Chionides won a large number of
victories. Sir William Ridgeway (Dramas, &c., p. 410) appears not to
have considered the evidence in regard to these dates.

[1] Athen. iv. 137 e, xiv. 638 d.

[2] C.I.A. ii. 971 b (Wilhelm, Urkunden, pp. 16 ff.). Capps' calculations
(l. c., pp. 14–22) fix the date with certainty, and he disposes easily of the
reasons which used to be given for a later date. The choregus was
Pericles, and earlier scholars assumed that he would have been too young
to undertake the choregia in 472 B.C.: but a very young man might
be called upon if he were rich enough, and the choregia did not depend
upon, or lead to, political eminence. In Lysias xxi. 1 we find a choregus
of eighteen years of age. Suidas' statement that Magnes ἐπιβάλλει
'Επιχάρμῳ νεὸς πρεσβύτῃ causes no difficulty (see below, p. 355, n. 1); but
Sir William Ridgeway can hardly be right in translating ἐπιβάλλει by
'attacked'. The word sometimes means to succeed or follow; and so
here it practically means to overlap.

to connect him with Susarion and Thespis. Aristophanes
(*Knights* 518 ff.) tells us that he fell out of favour in his
old age :

ὑμᾶς τε πάλαι διαγιγνώσκων ἐπετείους τὴν φύσιν ὄντας,
καὶ τοὺς προτέρους τῶν ποιητῶν ἅμα τῷ γήρᾳ προδιδόντας·
τοῦτο μὲν εἰδὼς ἅπαθε Μάγνης ἅμα ταῖς πολιαῖς κατιούσαις,
ὃς πλεῖστα χορῶν τῶν ἀντιπάλων νίκης ἔστησε τροπαῖα,
πάσας δ' ὑμῖν φωνὰς ἱεὶς καὶ ψάλλων καὶ πτερυγίζων
καὶ λυδίζων καὶ ψηνίζων καὶ βαπτόμενος βατραχείοις
οὐκ ἐξήρκεσεν, ἀλλὰ τελευτῶν ἐπὶ γήρως, οὐ γὰρ ἐφ' ἥβης,
ἐξεβλήθη πρεσβύτης ὤν, ὅτι τοῦ σκώπτειν ἀπελείφθη.

The titles of his plays, according to Suidas' notice, were
Βαρβιτισταί (hence ψάλλων), Ὄρνιθες, Λυδοί, Ψῆνες, Βάτραχοι.
The significance of these titles, and particularly of the animal-
choruses, has already been referred to.[1]

Plays called Διόνυσος and Ποάστρια (' the Haymaker ') were
also ascribed to him,[2] but the critics of the early centuries A.D.
were aware that the extant plays bearing his name were either
spurious or had been revised and greatly altered.[3] Probably
not a line really written by Magnes survives ; the fragments,
even if genuine, are quite trivial.

Sir William Ridgeway[4] appears to go beyond the evidence
when he says that ' we know from Aristophanes that Magnes
continued to adhere to the old Megarean farce'. Neither our
knowledge of Magnes nor our knowledge of the Megarean
farce can justify such a statement. It seems much more
probable that Magnes followed the lines of a native Athenian
κῶμος, including choruses dressed as animals, though even this
is no more than a conjecture.

§ 3. The last of the poets who appeared before the great
period of Attic comedy opened with Cratinus is Ecphantides.

[1] Above, p. 247.
[2] Athen. ix. 367 f ; xiv. 646 e ; Schol. Platon. Bekk. 336.
[3] Athen., ll. cc. ; Hesych. Λυδίζων· χορεύων· διὰ τοὺς Λυδούς, οἳ σώζονται
μέν, διεσκευασμένοι δ' εἰσίν : Phot. Λυδίζων· Λυδοὶ Μάγνητος τοῦ κωμικοῦ
διεσκευάσθησαν.   [4] *Dramas*, &c., p. 410.

3182   U

In the list of comic poets victorious at the City Dionysia [1] his
name appears to be correctly restored, with four victories,
before that of Cratinus, and after that of Euphronius (of
whom nothing more is known). His first victory must have
been won in or shortly before 454 B.C. A scholiast [2] describes
him as παλαιότατος ποιητὴς τῶν ἀρχαίων, and Körte takes this
to imply that he was the oldest comic poet of whom any play
was preserved; this, however, appears hardly certain. The
contempt of Ecphantides for Megarean comedy has already
been mentioned, and he may have attempted to produce something more refined. The only title of a play of Ecphantides
which has been preserved is Σάτυροι, a line of which, referring
to boiled pigs' trotters, is quoted by Athenaeus.[3] In addition
we have only a salutation to Bacchus, and the superlative
κακηγορίστατος. The scholiast on Aristophanes' *Wasps*, 1187,
states that, like Cratinus, Telecleides, and Aristophanes, he
attacked a certain Androcles.[4] Aristotle refers [5] to a tablet
dedicated by Thrasippus, who had been choregus to Ecphantides, and from the context the date of the dedication appears
to have been a considerable time after the Persian Wars.
Ecphantides is said to have been nicknamed Καπνίας,[6] though

---

[1] *C.I.A.* ii. 977 i (Wilhelm, *Urkunden*, pp. 106 ff.).   See Geissler,
Chronol. der altatt. Kom., p. 11.

[2] See above, p. 287; cf. Körte in Pauly-W. *Real-Enc.* xi, col. 1228.

[3] Athen. iii. 96 b, c.

[4] Ἀνδροκλέα δὲ Κρατῖνος Σεριφίοις φησι δοῦλον καὶ πτωχόν, ἐν δὲ Ὥραις
ἡταιρηκότα Ἀριστοφάνης τὸν αὐτόν, Τηλεκλείδης δὲ ἐν Ἡσιόδοις καὶ Ἐκφαντίδης
βαλλαντιοτόμον.

[5] *Pol.* VIII. vi. 1341 a 36.

[6] Hesych., s. v. καπνίας, says of Ecphantides that καπνίας ἐπεκαλεῖτο διὰ
τὸ μηδὲν λαμπρὸν γράφειν, adding, καὶ οἶνος δὲ καπνίας λέγεται ὁ κεκαπνισμένος.
Schol. Ven. on Aristoph. *Wasps* 151 says : τὸν ὑπεκλυόμενον οἶνόν φασί τινες
καπνίαν λέγεσθαι, ἐν δὲ τοῖς περὶ Κρατίνου διώρισται ὅτι τὸν ἀπόθετον καὶ
παλαιόν, διὸ τὸν Ἐκφαντίδην Καπνίαν καλοῦσι. Either the nickname meant
'obscure', 'dull', without reference to the οἶνος καπνίας at all, but only
to καπνός, a word not uncommonly used as a nickname ; or there is a
reference to the wine. But the meaning of καπνίας as applied to wine
was disputed in the time of the *grammatici*. Some explain it by the
grape κάπνη (εἶδος ἀμπέλου ξηρότατον καὶ δριμύτατον οἶνον ποιούσης, ὁμοίως
καπνῷ ποιοῦντα δάκρυα), and this would suit Pherecr. fragm. 132 K., but

different reasons for the name are given. Hesychius preserves a story that he was helped in the composition of his plays by his slave Choerilus.[1]

would only suit Anaxandrid. fragm. 41, l. 70 γλυκὺς αὐθιγενὴς ἡδὺς καπνίας, if the expression is ironical (as is just possible). Others think it means 'old, choice wine', long accustomed *fumum bibere*, and this is the sense of the second view mentioned by the scholiast. Others (also referred to by the scholiast) thinks it means 'flat'.

[1] s. vv. ἐκκεχοιριλωμένη and Χοιρίλον Ἐκφαντίδους. See above p. 97.

APPENDIX A

ON THE FORM OF THE OLD COMEDY

§ 1.

It was argued above that the extant comedies of Aristophanes show clear traces of an original κῶμος-sequence, which may for convenience sake be summed up as Parodos-Agon-Parabasis, or Parodos-Proagon-Agon-Parabasis, all of these elements showing, with different degrees of completeness and symmetry, the same type of metrical structure. Part of the business of this Appendix will be to illustrate and amplify this statement. But in the extant plays this sequence is combined with scenes of another type, in iambic trimeters, separated by choral odes, and (at least in many plays) of an 'epeisodic' character, only slightly connected with the plot which has come to some kind of conclusion with the decision of the agon, but usually at least illustrating the results of that decision; very often these form simply a series of farcical scenes, in which one ridiculous character after another tries to impose upon the victor, and is driven off with scorn or violence. The plays of Aristophanes show a gradually increasing success in welding these two main elements in the play, the epirrhematic and the iambic, into a whole. In all the plays there is an introductory scene or prologue which serves as a bond of unity (and this, in its known form, may have been the invention of Aristophanes himself); and there is often an iambic scene between the agon and the parabasis, inserted evidently to prepare for the scenes which are to follow the parabasis. Aristophanes also, especially in the later plays, while adhering more or less to the general outline which has been indicated—Prologue, Parodos, Proagon, Agon, Transition scene (if any), Parabasis, Iambic scenes, Exodos—introduces many variations, as the accompanying analysis of his plays will show, and in particular he sometimes introduces among or near the end of the iambic scenes a second parabasis or a second agon, of a shorter form than the parabasis or agon proper. It cannot be too plainly stated that the poet is not bound by these conventional forms; he evidently stands at the end of the development of the Old Comedy, and, especially in the latter part of his career, he experiments freely; but it is obvious that he is conscious of them to the end.

No discussion of the form of the plays of Aristophanes can begin without an acknowledgement of the debt which all students of the subject owe to Zielinski,[1] whose thorough and ingenious discussion is necessarily the basis of all other work; the discussion was carried further by Mazon,[2] and contributions to it have been made from time to time by others. But both Zielinski and Mazon appear to postulate too rigid a structure for comedy, and to leave too little freedom to the poet; and Zielinski in particular is led to frame a number of very unconvincing theories, partly in regard to the revision of particular plays, partly in regard to metre and delivery, to account for our text being at certain points divergent from the assumed structure. These theories we shall have to reject, but the poet's consciousness of something like a normal sequence of scenes of certain definite types appears nevertheless to be certain.

The number of elements in the simplest complete epirrhematic scene is four—ode (a), antode (a'), epirrhema (b), antepirrhema (b'), and the order of these may be $aba'b'$, $bab'a'$, $abb'a'$, $aa'bb'$, and perhaps $bb'aa'$. Such a fourfold scene has, since the appearance of Zielinski's work, been called an epirrhematic syzygy. This structure may be enlarged (1) by the prefixing of two (or sometimes more) lines to the epirrhema or antepirrhema, usually containing a command or encouragement to each party to state his case; these are the κατακελευσμός and ἀντικατακελευσμός, (2) by appending to the epirrhema and antepirrhema, which are always in tetrameters (anapaestic, iambic, or trochaic), a number of dimeters of the same type, sometimes (when delivered by one speaker) termed πνῖγος (probably

---

[1] *Die Gliederung der altattischen Komödie*, 1885.
[2] *Essai sur la composition des comédies d'Aristophane*, 1904.

because of the pace at which they were delivered in one breath)
or μακρόν, and often introducing language of a more violent
or vulgar character than the tetrameters, as a kind of climax.
It is convenient to use the term 'antipnigos', for the dimeters
of the antepirrhema.[1] The whole may be preceded by an
invocation or prelude, and rounded off by a σφραγίς or conclusion, emphasizing the issue.

Except in the parabasis, the epirrhemata and πνίγη may be
shared between several speakers, of whom one may be the
leader of the chorus or of one of the semi-choruses composing it,
and the ode and antode may be entirely given to the chorus,
or may be shared by the actors or interrupted by 'mesodic'
tetrameters or other lines not strictly lyric. But in the
parabasis there are no such divisions; the ode and epirrhema
belong to one semi-chorus and its leader, the antode and antepirrhema to the other semi-chorus and leader.

The ode and antode always correspond exactly, as strophe
and antistrophe. In the parabasis the epirrhema and antepirrhema also correspond exactly, and the number of lines in
each is always a multiple of four (usually sixteen); but in other
epirrhematic scenes there may or may not be such exact
correspondence, and we shall have to discuss various cases
separately.

It will be best to begin our consideration of the normal
elements in comedy with the parabasis, which adheres far
more strictly to type than the other varieties of epirrhematic
scene. In the parabasis, in its complete form, the epirrhematic
syzygy, in which the epirrhema and antepirrhema are always
in trochaic tetrameters, is preceded by (1) the κομμάτιον, a
brief farewell to the persons who are quitting the scene, or
a 'word of command' to the chorus to begin the parabasis,
(2) the 'anapaests' regularly so called, though sometimes the
Eupolidean or other metres are employed[2]—an address,

---

[1] For the terminology and the authority for it in antiquity see Körte in
Pauly-W. Real-Enc. xi. 1242. The words ἀντικατακελευσμός and antipnigos have no ancient authority, but are conveniently coined.

[2] Körte, in Pauly-W. Real-Enc. xi, col. 1243, finds evidence of about
twenty parabases of lost plays in metres other than the anapaestic, and

normally in anapaestic tetrameters, by the leader of the chorus
to the audience, usually and originally in the poet's name and
interest, and concluding with (3) a πνῖγος in the same metre.
(2) and (3) are sometimes called the 'parabasis' in the
narrower sense of the word.

§ 2. *The Parabasis.*

The parabasis is found in its complete form in the
Acharnians, Knights, Wasps, and *Birds,* and (except for the
absence of the πνῖγος) in the *Clouds.* In the *Lysistrata* the
chorus is divided into two semi-choruses (of men and women
respectively) throughout, and all the parts of the parabasis
are accordingly duplicated (see analysis). In the *Frogs* the
epirrhematic syzygy is complete, but there are no κομμάτιον,
anapaests, or πνῖγος. In the *Peace* there are the κομμάτιον,
anapaests, πνῖγος, ode and antode, but no epirrhemata. In
the *Thesmophoriazusae* we find the κομμάτιον, anapaests,
πνῖγος, and epirrhema only. The only plays without a parabasis are the two fourth-century plays, the *Ecclesiazusae* and
Plutus.

In the *Knights, Peace,* and *Birds* there is a second parabasis
in the form of a simple epirrhematic syzygy, the only variation
being the termination of the epirrhema and antepirrhema in the
Peace by a short πνῖγος. In the *Clouds* a single epirrhema of
sixteen lines addressed to the judges takes the place of a
second parabasis. In the *Wasps* (1265-91) is a second parabasis of irregular shape.

These facts are sufficient evidence of the normality of a
parabasis.

thinks that as practically all of these are based on the popular chori-
ambic dimeter metre, they may be older (in Attic comedy) than, and
may have been ousted by, the anapaestic tetrameter used by Epicharmus.
But the strong predominance of the anapaestic metre makes this very
doubtful, and the ascription to the parabasis proper of some of the
passages to which he refers is very uncertain. The majority of the
passages are in Eupolideans, but a parabasis of Eupolis' Ἀστράτευτοι
in the *metrum Cratineum* is certain, and fr. 30, 31 in a choriambic-
iambic metre are probably from the parabasis proper of Aristophanes'
Amphiaraus.

In the extant parabases the epirrhema and antepirrhema always contain sixteen or twenty lines each, and are of the same length; except that in the *Lysistrata* there are two epirrhemata and two antepirrhemata, each of ten lines. There is no direct evidence as to the way in which these portions were delivered; but it may be taken as almost certain that the epirrhema and antepirrhema were delivered in recitative by the leaders of the two semi-choruses, and that they were accompanied by dancing movements[1]—perhaps executed by the semi-chorus whose leader was not reciting, as its formation would be complete, whereas if the other semi-chorus were dancing we should have to suppose either that it danced without its leader, in incomplete formation, or that he delivered his address while in motion; neither of these things is impossible, but both seem improbable. The exact symmetry of the structure (as compared with that of some other epirrhematic scenes) is probably due to the necessity of conformity with the orderly evolutions of the dancers.

The parabasis inevitably makes a break in the action of the play, and the facts suggest that at first the action—or at least *an* action—was virtually complete before the parabasis began. In the *Acharnians*, Dicaeopolis has already got his Peace, and the subsequent scenes only show its farcical consequences; in the *Wasps*, Philocleon has submitted, and the scenes after the parabasis do not really touch the main issue of the play; in the *Peace*, the corresponding scenes only show the consequences of the newly-recovered Peace; and those in the *Birds* display Peithetaerus in the City of the Birds which he has won before the beginning of the parabasis, though the final settlement with the gods is left over to the end of the play. There can, of course, be no doubt that Aristophanes attempted, and with greater success as time went on, to make his plays a unity and to include the parabasis itself within the whole; and in the *Knights, Clouds, Lysistrata, Thesmo-*

---

[1] There is no direct evidence of this, except in the *Lysistrata*; but the fact that the chorus prepared for the parabasis by shedding some of its garments would be meaningless otherwise (e. g. *Ach.* 627, &c.); the ode and antode are always very brief and would not be worth stripping for.

phoriazusae, and *Frogs* (the latter perhaps the most artistic play and the completest unity of all, as well as the most free in its handling of traditional forms) the plot extends over the whole play and the issue is not decided until the end. But unless the parabasis had originally involved a breaking off from an action already decided, it is hardly conceivable that any poet would have invented or accepted such a break in the middle of his play.

The parabasis makes a break, not only in the action, but in the dramatic function of the chorus.[1] In the first five extant plays the ' anapaests ' are an address of the poet to the audience in his own defence,[2] and have nothing to do with the play, though the chorus resumes its stage character in part in the epirrhema and antepirrhema. Again the poet strives for greater unity, and in the *Birds* the anapaests also are in character, expounding the ' new theology ' associated with the government of the Birds; in the *Lysistrata* and *Thesmophoriazusae* the dramatic character of the chorus is maintained throughout, and there is nowhere any marked divergence from the subject of the play; in the *Frogs* the mystae retain their character in the epirrhema and antepirrhema, though the ode and antode consist of satire directed against Cleophon and Cleigenes. In the first four of the six plays which have a second parabasis, the subject of it is independent of the plot; in the *Peace* the rustics sing of the country and country-life at different seasons; in the *Birds* the chorus remain in character except for an address to the judges in the antepirrhema.

The natural conclusion from these facts is that the parabasis was originally a semi-dramatic, or even a non-dramatic, sequel to the dramatic action of the agon by the κωμασταί.[3]

---

[1] The recovery from this break is sometimes very imperfect. Many of the odes which separate the epeisodic scenes, after the parabasis, might be sung by any chorus, and no one would suspect (from their contents) that they were sung by *Knights* or *Wasps* or *Birds*. (See later.)

[2] That this had been their use before Aristophanes seems to be implied by his statement in the *Acharnians* that that play was the first in which he himself had used them for the purpose.

[3] See above, p. 241. Mr. Cornford's idea that an agon between two semi-choruses (as in the *Lysistrata*) was itself the original form of parabasis is

§ 3. *The Agon.*

It is convenient to confine the use of the name 'agon' to the formal or set debate between two parties which is so common in Aristophanes, and to treat the preliminary conflicts which lead up to it under other heads.

The facts may be briefly stated as follows. We find an agon in regular form, including an epirrhematic syzygy, and presenting only slight variations in other respects, in the first part (i.e. before the parabasis) in the *Knights, Wasps, Birds,* and *Lysistrata,* and in the second part in the *Knights* (on a larger scale than the first agon), the *Clouds* (where there are two such contests after the parabasis), and the *Frogs* (though in this play there is some irregularity as regards the odes). In the *Peace* there is not, strictly speaking, an agon as regards either matter or form, perhaps because it would have been dangerous to discuss seriously the policies of war and peace ; but in form there is a fragment of an agon (601–56) including katakeleusmos and epirrhema, and the epirrhema is certainly contentious in matter. (Hermes gives a paradoxical account of the causes of the war.) In an earlier scene (346–430) there is more of the agon as regards the matter, where Trygaeus persuades Hermes not to tell Zeus of the plan for raising Peace, and as regards form, this scene gives us a strophe and anti-strophe, each succeeded by what, but for its being in the iambic trimeter metre, would be respectively an epirrhema and antepirrhema of almost equal length, and the whole concluded by a σφραγίς in trochaic tetrameters. It is clear that if it was a general rule that the first half of the play should contain something like an agon, the *Peace* is not a very violent exception, and there seems to be no need for Zielinski's strange theory as to the nature of the play.[1]

In the *Clouds* it is remarkable that both contests are postponed to the second half of the play ; the natural place of the

rendered improbable by the fact that, except in the *Lysistrata,* a play in many ways unique, there is scarcely any trace of opposition between the semi-choruses in the parabasis (see above, p. 242).

[1] op. cit., pp. 63–78.

agon in the first half is taken by Socrates' instruction of Strepsiades in the new religion. But it is practically certain that the *Clouds* as we have it is neither the play in its original form nor yet a completed revision, and Zielinski may be right [1] in thinking that in the first edition this scene may have been more like a formal agon. The discussion between Socrates and the incredulous Strepsiades would certainly lend itself to this; and one or both of the existing agones may belong to the unfinished second edition of the play.

There are two plays in which the matter in the first part of the play is exactly of the kind to make a good agon, but in which the form is abnormal—the *Acharnians* and the *Thesmophoriazusae*. In both these the place of the epirrhemata is taken by set speeches in iambic trimeters, and the reason is obvious,—that the speeches are parodies of the orations delivered in the law-courts (*Acharnians*) or the assembly (*Thesmophoriazusae*), and the iambic trimeter was the metre conventionally appropriated to such set speeches on the stage; in the *Acharnians* also there is obvious burlesque of the ' forensic contests ' of tragedy. So in the *Acharnians* there is first a kind of proagon (358–92) with symmetrical semi-lyric odes and a κατακελευσμός (364, 5), but with the first epirrhema replaced by Dicaeopolis' first defence in iambic trimeters (366–84) while for the second, which we expect after l. 392, is substituted the farcical scene between Dicaeopolis and Euripides. Then follows what in matter is a real agon, with short semi-lyric odes,[2] Dicaeopolis' defence for epirrhema, and for antepirrhema the presentation of the other side *pour rire* in the person of Lamachus. This is of course only an imperfect substitute for the proper epirrhematic structure, but it is near enough to it to be regarded as a deliberate variation of it. In the *Thesmophoriazusae*, in addition to the substitution of a debate

---

[1] ib., pp. 34-60. The details of his reconstruction of the original play are not at all convincing.

[2] These odes do not perfectly correspond in our texts. In ll. 490-6 there are two pairs of dochmiac lines separated by two iambic trimeters, in ll. 566-71 there are six dochmiacs; but the difference is not very noticeable.

in iambic trimeters, there is the further irregularity that the kind of 'battle-scene',[1] which usually leads up to the agon, in this play follows the quasi-agon or debate, and in fact the whole structure of the first half of this play is very formless, though as a plot the play hangs together well, and there is no reason to suspect any loss or displacement, granted that the poet was not rigidly tied down by conventions.

The postponement of the agon in the *Frogs* to the second half was plainly necessitated by the nature of the plot, which covers the whole play.

When all exceptions are allowed for, it may fairly be said that in Aristophanes' plays there is a marked preference for an agon, regular or modified, before the parabasis, and there can be little doubt that this was its normal place, though the poet did not hesitate to modify both the position and the epirrhematic structure of the contest, if his plot demanded it. The structure may be preserved, even if the matter (as in the *Birds*) is less that of an actual contest than an exposition to the incredulous of a paradoxical thesis, and if in consequence the leading part in the epirrhema and antepirrhema cannot be assigned to two different parties.

It has already been noticed that the symmetry between epirrhema and antepirrhema, which is observed without exception in the parabasis, is not so strict in the agon. The two are not always in the same metre, though the metre is always some species of tetrameter.[2] In the first agon in the *Knights* the symmetry is perfect, except that six mesodic trochaic tetrameters (391–6) in the antode correspond to eight such lines (314–21) in the ode; it is at least possible that two lines may have been lost, though the irregularity is not so

---

[1] The term is borrowed from Mazon.

[2] The species seems to be chosen, at least sometimes, with a view to the character of the contestant. The better side tends to be given anapaestic tetrameters (the Just Argument, Aeschylus), and this metre generally goes with an elevated or mock-heroic argument (the proof of the divinity of the *Clouds* or the *Birds*, &c.); while the iambic tetrameter generally suggests something more degraded (the Unjust Argument, Euripides, Pheidippides' justification of mother-beating, Cleon, &c.). But the distinction is not quite constant.

surprising as a want of correspondence between the lyric portions of the ode would be. In the second agon in the same play (756–941) 61 lines of epirrhema are answered by 68 of antepirrhema. In the *Birds* there is exact correspondence; the epirrhema and antepirrhema have each 61 lines. In the *Lysistrata* each has 47 lines, and the symmetry is thus complete. In the *Wasps* the 69 lines of the antepirrhema just fail to correspond with the 72 lines of the epirrhema. In both contests in the *Clouds* the correspondence is slightly inexact (epirrhema of 47 lines, antepirrhema of 49 lines in the first; in the second 33 and 46 lines respectively; and slight differences in the πνίγη). In the *Frogs* the lines of the epirrhema and antepirrhema are 64 and 71 respectively. Thus the symmetry, though, as a rule, roughly observed (as would be natural in a fairly ordered debate, and in a structure freely adapted from that of the parabasis) is not rigorously exact; the chorus (though they may begin as partisans) are judges, or at least 'keepers of the ring' in the agon: they are accordingly not dancing but listening, and there would therefore be no need to provide for symmetrical evolutions of the chorus during the discussion by the litigants.[1] In one agon only, so far as can be seen, were the chorus in motion; in the *Lysistrata* (539–42) the singers in the women's chorus exhort each other to move and help their friends, and declare that dancing will never tire them (ἔγωγε γὰρ ἂν οὔποτε κάμοιμ' ἂν ὀρχουμένη). Zielinski argues (and though the argument is not conclusive, he may be right) that this cannot refer to the brief dance during the antode,

---

[1] Zielinski's argument from the Schol. on Aristoph. *Clouds* 1352 is most inconclusive. The scholium runs: χρὴ δὴ λέγειν πρὸς τὸν χορόν· οὕτως ἔλεγον πρὸς χορὸν λέγειν, ὅτι τοῦ ὑποκριτοῦ διατιθεμένου τὴν ῥῆσιν ὁ χορὸς ὠρχεῖτο. διὸ ἐκλέγονται ὡς ἐπὶ τὸ πλεῖστον ἐν τοῖς τοιούτοις τὰ τετράμετρα, ἢ τὰ ἀναπαιστικὰ ἢ τὰ ἰαμβικά, διὰ τὸ ῥᾳδίως ἐμπίπτειν ἐν τούτοις τὸν τοιοῦτον μέτρον. The scholium is nonsense as an explanation of the passage, which simply means 'to tell the chorus'; but it may have some meaning if applied not, as Zielinski suggests, to the agon, but to some of the scenes before it, in which the chorus are often in violent motion. (The mention of the ὑποκριτής excludes the parabasis.) But it seems doubtful whether any importance at all should be attached to so confused and obscure a scholium.

but must mean that they will dance through the antepirrhema,
as the men's chorus has (*ex hypothesi*) just danced through the
epirrhema.   But if the phrase 'dancing never tires me' does
not refer to the antode or is not perfectly general—if it means
that the chorus danced throughout—we have here one of those
exceptions which prove a rule.   For in this agon the two semi-
choruses do not pretend to be judges, but are keen partisans;
they have no judicial calm, and may quite well be in movement
all the time.   (The contest is left drawn, when the Proboulos and
Lysistrata divide the σφραγίς between them.)   It is confirmatory of this that the agon is perfectly symmetrical.

Zielinski however wishes to impose exact symmetry everywhere, and to raise the number of lines in every epirrhema
and antepirrhema to a multiple of four; and to accomplish
this he has to assume pauses of from one to four lines' length
in many places,[1] and to suppose that these were filled with
instrumental music to which the chorus danced.   But the
distribution of these pauses is very unconvincing; in some
places the suggested pause is not only unnecessary but
unnatural, nor is there anything in the matter to account
for the varying lengths of these pauses.   The explanation
above given of the want of symmetry, namely that symmetry
was unnecessary to the performance, because the words of the
agon had not to be correlated with dancing movements of
the chorus, seems much more likely.

§ 4.   *The Preparatory Scenes.*

The scenes between the prologue (or introductory iambic
scene) and the agon vary much more in form than those
which we have been considering, and if we were right in

---

[1] e. g. in the second agon of the *Knights* he makes up the epirrhema
and antepirrhema to multiples of four, with pauses of three lines' length
at ll. 780 or 784, 867 and 880; of four lines' at 889: of one line's at
849 and 905.   Again, pauses are inserted at *Clouds* 1429, 1436, and the
epirrhema cut down to thirty-two lines by joining l. 1385 to the πνῖγος.
In the *Wasps* also epirrhema and antepirrhema are raised to eighty
lines each, with pauses of four lines' length at 559; two lines' at 695
and 699; three lines' at 706; and one line's at 577, 589, 600, 615, 649, 663,
703 (some of these are most improbable).

deriving them from an original κῶμος-sequence there is
nothing unnatural in this; a band of revellers breaking in
upon the scene might behave very freely and variously before
coming at length to the conventional agon and parabasis.
But one of the commonest types of scene which we find in
this place in Aristophanes is that which Zielinski conveniently
terms a 'proagon' (though the technical use of the word in
antiquity was different) and which often takes the form which
Mazon calls a 'scène de bataille'. The business of this scene
is to single out and present the disputants in the coming agon
to the audience, to calm them (and often the chorus which at
first sides with one of them) down to the debating point, and
generally to arrange the terms of the debate, to which, often
after a violent beginning, the scene leads. The proagon often
includes symmetrical elements of an epirrhematic type, at
least in the earlier plays. Thus in the *Acharnians* 280–357,
there is a completely symmetrical epirrhematic scene, of the
abb'a' form, with κατακελευσμός and σφραγίς: the chorus are
evidently in energetic movement all the time.[1] In the
Knights it is difficult to distinguish proagon from parodos
(242–302); the scene is all in trochaic tetrameters, but after
the κατακελευσμός or invocation by Demosthenes, the speeches
(247–68) are symmetrically arranged, though the dialogue
afterwards becomes unsymmetrical until it terminates in a
πνῖγος (284–302). In the first part of the *Clouds* there is no
distinct proagon: but in the *Wasps* there is a long and
elaborate scene (317–525), portions of which are plainly of
the (roughly) symmetrical epirrhematic type (see Analysis),
e. g. 333 to 388 or 402, and 403–525.[2] In the *Peace* the
preparatory scenes are very freely constructed, but there are
marked symmetrical elements, viz. 346–430 (strophe and

---

[1] The schol. says they are dancing a κόρδαξ, but was this a choral
dance at all?

[2] 403-4 correspond with 461-2; 405-29 correspond with 463-87,
except that the latter part of the antode (463-71) is not exactly in
accordance with that of the ode (405-14); there is an epirrhema
(430-60) of thirty-one lines, and an antepirrhema (488-525) of thirty-
eight lines.

antistrophe with iambic scenes, almost equal, for epirrhemata, and σφραγίς) and 459–511 (a similar though not exactly correspondent structure) ; the whole passage from 346–600 leads up, by its vigorous action (the raising of Peace), to the half-agon (601–656). In the *Birds* the 'battle-scene' (352–432) which succeeds the parodos is not epirrhematic; nor are the scenes in iambic tetrameters (350–81, with πνῖγος 382–6) and trimeters (387–466) which precede the agon in the *Lysistrata*. In the *Thesmophoriazusae* and the *Frogs* (in which the agon is postponed) there is no proper proagon, though in the second part of the *Frogs* the iambic scenes from 830 to 904 deserve the name ; and in the *Ecclesiazusae* (520–70) and the *Plutus* (414–86) the same purpose is again served by an iambic scene. In plays in which an agon occurs in the second half of the play, it may also be preceded by a scene which is recognizably of the proagon-type, at least as regards matter, e. g. *Clouds* 1321–44; *Knights* 611–755, which is also in syzygy form, but with iambic scenes (nearly equal) in place of epirrhema and antepirrhema; *Frogs* 830–94. The first agon in the *Clouds* is preceded by a preliminary contest in anapaestic dimeters between the two Λόγοι (889–948).

The term 'Parodos' is nowhere defined in ancient writers with reference to comedy,[1] and its use by modern writers on the subject varies, and that almost inevitably : for the actual entrance-song of the chorus is so closely connected in many plays with passages which follow it (and more rarely, as in the *Birds*, with passages which precede it), that to separate them would be unnatural, so that for convenience sake the term may well be used to cover these. In the *Acharnians* the parodos proper or entrance-scene (ll. 204–41) is quite symmetrical in structure, and the first part epirrhematic (*bab'a'*); the parodos in the wider sense includes Dicaeopolis' celebration of the Rural Dionysia, after which the battle-scene or proagon follows. The parodos (or proagon) of the *Knights* with its symmetrical opening has already been mentioned. In the *Clouds* the parodos proper consists of an ode and antode sung by the

---

[1] The definition which Aristotle (*Poet.* xii) gives of it for tragedy is clearly inapplicable to Comedy.

chorus unseen, with an invocation in anapaestic tetrameters
preceding them and a brief dialogue in the same metre
dividing them, the whole section (263–313) forming a rough
epirrhematic syzygy of the form $bab'a'$: in the wider sense
the parodos will include the dialogue which follows, down to
the exchange of greetings between Socrates and the now
visible chorus (356–63). In the *Wasps* the chorus enter
stumbling and talking (230–72) in iambic tetrameters (only
exchanging a few words with the 'link-boy' who is lighting
their way); they then sing an ode, in strophe and antistrophe
(273–89), and take part in a quaint antistrophic κομμός with
the boy (290–316); but strictly epirrhematic structures do
not appear till the next scene, which we have treated as part
of the proagon. The parodos of the *Peace* (301–45) is in
trochaic tetrameters with a πνῖγος; it would be unnatural
to include the next scene, which is essentially a discussion
between Hermes and Trygaeus. The parodos of the *Birds* is
elaborate and beautiful. The invocation-scene (209–66) is
really an integral part of it; each song of the Epops is succeeded by four iambic trimeters: the parodos proper begins
with the trochaic dialogue at 268, during which the birds
enter one by one, till they join in the ode and antode
(separated by a few trochaic lines), and then bring on the
'battle-scene'. In the *Lysistrata* the divided chorus enters
in two semi-choruses, the men (ll. 254–318) with a long speech
which (after a κατακελευσμός) falls into the form of an
epirrhematic syzygy, followed by a strophe and antistrophe
and thirteen iambic tetrameters. The women (319–49) are
content with a κατακελευσμός, strophe and antistrophe. In
the *Thesmophoriazusae* the chorus enter as the herald makes
the proclamation opening the assembly; they sing an ode;
another proclamation follows, and an ode which does not
correspond exactly with the preceding one, and the herald
reads the notice convening the meeting and calls for speakers.
The parodos of the *Frogs*, containing the incomparable lyrics
of the mystae, is quite unique, an d may be, as Zielinski
suggests, founded upon the actual pr ocession of the initiated
to Eleusis, with the accompany ing σκώμματα. The parodos

of the *Ecclesiazusae* consists of a few iambic tetrameters followed by lyrics; that of the *Plutus* of a dialogue in iambic tetrameters between the chorus and Cario, followed by five lyric strophes, which the chorus and Cario sing alternately.

This summary illustrates the predominance of tetrameter metres in the first scenes after the prologue, and the occasional occurrence of definitely epirrhematic structures, as well as the possibility of great variety of form in this part of the play.

§ 5. *Iambic Scenes.*

Having now reviewed the scenes which we have regarded as probably derived from the κῶμος, we may conveniently consider the iambic scenes which form the greater part of the last half of each play, i. e. of that portion of the play which succeeds the parabasis, when there is one.

These scenes are treated by the poet in two different ways. (1) They may be paired, and associated with a parallel ode and antode, so as to form what (when dealing with epirrhematic scenes) we called a syzygy. In such cases it is usual to find that there is an evident relation in subject-matter between the coupled scenes, and that (as in an epirrhematic syzygy) they are not interrupted by lyrics (whether original or parodied), or by the entry and exit of speakers.[1] It would probably be right to think of these iambic syzygies (if the term may be used) as modelled on the epirrhematic, but affected also by the structure of tragedy, the influence of which upon Aristophanic comedy is very plain. (2) On the other hand, we find iambic scenes strung together without any structural relationship, and divided from one another, not by a corresponding ode and antode, but by a χορικόν or στάσιμον complete in itself and including both strophe and antistrophe

---

[1] The facts, as regards Aristophanes, have been carefully worked out by Zielinski. He points out that where the scenes are parallel in matter, or form two stages of the same action, and yet are not grouped in syzygies, it is usually because the poet wished to introduce lyrics into the dialogue. He considers (*Gliederung*, p. 219) the two or three apparent exceptions to the rule against introducing such lyrics into iambic syzygies.

together (whereas the separated ode and antode form a separate strophe and antistrophe). Several virtually separate scenes of this kind may follow in succession without any choral interlude. In these epeisodic scenes (as scenes of this class have been termed) casual lyrics may be introduced where required, and there is no restriction on entrance and exit. Writers on the subject [1] often add that the choral odes which separate these iambic scenes are irrelevant to the subject of the play. It is, however, only a limited number of the odes which are thus irrelevant, so that this supposed irrelevance cannot be used to prove the original distinctness of the iambic scenes from the epirrhematic, in which the choral odes are relevant; and indeed their distinctness is plain enough without.

As regards the relation of the scenes which follow the parabasis to the plot of the play, it occasionally happens (as has already been said) that the main plot is carried over the whole play, and the issue not finally decided till the end. This is certainly so in the *Knights* and the *Frogs*, and (in a smaller degree) in the *Thesmophoriazusae*, in which indeed the discomfiture of Mnesilochus by the women is complete by the middle of the play, but the question whether he will or will not escape remains open to the last. But in general the second half of the play, though it may include some

---

[1] e. g. Cornford, op. cit., p. 108. The lyric interludes between the iambic scenes have been carefully studied by Wüst, in *Philologus*, lxxvii (1921), pp. 26–45. He distinguishes (*a*) a type closely modelled on the σκόλιον (as known from Athen. xv, pp. 693 ff.) and composed in short, similar stanzas, usually of four lines, relevant to the action and scarcely ever including any attack upon contemporaries; (*b*) a type composed usually in 10- or 11-line stanzas, irrelevant to the action, containing satire on individuals, and commonly ending with a σκῶμμα παρὰ προσδοκίαν —a type derived, as he supposes, from the γεφυρισμοί or σκώμματα ἐκ τῶν ἀμαξῶν of Athenian processions (the Lenaean among others). His classification is not exhaustive, and there are some slight overlappings between the two types, while the derivation of the second from γεφυρισμοί is not more than a conjecture; but on the whole the distinction which he draws corresponds to the facts. Neither type is found (except for special reasons) in the first half of the play. Typical instances of (*a*) are Aristoph. *Ach.* 929–51, *Eccles.* 938–45; of (*b*) *Ach.* 1150–73, *Knights* 1111–50, *Frogs* 416–33; but both occur in nearly all the plays.

minor action of its own, for the most part illustrates or carries somewhat further—it may be to a climax [1]—the results of the decision reached in the first half by means of the agon. This is so in the *Acharnians, Wasps, Peace, Birds,* and *Lysistrata,* as well as in the two plays which have no parabasis, the *Ecclesiazusae* and *Plutus.* [2]

In the early plays one particular type of iambic scene is particularly frequent,—that in which one ridiculous or pretentious character after another comes in, tries to 'get round' the victorious hero, and is driven away discomfited. Most of the iambic scenes in the *Acharnians,* the *Peace,* and the *Birds* are of this kind; so are the scenes between Strepsiades and Pasias and Amynias in the *Clouds* and the scenes in the *Wasps* (1387 ff., 1415 ff.) in which the Ἀρτόπωλις and the Κατή-γορος figure, and perhaps one scene (1216 ff.) in the *Lysistrata*; and though this kind of scene is not much employed by Aristophanes after the earlier plays, he reverts to it in the latter half of the *Plutus.* The characters who appear in this way belong to well-known contemporary types, and the farcical treatment of such types was just what we saw reason to connect with early Dorian buffoonery.

We sometimes find iambic scenes in the first half of the play, belonging both to the paired type and to the epeisodic; but usually there are special reasons for this. We have already seen the reason for the two iambic syzygies which replace the agon (and part of the proagon) in the *Acharnians.* In the *Wasps* (760-1008) there are two scenes, divided by a lyric interlude, which are epeisodic and precede the parabasis, and yet are not in principle exceptional, since they illustrate the consequences of Philocleon's submission. (The second half of the play is really a separate action, and represents his 'education' and its consequences.) In the *Peace* the iambic

---

[1] As in the *Acharnians,* where the last discomfiture is reserved for Lamachus himself, the incarnation of bellicosity; and still more in the *Birds* and the *Plutus,* where at last the results of the action are displayed as discomfiting the gods themselves.

[2] The *Clouds,* with its two contests in the second half, is peculiar in its present form. See above, p. 299.

scenes which (with the intervening lyrics) follow the parodos, are grouped in a more or less symmetrical structure. (This may be connected with the fact that they replace the epirrhematic scenes which would be normal.) So do those in the early part of the *Thesmophoriazusae* (e. g. 312–80, 433–530), though the analysis will show that this play is very irregular in form. In the *Frogs* the section of the play which precedes the parabasis forms a clear syzygy. Of the two fourth-century plays, the greater part (early as well as late) consists of iambic scenes, and the structure cannot be considered typical of the Old Comedy.

Separate mention must be made of one special kind of iambic scene—the transition-scene which often leads from the agon to the parabasis, e. g. in the *Knights*, *Clouds*, *Peace*, and *Birds*, and also in the *Lysistrata* (unless ll. 608–13 are more conveniently regarded as the σφραγίς of the agon). This scene owes its function mainly, perhaps, to the union of two originally distinct kinds of performance in Attic comedy, and serves to knit the two together, preparing, in the first half, for the action, or at least for the incidents, of the second half. Its structural value is obvious. In some of the later plays—the *Birds*, *Lysistrata*, *Ecclesiazusae*, and *Plutus*—there is a somewhat similar scene before the agon, making a break in the succession of tetrameters, and serving as a proagon or part of one.

§ 6. The Exodos.[1]

It is clear from the extant plays that there was no stereotyped method of concluding a comedy, though there are features which recur in several of the final scenes. Thus in the *Acharnians*, *Wasps*, *Birds*, and *Ecclesiazusae* the last stage of the play begins with a 'Messenger's Speech', evidently based on tragic models and announcing what is to follow. A messenger also appears in the *Knights*, and the servant in the *Ecclesiazusae* performs the same function.

---

[1] The word ought perhaps to be confined to the final utterance of chorus (cf. Tract. Coisl. ἔξοδός ἐστι τὸ ἐπὶ τέλει λεγόμενον τοῦ χοροῦ); but it has become usual to include under the term the whole final scene.

In several plays the last scene is marked by gross indecency, generally in connexion with a 'wedding'-scene (which in the *Birds* appears in a greatly refined form). The meaning of these scenes will be more conveniently considered in connexion with Mr. Cornford's theory of comedy; the plays in which such scenes—decent or indecent—occur at or near the end are the *Acharnians, Knights, Wasps, Peace, Birds,* and *Lysistrata.*

In some plays there is a song *of* victory or *for* victory. The *Acharnians* ends with the τήνελλα καλλίνικος, which is led by Dicaeopolis to celebrate his victory in the drinking-match, as the context makes plain.[1] In the *Birds* the strain of victory is blended with the wedding-hymn; in the *Lysistrata* also, while singing a wedding-hymn, the choruses dance ὡς ἐπὶ νίκῃ, and it is ὡς ἐπὶ νίκῃ that the two semi-choruses dance their way to the feast in the *Ecclesiazusae.* There can be little doubt that the victory of which the chorus sings in these three plays is their own anticipated success in the dramatic contest; otherwise the confusion of the hymeneal and triumphal songs would hardly be natural, and in fact the victory of the hero of the play is long past.

When there is not a wedding, there may still be a feast; even in the *Frogs* Pluto gives an invitation to a banquet. (We may well believe that ancient, as well as modern, seasonal κῶμοι ended in feasting.)

The chorus sometimes leaves the scene marching, but not dancing. This is clearly so in the *Acharnians* and *Clouds,* and probably was so in the *Peace, Birds, Thesmophoriazusae, Frogs,* and *Plutus.*[2] On the other hand, they depart dancing with extreme vigour in the *Wasps, Lysistrata,* and *Ecclesiazusae.* Occasionally, as in the *Clouds, Thesmophoriazusae,* and *Plutus,* the exit of the chorus follows very abruptly upon the termination of the action, and they only speak a few words of a more or less formal kind.

---

[1] In l. 1227 he says, 'See I have emptied the wine-skin—τήνελλα καλλίνικος', and the chorus join in ᾄδοντες σὲ καὶ τὸν ἀσκόν.

[2] The conclusion of the *Knights* is lost.

§ 7. *The Prologue or Introduction.*

We have left the Prologue or Introduction until last. It is, in Aristophanes, always a scene in iambic trimeters,[1] usually from 200 to 300 lines in length, and sometimes including a prologue in the narrower sense, modelled at times upon the tragic, and particularly upon the Euripidean, prologue.

The prologue in the wider sense constitutes (as Navarre has noticed) a relatively complete little action by itself, generally based on some paradoxical or fantastical idea,[2] which is just about to be carried into effect when it is rudely interrupted by the invasion of the chorus. The function of the prologue is to introduce the subject of the play to the audience (whether by a formal explanation, or by letting it reveal itself through the dialogue and action); to put them into a good humour by a number of jests, which may be unconnected with the subject of the play; and to bring the action up to the point required for the entrance of the chorus. As an iambic scene, coming before the epirrhematic parts of the play, while other iambic scenes follow them, it also serves to knit the whole together. This form of introduction may have been the invention, or at least a speciality, of Aristophanes himself. Certainly Cratinus did not always employ it. Its close dependence upon Euripides is very plain, whether it begins with a set speech,[3] or a dialogue followed by a set speech,[4] or a dialogue making the situation clear, but without any soliloquy or address to the audience.[5]

In the later plays Aristophanes, among other steps towards the introduction of greater unity into his plays, confines his prologues to what is relevant to the plot, and discards such irrelevant jests as appear (e. g.) in the *Wasps*.

[1] Lyrics are introduced occasionally, e. g. in the *Thesmophoriazusae* and the *Frogs*.

[2] A study of the lost plays of the Old Comedy makes it clear that many of them also were based on such ideas -- descents to Hades, voyages to Persia, to the wilds, &c.

[3] *Acharnians, Clouds, Ecclesiazusae, Plutus.*

[4] *Knights, Wasps, Peace, Birds.*

[5] *Lysistrata, Thesmophoriazusae, Frogs.*

ANALYSIS OF PLAYS

Acharnians.

Prologue, 1–203.

Parodos, 204–79.

 A. Parodos proper :

  (1) Epirrhema, 4 troch. tetr., 204–7. ⎫
   Ode (paeonic), 208–18.   ⎬ Chorus.
   Antepirrhema, 4 troch. tetr., 219–22. |
   Antode (paeonic), 223–33.   ⎭

  (2) Chorus, 3 troch. tetr., 234–6.   ⎫
   Dicaeop., 1 irregular line, 237. |
   Chorus, 3 troch. tetr., 238–40. |
   Dicaeop., 1 irregular line, 241.   ⎭

 B. Phallic procession (iambic scene and lyric monody), 242–79.

Battle Scene, 280–357.

 κατακελευσμός (2 troch. and 2 paeon. dimeters), 280–3.
 Ode (with troch. tetr. by Dicaeop. inserted), 284–301. ⎫
 Epirrhema (16 troch. tetr.), 302–18. |
 Antepirrhema (16 troch. tetr.), 319–34.   ⎬
 Antode (with troch. tetr. as in ode), 335–46. ⎭
 σφραγίς (11 iamb. trim. spoken by Dicaeop.), 347–57.

Proagon, 358–489.

 Ode, 358–63.   ⎫
 κατακελευσμός, 364–5. |
 Iambic scene (speech of Dicaeop. 19 iamb. |
  trim.), 366–84.   ⎬ Iambic syzygy
 Antode, 385–90. |
 ἀντικατακελ., 391–2. |
 Iambic scene (dialogue, 97 iamb. trim.), |
  393–489.   ⎭

Quasi-Agon, 490–625.

 Ode, 490–6.
 Iambic scene (70 ll.), 496–565. ⎫
 Antode, 572–625.   ⎬ Iambic syzygy.
 Iambic scene (53 ll.), 572–625. ⎭

Parabasis, 626–718.

κομμάτιον, 626–7.

Anapaests, tetrameters, 628–58.

πνῖγος, 659–64.

Ode, 665–75.

Epirrhema (16 troch. tetr.), 676–91.

Antode, 692–702.

Antepirrhema (16 troch. tetr.), 703–18.

Iambic Scenes and Lyric Interludes.

Iambic scene, 719–835.

Stasimon, 836–59.

Iambic scene, 860–928.

Lyric dialogue, 929–51.

Iambic scene, 952–70.

Stasimon, 971–99.

Iambic Syzygy, 1000–68.

Introduction (8 iamb. tetr.), 1000–7.

Ode, 1008–17.

Iambic scene (19 ll.), 1018–36. ⎫
Antode, 1037–46.   ⎬
Iambic scene (22 ll.), 1047–68. ⎭

Iambic Scene and Stasimon.

Iambic scene, 1069–1142.

Stasimon, 1143–73 (anap. dim. 1143–9, str. and ant. 1150–73).

Exodos, 1174–1233.

Messenger, 1174–89.

Finale, 1190–1233.

Notes.—(1) The passage from l. 347 to l. 489 might be differently
arranged as follows: [1]

> *Proagon,* 347–92.
>> Iambic scene (4 ll.), 347–57.
>> Ode, 358–65.
>> Iambic scene (19 ll.), 366–84.
>> Antode, 385–92.
>
> *Iambic Transition Scene,* 393–489.

(2) The ode and antode in the quasi-agon do not correspond
exactly, the two middle lines being iambic trimeters in the former
and dochmiacs in the latter.

[1] As by White, *The Verse of Greek Comedy,* p. 423.

Knights.

Prologue, 1–241.

Parodos, 242–302.

κατακελευσμός (5 troch. tetr.), 242–6.

Semi-chorus (8 troch. tetr.),
Cleon   (3 „   „), } 247–68.
Semi-chorus (8 „   „),
Cleon   (3 „   „),

Dialogue (15 troch. tetr.), 269–83. } ? Proagon.
        (19 troch. dim.) 284–302.

Agon I, 303–460.

Ode { str. α′, 303–13.
     { 8 mesodic troch. tetr., 314–21.
     { str. β′, 322–32.

κατακελευσμός (2 iamb. tetr.), 333–4.
Epirrhema (32 iamb. tetr.), 335–66.
πνῖγος (15 iamb. dim.), 367–81.

Antode { antistr. α′, 382–90.
       { 6 mesodic troch. tetr., 391–6.
       { antistr. β′, 397–406.

ἀντικατακελ. (2 iamb. tetr.), 407–8.
Antepirrhema (32 iamb. tetr.), 409–40.
ἀντιπνῖγος (16 ll.), 441–56.
σφραγίς (4 iamb. tetr.), 457–60.

Iambic Transition Scene, 461–97.

Parabasis I, 498–610.

κομμάτιον, 498–506.
Anapaests, tetrameters, 507–46.
πνῖγος, 547–50

Ode, 551–64.
Epirrhema (16 troch. tetr.), 565–80.
Antode, 581–94.
Antepirrhema (16 troch. tetr.), 595–610.

Iambic Syzygy, 611–755.

Introduction (5 iamb. trim.), 611–15.
Ode, 616–24.
Iambic scene (59 ll.), 624–82.
Antode, 683–90.
Iambic scene (65 ll.), 691–755.

Agon II, 756–941.

    Introduction (5 iamb. tetr.), 756–60.

    κατακελευσμός (2 anap. tetr.), 761–2.

    Epirrhema (61 anap. tetr.), 763–823.

          (12 anap. dim.), 824–35.

    Introduction and ἀντικατακελ. (7 iamb. tetr.), 836–42.

    Antepirrhema (68 iamb. tetr.), 843–910.

          (30 iamb. dim.), 911–40.

    σφραγίς, 941.

Iambic Scenes and Lyric Interludes.

    Iambic scene, 942–72.

    Stasimon, 973–96.

    Iambic scene, 997–1110.

    Lyric dialogue, 1111–50.

    Iambic scene, 1151–1263.

Parabasis II, 1264–1315.

    Ode, 1264–73.

    Epirrhema (16 troch. tetr.), 1274–89.

    Antode, 1290–9.

    Antepirrhema (16 troch. tetr.), 1300–15.

Exodos.

    Solemn anapaests (messenger and chorus), 1316–34.

    Iambic scene, 1335–1408.

    Finale (lost).

    Note.— In the first agon, the strict correspondence is only broken by the insertion of an iambic trimeter line (441) in the ἀντιπνῖγος, and by the fact that there are only six mesodic lines in the antode.

Clouds.

Prologue, 1–262.

Parodos, 263–363.

    Epirrhema, invocation (12 anap. tetr.), 263–74.

    Ode, 275–90.

    Antepirrhema dialogue (7 anap. tetr.), 291–7.

    Antode, 298–313.

    Scene in anap. tetrameters, 314–63.

Quasi-Half-Agon, 364–475.

    Dialogue in anap. tetr., 364–438.

    πνῖγος, 439–56.

    Ode (lyric dialogue), 457–75.

Transition Scene, 476–509.
  κατακελευσμός (2 anap. tetr.), 476–7.
  Iambic scene, 478–509.

Parabasis I, 510–626.
  κομμάτιον, 510–17.
  ' Anapaests ' (Eupolideans, without πνῖγος), 518-62.
  Ode, 563–74.
  Epirrhema (20 troch. tetr.), 575–94.   ⎫
  Antode, 595–606.   ⎬
  Antepirrhema (20 troch. tetr.), 607–26. ⎭

Iambic Syzygy, 627–813.
  Iambic scene (73 ll.), 627–99.   ⎫   ⎫
  Ode, 700–6.   ⎬   ⎪
  Dialogue in dimeters (mainly), 707–22. ⎬
  Iambic scene (81 ll.), 723–803. ⎫   ⎪
  Antode, 804–13.   ⎬   ⎭

Iambic Transition Scene, 814–88.

Proagon, 889–948.

Agon I, 949–1104.
  Ode, 949–58.
  κατακελευσμός, 959–60.
  Epirrhema (47 anap. tetr.), 961–1008.   ⎫
            (16 anap. dim.), 1009–23.   ⎪
  Antode, 1024–31.   ⎬
  ἀντικατακελ., 1032–5.   ⎪
  Antepirrhema (49 iamb. tetr.), 1036–84.   ⎪
            (4 iamb. trim. and 19 iamb. dim.), 1085–1104. ⎭

Iambic Transition Scene, 1105–13.

Parabasis II, 1114-30.
  κομμάτιον, 1114.
  Epirrhema (16 troch. tetr.), 1115–30.

Iambic Scenes and Lyric Interludes.
  Iambic scene, 1131–53.
  Lyrics (Strepsiades and Socrates), 1154–69.
  Iambic scene, 1170–1200.
  Lyrics (Strepsiades), 1201–13.
  Iambic scene, 1214–1302.
  Stasimon, 1303–20.

Iambic Transition Scene (or Proagon), 1321–1344.

Agon II, 1345–1451.
    Ode, 1345–50.
    κατακελευσμός, 1351–2.
    Epirrhema (33 iamb. tetr.), 1353–85.
              (5 iamb. dim.), 1386–90.
    Antode, 1391–6.
    ἀντικατακελ., 1397–8.
    Antepirrhema (46 iamb. tetr.), 1399–1444.
              (7 iamb. dim.), 1445–51.

Final Scene, 1452–1510.
    Iambic scene, 1452–1509.
    Choral exodos, 1510.

Notes.—(1) Lines 314–438 might be grouped together in the half-agon. In the present state of the play any analysis can only be tentative.

(2) The antode, 804–13, has two extra lines as compared with the ode, but otherwise corresponds ; and the dimeter dialogue after the ode is unusual. Possibly these things are due to imperfect revision.

(3) The mutual abuse (in dimeters) of the two Λόγοι, leading up to the formal agon, may be conveniently treated as a kind of proagon.

(4) The correspondence between the non-tetrametric parts of the epirrhema and antepirrhema of the agon is defective.

(5) Perhaps the whole passage from 1131–1302 should be treated as one iambic scene, with lyrics inserted ; the scenes 1212–1302, however, seems to consist of two short scenes of the primitive epeisodic type.

Wasps.

Prologue, 1–229.

Parodos, 230–316.
    A. Entry of chorus (18 iamb. tetr.), 230–47.
    B. Dialogue of boy and chorus (25 iamb. troch. ll.), 248–72.
    C. Choral ode (str. and antistr.), 273–89.
         (extra line), 290.
    D. Lyric dialogue (str. and antistr.), 291–316.

Proagon, 317–525.
    A. Lyric monody of Philocleon, 316–32.

   B. Ode (with mesodic troch. tetr.), 333–45.

       κατακελευσμός (2 anap. tetr.), 346–7.

       Epirrhema (10 anap. tetr.), 348–57.

                (7 anap. dim.), 358–64.

       Antode (with mesodic troch. tetr.), 365–78.

       ἀντικατακελ. (2 anap. tetr.), 379–80.

       Antepirrhema, (22 anap. tetr.), 381–402.

   C. (1) 2 troch. tetr. (chorus), 403–4.

       Ode, 405–14.

       3 troch. tetr., 415–17.

       2 ll. lyrics, 418–19.

       8 troch. tetr., 420–7.

       2 ll. lyrics, 428–9.

       Epirrhema (31 ll. troch. tetr.), 430–60.

     (2) 2 troch. tetr. (Bdelycl.), 461–2.

       Antode, 463–71.

       3 troch. tetr., 472–4.

       2 ll. lyrics, 475–6.

       8 troch. tetr., 477–85.

       2 ll. lyrics, 486–7.

       Antepirrhema (38 ll. troch. tetr.), 488–525.

Agon I, 526–727.

    Ode (with mesodic iamb. tetr.), 526–45.

    κατακελευσμός (2 anap. tetr.), 546–7.

    Epirrhema (72 anap. tetr.), 548–620.

             (13 anap. dim.), 621–30.

    Antode (with mesodic iamb. tetr.), 631–47.

    ἀντικατακελ. (2 anap. tetr.), 648–9.

    Antepirrhema (69 anap. tetr.), 650–718.

             (6 anap. dim.), 719–24.

    σφραγίς (3 anap. tetr.), 725–7.

Lyric and Iambic Scenes.

    Lyric transition scene, 729–59.   Strophe, 729–36.

                                    Anap. dim., 737–42.

                                    Antistrophe, 743–9.

                                    Anap. dim., 750–9.

    Iambic scene, 760–862.

    Lyric interlude, 863–90.

    Iambic scene, 891–1008.

Parabasis I, 1009–1121.

    κομμάτιον, 1009–14.

    Anapaests, tetrameters, 1015–50.

        πνῖγος, 1051–9.

    Ode, 1060–70.

    Epirrhema (20 troch. tetr.), 1071–90.

    Antode, 1091–1101.

    Antepirrhema (20 troch. tetr.), 1102–21.

Iambic Scene, 1122–1264.

Parabasis II, 1265–91.

Iambic Scenes, 1292–1449.

Stasimon, 1450–73.

Exodos, 1474–1537.

    Xanthias (as messenger), 1474–81.

    Dialogue, anap. dim., 1482–95.

        iambic scene, 1496–1515.

    Choral finale, 1516–37.

Notes.—(1) Lines 403-4 might be called a κατακελευσμός, but the corresponding ll. 461-2 are not such.

(2) The latter part of the antode, 463-71, does not correspond with that of the ode, 405-14, though the earlier part does.

(3) There are ten anap. dimeters in ll. 750-9, answering to seven in ll. 737-42; and before l. 750 there is a passage outside the structure, viz. ΦΙ. ἰώ μοί μοι. ΒΔ. οὗτος, τί μοι βοᾷς ;

(4) The second parabasis is quite irregular in form ; White (p. 435) regards it as a stasimon.

(5) The iambic scene, 1292-1449, falls into several parts or even separate scenes, viz. 1292-1325 (Xanthias as messenger), 1326-63 (Philocleon drunk), 1364-86 (Philocleon and Bdelycleon), 1387-1414 (the 'Αρτοπωλίς), 1415-41 (the Κατήγορος)—these two scenes being of the primitive epeisodic type—, 1442-9 Philocleon and Bdelycleon.

(6) The choral finale, 1516-37, consists of two anap. tetrameters, a short strophe and antistrophe, and seven hyporchematic prosodiacs.

Peace.

Prologue, 1–300.

Parodos, 301–45.   (In troch. tetr. with πνῖγος, 339–45.)

Series of Irregular Scenes, 346–600.

    I. Ode, 346–60.

        Iambic scene (24 ll.), 361–84. ⎫

        Antode, 385–99.   ⎬ Iambic syzygy.

        Iambic scene (26 ll.), 400–25. ⎪

        σφραγίς, troch. tetr., 426–30. ⎭

    II. Introduction, iambic scene, 431–58.

        Lyric dialogue (str.), 459–72 (the

           first attempt).

        Iambic scene (13 ll.), 473–85.

        Lyric dialogue (antistr.), 486–99   ⎬ Iambic syzygy.

           (the second attempt).

        Iambic scene (8 ll.), 500–7.

        σφραγίς, iamb. tetr., 508–11. ⎫

           iamb. dim., 512–19. ⎬ The final attempt.

    III. Iambic scene, 520–52.

        Scene in troch. tetr. and dim., 553–81. ⎱

    IV. Epode, 582–600 (corresp. to ode and antode in I).

Quasi-Half-Agon, 601–56.

    κατακελευσμός, 601–2.

    Epirrhema, troch. tetr., 603–50.

               troch. dim., 651–6.

Iambic Transition Scene, 657–728.

Parabasis I, 729–818.

    κομμάτιον, 729–33.

    Anapaests, tetram., 734–64.

        πνῖγος, 765–74.

    Ode, 775–96.

    Antode, 797–818.

Iambic Syzygy, 819–921.

    Iambic scene (37 ll.), 819–55.

    Ode, 856–67.   ⎫

    Iambic scene (42 ll.), 868–909. ⎬

    Antode, 910–21.   ⎭

Iambic Syzygy, 922–1038.

    Iambic scene (17 ll.), 922–38.

    Ode (with proodic and mesodic iamb. tetr.), 939–55.

    Iambic scene (17 ll.), 956–73.

    Anap. dim. dialogue, 974–1015.

    Iambic scene (7 ll.), 1016–22.

    Antode (with proodic and mesodic iamb. tetr.), 1024–38·

Iambic Scene (with hexameter passage), 1039–1126.

Parabasis II, 1127–90.

    Ode, 1127–39.

    Epirrhema, 16 troch. tetr., 1140–55.

               3 troch. dim., 1156–8.

    Antode, 1159–71.

    Antepirrhema, 16 troch. tetr., 1172–87.

               3 troch. dim., 1188–90.

Epeisodic Scenes, 1191–1304.

Exodos, 1305–56.

    Invitation to wedding (iamb. tetr. and dim.), 1305–15.

    Choral invocation (anap. tetr. and dim.), 1306–28.

    Wedding procession and song, 1329–56.

Note.—(1) The ode, ll. 582–600, treated above as an epode corresponding (as it does metrically) with the ode and antode, ll. 346–60
and 385–99, might (apart from this correspondence) be regarded as
the ode of the half-agon; but the whole of the scenes between the
parodos and the parabasis are difficult to schematize. (White,
pp. 436–7, treats them somewhat differently.)

    (2) White regards 1305–15 as a stasimon (1305–10=1311–15),
perhaps rightly.

Birds.

Prologue, 1–208.

Parodos, 209–351.

    A. Invocation, 209–66.   Lyric invocation, 209–22.

                            4 iamb. trim. 223–6.

                            Lyric invocation, 227–62.

                            4 iamb. trim. 263–6.

    B. Parodos proper, 267–351.

                        Irregular line, 267.

                        Dial. troch. tetr. (59 ll.), 268–326.

                        Ode, 327–35.

                        Dial. troch. tetr. (7 ll.), 336–42.

                        Antode, 343–51.

Battle Scene, 352–432.

> Dialogue, troch. tetr., 352–86.
> troch. dim., 387–99.
> Anap. dim. (chorus), 400–5.
> Lyric dialogue, 406–34.

Iambic Transition Scene, 435–50.

Agon, 451–637.

> Ode, 451–9.
> κατακελευσμός (2 anap. tetr.), 460–1.
> Epirrhema, 61 anap. tetr., 462–522.
> 16 anap. dim., 523–38.
> Antode, 538–47.
> ἀντικατακελ. (2 anap. tetr.), 548–9.
> Antepirrhema, 61 anap. tetr., 550–610.
> 16 anap. dim., 611–26.
> σφραγίς (anap. tetr. and dim.), 627–38.

Iambic Transition Scene, 639–75.

Parabasis I, 676–800.

> κομμάτιον, 676–84.
> Anapaests, tetram., 685–722.
> πνῖγος, 723–36.
> Ode, 727–52.
> Epirrhema (16 troch. tetr.), 753–68.
> Antode, 769–84.
> Antepirrhema (16 troch. tetr.), 785–800.

Iambic Syzygy, 801–902.

> Iambic scene (50 ll.), 801–50.
> Ode, 851–8.
> Iambic scene (35 ll.), 859–94.
> Antode, 895–902.

Series of Epeisodic Scenes, 903–1057.

Parabasis II, 1058–1117.

> Ode, 1058–70.
> Epirrhema (16 troch. tetr.), 1071–87.
> Antode, 1088–1100.
> Antepirrhema (16 troch. tetr.), 1101–17.

Iambic Syzygy, 1118–1266.
    Iambic scene (71 ll.), 1118–88.
    Ode, 1189–96.
    Iambic scene (65 ll.), 1197–1261.
    Antode, 1262–6.

Iambic Scenes and Lyric Interludes, 1269–1493.
    Iambic scene, 1269–1312.
    Lyric dialogue, Strophe, 1313–22.
                2 lines, Peithet., 1323–4.
                Antistrophe, 1325–34.
    Iambic scene, 1335–1469.
    Stasimon, 1470–93.

Iambic Syzygy, 1494–1705.
    Iambic scene (59 ll.), 1494–1552.
    Ode, 1553–64.
    Iambic scene (129 ll.), 1565–1693.
    Antode, 1694–1705.

Exodos, 1706–65.
    Messengers' speech, 1706–19.
    Wedding procession, 1720–65.

    Note.—The iambic scene, 1335–1469, consists of three typical epeisodic scenes.

Lysistrata.

Prologue, 1–253.

Parodos, 254–386.
    A. (Men's Chorus.)
    κατακελευσμός (2 iamb. tetr.), 254–5.
    Ode, 256–65.
    Epirrhema (5 iamb. tetr.), 266–70.
    Antode, 271–80.
    Antepirrhema (5 iamb. tetr.), 281–5.
    Ode, 286–95.
    Antode, 296–305.
    Quasi-κατακελ. (1 iamb. tetr.), 306.
    Epirrhema (6 iamb. tetr.), 307–12.
    Antepirrhema (6 iamb. tetr.), 313–18.
    B. (Women's Chorus.)
    κατακελευσμός (2 iamb. tetr.), 319–20.
    Ode, 321–34.
    Antode, 335–49.

Proagon, 350–86 (iamb. tetr. and dim.).

Iambic Scene, 387–466.

Agon, 467–613.

    A. Introd. (9 iamb. tetr.), 467–75.

        Ode, 476-83.

        κατακελευσμός (2 anap. tetr.), 484–5. ⎫

        Epirrhema (47 anap. tetr.), 486–531. ⎬

            (7 anap. dim.), 532–8. ⎭

    B. Introd. (2 iamb. tetr.), 539–40.

        Antode, 541-8.

        ἀντικατακελ., 549–50. ⎫

        Antepirrhema (47 anap. tetr.), 551–97. ⎬

            (10 anap. dim.), 598–607. ⎭

Iambic Transition Scene, 608–13.

Parabasis, 614–705.

    A. (Men.) κομμάτιον (2 troch. tetr.), 614–15. ⎫

        Ode, 616–25. ⎬ ⎫

        Epirrhema (10 troch. tetr.), 626–35. ⎭ ⎪

    (Women.) κομμάτιον (2 troch. tetr.), 636–7. ⎫ ⎬

        Antode, 638–47. ⎬ ⎪

        Antepirrhema (10 troch. tetr.), 648–58. ⎭

    B. (Men.) Ode, 659–70. ⎫ ⎫

        Epirrhema (10 troch. tetr.), 671–81. ⎬ ⎪

    (Women.) Antode, 682–95. ⎫ ⎬

        Antepirrhema (60 troch. tetr.), 696–705. ⎭ ⎭

Iambic Scenes and Lyric Interludes, 706–1013.

    Iambic scene, 706–80.

    Lyric dialogue (str. and antistr.), 781–829.

    Iambic scene, 830–953.

    Dial. in anap. dim., 954–79.

    Iambic scene, 980–1013.

Agon II (?).

    Dial. of semi-choruses (paeonic and troch. tetr.), 1014–42.

Iambic Syzygy, 1043–1215.

    Ode, 1043–71.

    2 anap. tetr. (chorus), 1072–3. ⎫

    Iambic scene (34 ll.), 1074–1107. ⎪ ⎫

    4 anap. tetr. (chorus), 1108–11. ⎬ ⎬

    Iambic scene (77 ll.), 1112–88. ⎪

    Antode, 1189–1215. ⎭

Iambic Scene, 1216-46.

Exodos, 1247-1319.

    Laced. chorus, 1247-70.

    Iambic trim. (Lysistrata), 1271-8.

    Athen. chorus, 1279-96.

    Laced. chorus, 1297-1320.

Notes.—(1) 608-13 might be treated as the σφραγίς of the agon.

    (2) 830-1013 might be treated as a single scene, with lyric interruption (as by White).

Prologue, 1-294.   *Thesmophoriazusae.*

Parodos, 295-380.

    Proclamation (prose), 295-311.

    Ode, 312-30.

    Proclamation (iamb. trim., 21 ll.), 331-51.

    Ode, 352-71 (not corresp. to ll. 312-30).

    Proclamation, &c. (iamb. trim., 9 ll.), 372-80.

Quasi-Agon, 381-530.

    κατακελευσμός (2 iamb. tetr.), 381-2.

    Iambic speech, 383-432.

    Ode, 433-42.

    Iambic speech, 443-58.

    Lyric interlude, 459-65.

    Iambic speech, 466-519.

    Antode, 520-30.

Iambic Tetrameter Scene, 531-73.

Iambic Trimeter Scene, 574-654.

Irregular Scene, 655-784.

    Chorus, 4 anap. tetr., 655-8.

        4 troch. tetr. and dim., 659-62.

        lyrics, 663-86.

        2 troch. tetr., 687-8.

    Iambic scene (10 ll.), 689-98.

    Lyrics, 699-701.

    Dial. troch. tetr. (5 ll.), 702-6.

    Lyric dialogue, &c., lyrics, 707-25.

        2 troch. tetr., 726-7.

    Iambic scene (37 ll.), 728-64.

    Mnesilochus' soliloquy, iamb. trim., 765-75.

        lyric, 776-84.

Parabasis (imperfect), 785-845.

κομμάτιον, 785.

Anapaests, tetram., 785-813.

πνῖγος, 814-29.

Epirrhema (16 troch. tetr.), 830-45.

Iambic Scenes and Stasima, 846-1159.

Iambic scene, 846-946.

Stasimon, 947-1000.

Iambic scene, 1001-1135.

Stasimon, 1136-59.

Exodos, 1160-1231.

Iambic scene, 1160-1226.

Choral finale, 1227-31.

Note.—655-764 might be treated as an irregular iambic syzygy and 765-84 as an iambic transition scene.

Frogs.

Prologue, 1-323 (or 315).

Parodos, 324 (or 316)-459.

Iambic Scenes, &c., 460-74.

Iambic scene, 460-533.

Dial. in troch. dim. (22 ll.), 534-48.

Iambic scene, 549-89.

Dial. in troch. dim. (22 ll.), 590-604.

Iambic scene, 605-73.

Parabasis, 674-737.

Ode, 674-85.

Epirrhema (20 troch. tetr.), 686-705). ⎫

Antode, 706-16. ⎬

Antepirrhema (20 troch. tetr.), 717-37. ⎭

Iambic Scenes and Stasima, 738-894.

Iambic scene, 738-813.

Stasimon, 814-29.

Iambic scene, 830-74.

Stasimon, 875-84.

Iambic scene, 885-94.

Agon, 895–1098.

    Ode, 895–904.

    κατακελευσμός (2 iamb. tetr.), 905–6.

    Epirrhema (64 iamb. tetr.), 907–70.

           (21 iamb. dim.), 971–91.

    Antode, 992–1003.

    ἀντικατακελ. (2 anap. tetr.), 1004–5.

    Antepirrhema (71 anap. tetr.), 1006–77.

           (21 anap. dim.), 1078–98.

Iambic Scenes and Stasima, 1099–1499.

    Stasimon, 1099–1118.

    Iambic scene, 1119–1250.

    Stasimon, 1251–60.

    Iambic scene, 1261–1369.

    Stasimon, 1370–7.

    Iambic scene, 1378–1481.

    Stasimon, 1482–99.

Exodos, 1500–33.

    Dial. in anap. dim. 1500–27.

    Choral finale (dactyl. hex.), 1528–33.

Notes.—(1) Evidently two of the three scenes, 460–673, might be grouped, with the two trochaic dimeter passages, as a syzygy; but the entrance of a new character in l. 503 is against such a treatment of the scene 460–533.

(2) The whole passage 830-94 might be regarded as a kind of proagon, though not in tetrameters; or the scene 885–94 might be taken as a transition-scene serving as introduction to the agon.

Ecclesiazusae.

Prologue, 1–284.

Parodos, 285–310.

Iambic Scenes, 311–477.

Second Parodos, 478–519.

    Iambic tetr. and dim. (chorus), 478–503.

    Iambic trim. (speech of Praxagora), 504–13.

    Dial. anap. tetr., 514–19.

Iambic Scene, 520–70.

Half-Agon, 571–709.
>   Ode, 571–81.
>   κατακελευσμός (2 anap. tetr.), 582–3.
>   Epirrhema, anap. tetram., 584–688.
>>   anap. dim., 689–709.

Iambic Scene, 710–29.

XOPOY.

Iambic Scenes, 730–1153 (with occasional non-choral lyrics).

Exodos, 1154–82.
>   Address to audience, 1154–62.
>   Choral finale, 1163–1182.

Plutus.

Prologue, 1–252.

Parodos, 253–321.
>   Dial. iamb. tetr., 253–289.
>   Lyrics, str. a′, antistr. a′. ⎫
>>   str. β′, antistr. β. ⎬ 290–321.
>>   epode.   ⎭

Iambic Scene, 322–414.

Iambic Scene (Proagon), 415–86.

Half-Agon, 487–618.
>   κατακελευσμός (2 anap. tetr.), 487–8.
>   Epirrhema, anap. tetr., 489–597.
>>   anap. dim., 598–618.

Iambic Scenes, 619–1207 (mainly of the epeisodic type).

Exodos, 1208–9.

APPENDIX B

MR. CORNFORD'S THEORY OF THE ORIGIN
OF COMEDY

§ 1. In a work on the Origin of Attic Comedy (1914), containing much that is interesting and illuminating, Mr. F. M. Cornford propounds an explanation of the main features of the Old Comedy by means of a supposed ritual sequence, which is closely parallel to that by which Professor Murray explains Attic Tragedy; indeed his conclusion is that comedy and tragedy arose from the same ritual—that of the agon, pathos or death, and resurrection of an 'Eniautos-Daimon'.

There was, however, more in the original ritual, according to Mr. Cornford, than the agon, death, and resurrection; how much more, is never quite clearly stated, since the summary which he gives (p. 103) does not include elements which (as we gather from other passages) must have formed part of the ritual. Before this ritual, as described on p. 103, begins, there must apparently have been enacted the birth of a miraculous infant, who developed with amazing rapidity; this infant was the son of the Earth-Mother. But all that remains of this part of the ritual is contained in the personality of a drunken old hag who appears in a number of plays, and it is not quite clear how this was related to the phallic procession and its incidents, to which most of the supposed ritual is said to have belonged. At a certain point in the phallic procession there was a sacrifice;[1] and in its primitive dramatic form this sacrifice took the shape of a conflict or agon between the representatives of two principles, ending in the simulated death of one of the combatants. Still earlier, it must have been his real death by

---

[1] In the *Acharnians*, the sacrifice is represented by an offering of soup and cake; presumably, however, Mr. Cornford imagines something more sanguinary.

σπαραγμός—the Good Spirit was slain, dismembered, cooked and eaten. But the personage thus slain was brought back to life—sometimes by a process of boiling, such as was practised by Medea upon Pelias. Then there followed the ἱερὸς γάμος, when he was restored to life and youth to be the husband of the Mother-Goddess, and the wedding was accompanied by a choral song of victory, while the adversary was expelled in the manner peculiar to the driving out of the Pharmakos at the Thargelia. This ritual, it is claimed, explains the phallic character of some of the actors, the invocations and abusive language (which belonged both to the parabasis and the phallic κῶμος), the agon, the exodos (which often ends in a marriage, a feast, and a song of triumph), and certain scenes which Mr. Cornford considers to be relics of the simulated death and resurrection of the Good Spirit. The series of scenes in which the preparations for the feast are rudely interrupted by one impostor or adversary after another are due to a multiplication of the agon between the Good and the Bad Spirit.

Thus the whole, or almost the whole, of Attic comedy grew out of one germ,—the enactment of the conflict, death, resurrection, and marriage of a Good Spirit. (The variations in the theory we shall notice at convenient points in the discussion.)

The question, whether there is any reason to suppose that this complex ritual ever really existed, is one which Mr. Cornford practically does not touch. It need only be said that it would require very strong evidence indeed to prove that one and the same rite included the birth of a wonder-child, his agon, death, and resurrection, a sacred marriage in which he took part, and the expulsion of a Pharmakos. The somewhat loose parallel with the modern folk-play at Viza (itself very variously explained) is not nearly good enough evidence; we certainly do not find these elements combined in any ancient Greek ritual about which we have information. But does the supposed ritual actually explain the plays?

§ 2. We will begin, as Mr. Cornford does, with the 'marriage', which (on the strength of the scenes in some plays in which the protagonist appears with a silent female figure) he concludes to have been the climax of the original ritual. We must ask

(1) Is a marriage so constant a feature of the closing scenes of the Old Comedy that it can best be explained as the survival of a ritual ἱερὸς γάμος, which was essential to the performance? (2) Who is the bridegroom? (3) Who is the bride? The questions cannot be kept entirely separate.

One point appears at once—that in several of the plays we have not *one* mute female figure in the place of the bride, but *two*, and that the protagonist is quite happy with both. In the *Acharnians*, Dicaeopolis has a courtesan on each arm; in the *Knights*, two are similarly offered to Demos as representing the Σπονδαί; in the *Peace* there are both Opora and Theoria, and though Trygaeus only proposes to marry the former, the other is there and has to be disposed of. (She is given to the president of the Council).[1] Surely these characters resemble, not the single female partner in a ἱερὸς γάμος (which was always, so far as our evidence goes, a solemn ceremony), but the much less reputable characters, who, as αὐλητρίδες, ὀρχηστρίδες, or what not, were adjuncts of the more licentious kinds of συμπόσια in Athens. A feast, as Mr. Cornford rightly points out, was the most frequent ending of a Greek Comedy, though it was not the invariable ending; and it may well have been the ending of the original κῶμος, if this was at all like modern occasions of the sort; and it is far more likely that these females came in as adjuncts of a feast in the Greek manner, than that they are survivals of a ritual marriage. The process of doubling is one which Mr. Cornford is fond of introducing; but it may be doubted whether these pairs of females in the early plays of Aristophanes got there by the doubling of the bride in a ἱερὸς γάμος.

Moreover, before we leave this topic, it should be observed that, though there is gross obscenity, Dicaeopolis does not suggest marriage with either of the ὀρχηστρίδες, who are part of the attractions of the feast to which the priest of Dionysus invites him: and that the utmost that Philocleon in the *Wasps* (1353) promises the αὐλητρίς is that if she is good, she shall be his concubine when his son his dead. It is really impossible to agree to the suggestion, which appears to be implied in Mr. Cornford's

---

[1] Probably the *Lysistrata* should be added to the list; see below.

remark (p. 11) that Philocleon 'enters singing the opening
words of Cassandra's mad Hymenaeal in the Troades',[1] that
this confirms his explanation of the scene as the relic of
a ἱερὸς γάμος. It is true that Philocleon begins a short lyric
with ἄνεχε πάρεχε, and that the Ravenna Scholiast says, ἐκ
Τρῳάδων Εὐριπίδου, οὗ Κασάνδρα φησίν· ἄνεχε, πάρεχε, φῶς
φέρε κτλ. But the passage in the *Wasps* has only two words
identical with Cassandra's, viz. ἄνεχε, πάρεχε; and it is very
doubtful whether these words were part of a specifically
hymenaeal cry at all, and are not merely a bacchic cry.[1]
Aristophanes parodies Euripides continually in the most
dissimilar contexts, and it cannot be inferred that, because the
words as used by Cassandra are part of a 'mad hymenaeal',
referring to a γάμος which was anything but a ἱερὸς γάμος,
the obscene passage in which Philocleon uses them was the
relic of a ritual marriage.

As to the other plays; there is no trace of any kind of
γάμος or indecency in the conclusion of the *Clouds*[2] or the *Frogs*,
and there is actually no feast in either, though in the *Frogs*,
Pluto invites Dionysus and Aeschylus to a meal before their
journey. In the *Lysistrata*, the heroine does indeed offer the
mute courtesan Διαλλαγή to the various ambassadors (1114 ff.);
and as the title of the play was once Λυσιστράτα ἢ Διαλλαγαί
it is just possible that more than one was offered, in which case
the play should be grouped with those previously discussed:
but it is surely unwarrantable to say that 'the reunion of men
and women in the final dance is itself a sort of remarriage', if
it is intended by this that the scene is the relic of a ritual
marriage (evidently much multiplied on this occasion).[3] The
reunion is necessitated by the considerations (1) that the *motif*

---

[1] *Troades* 308; cf. Eur. *Cyclops* 203, and Starkie on the *Wasps* 1326.
(The Schol. Ven., ad loc., is in agreement with the Ravenna Schol.)

[2] Or is Pheidippides' threat to beat his mother a faint relic of an
original marriage? If we are to be quite up to date, I suppose we must
call it a repressed Oedipus-complex.

[3] The suggested inferences (p. 14) from the mention of certain gods in
the choral song (1285 ff.) appear to be quite unwarranted; but I do not
want to discuss every point in detail.

of the play at the outset was a divorce, (2) that in comedies quarrels are wont to end well. In the *Thesmophoriazusae* there is no hint of a feast, and it is certainly not evident that the indecent scene in which Elaphion figures as a mute personage, to distract the Policeman's attention, is ' clearly an adaptation of the marriage motive '. In the *Ecclesiazusae* the mute courtesan is, according to Mr. Cornford, represented by the Θεράπαινα who is sent to Blepyrus by his wife, to summon him to the feast. The only reasons which he gives for this are ' that she is intoxicated alike with Thasian wine and with the unguents of the courtesan on her hair ', and that she swears νὴ τὴν Ἀφροδίτην. But the context does not show her to be intoxicated, though she recommends the wine which is in store for the feasters ; and it was not only courtesans who used unguents ; they were in common use at banquets. The oath by Aphrodite is certainly not conclusive in the context. The Θεράπαινα is surely the equivalent, not of the mute courtesan (whether one or two), but of the messenger who frequently recurs in the concluding scenes of Aristophanes' plays, and who describes the preparations for the feast, and invites people to join in it. The courtesans are in fact mentioned in l. 1138, and were almost certainly on the stage with her: and the fact that they are plural confirms the belief that they were simply adjuncts of a riotous feast.

The scene in the *Plutus* between the old woman and the young man who rejects her advances can hardly be made to prove anything as to a ritual marriage of the Old Year or Good Spirit with a (presumably) young woman: but the Old Woman is a subject for future consideration. The idea that Plutus, the new Zeus-Soter, is to be installed in the Opisthodomos of the Parthenon as the husband of Athena must rank with the wildest of conjectures; indeed its real basis seems to be itself a conjecture of Dr. Cook.[1]

---

[1] Dr. Cook's conjecture (unpublished) was that the double structure of the Erectheum and Parthenon was to be explained by the reservation of the western half of the building for the king or consort of the goddess, and that Peisistratus in driving into Athens with Athena, wished people to regard him as her consort. So Plutus here. It is true that Zeus-Soter

Our conclusion, therefore, is that in several plays there is no marriage at all; that in several there is simply gross indecency in the presence of one, or more often two, courtesans; and that these courtesans are there as common accompaniments of the feast, not as representing the female partner in a ritual marriage. If it be urged that a ritual marriage may not have had, in very primitive agrarian rites, the solemnity of the later ἱερὸς γάμος, we can only answer (1) that such ceremonies *are* solemn rites when we come across them in ancient Greece (and generally in the religion of primitive peoples), and that we have no hint of anything else; nor should we expect it to be otherwise, if such rites were a serious piece of agrarian magic; (2) that the modern folk-play at Viza, which is no longer the performance of a primitive people, and which contains elements drawn from Christian sources, and the seriousness of which as magic may be doubted, is no parallel; (3) that we still have to account for the fact that we have two females as often as one. The one play in which there really is a quasi-daemonic marriage is the *Birds*: but there the explanation is that, since the whole plot turns on the super-session of the gods by new rulers (a theme the reason for which will be suggested later), the provision of a queen for the supplanter of Zeus is practically inevitable, or, at least, is so natural as to require no ritual explanation.

What of the bridegroom? On p. 20 Mr. Cornford states that there can be little doubt that 'the protagonist in comedy must originally have been the spirit of fertility himself, Phales or Dionysus', and that it must have been he who originally led the final κῶμος as male partner in a marriage. The evi-dence for this does not appear; the fact that some Athenian actors wore the phallus (p. 183) certainly does not prove it. There is no trace of Phales as a character in any kind of

and Athena Soteira were worshipped together in certain cults both at Athens and in Delos: but this does not prove any nuptial relations between them. The idea that Athena was ever regarded as wedded is answered by Farnell, *Cults*, i, p. 303. The other arguments by which (pp. 26, 27) Mr. Cornford tries to force a 'sacred marriage' into the end of the *Plutus* seems to be equally untenable.

procession or drama in ancient Greece, though he is invoked in song, or represented by the phallus carried aloft; and Dionysus did not wear the phallus in art or drama. But, however this may be, how did Phales or Dionysus come to be replaced by the Old Rustic who acts the part of protagonist in almost every play? For Mr. Cornford himself emphasizes the fact that the final marriage is that of an *old* man; and this Old Rustic (whose real history is in fact fairly clear) is a very constant type in comedy from beginning to end. But in fact Mr. Cornford's account of the protagonist-bridegroom is somewhat fluctuating. Sometimes he is Phales or Dionysus; sometimes he is the Old Year, who becomes the New Year after rejuvenation; or the Old (subsequently the New) God or Zeus or King; sometimes he is equated with Summer, or with Life, or with the Good Principle; and the Antagonist varies similarly. (We shall find that these variations give trouble when we come to the agon.) In the *Thesmophoriazusae*, if Elaphion is the bride, the bridegroom must be the Scythian Policeman. It is important to note that the evidence for connecting a ἱερὸς γάμος with a phallic procession in any actual ancient Greek ritual is non-existent.

The 'bride' is naturally represented by a young female—the mute figure. How then does Mr. Cornford work in the Old Woman? 'In the Old Woman we must recognize the Earth-Mother'; she survives also in the Babo of the play at Viza, nursing the miraculous infant, who grows at an astonishing pace; and 'in the sordid pantomime of this first part of the play' we have 'a last survival of the supernatural birth and growth of Dionysus'.[1] If then, in the original

---

[1] This is perhaps right as regards the Viza play, and the comparison with the wonder-child in the *Ichneutae* is apposite. But the evidence (pp. 85, 86) that the Lenaea included an acted Anodos of Semele, bearing Iacchos, followed by the σπαραγμός of the now mature god and his resurrection is extremely weak (see above, pp. 209–10, and Farnell, *Cults*, v, pp. 171, 176, 209). There is in fact no evidence that the mother of Iacchos figured at all in the Lenaea, and the σπαραγμός was only mentioned in a hymn. And whatever may happen at Viza, we have no other evidence of a ritual sequence in ancient Greece combining anodos, birth, σπαραγμός, and resurrection.

ritual, the Old Woman was the mother of the bridegroom
(Phales or Dionysus), does she survive in comedy as the mother
of the Old Rustic ? In some plays she is his wife. But if, as
Mr. Cornford thinks likely, the first part of the ritual sequence
(containing the birth of the infant) dropped out, with the
growth of literary comedy, why should the Old Woman have survived at all ? and why as ' a drunken and amorous old hag, who
dances the cordax ' ? The truth seems to be that Mr. Cornford
has left out of sight the strong evidence which exists that
this Old Woman is a stock figure derived, not from any Anodos-
ritual (for in such ritual the mother does not appear to have
been either amorous or effete), but from very early Peloppon-
nesian cult-plays, as has been explained elsewhere.

§ 3. Mr. Cornford represents the bridegroom or the victor
in the agon as a New God, and therefore as the survival of
a divine figure in the original folk-play or ritual ; or at least
as a victorious king—the distinction between King and God
being, in primitive ritual, sometimes a vanishing one. Here
we must examine the evidence in detail. It is found mainly
in the exodoi.

In the *Acharnians* the victory which Dicaeopolis celebrates
appears to be a victory in a drinking-match,[1] not in any agon
which forms part of the main plot of the play. There is
nothing to suggest that he is made a king ; his inquiry for
the king of the feast, from whom he is to claim his prize,
suggests the opposite.

In the *Knights*, when the sausage-seller has defeated Cleon,
the chorus greets him with ὦ χαῖρε καλλίνικε (1254). Afterwards Demos, having been boiled back to youth by the
sausage-seller, is greeted by the chorus (1330) δείξατε τὸν τῆς
Ἑλλάδος ὑμῖν καὶ τῆς γῆς τῆσδε μόναρχον, and (1333) χαῖρ' ὦ
βασιλεῦ τῶν Ἑλλήνων : [2] and (1338) he is given the Σπονδαί—
two courtesans. (Apparently then Demos is the bridegroom,
though Agoracritus was the victor ; this scarcely fits Mr.
Cornford's theory.) Demos then gives Agoracritus a green

[1] See above, p. 310.
[2] These phrases are naturally taken as metaphors, used as Thucydides
uses expressions virtually synonymous about the Athenian supremacy.

robe (βατραχίς), which (according to Mr. Cornford)[1] implies that Agoracritus is a king. (That makes two kings in this play.) The end of the play is lost; but the fact that Demos refers to Cleon by the epithet φαρμακός (a word elsewhere used metaphorically in abusive contexts)[2] leads Mr. Cornford to suggest that Cleon was literally driven out in the manner of a Pharmakos; though it is not easy to see how this is consistent with turning him into a sausage-seller, the fate actually proposed for him; the Pharmakos did not usually get off so easily.

Mr. Cornford's treatment of the *Clouds* is very difficult to follow. If his idea that the victor or bridegroom is also a New God or King is correct, we ought to find in the play the defeat of an antagonist by such a God or King, or else the defeat of the victor by the antagonist, followed by the victor's resurrection. Now the *Clouds* as it stands appears to be an imperfectly revised version, and it is uncertain between whom the agon was originally fought. The fact that it is Strepsiades who answers interrogations (627 ff.) makes it probable that it was originally Strepsiades who was instructed, after a preliminary agon with Socrates, and that the instruction of Pheidippides and his agon with his father, belonged only to the second edition. Whichever was the case, the agon was at least between two characters in the play. But Mr. Cornford apparently regards the play as in effect an agon between Zeus and the usurping Dinos, in which the antagonist first wins, but is afterwards defeated again. This seems to exaggerate out of all proportion the one or two lines which give colour to such a theory. The subject of the play is, of course, in part the contrast of older and newer religious ideas—a subject chosen, not as keeping up an ancient ritual sequence, but as a topic of burning interest at the time; these passages arise naturally

---

[1] Relying on Pollux, iv. 116, but there is no suggestion in Pollux that this was a *royal* robe.

[2] e.g. Aristoph. fr. 634 (K.). [Dem.] *in Aristog.* i, § 80; Lys. *in Andoc.* § 53. cf. Bekk. Anecd. Gr. I. 315. 22. Mr. Cornford's comparison of the *Knights* with St. Paul's words in 1 Cor. iv. 6 appears to be peculiarly far-fetched.

out of the subject, and require no ritual sequence to explain them. On what principle, again, does Mr. Cornford suddenly transfer the idea of kingship from the protagonist in the play (to whom, on his general theory, it ought to be attached), to a god who is merely mentioned among other subjects of discussion? If any one is to be King or God, it ought to be Strepsiades or Pheidippides.

In the *Wasps* there is no suggestion of kingship or godhead being attributed to Philocleon—only a challenge on his part to a dancing match. There is no mention of victory, except his warning that at Olympia the older competitor sometimes won.[1]

The *Peace* is said (p. 28) to present the 'New Zeus' motive in a milder form. It would be truer to say that it does not present it at all. For the intention of Trygaeus to go up and question Zeus as to his meaning cannot possibly be construed as making Trygaeus a New Zeus. Mr. Cornford's reference (p. 28) to Salmoneus also seems very far-fetched. Apparently the implied argument is that since Trygaeus looked up to heaven and abused Zeus, as Salmoneus does on a vase-painting, Trygaeus is a 'thunder-king' like Salmoneus. There could not be a clearer case of 'undistributed middle term'; and besides, Trygaeus (ll. 56 ff.) does not abuse Zeus, but questions and entreats. He is never called a victor.

The *Birds* is Mr. Cornford's trump card. Here Peithetaerus is really the New Zeus. The supersession—not of Zeus in particular, but of all the gods—is the theme of this play; and it can hardly be doubted that the recurrence of this theme during the Peloponnesian War is a comic reflex of the feeling which became manifest, that there was no moral government in the world, that the gods' régime had broken down, and that (as Thucydides expressed it) it was ἐν ὁμοίῳ καὶ σέβειν καὶ μή. We find such discontent with the gods in the *Peace* and in the *Birds*, and also in the *Plutus*, in which the poet, in his senile period, dishes up many of his old ideas in a more frigid collation. The treatment of Peithetaerus as the New Zeus is simply a necessary part of the working out of this general idea, not the survival of a ritual performance, though naturally

[1] ll. 1381 ff.

some ideas are borrowed from the thunder-kings, &c., of the legends, in some of which primitive religious 'king-choosings' may be reflected; Peithetaerus is therefore quite naturally hailed with the καλλίνικος song, as victor, king, and god.

In the *Lysistrata* there is no hint of king or god—only an anticipation in one line (1293) of a dramatic victory. In the *Thesmophoriazusae* there is not even this.

In the *Frogs* there is the contest for the 'throne of tragedy'; but it is quite plain (though Mr. Cornford thinks otherwise) that it was *not* thought of as a royal throne. The privileges of the supreme poet are

$$\sigma\acute{\iota}\tau\eta\sigma\iota\nu \ \alpha\grave{\upsilon}\tau\grave{\upsilon}\nu \ \grave{\epsilon}\nu \ \pi\rho\upsilon\tau\alpha\nu\epsilon\acute{\iota}\psi \ \lambda\alpha\mu\beta\acute{\alpha}\nu\epsilon\iota\nu,$$
$$\theta\rho\acute{\upsilon}\nu\upsilon\nu \ \tau\epsilon \ \tau\upsilon\hat{\upsilon} \ \Pi\lambda\upsilon\upsilon\tau\hat{\omega}\nu\upsilon\varsigma \ \acute{\epsilon}\xi\eta\varsigma.$$

It is fallacious to urge that the Prytaneum was a survival of the king's palace, and that there is an analogy with the Olympic victor who was feasted in the Prytaneum. These facts cannot by any legitimate means be used to prove that the mention of σίτησις ἐν πρυτανείῳ implies that the person feasted owes his place in comedy to the fact that he is a relic of a primitive ritual of king-making.[1] Are we to assume that (e. g.) the proceedings in the Assembly and the Prytaneum on the return of an ambassador come down from times when the ambassador was made a king? If *only* the Olympic victor was even fed at the public expense, and if he were really treated as a king (a point which is more than doubtful), there might be something to be said for Mr. Cornford's theory; but it is not so.

In the *Ecclesiazusae* there is no hint of god or king, but only the same cries which have been quoted from the *Lysistrata*, and which (as has already been suggested)[2] do

---

[1] An equally inadmissible argument is that on the same page (p. 32), that, because Pericles was accused of being a tyrant and was nicknamed ὁ σχινοκέφαλος Ζεύς, the play in which he occurred must be descended from a ritual in which a king figured. Surely no one can take the current comparisons of Pericles to Zeus as anything but metaphors, evoked by his strong and domineering character and certain facts in his history. (The same reply is to be made, *mutatis mutandis*, to the foot-note on p. 31.)   [2] See above, p. 310.

not really imply that any one in the play is a victor, but are simply a joyful anticipation by the chorus of their own victory in the Dionysiac competition.

We have lastly to consider the *Plutus*. The amazing conjecture that *Plutus* is installed in the Opisthodomus of the Parthenon as consort of Athena, thus replacing Zeus Soter in the same capacity, has already been mentioned [1], and a reply given to it. It is, of course, true that Plutus virtually brings to an end the rule of Zeus, and Chremylus says of Plutus (l. 1189)

$$\text{ὁ Ζεὺς ὁ σωτὴρ γὰρ πάρεστιν ἐνθάδε}$$
$$\text{αὐτόματος ἥκων.}$$

But the latter expression is naturally taken as a strong metaphor, like οἷς Ποσειδῶν ἀσφαλεῖός ἐστιν ἡ βακτηρία: [2] and, once more, the idea of the replacement of the gods by a juster government is a reversion to the frame of mind generated by the Peloponnesian War and given far more brilliant expression in the *Birds*.

What is the result? In two plays the theme of the play is the supersession of the gods, and it is not very strange to find the leader of the revolt acclaimed as the New Zeus. It would be strange if it were otherwise. In the *Knights* there is some metaphorical use of the idea of kingship, applied *not* to the victor in the agon, but to Demos; this hardly helps Mr. Cornford's theory, and there is little else that does so. For no one can take seriously the argument that because in two or three plays the victor in the contest is greeted with the same cry as an Olympic victor, and because (according to one much-disputed theory) [3] the Olympic victor is the descendant of a king chosen by competition, comedy itself is descended from such a competition. The only conclusion which we can draw is that the ideas of the New Zeus and New King occur so rarely in comedy and are applied, as a rule, in so metaphorical a manner, that it may be taken as certain that they were not

---

[1] p. 333. [2] *Acharnians* 672.

[3] The theory is propounded by Mr. Cornford in Miss Harrison's *Themis*, ch. vii. In the *B. S. A. Annual*, vol. xxii, pp. 85 ff., Dr. E. N. Gardner gives what seems to be a conclusive reply.

ideas implicit in any ritual from which comedy sprang, but have a simple and sufficient explanation where they occur.

§ 4. It is not clear in what way the Pharmakos-ritual is supposed to have formed part of the original ceremony imagined in Mr. Cornford's theory. It is quite true that the rite of the expulsion of the Pharmakos existed, and must have existed from primitive times, in Athens. But was it part of a larger ritual typifying the change from the Old to the New Year? There is no evidence of this. The ceremony took place on the sixth of Thargelion; but the fact that Socrates' birthday-feast was also celebrated on that day [1] surely cannot mean that 'Socrates, the purifier of men's souls, who suffered an unjust death, was regarded as a Pharmakos, who bore the sins of Athens on his innocent head'; [2] there is nowhere the vestige of a hint of such a notion in antiquity; and that the *Clouds* ended with the expulsion of Socrates as Pharmakos [3] is a conjecture unsupported by a single word of the text. It is also mere conjecture that the driving out of Penia in the *Plutus* is based on the Pharmakos-ritual, as the bringing-in of Plutus is on the Eiresione ceremony.[4] Nothing in the text suggests this. The application of the word φαρμακός as an abusive epithet to Cleon needs no ritual basis. There is no other reference to the idea in Aristophanes at all.[5]

§ 5. We have now to consider more particularly the nature of the agon, and its origin as conceived by Mr. Cornford. The agon stands [6] in a fixed relation to the concluding marriage, such that the bridegroom in the marriage is usually the victor in the agon. We have in the agon the agonist—the ultimate victor and bridegroom—and his antagonist: these, it would seem (at least in some of Mr. Cornford's chapters), represent the Old and New Year, and the Old Year must therefore have originally been killed; but, since he has to be the bridegroom, he must, if killed, be resuscitated. We have therefore to look

---

[1] Plut. *Symp.* VIII. i, § 1.   [2] Cornford, p. 55.
[3] ibid., p. 11.   [4] ibid., pp. 56, 82.
[5] Mr. Cornford's note on p. 77 seems to be full of the most doubtful matter.
[6] ibid., p. 70.

into the plays to find traces (1) of the ultimate victor being killed in the agon, (2) of his being resuscitated. As to the killing, Mr. Cornford sums up his case on p. 83 : 'In five plays (*Acharnians, Knights, Wasps, Birds, Lysistrata*) the chorus before the agon make a violent assault upon one or other of the adversaries and threaten him with death. In the *Acharnians* and *Lysistrata* the two halves of the chorus also quarrel among themselves.' (The latter fact proves nothing as to the death of the agonist.) ' After the agon, one or other of the adversaries is wounded (finale of the *Acharnians*), is beaten by his adversary and the chorus, and finally degraded and expelled as if he were a Pharmakos (*Knights*); endures the terrors of a descent into the cave of Trophonius (*Clouds*); faints almost to death and is recalled to life, after threatening to kill first himself and then his son (*Wasps*); is adorned for burial (*Lysistrata*); tied to a plank and only saved from death by a ruse (*Thesmophoriazusae*); 'left for dead' in Hades, while his adversary is brought back to life (*Frogs*); driven away with curses, as Hunger or Death was driven out, while Wealth is brought in instead.' Mr. Cornford proceeds: ' The strength of this evidence may be variously estimated. No one instance taken by itself would have much weight: but when all are taken together, and it is seen how constant this motive is, it appears to me that the probability that we have here survivals of an original simulated death of one or other adversary is considerably stronger than we should expect to find it even if we knew on other grounds that the hypothesis was true.'

Let us now examine the instances and see whether they really lend colour to the theory of an original simulated death.

It is, indeed, difficult to know exactly what we are to look for. Apparently if *either* combatant—the final victor or his antagonist—undergoes something like death, Mr. Cornford is satisfied, though strictly no one ought to be killed but the representative of the Old Year or Good Spirit in the original ritual.[1] That, however, would make the wounding of

---

[1] In fact the identification of the Old Year with the Good Spirit sometimes leads to difficulties. In a ritual agon the New Year would

Lamachus pointless, and also the leaving of Euripides in Hades. At the same time, the 'something like death' need not be so very like it, as a perusal of Mr. Cornford's list will show. But, passing over these difficulties, let us grapple with his instances.

In five plays there is a violent assault upon one or other of the adversaries, and he is threatened with death. In the *Acharnians* the attack upon Dicaeopolis is sufficiently explained by the strong feelings current upon political questions early in the war. But apparently the wounding of Lamachus (not, it is to be noted, by Dicaeopolis) is also a point in Mr. Cornford's argument. If so, Lamachus ought to represent the Old Year or the Good Spirit; whereas it is Dicaeopolis who is the Old Year and is rejuvenated at the end of the play.

In the *Knights* there are of course violent threatenings of one combatant by another, but nothing that suggests an original ritual slaughter or simulated death ; to argue from the fact that when Cleon is taken indoors (l. 1250) he parodies the words of the dying Alcestis is really almost ridiculous. And there is again the difficulty that while Agoracritus is the victor and Cleon the victim, it is Demos who is rejuvenated, and not either combatant.

In the *Wasps* the chorus attack Bdelycleon, but the supposed traces of simulated death in this play are slight indeed. The first (p. 79) is Philocleon's mock-heroic demand (l. 522) for a sword, upon which he may fall, like Ajax, if he is defeated ; the second is, apparently, his threat to murder Bdelycleon, if he is not defeated. (We may well ask to *whose* simulated death these contrary indications point.) The third is Philocleon's collapse when Bdelycleon wins—a scene described by Mr. Cornford in language which greatly exaggerates the mock-heroic text. 'Bdelycleon's exposure', he says, 'of the slavery that is masked as democratic freedom reduces the old man to a fainting condition. The sword drops from his nerveless hand. Already his eyes are fixed on a better land of everlast-

naturally be the Good Spirit and would kill the Old; but this is not easily combined with the rejuvenation or resurrection of the Old as the New.

ing service on the jury, and his soul is taking flight, when his
son coaxes him back to life with the promise of a private law-
court at his own fireside. Philocleon's words are full of
reminiscences of the languishing heroes and heroines of
Euripides. In this passage we come as near as possible to
a sort of simulated death and revival.' This is surely more
than forced. Philocleon of course performs a mock-tragic
collapse—he parodies the behaviour and language of tragedy
all through the play, and he parodies Euripides in particular;
but the scene needs no ritual death and revival to explain it—
nothing but a study of the cleverly drawn character of
Philocleon, and a sense of humour.

The pitched battle in the *Birds* is of the typical kind. But
there is a difficulty about the meaning of the agon. According
to Mr. Cornford (p. 80) the contest between the Epops and
Peithetaerus is a contest between the Old and the New King,
and we are reminded that the Hoopoe 'is the metamorphosis
of one of the ancient kings of Athens'. But at an earlier
point in the book, Zeus was the Old King, not the Epops. Or
have we here another of Mr. Cornford's ever-ready doublings?

In the *Lysistrata* there are fights between the semi-choruses,
and between the Proboulos and Lysistrata, each with their
supporters. These will be dealt with presently. But, according to Mr. Cornford, there is a quasi-death of the Proboulos.
Lysistrata interrupts his reply to her with the words (599 ff.),
σὺ δὲ δὴ τί μαθὼν οὐκ ἀποθνήσκεις; and offers him a cake for
Cerberus, and puts a funeral wreath on him; and as he goes
off she adds:

μῶν ἐγκαλεῖς ὅτι οὐχὶ προὐθέμεσθά σε;
ἀλλ' εἰς τρίτην γοῦν ἡμέραν σοὶ πρῴ πάνυ
ἥξει παρ' ἡμῶν τὰ τρίτ' ἐπεσκευασμένα.

Surely this is no more than a jeer at his old age and his
out of date views; and any street-boy could have invented
such a piece of rudeness without the compulsion of a ritual
origin.

It is true that the five plays which have just been discussed
all begin the dispute with a violent quarrel. But it seems far

easier to explain this by the comparatively simple form of κῶμος which has been suggested in Ch. III of the present book (or, if Navarre's theory be preferred, by a contest arising between the phallic κῶμος and the spectators) than by the elaborate ritual which Mr. Cornford imagines and which would fit in very badly with any recorded form of κῶμος.

Some other points in Mr. Cornford's argument may be briefly mentioned. The supposed expulsion of Cleon as a Pharmakos has already been disposed of; his conversion into a sausage-seller cannot be interpreted as pointing back to a simulated death. The sham initiation of Socrates is only a way of deriding the hocus-pocus connected alike with his pretentious doctrines and with some current kinds of mystery. The treatment of Mnesilochus in the *Thesmophoriazusae* would certainly not have suggested a ritual death and resurrection to any one but Mr. Cornford. In the *Frogs* Euripides is 'left for dead': but the resurrection is that of Aeschylus. In the *Plutus* the death of the god is represented (p. 100) by 'the painful therapeutics of the god of medicine'. They were not painful to Plutus, but only to Neocleides. Need we go further? The scenes on which Mr. Cornford relies arise naturally out of the dramatic situation: except the *mêlées* after the Parodos, they conform to no one pattern; they are mostly parodies of tragedy, bits of original humour: there is not one of which Mr. Cornford's explanation is the natural one, or in which the genius of the poet, drawing illustrations from all sources, is not an adequate one. The necessity for some kind of agon the poet certainly did feel; there is no reason to suppose that he was under any such obligation to introduce a simulated death, or that if he had done so, the traces of it would have remained undiscovered for twenty-three centuries.

§ 6. We are in equal difficulties when we come to study Mr. Cornford's proof that the original ritual contained the rejuvenation of the Old Year, combined with, or as an alternative to, the expulsion of the adversary by the New Year. The combination, indeed, is very difficult to imagine. If the Old Year was killed or expelled by the New, we should have to postulate a rite with two New Years, one of whom is (or has

been) expelled as a Pharmakos. So, instead of the killing of
the Old Year by the New, Mr. Cornford substitutes [1] the expulsion of the Evil Principle by the Good (dropping all mention
of the year). The Good Principle could of course be subsequently rejuvenated; though our idea of what the original
ritual is supposed to have been is somewhat blurred by this
substitution. The rejuvenation may be a resurrection, or a
rejuvenation by cooking, as when Medea professed to renew
the youth of Pelias.

The only play which ends in an actual resurrection of the
Good Adversary is (as Mr. Cornford remarks) the *Frogs*. 'This
is also' (he adds) 'the only play in which Dionysus takes a
leading part; but' (he continues very candidly) 'it is hardly
fair to lay much stress upon it, because the whole conception
of the plot demands that it should be modelled upon a descent
into Hades.' Yet he cannot give up the case altogether. 'In
the ritual that underlay these descents—or one form of that
ritual—it was the male power of fertility who went down to
bring back from the underworld either his mother or his
bride.' He instances the recovery of Alcestis by Heracles, and
of Semele by Dionysus (at Lerna), and a scene in the modern
play at Viza. But what has this to do with the *Frogs*, even
though Dionysus had to cross a lake (part of the regular
topography of Hades) in the *Frogs* as in the Lernaean tale?
Does Aeschylus represent the mother or the bride of Dionysus?
and which was represented by the poets in the *Gerytades*, and
the statesmen who were recalled to life in the $\Delta\hat{\eta}\mu o\iota$ of Eupolis?
Surely the idea of bringing back the dead to help or advise
their degenerate successors is not so far beyond the imagination
of a brilliant poet, particularly with the Odyssey to help him,
as to require an original ritual to explain it. [2]

As to the rejuvenation of Demos in the *Knights*, when the

[1] p. 84.

[2] That the scene in the *Peace* in which Eirene is hauled up by Trygaeus
is modelled on the Anodos-scenes which appear on certain vases, and
which may (though this is very uncertain) have been enacted at some
festival, is very probable; and Mr. Cornford does well to call attention to
Robert's interpretation of the scene in this sense.

sausage-seller claims to have 'cooked him young again', Mr. Cornford overstates the case; and it is not likely that many readers will agree with him that 'the trade of the sausage-seller, who is repeatedly called a cook (μάγειρος), has, in fact, been chosen solely in order that he may render this last brilliant service to Demos'—solely, that is, with a view to l. 1321, τὸν Δῆμον ἀφεψήσας ὑμῖν καλὸν ἐξ αἰσχροῦ πεποίηκα. (His trade simply marks him as representing the lowest of the people.) The rejuvenation by cooking is surely no more than a reminiscence of the story of Medea and Pelias in a comic context—a variation on the rejuvenation of an elderly person which certainly does occur in several plays, and is natural enough in a comedy in which the old rustic was a traditional character and would be granted his heart's desire best by becoming young again. It needs no ritual to explain this.

§ 7. Mr. Cornford points out quite truly that there is sometimes a sacrifice shortly before the end of the play. His arguments, however, to prove the occurrence of such a sacrifice are not always convincing. In the *Acharnians* the series of scenes in which Dicaeopolis holds his market are said [1] to be preparations for sacrifice and feast; but the Megarean's statement that his pigs are old enough Ἀφροδίτᾳ θύειν hardly proves it. There is no sacrifice in the *Clouds*, only 'the initiation scene which the neophyte mistakes for a sacrifice'; in the *Thesmophoriazusae* only the 'sacrifice' of the sham baby (the wine-skin) hardly a ritual relic; in the *Ecclesiazusae* no sacrifice, but a 'curious scene' out of which Mr. Cornford vainly tries to squeeze reminiscences of one. In the *Frogs* the sacrifice precedes the agon instead of following it as it ought to do if it is either the victor's thank-offering or a relic of the ritual death of the defeated combatant. The clear scenes of sacrifice and feast are those of the *Knights, Peace, Birds,* and *Plutus*; and we may well be content to regard such scenes as the natural way of celebrating the victory of the successful party in the agon, without laying such stress as Mr. Cornford does upon the parallelism with the proceedings of the victor in the Olympic games. In both cases the victor

[1] p. 94.

offers a sacrifice and leads a κῶμος, and there the parallelism ends.

It is certainly not possible to accept Mr. Cornford's further (or alternative) explanation that the sacrifice was once the rending, or omophagy, or scattering of the Good Principle—the Principle represented in the plays by Demos, Philocleon, Mnesilochus (!), Aeschylus, Plutus. It is only necessary to read § 47 of his book to see how strained this interpretation is.

Whether the scattering of nuts or cakes to the spectators has any connexion with phallic rites and the scattering of emblems of fertility [1] may be left an open question. But we may be sure that it was never the scattering of portions of the slain god; for there is no evidence at all that the god was ever slain in any ritual with which comedy can be connected; and the idea that the agon arose from a ritual in which an Eniautos-Daimon or Good Principle underwent a simulated death must be pronounced wholly unproved.

§ 8. Some points of detail in regard to Mr. Cornford's treatment of the 'Impostors' have already been noticed. They are probably not due to the multiplication of the antagonist, but spring from a different source. They are by no means all impostors, though they are highly inconvenient people.

Probably Mr. Cornford would have modified in some degree his treatment of the stock masks of comedy, had he been able to study Robert's important work, which, though dealing primarily with the New Comedy, throws much light incidentally on the Old. Mr. Cornford explains the fact that certain types seem to have been common to Athens, Megara, Sparta, Syracuse, and Tarentum by the hypothesis that the masks were 'the set required for the fertility drama of the Old Year transformed into the New, that marriage which is interrupted by the death and revival of the hero'. It would not be difficult to show that he exaggerates the fixity of the types, owing to his desire to prove that they were the masks of a troupe of actors who came into existence as the actors of a fixed plot. But in fact the existence of such troupes of actors seems to be a late, not an early phenomenon in the history of the Greek

[1] pp. 100-2.

drama, and there is far more variety, especially in the scenes
of the second half of Aristophanes' comedies, than can be
explained on these lines. There are also difficulties of detail,
e. g. his treatment of the *Miles Gloriosus* as originally the
antagonist of the bridegroom in the ἱερὸς γάμος—an idea
which does not seem to correspond to anything in the actual
plays.

In the last chapter of the book Mr. Cornford tries to show
that his supposed ritual was indigenous to Attica. As it is
more than doubtful whether such a ritual existed at all, we
need hardly discuss this point, but may be content to refer
back to the reasons already given for ascribing to Dorian
peoples some share in the origination of the Attic Comedy.
(These reasons are not exactly those which he discusses.)
What the native elements in Attic Comedy probably were, the
present chapter has attempted to show.

IV

EPICHARMUS

ANALYSIS OF CHAPTER IV

IV

EPICHARMUS

I

Life, etc., of Epicharmus.

ALL that can be said with certainty about the life of
Epicharmus can be stated in a few lines. He wrote comedies at
Syracuse in the reigns of Gelo (485–478 B.C.) and Hiero (478–
467 B.C.), and must have been writing for many years before
487/6 B.C.—the year of Chionides' first appearance in Athens,
since Aristotle records that he was πολλῷ πρότερος Χιωνίδου
καὶ Μάγνητος.[1] It may also be taken as certain that he wrote
comedies at Megara Hyblaea before he did so at Syracuse;
the Megarean claim to have originated comedy (recorded by
Aristotle) was based on the fact that Epicharmus belonged to
Megara Hyblaea, and the claim would have been pointless
unless he had actually written there. (Megara Hyblaea was
destroyed by Gelo in 483 B.C.) These statements can be
legitimately inferred from the following passages:

ARISTOTLE, *Poet.* iii. 1448 a 30 ff. διὸ καὶ ἀντιποιοῦνται τῆς
τε τραγῳδίας καὶ τῆς κωμῳδίας οἱ Δωριεῖς· τῆς μὲν γὰρ κωμῳδίας
οἱ Μεγαρεῖς οἵ τε ἐνταῦθα ὡς ἐπὶ τῆς παρ' αὐτοῖς δημοκρατίας
γενομένης καὶ οἱ ἐκ Σικελίας· ἐκεῖθεν γὰρ ἦν Ἐπίχαρμος ὁ
ποιητής, πολλῷ πρότερος ὢν Χιωνίδου καὶ Μάγνητος.

ibid. v. 1449 b 5 ff. τὸ δὲ μύθους ποιεῖν Ἐπίχαρμος καὶ
Φόρμις· τὸ μὲν ἐξ ἀρχῆς ἐκ Σικελίας ἦλθε. (The passage is
variously emended, but there is no reason to doubt that it
connected the origination of comic plots of general, as opposed
to personal, interest with Epicharmus' work in Sicily.)

MARM. PAR. *Ep.* 71 ἀφ' οὗ Ἱέρων Συρακουσσῶν ἐτυράννευσεν
ἔτη HHΠIII ἄρχοντος Ἀθήνησι Χάρητος (i.e. 472/1 B.C.). ἦν δὲ
καὶ Ἐπίχαρμος ὁ ποιητὴς κατὰ τοῦτον.

---

[1] On Wilamowitz's objection to this statement see below (p. 355).

ANON. DE COM.[1] (Kaibel, *Com. Graec. Fr.*, p. 17) ⟨'Επίχαρμος
Συρακόσιος⟩. οὗτος πρῶτος διερριμμένην τὴν κωμῳδίαν ἀνεκτήσατο πολλὰ προσφιλοτεχνήσας. χρόνοις δὲ γέγονε [2] κατὰ τὴν
ογ΄ 'Ολυμπιάδα (73rd, i.e. 488–485 B.C.), τῇ δὲ ποιήσει γυμνικὸς
καὶ εὑρετικὸς καὶ φιλότεχνος. σῴζεται δὲ αὐτοῦ δράματα μ΄,
ὧν ἀντιλέγονται δ΄.

CLEM. AL. *Strom.* i. 64 τῆς δὲ 'Ελεατικῆς ἀγωγῆς Ξενοφάνης
ὁ Κολοφώνιος κατάρχει, ὅν φησι Τίμαιος κατὰ 'Ιέρωνα τὸν
Σικελίας δυνάστην καὶ 'Επίχαρμον τὸν ποιητὴν γεγονέναι,
'Απολλόδωρος δὲ κατὰ τὴν τεσσαρακοστὴν 'Ολυμπιάδα (i.e. 620–
617 B.C.) γενόμενον παρατετακέναι ἄχρι Δαρείου τε καὶ Κύρου
χρόνου.

SUIDAS s.v. 'Επίχαρμος· Τιτύρου ἢ Χιμάρου καὶ Σικίδος
Συρακούσιος ἢ ἐκ πόλεως Κραστοῦ τῶν Σικανῶν· ὃς εὗρε τὴν
κωμῳδίαν ἐν Συρακούσαις ἅμα Φόρμῳ. ἐδίδαξε δὲ δράματα νβ΄,
ὡς δὲ Λύκων φησι, λε΄. τινὲς δὲ αὐτὸν Κῷον ἀνέγραψαν τῶν
μετὰ Κάδμου εἰς Σικελίαν μετοικησάντων, ἄλλοι Σάμιον, ἄλλοι
Μεγαρέα τῶν ἐν Σικελίᾳ. ἦν δὲ πρὸ τῶν Περσικῶν ἔτη ἐξ
διδάσκων ἐν Συρακούσαις· ἐν δὲ 'Αθηναῖς Εὐέτης καὶ Εὐξενίδης
καὶ Μύλλος ἐπεδείκνυντο. καὶ 'Επιχάρμειος λόγος, τοῦ
'Επιχάρμου.

[Various points in Suidas' notice will be discussed later.
The last sentence but one, however, gives as a fact, without
any alternative tradition, the same date as the Anonymous
writer. We do not know what their authority was, or on
what computation the date was based.

The expression ἅμα Φόρμῳ may also be compared with
Suidas' account of Φόρμος (s.v.) as Συρακούσιος, κωμικός,
σύγχρονος 'Επιχάρμῳ, οἰκεῖος δὲ Γέλωνι τῷ τυράννῳ Σικελίας
καὶ τροφεὺς τῶν παίδων αὐτοῦ: and of Deinolochus (s.v.) as
Συρακούσιος ἢ 'Ακραγαντῖνος· κωμικὸς ἦν ἐπὶ τῆς ογ΄ 'Ολυμπιάδος
(488–485 B.C.) υἱὸς 'Επιχάρμου, ὡς δέ τινες μαθητής.]

SCHOL. PIND. *Pyth.* i. 98 ὅτι δὲ 'Αναξίλαος Λοκροὺς ἠθέλη-
σεν ἄρδην ἀπολέσθαι καὶ ἐκωλύθη πρὸς 'Ιέρωνος, ἱστορεῖ

---

[1] On the value of this authority see Kaibel, Prolegomena περὶ κωμῳδίας.
[2] Rohde (*Rhein. Mus.* xxxiii, p. 165) has shown that γέγονε does not
mean 'was born' in most cases where it occurs in such notices, but
= ἠκμάζετο or *floruit*.

Ἐπίχαρμος ἐν Νάσοις. (The event referred to took place in 476 B.C., or between 478 and 476 B.C.)

Other writers, such as Diogenes and Iamblichus, who did not think of Epicharmus primarily as a comic poet, also mention his residence at Syracuse, and this, and the facts that he was associated with Hiero and wrote comedies, are all that is beyond dispute.

How far his life can be carried back beyond the reigns of Gelo and Hiero depends

(1) upon the interpretation put upon Aristotle's expression πολλῷ πρότερος Χιωνίδου καὶ Μάγνητος. It is clear that the later authorities quoted date Epicharmus by his association with Hiero and not by anything earlier, though Suidas may give as his *floruit* the date of his actual or supposed migration to Syracuse,[1] and seems to have an independent tradition about Epicharmus' contemporary, Phormus, as a friend of Gelo. But to alter Aristotle's phrase to οὐ πολλῷ πρότερος[2] does not seem to be justifiable, and the number of 'plays' ascribed to Epicharmus implies a long period of activity.

(2) upon the view taken of the tradition, which we must now consider, that Epicharmus was a hearer of Pythagoras. Pythagoras is said to have arrived at Croton in 530 B.C., and the persecution of the Pythagoreans in Magna Graecia seems to have begun about 510 B.C. If the tradition is true, it is fairly probable that Epicharmus' attendance on Pythagoras would have been earlier than 510 B.C., and that he would have been born at least by 530 B.C. If he began writing plays while young (as e.g. Aristophanes did) he might well be described as πολλῷ πρότερος Χιωνίδου, who (according to Suidas) appeared first in 487/6 B.C. ἔτεσιν ὀκτὼ πρὸ τῶν Περσικῶν.[3]

---

[1] As suggested by Wilamowitz, *Gött. Gel. Anz.* 1906, p. 620.

[2] This was done by Butcher in his first edition, and approved by various scholars : but he afterwards abandoned the emendation.

[3] Assuming with Capps that the year of the 'Persian Wars' was 480/79 B.C., and the reckoning inclusive (though 488/7 B.C. must be admitted to be possible). Wilamowitz is not convincing when he attempts (*Gött. Gel. Anz.* 1906, pp. 621–2) to prove that the dating of Epicharmus

The tradition of Epicharmus as a Pythagorean and a 'wise man' is recorded by various writers:

PLUTARCH, *Vit. Numae*, viii Πυθαγόραν Ῥωμαῖοι τῇ πολιτείᾳ προσέγραψαν, ὡς ἱστόρηκεν Ἐπίχαρμος ὁ κωμικὸς ἔν τινι λόγῳ πρὸς Ἀντήνορα γεγραμμένῳ, παλαιὸς ἀνὴρ καὶ τῆς Πυθαγορικῆς διατριβῆς μετεσχηκώς.

[But the Λόγος πρὸς Ἀντήνορα was certainly a spurious work.]

CLEM. AL. *Strom.* v, § 100 πάλιν τὸ δυνατὸν ἐν πᾶσι προσάπτουσιν καὶ οἱ λογιμώτατοι τῷ θεῷ, ὁ μὲν Ἐπίχαρμος (Πυθαγόρειος δ᾽ ἦν) λέγων . . . (fragm. 266, Kaib.).

[But Clement elsewhere quotes the certainly spurious Πολιτεία of Epicharmus as genuine.]

DIOG. LAERT. i. 42 Ἱππόβοτος δ᾽ ἐν τῇ τῶν φιλοσόφων ἀναγραφῇ· Ὀρφέα, Λίνον, Σόλωνα, Περίανδρον, Ἀνάχαρσιν, Κλεόβουλον, Μύσωνα, Θαλῆν, Βίαντα, Πιττακόν, Ἐπίχαρμον, Πυθαγόραν.

[Hippobotus lived at the end of the third or beginning of the second century B.C.]

ibid. viii. 78 Ἐπίχαρμος Ἡλοθαλοῦς Κῷος.[4] καὶ οὗτος ἤκουσε Πυθαγόρου. τριμηνιαῖος δ᾽ ὑπάρχων ἀπηνέχθη τῆς Σικελίας εἰς Μέγαρα, ἐντεῦθεν δ᾽ εἰς Συρακούσας, ὥς φησι καὶ αὐτὸς ἐν τοῖς συγγράμμασιν. καὶ αὐτῷ ἐπὶ τοῦ ἀνδρίαντος ἐπιγέγραπται τάδε·

> εἴ τι παραλλάσσει φαέθων μέγας ἅλιος ἄστρων
> καὶ πόντος ποταμῶν μεῖζον᾽ ἔχει δύναμιν,
> φαμὶ τοσοῦτον ἐγὼ σοφίᾳ προέχειν Ἐπίχαρμον
> ὃν πατρὶς ἐστεφάνωσ᾽ ἅδε Συρακοσίων.

by Aristotle (implied also in Plato, *Theaet.* 152 d, e, vid. infr.) is inconsistent with the date given by Suidas and the 'grammatical' tradition. The two are quite reconcilable if we suppose that he was composing at Megara long before he was famous at Syracuse, and Suidas' statement that Magnes' ἐπιβάλλει Χιωνίδη νέος πρεσβύτῃ is absolutely consistent with the facts that Epicharmus was writing in 476 B.C. and that the first (recorded) mention of a victory by Magnes is in 472 B.C.

[4] A very confused passage of Diogenes (vii. 7) about supposed writings of Pythagoras also mentions Ἡλοθαλῆ τὸν Ἐπιχάρμου τοῦ Κῴου πατέρα.

οὗτος ὑπομνήματα καταλέλοιπεν ἐν οἷς φυσιολογεῖ, γνωμολογεῖ,
ἰατρολογεῖ. καὶ παραστιχίδια ἐν τοῖς πλείστοις τῶν ὑπομνη-
μάτων πεποίηκεν, οἷς διασαφεῖ ὅτι ἑαυτοῦ ἐστὶ τὰ συγγράμματα.
βιοὺς δ' ἔτη ἐνενήκοντα κατέστρεψεν.

[The comedies are not here mentioned, but in a passage to be
considered later (iii. 12) Diogenes, while still thinking of
Epicharmus' contributions to philosophy, calls him ' the comic
poet ': πολλὰ δὲ καὶ παρ' Ἐπιχάρμου τοῦ κωμῳδιοποιοῦ προσωφέληται (sc. Πλάτων) κτλ.

Lucian, Μακρόβιοι, § 25, has a similar tradition about the
poet's great age : καὶ Ἐπίχαρμος δὲ ὁ τῆς κωμῳδίας ποιητὴς
καὶ αὐτὸς ἐνενήκοντα καὶ ἑπτὰ ἔτη λέγεται βιῶναι.]

Theocritus' Epigram (18) also evidently thinks of the statue
erected in the theatre at Syracuse as a recognition of Epicharmus' wisdom :

ἅ τε φωνὰ Δώριος χὠνὴρ ὁ τὰν κωμῳδίαν
    εὑρὼν Ἐπίχαρμος·
ὦ Βάκχε, χάλκεόν νιν ἀντ' ἀλαθινοῦ
    τὶν ὧδ' ἀνέθηκαν
τοὶ Συρακόσσαις ἐνίδρυνται πελωρισταὶ πόλει,
    οἷ' ἀνδρὶ πολίτᾳ
σοφῶν ἔοικε ῥημάτων μεμναμένους[1]
    τελεῖν ἐπίχειρα.
πολλὰ γὰρ πὸτ τὰν ζόαν τοῖς πᾶσιν εἶπε χρήσιμα·
    μεγάλα χάρις αὐτῷ.

ANON. *in Plat. Theaet.* 152 e (Berl. Klass. Texte ii, col. 71. 12)
Ἐπίχαρμος ὁ ⟨ὁμιλή⟩σας τοῖς Πυθα⟨γορείοις⟩ ἄλλα τέ τινα
ἐ⟨πινενόη⟩κεν δεινὰ κτλ.   (See below, p. 375.)

IAMBLICHUS, *Vit. Pythag.* 166 περὶ τῶν φυσικῶν ὅσοι τινὰ
μνείαν πεποίηνται, πρῶτον Ἐμπεδοκλέα καὶ Παρμενίδην τὸν
Ἐλεάτην προφερόμενοι τυγχάνουσιν, οἵ τε γνωμολογῆσαί τι τῶν
κατὰ τὸν βίον βουλόμενοι τὰς Ἐπιχάρμου διανοίας προφέρονται,
καὶ σχεδὸν πάντες αὐτὰς οἱ φιλόσοφοι κατέχουσι.

ibid. 226 τῶν δὲ ἔξωθεν ἀκροατῶν γενέσθαι καὶ Ἐπίχαρ-

---

[1] Editors differ much in their readings of this line and the lines which
precede and follow it, but it would be beside the point to discuss the
readings here.

μον, ἀλλ' οὐκ ἐκ τοῦ συστήματος τῶν ἀνδρῶν, ἀφικόμενον δὲ
εἰς Συρακούσας διὰ τὴν Ἱέρωνος τυραννίδα τοῦ μὲν φανερῶς
φιλοσοφεῖν ἀποσχέσθαι, εἰς μέτρον δ' ἐντεῖναι τὰς διανοίας τῶν
ἀνδρῶν, μετὰ παιδιᾶς κρύφα ἐκφέροντα τὰ Πυθαγόρου δόγματα.
ibid. 241 Μητρόδωρός τε ὁ Θύρσου τοῦ πατρὸς 'Επιχάρμου
καὶ τῆς ἐκείνου διδασκαλίας τὰ πλείονα πρὸς τὴν ἰατρικὴν
μετενέγκας, ἐξηγούμενος τοὺς τοῦ πατρὸς λόγους πρὸς τὸν
ἀδελφόν φησι τὸν 'Επίχαρμον καὶ πρὸ τούτου τὸν Πυθαγόραν
τῶν διαλέκτων ἀρίστην λαμβάνειν τὴν Δωρίδα.

[The reading is very doubtful and the corrections uncertain.
Wilamowitz, reading ὁ Θύρσου τοῦ [πατρὸς] 'Επιχάρμου makes
Metrodorus grandson of Epicharmus : Diels reads ὁ Θύρσου
⟨ἀδελφὸς ἐκ τῆς⟩ τοῦ πατρὸς 'Επιχάρμου. It is also uncertain
who is meant by ἐκείνου—Thyrsus, Epicharmus, or, as Diels
thinks, Pythagoras. But as was pointed out by Rohde,[1] and
as is agreed by Kaibel and Diels, Metrodorus cannot have
lived until after Aristoxenus, whose musical theories are presupposed in other remarks ascribed to him by Iamblichus ;
and the passage, which after all says nothing about Epicharmus except that he wrote in Doric, may be neglected.]

It is clear that in these passages two traditions are to be
distinguished. The first is that of the introduction of
philosophical ideas into the comedies of Epicharmus ; the
second, which only occurs distinctly in Diogenes, viii. 78,
affirms that he wrote ὑπομνήματα—treatises on Nature and
Medicine, as well as gnomic wisdom. The first tradition is all
that can be extracted with certainty from Iamblichus, and
fortunately (since the authority of the work which passes
under the name of Iamblichus, and particularly of this part of
it, is very weak) it does not need his support. We shall
return shortly to the subject of the γνῶμαι of Epicharmus.
The second tradition proves its own worthlessness, when it
records that most of the 'treatises' contained acrostics showing Epicharmus to be the author. The acrostic does not
appear before the Alexandrian age,[2] and the writings before
Diogenes (or his source) were plainly spurious.

---

[1] *Rhein. Mus.* xxvii, p. 40.   [2] See Pascal, *Riv. di Filol.* 1919, p. 58.

The statement that Epicharmus was a hearer or follower of Pythagoras, though not one of his intimate disciples, may or may not be true; though the authority for it is very weak, there is nothing unlikely in it; but we shall see that there is nothing in the extant fragments of a 'philosophical' kind which proves more than that the poet was generally acquainted with the discussions of contemporary thinkers about Change and Permanence—a point which is also sufficiently proved by Plato, *Theaet.* 152 d, e ἔκ τε δὴ φορᾶς καὶ κινήσεως καὶ κράσεως πρὸς ἄλληλα γίγνεται πάντα ἃ δή φαμεν εἶναι, οὐκ ὀρθῶς προσαγορεύοντες· ἔστι μὲν γὰρ οὐδέποτ' οὐδέν, ἀεὶ δὲ γίγνεται. καὶ περὶ τούτου πάντες ἑξῆς οἱ σοφοὶ πλὴν Παρμενί-δου συμφερέσθων, Πρωταγόρας τε καὶ Ἡράκλειτος καὶ Ἐμπεδο-κλῆς, καὶ τῶν ποιητῶν οἱ ἄκροι τῆς ποιήσεως ἑκατέρας, κωμῳδίας μὲν Ἐπίχαρμος, τραγῳδίας δὲ Ὅμηρος, ὃς εἰπών, "Ὠκεανόν τε θεῶν γένεσιν καὶ μητέρα Τηθύν," πάντα εἴρηκεν ἔκγονα ῥοῆς τε καὶ κινήσεως. The reference to Homer shows that Plato was not thinking only of set philosophical discussions, and if he had known of any treatises of Epicharmus' περὶ φύσεως, it is not likely that he would have referred to him simply as a comic poet. The question of Epicharmus' relation to Pythagoras, and therewith the question how far back he may be dated, must therefore be left open. All that can be said is that there is nothing to contradict Aristotle's statement that he was long before Chionides and Magnes. We do not know when he died.

The notices are at variance as regards the poet's parentage and birthplace. The matter is not of great importance, and may be discussed briefly. Diogenes (viii. 7), who is interested in Epicharmus as a 'wise man', makes him the son of Helothales, who in a confused way is also brought into some relation to Pythagoras. Diogenes also makes him a native of Cos, the seat of a great medical school, with which perhaps he desired to connect Epicharmus on account of the spurious medical writings. A variety of this account appears in Suidas, who says that 'some have made him a native of Cos, one of those who migrated to Sicily with Cadmus'. Cadmus was a tyrant of Cos, who, according to Herodotus (vii. 164)

abdicated owing to conscientious objections to tyranny, and
migrated to Zancle (afterwards called Messene) with certain
exiles from Samos. But this took place after the fall of Miletus
in 494 B. C. (Herod. vi. 22–5) ; and it is scarcely possible that
Epicharmus should have arrived in Sicily as late as this, if he
was producing plays at Syracuse in 483 B. C. and in Megara
Hyblaea long enough before that to be called 'much earlier than
Chionides'. This account would also make it very improbable
that he should have been a hearer of Pythagoras, but not much
stress can be laid upon this. Nor need we be troubled by the
statement of Diomedes (about the end of the fourth century A. D.)
'sunt qui velint Epicharmum in Co insula exulantem primum
hoc carmen frequentasse, et sic a Coo comediam dici '.[1] It
remains quite possible that the poet was born at Cos, and
taken to Sicily in infancy, as Diogenes says; but in view of
the uncritical character of Diogenes' notice, the question must
at least be left open; and the συγγράμματα on which Diogenes
drew must be assumed to be the spurious ones. The theory
mentioned by Suidas, that he was a native of Samos, may
have been intended to bring him into early relations with
Pythagoras, or to account for the supposed association of the
poet (along with other Samians) with Cadmus.

But another tradition makes Epicharmus a Sicilian from
the first. One of the alternatives mentioned by Suidas makes
his birthplace Krastos, a Sicanian town; but Suidas probably
got this from Neanthes' περὶ ἐνδόξων ἀνδρῶν. (Neanthes lived
under Attalus I of Pergamum, who reigned 241–197 B.C.) As
Neanthes in the same breath made Krastos the birthplace of
the famous ἑταίρα Lais, who is known (from Polemo ap. Athen.
xiii, p. 588 b) to have been born at Hykkara, no weight can
be attached to the story.[2] The other account mentioned by

---

[1] Kaibel, *Com. Fr.* i, pp. 58, 88. Grysar (*de Doriensium Comoedia*,
Cologne, 1828) builds on this an elaborate theory that Epicharmus was
driven into exile by the persecution of the Pythagoreans about 510 B. C.,
but returned with Cadmus to Sicily in 494 B.C.

[2] Steph. Byz., p. 382. 13 Κραστός, πόλις τῶν Σικανῶν. Φίλιστος Σικελικῶν
τρισδεκάτῳ. ἐκ ταύτης ἦν Ἐπίχαρμος ὁ κωμικὸς καὶ Λαὶς ἡ ἑταίρα, ὡς Νεάνθης
ἐν τῷ περὶ ἐνδόξων ἀνδρῶν. Plutarch, *Symp. Quaest.* I. x. 2, animadverts

Suidas makes Epicharmus a Syracusan ; and he was probably also claimed by the Megareans. The only possible conclusion is that we cannot tell where he was born.

The futility of some of Suidas' sources is illustrated by his description of Epicharmus as son of Tityrus or Chimaros— evident inventions like those (also reported by Suidas) which made Phrynichus son of Minyras or Chorocles, and Arion son of Κυκλεύς. In the text of Suidas his mother's name is given as Sikis (καὶ Σικίδος). This has been emended by some to Σηκίδος, in which case the name would be a false inference on some one's part from fragment 125 (Kaibel) ;[1] by Welcker to Σικιννίδος, the σίκιννις being a satyric dance, and the name at least as appropriate for a parent of Epicharmus as Tityrus or Chimaros. Once more we can only conclude that we cannot tell who the poet's parents were any better than the early grammarians could.[2]

Of the poet's relations to Hiero we know nothing apart from one or two anecdotes. The statement of Iamblichus that Epicharmus was a philosopher who was driven by fear of Hiero's tyrannical character to veil his philosophy under the forms of comedy is not likely to be true ; for though on one occasion the poet got into trouble for an indecent remark made in the presence of Hiero's wife (Plut. *Apophth. Reg.*, p. 175 c), another story shows that he could give himself considerable freedom : viz. Plut. *Quomodo quis adulatorem distinguat ab amico*, p. 68 a Ἐπίχαρμος, τοῦ Ἱέρωνος ἀνελόντος ἐνίους τῶν συνηθῶν καὶ μεθ' ἡμέρας ὀλίγας κελεύσαντος ἐπὶ δεῖπνον αὐτόν, Ἀλλὰ πρῴην, ἔφη, θύων τοὺς φίλους οὐκ ἐκάλεσας. Aelian (*Var. Hist.* ii. 34) narrates another anecdote : Ἐπίχαρμόν φασι

on the unreliability of Neanthes, and Polemo Periegetes wrote a work called Ἀντιγραφαὶ πρὸς Νεάνθην (Athen. xiii, p. 602 f).

[1] Schol. Ar. *Peace* 185 (explaining the thrice-repeated μιαρώτατος of Trygaeus) τοῦτο ... τὸ ἀληθὲς τὴν ἀφορμὴν ἐκ τοῦ Σκίρωνος παρ' Ἐπιχάρμου ἔχει, ἐπεὶ κἀκεῖνος πεποίηκε τὸν φορμὸν ἐρωτηθέντα " τίς ἐστι μήτηρ " ; ἀποκρινό-μενον ὅτι " Σηκίς ", καὶ " τίς ἐστι πάτηρ " ; εἰπόντα " Σηκίς ", καὶ " τίς ἀδελφός " ; ὁμοίως Σηκίς.

[2] *Phot. Biblioth.*, p. 147 a (Bekker), states (after Ptolemaeus, son of Hephaestion, late second century A. D.) that Epicharmus was descended from Achilles, son of Peleus.

πάνυ σφόδρα πρεσβύτην ὄντα μετὰ τῶν ἡλικιωτῶν ἐν λέσχῃ
καθημένων, ἐπεὶ ἕκαστος τῶν παρόντων ἔλεγεν, ὁ μέν τις, Ἐμοὶ
πέντε ἔτη ἀπόχρη βιῶναι· ἄλλος δέ, Ἐμοὶ τρία· τρίτου δὲ
εἰπόντος, Ἐμοὶ τέσσαρα· ὑπολαβὼν ὁ Ἐπίχαρμος, ὦ βέλτιστοι,
εἶπε, τί στασιάζετε καὶ διαφέρεσθε ὑπὲρ ὀλίγων ἡμερῶν; πάντες
γὰρ οἱ συνελθόντες κατά τινα δαίμονα ἐπὶ δυσμαῖς ἐσμέν· ὥστε
ὥρα πᾶσιν ἡμῖν τὴν ταχίστην ἀνάγεσθαι πρὸ τοῦ τινος καὶ
ἀπολαῦσαι κακοῦ πρεσβυτικοῦ. We are also told that he
laughed at Aeschylus for his fondness for the word τιμαλφεῖν : [1]
and we may regret that we can only imagine the life of the
brilliant literary circle of Hiero's court, frequented as it was
by Aeschylus, Pindar, Simonides, and Bacchylides, and enter-
tained by the performance of their works.[2] A good deal is
sometimes made (after the example of Lorenz, pp. 92 ff.) of
the supposed influence of the social and intellectual habits
of the Sicilians, and of the Syracusans in particular, upon
Epicharmus and so upon Greek Comedy in general.   There
may be some truth in the statement commonly made that the
Sicilians were naturally a witty people.   Plato (*Gorgias* 493 a)
speaks of κομψὸς ἀνήρ, ἴσως Σικελός τις ἢ Ἰταλικός, and Cicero
(II *Verr.* iv, § 95) writes 'numquam tam male est Siculis, quin
aliquid facete et commode dicant'; and they may well have
been as witty in the prosperous days of Gelo and Hiero as they
were under Dionysius and Verres.   The rise of Rhetoric in
Sicily belongs to the generation after Hiero; but the attribution of certain rhetorical tricks to Epicharmus himself shows
that such cleverness could be appreciated in his day as well as
later.   But when Lorenz and others attribute to the influence
of the proverbial luxury of the Syracusans [3] the fact that
Epicharmus could write long passages of 'patter' containing
little but the names of fish and other eatables, it is natural to

---

[1] Schol. Aesch. *Eum.* 402.

[2] Apart from the epinikian odes of the great lyric poets we know that
the Αἰτναῖαι of Aeschylus was composed in honour of Hiero's newly
founded city of Aetna (*Vit. Aeschyli*; Plut. *Vit. Cim.* viii), and that the
Persae was reproduced at Syracuse (*Vit. Aesch.*; Schol. Ar. *Ran.* 1028).

[3] Cf. Plat. *Rep.* iii. 404 d and *Gorg.* 518 b; Hor. *Od.* III. i. 18; Strabo
VI. ii. 4; Schol. Ar. *Knights*, 1091; Athen. iii, p. 112 d; vii, pp. 282a, 352 f;
xii, p. 518 c; xiv, pp. 655 f, 661 e, f; and Suidas, *s. v.* Σικελικὴ τράπεζα.

ask whether such things do not belong to popular comedy everywhere and are not more likely (if they were derived from anywhere) to be derived from the mime-like performances in the Peloponnese to which both Sicilian and Athenian Comedy owed some of their characteristic features. The dances—chiefly of a mimetic kind—which were in vogue in Sicily are enumerated by Athenaeus, and no doubt contributed something to comedy, though few definite points of contact can be discerned.[1] It need only be observed here that such indications as there are suggest that Syracuse provided the comic poet with an atmosphere in which comedy might easily flourish. If we ask why there was no political comedy in Sicily, we need not have recourse to Hiero's temper or to the dangers of life under a monarch for an explanation.[2] The simple reason seems to be that the earlier kinds of performance out of which Sicilian Comedy developed were entirely non-political, and that political comedy was a special extravagance peculiar to Athens and does not lie in the main stream of the development of the art.

II

The spurious writings ascribed to Epicharmus.

§ 1. The vestiges of the Ψευδεπιχάρμεια are collected and the problems to which they give rise are discussed in Kaibel's edition of the fragments.[3] Besides the statement of Diogenes about the ὑπομνήματα of Epicharmus ἐν οἷς φυσιολογεῖ, γνωμολογεῖ, ἰατρολογεῖ (the spuriousness of which is proved by the acrostics which Diogenes found in them), the chief evidence (apart from fragments) is that of Athenaeus xiv. 648 d τὴν μὲν ἡμίναν οἱ τὰ εἰς ᾿Επίχαρμον ἀναφερόμενα ποιήματα πεποιηκότες οἴδασι, κἂν τῷ Χίρωνι ἐπιγραφομένῳ οὕτως λέγεται·

κ α ὶ π ι ε ῖ ν ὕ δ ω ρ δ ι π λ ά σ ι ο ν χ λ ι α ρ ό ν , ἡ μ ί ν α ς δ ύ ο .

---

[1] Athen. xiv. 629 e, f. Cf. also Pollux iv. 101–3; see above, pp. 233, 257. On the dance of Artemis Χιτωνέα, which Athenaeus mentions first as specially Syracusan, see below (p. 392).

[2] For the few traces of political allusions in Epicharmus, see below, p. 396.   [3] pp. 133 ff.

τὰ δὲ ψευδεπιχάρμεια ταῦτα ὅτι πεποιήκασιν ἄνδρες ἔνδοξοι
Χρυσόγονός τε ὁ αὐλητής, ὥς φησιν Ἀριστόξενος ἐν ὀγδόῳ
Πολιτικῶν Νόμων, τὴν Πολιτείαν ἐπιγραφομένην. Φιλόχορος
δ᾽ ἐν τοῖς περὶ μαντικῆς Ἀξιόπιστον τὸν εἴτε Λοκρὸν γένος εἴτε
Σικυώνιον τὸν Κανόνα καὶ τὰς Γνώμας πεποιηκέναι φησίν.
ὁμοίως δὲ ἱστορεῖ καὶ Ἀπολλόδωρος.

Chrysogonus flourished in the last part of the fifth century
B.C.;[1] but though the spuriousness of the Πολιτεία was known
to Aristoxenus in the latter part of the fourth century, and to
Apollodorus of Athens in the second, it is still quoted without
any hint of spuriousness by Clement of Alexandria in the
second century A.D. Ten lines or so from the poem have thus
been preserved.[2]

The *Chiron* is conjectured by Kaibel to have contained
medical instruction, placed in the mouth of the centaur
Chiron, who was, in mythology, acquainted with the healing
art; and the line above quoted is consistent with this.
Whether the various prescriptions for men and animals
attributed to Epicharmus by Roman writers[3] came from this
poem cannot be stated; it is at least likely.[4] If, as is conjectured with great probability by Susemihl,[5] the Ὀψοποιία

[1] Athen. xii. 535 d.   [2] Fragm. 255–7 (Kaibel).

[3] Colum. VIII. iii. 6; Pliny, *N. H.*, xx.89 and 94. Columella I. i. 8
may refer to such prescriptions (for animals) when he writes: Siculi
quoque non mediocri cura negotium istud (sc. res rusticas) prosecuti
sunt, Hiero et Epicharmus discipulus, Philometor et Attalus. (The text
is perhaps wrong; the agriculturally minded Hiero was a later one than
the patron of Epicharmus, and 'Epicharmus discipulus' can hardly be
right.) Comp. Statius, *Silv.* IV. iii, l. 150 quantumque pios ditavit
agrestes | Ascraeus Siculusque senex. Censorinus, *De die natali*, vii. 5,
also refers to Epicharmus' views on the period of gestation (in human
beings). Whether or not the *Chiron* discussed this cannot be said; Kaibel
thinks the reference is to a poem Περὶ φύσεως.

[4] Pascal, *Riv. di Filol.* 1919, p. 62, collects the evidence for the association of veterinary writings in the Roman age with the name of Chiron,
when the title *Mulomedicina Chironis* was given to such writings; and
cf. Veget. *Praef.* 3. In the second century A. D. a medical work in forty
books of verse was written by Marcellus Sidites, of whom *Anth. Pal.* VII.
clviii, ll. 8, 9, speaks: ἡρώῳ μέλψαντι μέτρῳ θεραπήϊα νούσων | βίβλοις ἐν
πινυταῖς Χειρωνίσι τεσσαράκοντα.

[5] *Philologus*, liii, p. 565; cf. Kaibel on fr. 290.

of 'Epicharmus'[1] was actually the *Chiron*, or part of the *Chiron*, there may be a reference to this in Alexis, fragm. 135 (K.). From the fact that the *Canon* was mentioned by Philochorus in his Περὶ μαντικῆς, and from the statement of Tertullian[2] 'ceterum Epicharmus etiam summum apicem inter divinationes somniis extulit cum Philochoro Atheniensi', Kaibel naturally supposes that divination may have been one of the subjects treated in the poem.

§ 2. The treatment of Nature (φυσιολογεῖ) in the Ψευδεπιχάρμεια is a more difficult subject. Kaibel[3] believes that there was a poem Περὶ φύσεως bearing the name of Epicharmus at a date early enough to have enabled Euripides to read it. The argument, stated briefly, is that lines are found in Euripides which are closely parallel to lines of Ennius quoted by Varro, and referred by scholars, with great probability, to the *Epicharmus* of Ennius. It is urged that it is more likely that Ennius should have imitated a connected poem (as he did in the *Hedyphagetica* and *Euhemerus*) than that he should have collected references to scientific matters from the plays of Epicharmus, particularly as the tone of the philosophical passages which do come from plays is that of parody, and is alien from the grand seriousness of some of the lines of a philosophical type, which are quoted as from Epicharmus, and (according to Kaibel) are probably to be ascribed to the supposed poem Περὶ φύσεως—lines such as νᾶφε καὶ μέμνασ' ἀπιστεῖν, and νοῦς ὁρῇ καὶ νοῦς ἀκούει, &c.

Kaibel's argument is not perfectly convincing. It is true that of the two Euripidean passages quoted, one is from the *Bacchae* (276-8), one of Euripides' latest plays, and that the unknown play from which the other comes (fragm. 941, Nauck, ed. 2) *may* have been late; and this partly meets the difficulty of supposing that an important poem would be forged in the name of Epicharmus sufficiently soon after his death (which may have taken place about 470 B.C. or some time later) to be familiar to Euripides. But it remains easier to suppose that if Ennius did adapt some entire poem passing under the name of

---

[1] Antiatt. Bekk. 99. 1.   [2] *De anima*, 46.

[3] *Com. Graec. Fragm.*, pp 134-5.

Epicharmus, it was a forgery of later date, and that the resemblances to Euripides in Ennius' poem (if substantiated) are due to reminiscences of Euripides by Ennius himself (for he certainly knew Euripides as well as he knew Epicharmus) or by the forger. In fact, however, the resemblances to Euripides are not themselves convincing, and without them the whole argument for a fifth-century forgery fails. The passages are as follows:

(1) Eur. fr. 941 (Nauck):

$$\text{ὁρᾷς τὸν ὑψοῦ τόνδ' ἄπειρον αἰθέρα}$$
$$\text{καὶ γῆν πέριξ ἔχονθ' ὑγραῖς ἐν ἀγκάλαις·}$$
$$\text{τοῦτον νόμιζε Ζῆνα, τόνδ' ἡγοῦ θεόν.}$$

Cf. Varro, De ling. Lat. v. 65 'idem hi dei caelum et terra Iupiter et Iuno, quod, ut ait Ennius,

istic est is Iupiter quem dico, quem Graeci vocant
aerem, qui ventus est et nubes, imber postea,
atque ex imbre frigus, ventis post fit aer denuo.
haece propter Iupiter sunt ista quae dico tibi,
quando mortalis atque urbes beluasque omnes iuvat'.

The only common point between the two passages is the identification of Zeus or Jupiter with the sky, and this doctrine was not peculiar to Epicharmus. (Ennius may have got it from Euripides.)

(2) Eur. Bacch. 276:

$$\text{Δημήτηρ θεά·}$$
$$\text{γῆ δ' ἐστίν, ὄνομα δ' ὁπότερον βούλῃ κάλει·}$$
$$\text{αὕτη μὲν ἐν ξηροῖσιν ἐκτρέφει βρότους.}$$

Cf. Varro, De ling. Lat. v. 64 'Terra Ops, quod hic omne opus et hac opus ad vivendum, et ideo dicitur Ops mater quod Terra mater. Haec enim

terris gentis omnis peperit, et resumit denuo
quae dat cibaria'.

But the points of the passages are clearly quite different. All that is common is the statement that the earth gives food to men, and this need not be derived from Epicharmus.

It may be added that, while these passages are quoted

by Varro from Ennius, they are not in fact stated to come
from the *Epicharmus* (though passages, to which there is no
Euripidean parallel, are ascribed to that poem in chs. 59 and
68 of the same book); that the *Epicharmus* was not the only
poem in which Ennius used this metre; and that the quotations may well be from the tragedies of Ennius, copying the
tragedies of Euripides.

It may be suggested,[1] as an alternative to Kaibel's theory,
that if there was a forged physiological poem [2] bearing the
name of Epicharmus and used by Ennius it was forged very
late in the fifth or else during the fourth century, by some one
well acquainted with Euripides, or at least with the scientific
theorists from whom Euripides drew. This would equally
account for a third pair of passages quoted by Kaibel:

Eur. *Suppl.* 531:

$$\text{ἐάσαθ' ἤδη γῆ καλυφθῆναι νεκρούς,}$$
$$\text{ὅθεν δ' ἕκαστον εἰς τὸ σῶμ' ἀφίκετο}$$
$$\text{ἐνταῦθ' ἀνελθεῖν, πνεῦμα μὲν πρὸς αἰθέρα,}$$
$$\text{τὸ σῶμα δ' εἰς γῆν.}$$

Epich. fr. 245:

$$\text{συνεκρίθη καὶ διεκρίθη κἀπῆλθεν ὅθεν ἦλθεν πάλιν,}$$
$$\text{γᾶ μὲν εἰς γᾶν, πνεῦμα δ' ἄνω· τί τῶνδε χαλεπόν; οὐδὲ ἕν.}$$

Both writers evidently draw on the same ideas, which seem to
be those of Anaxagoras, but in fact neither need be supposed
to derive them from the other. The hypothesis of a fourth-
century forgery would also account for the reference to
'Epicharmus' by Menander fr. 537 (Kock):

$$\text{ὁ μὲν Ἐπίχαρμος τοὺς θεοὺς εἶναι λέγει}$$
$$\text{ἀνέμους, ὕδωρ, γῆν, ἥλιον, πῦρ, ἀστέρας—}$$

a doctrine also ascribed to Epicharmus by Vitruvius viii,
Praef. 1, and to Ennius by Varro, *de Re Rustica,* i. 4, though

---

[1] Almost the same suggestion was made by Susemihl, *Philolog.* liii,
pp. 564 ff., which I had not seen until after the above was written.

[2] Whether, if there was such a poem, it was identical with the Πολιτεία
forged by Chrysogonus, as Wilamowitz thinks, cannot be stated in view
of the want of evidence. It is not safe to base arguments on the few
lines (fr. 255-7) quoted by Clement from the Πολιτεία.

it does not seem at all impossible that the reference should be to some passage in the comedies of Epicharmus.

In fact, the case for the existence of an independent physiological poem is not at all strong. A considerable number—if not all—of the fragments ascribed by scholars to this supposed poem are passages which it is not impossible to think of as occurring in comedies. Fragment 250, on which Kaibel lays some stress, νᾶφε καὶ μεμνᾶσ' ἀπιστεῖν· ἄρθρα ταῦτα τᾶν φρενῶν is as suitable to a comedy as to a poem Περὶ φύσεως. The line νοῦς ὁρῇ καὶ νοῦς ἀκούει· τἆλλα κωφὰ καὶ τυφλά (fr. 249),[1] which is quoted by a number of writers, may well be genuine. We know that Epicharmus had some kind of controversy with Xenophanes, and the line may have been some speaker's reply to Epicharmus' οὖλος ὁρᾷ, οὖλος δὲ νοεῖ οὖλος δὲ τ' ἀκούει. (The familiarity of Epicharmus with Xenophanes is plain from fr. 173; and Aristotle, Met. iii. 1010 a 5, refers to a remark of Epicharmus against Xenophanes—fr. 252, Kaibel—which Alexander of Aphrodisias, p. 670. 1, explains ὡς 'Επιχάρμου τοῦ τῆς κωμῳδίας ποιητοῦ εἰς Ξενοφάνην βλασφημότερά τινα καὶ ἐπηρεαστικὰ εἰρηκότος, δι' ὧν εἰς ἀμαθίαν καὶ ἀγνωσίαν τῶν ὄντων σκώπτων διέβαλεν αὐτόν.) Nestle[2] greatly enlarges the list of parallels between Euripides and Epicharmus, and ascribes nearly all the fragments to the real Epicharmus. We may indeed doubt whether Euripides was really imitating or remembering Epicharmus in very many of these passages; the sentiments mostly belong to the common stock of fifth-century ideas or are such that they might easily occur to two writers independently; but he is obviously right in rejecting as a mere petitio principii,[3] and, we may add, as rather futile in itself, the statement of Kaibel that Euripides would not have quoted comedies: and it is in fact impossible to lay down a priori that this passage or that could not have found a place in the comedies of Epicharmus, who obviously was well acquainted with the

---

[1] On the history of the quotations of this line by subsequent writers, see Gerhard, Cercidea (Wiener Stud. xxxvii (1919), pp. 6–14).

[2] Philologus, Suppl. Bd. viii, 601 ff.

[3] On this see also Rohde, Psyche, ii². 258.

thoughts of the philosophers of his time. (Nestle shows
how closely some of the shorter fragments correspond with
fragments of Heracleitus; the longer ones will be discussed
later.) Kaibel's argument that Ennius is most likely to have
copied an entire poem passing under the name of Epicharmus
loses its force, when we observe that Ennius borrows
from authors as he wants them (from Epicharmus himself,
probably, fr. 172, in the *Annals*, fr. 12), and reflect that if, as
appears to have been the case, the setting of his *Epicharmus*
was a visit in a dream to the lower world, this at least is not
likely to have been the setting of the supposed physiological
poem.

On the whole, the existence of the supposed poem[1] seems
to be an unnecessary hypothesis. The parallels with Euripides,
and also all that Diogenes records of the (spurious) works,
are accounted for without it. The extant fragments of the
Πολιτεία show us at any rate that some 'physiology' was
included in the poem, and the same may have been the case
with the *Canon*; the explanation of ἰατρολογεῖ already has
been discussed.

§ 3. With regard to Diogenes' γνωμολογεῖ and Axiopistus'
forgery in the fourth century of a book of Γνῶμαι in the
name of Epicharmus, it may be safely conjectured that such
forgery was rendered plausible by the occurrence of many
sententious maxims in the comedies themselves. The fragment quoted by Diogenes Laertius iii. 12,[2] together with
a fragment[3] unknown to Kaibel, probably come from the
introduction to some similar collection or perhaps even from
a copy of Axiopistus' own book:

τεῖδ' ἔνεστι πολλὰ καὶ παντοῖα, τοῖς χρήσαιό κα
ποτὶ φίλον, ποτ' ἐχθρόν, ἐν δίκᾳ λέγων, ἐν ἁλίᾳ,

---

[1] There is no hint in antiquity of any forgeries besides the three
attributed to Chrysogonus and Axiopistus, and no doubt treated as
forgeries by Apollodorus.

[2] After, but not among, the quotations furnished by Alcimus; see
p. 372, below.

[3] *Hibeh Papyri*, I. i. The date of the papyrus is between 280 and 240 B.C.
I take the text of the fragment almost exactly from Diels, *Vorsokr.*[3],
p. 116.

B b

ποτὶ πονηρόν, ποτὶ καλόν τε κἀγαθόν, ποτὶ ξένον,
ποτὶ δύσηριν, ποτὶ πάροινον, ποτὶ βάναυσον, εἴτε τις
5 ἀλλ᾽ ἔχει κακόν τι. καὶ τούτοισι κέντρα τεῖδ᾽ ἔνο,[1]
ἐν δὲ καὶ γνῶμαι σοφαὶ τεῖδ᾽, αἷσιν εἰ πίθοιτό τις,
δεξιώτερός τε κ᾽ εἴη, βελτίων τ᾽ ἐς πάντ᾽ ἀνήρ.
κού τι πολλὰ δεῖ λέγειν, ἀλλ᾽ ἒμ μόνον, τοῦτ᾽ ὦν ἔπος
ποττὸ πρᾶγμα ποτιφέροντα τῶνδ᾽ ἀεὶ τὸ συμφέρον.
10 αἰτίαν γὰρ ἦχον, ὡς ἄλλως μὲν εἴην δέξιος,
μακρολόγος δ᾽ οὔ κα δυναίμαν ἐμ βραχεῖ γνώμας λέγειν.
ταῦτα δὴ γῶν εἰσακούσας συντίθημι τὰν τέχναν
τάνδ᾽, ὅπως εἴπῃ τις, ᾽Επίχαρμος σοφός τις ἐγένετο,
⟨πόλλ᾽ ὃς εἶπ᾽⟩ ἀστεῖα καὶ παντοῖα καθ᾽ ἓν ⟨ἔπος⟩ λέγων,
15 ⟨πεῖραν⟩ αὑταυτοῦ διδούς, ὡς καὶ β⟨ραχέα λέγειν ἔχει⟩.

Crönert[2] restores the last line somewhat differently, and
expands some very fragmentary lines which follow to suit the
context. He has no difficulty in showing that the extant
γνῶμαι attributed to Epicharmus can easily be distributed
under the headings mentioned in the early lines of this
passage, and he supposes that most of them come from this
poem. The fragment (fr. 254) quoted by Diogenes is in the
same style, and perhaps concluded the introduction:

ὡς δ᾽ ἐγὼ δοκέω—δοκέων γὰρ σάφα ἴσαμι τοῦθ᾽ ὅτι
τῶν ἐμῶν μνάμα ποκ᾽ ἐσσεῖται λόγων τούτων ἔτι.
καὶ λαβών τις αὐτὰ περιλύσας τὸ μέτρον ὃ νῦν ἔχει,
εἶμα δοὺς καὶ πορφύραν, λόγοισι ποικίλας καλοῖς,
δυσπάλαιστος αὐτὸς ἄλλους εὐπαλαίστους ἀποφανεῖ.[3]

There is no reason why such a collection should not have
contained many genuine γνῶμαι of Epicharmus, but we have
now no sure test for distinguishing the true from the false,
and Crönert's inclination to regard almost all as genuine does
not rest upon proof.[4]

---

[1] ἔνο = ἔνεστι: cf. ἔξο, Anecd. Ox. i. 160. 26.
[2] Hermes, xlvii, pp. 402 ff.
[3] Cholmeley, Theocr.², p. 421, reads ἄλλος εὐπάλαιστος.
[4] The metrical investigations of Kauz (De tetrametro trochaico, Darm-
stadt, 1913) show that in the Ψευδεπιχάρμεια taken as a whole (he
examined 69 lines) there are far fewer non-trochaic feet, and much less

III

' *Philosophical* ' *Fragments.*

It will be convenient to consider next four fragments
preserved by Diogenes Laertius which have some reference
to philosophical questions. Diogenes is quoting from the
treatise of Alcimus πρὸς Ἀμύνταν. It is generally believed
that the Alcimus quoted is the Sicilian rhetorician and
historian of the name, who was the pupil of Stilpo [1] and lived
about the end of the fourth and the beginning of the third
centuries B.C.; and that he is addressing (or controverting)
Amyntas of Heracleia, who had been a pupil of Plato and was
a mathematician. The object of Alcimus was to show that
some of Plato's most characteristic doctrines were derived
from Epicharmus—a conclusion in itself most improbable,
though Epicharmus was no doubt travestying theories which
were afterwards considered by Plato in a more developed
form. The assertion of Wilamowitz [2] that the fragments
imply a knowledge of Plato's fully developed Theory of
Ideas, and that Alcimus was therefore deceived in thinking
them the work of Epicharmus, can hardly be accepted. In

irregularity as regards caesura, than in the 116 lines certainly derived
from comedies. But of course the test is based on far too small a
number of lines in all to be of much value. Out of the 116 lines from
comedies there are 44 without any non-trochaic feet. But great caution
is necessary in making statements about the metrical technique of
Epicharmus, in view of the uncertainty of the text, especially as regards
the restored or conjectural Doric forms. Kauz does, however, disprove
successfully the suggestion of Hoffmann (*Gesch. der Gr. Sprache*, pp. 126 ff.)
that Epicharmus got his tetrameter from Phrynichus and Aeschylus, who
in fact follow different and much stricter rules. Kauz thinks that Epicharmus used the metre as he found it in popular songs.

[1] This view seems more probable than the conjecture that he was
an unknown Neoplatonist, which rests only on the fact that the Neo-
platonists tried to discover Plato's doctrines in many earlier writers.
Alcimus is mentioned as an historian by Athen. vii, p. 322 a; x, p. 441 a, b.
Schwartz (in Pauly-W. *Real-Enc.* i, col. 1544) refuses to identify the
historian with the rhetorician (Diog. II. xi. 114), and not more than high
probability can be claimed for the identification.

[2] *Gött. Gel. Anz.* 1906, p. 622.

fact the fragments, when carefully studied, do not seem to
be really parallel to Plato at all. That the quotations given
by Alcimus were taken from the comedies of Epicharmus, and
not from a separate philosophical poem, is, if not proved, at
least strongly suggested by the facts (1) that they are in
dialogue; (2) that something like parody is discernible in
them; (3) that Diogenes calls the author 'Epicharmus the
comic poet', while an anonymous commentator on Plato's
Theaetetus[1] also uses the word ἐκωμῴδησεν of the illustration
which he gives from Epicharmus of the point which is also
elaborated in the long fragment quoted by Alcimus.

§ 1. This first fragment (fr. 170), which deals mainly with
the problem how that which changes can yet retain its identity,
is given as one fragment in the text of Diogenes,[2] but Diels
divides it into two, the first of which ends with l. 6 and
speaks of the eternity of the gods and the unchangingness of
νοητά, while the second emphasizes the ceaseless mutability
of all particular things, which is such that nothing remains
itself from one moment to another. Diels thinks that the
first alludes to the theory of the Eleatics, the second to that
of Heracleitus, whereas most scholars have been content to
treat the whole as alluding to Heracleitus, and Rostagni[3]
thinks that it is Pythagorean doctrine which is travestied.
The truth seems to be (as this diversity of views suggests)
that the allusions are not sufficiently specific to be definitely

---

[1] *Berliner Klassikertexte*, ii, p. 47 (below, p. 375, n. 2).

[2] Diog. Laert. III. xii πολλὰ δὲ καὶ παρ' Ἐπιχάρμου τοῦ κωμῳδιοποιοῦ
προσωφέληται (sc. Πλάτων) τὰ πλεῖστα μεταγράψας, καθά φησιν Ἄλκιμος ἐν
τοῖς πρὸς Ἀμύνταν, ἅ ἐστι τέτταρα. ἔνθα καὶ ἐν τῷ πρώτῳ φησὶ ταῦτα, Φαίνεται
δὲ καὶ Πλάτων πολλὰ τῶν Ἐπιχάρμου λέγων· σκεπτέον δέ. ὁ Πλάτων φησὶν
αἰσθητὸν μὲν εἶναι τὸ μηδέποτε ἐν τῷ ποιῷ μηδὲ ἐν τῷ πόσῳ διάμενον, ἀλλ' ἀεὶ
ῥέον καὶ μεταβάλλον· ὡς ἐξ ὧν ἄν τις ἀνέλῃ τὸν ἀριθμόν, τούτων οὔτε ἴσων οὔτε
τινῶν οὔτε ποσῶν οὔτε ποιῶν ὄντων. ταῦτα δ' ἐστὶν ὧν ἀεὶ γένεσις, οὐσία δὲ
μηδέποτε πέφυκε. νοητὸν δὲ ἐξ οὗ μηδὲν ἀπογίγνεται μηδὲ προσγίγνεται. τοῦτο
δ' ἐστὶν ἡ τῶν ἀϊδίων φύσις, ἣν ὁμοίαν τε καὶ τὴν αὐτὴν ἀεὶ συμβέβηκεν εἶναι.
καὶ μὴν ὅ γε Ἐπίχαρμος περὶ τῶν αἰσθητῶν καὶ νοητῶν ἐναργῶς εἴρηκεν. " ἀλλ'
ἀεί κτλ." Plato himself refers to Epicharmus' discussion of the subject in
Theaet. 152 d, e (quoted above, p. 359).

[3] *Il verbo di Pitagora*, chs. ii, iii. See above, p. 359.

referred to any one school. As regards the second portion
(lines 7 ff.), all schools of philosophy or science were familiar
with the spectacle of continual change. Heracleitus had, no
doubt, particularly emphasized this, and many of his fragments are variations on the theme πάντα χωρεῖ καὶ οὐδὲν
μένει: but, as Rostagni points out, Heracleitus admits no
exceptions to the general flux and interchange of opposites,
not even the gods, and at the same time he points to an
underlying and permanent ἁρμονία, whereas in Epicharmus
the gods and τάδε (the meaning of which we shall presently
discuss) are exceptions to the flux, and there is no hint
(though in view of the fragmentary nature of the passage
no stress must be laid on this) of any ἁρμονία.[1] So far as
any contrast of αἰσθητά and νοητά, such as Alcimus had in
view, had been formulated at this time, it may be found either
(as Rostagni thinks) in the Pythagorean theory of numbers or
(as Diels supposes) in the Eleatic contrast of Appearance and
Reality: but probably the contrast, like the perception of the
mutability of αἰσθητά, was a common topic in the discussions
of all schools. In the first part of the fragment (lines 1–6) the
principal speaker denies some of the statements of poetical
cosmogonies, and affirms the eternity of the gods and of τάδε
in l. 2. The text of the fragment is as follows:[2]

A. ἀλλ' ἀεί τοι θεοὶ παρῆσαν, χὐπέλιπον οὐ πώποκα,
  τάδε δ' ἀεὶ πάρεσθ' ὁμοῖα, διά τε τῶν αὐτῶν ἀεί.
B. ἀλλὰ λέγεται μὰν χάος πρᾶτον γενέσθαι τῶν θεῶν.
A. πῶς δέ κα; μὴ ἔχον γ' ἀπὸ τίνος μηδ' ἐς ὅ τι πρᾶτον
  μόλοι.

---

[1] The attempt of Rostagni to show that Heraclitus' book could not
have been published until shortly before Epicharmus' death is not conclusive. It rests on the assumption, made first by Zeller, that Hermo-
dorus, whose exile from Ephesus is mentioned by Heracleitus, would not
have been exiled before the collapse of the Persian supremacy—an
assumption to which Burnet (*Early Gk. Phil.*[3], p. 130) sufficiently replies—
together with the further assumption that Epicharmus cannot have lived
beyond 470 B.C. and must have been born some ninety years earlier.

[2] I print the text almost as given by Diels, *Vorsokr.*[3], pp. 113-14, with
a few necessary critical notes.

B. οὐκ ἄρ' ἔμολε πρᾶτον οὐθέν;
5 A.   οὐδὲ μὰ Δία δεύτερον
τῶνδε γ' ὧν ἀμὲς νῦν ὧδε λέγομες, ἀλλ' ἀεὶ τάδ' ἦς . . .
⟨αἰ⟩ πὸτ ἀριθμόν τις πέρισσον, αἰ δὲ λῆς πὸτ ἄρτιον,
πότθεμεν λῇ ψᾶφον ἢ καὶ τᾶν ὑπαρχουσᾶν λαβεῖν,
ἦ δοκεῖ κά τοί γ' ⟨ἔθ'⟩ ὡὐτὸς εἶμεν;
B.   οὐκ ἐμίν γά κα.
10 A. οὐδὲ μὰν οὐδ' αἰ ποτὶ μέτρον παχυαῖον πότθεμεν
λῇ τις ἕτερον μᾶκος ἢ τοῦ πρόσθ' ἐόντος ἀποταμεῖν,
ἔτι χ' ὑπάρχοι κῆνο τὸ μέτρον;
B.   οὐ γάρ.
A.   ὧδε νῦν ὅρη
καὶ τὸς ἀνθρώπως· ὁ μὲν γὰρ αὔξεθ', ὁ δέ γα μὰν φθίνει,
ἐν μεταλλαγᾷ δὲ πάντες ἐντὶ πάντα τὸν χρόνον.
15 ὃ δὲ μεταλλάσσει κατὰ φύσιν κοὔποκ' ἐν ταὐτῷ μένει
ἕτερον εἴη κα τόδ' ἤδη τοῦ παρεξεστακότος.
καὶ τὺ δὴ κἀγὼ χθὲς ἄλλοι καί νυν ἄλλοι τελέθομες,
καὖθις ἄλλοι κοὔποχ' ὡὐτοὶ καττὸν ⟨αὐτὸν αὖ⟩ λόγον.

Notes. 2. διὰ δὲ Kühn : διά τε MSS. 4. textum G. Hermann : πῶς δέ
κ' ἀμήχανον γ', MSS. 6. ἀλλ' ἀεὶ ταδ' ἦς, Bergk : μέλλει ταδ' εἶναι vel ἦναι
MSS., ἦναι ex ἦς καὶ ortum fuisse putat Diels, hoc autem καὶ fragmentum
alterum introduxisse. 7. πὸτ Bergk : τὸν MSS. 9. κά τοί γ' ⟨ἔθ'⟩
ὡὐτὸς, Kaibel : κάτοικ' ἑαυτός vel κάτοι καὶ ὁ αὐτός MSS. 16. κά τόδ' ἤδη,
Cobet : ωδὴ vel κατοδὴ vel καὶ τὸ δ' εἰ MSS.

As regards the two difficulties—the meaning of τάδε, and
the division of the fragment—a few words will suffice.
(1) Diels thinks that τάδε are αἰσθητά—'die Vorgänge hier
(in der Natur)'. But the words of Alcimus strongly suggest
that τάδε must be τὰ ἀΐδια or νοητά, and the only difficulty in
this is the δέ, which seems to involve a contrast with the
previous line : there may, however, be a contrast between the
gods and the other ἀΐδια—a contrast perhaps carried over
from the preceding context; or the δέ may be quasi-infer-
ential, 'and so'. The contrast cannot really be between gods
and αἰσθητά, for in reference to the latter the line would be
plainly untrue and inconsistent with the second part of the
fragment. (Hence some scholars prefer to emend to τάδε δ'

οὔποκα πάρεσθ' ὅμοια : but then διά τε or διὰ δέ for οὐδὲ διά
is very awkward.) If δέ is really felt to be an objection, it
would be easy to read τάδε τ' ἀεὶ πάρεσθ' ὅμοια.[1]

(2) Diels' suggestion that the ἧναι of some MSS. arises out
of ἧς (belonging to l. 6) and καί (belonging to the prose of
Alcimus) is ingenious and may be right. It certainly gets rid
of a rather abrupt transition; but the text of the line is
really very uncertain, and it seems best to suspend judgement on the proposed division.

It happens that the point of this passage of Epicharmus is
made plain by Plutarch[2] and by the anonymous commentator

---

[1] διὰ τῶν αὐτῶν ἀεί is perhaps more easily interpreted as ὡσαύτως ἔχοντα
ἀεί than as implying causation. This interpretation was first suggested
by Leopold Schmidt, *Quaestiones Epicharmeae*, pp. 29, 30, who finds
parallel usages in Hippocrates, though it is not approved by Lorenz,
p. 109. Lorenz, however, is clearly right in rejecting the interpretation
of τάδε as meaning the four elements.

[2] Plut. *de sera num. vind.*, p. 559 b μᾶλλον δ' ὅλως ταῦτά γε τοῖς Ἐπι-
χαρμείοις ἔοικεν, ἐξ ὧν ὁ αὐξανόμενος ἀνέφυ τοῖς σοφισταῖς λόγος· ὁ γὰρ λαβὼν
πάλαι τὸ χρέος νῦν οὐκ ὀφείλει γεγονὼς ἕτερος. ὁ δὲ κληθεὶς ἐπὶ δεῖπνον ἐχθὲς
ἄκλητος ἥκει τήμερον· ἄλλος γάρ ἐστιν. Cf. *de comm. notit.*, p. 1083 a ὁ τοίνυν
περὶ αὐξήσεως λόγος ἐστὶ μὲν ἀρχαῖος· ἠρώτηται γάρ, ὥς φησι Χρύσιππος, ὑπ'
Ἐπιχάρμου. Plutarch's language a few lines after the last quoted passage
is very like that of Epicharmus : ὁ μὲν γὰρ λόγος ἁπλοῦς ἐστι καὶ τὰ λήμματα
συγχωροῦσιν οὗτοι (sc. οἱ Στωικοί), τὰς ἐν μέρει πάσας οὐσίας ῥεῖν καὶ φέρεσθαι,
τὰ μὲν ἐξ αὐτῶν μεθιείσας, τὰ δέ ποθεν ἐπιόντα προσδεχομένας· οἷς δὲ πρόσεστι
καὶ ἄπεισιν ἀριθμοῖς ἢ πλήθεσιν ταὐτὰ μὴ διαμένειν, ἀλλ' ἕτερα γίγνεσθαι ταῖς
εἰρημέναις προσόδοις ἐξαλλαγὴν τῆς οὐσίας λαμβανούσης· αὐξήσεις δὲ καὶ
φθίσεις οὐ κατὰ δίκην ὑπὸ συνηθείας ἐκνενικῆσθαι τὰς μεταβολὰς ταύτας λέγεσθαι,
γενέσεις δὲ καὶ φθορὰς μᾶλλον αὐτὰς ὀνομάζεσθαι προσῆκον, ὅτι τοῦ καθεστῶτος
εἰς ἕτερον ἐκβιάζουσιν. For the special application of the λόγος to human
existence, see Plut. *de tranq. anim.*, p. 473 d οἱ μὲν γὰρ ἐν ταῖς σχολαῖς τὰς
αὐξήσεις ἀναιροῦντες, ὡς τῆς οὐσίας ἐνδελεχῶς ῥεούσης, λόγῳ ποιοῦσιν ἡμῶν
ἕκαστον ἄλλον ἑαυτοῦ καὶ ἄλλον. Plut. also states (*Vit. Thes.* xxiii) that
philosophers used to illustrate the λόγος by the ship which Theseus
repaired with so many new planks that some said it was no longer the
same ship. The Ἐπιχάρμειος λόγος (Suidas, s. v.) was probably the
αὐξανόμενος λόγος under another name. The anonymous commentator
on the *Theaetetus* 152 e (*Berl. Klass. Texte*, ii, col. 71. 12 ff.) writes: Ἐπίχαρμος ὁ (ὁμιλή)σας τοῖς Πυθα(γορείοις) ἄλλα τε ἐπινενόηκεν δ(εινὰ τ(όν τε
περὶ το)ῦ αὐξο(μένου λόγον) ἐφοδ(εύει). The next few lines are very fragmentary; then (l. 24) he goes on: οὐσίαι ἄλλ(οτε ἄλλαι) γίνονται (κατὰ

on the *Theaetetus*, who enable us to see how such a passage could have got into a comedy. Epicharmus, we are told, used, and in fact invented, the αὐξανόμενος λόγος—the 'fallacy of the sorites' of later logicians, so called from the use of a heap (σωρός) of corn as the favourite illustration of it. (How many grains of corn must be taken away before a heap of corn will cease to be a heap? What if that number less one be taken away? and so on.) Epicharmus applied it to personality. How much change will make a man a different person? And he appears to have argued that a debtor who borrowed money yesterday does not owe it to-day, since he is already a different man from the borrower; and that the man whom you invited yesterday to dinner may be turned away when he arrives to-day, ἄλλος γάρ ἐστιν: while the commentator on the *Theaetetus* tells the story of a man who refused to pay a promised subscription on the ground that he was a different person : the would-be collector struck him and demanded the debt, but he rejoined that the man who had struck him was no longer the same as the claimant. It is obvious that there is here some pretty material for comedy. We have a quack-philosopher using subtleties of argument to justify him in playing tricks on his neighbours—a character very like Socrates in the *Clouds* of Aristophanes, and still more like what Socrates makes of Strepsiades; and there is reason to think that such a character-type persisted from the time of the old Peloponnesian buffoonery, which contributed much both to Attic and to Syracusan comedy, down to the Middle Comedy, when the philosopher was frequently presented in this guise.[1]

συν)εχῆ ῥύσιν. καὶ ἐκωμῴδησεν αὐτὸ ἐπὶ τοῦ ἀπαιτουμένου συμβολὰς καὶ ἀρνουμένου τοῦ αὐτοῦ εἶναι διὰ τὸ τὰ μὲν προγεγενῆσθαι τὰ δὲ ἀπεληλυθέναι, ἐπεὶ δὲ ὁ ἀπαιτῶν ἐτύπτησεν αὐτὸν καὶ ἐνεκαλεῖτο, πάλιν κἀκείνου φάσκοντος ἕτερον μὲν εἶναι τὸν τετυπτηκότα, ἕτερον δὲ. τὸν ἐγκαλούμενον. Both Plato and his commentator are plainly thinking of the comedies of Epicharmus, not of a philosophical poem.

[1] Another rhetorical figure, ἐποικοδόμησις, is said to have been invented by Epicharmus (*Arist. Rhet.* i, p. 1365 a 10 ; *De Gen. An.*, i, p. 724 a 29). It is illustrated by fragm. 148 (Kaibel). See below, p. 400.

It should be added that the attempt made by some scholars [1]
to prove this fragment to be a Sophistic forgery is rightly
answered by Körte,[2] who points out the contrast of this
vigorous and dramatic dialogue with the tone of the spurious
γνῶμαι of later forgers.

§ 2. The second fragment (fr. 171) which Alcimus quoted
he supposed to foreshadow the Platonic theory of ideas and
of the Idea of Good.[3] The chief speaker does in fact speak
of 'the Good' as a 'thing in itself'; not, however, in the
Platonic sense of a self-existent Idea, but simply in the sense
of something distinguishable from the person who knows
what 'good' is, just as any art is distinguishable from the
artist.

A. ἆρ' ἐστὶν αὔλησίς τι πρᾶγμα;   B. πάνυ μὲν ὦν.
A. ἄνθρωπος ὦν αὔλησίς ἐστιν;   B. οὐδαμῶς.
A. φέρ' ἴδω, τί δ' αὐλητάς; τίς εἶμέν τοι δοκεῖ;
   ἄνθρωπος, ἢ οὐ γάρ;   B. πάνυ μὲν ὦν.   A. οὐκῶν
   δοκεῖς
5 οὕτως ἔχειν καὶ περί ⟨γα⟩ τὠγαθοῦ; τό γα
   ἀγαθὸν τὸ πρᾶγμ' εἶμεν καθ' αὐθ', ὅστις δέ κα
   εἰδῇ μαθὼν τῆν', ἀγαθὸς ἤδη γίγνεται.
   ὥσπερ γάρ ἐστ' αὔλησιν αὐλητὰς μαθὼν
   ἢ ὄρχησιν ὀρχηστάς τις ἢ πλοκεὺς πλοκὰν
10 ἢ πᾶν γ' ὁμοίως τῶν τοιούτων ὅ τι τὺ λῇς,
   οὐκ αὐτὸς εἴη κα τέχνα, τεχνικός γα μαν.

(In l. 6 τὸ πρᾶγμα is Kaibel's correction for τὸ δὲ πρᾶγμα:
perhaps τι πρᾶγμ' is what Epicharmus wrote.)

We have here no Plutarch to guide us to Epicharmus' point:
the argument is in part not unlike some passages in Plato's
Hippias Maior (e. g. 287 c), and Diels thinks that the fragment, though not open to suspicion so far as its language is

---

[1] e. g. Schwartz, in Pauly-W. *Real-Enc.* i. 1543.
[2] Bursian's *Jahresber.* 1911, pp. 230 ff.
[3] Diog. Laert. l. c. διὸ καί φησιν (sc. Πλάτων) ἐν τῇ φύσει τὰς ἰδέας ἑστάναι
καθάπερ παραδείγματα, τὰ δ' ἄλλα ταύταις ἐοικέναι, τούτων ὁμοιώματα καθε-
στῶτα. ὁ τοίνυν Ἐπίχαρμος περί τε τἀγαθοῦ καὶ περὶ τῶν ἰδεῶν οὕτω λέγει,
"ἆρ' ἐστὶν κτλ."

concerned, is possibly (in view of its contents and its catechetical form) the work of a fourth-century writer; he
suggests that it is an interpolation inserted by Dionysius in
the comedies of Epicharmus which he had reproduced on the
stage for Plato's benefit. (Dionysius' interest in Epicharmus
is reflected in Suidas' statement that he wrote περὶ τῶν
ποιημάτων Ἐπιχάρμου.) But though the dialogue is very
like some of those put in the mouth of Socrates, it is
certainly not one which Epicharmus could not have written:
the parallelism with Plato's *Apology* 27 b, which Diels thinks
the forger had in mind, is really very superficial, if carefully
examined, and the points of the externally parallel phrases
are not the same. There seems to be no sufficient reason for
judging the fragment to be spurious, and it is scarcely likely
that, if this or any of the other fragments had been forged
after the publication of Plato's writings, they could have
imposed upon writers so little junior to Plato, and so well-
versed in the literature of the time as presumably both
Alcimus and Amyntas must have been. It is tempting to
suppose that the argument in the fragment led to some
subtle travesty of the theory that knowledge produces virtue;
but it would probably be an anachronism to date the discussion
of this topic so far back as the time of Epicharmus, and for
the present we must be content to be ignorant of the context.

§ 3. The two other fragments were quoted by Alcimus as
parallels to Plato's theory of animal life and instinct:[1]

fr. 172 (Kaibel):

> Εὔμαιε, τὸ σοφόν ἐστιν οὐ καθ᾽ ἓν μόνον,
> ἀλλ᾽ ὅσσαπερ ζῇ, πάντα καὶ γνώμαν ἔχει.
> καὶ γὰρ τὸ θῆλυ τῶν ἀλεκτορίδων γένος,

---

[1] Diog. Laert. l. c. Πλάτων ἐν τῇ περὶ ἰδεῶν ὑπολήψει φησίν, "Εἴπερ ἐστὶ μνήμη,
τὰς ἰδέας ἐν τοῖς οὖσιν ὑπάρχειν διὰ τὸ τὴν μνήμην ἠρεμοῦντός τινος καὶ μένοντος
εἶναι· μένειν δὲ οὐδὲν ἕτερον ἢ τὰς ἰδέας. τίνα γὰρ ἂν τρόπον, φησί, διεσώζετο
τὰ ζῷα μὴ τῆς ἰδέας ἐφαπτόμενα, καὶ πρὸς τοῦτο τὸν νοῦν φυσικῶς εἰληφότα; "
νῦν δὲ μνημονεύει τῆς ὁμοιότητός τε καὶ τροφῆς, ὁποία τίς ἐστιν αὐτοῖς, ἐνδεικνύ
μενα διότι πᾶσι τοῖς ζῴοις ἔμφυτός ἐστιν ἡ τῆς ὁμοιότητος θεωρία· διὸ καὶ τῶν
ὁμοφύλων αἰσθάνεται. πῶς οὖν ὁ Ἐπίχαρμος; (the two fragments follow).
Alcimus supposes Epicharmus to foreshadow Plato, *Parmen.*, p. 129; of

αἰ λῆς καταμαθεῖν, ἀτενὲς οὐ τίκτει τέκνα
5 ζῶντ᾿, ἀλλ᾿ ἐπῴζει καὶ ποιεῖ ψυχὰν ἔχειν.
τὸ δὲ σοφὸν ἀ φύσις τόδ᾿ οἶδεν ὡς ἔχει
μόνα· πεπαίδευται γὰρ αὐταυτᾶς ὕπο.

fr. 173 (do.) :

θαυμαστὸν οὐδὲν ἀμὲ ταῦθ᾿ οὕτως ἔχειν
καὶ ἀνδάνειν αὐτοῖσιν αὐτοὺς καὶ δοκεῖν
καλῶς πεφύκειν· καὶ γὰρ ἀ κύων κυνὶ
κάλλιστον εἶμεν φαίνεται, καὶ βῶς βοΐ,
ὄνος δ᾿ ὄνῳ κάλλιστον, ὗς δὲ θὴν ὑΐ.

The fragments affirm the possession of reason or instinct by
animals, and the attraction of like to like—neither point
requiring any great depth of philosophical thought; the
second seems to be reminiscent of Xenophanes, fr. 16,

ἀλλ᾿ εἰ χεῖρας ἔχον βόες ἠδὲ λέοντες,
ὡς γράψαι χείρεσσι καὶ ἔργα τελεῖν ἅπερ ἄνδρες,
καί κε θεῶν ἰδέας ἔγραφον καὶ σώματ᾿ ἐποίευν
τοιαῦθ᾿, οἷόν περ καὐτοὶ δέμας εἶχον ⟨ἕκαστοι⟩,
ἵπποι μέν θ᾿ ἵπποισι, βόες δέ τε βουσὶν ὅμοια.

The vein of parody in the two fragments is clear enough,
and the mention of Eumaeus in the first has led to the
natural conjecture that it, or both, came from the Ὀδυσσεὺς
Ναυαγός. There is obviously no difficulty in supposing that
the two passages fitted well into the dialogue of one of
Epicharmus' plays, and possibly the speaker again may have
been some one in the character of a quack wise-man, as is even
more probable in the case of the two other fragments.

course he does not really do so. The first passage is perhaps imitated
by Ennius, *Annals*, i, fr. 12 (Vahlen):

> Ova parire solet genus pinnis condecoratum,
> non animam ; et post inde venit divinitus pullis
> ipsa anima.

IV

The Plays and Fragments.

Before attempting any general description of the Comedy of Epicharmus it will be well to survey briefly the extant remains.

§ 1. A large number of the plays were evidently mythological burlesques, and it is clear that the two favourite heroes were Odysseus and Heracles; cunning and violence (the latter combined with voracity) are natural themes for comedy of a simple type.

The Ὀδυσσεὺς Αὐτόμολος dealt probably with the story of Odysseus' entry into Troy, disguised as a beggar, in order to obtain information from the enemy—a task which (according to *Odyssey* iv. 240–64) he performed, thanks to Helen's connivance, with great success. In the version of the story given by Epicharmus, Odysseus seems to have been less heroic, i. e. if the papyrus fragment which Kaibel prints as fr. 99 is really from this play.[1] According to this it appears that the Achaeans had commissioned him to go into Troy as a spy, but thinking discretion the better part of valour, he proposed to pretend to have gone there, and to give an eloquent account of what he professed to have seen. The text, as printed by Kaibel, is as follows:

τῆλ' ἀπε]νθὼν τεῖδε θωκησῶ τε καὶ λεξοῦ[μ' ὅπως
πιστά κ' ε]ἴμειν ταῦτα καὶ τοῖς δεξιωτέροι[ς δοκῇ.
"τοῖς θεοῖς] ἐμὶν δοκεῖτε πάγχυ καὶ κατὰ τρόπ[ον
καὶ ἐοικό]τως ἐπεύξασθ', αἴ τις ἐνθυμεῖν γ[α λῇ,
ὅσσ' ἐγών] γ' ὤφειλον ἐνθ[ὼ]ν ὗσπερ ἐκελή[σασθ' ἐμὲ
τῶν παρ' ὑμέ]ων ἀγαθικῶν κακὰ προτιμάσαι θ' [ἅμα
ἅμα τε κίν]δυνον τελέσσαι καὶ κλέος θεῖον [λαβεῖν
πολεμίω]ν μολὼν ἐς ἄστυ, πάντα δ' εὖ σαφα[νέως
πυθόμε]νος δίοις τ' Ἀχαιοῖς παιδί τ' Ἀτρέος φί[λῳ
ἂψ ἀπαγγ]εῖλαι τὰ τηνεῖ καὐτὸς ἀσκηθὴς [μολεῖν.

---

[1] Gomperz, *Pap. Erzherzog Rainer*, v. 1, first printed the fragment: Blass (*Fleck. Jahrb.* 1889, p. 257) discusses it and the scholia attached. The latter are very defective, but the words πόρρω καθεδοῦμαι καὶ προσποιήσομαι πάντα διαπεπρᾶχθαι appear to be certain.

In this fragment the hero is evidently delivering a soliloquy in which he is rehearsing his speech; but the course of the argument can only be conjectured.

Another fragment of the play (fr. 100) is interesting as showing that the introduction of contemporary allusions into a heroic setting, which was so favourite a device of the Old and Middle Comedy at Athens, was one of the resources of Epicharmus:

> δέλφακά τε τῶν γειτόνων
> τοῖς Ἐλευσινίοις φυλάσσων δαιμονίως ἀπώλεσα,
> οὐχ ἑκών· καὶ ταῦτα δή με συμβολατεύειν ἔφα
> τοῖς Ἀχαιοῖσιν προδιδόμειν τ' ὤμνυέ με τὸν δέλφακα.

The speaker has lost the sucking-pig which he was rearing for the Eleusinian mysteries, and complains that he is accused of betraying it to the Achaeans. (συμβολατεύειν apparently means 'to barter', see Hesych. s. v.) In fr. 101 we have personifications of Peace and Moderation:

> ἁ δ' Ἀσυχία χαρίεσσα γυνὰ
> καὶ Σωφροσύνας πλατίον οἰκεῖ.

(πλατίον = Attic πλησίον.) The fragment is interesting as attesting the use of anapaestic dimeters in the play.

No fragment of the Ὀδυσσεὺς Ναυαγός is preserved, unless fr. 172, 173, in the first of which the name of Eumaeus is preserved, belonged to this play, and the only information we have about it is to the effect that the poet mentioned in it (as also in the Ἀλκυονεύς) the name of Diomos, a Sicilian shepherd who invented βουκολιασμός (Athen. xiv, p. 619 a, b). But the character of the shipwrecked Odysseus persisted in the West, and Athenaeus, i. 20 a, mentions an Italian mimus (no doubt a φλύαξ)[1] ὃς καὶ Κύκλωπα εἰσήγαγε τερετίζοντα καὶ ναυαγὸν Ὀδυσσέα σολοικίζοντα.

---

[1] Cf. Reich, *Mimus*, i, p. 233. Whether the vase-painting reproduced by Heydemann, Phlyaken Darstellungen (*Arch. Jahrb.* i, p. 299), and von Salis, *de Doriensium ludorum in Comoedia Attica vestigiis*, p. 10, really represents Odysseus shipwrecked is uncertain. Von Salis thinks it represents his welcome by the Phaeacian king and queen. If so, either it does not depict the same event as the play of Epicharmus, or

Odysseus was also the hero of the Σειρῆνες. A hexameter parody-line (fr. 123), quoted as from Epicharmus by the on scholiast Homer, *Iliad* xix. 1, probably belongs to this play:

λαοὶ τοξοχίτωνες, ἀκούετε Σειρηνάων,

though it is difficult to assign any meaning to τοξοχίτωνες. Besides this, only a few lines of dialogue remain, in which one speaker enumerates the luxuries which he had enjoyed (perhaps in the Siren's island), and is interrupted by ejaculations of misery from his companion, probably at the thought of what he had missed. (The association of some such luxuries with the Sirens is attested also by the fragments of the Σειρῆνες of the comic poets Theopompus and Nicophon.) The fragment (fr. 124) [1] runs:

A. πρωὶ μέν γ᾽ ἀτενὲς ἀπ᾽ ἀοῦς ἀφύας ἀπεπυρίζομες
   στρογγύλας, καὶ δελφακίνας ὀπτὰ κρέα καὶ πωλύπους,
   καὶ γλυκύν γ᾽ ἐπ᾽ ὦν ἐπίομες οἶνον.
B.   οἰβοιβοῖ τάλας.
A. περί γά μαν αἴκλου τί κά τις καὶ λέγοι;
B.   φοῦ τῶν κακῶν.
A. †ὃ καὶ† πάρα τρίγλα τε μία παχεῖα κἀμίαι δύο
   διατετμαμέναι μέσαι, φάσσαι τε τοσσαῦται παρῆν
   σκόρπιοί τε.

The principal speaker may have been Odysseus, who, in that case, must have passed some time with the Sirens. Another possibility is that the ejaculations came from the hero bound to the mast, and that the other speaker is a Siren.

The Φιλοκτήτας is represented only by one intelligible line, οὐκ ἔστι διθύραμβος ὄκχ᾽ ὕδωρ πίῃς (fr. 132),[2] and two which are corrupt; probably the cunning Odysseus had some part in it: but how the dithyramb came in we cannot tell.

the fragment in which Eumaeus is mentioned does not belong to the play.

[1] ap. Athen. vii, p. 277 f. If ἀφύαι were στρογγύλαι, 'rounded' or 'spherical', they must have been something different from any of the fishes usually identified with ἀφύαι (anchovy, sardine, *Motella glauca*, &c.).

[2] Vid. supr., p. 19.

Of the Κύκλωψ only three scraps survive:

— ναὶ τὸν Ποτιδᾶν, κοιλότερος ὄλμου πολύ (fr. 81, readings
   uncertain)
— χορδαί τε ἁδύ, ναὶ μὰ Δία, χὠ κωλεός (fr. 82)
— φέρ' ἐγχέας εἰς τὸ σκύφος (fr. 83),

of which the last may be the words of the Cyclops to
Odysseus.

The subject of the Τρῶες is unknown, and the text of the
two short fragments is quite uncertain. As given by Kaibel
they are as follows:

fr. 130 Ζεὺς ἄναξ, ἀν' ἄκρα ναίων Γαργάρων ἀγάννιφα.[1]
fr. 131   ἐκ παντὸς ξύλου
κλοιός τέ κα γένοιτο κῆκ τωὐτοῦ Θεός.

The first may be reminiscent of Homer; the second seems to
be a proverb.

§ 2. Five plays were constructed out of the stories about
Heracles.

The Ἀλκυονεύς treated in some way the story of Heracles'
struggle with the giant Alcyoneus; of this there were various
versions,[2] but there is nothing to show which Epicharmus
followed. The herdsman Diomos, who was credited with the
invention of βουκολιασμός, was mentioned in the play,[3] but
that he was introduced as the herdsman of Alcyoneus, as
Kaibel suggests, is only a conjecture. A local legend made
Diomos the father of Alcyoneus.[4]

The Βούσιρις dealt with a story found in Apollodorus
(II. v. 11). Busiris, son of Poseidon, was a king of Egypt,
who was recommended by a Cyprian prophet, named Phrasios
or Thrasios, to obtain prosperity after many unfruitful years

---

[1] On Zeus and Gargara see Cook's *Zeus*, ii, pp. 949 ff.

[2] See Robert, *Hermes*, xix, pp. 473 ff., and art. Alkyoneus in Pauly-W.
Real-Enc. i, col. 1581.

[3] Athen. xiv, p. 619 a, b. Here, and also in Apollon. *de pron.*, p. 80 b
(where fragment 5, αὐτότερος αὐτῶν, is quoted), the MS. reads ἐν Ἀλκυόνι,
but as no legend of Ἀλκύων is known, O. Jahn's emendation ἐν Ἀλκυονεῖ
is generally accepted.

[4] Nicander ap. Anton. Liberal. 8.

by the annual sacrifice of a stranger; Busiris promptly sacrificed the Cyprian prophet, and later on, when Heracles visited
Egypt on his way to the Hesperides, tried to make a victim
of him also: but Heracles broke his bonds and killed Busiris.
In the play he doubtless satisfied his appetite from the late
king's stores,[1] and a fragment (fr. 21)[2] describes him while
eating:

πρᾶτον μὲν αἴ κ' ἔσθοντ' ἴδοις νιν, ἀποθάνοις·
βρέμει μὲν ὁ φάρυγξ ἔνδοθ', ἀραβεῖ δ' ἀ γνάθος,
ψοφεῖ δ' ὁ γομφίος, τέτριγε δ' ὁ κυνόδων,
σίζει δὲ ταῖς ῥίνεσσι, κινεῖ δ' οὔατα.

Of the "Ηβας Γάμος, which was reproduced in a revised
form under the title of Μοῦσαι,[3] there are a good many
fragments, nearly all, however, consisting of little more than
a string of names of fish and other good things, taken
evidently from a narrative, delivered by one of the gods, of
the wedding-feast of Heracles and Hebe. To this feast,
apparently, came seven Muses; these Muses were named
after seven great rivers or lakes,[4] and probably brought the
fish of their rivers with them; they were represented as the
daughters of Pieros and Pimpleis—'Fat' and 'Fill'—if we
may distort two classic names of English poetry as Epicharmus
did those of the Pierides and Pimpleides; there is no ground
for thinking (with Welcker, Kl. Schr. i. 289 ff.) that they
appeared on the stage. Poseidon also brought cartloads of
fish in Phoenician merchant-ships (fr. 54), and Zeus had the
one specimen of the ἔλοψ, a fish of particular delicacy,
specially served for himself and his queen (fr. 71). The
Dioscuri sang (or danced) a martial strain, accompanied by

---

[1] Epicharmus is said to have used the Siceliot word ῥογοί for 'granaries'
(σιτοβόλια) in this play (Pollux, ix. 45).

[2] ap. Athen. x, p. 411 a, b. Figs. 47–9 illustrate the story.

[3] Athen. iii, p. 110 b Ἐπίχαρμος ἐν "Ηβας Γάμῳ κἀν Μούσαις· τοῦτο δὲ
τὸ δρᾶμα διασκευή ἐστι τοῦ προκειμένου.

[4] Tzetzes ad Hesiod. Op. 6 (and Cramer, Anecd. Ox. 424) Ἐπίχαρμος δὲ
ἐν τῷ "Ηβας Γάμῳ ἑπτὰ λέγει (sc. τὰς Μούσας), θυγατέρας Πιέρου καὶ Πιμπληΐδος
νύμφης, Νειλοῦν, Τριτώνην, Ἀσωποῦν, Ἑπτάπορɩν, Ἀχελωΐδα, Τιτοπλοῦν (Τιτω-
νοῦν, Kaibel) καὶ Ῥοδίαν.

FIGS. 47–48. HERACLES AND BUSIRIS

Fig. 49. HERACLES AND BUSIRIS

Athena on the flute,[1] an instrument which in more orthodox legend she had flung away in disgust.[2] Again we do not know if this took place on the stage; it is very probable that the 'comedy' was nothing but a comic narrative,[3] as, at a later time, a mime might be. Some of the descriptions of the fish and shell-fish show that the writer was an interested and accurate observer. The following will serve as specimens:

fr. 42 ἄγει δὲ παντοδαπὰ κογχύλια,
λεπάδας, ἀσπέδους, κραβύζους, κικιβάλους, τηθύνια,
κτένια, βαλάνους, πορφύρας, ὄστρεια συμμεμυκότα,
τὰ διελεῖν μέν ἐντι χαλεπά, καταφαγῆμεν δ' εὐμαρέα,
5 μύας ἀναρίτας τε κάρυκάς τε καὶ σκιφύδρια,[4]
τὰ γλυκέα μέν ἐντ' ἐπέσθειν, ἐμπαγῆμεν δ' ὀξέα,
τούς τε μακρογογγύλους σωλῆνας· ἁ μέλαινά τε
κόγχος, ἅπερ κογχοθηρᾶν παισὶν †ἐστρισώνια†·[5]
θάτεραί τε γαῖαι κόγχοι τε κἀμαθίτιδες,
10 ταὶ κακοδόκιμοί τε κηΰωνοι, τὰς ἀνδροφυκτίδας
πάντες ἀνθρώποι καλέονθ', ἁμὲς δὲ λεύκας τοὶ θεοί.

fr. 53 καρκίνοι θ' ἵκοντ' ἐχῖνοι θ', οἳ καθ' ἁλμυρὰν ἅλα
νεῖν μὲν οὐκ ἴσαντι, πεζᾷ δ' ἐμπορεύονται μόνοι.

fr. 57 ἐντὶ δ' ἀστακοὶ κολύβδαιναί τε χὡς τὰ πόδι' ἔχει
μικρά, τὰς χεῖρας δὲ μακράς, κάραβος δὲ τοὔνομα.

fr. 58 καὶ σκιφίας χρόμις θ', ὃς ἐν τῷ ἦρι κὰτ τὸν Ἀνάνιον[6]
ἰχθύων πάντων ἄριστος, ἀνθίας δὲ χείματι.

---

[1] Athen. iv, p. 184 f καὶ τὴν Ἀθηνᾶν δέ φησιν Ἐπίχαρμος ἐν Μούσαις ἐπαυλῆσαι τοῖς Διοσκούροις τὸν ἐνόπλιον; cf. Schol. Pind. *Pyth.* ii. 127.

[2] vid. supr. (ch. i, pp. 56, 70.).

[3] The use of the phrase αἱ δὲ λῇς, evidently as a 'deictic' formula, in fr. 55 does not necessarily imply that there was a second person on the stage.

[4] = ξιφύδρια, perhaps 'razor-shells'. Their other name was τελλίνη. Some also think that σωλῆνες were razor-shells. There is not enough evidence to settle the point.

[5] In the Μοῦσαι this line ran, κόγχος, ἂν τέλλιν καλέομες· ἐστὶ δ' ἄδιστον κρέας (Athen. iii, p. 85 e).

[6] The ξιφίας or σκιφίας was the sword-fish. The Ananios thus referred to as an authority on the seasons for fish was an early writer of choliambi; his exact date is uncertain; he seems to have anticipated Epicharmus (fr. 25) in using the oath 'By the Cabbage', ναὶ μὰ τὴν κράμβην (Athen. ix, p. 370 b).

C C

There are altogether more than fifty lines in this style remaining, all preserved by Athenaeus.

Only two lines remain of the Ἡρακλῆς ὁ ἐπὶ τὸν ζωστῆρα, but those not without interest (fr. 76):

⟨ὁ⟩ Πυγμαρίων λοχαγὸς ἐκ τῶν κανθάρων
τῶν μεζόνων, οὕς φαντι τὰν Αἴτναν ἔχειν.[1]

This is the earliest mention in literature both of the Pygmies and of the Αἰτναῖος κάνθαρος, which Aristophanes employed as the Pegasus of Trygaeus in the Peace. The interpretation of the phrase Αἰτναῖος κάνθαρος was uncertain in antiquity, and is still disputed. On line 73 of the Peace— εἰσήγαγ᾽ Αἰτναῖον μέγιστον κάνθαρον—the scholiast in Codex Venetus writes as follows:

ὑπερμεγέθη· μέγιστον γὰρ ὄρος ἡ Αἴτνη. ἢ ὅτι διάφοροι κάνθαροι ἐκεῖ εὑρίσκονται. ἄλλως. μεγάλοι λέγονται εἶναι κατὰ τὴν Αἴτνην κάνθαροι, μαρτυροῦσι δὲ οἱ ἐπιχώριοι. Ἐπίχαρμος ἐν Ἡρακλεῖ τῷ ἐπὶ τὸν ζωστῆρα·

⟨ὁ⟩ Πυγμαρίων λοχαγὸς ἐκ τῶν κανθάρων
τῶν μειζόνων, οὕς φαντι τὴν Αἴτνην ἔχειν.

τρόπον δέ τινα καὶ Αἰσχύλος ἐπιχώριος· λέγει δ᾽ ἐν Σισύφῳ Πετροκυλίστῃ (fr. 233),

Αἰτναῖός ἐστι κάνθαρος βίᾳ πονῶν.

Σοφοκλῆς Δαιδάλῳ·

ἀλλ᾽ οὐδὲ μὲν ἂν κάνθαρος τῶν Αἰτναίων πάντων.[2]

λέγει δὲ πάντα εἰκάζων εἰς μέγαν. Πλάτων ἐν Ἑορταῖς·

ὡς μέγα μέντοι πάνυ τὴν Αἴτνην ὄρος εἶναί φασι,
τεκμαίρου·[3]
ἔνθα τρέφεσθαι τὰς κανθαρίδας τῶν ἀνθρώπων λόγος
ἐστιν
οὐδὲν ἐλάττους.

[1] Van Leeuwen, Mnemos. xxxv (1907), p. 273, suggests πυγμάριον εἰ λοχαγὸς κτλ., and no doubt the restoration of the missing syllable is uncertain. ⟨ὁ⟩ Πυγμαρίων is due to Crusius.
[2] Pearson, Soph. fr. 162, gives the original text of the fragment as ἀλλ᾽ οὐδὲ μὲν δὴ κάνθαρος | τῶν Αἰτναίων γε πάντως.
[3] The last three words of the line are evidently corrupt.

ἢ ἀντὶ τοῦ μέγαν ὡς τὴν Αἴτνην· ἢ ὅτι οἱ Αἰτναῖοι ἵπποι
διαβόητοι καὶ τὸν δρόμον ἀξιόλογοι, καὶ τὰ ζεύγη ἐπαίνετα.[1]
καὶ Πίνδαρός φησι

ἀλλ᾽ ἀπὸ τῆς ἀγλαοκάρπου Σικελίας ὄχημα.

To the passages quoted by the scholiast must be added
Soph. *Ichneutae* 300:

ἀλλ᾽ ὡς κεράστης κάνθαρος δῆτ᾽ ἐστὶν Αἰτναῖος φύην;

The scholiast evidently hesitates between the interpretation
'as big as Aetna', or 'as fine as an Aetnaean horse'; and
modern writers improve on the second suggestion by supposing
κάνθαρον in Aristophanes to be παρὰ προσδοκίαν for κανθήλιον
or κάνθωνα.[2] If the phrase only occurred in Aristophanes this
would be possible, but the passage of Epicharmus excludes
this interpretation, while κεράστης in the *Ichneutae* cannot
be explained by any reference to horses, and is very appropriate to certain large beetles. And further, the association
of a real beetle (not merely a pun-beetle) with the town—not
the mountain—of Aetna is proved by the occurrence of a
scarab on a tetradrachm of Aetna, between 476 and 461 B.C.[3]
But why such a beetle should have been especially associated
with the town of Aetna we do not know. It is conjectured by
von Vürtheim[4] that a city, whose inhabitants were connected
by origin with Chalcis and Naxos, would, like those cities,
have been devoted to Dionysus and to the Libyan Ammon,
and that the κάνθαρος, or wine-cup, which appears on the
coins of those cities, was replaced on the coinage of Aetna
through a kind of insulting jest on the part of Hiero, by a
scavenger-beetle; but this seems very far-fetched and improbable. It is perhaps more likely that the place may have
been (perhaps only temporarily) inhabited by large scavenger

[1] So van Leeuwen for ἐπαίνετοι.
[2] Van Leeuwen, l. c.; cf. Pearson, l. c. That Soph. *Oed. Col.* 312
describes Ismene as Αἰτναίας ἐπὶ | πώλου βεβῶσαν has not, I think, any
necessary bearing on the point. There was no doubt a fine breed of
horses associated with Aetna; but it may be doubted whether they were
ever called κανθήλιος or κάνθων, which seems to mean a 'pack-ass'.
[3] Hill, *Historical Greek Coins*, p. 43, pl. iii. 22, &c.
[4] *Mnemosyne*, xxxv (1907), pp. 335-6.

beetles, possibly imported by accident or design from Africa, and that the fact may have been notorious just at this time. This seems rather more likely than that there was a special breed of scarabaei at Aetna, as Jebb suggests;[1] if there was such a breed it is now extinct.

Crusius conjectures that Heracles in this play was presented or described as fighting with a race of pygmies, riding on beetles' backs, and refers to Philostratus,[2] by whom the story is told, how the pygmies in Libya set upon Heracles in his sleep after his victory over Antaeus, and how he swept them all into his lion-skin and carried them off. There is no mention of beetles as steeds in Philostratus, and Athenaeus[3] quotes a story to the effect that 'that small infantry warred on by cranes' in India rode on partridges; but it is quite possible that Epicharmus used some early variety of the tale, or invented one for himself.

It is uncertain where the scene of the play was laid. It is generally assumed to have been in Sicily, not in Libya; and Epicharmus is supposed to have invented a Sicilian pygmy race on the analogy of the African; and this is not impossible, though it would have been as easy for him to transport an Αἰτναῖος κάνθαρος to Libya, as for Aristophanes to bring one to Athens. It is commonly believed that the 'girdle' of which Heracles was in quest was the girdle of Hippolyte, queen of the Amazons, which Heracles obtained by violence at the bidding of Eurystheus; the scene of that adventure was on the Thermodon or in Scythia. But it is possible that Epicharmus was thinking of the girdle of Oeolyce, daughter of Briareus, the seizure of which was treated by Ibycus;[4] and that the scene of Heracles' exploit was laid in the West.[5]

---

[1] On Soph. *Oed. Col.* 312.   [2] *Imag.* ii. 22.   [3] ix, p. 390 b.

[4] Schol. Apoll. Rhod. ii. 777 πολλοὶ δὲ λόγοι περὶ τοῦ ζωστῆρός εἰσιν· τινὲς μὲν γὰρ Ἱππολύτης, ἄλλοι δὲ Δηϊλύκης, Ἴβυκος δὲ Οἰολύκης ἰδίως ἱστορῶν τῆς Βριαρέω θυγατρός φησιν.

[5] The conjecture of Wilamowitz that the name of Ἀφανναί, an obscure Sicilian town, used proverbially for the other end of the world, came in this play is quite probable, but does not settle the scene of the play. (Antiatt. Bekk. 83. 28 has Ἀφανναί· Ἐπίχαρμος Ἡρακλεῖ τῷ . . .)

The last of the Heracles-plays, Ἡρακλῆς ὁ πὰρ Φόλῳ, doubtless presented or narrated the story[1] of Heracles' fight with the centaurs over the cask of old wine which Dionysus had entrusted to Pholos, with the injunction that it was not to be opened until Heracles came. The only two lines which remain are quoted by Eustratius[2] for the sake of the proverb which they contain :

ἀλλὰ μὰν ἐγὼν ἀνάγκᾳ ταῦτα πάντα ποιέω·
οἴομαι δ' οὐδεὶς ἑκὼν πονηρὸς οὐδ' ἄταν ἔχων.

The words may have been spoken by Heracles with reference to his enforced labours.

§ 3. Of the other plays which presented legendary subjects, the Ἄμυκος dealt with the boxing-match of Polydeuces with the giant Amycus, son of Poseidon, who tried to prevent the Argonauts from getting water, when they landed in the territory of the Bebrykes. The scholiast on Apoll. Rhod. ii. 98 says that Epicharmus, like Peisander, made Pollux bind the giant after defeating him, whereas in Apollonius he slew him ; and perhaps a few words (fr. 7) preserved by lexicographers[3] refer to the 'packing-up' of Amycus :

† εἴ γε μὲν † ὅτι
ἐγκεκόμβωται καλῶς.

Fragment 6 is more interesting :

Ἄμυκε, μὴ κύδαζέ μοι
τὸν πρεσβύτερον ἀδελφέον.

---

[1] For the story and its varieties see Gruppe in Pauly-W. *Real-Enc.*, Suppl. iii, col. 1045 ff.

[2] On Aristot. *Eth. N.* III. v, § 4. He gives the title as Ἡ. παρὰ Φόλῳ, but see Wilamowitz, *Hermes*, xxxvii (1902), p. 325. πονηρός does not mean 'bad' (as Diels, *Vorsokr.*[3] i, p. 122, takes it), but 'beset with toil' ; cf. Solon fr. 14 (Bergk[4]) οὐδὲ μάκαρ οὐδεὶς πέλεται βρότος ἀλλὰ πονηροὶ πάντες ὅσους θνητοὺς ἠέλιος καθορᾷ. The meaning of the word (and of the proverb) is different in Aristotle, who quotes the proverb as οὐδεὶς ἑκὼν πονηρὸς οὐδ' ἄκων μάκαρ.

[3] *Etym. Magn.* 311. 8; Photius, *Epist.* 156 (p. 210). Blomfield's εὖ γα μᾶν ὅτι may be right. Hesychius explains ἐγκεκόμβωται as ἐνείληται. This version of the story was followed by the artist of the Ficoroni Cista: see Robert, *Archäol. Hermen.*, pp. 105-16.

The words must have been addressed by Castor to Amycus, and show that the play must have included three persons taking part in the same dialogue. The fragment, slight as it is, reminds us of the scenes of dispute which in Attic comedy led up to the agon; and it is at least possible that the play consisted of a wrangle, a boxing-match, and a scene in which the giant was safely tied up. The occurrence of the word ἡμιόγκιον in the play [1] shows that the language was not confined to words suitable to the Argonautic expedition; but the suggestion of Welcker [2] that the word shows that the quarrel arose out of an attempt of the Argonauts to buy provisions is a mere guess. Sophocles wrote a satyric play on the same subject.

The Κωμασταὶ ἢ ʺΗφαιστος is shown by a note of Photius [3] to have dealt with a story which was a favourite subject of vase-painters and other artists [4] in the sixth and fifth centuries B. C. in all parts of Greece. Wilamowitz [5] thinks that it was probably the subject of an Ionian ' Hymn ' of the same type as the extant Homeric Hymns; [6] and it was the subject of a poem of Alcaeus; [7] but both literature and art

---

[1] Bekker, *Anecd. Gr.* i. 98.   [2] *Kleine Schriften*, i, p. 299.

[3] ʺΗρας δεσμοὺς ὑπὸ υἱέος· παρὰ Πινδάρῳ, ʺΗρα ὑπὸ ʹΗφαίστου δεσμένεται ἐν τῷ ὑπ᾽ αὐτοῦ κατασκευασθέντι θρόνῳ, ὅ τινες ἀγνοήσαντες γράφουσιν ὑπὸ Διός. Κλήμης· ἡ ἱστορία καὶ παρὰ ᾽Επιχάρμῳ ἐν Κωμασταῖς ἢ ʹΗφαίστῳ. The story is told by Libanius, iii. 7, and Pausan. I. xx, § 3.

[4] e. g. in the temple of Athena Χαλκίοικος at Sparta (Paus. III. xvii, § 3), on the throne of Apollo made by Bathycles at Amyclae (ib. III. xviii, § 8), and in the oldest temple of Dionysus at Athens (ib. I. xx, § 3).

[5] *Gött. Nachr.* 1895, pp. 217 ff.

[6] Prof. J. D. Beazley tells me that the representation of the story on the François vase (*Furtw.-Reichold, Gr. Malerei*, pl. 11, 12) also suggests dependence upon some epic treatment, and that the treatment of it on this vase reappears, in its general lines, on most later vases. The earliest extant representation of the story happens to be on a Corinthian vase, which is often figured (*Ath. Mitt.* xix, p. 510, pl. 8; cf. Bieber, *Denkm. zum Theaterwesen*, Abb. 122, p. 129), but this does not mean that the story is specially Dorian: it is found on sixth-century Ionic and Attic vases (e. g. one in the Ashmolean Museum, of about 550 B. C.). See above, p. 264.

[7] Traces survive in fragm. 9, 9 A, and 133 (Diehl).

seem to have lost interest in the story after the fifth century.[1]
Hera, annoyed at the lameness of Hephaestus, had cast him
out of heaven, and in revenge he sent her a golden chair so
contrived that no one but himself could release her from it.
Ares tried and failed; and all attempts to induce Hephaestus
to return to heaven were unsuccessful, until Dionysus made
him drunk and transported him back in that condition,
accompanied (on the vases at least) by a κῶμος of satyrs.
(Dionysus' share in the story is perhaps not an original part
of it; Wilamowitz conjectures that the two gods may have
been brought into connexion at Naxos, where both were
worshipped. He also suggests that the story of the fettered
goddess may be connected with some cult in which the statue
or the aniconic idol was fettered, as it was in the cult of Hera
at Samos.) Unfortunately the fragments of the play are quite
insignificant.

The problem set by the titles Πύρρα καὶ Προμαθεύς (Athen.
iii, p. 86 a, and probably Pollux, x. 82), Πύρρα (Athen. x,
p. 424 d), Προμαθεύς (*Etym. Magn.* 725. 25), Δευκαλίων
(Antiatt. Bekk. 90. 3), Πύρρα ἢ Λευκαρίων (*Etym. Magn.* s. v.
Λευκαρίων), has not been completely solved. One or more of
these titles may belong to revised editions of plays originally
bearing other titles in the list. Wilamowitz has made the
brilliant conjecture that Epicharmus presented Pyrrha and
Leucarion (a play on Deucalion) — 'Red-hair' and 'White-
hair' — as husband and wife. This would suit fragment 117,
Πύρραν γα μῶται Λευκαρίων (where μῶται = ζητεῖ), and the
remark of the scholiast on a passage of Pindar (*Olymp.* ix. 68)
referring to Pyrrha and Deucalion, καὶ ὁ μὲν Ἐπίχαρμος ἀπὸ
τῶν λάων τῶν λίθων, λαοὺς τοὺς ὄχλους φησὶν ὠνόμασθαι. Doubtless the play referred to in some way travestied the creation of
men from stones by Deucalion and Pyrrha after the flood, and

---

[1] Welcker conjectured that the satyric play *Hephaestus* of Achaeus
treated the subject, but Wilamowitz (l.c.) shows that this is very doubtful;
and the scene on a phlyakes-vase (Heydemann, *Jahrb. Arch. Inst.* i. 290),
in which Daedalus and Enyalios are fighting in the presence of the
seated Hera, can only be brought into connexion with the story if a
number of doubtful hypotheses are granted.

there may possibly have been two plays, or two versions of
the same play, entitled (e.g.) Πύρρα καὶ Προμαθεύς and Πύρρα
ἤ (or καὶ) Λευκαρίων. Whether there was a serious legend of
Leukarion, as well as of Deucalion, may be doubted. Some
writers [1] think they have found such a legend connected with
Opuntian Locris, but the evidence rests upon very unconvincing
hypotheses, and it is much more likely that if the word
Leukarion is correct at all, it was due to a pun of Epicharmus.
The few fragments of the play give no information as to the
treatment of the subject.

The Σκίρων must have dealt with the story of the highway-
man who gave his name to the Scironian rocks, where, until
Theseus overcame him, he threw the passers-by over the
rocks, to feed a gigantic tortoise: but the only connected
fragment is a passage (fr. 125) quoted by the scholiast on
Aristophanes, Peace 185 ff., where a somewhat similar verbal
repetition is employed: [2]

> A. τίς ἐστι μάτηρ;   B. Σακίς.   A. ἀλλὰ τίς πατήρ;
> B. Σακίς.   A. τίς ἀδελφεὸς δέ;   B. Σακίς.

(The first speaker, according to the scholiast, was a basket
(φορμός) and σακίς means a maidservant, but may also be a
proper name.)

Of the Σφίγξ nothing is known except the title and a couple
of lines, in one of which (fr. 127) the speaker calls for a tune
proper to Artemis Χιτωνέα (καὶ τῆς Χιτωνέας αὐλησάτω τίς
μοι μέλος); the text of the other, which mentioned a species of
figs, is uncertain. A comic treatment of the story of Oedipus
and the Sphinx appears also on a vase painting from South

---

[1] See Reitzenstein, Philologus, lv (1896), pp. 193 ff., and Tümpel in
Pauly-W. Real-Enc. v, col. 265.

[2] The restoration of the fragment is not perfectly certain (see p. 361).
It is still less certain whether Aristophanes really 'imitated' it. The
lines from the Peace are as follows:—

> EP. τί σοί ποτ' ἔστ' ὄνομ'; οὐκ ἐρεῖς; TP. μιαρώτατος.
> EP. ποδαπὸς τὸ γένος δ' εἰ; φράζε μοι. TP. μιαρώτατος.
> EP. πάτηρ δέ σοι τίς ἐστ'; TP. ἐμοί; μιαρώτατος.

A comparison with Aristotle, Ath. Pol. lv. 3, shows that Hermes is
parodying the interrogation which took place at a δοκιμασία.

Italy which was probably influenced by the performances of
the φλύακες.[1]

There are references in ancient authorities to three plays
bearing the plural titles Ἀταλάνται, Βάκχαι, and Διόνυσοι. No
significant fragment of any of these survives, nor any hint of
the plot: but the first is probably ascribed to Epicharmus in
error,[2] as the play seems to have referred to some of the
victims of the Attic comedy of the last half of the fifth
century.

§ 4. A few plays bear titles which may (but do not
necessarily) imply the portraiture of a character-type. Of the
Ἀγρωστῖνος or 'Rustic' the only significant words (fr. 1) refer
to an athletic trainer named 'Fisticuffs':[3]

ὡς ταχὺς
Κόλαφος περιπατεῖ δεινός.

Of the Ἁρπαγαί there are two fragments, of which one
(fr. 9) speaks of fraudulent soothsaying-women, and both
mention a number of Sicilian coins. The first runs as
follows:

ὡσπεραὶ πονηραὶ μάντιες,
αἵθ' ὑπονέμονται γυναῖκας μωρὰς ἀμ πεντόγκιον
ἀργύριον, ἄλλαι δὲ λίτραν, ταί δ' ἀν' ἡμιλίτριον
δεχόμεναι, καὶ πάντα γινώσκοντι τῷ . . . λόγῳ.

The attempt of Crusius[4] to connect the title of the play
with a Sicilian feast of Cotytto, at which a half-ritual, half-
sportive ἁρπαγή of cakes and acorns took place, is very
unconvincingly argued.

Of the Ἐπινίκιος (the Victorious Athlete) and the Χορεύοντες
we know nothing beyond the statement of Hephaestion[5] that

---

[1] Hartwig, *Philologus*, lvi, pl. 1.

[2] Athen. xiv, pp. 618 d, 652 a; *Etym. Magn.* 630. 48. Others, e.g.
Hesychius and Schol. Ven. Ar. *Birds* 1294, only speak of the writer as
ὁ τὰς Ἀταλάντας συνθείς or γράψας.

[3] Hesych. s.v. κόλαφος· κόνδυλος. παρὰ δ' Ἐπιχάρμῳ ἐν Ἀγρωστίνῳ καὶ
παιδοτρίβου ὄνομα. The quotation is given in *Etym. Magn.* 525. 8.

[4] *Philologus*, Suppl.-Bd. vi. 285.

[5] *De Metris*, ch. viii, p. 25 (Consbr.)

both were written in anapaestic tetrameters throughout;
which shows at least that they were 'plays' of a very different
kind from those of Attic comedy.

The Θεαροί or 'Temple-visitors' takes its place in a series of
Greek poems representing or describing visitors who are study-
ing the beauties of a temple—in this case the temple of Apollo
at Delphi.[1] The fragment is like parts of Herodas' fourth mime,
in which two women are portrayed while visiting the temple
of Asklepios; and Sophron is known to have written a mime
which was said to have been the original of the Ἀδωνιάζουσαι
of Theocritus, itself a poem of kindred subject to those
mentioned.[2] It is quite likely that such subjects may have
been a favourite theme from very early times in Dorian towns.
The extant fragment (fr. 94) of the Θεαροί is as follows:

> κιθάραι, τρίποδες, ἄρματα, τράπεζαι χάλκιαι,
> χειρόνιβα, λοιβάσια, λέβητες χάλκιοι,
> κρατῆρες, ὀδελοί· τοῖς γα μὰν ὑπωδέλοις
> † καιλωτε † βαλλίζοντες † σιοσσον χρῆμ' εἴη.†[3]

It is to be noted that the objects enumerated belong partly
to the interior of the temple, and probably therefore the
speaker had come actually to consult the oracle, after offering
the necessary sacrifice, to which the few other words of the
play which have been preserved may refer—ὀσφύος τε πέρι
κήπιπλόου.

The Μεγαρίς (the 'Megarean Woman') is represented only
by an uncomplimentary and partly unintelligible description,
perhaps of a certain Theagenes (fr. 90):

> τὰς πλευρὰς οἶόνπερ βατίς,
> τὰν δ' ὀπισθίαν ἔχεις, Θεάγενες, οἶόνπερ βάτος,

---

[1] Athen. viii, p. 362 b, cf. ix, p. 408 d.

[2] The title of Aeschylus' Θεωροὶ ἢ Ἰσθμιασταί suggests a similar subject.
The title of Sophron's mime is conjecturally given by Kaibel as ταὶ
Θάμεναι τὰ Ἴσθμια. Compare the first chorus of Eurip. *Ion* and Eurip.
Hypsipyle, fr. 764.

[3] ὀδελοί = ὀβελοί (spits) and ὑπωδέλοι are probably 'stands for spits';
vid. Friedländer, *Joh. von Gaza*, pp. 26 ff.

τὰν δὲ κεφαλὰν ὀστέων οἴωνπερ ἔλαφος οὐ βατίς,
τὰν δὲ λαπάραν σκορπίος † παῖς † ἐπιθαλάττιος τεοῦ,¹
and a pleasanter account of some one whose name does not
appear:

εὔυμνος καὶ μουσικὰν ἔχουσα πᾶσαν, φιλόλυρος.²

The title in itself tells no more than the many similar titles
of plays of the Middle and New Comedy.³

The title of the Περίαλλος is given only by Athenaeus, who
mentions it twice;⁴ it has been suspected, but it may be a
word coined by Epicharmus, and may possibly, as Lorenz
suggests, mean 'the Superior Person' (ὁ περὶ τῶν ἄλλων).
The only fragment (fr. 109) which certainly comes from the
play is as follows:

Σεμέλα δὲ χορεύει,
καὶ ὑπαυλεῖ σφιν † σοφὸς † κιθάρᾳ παριαμβίδας· ἃ δὲ
γεγάθει
πυκινῶν κρεγμῶν ἀκροαζομένα.⁵

This tells us nothing of the meaning of the word. But the
possibility that it may have had an indecent signification
cannot be entirely excluded. Arcadius⁶ gives the meaning of
περίαλλος as τὸ ἴσχιον, and Meineke, writing on Alciphron,
Ep. i. 39, § 6, makes a strong case for the restoration of the
word in the text of Alciphron, and for connecting it (in an
obscene sense) with other words of almost similar formation.

Whether Πίθων, as the title of a play by Epicharmus,
meant a 'cellar' (as in some fragments⁷ of the Old Comedy)

¹ The text is very uncertain. In l. 2 ἔχεις, Θεάγενες, is Kaibel's emendation for ἔχησθ' ἀτενές: in l. 3 οἴωνπερ is a suggested emendation for
οἰόνπερ. The quotation is given by Athen. vii, p. 286 c.
² Quoted by Hephaestion, p. 6, l. 7 (Consbr.), on account of the short
ὔ before -μν- in εὔυμνος.
³ Ἀχαιίς, Βοιωτίς, Ἑλληνίς, Δωδωνίς, Μεγαρική, Ἀνδρία, Περινθία, Σαμία,
κτλ. See below, p. 411, n. 6.
⁴ iv, p. 139 b, 183 c.
⁵ σοφός gives a syllable too few; perhaps a proper name originally
stood here. παριαμβίδες were a species of κιθαρῳδικοὶ νόμοι οἷς προσηύλουν
(Phot., &c.).
⁶ Arcadius περὶ τόνων, p. 54. 10, ed. Barker.
⁷ Pherecr. fr. 138 (K.), Eupolis fr. 111 (K.),

or a 'monkey' (as once in Pindar [1]), no one can tell. The few words preserved do not help.

Two plays need only (and in fact can only) be mentioned by name—the Μῆνες (the title of which recalls the Μῆνες of Pherecrates), and the Τριακάδες. Nothing is known of these. Offerings to Hecate were made on the 30th day of the month; but the τριακάς was also a political division of the state at Sparta, and may have been so in Syracuse. In either sense the title Τριακάδες could be paralleled from Old Comedy plays such as the Νουμηνίαι of Eupolis, and the Δωδεκάτη of Philyllius, or the Δῆμοι of Eupolis.

The word Ὀρύα or Ὀρούα means 'a sausage'; [2] an obscure gloss of Hesychius [3] suggests that the play may have contained some political allusions. The Πέρσαι has only its title to speak for it; but this, and the certainty [4] that the Νᾶσοι referred to a political event of 477/6 B.C., imply that political subjects were not altogether barred to Sicilian comedy. The event was the attempt to destroy Locri, made by Anaxilas of Rhegium and prevented by Hiero. Otherwise all that is known of the play is that it contained a mention of the proverb ὁ Καρπάθιος τὸν λάγων. [5] The Χύτραι is conjectured by Crusius [6] to have presented a poor potter building castles in the air; but the evidence for this will not bear inspection.

§ 5. There are three plays which are generally supposed to have consisted mainly of a conflict or debate between two characters. These are Γᾶ καὶ Θάλασσα, Λόγος καὶ Λογίνα, and Ἐλπὶς ἢ Πλοῦτος.

---

[1] *Pyth.* ii. 73.   [2] Athen. iii, p. 94 f.

[3] Ὀρούα· χορδή, καὶ σύντριμμα πολιτικόν, εἰς ὃ Ἐπιχάρμου δρᾶμα. σύντριμμα might be used of 'sausage-meat' pounded up together, and metaphorically of a political 'hash'; cf. Aristoph. *Knights* 214 τάραττε καὶ χόρδευ' ὁμοῦ τὰ πράγματα. Dieterich (*Pulcinella*, p. 79) thinks that the title may be equivalent to *satura* or *farsa*; but this seems less likely.

[4] Schol. Pind. *Pyth.* i. 98.

[5] The Carpathians introduced hares into the island, and they multiplied so rapidly (like the rabbits introduced into Australia) that they devoured all the produce of the island (*Prov. Bodl.* 731, Gaisf.). The title of the play is given in Athen. iv, p. 160 d as Ἑορτὰ καὶ Νᾶσοι, but Kaibel has shown that this is probably a misreading.

[6] *Philologus*, Suppl.-Bd. vi, p. 293.

The first of these may have presented the rival claims of
Land and Sea to have benefited mankind most, particularly
by their edible produce. The very slight fragments contain
several names of fish, and Aelian [1] states that many fish were
named in the play. (This theory of the play, though only a
conjecture, seems more probable than the suggestion of Welcker
that Γᾶ καὶ Θάλασσα were two courtesans, even though such
names of courtesans are known in Attic comedy.) It is
interesting to compare the apparent subject of the play with
that of a late poem [2] presenting a contest of the Nile and the
Sea :

> ναῦται βαθυκυματοδρόμοι,
> ἁλίων Τρίτωνες ὑδάτων,
> καὶ Νειλῶται γλυκυδρόμοι
> τὰ γελῶντα πλέοντες ὑδάτῃ,
> τὴν σύγκρισιν εἴπατε, φίλοι,
> πελάγους καὶ Νείλου γονίμου.

The dispute of the fisherman with the rustic, which must
have been the subject of Sophron's mime Ὡλιεὺς τὸν ἀγροιώταν
may have been of the same type. (Wilamowitz conjectures
that the fifth poem of Moschus was based on this.) The words
of fragm. 24 οὐδ᾽ ἁμαμάξυας [3] φέρει may be part of the
depreciation of Sea by Land; otherwise the fragments contain
nothing more interesting than the oath, ναὶ μὰ τὰν κράμβαν,
'By the Cabbage', which Athenaeus [4] states to have been
invented by Ananios, a writer of iambi who was quoted in the
Ἥβας Γάμος.[5]

The Λόγος καὶ Λογίνα [6] is conjectured to have contained
a contest between the Masculine and the Feminine Reason,
and so to have been parallel to the argument of the Just
and Unjust Reason in Aristophanes' *Clouds*. But we know

[1] *Nat. Hist. An.* 13. 4.
[2] *Oxyrh. Pap.* iii. 425 (p. 72).   [3] 'Climbing-vines.'
[4] ix, p. 370 b.   [5] See above, p. 385.
[6] The fragments are all quoted as ἐν Λόγῳ καὶ Λογίνᾳ. That the
nominative is the feminine Λογίνα, and not (as Welcker supposed)
Λογίνας is shown by *Anecd. Oxon.* ii. 114; and there seems to be no
justification for the form Λόγιννα which some scholars have adopted.

nothing significant of the play, except that it contained in fr. 88 a mention of an earlier poet, Aristoxenus of Selinus:

οἱ τοὺς ἰάμβους καὶ τὸν † ἄριστον † τρόπον
ὃν πρᾶτος εἰσηγήσαθ' ὠριστόξενος,

and, in fr. 87, a pun of the kind which is common in the Old Attic comedy, and which occurred in a dialogue:

A. ὁ Ζεύς μ' ἐκάλεσε, Πέλοπί γ' ἔρανον ἱστιῶν.
B. ἦ παμπόνηρον ὄψον, ὦ τάν, ὁ γέρανος.
A. ἀλλ' οὐχὶ γέρανον, ἀλλ' ἔρανον ⟨γά⟩ τοι λέγω.

The interest of this fragment lies in the fact that it shows that the characters were mythological; and it is not quite clear how the Masculine and Feminine Reason fitted in with these.

From the Ἐλπὶς ἢ Πλοῦτος, if that was the title, we have one of the few long and important fragments of Epicharmus that have survived. It is in two parts (fr. 34, 35), in the first of which a speaker notices a parasite following on the heels of another character (again showing that there must have been at least three persons on the stage), while in the second the parasite describes his life in answer to inquiries. (It is not certain whether the name παράσιτος was used in the play; the evidence as to the date when the word came into use is contradictory;[1] but there is no mistaking the character):

(*a*) ἀλλ' ἄλλος ἔστειχ' ὧδε τοῦδε κατὰ πόδας,
     τὸν ῥᾳδίως λαψῇ τυ καὶ τὸ νῦν γὰ θὴν
     εὔωνον ἀείσιτον· ἀλλ' ἔμπας ὅδε,
     ἄμυστιν ὥσπερ κύλικα πίνει τὸν βίον.

(*b*) συνδειπνέω τῷ λῶντι, καλέσαι δεῖ μόνον·[2]
     καὶ τῷ γα μὴ λεῶντι, κοὐδὲν δεῖ καλεῖν.
     τηνεὶ δὲ χαρίεις τ' εἰμὶ καὶ ποιέω πολὺν
     γελῶτα καὶ τὸν ἱστιῶντ' ἐπαινέω·
5   κάί κα τις ἀντίον ⟨τι⟩ λῇ τήνῳ λέγειν,
     τήνῳ κυδάζομαί τε κἀπ' ὧν ἠχθόμαν.
     κἤπειτα πολλὰ καταφαγών, πολλ' ἐμπιών,

---

[1] Athen. vi, pp. 235 e, f, 236 b, e, 237 a; Pollux, vi. 35; Schol. on *Il.* xvii. 577; cf. Mein. *Hist. Crit.*, pp. 377 ff.

[2] συνδειπνέω is Casaubon's emendation for συνδειπνέων.

ἄπειμι· λύχνον δ' οὐχ ὁ παῖς μοι συμφέρει,
ἕρπω δ' ὀλισθράζων τε καὶ κατὰ σκότος
10 ἔρημος· αἴ κα δ' ἐντύχω τοῖς περιπόλοις,
τοῦθ' οἷον ἀγαθὸν ἐπιλέγω τοῖς θεοῖς, ὅτι
οὐ λῶντι πλεῖον ἀλλὰ μαστιγοῦντί με.
ἐπεὶ δέ χ' εἴκω οἴκαδις καταφθερείς,
ἄστρωτος εὕδω· καὶ τὰ μὲν πρᾶτ' οὐ κοῶ,
ᾆς κά μ ⟨ἔχ⟩ων ὤκρατος ἀμφέπῃ φρένας.

We have here the first of many such descriptions in Greek
comedy; and fr. 37 contains a scrap of a remark addressed to
a parasite :

ἐκάλεσε γάρ τύ τις
ἐπ' αἶκλον ἀέκων· τὺ δὲ ἑκὼν ᾤχεο τρέχων.

(αἶκλον = δεῖπνον.)

But the place of the parasite in the play is quite uncertain.
It is tempting to suppose that Hope was represented by the
parasite, always on the look-out for an invitation, and Πλοῦτος
by one of his patrons (or victims) very unwilling to invite
him; and this really seems more natural than the more
elaborate theory of Birt,[1] who thinks that there was an ἀγών
(like that of Πλοῦτος and Πενία in Aristophanes) between
Hope and Riches, and that Hope was personified in a Fisherman. There is really no proof of the latter suggestion, except
that in Greek and Roman comedy and other literature the
hope which buoys up the poor is often found in the fisher-
class, that this was so in Theocritus, and that an epigram of
Theocritus shows that he was familiar with the works of
Epicharmus; and this is no proof at all. It is perhaps more
likely that the plot consisted of a series of farcical encounters
between the parasite and the rich men who tried to shake
him off.

It is hardly worth while to lay stress, as some would do,[2] on
the contrast between the καί in the titles of Γᾶ καὶ Θάλασσα,
Λόγος καὶ Λογίνα, and the ἤ in Ἐλπὶς ἢ Πλοῦτος. Either

---

[1] Birt, *Elpides*, pp. 28 ff.
[2] ibid., p. 106, n. 92. Birt compares the title of a discussion of
Antisthenes, περὶ φρονησέως ἢ ἰσχύος, &c.

would be intelligible in a title denoting a conflict of interests; but the possibility cannot be excluded that the original title was simply Ἐλπίς (words are several times quoted from the play as ἐν Ἐλπίδι Ἐπιχάρμου), and that Πλοῦτος was the name given to a second edition (such as there was of some other plays of Epicharmus). Much therefore remains uncertain.

§ 6. Of the fragments which are not taken from any named play, few, except those quoted from Alcimus,[1] are of much interest. In one (fr. 148) there is an example of the rhetorical figure ἐποικοδόμησις, and quoted as such by Aristotle,[2] though he only paraphrases it. What seems to be nearer the original text is given by Athenaeus :[3]

A.   ἐκ μὲν θυσίας θοῖνα,
    ἐκ δὲ θοίνας πόσις ἐγένετο.

B.   χαρίεν, ὡς γ' ἐμὶν ⟨δοκεῖ⟩.

A. ἐκ δὲ πόσιος μῶκος,[4] ἐκ μώκου δ' ἐγένεθ' ὑανία,
    ἐκ δ' ὑανίας ⟨δίκα ... ἐκ δίκας δὲ κατα⟩δίκα,
    ἐκ δὲ καταδίκας πέδαι τε καὶ σφαλὸς[5] καὶ ζαμία.

Another fragment (fr. 149) presented a riddle which needed Oedipus to solve it. (The last line is corrupt.)

A. τί δὲ τόδ' ἔστι;

B.   δηλαδὴ τρίπους.

A.   τί μὰν ἔχει πόδας
    τέτορας; οὐκ ἔστιν τρίπους, ἀλλ' ⟨ἐστὶν⟩ οἶμαι τετράπους.

B. ἔστιν ὄνομ' αὐτῷ τρίπους, τέτοράς γα μὰν ἔχει πόδας.

A. Οἰδίπους τοίνυν † ποτ' ἦν αἴνιγμα τοι νοεῖς †.[6]

---

[1] See above, pp. 371 ff.

[2] De Gen. An., i, p. 724. 28; Rhet. i, p. 1365 a 10.

[3] ii, p. 36 c, d.

[4] μῶκος ... μώκου Mein. for κῶμος, κώμου codd. Athen. μῶκος is confirmed by Aristotle's paraphrase (λοιδορία or διαβολή).

[5] σφαλός Bochart, which the lexicographers explain as ξύλον ποδῶν δεσμωτικόν. (The σφάκελλος of the codd. will not scan.)

[6] Perhaps we should read Οἰδίπου τοίνυν τὸ τὴν' αἴνιγμα τοὶ νοεῖν. A similar tame joke appears in Aristoph. fr. 530 A. τράπεζαν ἡμῖν εἴσφερε | τρεῖς πόδας ἔχουσαν, τέτταρας δὲ μὴ 'χέτω· | B. καὶ πόθεν ἐγὼ τρίπουν τράπεζαν λήψομαι;

One or two lines are apparently of a gnomic or proverbial type; e. g.

fr. 165 ἀλλὰ καὶ σιγῆν ἀγαθόν, ὅκκα παρέωντι κάρρονες.[1]

fr. 168 οἵαπερ ἁ δέσποινα, τοία χἁ κύων.[2]

fr. 216 ὅκκ᾽ ἀργύριον ᾖ, πάντα θεῖ κἠλαύνεται.[3]

fr. 221 ἔνθα δέος, ἐνταῦθα καἰδώς.[4]

fr. 229 ἐν πέντε κριτῶν γούνασι κεῖται.[5]

The following γνῶμαι, among others, are definitely ascribed to Epicharmus by the writers who quote them; but we cannot tell which of them may be forgeries by Axiopistus, nor whether Crönert is right in grouping them all with others as parts of one gnomic poem.[6]

fr. 265 εὐσεβὴς νόῳ πεφυκὼς οὐ πάθοις κ᾽ οὐδὲν κακὸν
κατθανών· ἄνω τὸ πνεῦμα διαμένει κατ᾽ οὐρανόν.

fr. 266 οὐδὲν ἐκφεύγει τὸ θεῖον· τοῦτο γινώσκειν τυ δεῖ·
αὐτὸς ἔσθ᾽ ἁμῶν ἐπόπτας, ἀδυνατεῖ δ᾽ οὐδὲν θέος.

fr. 267 ὡς πολὺν ζήσων χρόνον χὢς ὀλίγον, οὕτως διανοοῦ.

fr. 268 ἐγγύας ἄτα (῎στι) θυγάτηρ, ἐγγύα δὲ ζαμίας.

fr. 269 καθαρὸν ἂν τὸν νοῦν ἔχῃς, ἅπαν τὸ σῶμα καθαρὸς εἶ.

fr. 270 αἴ τί κα ζατῇς σοφόν, τᾶς νυκτὸς ἐνθυμητέον.

fr. 271 πάντα τὰ σπουδαῖα νυκτὸς μᾶλλον ἐξευρίσκεται.

fr. 272 οὐ λέγειν τύγ᾽ ἐσσὶ δεινός, ἀλλὰ σιγῆν ἀδύνατος.

fr. 273 ἁ δὲ χεὶρ τὰν χεῖρα νίζει· δός τι καὶ λάβ᾽ αἴ τι
(λῇς).

fr. 274 οὐ φιλάνθρωπος τύγ᾽ ἐσσ᾽· ἔχεις νόσον, χαίρεις
διδούς.

---

[1] κάρρονες is a Doric form = κρείσσονες (vid. Bechtel, *Gr. Dial.* ii, p. 235).

[2] It is not certain that this is a line of Epicharmus, but Kaibel's conjectural ascription of it to him is very probable. It is quoted by Clem. Alex. *Paed.* III. xi, p. 296, and there are other references to it.

[3] The ascription to Epicharmus is a conjecture of Kaibel. The quotation is in Schol. Aristoph. *Eccl.* 109.

[4] Schol. Soph. *Aj.* 1074.

[5] This is ascribed to Epicharmus by Zenob. iii. 64 εἴρηται δ᾽ ἡ παροιμία παρόσον πέντε κριταὶ τοὺς κωμικοὺς ἔκρινον, ὥς φησιν Ἐπίχαρμος. But see below, p. 410.

[6] See above, p. 369.

D d

fr. 277 πρὸς ⟨δὲ⟩ τοὺς πέλας πορεύου λαμπρὸν ἱμάτιον ἔχων,
      καὶ φρονεῖν πολλοῖσι δόξεις, τυχὸν ἴσως ⟨οὐδὲν φρονῶν⟩.

fr. 280 οὐ μετανοεῖν ἀλλὰ προνοεῖν χρὴ τὸν ἄνδρα τὸν
      σοφόν.

fr. 281 μὴ 'πὶ μικροῖς αὐτὸς αὐτὸν ὀξύθυμον δείκνυε.

fr. 282 ἐπιπολάζειν οὔ τι χρὴ τὸν θυμὸν ἀλλὰ τὸν νόον.

fr. 283 οὐδὲ εἷς οὐδὲν μετ' ὀργᾶς κατὰ τρόπον βουλεύεται.

fr. 284 ἁ δὲ μελέτα φύσιος ἀγαθᾶς πλέονα δωρεῖται φίλοις.

fr. 285 τίς δέ κα λώῃ γενέσθαι μὴ φθονούμενος φίλοις;
      δῆλον ὡς ἀνὴρ παρ' οὐδέν ἐσθ' ὁ μὴ φθονούμενος·
      τυφλὸν ἠλέησ' ἰδών τις, ἐφθόνησε δ' οὐδὲ εἷς.

fr. 286 σώφρονος γυναικὸς ἀρετὰ τὸν συνόντα μὴ ἀδικεῖν.

fr. 287 τῶν πόνων πωλοῦσιν ἁμῖν πάντα τἀγαθ' οἱ θεοί.

fr. 288 ὦ πονηρέ, μὴ τὰ μαλακὰ μῶσο, μὴ τὰ σκλήρ'
      ἔχῃς.

A few of these seem to bear the true Epicharmean stamp; such are Nos. 268, 270, 272, 273, 274, 288 : but most of them have nothing witty or characteristic about them. Some, if genuine, have become Atticized in the course of repitition. It is certain, however, that works of the kind to which mimes and primitive comic performances generally belong constantly contain such moral and sententious maxims, and it is such maxims which form a considerable part of the fragments of the Roman mime-writer, Publilius Syrus. Sometimes, perhaps, they pointed a moral, and sometimes travestied the moralizing temperament.

V

The Character of Epicharmus' Comedy.

§ 1. The Anonymus Estensis (quoted at the beginning of this chapter) says of Epicharmus, οὗτος πρῶτος διερριμμένην τὴν κωμῳδίαν ἀνεκτήσατο, πολλὰ προσφιλοτεχνήσας, and that he was τῇ ποιήσει γυμνικὸς καὶ εὑρετικὸς καὶ φιλότεχνος. The writer is no doubt condensing or repeating statements which had become traditional, and had no knowledge of the works of Epicharmus at first hand, but his words sum up conveniently the general impression which a study of the fragments makes,

though the suggestion in the word ἀνεκτήσατο, that comedy
had already existed in some organized form but had been
broken up and was put together again by Epicharmus, is
probably misleading. There is no trace, at least, of any
organized comedy before him; but he did unite various
elements into a structure which was sufficiently coherent to
be regarded as the beginning of an artistic comedy. What
these elements were will be presently considered: but first it
will be well to deal briefly with a point of which some writers
perhaps make too much [1]—the fact that the plays of Epicharmus are never in antiquity actually called κωμῳδίαι.
This seems to be true, but it is probably an accident;
Aristotle, *Poet*. v, evidently thinks of his writing as properly
called κωμῳδία : Plato speaks of οἱ ἄκροι τῆς ποιήσεως ἑκατέρας,
κωμῳδίας μὲν 'Επίχαρμος, τραγῳδίας δὲ "Ομηρος : late writers
call him κωμικός, κωμῳδιογράφος, κωμῳδιοποιός : and it seems
hard to believe that if all these and other writers could use
the word κωμῳδία to describe the species of poetry which he
composed, they would not, if they had wished, have spoken of
the single plays as κωμῳδίαι. (In fact the plays are seldom
referred to distributively. They are spoken of as δράματα by
Athen. iii, p. 94 f., Hesych. s. v. ὀρούα, and Hephaest., p. 25.
15 Consbr. The word δρᾶμα appears not to be used in Attic
of the classical period in application to Attic Comedy, but in
a fragment of Ecphantides there is a mention of a δρᾶμα
Μεγαρικόν, which was evidently a comic performance, and it
is possible that the word was also used of comedy and similar
performances in Sicily. This would agree with Aristotle's
statement in *Poet*. iii that some people regarded δρᾶμα as a
Dorian word.[2]) What is highly probable, is that the performances of Epicharmus were not especially associated with
a Dionysiac κῶμος, and that there would accordingly have
been no ground for calling them κωμῳδίαι in Sicily itself; but
that the ancients recognized them as belonging to the same
general type as κωμῳδίαι can hardly be disputed.

[1] Wilam. *Einl. in die Gr. Trag.*, pp. 54–5 ; Kaibel, in Pauly-W. *Real-Enc.*
vi, col. 36 ; Radermacher, Aristoph. *Frösche*, p. 15.
[2] See above, pp. 144–5.

§ 2. It is clear that in the opinion of Aristotle,[1] who evidently knew of no written comedy in Sicily before Epicharmus, the essence of the work of Epicharmus was the composition of plots of general, as distinct from personal, interest; and Aristotle would hardly have given the title of μῦθοι to any but more or less connected and coherent structures. But he does not say that all the works of Epicharmus were alike or possessed these merits in equal degrees, and it seems very probable that it was not so, but that there were 'plays' of several different types included among his works. We have found traces of dialogues in which at least three speakers took part, in the Ἄμυκος and the Ἐλπὶς ἢ Πλοῦτος : of narrative speeches, something like those of the messenger in Attic tragedy and comedy, in the Βούσιρις and the Ἥβας Γάμος: of monologue in the Ὀδυσσεὺς Αὐτόμολος. In the Ἄμυκος there was probably a quarrel, a boxing-match, and a scene in which the giant was tied up : in the Θεαροί there may have been a scene (and this may have been the whole play) like that of Theocritus' Ἀδωνιάζουσαι and of certain mimes: the Ἐπινίκιος and the Χορεύοντες were composed entirely in anapaestic tetrameters: some plays perhaps consisted mainly (or at least in part) of an agon or set debate,[2] though apparently without a chorus standing by, or any

---

[1] *Poet.* v.

[2] The attempt of Sieckmann (*de Comoediae Atticae primordiis*, 1906) to prove that something like an agon occurred in nearly all the plays of Epicharmus comes to very little. He shows that most plays included more than one speaker; that the anapaestic tetrameter, one of the regular metres of the Attic agon, was common in Epicharmus, and that in the extant fragments (as in the epirrhematic portions of Attic comedy) there are virtually no traces of characters entering or leaving the scene. But this is a very different thing from proving that most plays consisted of an agon, with (in some) a prologue or epilogue in iambics. That the comedies of Epicharmus were (as he believes) of about the same length as an agon of Aristophanes also proves nothing, and a general review of the fragments is sufficient to dispose of his theory. (I find that a reply to Sieckmann, on the same lines, was given by Süss in the *Berl. Phil. Woch.* 1907, pp. 1397 ff.) The further suggestion of Sieckmann, that the agon of Attic comedy was of Dorian rather than of native origin, seems to be equally groundless. (See above, pp. 240 ff.)

other judge, so far as our evidence goes: in some plays an ἀλαζών (and possibly more than one) was made a fool of or else outwitted his neighbours. Some of the plays on mythological subjects may have had plots of several scenes; e. g. the Κωμασταὶ ἢ Ἥφαιστος, and some of the Heracles-plays, though it is uncertain how much was acted and how much narrated. Now and then the action may have been interrupted by a dance or assisted by an instrumental performance: a flute solo in the Ἥβας Γάμος, accompanying a dance by two performers, and a μέλος associated with Artemis Χιτωνέα[1] in the Σφίγξ, are well attested (unless indeed the first-named play was entirely narrative); and there is some reason for the conjecture that a πυκτικὸν μέλος accompanied the boxing-match in the Ἄμυκος.[2]

There was probably no uniform or prescribed structure in the plays of Epicharmus and his contemporaries. That such a set form was so closely adhered to in Attic comedy was largely the result of the presence of the chorus; and of a chorus, at least as a regular element in the play, there is, in the fragments of Epicharmus, no distinct trace. There may have been some kind of κῶμος in the Κωμασταὶ ἢ Ἥφαιστος: and the Seven Muses may have sung together in the Ἥβας Γάμος, though they may only have figured in the narrative of the feast. It cannot be inferred from the title Σειρῆνες (or even from the expression ἀκούετε Σειρηνάων in fr. 123) that there was a chorus of Sirens, or that more than one was actually a character in the play. Nor do the plural titles of the Ἀταλάνται (if genuine), Βάκχαι, and Διόνυσοι necessarily imply a chorus.[3] It is sometimes argued that Epicharmus

---

[1] A specially Syracusan dance and tune of this kind are mentioned by Athen. xiv, p. 629 e. See above, p. 392.

[2] See Pollux, iv. 56, where πυκτικόν τι μέλος seems to be a certain correction of ποιητικόν, and Kaibel on fr. 210. But it cannot be inferred (as Lorenz, p. 90, seems to infer) from the mere use of the word σκωλοβατίζειν in the Πέρσαι (fr. 112) that there was a dance in which the performer stood on one leg; nor from the corrupt fr. 79 that there was a scene of βαλλισμός in the Θεαροί.

[3] Cratinus' Ὀδυσσεῖς, Ἀρχίλοχοι, and Κλεοβουλῖναι and Teleclides' Ἡσίοδοι need not have been so named owing to the presence of the

employed a chorus, on the strength of a note in Pollux[1] that
he called the dramatic training-school χορηγεῖον. But the use
of χορηγεῖον for διδασκαλεῖον may well have been derived
from the training of the tragic chorus there, or some chorus
other than the comic, and so Epicharmus might naturally
use the word, even if he had no chorus himself.[2]

The poems were probably short, like the mimes and their
earlier predecessors in Dorian lands. (The want of a chorus
and the variability of the form would be further points of
resemblance.) We are told that Apollodorus divided the
plays of Epicharmus into ten volumes:[3] Birt (followed by
several scholars since) argues[4] that as apparently each
Aristophanic comedy constituted a τόμος, such a τόμος would
contain about 1,500 lines, and the plays of Epicharmus (which
he counts as 35) would therefore average between 300 and
400 lines each. The argument itself is not quite satisfactory.
It postulates an unnatural uniformity (disproved in fact by
Birt himself) in the size of volumes; and we do not know
how much (if any) of the spurious works Apollodorus may
have included in the ten volumes: the fact that he distinguished the genuine from the spurious does not prove that
he excluded the latter from his edition. Nor is a statement
in the *Liber glossarum* quoted by Kaibel (p. 72), to the effect
that the early comedies did not exceed 300 lines,[5] of great
weight, since we do not know its authority, and it appears to

chorus. The titles may mean either 'persons like Odysseus &c.' or
'Odysseus &c. and their companions'.

[1] ix. 41, 42 ἐκάλουν δὲ τὸ διδασκαλεῖον καὶ χορόν (χορηγεῖον, Kaibel),
ὁπότε καὶ τὸν διδάσκαλον χορηγόν, καὶ τὸ διδάσκειν χορηγεῖν, καὶ μάλιστα οἱ
Δωριεῖς, ὡς Ἐπίχαρμος ἐν Ὀδυσσεῖ Αὐτομόλῳ· ἐν δὲ Ἁρπαγαῖς χορηγεῖον τὸ
διδασκαλεῖον ὠνόμασεν. Comp. Hesych. χοραγ⟨ε⟩ίων· διδασκαλείων.

[2] On the probable absence of a chorus from Dorian comedy, see also
Reich, *Mimus*, i, pp. 503-4.

[3] Porphyr. *Vit. Plotin.* 24 μιμησάμενος δ' Ἀπολλόδωρον τὸν Ἀθηναῖον καὶ
Ἀνδρόνικον τὸν Περιπατητικὸν ὢν ὁ μὲν Ἐπίχαρμον τὸν κωμῳδιογράφον εἰς δέκα
τόμους φέρων συνήγαγεν κτλ.

[4] *Antike Buchwesen*, pp. 446, 496.

[5] 'Sed prior ac vetus comoedia ridicularis extitit . . . Auctor eius
Susarion traditur. Sed in fabulas primi eam contulerunt non magnas,
ita ut non excederent in singulis versus trecenos.'

refer to Attic comedy as composed by Susarion and others.[1] But that the plays were actually short is rendered likely from the slight nature of their subject-matter, so far as we can trace it, and by their apparent resemblance to the mime; and although the statement about Apollodorus' edition cannot be made the basis of a numerical calculation, it does suggest comedies much shorter than those of Aristophanes.

Apart from the kind of farce and horseplay that is always an element of popular comedy of a not very advanced type, the great interest of Epicharmus' work seems to have lain in its presentation of character. We are already familiar with the Parasite as depicted by him; Körte's conjecture[2] that with the Parasite there appeared also his companion in so many Athenian plays, the Boastful Soldier, while not substantiated by evidence, is probable in itself, and no doubt the mercenary captains employed by Sicilian tyrants could have provided specimens of the type. We have seen also the ingenious philosopher—the ἀλαζὼν σοφός, in a guise very like that in which he appears in Attic Comedy, and traces of various other types flit across the scene in the fragments—the Trainer, the Sight-seer, the Victorious Athlete, and many others. Athenaeus asserts[3] that Epicharmus was the first to bring a drunkard on the stage (and was followed by Crates in the Γείτονες), and probably many of his personages were in one way or another connected with the pleasures of the table. It must also be admitted that the fragments are not free from traces of those indecencies which the hearers of the earlier Greek comedies everywhere enjoyed,[4] though Crusius[5] goes beyond the evidence in supposing that these traces show that the actors of Epicharmus wore the gross phallic costume which was adopted by Attic actors, and which is seen also on

---

[1] Cf. Usener, *Rhein. Mus.* xxviii. 418; Kaibel, *Die Proleg.* περὶ κωμῳδίας, p. 46, who rightly rejects the authority of this late passage for facts upon which Aristotle was unable (*Poet.* iv) to obtain information.

[2] *Die griechische Komödie*, p. 13, and in Pauly-W. *Real-Enc.* xi, col. 1225.

[3] x, p. 429 a.   [4] fr. 191, 235.

[5] *Philologus*, Suppl.-Bd. vi, p. 284.

the vases which depict the performances of the φλύακες. It may have been so, but it is not proved. Traces of contemporary allusions are very rare; but we have seen that there was certainly an instance in the Νᾶσοι, and the reference to the Eleusinian Mysteries in the Ὀδυσσεὺς Αὐτόμολος exhibits the same kind of incongruity as was common in both the Old and the Middle Comedy of Athens.

Besides the comic character of the plot and the drawing of the personages, much of the amusement of the audiences of Epicharmus must have been derived from the language. In this the stock devices of Greek comedy are already apparent —parody,[1] word-play,[2] the coinage of long-words,[3] diminutives,[4] and significant proper names,[5] and the rattling off of lists of the good things of the feast. The rapidity of his 'patter', or perhaps of the interchange of question and answer, may be referred to by Horace [6]

Plautus ad exemplar Siculi *properare* Epicharmi (*sc.* dicitur).

§ 3. It is not easy for us to judge broadly of the effect of the Dorian dialect when used on a large scale; the first impression of awkwardness and inelegance is no doubt superficial and due to the comparative strangeness of the Doric forms to our eyes; there is certainly no reason for supposing that the sounds were harsh or unmusical. The dialect employed by Epicharmus is in the main that of Corinth and its colonies, of which Syracuse was one, and which in general form a homogeneous group; but Bechtel has shown that in Epicharmus this is modified in two ways. There are elements in his language which seem to be Rhodian,[7] and these he

---

[1] fr. 123, 130; cf. Athen. xv, p. 698 c εὑρετὴν μὲν οὖν τοῦ γένους (sc. τῆς παρῳδίας) Ἱππώνακτα φατέον τὸν ἰαμβοποιόν . . . κέχρηται δὲ καὶ ὁ Ἐπίχαρμος ὁ Συρακόσιος ἔν τινι τῶν δραμάτων ἐπ᾽ ὀλίγον.

[2] fr. 87.   [3] e. g. μακροκαμπυλαύχενες in fr. 46.

[4] Πριαμικύδριον in fr. 142.   [5] Κόλαφος in the Ἀγρωστῖνος.

[6] *Epp.* II. i. 58.

[7] Especially (1) the accus. plur. in -ŏς and -ăς, e. g. καὶ τὸς ἀνθρώπους (fr. 170), μωρᾱς (fr. 9), τᾱς ἀνδροφυκτίδας (fr. 49), πλευρᾱς (fr. 90), ἀφύᾱς (fr. 124); cf. καλὰς ὥρας ἄγουσα in the Rhodian swallow-song; and (2) the infin. in -μειν, e. g. εἶμειν (fr. 99 and 182), προδιδόμειν (fr. 100), ποτθέμειν (fr. 170).

ascribes, as Ahrens did, to the influence of the citizens of
Gela (a colony of Rhodes), whom Gelo settled in Syracuse,[1]
and who would naturally be found about the court of Gelo
and Hiero: and there are also words[2] taken entirely or in
part from Latin, as is natural enough. But, as Kaibel has
well pointed out, the language is not merely that of the street,
but is full of allusions and turns of wit and argument, which,
despite occasional slang and vulgarity, presuppose an alert
and educated audience.

In handling his metres Epicharmus secures a vigorous
movement and a certain liveliness by allowing free resolution
of long syllables, as well as changes of speakers in the middle
of the line—a licence not allowed in early tragedy, but found
in the satyric Ἰχνευταί of Sophocles. There is no trace of
lyric metres in the fragments; only fr. 101 comes from an
anapaestic dimeter-system. In a few fragments only[3] we
find anapaestic tetrameters, but we are told (as has already
been noticed) that the Ἐπινίκιος and the Χορεύοντες were
composed entirely in this metre.[4] There is one line of parody
in hexameters.[5] The metres chiefly represented in the fragments are the trochaic tetrameter (which Marius Victor calls
the *metrum Epicharmeum*)[6] and the iambic trimeter; the
former was probably already in use in popular songs as well
as in earlier literature; the latter had a long history before
Epicharmus.

---

[1] Herod. vii. 156.

[2] e. g. κυβιτίζειν, κύβιτος (fr. 213), πεντόγκιον (fr. 9), ὀγκία (fr. 203),
ἡμιόγκιον (fr. 8).

[3] fr. 109, 111, 114, 152.

[4] It is probable that the metre was of Dorian origin. It was certainly
associated with the Spartan ἐμβατήρια, or marching-songs, and a special
variety of it was termed Λακωνικόν (Hephaestion, *de Metris*, viii, p. 25. 22
Conbr,). Hephaestion quotes a line in the metre from Aristoxenus of
Selinus (who was earlier than Epicharmus); but Kaibel and others doubt
its genuineness (see Bergk, *Poet. Lyr.*[4], ii, p. 21; Cic. *Tusc. Disp.* II. xvi,
§ 37, &c.). There is no instance of its use in dialogue before Epicharmus,
and it was no doubt originally a marching-rhythm.

[5] fr. 123.

[6] For the theories of Hoffmann and Kauz on Epicharmus' use of this
metre, see above, p. 370, n. 4.

§ 4. It has already been stated that we have no reason for
associating the plays of Epicharmus, any more than the
mimes which they so closely resemble, or their Peloponnesian
ancestors, with a Dionysiac κῶμος ; and in fact we know
nothing of the external conditions of their performance, nor
whether they formed part of a contest, as at Athens. If
Aelian [1] is right in speaking of Deinolochus as ἀνταγωνιστὴς
Ἐπιχάρμου, some kind of contest is probably implied. The
proverb ἐν πέντε κριτῶν γούνασι κεῖται is quoted by Zenobius,[2]
and both he and Hesychius [3] state or imply that five judges
decided between the comic poets in Sicily ; but this may
possibly be a mere inference from the occurrence of the
proverb in Epicharmus, if indeed it is quoted from the real
Epicharmus at all. Tragedy was very probably performed in
competition before five judges, this custom, like tragedy itself,
being imported from Athens ; but the custom may or may not
have been adopted for comedy, and the proverb itself may
have been imported with the custom.

§ 5. The precise degree to which Epicharmus influenced
Attic comedy cannot be determined ; it is difficult to agree
either with Zielinski,[4] who does not think that the plays of
Epicharmus were known to the early Attic comic poets, or
with those who, like von Salis,[5] find the influence of Epicharmus everywhere. It is clear that many features are common
to Epicharmus and the Old Comedy—the characters of the
philosopher, the parasite, the drunkard, the rustic, the voracious
and turbulent Heracles, the crafty Odysseus, the burlesqued
gods ; but Athens may well have derived most of these (in so
far as they were borrowed at all) from Dorians nearer home.
The agon was also probably home-grown in Attica. Nor

[1] *Nat. Hist.* vi. 51.
[2] iii. 64 εἴρηται δ’ ἡ παροιμία παρόσον πέντε κριταὶ τοὺς κωμικοὺς ἔκρινον,
ὥς φησιν Ἐπίχαρμος, ἐν πέντε κριτῶν γούνασι κεῖται.
[3] Ἐν πέντε κριτῶν· ἐν ἀλλοτρίᾳ ἐξουσίᾳ ἐστίν. πέντε δὲ κριταὶ τοῖς κωμικοῖς
ἔκρινον : and also πέντε κριταί· τοσοῦτοι τοῖς κωμικοῖς ἔκρινον, οὐ μόνον
Ἀθήνησιν, ἀλλὰ καὶ ἐν Σικελίᾳ.
[4] *Glied. der altatt. Köm*, p. 243 ; cf. Bethe, *Proleg.*, p. 61.
[5] op. cit.

would Athenian poets need to go to Sicily for the use of
parody, of word-play in countless forms, and of 'patter' containing long lists of the good things of the feast. We have
seen reason to doubt whether the scholiast was right, who
found an imitation of Epicharmus in Aristophanes, *Peace*
185 ff.[1] It is also very unsafe to infer direct imitation in lines
of Aristophanes in which common and colourless words occupy
the same place as in lines of Epicharmus.[2] The puzzle about
a τρίπους τράπεζα in Aristophanes, fr. 530[3] may or may
not have been suggested by Epicharmus, fr. 149; the same
is the case with the conceit employed in the *Peace*, when
Trygaeus rides on an Αἰτναῖος κάνθαρος. (The creature was
proverbial, but its use as a steed is not found before Epicharmus.[4]) The use of the anapaestic tetrameter in comedy by
Cratinus and his successors *may* have been suggested by
Epicharmus, but this would hardly account for its regular and
predominant use in what appear to have been native elements
in Attic comedy, the agon and parabasis; and in any case
the Athenians could have borrowed the metre from the
Peloponnesian Dorians.

The enumeration of parallel lists of titles of plays from
Epicharmus and from Attic comedy undoubtedly suggests
that the two had many subjects in common;[5] but against this
must be set the extraordinary difference of treatment in choral
and non-choral comedy respectively. The close resemblance

---

[1] See above, p. 392, n. 2.

[2] Von Salis compares Epich. fr. 171 ἆρ' ἐστὶν αὔλησίς τι πρᾶγμα; πάνυ
μὲν ὦν with Aristoph. *Plut.* 97, 1195, in which πάνυ μὲν οὖν similarly ends
the line; and fr. 171, l. 2, and fr. 128, with Aristoph. *Frogs* 56, *Lysistr.*
916, and Pherecr. fr. 69, l. 4, in which οὐδαμῶς or μηδαμῶς is similarly
placed. Other instances which he gives (p. 41) are even less convincing.

[3] See above, p. 400.   [4] See above, p. 388.

[5] Von Salis compares the Μεγαρίς with plays entitled Ἀχαιίς, Ἕλληνις,
Βοιωτίς, Δωδωνίς, Περσίς, Μεγαρική, &c.; and points to Attic comedies
called Κύκλωψ, Βούσιρις, Σκίρων, Φιλοκτήτης, Νῆσοι, Μῆνες, Βάκχαι, Μοῦσαι,
Σειρῆνες, Κωμασταί, &c. The Ἡρακλῆς γαμῶν of Archippus may have had
the same subject as the Ἥβας Γάμος, and the Δράματα ἢ Κένταυρος of
Aristophanes may have resembled the Ἡρακλῆς ὁ πὰρ Φόλῳ (cf. Kaibel,
Hermes, xxiv, pp. 54 ff.; Prescott, *Class. Phil.* xii, pp. 410 ff.).

between the parasite in Eupolis' Κόλακες[1] and the same
character in Epicharmus may well have been due to the fact
that both drew from the same type in real life; and although
there is some parallelism of subjects between Epicharmus and
the Middle Comedy, the explanation is probably to be found
in a common mythology and a similar social life.

It is dangerous, therefore, to exaggerate resemblance into
imitation; and the tricks of comic poets and performers are
much the same all the world over; but to suppose that the
Attic poets were unacquainted with Epicharmus, and derived
no suggestion or inspiration from him seems to be at least
equally extravagant; and if Plato knew and admired him, it
is unlikely that he was quite unknown to the generation
before Plato.

In the same way it is impossible to trace in detail the
influence which Epicharmus may have had on the comic
performances of later times in Magna Graecia, though that
influence is not likely to be disputed. The subjects of his plays
and those of the paintings on the φλύακες-vases are noticeably
alike, though the performances of the φλύακες are never
classed as comedies. Among the mimes of Sophron (also
never called comedies[2]) are some, the titles of which resemble
those of plays of Epicharmus, such as Ἀγροιώτης, ταὶ Θάμεναι
τὰ Ἴσθμια (if that was the title), Προμαθεύς, and in his
travesty of heroic stories he may have affected the ἱλαροτρα-
γῳδία of Rhinthon.

But whatever may be conjectured where so much is uncertain, it remains the outstanding merit of Epicharmus, as
Aristotle saw, that he created a type of comedy which turned
largely upon topics of general interest; and so he was the
forerunner not only of the later comedies which travestied

---

[1] 159 (K.).

[2] At least not before Suidas (s. v. Σώφρων κωμικός). I think Reich,
Mimus, i, p. 269, overstates the extension of the word κωμῳδία to mimes,
&c. It is doubtful whether Athen. ix, p. 402 b, in speaking of Ἰταλικὴ
καλουμένη κωμῳδία written by Sciras of Tarentum refers to the φλύακες.
In any case both Athenaeus and Suidas are very late, and Athenaeus'
expression shows that the name was not used in its strict sense.

heroic legend, but of the comedy of social life and manners which has never entirely disappeared, and has sometimes taken shape in literature of the first order.

VI

Phormus and Deinolochus.

It is convenient to append here a note on the little that is known about Epicharmus' fellow-poets, Phormus and Deinolochus.

Phormus is known to us only from a few scattered notices of Athenaeus and Suidas, as a contemporary of Epicharmus, and with him the 'inventor' of comedy, and as the friend of Gelo and tutor of his children.[1] With regard to the titles of his comedies, which are more in number than six (the number given by Suidas) there is a difficulty which cannot be solved, even if it were worth solving;[2] but it is evident that most or all of the plays were mythological burlesque, probably of the same type as those of Epicharmus.

Suidas states also that he introduced a robe, reaching to

---

[1] Suidas, s. v. Ἐπίχαρμος . . . ὃς εὗρε τὴν κωμῳδίαν ἐν Συρακούσαις ἅμα Φόρμῳ: and s. v. Φόρμος· Συρακούσιος, κωμικός, σύγχρονος Ἐπιχάρμῳ, οἰκεῖος δὲ Γέλωνι τῷ τυράννῳ Σικελίας καὶ τροφεὺς τῶν παίδων αὐτοῦ. ἔγραψε δράματα ζ', ἅ ἐστι ταῦτα· Ἄδμητος, Ἀλκίνοος, Ἀλκύονες, Ἰλίου πόρθησις, Ἵππος, Κηφεὺς ἢ Κεφάλαια, Περσεύς. ἐχρήσατο δὲ πρῶτος ἐνδύματι ποδήρει καὶ σκηνῇ δερμάτων φοινικῶν. μέμνηται δὲ καὶ ἑτέρου δράματος Ἀθηναῖος ἐν τοῖς Δειπνοσοφισταῖς, Ἀταλάντης (cf. Athen. xiv, p. 652 a φοίνικα δὲ τὸν καρπὸν καὶ Ἑλλάνικος κέκληκεν . . . καὶ Φόρμος ὁ κωμικὸς ἐν Ἀταλάνταις). Aristotle, *Poet.* v, gives the poet's name as Φόρμις, but the reading of the passage is in any case very uncertain.

[2] Ἰλίου πόρθησις and Ἵππος may have been the same play in different versions or with an alternative title ; so may Κηφεύς and Περσεύς and Κεφάλαια (one MS. has ἤ before Περσεύς). Κεφάλαια may have some reference to the Gorgon's head which figured in the story of Perseus. Lorenz suggests that Ἀλκύονες is a dittography from Ἀλκίνοος, though the name is in itself unsuspicious. It is very doubtful whether either Epicharmus or Phormus wrote an Ἀταλάνται (vid. Kaibel Fragm., p. 93).

the feet, for his actors, and decorated his stage with purple
hangings.[1] Pausanias[2] mentions a Phormis who came from
Arcadia to Syracuse and did good service both to Gelo and to
Hiero by his brilliant generalship, and whose statue was
erected at Olympia both by himself and by his friend Lycortas
of Syracuse. Some writers have assumed without question
that the comic poet and the general were identical; but, apart
from the difficulty in regard to the termination of the name,
there is no evidence which clearly connects the two. No
fragment of Phormus survives.

Deinolochus is described by Suidas[3] as of Syracuse or
Acragas, and the son or pupil (Aelian says the rival[4]) of
Epicharmus. The titles of his plays which have been preserved are *Althaea*, *The Amazons*, *Medea*, *Telephus*, and Κωμῳ-
δοτραγῳδία. The last is only known as the title of plays by
much later writers, such as Alcaeus and Anaxandrides; but
there is no reason why Deinolochus, who must have seen
tragedies acted at Syracuse, should not have travestied them
under such a title. The fragments are very meagre[5] and tell
us nothing of his work, except that he made use of proverbs
and of local (as opposed to literary) words. Aelian[6] says that
Deinolochus, like some other poets, treated a quaint story to
the effect that when Prometheus had stolen fire, Zeus offered
to give any one who detected the theft a drug which would
keep off old age. Those who earned this reward took it away
tied on to a donkey's back. The donkey grew thirsty, and

---

[1] Bernhardy emends σκήνη to σκευῇ; but Ar. *Eth. N.* iv. ii illustrates
extravagant μεγαλοπρέπεια by instancing a man ἐρανιστὰς γαμικῶς ἑστιῶν,
καὶ κωμῳδοῖς χορηγῶν ἐν τῇ παρόδῳ πορφύραν εἰσφέρων, ὥσπερ οἱ Μεγάρεις :
on which Aspasius comments συνηθὲς ἐν κωμῳδίᾳ παραπετάσματα δέρρεις
ποιεῖν, οὐ πορφυρίδας. Possibly Phormus, like the Megareans, hung purple
fabrics (which might loosely be called σκήνη) at the stage-entrances for
the sake of display.

[2] V. xxvii, § 7.

[3] Δεινόλοχος· Συρακούσιος ἢ ᾿Ακραγαντῖνος· κωμικὸς ἦν ἐπὶ τῆς ογ (73rd)
᾿Ολυμπιάδος, υἱὸς ᾿Επιχάρμου, ὡς δέ τινες μαθητης. ἐδίδαξε δαάματα ιδ' Δωρίδι
διαλέκτῳ.

[4] *N. H.* vi. 51 Δεινολόχος ὁ ἀνταγωνιστὴς ᾿Επιχάρμου.

[5] They are collected by Kaibel, pp. 149-51.   [6] l.c.

went to a spring to drink ; but the snake which guarded the spring would only let the donkey drink, if he gave him the drug in exchange. So the snake got free of old age, but received in addition the thirst of the donkey.

The only interest of these two writers lies in the evidence they afford of the existence of a small school of comic poets at Hiero's court.

ADDENDA

I (p. 124)

To the passages illustrating the meaning of ἐξάρχειν may be added the following, which show its use in prose at a date nearer to that of Aristotle:

Xenoph. *Cyrop.* III. iii. 58. ἐξῆρχεν αὐτοῖς ὁ Κῦρος παιᾶνα τὸν νομιζόμενον, οἱ δὲ θεοσεβεῖς πάντες συνεπήχησαν μεγάλῃ τῇ φωνῇ.
Id. *Anab.* V. iv. 14. ἐξῆρχε μὲν αὐτῶν εἷς, οἱ δ' ἄλλοι ἅπαντες ἐπορεύοντο ᾄδοντες ἐν ῥυθμῷ.

II (p. 148)

Since the sections of this work which deal with the dialect of Tragedy were printed, a fresh attempt has been made by G. H. Mahlow (*Neue Wege durch die Griechische Sprache und Dichtung*) to rehabilitate the view that Tragedy contains nothing that is not Attic, old or new, and that the many words and forms which seem to be Epic (Ionic) or Doric are not really such, but are forms which were current in Athens (the population of which was of mixed origin) alongside of those which grammarians regard as Attic; these were gradually falling out of use in the sixth and fifth centuries, but were still employed by poets to give a certain distinction to their style; in the fourth century they had practically disappeared, and early scholars and grammarians based their conception of Attic on the prose of the fourth century, when a kind of stabilized Attic was produced as the result of school education. Solon employed more of these forms and words than the Tragic poets, but none strayed beyond the limits of genuine Attic. Two kinds of argument are used to support this view, and to discredit the theory adopted in this book, that the explanation of these forms (whether Epic or Doric) is mainly to be found in the persistence of literary conventions based, first, on Homer, and then on the practice of the lyric poets.

In the first place, Mahlow denounces with some scorn the notion that poets addressing Athenian audiences would suddenly introduce a word or form from Ionic here, from Doric there. But the supposed absurdity is reduced to the vanishing point, if we reflect that the conditions were entirely different from those under which modern poets work. (In fact even modern poets do things very like this at times.) The earliest Athenian poets had very little behind them except Homer, and the writers of the choruses of tragedy had practically nothing behind them except lyric poems written in non-Attic dialects. The sense of the remoteness of the poet from everyday life seems also to have been distinctly greater then than now, and a certain remoteness in his language would probably

E e

have seemed far from absurd. (The support for his view which Mahlow draws from the fact that Solon wrote many years before the institution of public Homeric recitations at the Panathenaea is surely very frail. Very many Athenians must have known their Homer long before the recitations were publicly ordained.) The Ionic forms in Thucydides and Antiphon are at least as likely to be survivals in prose of the conventions of poetry, which was once the only form of literature, as to have been spoken forms, coexisting with those which we have learned to think normal. It should be added that the argument *ab absurdo* is also applied by Mahlow to non-Attic poets. Theognis was an Ionian, not a Dorian; so was Tyrtaeus, though politically a Spartan; Pindar wrote as he spoke at home; Hesiod was not a Boeotian but an Ionian from Kyme, and wrote, not in ' Epic ', but in his own home-dialect; Empedocles too was an Ionian, not a Dorian. It may be doubted whether these paradoxes (and even more whether his treatment on similar lines of Homer) help his theory.

But, in the second place, in addition to his *a priori* argument, Mahlow examines very elaborately a large number of the main characteristics which differentiate the language of Attic poetry from 'normal Attic', with a view to showing that e. g. the use of *a* for *η* was really current in spoken Attic, alongside of the use of *η*, and that there was no fixed rule in regard to the poets' use of these parallel forms. He does of course show that the poets are not at all consistent, and that the use of these vowels in words used in prose as well as in poetry cannot be reduced to uniform rules. (In fact, no one would expect a living language to conform to such rules.) But it remains possible that the far greater use of the *a*-forms in poetry as compared with prose may have been due to the influence on the poets of earlier lyric poetry; and the fact that their usage is inconsistent and even capricious is at least as natural if they were forms borrowed (perhaps half unconsciously), as the poet's mood or metre suggested, from the poetic tradition, as it would be if they were due to the mixture of the *a* and *η* forms in current speech. (*Mutatis mutandis* the same argument will apply to the use of Ionic forms like ξεῖνος, μοῦνος, &c., and to the other poetic usages which are discussed).

It is impossible in a note, written just before the final proofs of the present book were going to press, to discuss all Mahlow's instances at length; he contributes something to the history of certain usages; but when he uses this history to prove the ' Old-Attic ' theory, it is practically always possible to find an explanation consistent with the rival view.

III (*p. 199*)

Since the foregoing pages were in proof, I have seen a well-preserved Corinthian vase in the Fitzwilliam Museum at Cambridge, on which are very typical specimens of padded figures of the kind referred to on p. 199. This is reproduced (thanks to the kindness of Dr. A. B. Cook) in the Frontispiece.

IV (*p. 16*)

I have just heard (May 26, 1927) from Professor Calder that he has found a Phrygian inscription of about A. D. 250 on which Διούνσις (i. e. Dionysus) is mentioned in a way which implies his guardianship of the tomb. Combining this with the fact that διθρερα = tomb (which, he now tells me, is certain), he interprets διθύραμβος as = διθρερáνβας, 'lord of the tomb', the suffix -βας being construed 'lord' (in this and other Anatolian words) with ν inserted (as frequently in Anatolian before β and δ). From this he concludes that the dithyramb was originally both Dionysiac and funereal. He makes out a strong case; but I still feel the difficulty of inferring, from the existence of a διθρερα under the care of Dionysus (the two are not expressly connected in any one inscription, but the inference is perhaps permissible) in the third century A.D., the funereal character of Dithyramb, perhaps a thousand years earlier, in face of the fact that there is not a trace of funereal character about anything that is called dithyramb in Greece. We know so little of the reciprocal relations of Greek and Phrygian religion and ritual during that thousand years, and even less of the history of Phrygian beliefs. So I can still only suspend judgement. I am not competent to discuss the questions in comparative philology which he raises, but I am not sure whether his theory of -αμβος accounts sufficiently for all the Greek words of that and allied terminations. (There is also a difficulty still about the ῑ of διθύραμβος, and of διθρερα, if the syllable δῑ- means 'double', as he supposes.)

E e 2

INDEX I

Actors and Acting: 100, 109 ff., 122 ff., 162, 166.
Actor's costume (comic): 237, 261 ff., 337.
Actor's costume (tragic): 110 ff., 149 ff.
Adrastus: 136 ff.
Aegae: 181, 182.
Aeschylus: chorus in, 88; use of trochaic tetrameter, 112, 129; aetiology in, 197.
Plays: Aegyptii, 87 ff.; Bassarai, 183, 187; Choephoroe, 178, 179, 194, 200; Danaides, 87 ff., 191, 199; Eumenides, 178, 189–91: Oresteia, 193, 200; Persae, 89, 129, 178, 193, 200; Prometheus Πυρκαεύς, 154; Prometheus trilogy, 190, 191, 193, 200; Septem, 179, 194, 197, 200; Supplices, 87 ff., 126, 177, 193–5; Sphinx, 190; Θεωροὶ ἢ Ἰσθμιασταί, 394.
Aetiology in Tragedy: 195 ff.
ἀγωγή: 23, 24, 49.
Agon in Tragedy: 161, 162, 192 ff.; in Comedy: see Comedy.
ἀγῶνες χύτρινοι: 171, 216.
Agonothetes: 76, 79.
Agyieus-stones: 175, 176.
Αἰτναῖος κάνθαρος: 386 ff., 411.
ἀλαζών: 270 ff.
Alcaeus (comicus): 230.
Alcimus: 371 ff.
Alexander the Great: 71, 73, 181.
Ἄμβας: 15.
Amyntas: 371.
ἀναβολαί: 55, 60, 74.
Anagnorisis (in Tragedy): 187, 194.
Anaxandrides: 71, 291.
Antheas: 227.
Anthesteria: 141, 170–2, 213 ff.
Antigenidas: 64, 73.
Apollo Agyieus: 140.
Apollo, dithyrambs to: 9, 10 (see also Thargelia).
Apollonia (at Delos): 9, 77.
Archestratus: 72.

Archilochus: 5, 18, 19, 21.
Archippus: 247.
Arion: 7, 19–22, 50, 126, 131 ff., 143, 145.
Aristarchus: 72.
Aristias: 31.
Aristophanes: on new music, &c., 54, 59, 60; abjured stock devices, 259, 277; characters, see Comedy; use of Prologue, 311; animal choruses, 247; form and structure of plays, 292 ff., and see Comedy; analysis of plays, 312 ff.
Plays: (see also Index II) Acharnians, 238 ff., 277, 295–310, 312, 313, 329, 331, 336, 342, 343, 347; Babylonians, 251; Birds, 295–310, 321–3, 338, 342, 344, 347; Ecclesiazusae, 295, 304, 309, 310, 327, 328, 333, 339, 347; Frogs, 295–310, 326, 327, 332, 339, 342, 345–7; Gerytades, 346; Knights, 277, 289, 295–310, 314, 315, 331, 336, 340, 342, 343, 346; Lysistrata, 242, 261, 295–310, 323–5, 332, 339, 342, 344; Peace, 277, 295–310, 320, 321, 331, 332, 338, 347; Plutus, 277, 295, 297, 309, 310, 328, 333, 340, 342, 347; Thesmophoriazusae, 295–310, 325, 326, 333, 342, 345, 347; Wasps, 277, 295–310, 317–19, 331, 338, 342, 343.
Aristotle: on beginnings of Tragedy, 109, 110, 112, 121 ff.
on beginnings of Comedy, 225 ff., 240.
on dithyramb, 22, 55.
Aristoxenus: 31, 71, 81, 96, 116, 118.
Artemis Κορδάκα: 260; Λυαία, 248; Orthia, 254 ff.; Orthosia, 275; Χιτωνέα, 258, 363, 392, 405.
Asclepius: 10, 12, 79, 173.
ἀσκωλιασμός: 102 ff., 213.

E e 3

INDEX II

PASSAGES QUOTED AND REFERRED TO